The Daily Telegraph

FORMULA ONE

YEARS

Acknowledgements

Any book of this scale is impossible without recourse to a wide variety of previous reference works including the *The Complete Encyclopedia of Formula One* by Bruce Jones, Jacques Deschenaux's *Grand Prix Guide*, Steve Small's *Grand Prix Who's Who* and Trevor R. Griffiths' *Grand Prix*, all of which were invaluable, and a wide range of newspapers, magazines and websites. The specialist Formula One websites, like Inside F1 and Atlas-F1, deserve a special mention, the former in particular for its excellent encyclopedia. To list every source read, gleaned from or inspired by would be too lengthy. The drivers, teams, historians, media and paddock folk in the sport have all helped and deserve acknowledgement, too. The brunt of the heavy load of work in researching, reporting and writing this book was done by a group of people who all deserve praise and thanks. They are the Collings Sport team of Will Gray, Will Spong, Gary Emmerson and Marcus Lee, all of whom performed small miracles and worked long hours, and Vanessa Daubney, of Carlton Books, who cajoled and encouraged as appropriate and when required.

THIS IS A CARLTON BOOK

This edition published 2004 for Carlton Books Ltd

First edition published 2001

10 9 8 7 6 5 4 3 2 1

A CIP catalogue for this book is available from the British Library.

ISBN 1 84442 542 8

Executive Editor: Vanessa Daubney
Project Art Direction: Mark Lloyd, Jim Lockwood
Design: Anthony Cohen & Karen Kloot
Jacket Design: Simon Osborne
Picture Research: Debora Fioravanti
Production: Lisa French

The Daily Telegraph
FORMULA ONE
YEARS

TIMOTHY COLLINGS AND SARAH EDWORTHY

CARLTON

Contents

DENIM

MAGNETI MARELLI
Agip

Mobil
Lucent
Bell Labs
BRIDGESTONE
SPALT
SPALT
SPALT
MasterCard
Pilsen

Foreword

I sometimes wonder where the years have gone to when I reflect on the fact that my team has raced in Formula One for 10 years never mind that the World Championship has been in existence for half a century. During that time the sport has changed in many ways, the majority for the good – such as improvements in safety, the access to Formula One for billions of TV viewers across the globe and the creation of a highly successful industry – and some to its detriment – the professional jealousies and politics that exist today and the fact that for many fans the business and technology leave little for pure racers.

At the same time some things remain fundamentally unaltered – the fascination of seeing incredible machinery being raced wheel-to-wheel by the best drivers in the world and the appealing imagery of speed, technology, glamour and courage which strike such a chord with people the world over.

I did not even become interested in Formula One until the late 1960s, but for over thirty years I have been lucky enough to follow and then become involved in this intriguing sport. I have to admit that for me the business side is just as exciting as the racing which proves that Formula One holds something for everyone. I trust you will enjoy this book. By reading it you will gain a keen insight into the high drama, passion, highs and lows that have made Formula One such a compelling spectacle.

Eddie Jordan 2001

Introduction

The sound and the splendour of a Formula One Grand Prix motor race is one of sport's unrivalled sensations. Literally. It can leave you deafened temporarily or dazzled by the colour and the movement. At close quarters, on a hot day in central Europe, it can be daunting and exhausting. Yet it is a circus event, which remains enduringly popular for a growing number of live fans at the circuits each year and, across the world, for an increasingly large television audience. Most of the spectators, furthermore, remain "hooked" on their new sport after the first experience and go on to become intrigued by the history, tradition and statistical depth.

This book, *The Daily Telegraph Formula One Years,* is written to give those many fans a chance to dip into past seasons and to compare the stars of the past with those of the present. Readers can revisit the golden era of Stirling Moss, Mike Hawthorn, Peter Collins and the BRMs and Vanwalls or submerge themselves in the legal and technological arguments of later decades. Races from the past are reported again, drivers are profiled and seasons described. Juan-Manuel Fangio and his wonderful feats are recalled as are those of Ayrton Senna and Michael Schumacher. But who is the greatest?

The answer is not obvious. It is subjective. It is the source of arguments and opinions. This is a book to stimulate all of these things and to encourage the reader to check a fact, to recall a move or a result and to enjoy a private memory which had been left unprompted for too long.

It has been difficult selecting certain drivers and not others for special mention and highlighting some years, seasons or decades. Without doubt, some figures stand tall in the Formula One hall of fame. Fangio, Moss, Jim Clark, Jackie Stewart, Alain Prost, Senna, Michael Schumacher and, certainly, others are more than worthy of mention. Some seasons,

Ardent fans: the tifosi of Ferrari.

too. But for those of the generation which began to experience Formula One on a regular basis in the last 20 years of the 20th century, one year stands out above all others: 1994.

In that sombre and incident-packed year, Formula One plunged to the depths and rose to the heights. Death, grief, serious injury and controversy were followed by competitive racing and acrimony. Interest in the sport reached an all-time high. As the old adage goes, there is no such thing as bad publicity. The passing of Ayrton Senna and Roland Ratzenberger was too high a price to pay, but their deaths did stimulate a period of introspection and attention to safety and security that survives today.

The legend of Senna lives on, even if now all his records bar one, his astonishing tally of pole positions, have been superseded by the man who came out of his shadows on that fateful day at Imola in 1994, Michael Schumacher. The tenth anniversary of Senna's passing, commemorated at Imola in 2004 with an emotional run by his old friend and team-mate Gerhard Berger in the Lotus car the great Brazilian drove to his first Grand Prix victory, recalled comparisons amongst the greats. Some chose Senna, some chose Fangio, some chose Schumacher. Statistically, Schumacher is best. But in truth, well, take your pick. Different eras, different legends. That is what makes Formula One what it is.

In modern times, the sport has changed, of course, from the rosy days of being a fun-filled sport for wealthy amateurs into a serious global business. The big car manufacturers are involved deeply now. The stakes are high. The worldwide audience is huge. Despite recent dominance by Ferrari and "Team Schumacher", it is a sport that commands the back and the front pages of newspapers everywhere.

The stars are internationally recognized. The team owners are millionaires, the sport's owner a billionaire. But the racing remains just a part of a sequence of events, a pattern of results, which has built up a reputation for glamour, speed, excitement and intrigue lasting more than 50 years. That tradition and history is reflected in this book to prompt memories, inspire ambitions and settle arguments once and for all.

Jackie Stewart leads Jochen Rindt in the 1969 Italian Grand Prix.

The Origins of Formula One

Despite the claims of Britain and Germany, it is the French who can boast that they are the creators of Grand Prix motor racing. While the idea of cars racing on roads was banned in the countries that gave birth to the Industrial Revolution and the four-stroke internal-combustion engine, respectively, it was embraced warmly in France. All the more pity, then, that the French have struggled to muster a competitive Formula One team in recent years.

But top-class racing on roads anywhere was little more than a dream until 1887, when the first organized event was planned, but failed to take place. The failure was a short trial, organized by a journal known as *Le Vélocipède*, which owing to the presence of only one willing competitor quite simply could not happen. Not even the French could feel satisfied with a race comprising a solitary entry! The Parisians, however, folk who were keen on sport and organising sporting competitions (they created the Jules Rimet trophy which later became the World Cup for football), and who sparked many other tournaments, were not to be daunted.

Another event was organized. This was a reliability trial, run from Paris to Rouen, in 1894. The distance for the event was only 126 kilometres, but for that era it was enough of a challenge. The event, which included a break for lunch, was organized by Pierre Gifard of *Le Petit Journal* newspaper and the criteria for entries included notes declaring that the victorious "horseless carriage" had to be "safe, easily controllable and reasonably economical to run". Finally, a total of 21 competitors left Paris on 22 July for a race widely recognized today as the forerunner of modern Formula One. The first finisher, controlling a steam-driven De Dion tractor, was the Comte

The first "Grand Prix", organized by the Automobile Club de France, was held at Le Mans in 1906.

de Dion. Unfortunately, however, the judges decided to over-rule his success – because his vehicle was not considered to be a practical road vehicle – and award victory instead to the next two cars to finish, a Peugeot and a Panhard-Levassor. They shared the prize.

At this early time, the races were run without regulations. They were epic events of endurance covering long distances: from Paris to Bordeaux, or from Paris to Vienna and Amsterdam, and back. Spectators lined the routes, which were also carrying normal everyday traffic. Enthusiasm for the sport grew rapidly in France, where there were many long, straight roads, and an intense rivalry began to develop between manufacturers like Panhard-Levassor and Peugeot. At this time, too, steering wheels were still awaiting their invention and the cars were directed by a lever or a handlebar.

It was, of course, a recipe for trouble and, in due course, motor racing was banned briefly in France until a lobby of manufacturers succeeded in overturning the decision. They had enjoyed the racing and its benefits, particularly such famous events as the Paris-Bordeaux return. In 1895 Emile Levassor, driving a two-cylinder Panhard-Levassor, was the winner. He kept on the road virtually non-stop for 48 hours and 48 minutes. But, though he finished first at Porte Maillot, because his car had only two seats instead of four, he was denied the victors' prize of 31,000 Francs.

Another interesting entrant in this race was a Peugeot, driven by André Michelin. Unsurprisingly, thanks to the gift of hindsight, his car used pneumatic tyres, a revolutionary move at a time when the wheels on most other vehicles were either made of iron or solid rubber. At first, equally predictably, these early "air tyres" were ridiculed as impractical. Indeed, poor Michelin suffered many punctures, caused by the poor condition of the roads. He persevered, however, and his legacy is the company which returned to supply tyres in Formula One at the start of 2001.

In 1896, however, Michelin was a pioneer and motor racing was an embryonic sport and in the same year the Automobile Club de France (ACF), which had been created the previous year, held a return race from Paris to Marseilles. The following year, racing cars emerged as something different to road cars – mudguards, seat cushions and other items of luxury were removed in the interests of speed. The increased speeds, however, together with the increased intensity of the racing, led inevitably to the first fatal accident. This came soon after the start of the 1898 Paris-Nice race when the Marquis de Montariol, driving a Benz, waved his friend, the Marquis de Montaignac, through; Montaignac, lifting his hand to wave back, lost control of the tiller on his car and swerved off the road, colliding with De Montariol's vehicle. Both drivers were thrown clear and escaped injury, but a mechanic died from grievous head injuries.

André Michelin, aspiring racer and, with his brother Edouard, the pioneer of pneumatic tyres.

In 1900, (John) Gordon Bennett, a British newspaper proprietor and owner of the *New York Herald*, decided it was time the British motor industry became involved. He established a series of races bearing his name. Each nation had a team of three cars chosen by each national automobile club and the events were run alongside the great town-to-town races in France before, in 1904, a Bennett race was run in Germany for the first time. The French, unhappy that entries were limited in the Gordon Bennett races, killed it off in 1906 when they refused to allow it to take place alongside their own new event, the Grand Prix of the ACF, held at Le Mans.

In a bid to improve speeds in the years of these first forays, the engines used were rapidly increasing in size. Before long, seven- and eight-litre engines became common. Chassis design and development, brakes and tyres did not maintain the same progress, but in 1901 the arrival of the 35-horsepower Mercedes car changed that. It was the first sports racing car to feature a four-cylinder engine with mechanical valves, a "honeycomb" radiator, a steel chassis, pneumatic tyres and magneto ignition. After solving early reliability problems, it became a consistent race winner. In effect, the battle for supremacy on the track, which now prevails among the major manufacturers of the world, had begun.

In 1902, Mors introduced spring dampers which resulted in dramatically improved road-holding. With the cars now approaching speeds of 100 mph the races, held on open roads, resulted in several fatal accidents, some of which included spectators. In 1901, for example, at the Paris-Berlin event, a boy was killed when he stepped into the road to watch a passing car and the next vehicle knocked him down.

Brooklands racing circuit, designed by Hugh F. Locke-King and built on his land in Surrey in 1907.

The French government banned racing, briefly, but relented, only to ban it again after a spate of further accidents on the ill-fated Paris-Bordeaux-Madrid marathon in 1903, which attracted three million spectators. In this race Louis Renault averaged 65 mph on the first leg, but the event was cancelled in Bordeaux due to the dangers.

Once more the French government relented, providing the racing took place in safe, sparsely populated areas and on roads closed by barriers. It was the start of "circuit racing" as it is now known and it was pioneered, of course, by the French, whose ACF drew up regulations for the race widely regarded as the first "Grand Prix", the contest at Le Mans in 1906.

A total of 32 cars started this race, but after 12 laps over two days only 11 remained. The winner was a Hungarian, Ferenc Szisz, driving a 90-horsepower Renault which introduced the novelty of the times, detachable wheel-rims; created, of course, by Michelin. This meant that he had the distinct advantage of being able to stop and change his tyres in two or three minutes instead of the usual 15 minutes. It was another technical advance which remains in common use nearly 100 years later.

That year also saw the first running of the Targa Florio, across mountain roads in Sicily, organized by the wealthy Vicenzo Florio, and, in 1907, the Germans organized an event for touring cars limited to eight-litre engines. The Kaiserpreis was won by a Fiat driver, Nazzaro, a fact which proved international racing was by then established and thriving. This was endorsed in the years before the First World War when the French Grand Prix became a particular scrap for honours involving Peugeot, which entered three cars, and Mercedes, which

entered five. To the dismay of the big French crowd at Lyons, the Germans claimed the first three places. This was, effectively, the last Grand Prix before the Great War and forced several top drivers to go to the United States, where they competed in the Vanderbilt Cup, at Indianapolis, to find continued success on the track.

Britain, by then, was catching up. As British law had not allowed racing on public roads, it had been necessary to build a circuit. Brooklands, designed by Hugh F. Locke-King, was built on his own land in Surrey in 1907. It was an oval with banked corners and its example was followed after the war, in Italy, when the Autodromo Monza, which incorporated a 2.8-mile, banked oval into a 3.4-mile road track, was built. The enthusiasm of the Fiat entrants and Italy's natural love of sport helped attract crowds of more than 100,000 to the circuit. However, the ravages of war and economic recession had held European racing back and the Americans, with more advanced machinery, were showing the way. This was demonstrated particularly at the 1921 French Grand Prix at Le Mans when the visiting Americans dominated easily.

Further developments were inevitable and these followed with the creation of such circuits as the Miramas, near Marseilles in France, and the sprawling Spa-Francorchamps circuit in Belgium. The street circuit in Monte Carlo hosted the first Monaco Grand Prix in 1929, which was won by William Grover Williams in a Bugatti. As the sport developed, more and more Grands Prix were held with the classic events in France, Italy, Germany and Britain becoming the most established, before the formalization of the Formula One World Championship followed in 1950.

William Grover Williams, the winner of the first Monaco Grand Prix in 1929.

1950
Alfa dominates competition

Giuseppe Farina leads the grid at the start of the British Grand Prix.

TALKING POINT
ALFA'S THREE F'S

Fangio, Farina, and Fagioli made a formidable team which helped put the updated post-war Alfa 158 in a class of its own.

With the exception of the Indianapolis 500, the Alfa team won every one of the races in the 1950 Championship season, and between the team's three drivers Alfa amassed a total of 81 World Championship points – a massive chunk of the points available – and took the top three places in the series.

The team had withdrawn from racing in 1949, one year before the Championship began, after the deaths of its three drivers. The talent of their three replacements, along with the fact that Alfa was well prepared for the 1950 season, gave the team a head start which proved too much for their rivals.

The newly-formed Formula One World Championship aimed to bring together the world's best teams and drivers to compete in the most prestigious motor races. Very much in its infancy, however, the Championship only included one race out of Europe – the Indianapolis 500 – and that turned out to be a Championship race by definition only.

The Championship drew back the Alfa team from a short exile and saw a newly-born Ferrari team, which had begun racing in 1949, attempt to tackle the might of their Italian rivals. For the famous red marque, however, the season was not to turn out the way they'd hoped, as the Alfas completely annihilated the rest of the field.

The battle for the Championship went down to the wire, with just two points separating the leaders coming into the final round. The title eventually went to Giuseppe Farina, but Juan Manuel Fangio did not go down without a fight, taking over a team-mate's car in an ultimately doomed bid to overhaul his rival.

The Formula One World Championship came into being on 13 May, 1950 with the British Grand Prix at Silverstone. On a sunny afternoon at the usually windswept aerodrome, King George VI and Queen Elizabeth were present to watch the cars in the new "Formula One" category hit the track.

The technical regulations allowed both supercharged and normally-aspirated cars to enter the series. The trend of the season was set in the first race, when the works Alfa Romeo team filled the first three spots on the grid.

Alfa's Fangio had won the two main non-championship events prior to the season-opener, and other factory drivers Farina, Luigi Fagioli and Briton Reg Parnell joined him at Silverstone. Ferrari, who had raced in previous minor events, were not present, but both Maserati and Talbot Lago sent factory cars to the Northamptonshire circuit.

The 23-car field included Thai Prince Bira on the second row as the first non-Alfa runner. As the race began, Farina pulled into the lead and, after a frantic battle in the early laps, went on to take victory 2.5 seconds ahead of team-mate Fagioli. Parnell, who had been invited to take part by Alfa Romeo, finished a distant third as the leading Italian pair dominated. The closest non-Alfa driver, Frenchman Yves Giraud-Cabantous in the Talbot Lago, ended the race two laps down.

Fangio dominates in Monaco

Eight days later, the field moved to the glamorous setting of Monte Carlo. This time Ferrari joined the fray, and Alfa saw a more difficult task ahead.

Although Alfa still took the first two places on the grid, it was clear they had more to worry about this time as Argentine José Froilan Gonzalez powered his Maserati into third spot.

The start was clean, but as the cars piled into Tabac corner, midway through the first lap, Farina's second-placed Alfa spun on a wet track. Unusual winds had whipped up and sprayed water from the harbour on to the track and the conditions caused

Froilan Gonzalez to hit the rotating Farina. A multi-car pile-up ensued, putting nine cars out and reducing the field to 10. The crash put two of Fangio's Alfa team-mates out, and saw Gonzalez badly burned after fuel from a split tank ignited.

When Fangio returned on the next lap, he had to wind his way through the wreckage. He managed, but second-placed Luigi Villoresi was not so successful and stalled as he slowed. This put the Ferrari 125 of Italian Alberto Ascari into second place.

But Ascari's team-mate Villoresi refused to give up and stormed through from the back to regain second place. However, Villoresi's progress was thwarted on lap 62 with a rear axle problem.

His retirement left Fangio well out in front and the Argentine came across the finish line one full lap ahead of Ascari. Local driver Louis Chiron claimed third place in a Maserati, a further lap adrift.

Europeans ignore Indy

Indianapolis was the next round on the Grand Prix circuit, but proved irrelevant to the Championship as none of the leading teams or drivers turned up.

The famous American oval track was introduced into the World Championship because of its classic stature, but that did not entice the top European marques to travel across the Atlantic. Instead it was left mainly to Americans, and the field was filled with Offenhauser-engined cars.

The race was to be a 500-miler, but was shortened to 345 miles when a cloudburst sent torrential rain on to the circuit. Several cars spun in the conditions and common sense prevailed as the race was ended before more serious damage could be done.

Californian Johnny Parsons secured victory in a Wynn's Kurtis-Offenhauser, and fellow-American Bill Holland took second. It was only discovered later that Parsons' engine block was cracked, and he would have struggled to complete the full distance.

In a rapidly-advancing World Championship, the fourth round took place just three weeks after the first at the Swiss circuit of Bremgarten. Once again it was Alfa versus Ferrari, the Alfas getting the upper hand in qualifying.

The factory Alfa 158s of Fangio and Farina lined up on row one, and their qualifying times were well up on those of the third works Alfa man Luigi Fagioli and the Ferraris of Villoresi and Ascari on row two. Froilan Gonzalez was out of action after his Monaco crash, as was Maserati's Franco Rol.

Ascari's good start saw him break the Alfa stranglehold, but his Ferrari 125 was unable to maintain the pace, and the Alfas soon moved back in front.

Fangio and Farina proved they were in a class of their own, and pulled away from Fagioli as they battled for the lead. Farina made a decisive break as Fangio eventually retired with electrical problems.

The two Ferraris lacked both speed and reliability and both Ascari and Villoresi were out by the end of lap nine. Ten laps later Frenchman Eugene Martin, a factory Talbot-Lago driver, suffered serious injuries when he was thrown from his car after a heavy crash.

Farina eventually won by just 0.4 seconds from

Luigi Fagioli, Reg Parnell and Giuseppe Farina on the podium at Silverstone.

RACE BY RACE DETAILS

ROUND 1 – BRITAIN
Race Giuseppe Farina
Pole Giuseppe Farina
Fastest lap Giuseppe Farina

ROUND 2–MONACO
Race Juan Manuel Fangio
Pole Juan Manuel Fangio
Fastest lap Juan Manuel Fangio

ROUND 3–INDIANAPOLIS
Race Johnny Parsons
Pole Walt Faulkner
Fastest lap Johnny Parsons

ROUND 4–SWITZERLAND
Race Giuseppe Farina
Pole Juan Manuel Fangio
Fastest lap Giuseppe Farina

ROUND 5–BELGIUM
Race Juan Manuel Fangio
Pole Giuseppe Farina
Fastest lap Giuseppe Farina

ROUND 6–FRANCE
Race Juan Manuel Fangio
Pole Juan Manuel Fangio
Fastest lap Juan Manuel Fangio

ROUND 7–ITALY
Race Giuseppe Farina
Pole Juan Manuel Fangio
Fastest lap Juan Manuel Fangio

The first-lap pile-up on Tabac Corner during the Monaco Grand Prix. Water from the harbour was whipped up by high winds and sprayed on to the track making conditions hazardous.

team-mate Fagioli, with the Talbot-Lago of Louis Rosier one lap back in third. Prince Bira headed a group of four Maseratis in fourth after moving up from eighth on the grid.

Championship pressures take their toll

The picturesque Ardennes forests provided the setting for the next round, at Spa Francorchamps in mid-June. However, accidents and problems in previous races coupled with the regularity of the events – it was the fifth Championship event in as many weeks – meant that dwindling numbers saw just 14 cars make it to the Belgian track.

The top two teams were still going strong, and all three Alfa drivers made it on to the grid, although Ferrari could only provide two cars, a standard 125 for Villoresi and a new V12-engined car for Ascari.

Further down the grid Talbot-Lago brought three cars, for Yves Giraud-Cabantous, Rosier, and Philippe Entancelin, racing for the sidelined Martin.

True to form, Farina and Fangio ended qualifying on the front row, Fagioli again slowest of the Alfa bunch in third. However, the surprise came from the old Talbot-Lago of privateer Raymond Sommer, which split the Ferraris of Villoresi and Ascari.

As soon as the race began a familiar pattern emerged. The Alfas sped away from the field while behind them Sommer was battling it out with the works Ferraris for the minor places.

Fuel stops for the Alfas added an element of confusion and Sommer found himself in the lead. Soon after wards, however, his engine blew and Ascari's Ferrari moved to top the lap sheets. But normal order was restored when Ascari pitted to take on more fuel and Fangio, Farina and Fagioli moved through.

The only blot on Alfa's copybook was transmission problems for Farina, which sent him back to fourth and allowed the Talbot-Lago of Rosier to spoil the Alfa one-two-three.

After a two-week break the Formula One Championship contenders reconvened at Reims-Gueux for the French Grand Prix. Ferrari drivers Ascari and Villoresi now had the new V12 engine, and Ascari was in an interim 3.3-litre Ferrari 375.

However, the team found the smaller capacity a major problem and, in an unprecedented move by modern standards, the Italian marque withdrew both cars after practice because they were uncompetitive!

That left the Alfas to dominate once again, but this time at a level not been seen before as they finished three laps clear of their rivals.

They lined up in the order Fangio, Farina, Fagioli, with Fangio significantly quicker than the other two.

SHORTS

The 158 Alfetta was very much a pre-war car, but its availability – seven of them had been carefully stored in a cheese factory – meant that Alfa Romeo found their post-war feet much faster than anyone else. The team went on to win not only the opening Grand Prix of F1's inaugural season – The British Grand Prix at Silverstone – but also filled the top three spots in the Drivers' World Championship.

Juan Manuel Fangio in his car at Silverstone on 27 August 1950.

1950 DRIVERS' CHAMPIONSHIP

DRIVER	TEAM	POINTS
Giuseppe Farina	Alfa Romeo	30
Juan Manuel Fangio	Alfa Romeo	27
Luigi Fagioli	Alfa Romeo	24
Louis Rosier	Talbot-Lago	13
Alberto Ascari	Ferrari	11
Johnny Parsons	Kurtis Kraft	8
Bill Holland	Deidt	6
B Bira	Maserati	5
Louis Chiron	Maserati	4
Reg Parnell	Alfa Romeo	4
Mauri Rose	Deidt	4
Peter Whitehead	Ferrari	4
Philippe Etancelin	Talbot-Lago	3
Yves Giraud-Cabantous	Talbot-Lago	3
Cecil Green	Kurtis-Kraft	3
Robert Manzon	Simca-Gordoni	3
Dorino Serafini	Ferrari	3
Raymond Sommer	Ferrari	3
Felice Bonetto	Maserati	2
Tony Bettenhausen	Kurtis-Kraft	1
Eugene Chaboud	Talbot-Lago	1
Joie Chitwood	Kurtis-Kraft	1

Behind them, the works Talbot-Lagos enjoyed an unfamiliar second-row placing, while the Maseratis, private Talbot-Lagos and a lone Simca-Gordoni filled the rest of the grid.

Farina got the better of Fangio early in the race, but fuel problems sent him to the back of the field, leaving Fangio to take an unchallenged victory 20 seconds ahead of his team-mate Fagioli.

The works Talbot-Lagos faltered and it was the privateer Ferrari 125 of Peter Whitehead which picked up third, while Frenchman Robert Manzon claimed an impressive fourth in the Simca-Gordoni, better suited to low-speed circuits.

With one round remaining, the Alfas were clearly dominating, and the French result left Fangio with a two-point Championship lead over Farina.

Alfa confirms dominance

After a closely-packed first six races, it was two months before the Championship was decided in the seventh and concluding round of the series at Monza.

Although there was a World Championship break there were still plenty of races going on, as Alfa continued their dominance in non-championship events throughout Europe.

Farina had taken two wins, at Silverstone and Bari, while Fangio won at Pescara and the Grand Prix des Nations in Geneva, the latter more noted for the crash in which Villoresi was seriously injured and three spectators were killed.

The Talbot-Lagos had taken victories with Rosier in Albi and the Dutch circuit of Zandvoort. Ferrari, meanwhile, had something of a lean spell, being beaten by Rosier in Holland but still clocking up a win with Ascari at the Nurburgring in Germany.

When the teams returned to Championship action it was Ferrari creating the interest, with a new 4.5-litre machine, the 375...and it was fast. The new car caused a stir when it split the Alfas in practice, and immediately Alfa responded by sending Farina out in a modified 159.

However, Fangio did not need modifications to beat the Ferraris, and duly took pole ahead of Ascari and the slower but newer Alfa of Farina. Another Alfa 158, this time driven by Consalvo Sanesi, took the final place on the front row of a 4–4–4 formation grid, while Villoresi's substitute at Ferrari, Dorino Serafini, could only manage sixth.

Although the works Talbots had not made it to the final race of the season, the rest of the field was filled with Talbot Lagos and Maseratis, along with two Simca-Gordonis, and a rather unusual Jaguar-engined Ferrari!

After months of revision Ferrari took the race to Alfa as Ascari battled hard with Fangio and Farina at the head of the field until his new Ferrari came to a halt with an overheating engine.

But that was not the end for Ascari, as the rules allowed him to call in a team-mate and go back out. Meanwhile, Fangio had also retired with a gearbox problem and did the same thing, calling in Piero Taruffi to take over his 158.

Ascari went on to finish second behind Farina and claim the title as a despondent Fangio retired his Alfa.

1951
Fangio crowned Champion

TALKING POINT

ASCARI THE GENTLEMAN

Alberto Ascari proved he was a gentleman racer at Silverstone when he turned down the chance of taking a victory to allow his team-mate José Froilan Gonzalez, who had done all the hard work, to take the first-ever race win for Ferrari.

The team had been working hard after a drubbing from their Italian rivals Alfa Romeo in 1950, and the new Ferrari 375 took the challenge to the Alfas to break their stranglehold of the sport.

It was five races into the season when Gonzalez battled hard with Fangio for the lead in the absence of the retired Ascari. The team leader could have taken over Gonzalez's car, but he waved his team-mate on and watched him take a landmark first victory for an emerging Ferrari team.

It was the British Grand Prix, five races into the season, when the monumental moment happened. Gonzalez had battled hard with Fangio while Ascari had retired. Ascari, being the team leader, could have taken over Gonzalez' car, but he waved his team-mate on and watched him take the victory.

Juan Manuel Fangio and Giuseppe Farina get away first at the French Grand Prix.

Once again it was Alfa Romeo's year, with Juan Manuel Fangio taking his first world drivers' crown. The team left the Formula One at the end of the year, and Fangio's win sent the team out on a high.

The 1951 Championship, however, was far removed from the Alfa-domination of the previous year, as Ferrari gained momentum and became serious challengers towards the end of the season, proving themselves ready to take over Alfa's mantle.

The ageing Alfas had been modified to their limit, while the Ferraris were a new design.

It was the usual cast in the usual top cars as the field arrived in Switzerland for the first race of the season at the end of May. Fangio and Giuseppe Farina were back with new Alfa 149s, while at Ferrari Alberto Ascari was joined once more by team-mate Luigi Villoresi.

Fangio starts year in style

Ferrari had dominated three non-championship events before Switzerland in which the Alfas had not turned up. When they did, at the International trophy in Silverstone, they won the heats but Reg Parnell won a wet final in the Thinwall Special. But in Bremgarten, when it mattered, Fangio took the spoils in a wet race that was dominated by the Alfas.

Fangio and Farina powered away from the front whilst Piero Taruffi pulled his Ferrari up to third. He challenged for the lead, but could not get past the Alfas. Fangio decided to pit, but Farina tried to go through the whole race without a stop. The plan did not work, and the faster Fangio passed the Italian to take the victory. The Ferrari of Taruffi also made it past Farina to finish the race in second – although the dominance of the Alfas was such that the Argentine was almost a whole minute ahead of their nearest challenger.

The second place of Taruffi split the Alfa quartet as their two remaining cars settled for fourth and fifth. Reigning champion Ascari was way back in sixth as he returned bravely to the cockpit after he suffered burns in a crash at a Formula Two race in Genoa a week before.

A bizarre decision to hold the Indy 500 just

three days after the Swiss Grand Prix meant that the leading teams again boycotted America's great race.

New Yorker Lee Wallard drank the milk on Victory Road after a tight battle during the 500-mile race. His Belanger Special eventually crossed the line nearly two minutes ahead of nearest challenger Mike Nazaruk.

Pole man Duke Nolan ended the race on lap 151 when he stalled, but three-time Indy victor Mauri Rose, who had qualified fifth, had a more dramatic end. The wheel of his Pennzoil Special collapsed and sent him into a spin and the car overturned. He was lucky to escape unhurt.

Wallard's win enabled him to finish seventh overall in the drivers' standings, without racing in another round.

The leading title contenders returned to the track at Spa and Farina maintained Alfa's form, securing a win by a three-minute margin.

There were just 13 cars on the grid, and Villoresi's Ferrari sprang a surprise at the start of the race by jumping the two Alfas ahead of him and taking the lead. It was to last just two laps, however, as Farina powered past the Italian and into the lead.

Fangio took the lead on lap 15, but when he pitted his wheel stuck and he dropped to the back of the field. It lost the Argentinian a whole 15 minutes in the race, and there was no way back. Despite a vain attempt to land some Championship points, his speed earned him a fastest lap as he finished last of the finishers in ninth.

Once Fangio was gone, Farina had an easy cruise to the finish, and the Alfa driver beat the Ferraris by almost three minutes. Ascari was back on form as he claimed second, while Villoresi was a further 90 seconds back. The rest of the field finished a further two laps behind.

The French Grand Prix saw Ferrari moving close to the pace of the Alfas, and the race witnessed spectacular pace from Fangio and Ascari. But a win was not to be for either man and, despite taking over other machinery when theirs failed, it was Alfa's third man Luigi Fagioli, in his first race of the season, who eventually took the spoils.

Top two continue battle

All guns were blazing as Alfa took four 159s to France and Ferrari responded by fielding three 375s and a Thinwall Special for Brit Reg Parnell.

Fangio and Farina gave Alfa a one-two on the grid once again, with Ascari close behind as Ferrari kept their Italian rivals at close quarters.

For the second race in succession Ferrari stormed into the lead as Ascari powered off the line. Fangio followed, but it was not long before both drivers were forced out with car troubles and Farina took the lead.

Behind him, José Froilan Gonzalez moved up to second with Fagioli back in third, but for these two men, the race was about to end. The sidelined Fangio took over Fagioli's car while Ascari stole the Ferrari from Gonzalez and went off in pursuit of the Argentine.

The two title favourites seemed to be too far back to catch Farina, but when his Alfa began to have mechanical problems he dropped back towards the pair. Fangio cruised past and, with Ascari suffering late-race brake problems, the Argentinian ended the race a minute clear.

As the Formula One circus moved back to Silverstone, the scene of the first-ever Championship race, the Alfa stranglehold was finally broken. A Ferrari win had looked to be on the cards for some time and at last, in a thrilling race, the team managed to overhaul their Italian rivals and take a historic victory.

The race was also noted for the debut of the BRM team. Driven by Parnell and Peter Walker, the new British team did not make it to practice, but they were still allowed to start from the back of the grid.

RACE BY RACE DETAILS

ROUND 1 – SWITZERLAND
Race Juan Manuel Fangio
Pole Juan Manuel Fangio
Fastest lap Juan Manuel Fangio

ROUND 2 – INDIANAPOLIS
Race Lee Wallard
Pole Duke Nolan
Fastest lap Lee Wallard

ROUND 3 – BELGIUM
Race Giuseppe Farina
Pole Juan Manuel Fangio
Fastest lap Juan Manuel Fangio

ROUND 4 – FRANCE
Race Luigi Fagioli
Pole Juan Manuel Fangio
Fastest lap Juan Manuel Fangio

ROUND 5 – BRITAIN
Race José Froilan Gonzalez
Pole José Froilan Gonzalez
Fastest lap Giuseppe Farina

ROUND 6 – GERMANY
Race Alberto Ascari
Pole Alberto Ascari
Fastest lap Juan Manuel Fangio

Round 7 – ITALY
Race Alberto Ascari
Pole Juan Manuel Fangio
Fastest lap Giuseppe Farina

ROUND 8 – SPAIN
Race Juan Manuel Fangio
Pole Alberto Ascari
Fastest lap Juan Manuel Fangio

José Froilan Gonzalez in action at the British Grand Prix.

Alberto Ascari wins the Italian Grand Prix.

1951 DRIVERS' CHAMPIONSHIP

DRIVER	TEAM	POINTS
Juan Manuel Fangio	Alfa Romeo	31
Alberto Ascari	Ferrari	25
José Froilan Gonzalez	Ferrari	24
Giuseppe Farina	Alfa Romeo	19
Luigi Villoresi	Ferrari	15
Piero Taruffi	Ferrari	10
Lee Wallard	Kurtis-Kraft	9
Felice Bonetto	Alfa Romeo	7
Mike Nazaruk	Kurtis-Kraft	6
Reg Parnell	BRM/Ferrari	5
Luigi Fagioli	Alfa Romeo	4
Louis Rosier	Talbot-Lago	3
Consalvo Sanesi	Alfa Romeo	3
Andy Linden	Shermann	3
Jack McGrath	Kurtis-Kraft	2
Manuel Ayulo	Kurtis-Kraft	2
Bobby Ball	Schroeder	2
Emmanuel de Graffenried	Alfa Romeo	2
Yves Giraud-Cabantous	Talbot-Lago	2

Up front it was a Ferrari on pole. The Alfa team was shocked when Ferrari star Gonzalez topped the times in qualifying and planted himself firmly on pole position. Fangio was alongside him, but it was a telling chink in the Alfa armour, and a prelude to the team's performance on raceday.

Felice Bonetto made a stunning start in his Alfa, moving from seventh on the grid to sweep around the front row and take the lead. But Gonzalez and then Fangio moved, to head the field before the 10th lap.

The chase was on, and the battle was hard-fought. For once Gonzalez's Ferrari had the goods to do the job, and he re-passed Fangio's Alfa on lap 39. But the two were closely matched, and Fangio soon fought back.

The two leaders pitted, and Ascari, the senior member of the Ferrari team who had retired earlier, had the chance to take Gonzalez's car and go for the win. But in a selfless gesture, Ascari waved on Gonzalez as he took his team's maiden World Championship win.

The pressure from Fangio fell away in the latter stages as his compatriot Gonzalez won by 50 seconds.

Despite starting from the back of the grid, BRM finished a respectable fifth and seventh, with their heroic pilots suffering burns from overheating cockpits as they battled to drive their cars home.

Ferrari accepts mantle

By the time the Grand Prix teams reached the sixth race of the season in Germany, it was all change at the front with the previously all-conquering Alfas being pummelled into submission by Ferraris that had found a fantastic turn of pace. Five of the scarlet cars in the top six was enough to warn Alfa that their time at the top of Grand Prix racing was coming to an end, and it was only the genius of Fangio that prevented a Ferrari whitewash.

Farina pulled his Alfa off the grid quickest, despite the two Ferraris and Fangio being ahead of him – but he could not hold the lead for long, and he was passed by Fangio, Ascari, and Gonzalez before the end of the opening lap.

Local hero Paul Pietsch delighted the crowds by moving up to fifth behind the works Alfa cars, but then threw it all away with an off-track excursion which sent him to the back of the pack. Nine laps later he was off again, and this time it was serious – he was lucky to escape injury when his car flew backwards over an embankment.

The Alfas suffered overheating problems, and Farina retired to leave Fangio their only runner with the Ferraris. The Alfas had to have two pit-stops compared to Ferrari's one, and this proved to be the crucial factor in the race, as Ascari was left in the clear once all of the pit lane action was completed.

The Italian had to pit late in the race for a tyre change, but Fangio's Alfa was suffering engine problems and could not keep up enough pace to disturb leader Ascari, who headed a Ferrari 1-3-4-5-6.

The Ferrari team remained on a roll at their home Grand Prix in Italy, even though Alfa turned up to claim pole at Monza with a modified 159M.

The front row of the grid pitched the two top Alfas of Fangio and Farina alongside the Ferraris of Ascari and Gonzalez. BRM had turned up with three cars, but only Parnell made the start, and he was withdrawn with lubrication problems.

Fangio scorched into the lead from pole, but relinquished it to Ascari on lap four. They fought between themselves for some time before Fangio pitted for fresh tyres. With Farina and fellow Alfa driver Baron Emmanuel de Graffenried forced into retirement Gonzalez followed his team-mate in second place. But when Fangio's car began to misfire, Farina was left to fight Alfa's cause in Bonetto's car as he moved up to third. A leaking fuel tank ended any hopes of victory as Ascari took the chequered flag to delight his fans on home soil.

Although Fangio was still ahead in the Championship, the Ferraris were now hot on the trail of his slender three-point lead. One month after the Italian race, the Championship decider was battled out at the Pedralbes street circuit in a suburb of Barcelona. Considering its unusually long straight, the Ferrari team took the decision to go for thin, low-drag tyres, and it was a decision that ultimately cost them the World Championship title.

It was Ferrari, Alfa, Ferrari, Alfa on row one, and Ascari led from pole but Fangio took him on lap four and was never headed. The Ferraris, which had gone well in the last few races, suffered for their tactical decision and their cars had to make at least one time-consuming tyre stop due to the overheating of their reduced tread.

Ferrari's error proved crucial and paved the way for Fangio to cruise to victory for his first World Championship crown and Alfa's last.

SHORTS

The Swiss Grand Prix at Bremgarten was notable for the Championship debut of Britain's young hopeful Stirling Moss. However, it was a far from perfect race for the young charger as his HWM Formula Two car ran out of fuel on the last lap. He was classified eighth. Moss finished his first season in Formula One without a Championship point but his tenacity behind the wheel signalled there was much more to come.

Ferrari gambled with their choice of tyres in Spain – and it cost them the World Championship title.

Alberto Ascari

IN ALBERTO ASCARI'S COLOURFUL CAREER lies the template of most motorsport legend. A double World Champion, he was the only driver to compete consistently on the same level as Fangio in the early 1950s.

CAREER DETAILS

1918	Born 13 July, in Milan, Italy
1925	Learns of his father's death in French Grand Prix
1940	Makes transition from motorcycle to car racing. Drives the first Ferrari T815 in Mille Miglia and makes a big impression
1947	First experience of Grand Prix racing
1948	Victory in the San Remo Grand Prix rendered him hot property
1949	Begins year with victory for Maserati in Argentina, before switching with Luigi Villoresi to Ferrari and, with three Grand Prix wins immediately, the Ascari legend is born
1950	Leads Ferrari team in inaugural Formula One season, and finishes fifth
1952	Wins world title for Ferrari
1953	Wins consecutive world title for Ferrari Performs the unrepeated feat of scoring in nine consecutive Grands Prix
1955	Killed testing a Ferrari sportscar at Monza

Alberto Ascari became a legend in 1949 with Ferrari.

FORMULA ONE RECORD

Year	Team	Wins	Poles	Fast laps	Pts
1950	Ferrari	0	0	0	11
1951	Ferrari	2	2	0	25
1952	Ferrari	6	5	5	36
1953	Ferrari	5	6	4	34.5
1954	Maserati	0	0	1	-
	Ferrari	0	0	0	-
	Lancia	0	1	1	1
1955	Lancia	0	0	0	0

Alberto Ascari was the first successful second-generation Grand Prix driver. Like the Andretti, Fittipaldi, Hill and Villeneuve dynasties that were to follow, the son's career was inevitably seen in the context of the father's – poignantly so, in Ascari's case.

His father Antonio, a car dealer who became a star of the 1920s racing scene, died aged 36 in an accident at the Montlhery track near Paris while racing for Alfa Romeo in the 1925 French Grand Prix. Alberto was six. Thereafter he grew up to be obsessed with his father's fate and with notions of predetermination and coincidence. He relied on a lucky helmet, lived to particular routines and looked to St Anthony for courage (the saint also died at 36).

In 1955 Alberto died, just like his father, on the 26th of a month, at the same age to the month, when testing a sports car at Monza. He had been wearing a borrowed helmet. Two long skid marks led up to the scene of his fatal impact, but the reason behind his loss of control remains a mystery.

Posthumously tagged Mr Superstition, the genial Italian was nicknamed "Cicco", meaning "chubby", throughout his career. He began his racing career on Bianchi motorcycles in his late teens. In 1940 he progressed to cars, competing in the curtailed Mille Miglia road race for Ferrari whose team patron, Enzo Ferrari, a former team-mate of his father, entrusted him with one of his new Tipo 815 straight-eight 1.5-litre sports racers.

In 1947 he made his debut in Grand Prix racing and by the time modern-day Formula One was established in 1950, he had won several Grand Prix. "Like my father, like all those who embrace this career, I only obey my instinct. Without it, I would not know how to live, I would not succeed in making any sense of my days," he said on the inevitability of his racing life.

An obvious choice to lead the Ferrari team in the 1950 World Championship, he finished the season fifth. In 1951 he won the German and Italian Grands Prix in the Ferrari 375 and finished the season runner-up to Juan Manuel Fangio. By this stage it was clear his sheer speed (Mike Hawthorn reckoned he was faster than Fangio) and sublime skill at the wheel would render him the only driver consistently on the same plane of performance as the Argentinian.

"When he put his goggles on, those warm and friendly eyes suddenly became like steel, intense and concentrated."

Fellow-Italian driver Luigi Villoresi admires the amiable Ascari.

"When he put his goggles on, those warm and friendly eyes suddenly became like steel, intense and concentrated," remarked fellow-Italian driver Luigi Villoresi. Lining up for the start, his competitors could only hope he would suffer a racing misfortune because he was notably less impressive in adversity.

"He was a man who had to lead from the start. In that position he was hard to overtake, almost impossible to beat. Alberto was secure when playing the hare. That was when his style was at its most superb. In second place, or further back, he was less secure," opined Enzo Ferrari.

In 1952 – with a change in the rules that meant Formula One was run to two-litre regulations – Ferrari were in a strong position. Alberto missed the first race, in which team-mate Piero Taruffi was victorious in the Ferrari 500, but won six races and his first World Championship title. In the absence of Fangio (out for seven races owing to severe neck injuries), Giuseppe Farina and Taruffi were his rivals.

In 1953 Alberto blitzed the opposition at the first three races and went on to secure a consecutive world title. Of the 33 races entered in 1952 and 1953, Ferrari won a total of 30. Ascari, the double World Champion, won 19. In 1954 Ascari and Luigi Villoresi left Ferrari for Lancia – a move often described as the one of the biggest motor racing mistakes of all time. He raced for Maserati, to whom he had been loaned until the Lancia D50 was ready. It was not until early 1955 that the new car became available. At the Monaco Grand Prix Ascari was involved in another incident that posthumously denigrated his reputation for racing skill. In an incident that was immortalized in John Frankenheimer's 1966 movie *Grand Prix*, Ascari had to be fished out of Monaco harbour when his Lancia slid sideways and crashed through hay bales into the water.

Alberto was troubled by a foreboding. "My game is going wrong – the star is setting," he said to Fangio, following that underwater experience. Four days later he perished in a freak crash at Monza while "having a go" in the three-litre Ferrari sports car he was hoping to share with his protégé Eugenio Castelotti in the following weekend's Supercortemaggiore event. After four slow laps, the car overturned at the sweeping Curva Vialone left-hander, and Ascari was killed.

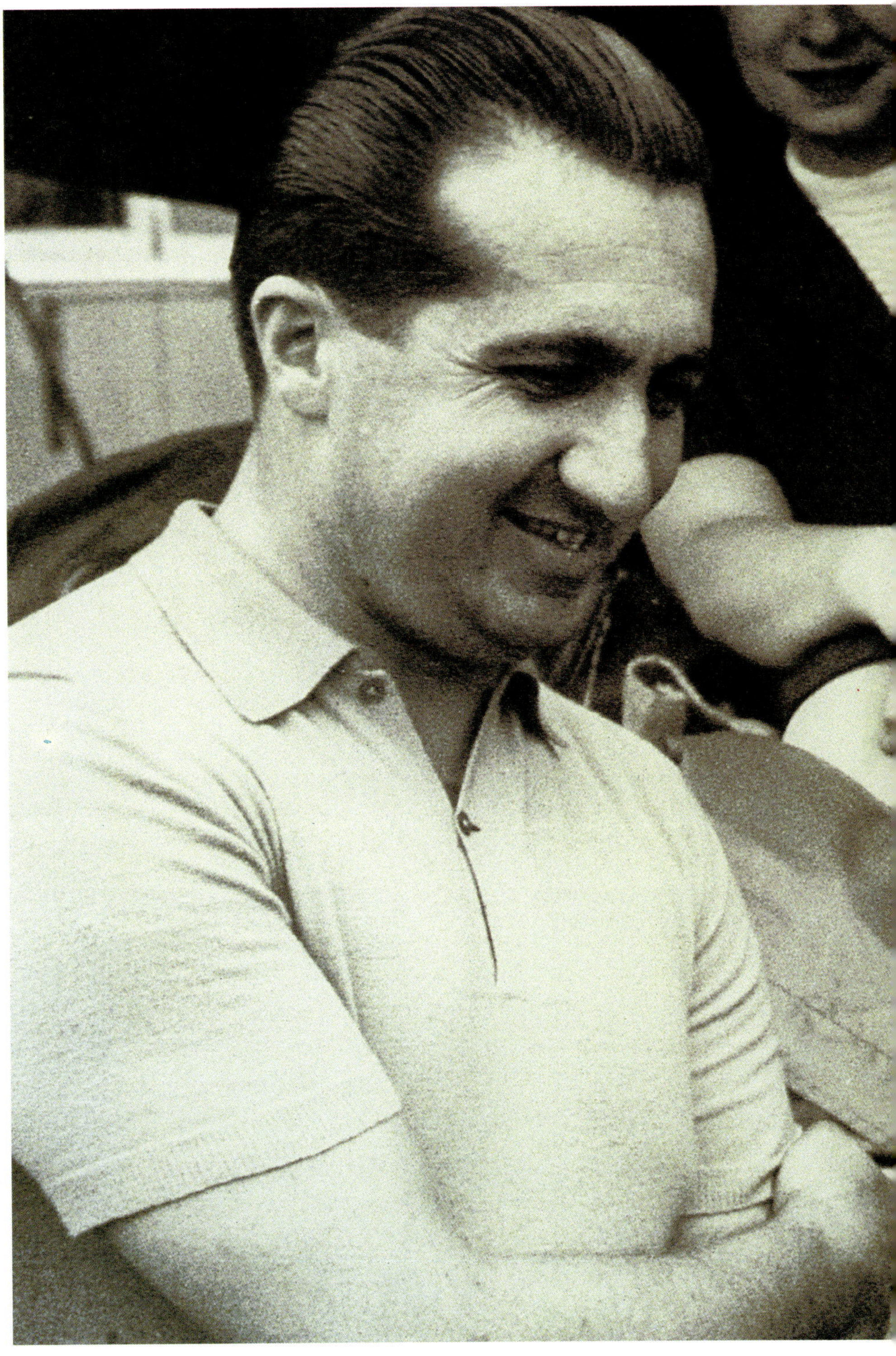

"My game is going wrong," said Alberto Ascari, four days before his death in an accident at Monza.

1952

Ascari wins one-sided race

TALKING POINT

AWESOME ASCARI

Alberto Ascari ruined the 1952 season! There was nothing he could do to stop it. His absolute dominance made races monotonous and predictable, and his clearly superior driving coupled with the sabbatical of reigning World Champion Juan Manuel Fangio left Formula One in serious need of some competition for the master.

The Italian could do nothing wrong during a season in which, race after race, he turned up, took pole, then won the race by a country mile. He was even brave enough to travel to America and take on the might of the continent in their own backyard and, although that trip could be seen as a blot on his copybook, he was unbeatable on the tracks he knew.

With the scoring system of the time he could only count his four best races, and with eight points for a win and one for fastest lap, there were 36 points available. He took victory in every World Championship event he entered on his home continent, and ended the season with a perfect score.

The withdrawal of Alfa from the series left a major void as Ferrari lost their only true challenger and the FIA's fledgling World Championship series was in danger of falling apart.

Something had to be done to expand the grid and restore some chance of competitive racing, and the FIA's solution was a change in regulations which would make it possible for more current cars to enter. They turned the World Championship over to their Formula Two category, and allowed two-litre (rather than 4.5-litre) unblown or 750cc (as opposed to 1.5-litre) supercharged machinery on to the grid.

A broken neck and serious back injuries sustained in a crash in a non-championship race at Monza denied Fangio the chance to retain his title and left Ascari and Ferrari with a licence to dominate.

Ferrari missed key personnel at the opening race of the season in Berne. The Italian favourites had snapped up Giuseppe Farina, and originally planned to field an unchanged line-up of Ascari and Villoresi in their other two cars – but only Farina made it to Switzerland.

Villoresi had been injured in a road accident, and Ascari had become the first major European top-level racer to cross the Atlantic and have a crack at the Brickyard classic in Indianapolis. Once again, the race schedules were tight, and his American challenge meant he would be forced to sit out the first Championship race of the season.

Ferrari chose Piero Taruffi and Andre Simon as stand-ins, and they were not disappointed as Taruffi went on to win the event. Farina slotted his Ferrari 500 on pole with Taruffi alongside, but it was not to be a one-two-three for the *scuderia* as Robert Manzon pulled his Gordoni up to the front row.

Behind were two more Ferraris, and the grid was awash with red. Peter Collins put his Alta-engined HWM on the third row, alongside the second Gordoni of Jean Behra and Baron Emmanuel de Graffenried in an old Maserati. Stirling Moss, who had made his Championship debut in a BRM the season before, was way back on the fourth row.

Farina led off the line from Taruffi until the team leader's Ferrari gave up the ghost, and the inevitable Scuderia victory was left for his team-mate. Farina took over Simon's Ferrari, and took it all the way up to second before that broke down too, and it was clearly not the Italian's day.

Piero Taruffi wins the British Grand Prix at Silverstone on 20 July 1952.

Luigi Villoresi pictured in his car.

Fischer ended up second in a privately-entered Ferrari, the only man to remain un-lapped by the flying Taruffi.

The series moved next to Indianapolis with a top European contender finally prepared to try his luck across the Atlantic. However, the Ferrari 375 of Ascari was clearly underpaced and he struggled to get to grips with the oval circuit, and once again, the Indy 500 failed to prove important in the overall Championship standings.

While Fred Agabashian topped the times in qualifying, Ascari was languishing in midfield with a lap speed average 4mph slower than the Americans' top man. Jack McGrath took the lead from third on the grid, but the Fuel Injection Special of Bill Vukovich soon moved up to the front – a position he would hold for nearly the entire race before disaster struck.

Just nine laps from the end, the unfortunate Californian's steering failed, he careered up the banking and smashed heavily into the wall.

By now, Ascari's European challenge had gone from dim and distant to non-existent after his Ferrari, which he had pulled up to ninth, suffered wheel failure on lap 40, and Vukovich's demise left Troy Ruttman to take an unexpected victory in his Agajanian Special.

Back in Europe, the usual suspects were taking wins all over the continent in non-championship races, and Ferrari's dominance was again never challenged when they arrived at Spa-Francorchamps in mid-June.

Taruffi headed an all-conquering front row for the Italian masters, with Farina and Ascari alongside, and the Gordonis of Jean Behra and Manzon sitting behind them hardly looked likely to provide a threat.

But Taruffi made a poor start and, struggling to cope with the wet conditions, he dropped right down the field. The other pair of Ferraris was also slow off the line, and no match for Behra's skills in the wet as the Gordoni moved up to first.

Stirling Moss had jumped the HWM ship to join ERA in Belgium, and made an awesome start. He drove a fantastic first half-lap before he crashed.

Ascari and Farina soon passed the Gordoni to take the lead, and Ascari was never challenged. Nor was Farina in second, and when Taruffi took Behra on lap 13 it looked an easy one-two-three for Ferrari. But Taruffi spun soon afterwards, and Behra hit him to take the pair of them out of the race.

It was left to Manzon to uphold Gordoni honour in third, while Championship new boy Mike Hawthorn nursed his fuel-leaking Cooper-Bristol to a credible fourth place.

Ferrari still on top

Les Essarts near Rouen was visited by the World Championship for the first time as the battle reached the fourth round, but although the circuit was magnificent, the race was not.

The crowd had hoped to witness the new works Maserati team taking the challenge to Ferrari, but when they did not turn up, the result was never in question. The Ferraris took a one-two-three on the grid, and the race. Ascari took a flag-to-flag victory, and his team-mates stayed in grid order until the end.

It was a dull race but the final positions do not tell the whole story. There was now clearly dominance within the Ferrari team, and in France Ascari

RACE BY RACE DETAILS

ROUND 1 – SWITZERLAND
Race Piero Taruffi
Pole Giuseppe Farina
Fastest Lap Piero Taruffi

ROUND 2 – INDIANAPOLIS
Race Troy Ruttman
Pole Freddie Agabashian
Fastest Lap Bill Vukovich

ROUND 3 – BELGIUM
Race Alberto Ascari
Pole Alberto Ascari
Fastest Lap Alberto Ascari

ROUND 4 – FRANCE
Race Alberto Ascari
Pole Alberto Ascari
Fastest Lap Alberto Ascari

ROUND 5 – BRITAIN
Race Alberto Ascari
Pole Giuseppe Farina
Fastest Lap Alberto Ascari

ROUND 6 – GERMANY
Race Alberto Ascari
Pole Alberto Ascari
Fastest Lap Alberto Ascari

ROUND 7 – HOLLAND
Race Alberto Ascari
Pole Alberto Ascari
Fastest Lap Alberto Ascari

ROUND 8 – ITALY
Race Alberto Ascari
Pole Alberto Ascari/José Froilan Gonzalez
Fastest Lap Alberto Ascari

truly showed his skills and speed. He finished having lapped not only all the other works teams and the privateers, but both team-mates on his way to an all-conquering victory.

Even behind the Ferraris it remained as expected, with the two Gordonis taking fourth and fifth, but the World Championship badly needed an injection of competition.

The World Championship had been dominated by the Italian muscle of Ferrari and Alfa since its conception in 1950, but the British Grand Prix gave the home fans something to shout about as Connaughts and Coopers came into force and gave the crowd hope of home success with some competitive-looking grid positions.

Ken Downing put his Connaught on the second row alongside the Cooper-Bristols of Parnell and Hawthorn. However, the formidable scarlet wall of Ferrari proved too much for the British hopefuls to get past as the Italians remained to the fore.

For once it was Farina ahead of Ascari on the front row of the grid and the crowd sensed that the seemingly-unbeatable Ascari might have some competition. But they were wrong, and it was Ascari who led Farina into the first corner as the cars got away.

Taruffi had a poor start yet again, and found himself in the unacceptable position of fighting through the Cooper-Bristols and Connaughts which were not even a match for the Ferrari.

Unsurprisingly he made it up to third, and when his team-mate Farina hit trouble and was forced to pit for some new sparkplugs he progressed up to second. Dennis Poore's Connaught was now up to third and the strong British showing was backed up by Mike Hawthorn's Cooper-Bristol. When Poore had to stop for fuel, the English gentleman Hawthorn was promoted to third, and went on to take his first podium two laps behind Ascari.

Germany brought another Italian challenger to take on the all-conquering Ferraris. Maserati had turned up with one of their new A6 GCMs for Bonetto, whilst there were another two in the field for privateers.

Bonetto, though, could only manage tenth on the grid for the Maserati debut, and with the British manufacturers not making the trip over it was left to the Gordonis of Maurice Trintignant and Behra, who had returned after being sidelined by a shoulder injury, to take the challenge to the Ferraris once more.

SHORTS

The Italian teams turned up at Monza – the 1952 season's finale – in droves, eager for a piece of the action in their home Grand Prix. The field was so oversubscribed that the organizers introduced a qualifying limit for the first time in a World Championship race. Eventually, just 24 of the 35 entries were granted a place on the grid with Ferrari – and Alberto Ascari – dominating proceedings.

Maserati disaster

Ascari and Farina were once again at the top of the grid, and they led the race from start to finish. The inconspicuous Maserati debut turned into a disaster right off the start-line when Bonetto spun and was disqualified for outside assistance.

It was not all plain sailing for Ascari, and when he hit trouble midway through the race he was forced to pit and let Farina past. Ascari, though, was not to be denied, and when he got back out he rapidly closed on his Ferrari team-mate and took victory by

The Connaughts in action at the British Grand Prix.

The Coopers are put through their paces at Silverstone.

an unusually slim margin of 14 seconds.

Taruffi got past the Gordonis to make it a Ferrari one-two-three, but he ran into trouble on the last lap and ended the race behind the privateer Ferrari of Rudolf Fischer, however all eyes were focused on the man at the top of Ferrari's tree. Ascari, in taking his fourth win of the season, had won the first title for the Italian marque with three races remaining, and his domination continued during the rest of the season.

Though it was a small field which turned up for the first World Championship race to be held in Holland, all but one of the major players were there. Maserati, after an inauspicious debut in Germany, had declined to turn up in an official capacity, although there were several of the cars present in privateer guise.

There was nothing anyone could do to prevent newly-crowned World Champion Ascari from underlining his superiority once again as he took a flag-to-flag victory and headed yet another Ferrari whitewash.

Ascari and Fangio double-act

The series was crying out for some competition for the Ferraris, but once again the other drivers were unable to prevent the awesome double-act of Ascari and Fangio from taking up their usual places on the front row of the grid.

The British teams were back in action again, and Hawthorn's Cooper-Bristol somehow managed to get up to the front row ahead of the returning Villoresi's Ferrari, which occupied the second row alongside Trintignant's Gordoni.

Hawthorn was on top form and out-dragged Farina off the line to slot in second behind Ascari's scarlet Ferrari. It was not to last long and although Hawthorn was the best of the rest he was still some way off the pace of the top trio.

Once the Ferraris were past the Englishman, who was helpless to do anything to stop them, the race turned into an absolute procession. The Ferraris completed a demonstration run, as they finished over three and a half minutes ahead of Hawthorn's Cooper-Bristol to show themselves a class above the rest.

Italy and Monza provided the venue for the final race of the season, and the home fans turned up in droves to see their beloved Ferrari team take an inevitable victory on home soil. Ferrari ran five factory cars, while Maserati were back with three, ready to put their disappointing debut behind them and make a fresh start.

The Italian teams had flocked to Monza for a piece of the action, and the field was so oversubscribed that the organizers introduced a qualifying limit for the first time in a World Championship Grand Prix.

Only 24 of the 35 entries were granted a place on the grid, but it basically meant the race lost most of the old privateers, and up front it was the same cast in the same roles. Ascari, Farina and Villoresi saw to it that Ferrari were in their usual positions when the curtain went up, while Trintignant's Gordoni played a side role on the front row.

Gonzalez put his Maserati on the second row, and he gave the team's dominant countrymen a fright by getting around the whole of the front row and making the first corner his. He stayed ahead until a slow pit stop let Ascari by to control the rest of the race.

Villoresi had also passed the pitted Maserati, but Gonzalez managed to reel him in, and spoiled the Ferrari party by taking second for his rival team. But even that could not hide the fact that it had been a season dominated by the scarlet Ferraris, and by taking his sixth victory in a row Ascari proved he was truly a worthy World Champion.

1952 DRIVERS' CHAMPIONSHIP

DRIVER	TEAM	POINTS
Alberto Ascari	Ferrari	36
Giuseppe Farina	Ferrari	24
Piero Taruffi	Ferrari	22
Rudi Fischer	Ferrari	10
Mike Hawthorn	Cooper-Bristol	10
Robert Manzon	Gordoni	9
Luigi Villoresi	Ferrari	8
Troy Ruttman	Kurtis-Kraft	8
Jose Froilan Gonzalez	Maserati	6.5
Jean Behra	Gordoni	6
Jim Rathmann	Kurtis-Kraft	6
Sam Hanks	Kuzma	4
Ken Wharton	Frazer	3
Dennis Poore	Connaught	3
Duane Carter	Lesovsky	3
Alan Brown	Cooper-Bristol	2
Paul Frere	HWM	2
Maurice Trintignant	Gordoni	2
Eric Thompson	Connaught	2
Felice Bonetto	Maserati	2
Art Cross	Kurtis-Kraft	2
Bill Vukovich	Kurtsi-Kraft	1

Juan Manuel Fangio

JUAN MANUEL FANGIO came to be known as "The Maestro". For many the greatest racing driver there has ever been, he won five World Championships in a career that spanned a mere eight full seasons.

CAREER DETAILS

1911 Born 24 June, in Balcarce, Argentina
1938 Begins career in road races in Argentina
1948 Travels to Europe and starts racing in single-seaters
1949 Despite doubts over safety he shows great talent and wins Libre races
1950 Drives for Alfa Romeo in inaugural F1 season and finishes runner-up to team-mate Nicola Farina, winning three races.
1951 Takes first World Championship with three wins in seven races
1952 Suffers a broken neck and misses season
1953 Moves to Maserati and is again second to an Italian, this time Alberto Ascari of Ferrari
1954 Joins Mercedes from Maserati after two races, but still goes on to clinch second World Championship, winning six races
1955 World Champion again, with four wins from six races
1956 Following Mercedes' withdrawal joins Ferrari, his fourth team, and wins title again
1957 Returns to Maserati and records what remains an unprecedented fourth consecutive World Championship, his fifth overall
1958 Following Maserati's withdrawal from F1 he drives in just two races, and retires following French GP, finishing fourth

FORMULA ONE RECORD

Year	Team	Wins	Poles	Fast laps	Pts
1950	Alfa Romeo	3	4	3	27
1951	Alfa Romeo	3	4	5	31
1952	DID NOT RACE				
1953	Maserati	1	2	2	28
1954	Maserati	2	1	0	–
	M. Benz	4	4	3	42
1955	M. Benz	4	5	3	40
1956	Ferrari	3	5	4	30
1957	Maserati	4	4	2	40
1958	Maserati	0	1	1	7

He won 24 out of 49 races he started and was in pole position 27 times. Alain Prost and Ayrton Senna both enjoyed victory in just over a quarter of their races; Fangio won nearly half of his – and he was 39 when he began his Formula One career. He remains the only five-times World Champion and a much-loved figure. As John Cooper said: "The great thing about him is that he won five world titles in four different cars and he never had a row with anyone."

Fangio, the son of Italian immigrants, grew up in Argentina in the inter-war period when cars where still far from common. His first love was football, but his fascination with cars grew when he began work as a mechanic. His introduction to racing came when he worked on one of the garage customers' Chevrolet. Over the next seven years he competed against Oscar Galvez for top national honours. After completing compulsory military service, Fangio opened up his own garage and started driving in road races in Argentina. The Second World War ended that.

In 1947 two Italian racing aces Achille Varzi and Luigi Villoresi arrived in Argentina and the Argentine Automobile Club bought two Maseratis to race against them. Fangio was entrusted with one and showed great aptitude.

Backed by both Maserati and the Peron government, he was sent to Europe in 1949 to race single-seaters, and enjoyed much success in Libre classes. He stunned Europeans by winning in San Remo, Perpignan, Marseilles, Pau, Albi and Monza in a Maserati 4CLT. Fangio's skill – if one can deconstruct something so sublime – was to remain unflustered, out of trouble, and call upon reserves of blinding speed if necessary.

In 1950, the birth of the Formula One World Championship saw Alfa Romeo offer Fangio a drive in their team, alongside Nino Farina. The team won six out of the seven races that first season (the other race was the Indianapolis 500), but it was 45-year-old Farina who came out on top of the 39-year-old Fangio by just three points.

A year later, Fangio was not to be denied, winning the world title ahead of Alberto Ascari's Ferrari. The team from Maranello were looking increasingly dangerous, and when Alfa pulled out of Formula One at the end of 1951 Fangio did not hesitate to join them. However he suffered a broken neck in a crash at Monza and sat out the season.

Fangio returned to action in 1953, back with Maserati, but Ascari and the Ferraris were almost unbeatable and second place for Fangio was a supreme performance. The arrival of Mercedes promised much, but Fangio did not join them until

Juan Manuel Fangio gets a kiss from his wife in 1956.

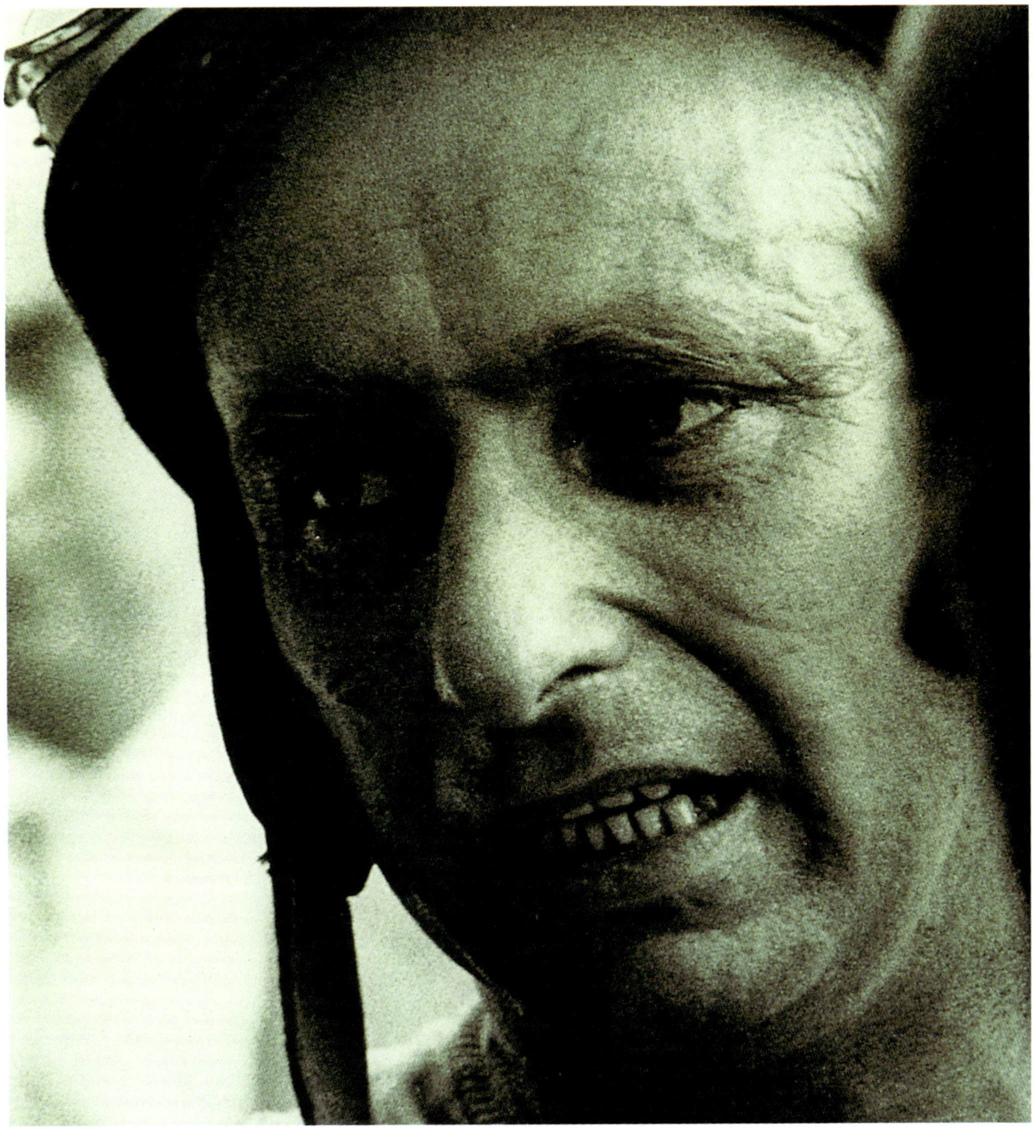

Juan Manuel Fangio was a fearless driver, and lived to the age of 84.

"In my day, it was 75 per cent car and mechanic, 25 per cent driver and luck. Today it's 95 per cent car."

the 1954 season was already under way, having driven the first two races for Maserati. The German cars proved very fast and Fangio went on to claim his second World Championship.

With Mercedes dominant again in 1955 Fangio and his team-mate Stirling Moss finished one-two in the Championship, but the German team withdrew before the 1956 season in the wake of the Le Mans disaster. Fangio, now in a Ferrari, and Moss, in a Maserati, finished one-two again, with Fangio securing the title by just three points.

The top two in the World Championship remained unchanged for a third season, and with different teams again. Fangio returned to Maserati while Moss moved to Vanwall. It was another fantastic season for Fangio whose fifth World Championship was to be his last.

The merry-go-round of teams continued in 1958. With Maserati now pulling out, Fangio drove in just a couple of races, at home in Argentina and in France. His car was not really competitive, so much so that Mike Hawthorn could have lapped him on the final lap, but did not do so out of deference to The Maestro who, at 47, finished fourth in both races.

With so many of his friends and rivals killed in crashes, it speaks volumes for Fangio's talent that he was able to survive so long. He drove only as fast as he needed to win and was the most successful driver in Formula One's formative years, helping to make it the great spectator sport it is today. His record of finishing first or second in every season he completed will probably never be matched.

Fangio retired to Argentina and set up business in Buenos Aires. Considered a great sportsman, he carried himself with a dignified air. "You must always aim to be the best, but you must never believe that you are," he said. Juan Manuel Fangio died on 17 July 1994, at the age of 84.

1953
Championship goes global

Alberto Ascari with the World Championship trophy.

TALKING POINT

TRAGEDY STRIKES

The 1953 season started under the shadow of tragedy with the first deaths in Formula One as nine spectators were killed and 40 injured when Giuseppe Farina lost control of his Ferrari after 30 laps of the season-opening Argentinian Grand Prix.

Farina had swerved to miss a spectator who had wandered on to the Buenos Aires track and ploughed into the bulging crowd, who in the early days were not protected by fencing or tyre walls.

The deaths were not Farina's fault, as thousands of fans had turned up at the circuit after Argentine president Juan Peron had attended the race on 18 January and declared entry free for everyone.

More spectators were fortunate to escape injury when wheels fell off two other cars in the eventful race.

Alberto Ascari, driving a Ferrari 500, dominated the 1953 season as the World Championship at last justified its tag as a worldwide sport with the season starting in the South American country of Argentina.

As in previous seasons the campaign featured a race at the Indianapolis Speedway but not all the top drivers from Europe travelled across the Atlantic to compete in the United States event.

Ascari won five of the eight races, excluding Indianapolis, to win his second successive world crown and the great Juan Manuel Fangio, making his return driving for Maserati after injuries had forced him to miss the whole of the previous season, was left in his dust.

Ascari was joined at Ferrari by Mike Hawthorn, Luigi Villoresi and Giuseppe Farina, while Maserati were spearheaded by Fangio, José Froilan Gonzalez and Onofre Marimon.

Spectator deaths

The only serious constructor competitors to Ferrari and Maserati were Gordoni, but Cooper Osca, HWM, Connaught, Veritas, AFM, EMW and BMW also had cars and drivers in the Championship.

Ascari got off to the best possible start at the tragedy-marred Argentinian Grand Prix as he raced to victory in hot conditions to defeat the challenge of local hero Fangio.

Nine spectators had died before Ascari took the chequered flag after his Ferrari team-mate Farina had ploughed into a packed crowd to avoid a spectator on the track.

Ascari had taken pole position for the race and lined up on the front row with Fangio, Farina and Villoresi. He quickly pulled away from the rest of the front row and dominated the race from start to finish to take the first win of the season.

At this time the World Championship was still being run to Formula Two regulations, but Maserati had an improved package and had shown promise the previous year. Needless to add, they were disappointed not to see bright prospect Fangio take the chequered flag in his homeland.

Fangio did not even finish, as he retired after 37 laps of the 97-lap race due to a fault with the propeller shaft in his car. Villoresi followed Ascari over the line in second place, while Fangio's Maserati team-mate Gonzalez was third.

Briton Hawthorn, newly-signed to the Ferrari team, showed his potential as he drove a comfortable race to hold off the challenge of Oscar Galvez in a Maserati to finish fourth in Buenos Aires.

The Formula One World Championship moved on to the second round in the United States as the prestigious endurance test of the Indianapolis 500 played its part in the season.

The Kurtis-Kraft cars battled it out at the front as the Europeans once again chose to remain within their own continent, and Bill Vukovich won after starting from pole and dominating the race in blisteringly hot conditions.

In fact, the end-of-May temperatures were so high on the track that one driver, Carl Scarborough, died of heat exhaustion after the stamina-zapping 200-lap race. Another racer, Andy Linden, exemplified the steamy conditions at the famous Brickyard circuit when he pulled out of the race after 107 laps and refused to resume because his cockpit was too hot. The race was also marred by five accidents as the drivers struggled to keep their cars on a track which contained a cramped 33 cars on the starting grid.

Five months after competing in Argentina, Ascari and his fellow top-level drivers returned to the World Championship with the third round in Holland at a recently-resurfaced Zandvoort.

Ascari stamps authority

Ascari, who had competed in some non-championship events across Europe while the World Championship continued in America, immediately stamped his authority on the series as he raced from pole to flag to claim a commanding victory.

Ascari's Ferrari team-mate Farina, now recovered following his crash in Argentina, pushed his colleague close and was just nine seconds behind Ascari as the cars crossed the finish line on a circuit where the surface had crumbled badly after the resurfacing work.

Ferrari driver Villoresi had challenged for second place, but he was forced to retire after 67 laps of the 90-lap race with a throttle problem.

Hawthorn again put in a steady performance and maintained his battle with Gonzalez as he finished fourth. Gonzalez retired after 22 laps with a rear axle problem but took over Maserati team-mate Felice Bonetto's car to beat Hawthorn to third place.

Gonzalez's Maserati team-mate Fangio still did not look back to his best and the Argentine driver failed to finish his second successive race as he retired in Holland after 36 laps with a rear axle fault.

Ascari won his third race of the season and ninth on the trot two weeks after the Dutch Grand Prix as the World Championship moved on to Belgium and the Spa-Francorchamps circuit. The Italian driver for once failed to gain pole as Fangio started to show promise to line up first on the grid.

Fangio's Maserati team-mate Gonzalez was also on the front row and he took the lead for the first 11 laps before his throttle pedal broke, to allow Fangio to take the lead in a Grand Prix for the first time during the season. But his spell leading the field lasted just two laps as mechanical problems again hindered the Maserati. This time the car's engine blew and the Argentine driver was forced to take over Belgian team-mate Johnnie Claes' car to rejoin the race.

In the meantime Ascari had taken full advantage and went on to dominate the race and take the chequered flag from team-mate Villoresi, who had started fifth on the grid and steered clear of trouble.

Fangio pushed the Ferraris hard and was on

Mike Hawthorn after winning the French Grand Prix.

RACE BY RACE DETAILS

ROUND 1 – ARGENTINA
Race Alberto Ascari
Pole Alberto Ascari
Fastest lap Alberto Ascari

ROUND 2 – INDIANAPOLIS
Race Bill Vukovich
Pole Bill Vukovich
Fastest lap N/A

ROUND 3 – HOLLAND
Race Alberto Ascari
Pole Alberto Ascari
Fastest lap Luigi Villoresi

ROUND 4 – BELGIUM
Race Alberto Ascari
Poled Juan Manuel Fangio
Fastest lap José Froilan Gonzalez

ROUND 5 – FRANCE
Race Mike Hawthorn
Pole Alberto Ascari
Fastest lap Juan Manuel Fangio

ROUND 6 – GREAT BRITAIN
Race Alberto Ascari
Pole Alberto Ascari
Fastest lap José Froilan Gonzalez

ROUND 7 – GERMANY
Race Giuseppe Farina
Pole Alberto Ascari
Fastest lap Alberto Ascari

ROUND 8 – SWITZERLAND
Race Alberto Ascari
Pole Juan Manuel Fangio
Fastest lap Alberto Ascari

ROUND 9 – ITALY
Race Juan Manuel Fangio
Pole Alberto Ascari
Fastest lap Juan Manuel Fangio

Juan Manuel Fangio celebrates after winning the Italian Grand Prix.

SHORTS

The Indianapolis 500 was dominated by extreme May temperatures that were so high on the track one driver, Carl Scarborough, died of heat exhaustion after the stamina-zapping 200-lap race. Another racer, Andy Linden, exemplified the steamy conditions at the Brickyard circuit when he pulled out of the race after 107 laps and refused to resume because his cockpit was too hot. The race was won by Bill Vukovich.

course to finish third before a high-speed crash on the final lap of the 36-lap race when his steering failed and sent him off the circuit. Marimon was classified third in his Maserati.

Hawthorn makes history

Hawthorn had once again gone about his business quietly in Belgium and finished sixth. But in July he made history in the next round of the Championship as he became the first British driver to win a Grand Prix in the French round of the series at Reims.

In his Ferrari, Hawthorn had a titanic battle with Fangio to deny the future five-time World Champion a win in what turned out to be one of the best races of all time.

The lead changed hands no fewer than 13 times between Hawthorn, Fangio and Gonzalez before the Briton eventually took the chequered flag of the 60-lap race by just one second from runner-up Fangio. Ascari was for once a bystander, despite having taken pole position, as Hawthorn and Fangio started from seventh and fourth places respectively and chased early leader Gonzalez, who had started with a light fuel load.

Gonzalez led for 29 laps before being forced to pit and Fangio took the lead and started his epic fight with Hawthorn over the remaining 31 laps. Hawthorn eventually won by slipstreaming Fangio and taking the Argentine just ahead of the finish.

Gonzalez finished third and Ascari was fourth, ahead of his Ferrari colleagues Farina and Villoresi.

Hawthorn's victory came at the perfect time; the Championship moved on to his homeland as Silverstone hosted the British Grand Prix in July, with spectator interest very high.

Expectation levels were growing for Hawthorn, but he failed to deliver and was left to reflect on a fifth-place finish as Ascari went on to win again. The Italian finished the 90-lap race a minute clear.

Fangio had led from the start in his Maserati, but after driving wide at the first corner, Ascari slipped through into the lead and never looked back as he was never headed up to the chequered flag.

Farina finished third to claim another podium finish ahead of the Maserati of Gonzalez, who had suffered an unfortunate race. After starting from second on the grid, Gonzalez was forced to come in by the marshals as he leaked oil on to the track.

It dropped him back to fourth place, and despite a spirited fightback the Ferrari of Farina overtook him in the closing laps.

August saw the Championship arrive at the Nurburgring in Germany for the seventh round of the series and once again Ascari was the centre of attention.

The Italian took pole position for the race, which was missing the Maserati of Gonzalez who had injured himself in a sports car race in the Portuguese capital of Lisbon the previous weekend.

But after leading the first four laps, Ascari lost a

José Froilan Gonzalez in a Maserati at the British Grand Prix on 18 July 1953.

1953 DRIVERS' CHAMPIONSHIP

DRIVER	TEAM	POINTS
Alberto Ascari	Ferrari	34.5
Juan Manuel Fangio	Maserati	28
Giuseppe Farina	Ferrari	26
Mike Hawthorn	Ferrari	19
Luigi Villoresi	Ferrari	17
Jose Froilan Gonzalez	Maserati	13.5
Bill Vukovich	Kurtis-Kraft	9
Emmanuel de Graffenried	Maserati	7
Felice Bonetto	Maserati	6.5
Art Cross	Kurtis-Kraft	6
Onofre Marimon	Maserati	4
Maurice Trintignant	Gordoni	4
Sam Hanks	Kurtis-Kraft	2
Duane Carter	Kurtis-Kraft	2
Oscar Galvez	Maserati	2
Hermann Lang	Maserati	2
Jack McGrath	Kurtis-Kraft	2
Fred Agabashian	Kurtis-Kraft	1.5
Paul Russo	Kurtis-Kraft	1.5

wheel on track and was forced to limp back to the pits, losing places along the way. He rejoined after a wheel change but then suffered an engine failure and had to take over team-mate Villoresi's car.

But his troubles were not over, as smoke billowed from the Ferrari in the latter stages and he came home in a disappointing eighth place.

Meanwhile, at the front of the field, Fangio and Hawthorn had once again embarked on a battle for the lead after their exploits in France.

As the pair fought neck-and-neck, Ascari and Hawthorn's team-mate Farina sneaked up, took the lead and then went on to dominate and bring home another Ferrari winner in the 18-lap race. Fangio was second and Hawthorn third.

Ascari victorious

Ascari clinched his second World Championship in the next race in Switzerland as there was no sign of Ferrari team orders at the Bremgarten circuit.

Fangio had claimed pole position, but Ascari was alongside him on the front row as he qualified second. The Italian driver took the lead from the start and seemed destined to cruise to victory and the title before fate made him work for the crown.

After leading for 40 laps, Ascari's engine started to misfire and he was forced to come into the pits. That gifted the lead to Ferrari team-mate Farina, who had taken second place from Fangio after his Maserati suffered valve problems. Fangio had battled on before taking over team-mate Bonetto's car on lap 29 as he fought to regain the lost ground.

Ascari rejoined the race in fourth place behind Farina, Hawthorn and Marimon, and after the latter retired with an engine problem on lap 46 he rose to third behind his two Ferrari team-mates.

Now in sight of another world crown, Ascari used his pure driving ability to reel in and overtake his team-mates to take the chequered flag and a deserved second Championship.

The season-ending race in Italy in September had a sense of anti-climax, with the title already in the safe grasp of Ascari, but in typical Formula One fashion the action continued unabated until the final race was over.

Fangio, for so long in the exhaust smoke of Ascari, at last won a Grand Prix as he dived through the last lap carnage involving the Italian to take Maserati's first win of the campaign.

Ascari had taken pole for the race, with Fangio second and Farina third in qualifying. The lead changed hands no less than 20 times between the three drivers. But with the chequered flag in sight and the perfect end to a season seconds away, Ascari was caught by Farina at the last corner and with both drivers side by side Ascari spun. Farina went wide on to the grass while Marimon ploughed into Ascari with nowhere to go. During the chaos around him, Fangio weaved through the accident to take the win. It was a dramatic end to a season which in so many ways exemplified the excitement and action which make Formula One a special sport.

Giuseppe 'Nino' Farina

CAREER DETAILS

1906	Born 30 October
1930s	Starts racing career in hill climbs, before progressing to circuit racing with Maserati under the tutelage of Tazio Nuvolari
1937	Wins the first of three consecutive Italian drivers' titles
1938	Wins Italian drivers' title in Scuderia Ferrari-entered Alfa 158
1939	Wins Italian drivers' title in same car
1950	Inaugural Formula One World Champion with Alfa Romeo
1951	Wins Belgian GP, but consistently eclipsed by team-mate Fangio. Finished fourth overall.
1952	Joined Ferrari
1953	Wins German GP at the Nurburgring, his first race win for Ferrari. Finished Championship in third place
1954	Second in Argentinian GP. Broke arm in the Mille Miglia. Severely burnt in sports car race at Monza
1955	Returns to racing, but retires because of pain
1966	Killed in a road accident on 30 June, on his way to watch the French Grand Prix

FORMULA ONE RECORD

Year	Team	Wins	Poles	Fast laps	Pts
1950	Alfa Romeo	3	2	3	30
1951	Alfa Romeo	1	0	2	19
1952	Ferrari	0	2	1	25
1953	Ferrari	1	0	0	26
1954	Ferrari	0	1	0	6
1955	Ferrari	0	0	0	10.3

GIUSEPPE FARINA, the inaugural World Champion, was a Doctor of Law whose near-brutal tactics were a precursor of what was to come in the 1980s and 1990s.

Giuseppe Farina pictured in his Alfa-Romeo on 26 August 1950.

At the age of 44 Giuseppe "Nino" Farina became the first World Champion, making dominant use of his Alfa Romeo to win three of the six races in the inaugural Championship in 1950. His best years were lost to the Second World War.

Fearless, extrovert, his distinctive outstretched arms method had many imitators (Stirling Moss perhaps the most prominent), but few could equal his skill. His approach was often characterized by bravery over technique.

"I could never help feeling apprehensive about him, especially at the start of a race and one or two laps from the end," remembered Enzo Ferrari.

At the start he was not unlike a highly strung thoroughbred, liable to break through the starting tape in its eagerness. Nearing the finish he was capable of committing the most astonishing follies although it must be admitted in all justice that he risked only his own safety and never jeopardized that of others. As a consequence he was a regular inmate of hospital wards."

The Motor magazine memorably described his third place in the 1951 Italian Grand Prix: "He finished the race with a fountain of fuel streaking along the road behind him – rather like driving a hand grenade with the pin out."

Farina, the suave and sophisticated scion of the family who founded the famous Farina coach-building company, began his competition career in the early Thirties in hill climbs. He progressed to circuit racing with Maserati and learned from the tutelage of the legendary Tazio Nuvolari.

He won the Italian drivers' title in 1937, 1938 and 1939 and the latter two years were spent at the wheel of the Ferrari-entered Alfa 158s, more than a decade before their derivates carried him to title glory. Three drivers' crowns put him in a strong position when the Second World War ended. He was duly rewarded in 1950, after keeping his hand in with a private Maserati and then a works Ferrari in the immediate post-war years.

He was a member of Alfa Romeo's squad but even in his title-winning year his star was on the wane. He was never quite a match for the pace of his team-mate Juan Manuel Fangio. The points-scoring system in 1950 was based on a driver's best four

"He was capable of committing the most astonishing follies although it must be admitted in all justice that he risked only his own safety."

Enzo Ferrari

results from seven races. Thus the first World Championship went down to the wire at Monza with Farina, Fangio and Fagioli all in with a chance. There was overwhelming patriotic fervour at Monza and a suspicion has lingered that Farina may have received preferential treatment in the Alfa camp over the bright young Argentinian star (at a non-championship race at Bari prior to the decider, Fangio had mysteriously run out of fuel while dicing for the lead while Farina's tank easily got him to the chequered flag).

In 1951 he won just the Belgian Grand Prix at Spa-Francorchamps, dropping to fourth overall. In 1952 he joined Ferrari but, again, he was consistently overshadowed by a team-mate, fellow-Italian Alberto Ascari. A race win did not come his way until the 1953 German Grand Prix at the Nurburgring. He finished the season in third place.

On the occasions when Fangio or Ascari fell awry, Farina's redoubtable fight and spirit pushed him to raise his game. Despite being one of the more accident-prone drivers among his peers, he showed the racing world on a number of occasions more than a glimpse of the skill that was lost to the war years.

He started 1954 as Ferrari's team leader and finished second to Fangio in the Argentinian Grand Prix. He broke his arm in an accident on the Mille Miglia but raced with it in plaster in the Belgian Grand Prix before being engulfed in flames in a sports car race at Monza. With severe burns to his legs, he was unable to return to the cockpit until 1955, again finishing second in Argentina, but he retired mid-season overwhelmed by the pain of racing, even though he dosed himself with painkillers.

He later dabbled with the Indy 500 but then retired, only to be killed in a road accident in 1966 when he skidded into a telegraph pole in the Savoy Alps on his way to watch the French Grand Prix, just a few months before his 60th birthday.

"All the drivers said that only the Holy Virgin was capable of keeping him on the track, because of the crazy way he used to drive, and that one day the Virgin would get tired of going along behind him," commented Fangio after Farina's death.

Giuseppe Farina and Princess De Rethy at the Italian Grand Prix on 14 September 1953.

1954

The Maestro wins for Mercedes

TALKING POINT

THE RETURN OF MERCEDES-BENZ

Mercedes-Benz returned to the revamped World Championship as the Formula Two rules were thrown by the wayside and replaced by new 2.5-litre regulations which promised to revolutionize the sport.

The German company had not been in Grand Prix racing since the Second World War and their return sparked a frenzy as drivers scrambled to earn a drive with the famous marque.

Juan Manuel Fangio, who won his first World Championship in 1951 with Alfa, had competed in 1953 with Maserati, but as soon as the new Mercedes-Benz was ready by the fourth race of the 1954 Championship he switched allegiances.

Alfred Neubauer, who had masterminded Mercedes-Benz dominance in the 1930s, was still at the helm and he hired Hans Herrmann and Karl Kling to team up with Fangio for their assault on the Championship.

Mercedes-Benz produced a W196 Silver Arrow car and in 1954, with Fangio at the wheel in determined mood, the German giants were unstoppable as the Argentinian driver claimed his second world crown.

In a way, the 1954 season eventually hinged on two decisions from undoubtedly two of the sport's most talented drivers. Juan Manuel Fangio was successful after making a calculated career move as he decided to swap from Maserati to Mercedes-Benz and went on to win his second World Championship.

Unfortunately Alberto Ascari, the man who had beaten Fangio for the past two seasons to win the World Championships in 1952 and 1953, got it wrong as he opted to leave Ferrari for the promise of a new car with Lancia.

Ascari was not to know that the new Lancia D50 would not be ready until the last race of the year in Spain, and he was forced to sit out a season in which a third world title could have been on the cards.

Lancia had also recruited Luigi Villoresi from Ferrari, while the Italian marque brought in Mike Hawthorn and José Froilan Gonzalez from Maserati to replace the departed Ascari and Villoresi. Maserati had hoped to keep Fangio for the entire season and had also retained the services of Onofre Marimon. But Fangio's departure to Mercedes-Benz provided a gap for the impressive Briton Stirling Moss to break on to the scene in dramatic style.

Once Fangio joined Mercedes-Benz it was clear everybody else was competing for second place. Fangio had already won two races before the Mercedes-Benz's introduction in the fourth round in France. He went on to win four of the remaining six races that season and claimed his second World Championship.

The season-opening Argentinian Grand Prix in January was run in indifferent conditions in Buenos Aires but it did not stop wet-race expert Fangio starting off his campaign with an inspired drive.

Fangio started from third on the grid, behind the Ferrari's of Farina and Gonzalez, who shared the lead over the first 32 laps before a storm broke out and caused chaos as drivers spun off.

Gonzalez, who had looked impressive in the opening laps fending off the challenges of Fangio and Hawthorn, was one of the first to spin off. He recovered, but from then on victory was never in the equation.

Hawthorn led for a few laps but he was eventually black-flagged for receiving outside help when he spun. But the biggest controversy was to follow as Ferrari and Maserati came to loggerheads.

Fangio came into the pits in his Maserati to get special hand-cut tyres put on his car and Ferrari team manager Nello Ugolini complained that the team had used too many mechanics during the stop.

Ugolini advised his two leading drivers Farina and Gonzalez to take it easy as he expected his

Juan Manuel Fangio in the new Mercedes.

SHORTS

Maserati, who had suffered the indignity of arriving late at the British GP, suffered again as Onofre Marimon, arguably their most exciting driver, was killed in an accident during practice in Germany, becoming the first driver fatality in Championship history. Argentine Marimon crashed on the downhill section before the bridge at Adenau. His death devastated the entire paddock, but particularly fellow countrymen Fangio and Gonzalez.

protest to be held up by the sport's governing body, the FIA. Fangio duly caught and overtook both drivers to take the chequered flag on the 87th lap. To Ferrari's dismay, the protest was rejected by the race stewards and by the FIA, so Fangio took the win and started his Championship-winning season in the best possible fashion.

Like the seasons before it, the World Championship once again included the Indianapolis 500 as its second round, despite none of the European teams making the trip to compete.

Bill Vukovich once again dominated the 200-lap race at the famous Brickyard circuit and he powered to his second successive victory in the event in his Kurtis-Kraft car.

The race in America in May was also notable for the performance of Jack McGrath, who became the first man to break the 140mph barrier in qualifying for the race in his Hinkle Special.

Belgian spectacular

The World Championship returned to Europe the following month and the big guns came back to race as the series moved to Belgium for what promised to be a 36-lap spectacular.

For the first time in a Grand Prix a car competed fitted with a camera, as Frenchman Emmanuel de Graffenried drove around the circuit.

Fangio wasted no time in reminding his competitors he was the man to beat as he claimed pole position in what was to be his last race with Maserati. The Ferraris of Farina and Gonzalez followed him on the grid.

Gonzalez's race lasted just a lap as he dropped out with an oil leak, and that left it as a straight battle between Farina and Fangio. Farina led for two laps before Fangio took over and stayed at the front until lap 10.

Farina pushed his Ferrari hard and overtook Fangio a lap later, but the exertion proved too much for his car as his engine failed on lap 14, gifting the lead and effectively the race win to Fangio.

Fangio won to beat the Ferrari of Maurice Trintignant into second place.

Promising British driver Moss finished third to highlight his potential for the first time during the season.

The World Championship moved on to France in July and it signalled the return of Mercedes-Benz, who would be spearheaded by the irrepressible Fangio. The German team wasted no time in making their mark on the sport as Fangio claimed pole for the 61-lap race at Reims.

Mercedes-Benz, in fact, occupied the first two places on the grid as German Karl Kling joined his team-mate Fangio on the front row. Kling started better, but for the entire race he battled with Fangio for the lead before losing out to the masterful driver on the penultimate lap.

Hans Herrmann had also looked impressive in his Mercedes-Benz before an engine problem ruled him out of the race on lap 16 after he had set the fastest lap, which remained despite the titanic battle between Fangio and Kling.

Mercedes-Benz were back, and everybody knew it. Ferrari limped on to the podium as Robert Manzon claimed third for the *tifosi*. It exemplified Ferrari's weekend after Farina had failed to compete and Gonzalez and Hawthorn had both been forced

RACE BY RACE DETAILS

ROUND 1 – ARGENTINA
Race Juan Manuel Fangio
Pole Giuseppe Farina
Fastest lap José Froilan Gonzalez

ROUND 2 – INDIANAPOLIS
Race Bill Vukovich
Pole Jack McGrath
Fastest lap N/A

ROUND 3 – BELGIUM
Race Juan Manuel Fangio
Pole Juan Manuel Fangio
Fastest lap Juan Manuel Fangio

ROUND 4 – FRANCE
Race Juan Manuel Fangio
Pole Juan Manuel Fangio
Fastest lap Hans Herrmann

ROUND 5 – BRITAIN
Race José Froilan Gonzalez
Pole Juan Manuel Fangio
Fastest lap Juan Manuel Fangio

ROUND 6 – GERMANY
Race Juan Manuel Fangio
Pole Juan Manuel Fangio
Fastest lap Karl Kling

ROUND 7 – SWITZERLAND
Race Juan Manuel Fangio
Pole José Froilan Gonzalez
Fastest lap Juan Manuel Fangio

ROUND 8 – ITALY
Race Juan Manuel Fangio
Pole Juan Manuel Fangio
Fastest lap José Froilan Gonzalez

ROUND 9 – SPAIN
Race Mike Hawthorn
Pole Albero Ascari
Fastest lap Alberto Ascari

Karl Kling at the French Grand Prix.

to retire with mechanical problems. But Fangio marched on.

As the Championship moved to Silverstone for the British Grand Prix, Mercedes-Benz were not so sure that their streamlined Silver Arrow car would perform as well at the Northamptonshire circuit as it did in France.

Early fears were allayed as Fangio set the fastest time in qualifying and started from pole position, but his close rival of the previous round, Kling, was back in sixth on the grid.

Maserati endured a miserable weekend as they failed to turn up in time for qualifying and were forced to start from the back of the grid. Marimon made the most of it and finished third eventually, but he never got close to the two Ferraris of Gonzalez and Hawthorn, who dominated the race as Fangio stuttered.

Gonzalez took the lead from the start and was never overtaken as Fangio battled to control his car on the corners and repeatedly hit oil drums set out to mark the circuit.

Fangio also suffered gearbox problems and Hawthorn battled with Moss for much of the race behind Gonzalez, much to the delight of the British crowd. Unfortunately for Moss, he dropped back in the latter stages due to a rear axle problem.

Ferrari restored some pride as they took a one-two finish, Gonzalez winning and Hawthorn second.

But their win brought Mercedes-Benz back to their best in their homeland as the German Grand Prix played host to the sixth round on a tragic week-end at the beginning of August, as Maserati driver Marimon was killed in practice (see Shorts).

Fangio, who had a new open-body Mercedes-Benz, somehow maintained his professional approach and delivered the perfect tribute to his compatriot by securing victory from pole.

Fangio had once again been threatened in the race by Kling, who had come from the back of the grid to challenge at the front, despite signals from the Mercedes-Benz pit to ease off Fangio.

Swiss win seals Championship

The German Grand Prix was also labelled the European Grand Prix, and three weeks later the Championship moved across the continent to com-pete in what turned out to be the last Swiss race.

The weather was bad for the race, but for once Fangio had been knocked off pole position as Ferrari's Gonzalez beat his compatriot to top spot at the Bremgarten circuit.

Fangio, however, did not waste any time in stamping his authority on the race and he led from start to finish as the others scrapped behind him for a podium spot. The win secured the Argentine the Championship.

Hawthorn had been one of the more impressive drivers in the chasing pack, but he was forced to pit due to a sticking throttle and eventually retired with

José Froilan Gonzalez and Juan Manuel Fangio at the Swiss Grand Prix.

Stirling Moss and Mike Hawthorn pictured on 3 October 1954.

1954 DRIVERS' CHAMPIONSHIP

DRIVER	TEAM	POINTS
Juan Manuel Fangio	Maserati/M-Benz	42
José Froilan Gonzalez	Ferrari	25.5
Mike Hawthorn	Ferrari	24
Maurice Trintignant	Ferrari	17
Karl Kling	Mercedes-Benz	12
Hans Herrmann	Mercedes-Benz	8
Bill Vukovich	Kurtis-Kraft	8
Roberto Mieres	Maserati	6
Luigi Musso	Maserati	6
Giuseppe Farina	Ferrari	6
Jimmy Bryan	Kuzma	6
Jack McGrath	Kurtis-Kraft	5
Stirling Moss	Maserati	4
Onofre Marimon	Maserati	4
Robert Manzon	Ferrari	4
Sergio Mantovani	Maserati	4
B Bira	Maserati	3
Luigi Villoresi	Maserati	2
Umberto Maglioli	Ferrari	2
Andre Pilette	Gordoni	2
Elie Bayol	Gordoni	2
Mike Nazurak	Kurtis-Kraft	2
Troy Ruttman	Kurtis-Kraft	1.5
Duane Carter	Kurtsi-Kraft	1.5
Alberto Ascari	Maserati/Lancia	1
Jean Behra	Gordoni	1

an oil pump problem after 30 laps of the 66-lap race.

Moss and Trintignant also retired with the same problem and that promoted Kling up into third place after he had battled through the field, but Fangio's team-mate was forced to retire with a fuel feed problem on lap 39 and Fangio was followed across the line by Gonzalez in second and Herrmann third.

Fangio relaxed

With the Championship already in the bag, Fangio arrived in Monza for the eighth round in Italy in a relaxed mood and went on to dominate proceedings despite a spirited performance from Moss.

Fangio took pole for the penultimate round of the Championship ahead of Ascari, who was back in his familiar Ferrari after being loaned from Lancia. Despite a quick start from Fangio's Mercedes-Benz team-mate Kling, Ascari and the new World Champion traded places at the front of the field after the third lap and the race seemed to be heading for a two-way battle.

But after starting from third on the grid, Moss powered ahead in his Maserati, took the lead after 45 laps and held Ascari and Fangio at bay.

A dream debut win beckoned for Moss before a cruel twist of fate shattered his hopes. Just 13 laps from the end of the 80-lap race the oil tank in Moss' car split and he lost speed, allowing Fangio through. Ascari had already retired himself as his Ferrari suffered a valve problem.

Moss limped home in 11th place as Fangio took the chequered flag after holding off the challenge of Hawthorn and Umberto Maglioli, who had started from 13th on the grid. Hawthorn did not have to wait long for his revenge on Fangio as he powered to his only victory of the season in the last race at the Pedralbes circuit in Spain in October.

The race had marked the long-awaited first appearance of the new Lancia car, and their top driver Ascari duly rewarded its introduction by claiming pole position for the 80-lap race.

Ascari, however, would be left frustrated as his new Lancia broke down after just 10 laps with a clutch problem, while he was leading at the time. New champion Fangio was never in the race, as his car was spraying oil into the cockpit. Hawthorn drove a steady race and bided his time before taking the lead after 24 laps to seal the race win. Maserati's Luigi Musso, was second ahead of a contented Fangio.

Jack Brabham

SHREWD, RUGGED and indefatigably spanner-in-hand, Sir Jack Brabham, a triple World Champion, remains the only driver to win a title in a car of his own manufacture.

CAREER DETAILS

1926	Born 2 April, in Hurstville outside Sydney
1946	Starts in Midget racing and progresses to hill climbs
1954	Finishes fourth in New Zealand GP and travels to Europe, beginning association with John Cooper
1955	Makes GP debut at Aintree
1958	Scores first F1 points with fourth place in the Monaco GP
1959	Cooper now real force in F1. World Driver's Champion
1960	World Champion again with Cooper scoring five straight wins at Zandvoort, Spa-Francorchamps, Reims, Silverstone and Oporto.
1961	Brabham forms Motor Racing Developments with Ron Tauranac
1962	First Brabham car makes its debut. Fourth place in US GP brings first points scored by driver in car of his own manufacture
1964	Brabham car wins first full GP at Rouen (driven by Dan Gurney)
1965	Goes into semi-retirement because of business demands
1966	Races full-time alongside Denny Hulme and wins third world driver's title in his own world constructors'-championship winning car Voted Australian of the Year
1967	Hulme beats his boss into second place. Brabham World Constructors' Champion. Awarded OBE
1979	Knighted for his services to motorsport

FORMULA ONE RECORD

Year	Team	Wins	Poles	Fast laps	Pts
1955	Cooper	0	0	0	0
1956	Maserati	0	0	0	0
1957	Cooper Cl	0	0	0	0
1958	Cooper Cl	0	0	0	3
1959	Cooper Cl	2	1	1	31
1960	Cooper Cl	5	3	3	43
1961	Cooper Cl	0	1	0	4
1962	Lotus Cl	0	0	0	–
	Brabham Cl	0	0	0	9
1963	Lotus Cl	0	0	0	–
	Brabham Cl	0	0	0	14
1964	Brabham Cl	0	0	1	11
1965	Brabham Cl	0	0	0	9
1966	Brabham Re	4	3	1	42
1967	Brabham Re	2	2	0	46
1968	Brabham Re	0	0	0	2
1969	Brabham Ford	0	2	0	14
1970	Brabham Ford	1	1	4	25

Jack Brabham in action in his Cooper.

John Arthur Brabham, a second-generation Australian whose grandfather came from Cockney East London, learnt to drive at the age of 12. He drove trucks belonging to his father, a greengrocer, around the yard in Hurstville, outside Sydney. The boy who started racing on the power-sliding dirt tracks of Australia went on to become a triple World Champion of the circuit-racing élite – and the only F1 driver to have won a world title in a car of his own construction, the BT19, which he drove to victory in 1966.

He was also the forerunner of the modern driver-cum-technician, and a significant nurturer and investor in young talent. In 1966 he was voted "Australian of the Year". In 1967 he was awarded the Order of the British Empire. In 1979 he became the first knight of motorsport – Sir Jack Brabham.

Brabham started wielding spanners as soon as he left school at 15. He found a job in a local garage and spent his evenings studying engineering at Kogarah Technical College.

In 1946, having served the statutory two years of National Service in the Air Force – where he maintained twin-engined Beaufighter fighter-bombers – Brabham opened a small repair business. He was introduced to Midget racing by an American expatriate named John Schonberg in 1947 who handed over his car after his wife had begged him to quit. Brabham won the New South Wales Championship in his first season. The South Australia Championship and the Australian Championship followed in 1948–49. During this time he formed a partnership with fellow-Australian Ron Tauranac that would continue into Formula One and Europe.

In 1955 he made his way to Europe. He drove with a distinctive head-down, opposite lock style that many of his rivals found over-aggressive. "He seemed to have forgotten that he was no longer on a dirt-track in Australia and insisted on coming round the corners sideways in a power slide," noted Stirling Moss.

Jack Brabham pictured at Brands Hatch in 1966.

After an abortive stint driving a private Maserati 250F he became a firmly-entrenched member of John Cooper's factory team, driving in Sports and Formula Two cars. That same year, he began his Formula One career. The partnership resulted in Brabham's first two Championship victories in 1959 and 1960. It was in the Cooper that he raced the very first rear-engined car at the Indianapolis 500, causing all manufacturers to switch from front-engined machines.

On 12 May 1959, Brabham won his first Formula One race, at Monaco, which helped propel him to his first World Championship in the Cooper with its 2.5-litre Coventry Climax engine. In 1960, he won five Grand Prix in a row, en route to his second consecutive title, with a new lowline model.

Finding his influence restricted at Cooper, Brabham decided to strike out on his own. In 1962, Sir Jack teamed up with Ron Tauranac to produce the first of the Brabham Marque. The new 1.5-litre engine limit in Formula One found the British teams scrambling for motive power. While the small-engined cars seemed tailor-made for Jim Clark and Lotus, Brabham's aggressive style seemed unsuited and he would not win a race during the 1500cc era. It was left to American Dan Gurney to take the team's maiden victory at Rouen.

For 1966 a new 3-litre formula came into existence. Brabham found an engine in his own backyard with the Australian Repco Company. The Brabham-Repco V8 would give Brabham a car with which he won the French, British, Dutch and German Grand Prix and that year's World Championship. The next year would see another Championship for the team; this time the title went to his team-mate Denis Hulme in the BT20.

In 1968, the year belonged to Lotus and Ford-Cosworth despite the tragic death of Jim Clark. For 1969 Brabham also had a Ford-Cosworth engine deal but a broken ankle during a test crash destroyed his title chances. In 1970 he had hoped to retire but finding all the top drivers unavailable he decided to continue himself. Rather than going through the motions – "If you have the right approach to racing and are reasonably fit, it doesn't matter what your age is," was his line – he won the season opener at the South African Grand Prix and led at Monaco until the final corner of the last lap while under pressure from the surging Jochen Rindt. The Mexican Grand Prix would be his last race at 44.

After retiring from driving he sold his interest in the team to Bernie Ecclestone and returned to Australia. Later Brabham would regret making such a clean break from Formula One. Besides maintaining his garage business, he still makes appearances at the various vintage races springing up everywhere.

> "His style may not satisfy the purist, but it is ruthlessly effective. The car is always under control."
>
> *Louis T. Stanley, 1965*

1955
Fangio wins back-to-back titles

TALKING POINT

TRAGEDY AT LE MANS

The Formula One World Championship continued to provide spectacular and exciting racing in 1955, but the season was overshadowed by the biggest tragedy in motor racing history.

As reigning World Champion Juan Manuel Fangio was joined at Mercedes-Benz by up-and-coming British driver Stirling Moss and the pair subsequently fought for the 1955 title, tragedy struck at the Le Mans 24-hour race in June.

More than 80 people were killed after Pierre Levegh lost control of his Mercedes-Benz in the classic French race and ploughed into the watching crowd with fatal results.

The accident had major repercussions in Formula One as race organizers cancelled the Grands Prix in France, Germany, Switzerland and Spain.

For Switzerland it marked a dismal finale to their appearance on the calendar as they never hosted another Grand Prix again.

More than 80 spectators were killed at Le Mans when Pierre Levegh lost control of his Mercedes Benz.

The season contrasted the brilliant driving talents of Juan Manuel Fangio and Stirling Moss with several tragedies scattered throughout one of the blackest years in motor racing history.

Even before the multiple deaths that shocked the world during the Le Mans 24-hour race in June, the Formula One World Championship had lost two drivers in accidents.

The double World Champion (1952 and 1953) Alberto Ascari died in an accident at Monza while testing sportscars in May and a few weeks later the dominant American driver Bill Vukovich, who had won the previous two Indianapolis 500 races, died in an accident in the 1955 race at the Brickyard circuit.

The tragedies at Le Mans had a great effect on the Formula One World Championship, as four races in Europe were cancelled. However, despite the magnitude of the disaster the racing had to go on.

Reigning champion Fangio stayed with Mercedes-Benz in 1955 and was joined by Moss. The Italian marque in turn signed Jean Behra as a replacement, while another major change saw Mike Hawthorn join the Vanwall team.

Ascari decided to stay with Lancia, who had only brought their new D50 car into the sport in the final race of the previous season and had big expectations and ambitions to catch Mercedes-Benz.

The heat was on Fangio to repeat his Championship success of 1954 and the Argentine driver did not fail to deliver as the season started in sweltering conditions in his homeland in January. Race day was extremely hot and several drivers were forced to change tyres several times or share cars with team-mates to take a break from racing in the heat.

Fangio and Robert Mieres, of Maserati, were the only two drivers to start and finish the race without having to use spare tyres.

The home crowd once again packed into the circuit, and were not disappointed as Argentine José Froilan Gonzalez claimed pole position in his Ferrari. The fans then went wild as Fangio took an early lead after starting from third on the grid.

Ascari pushed Fangio hard and took the lead on the third lap, but his Ferrari team-mate Gonzalez was also in the frame and he came back well from a slow start to take the lead a few laps later.

The lead swapped hands several times in the opening 20 laps between the three drivers and eventually the pressure told on Ascari as he crashed out on lap 22. His Lancia team-mate Luigi Villoresi had already retired on lap two with an oil-line problem.

Villoresi had taken over Eugenio Castellotti's car but, before Ascari could claim the car, Villoresi crashed on lap 35, ending the Lancia challenge.

The heat then began to play a major factor in the 96-lap race as drivers dropped out through heat exhaustion or mechanical failure with their cars. Moss dropped out of the race on lap 29 with a fuel problem and moments later Ferrari driver Maurice Trintignant dropped out with an engine failure.

Ferrari drivers Giuseppe Farina, Trintignant and Gonzalez all swapped drives as they took a break from the hot cockpit, but Fangio carried on to take the chequered flag with another brave drive.

Fangio was hot favourite to take victory in the next round as the World Championship returned to the street circuit of Monaco for the first time since 1950. Mercedes-Benz had produced two special short wheelbase cars for the twisty circuit which were used by Fangio and Moss while team-mate Hans Herrmann used the normal car, which was better on the quicker circuits with its streamline aerodynamics.

Herrmann was, in fact, involved in an accident after just eight laps of the race and was replaced by André Simon, who later retired with a valve problem after 24 laps. The race had started in familiar fashion with Fangio, Moss and Ascari all on the front row. Hawthorn made his first appearance of the season in his Vanwall as only 20 cars were permitted to start the event due to the lack of street space.

Fangio beat Ascari and Moss off the line and led for the first 49 laps before a transmission problem ended his race. His team-mate Moss, who had beaten off the challenge of Farina and Castellotti, took the lead and powered away with Ascari behind him.

Moss was 20 laps away from his first win of the season when his Mercedes-Benz engine blew. Ascari was the leader but it did not last long as he inexplicably went straight on at a chicane moments later and ploughed through hay bales before dropping into the harbour.

Ascari was unhurt and released himself from the car before swimming to safety, but all the action involving the top drivers had left Ferrari's Trintignant in the lead and he went on to win the 100-lap race.

F1 mourns Ascari

Four days after the Monaco Grand Prix, Ascari was killed in an accident while testing sportscars for Ferrari at Monza. His loss hit Formula One hard and soon afterwards his team, Lancia, announced their withdrawal from Formula One – just three races after the introduction of the D50 car into the sport.

In the wake of Ascari's death the other European drivers once again took a break as the Formula One World Championship went across the Atlantic to America for the third-round Indianapolis 500 at the end of May.

In an eventful season, Indianapolis was no exception, as two drivers died during the race weekend.

RACE BY RACE DETAILS

ROUND 1 – ARGENTINA
Race Juan Manuel Fangio
Pole José Froilan Gonzalez
Fastest lap Juan Manuel Fangio

ROUND 2 – MONACO
Race Maurice Trintignant
Pole Juan Manuel Fangio
Fastest lap Juan Manuel Fangio

ROUND 3 – INDIANAPOLIS
Race Bob Sweikert
Pole Jerry Hoyt
Fastest lap Bill Vukovich

ROUND 4 – BELGIUM
Race Juan Manuel Fangio
Pole Eugenio Castellotti
Fastest lap Juan Manuel Fangio

ROUND 5 – HOLLAND
Race Juan Manuel Fangio
Pole Juan Manuel Fangio
Fastest lap Robert Mieres

ROUND 6 – BRITAIN
Race Stirling Moss
Pole Stirling Moss
Fastest lap Stirling Moss

ROUND 7 – ITALY
Race Juan Manuel Fangio
Pole Juan Manuel Fangio
Fastest lap Stirling Moss

Argentine Grand Prix winner Juan Manuel Fangio receives his trophy from President Juan Domingo Perón.

Juan Manuel Fangio and Stirling Moss at the Monaco Grand Prix.

Manuel Ayulo suffered a bad accident in qualifying for the 200-lap race and later died of his injuries, while Bill Vukovich, the winner of the last two years' races, died in a spectacular accident on race day.

Vukovich had started the race well from fifth on the grid and was soon leading inside the first 50 laps before tragedy struck.

Rodger Ward lost control of his car in Turn Two and Al Keller and Johnny Boyd collided with it as they attempted to make the turn. Vukovich came around the bend at high speed and could not avoid the carnage across the track.

His car collided with one of the already-stricken vehicles and he was catapulted into the air before a series of cartwheels wrecked the car and sent it over a trackside wall in flames. Vukovich stood no chance.

Several drivers stopped to help Vukovich, but the race went on and Jimmy Bryan battled with Bob Sweikert for the lead. The latter eventually came out on top and took the chequered flag on a day when the field's thoughts were on Vukovich and his family.

In June, the World Championship returned to Belgium, and with Lancia missing from the field Eugenio Castellotti was allowed one last run in the D50 as a privateer. He impressed everyone by setting the fastest time in qualifying and taking pole position for the race.

Fangio was second on the grid and Moss third as Mercedes looked to get back to winning ways at the Spa-Francorchamps circuit.

At the start, Fangio took the lead from Castellotti and maintained it for the entire 36 laps, but behind him the action remained fast and frantic.

Ferrari's Behra crashed heavily on the third lap and suffered minor injuries. Castellotti also broke down with gearbox problems after 16 laps and Moss was left to challenge Fangio, but he had to settle for second place with Farina in third place for Ferrari.

Dutch event goes on

Before the next round in Holland all the Formula One teams were rocked by the events of the Le Mans 24-Hour race a few days earlier. Despite the high amount of fatalities, the Dutch race organizers decided to go ahead.

After dominating in Belgium, Mercedes-Benz once again took charge of proceedings at Zandvoort. Fangio claimed pole position, with his team-mates Moss and Karl Kling beside him on the front row.

Despite a shower of rain midway through the race, the event ran without incident as Fangio led from start to flag, with victory seemingly never in doubt. Moss followed up just behind his team-mate while Luigi Musso completed the podium positions with a third place finish in his Maserati.

Hawthorn finished seventh in the 100-lap race for Ferrari after abandoning his Vanwall project. But it was Fangio's day as he took charge in the Championship with his third win of the season.

With the French Grand Prix cancelled after the Le Mans tragedy, the sixth-round took place in Britain at Liverpool's Aintree racecourse.

The 90-lap Grand Prix was run on a track outside the famous steeplechase course which hosts the Grand National. Mercedes-Benz were again favourites to take glory and they did not disappoint, as the Championship race took a surprise turn.

Moss delighted his home fans by recording the fastest time in qualifying to take pole position and then embarked on an epic battle in the race with team-mate Fangio, who had qualified second.

Fangio led for two laps before Moss overtook and stayed at the front until lap 17. Fangio came back as the two drivers ran nose-to-tail and after holding the lead again for eight laps, Moss retook the lead on lap 26 and did not look back. The two Mercedes-Benz drivers were close throughout the remaining 64 laps, but Moss held on in front of his home crowd and took the chequered flag for his first win to take the Championship race to the last event.

Kling came home third while Piero Taruffi finished fourth to complete a memorable one-two-three-four finish for Mercedes-Benz. Hawthorn was Ferrari's best finisher in sixth. With Germany, Switzerland and Spain cancelled following the Le Mans tragedy there was only one race left as the Championship went to the wire in Italy.

Fangio and Moss' exciting battle for the Championship was overshadowed by Mercedes-Benz's announcement they would be leaving the sport at the end of the season.

SHORTS

The 1955 season saw two British drivers move teams in hope of greater success. Sterling Moss left Maserati, after capturing just four Championship points in '54, and joined Fangio at Mercedes-Benz.. Mike Hawthorn, who had finished third the previous year, left Ferrari for the England-based Vanwall team. The two men experienced conflicting fortunes, as Moss vaulted to a second-place Championship finish while Hawthorn struggled.

Fangio on pole

Despite the obvious pressure, Fangio claimed pole for the race with Moss second on the grid at the new-look Monza circuit. Before the September race the track had been lengthened from 3.9 miles per lap to 6.2 miles. High-banked curves had also been added to the circuit and they soon caused problems, as Farina suffered a big shunt early on after a tyre failed on his Ferrari.

Fangio led from the start, but was overtaken by Moss on lap eight as the top two promised a grandstand finish to the season. But Fangio fought back, regained the lead a lap later and never looked back as Moss suffered a series of unfortunate problems to end his race and Championship hopes.

Moss firstly had to come into the pits on lap 19 with a smashed windscreen and then after rejoining and battling back through the field his engine failed and he had to retire on lap 27. Moss' retirement meant Fangio did not even have to finish to win his second successive title; but in true Champion style, Fangio put the icing on a memorable season by taking the chequered flag ahead of team-mate Taruffi and Ferrari's Castellotti.

1955 DRIVERS' CHAMPIONSHIP

DRIVER	TEAM	POINTS
Juan Manuel Fangio	Mercedes-Benz	40
Stirling Moss	Mercedes-Benz	23
Eugenio Castellotti	Lancia/Ferrari	12
Maurice Trintignant	Ferrari	11
Giuseppe Farina	Ferrari	10⅓
Piero Taruffi	Mercedes-Benz	9
Bob Sweikert	Kurtis-Kraft	8
Roberto Mieres	Maserati	7
Jean Behra	Maserati	6
Luigi Musso	Maserati	6
Karl Kling	Mercedes-Benz	5
Jimmy Davies	Kurtis-Kraft	4
Paul Frere	Ferrari	3
Johnny Thompson	Kuzma	3
Tony Bettenhausen	Kurtis-Kraft	3
Paul Russo	Kurtis-Kraft	3
José Froilan Gonzalez	Ferrari	2
Cesare Perdisa	Maserati	2
Luigi Villoresi	Lancia	2
Carlos Menditeguy	Maserati	2
Umberto Maglioli	Ferrari	1⅓
Hans Herrmann	Mercedes-Benz	1
Walt Faulkner	Kurtis-Kraft	1
Bill Homeier	Kurtis-Kraft	1
Bill Vukovich	Kurtis-Kraft	1

Stirling Moss wins the British Grand Prix.

Peter Collins

PETER COLLINS, a front-rank driver, is best remembered for chivalrously surrendering his chances of the 1956 World Championship to team-mate Fangio "because he deserved it".

CAREER DETAILS

1931	Born 6 November
1952	Moves up to Formula Two with HWM and made World Championship debut in the Swiss Grand Prix aged 20
1954	Three outings for Vanwall team
1955	Rides with BRM
1956	Signed by Ferrari. Two wins in Belgian and French Grands Prix, three second-place finishes, third in Championship. Surrenders opportunity in 1956 World Championship by handing over his Ferrari to Fangio at Monza.
1957	No GP win, but victories in non-championship races at Syracuse and Naples
1958	Died 3 August, in a Ferrari at the German Grand Prix at Nurburgring

FORMULA ONE RECORD

Year	Team	Wins	Poles	Fast laps	Pts
1952	HWM	0	0	0	0
1953	HWM	0	0	0	0
1954	Vanwall	0	0	0	0
1955	Maserati	0	0	0	0
1956	Ferrari	2	1	0	25
1957	Ferrari	0	0	0	8
1958	Ferrari	1	0	0	14

Peter Collins with Mike Hawthorn.

Peter Collins spent much of his career racing alongside his great friend Mike Hawthorn (who called him "mon ami mate"). Both approached their careers with a certain boyish gaucheness. If there was little to split them in effectiveness on track, they had very different reputations among their peers. Collins was considered the more consistent, with Hawthorn the more likely to pull out an inspired performance.

According to Robert Daley, author of *Cars At Speed* (Foulis, 1961), an attitude problem prevented Collins from maximising his considerable potential. "A brash, smug young man...while he had the skill of a great driver, Collins never had the right emotions. He appeared to love the idea of being a famous racing driver, but he didn't want the responsibilities of being a great racing driver," he wrote.

Formula 500 racing was the launch pad for Collins' career. The tricks he learnt in that arena stood him in good stead and he made an immediate impact when he moved up to Formula Two with HWM in 1952. He made his World Championship debut at 20 in the Swiss Grand Prix at Bremgarten.

Stirling Moss and Lance Macklin were team-mates but the car's reliability problems meant finishes were few and far between, although the powers at Aston Martin saw his promise and signed him for their sports car team.

The next few seasons were unsatisfactory, with three outings for the Vanwall team in 1954 followed by a drive with BRM in 1955.

In 1956, however, he signed for Ferrari, the team for whom he would race for the rest of his career. With two wins in the Belgian and French Grands Prix and three second-place finishes, Collins finished third overall behind Juan Manuel Fangio and Stirling Moss, but the story could have been quite different.

The title fight went down to the wire, at the Italian Grand Prix. Fangio was well-placed on 30 points, but Collins and Jean Behra were eight behind (they could only capture the title by winning the race

> "I wanted things to go on just as they were, and so I handed my car over to Fangio."

and setting fastest lap with Fangio failing to score). During the race Fangio's hopes faded with steering trouble, but he was saved when Collins – who could still have won the title – stopped and handed his car over to him.

"All I could think of out there was that if I won the race and the Championship I would become an instant celebrity. I would have a position to live up to. People would make demands of me. I would be expected at all times to act like 'the champion'. Driving would not be fun any more. I wanted things to go on just as they were, and so I handed my car over to Fangio," he explained.

In 1957, despite team-mate Mike Hawthorn and himself starting the year with a one-two at Naples, his Lancia-Ferrari was consistently outclassed by the Maseratis and Vanwalls. Alongside Hawthorn, he played his part in one of the legendary drives in motor-racing history – a bit-part as it happened, in the famous scrap at the Nurburgring – when the Ferrari pair were passed by a scorchingly-quick Fangio on a mission to secure his fifth title (and Collins was lucky not to be blinded when the Argentinian's Maserati flicked a missile and broke his goggles).

Collins failed to win a Grand Prix, with a pair of third places his best results, although he did enjoy victories in the non-championship races at Syracuse and Naples.

Back to his best with the advent of Ferrari's classic Dino 246 Grand Prix car in 1958, he won the non-championship International Trophy race following a pair of sports car wins at Buenos Aires and Sebring. Sadly, just a fortnight after he stormed home ahead of Mike Hawthorn in the British Grand Prix at Silverstone, he was killed in the German Grand Prix at the Nurburgring when he clipped a bank and flipped while chasing Tony Brooks's Vanwall for the lead.

"I was just thinking of some choice words to say to him when we climbed out of two bent Ferraris when, without the slightest warning, fantastically quickly, his car just whipped straight over. I could not believe that it had happened. There was a blur as Pete was thrown out," said Hawthorn, after witnessing the death of his team-mate and close friend.

Peter Collins in his Ferrari on 29 May 1954.

1956
Fangio achieves three-peat

TALKING POINT

COLLINS GESTURE WINS IT FOR FANGIO

In one of the most remarkable moves in Formula One history, Briton Peter Collins sensationally sacrificed the chance of a maiden World Championship in his first year with Ferrari to give team-mate Juan Manuel Fangio the possibility of a fifth. Going into the final race of the season, the Italian Grand Prix at Monza, Collins, Fangio and Jean Behra could all win the title but after Fangio was forced out with a broken steering-arm, Collins sportingly handed over his car during a routine pit-stop. It was a move Fangio would never forget: it landed his fourth title and third in a row, as he ended second behind winner Stirling Moss.

Following his impressive third World Championship success the previous year, Juan Manuel Fangio switched to Ferrari after the departure of German manufacturer Mercedes-Benz. Fangio had guided Mercedes to the title in their two years of competition in 1954 and 1955, but he immediately set out to help the Ferrari team he had been forced to battle with in the past back to the top of the podium.

Ferrari had endured a difficult year in 1955 as Fangio strolled to success, but they acquired the old Lancia D50 chassis and put together a team comprising Fangio, Eugenio Castellotti, Luigi Musso and Peter Collins and were the competitive Ferrari of past days. Briton Mike Hawthorn had left in favour of BRM, while title contender Stirling Moss linked up with Maserati after he too was left out in the cold by Mercedes' withdrawal.

In the opening race of the season, the Argentinian Grand Prix in Buenos Aires, Moss's hopes of early success following his move to Maserati were hampered when his car was pushed over his foot prior to the race, but it had been the born-again Ferraris who had dominated the season-opening qualifying. Fangio, Castellotti and Musso sat alongside each other on the front row of the grid, with the Maserati of Frenchman Jean Behra joining them.

It was Musso who made the immediate impact at the start of the race but sacrificed the lead to Maserati's Jos´ Froilan Gonzalez, who in turn lost the advantage to his team-mate Carlos Menditeguy. Fangio failed to make an impact and was forced out of the race on lap 23 because of mechanical problems, while Gonzalez followed him two laps later. Italian driver Musso was forced to pit and hand over to Fangio, and race leaders Menditeguy, Castellotti and Moss all ran into problems, allowing the Argentine to close the gap.

And as Moss's Maserati trailed oil on to the circuit Fangio took the lead with over two-thirds of the race completed. The problem forced Moss to retire from the race and despite a spin, Fangio went on to win his home race ahead of Behra and Hawthorn, driving an Owen Racing Organisation Maserati. The works Maserati team protested against the eventual outcome, claiming Fangio had received a push-start after his spin, but the protest and a later appeal were turned down by the FIA.

Moss hits back

Moss gained revenge in the Monaco Grand Prix, despite a four-week break in action following Argentina, when he won the race ahead of Fangio. The Monte Carlo event featured a new-look chicane after Alberto Ascari's crash the previous year and would signal the arrival of BRM, although problems

Stirling Moss wins the Monaco Grand Prix.

Peter Collins and Juan Manuel Fangio.

RACE BY RACE DETAILS

ROUND 1 – ARGENTINA
Race ´Luigi Musso
Pole Juan Manuel Fangio
Fastest lap Juan Manuel Fangio

ROUND 2 – MONACO
Race Stirling Moss
Pole Juan Manuel Fangio
Fastest lap Juan Manuel Fangio

ROUND 3 – INDIANAPOLIS
Race Pat Flaherty
Pole Pat Flaherty
Fastest lap Eddie Russo

ROUND 4 – BELGIUM
Race Peter Collins
Pole Juan Manuel Fangio
Fastest lap Stirling Moss

ROUND 5 – FRANCE
Race Peter Collins
Pole Juan Manuel Fangio
Fastest lap Juan Manuel Fangio

ROUND 6 – BRITAIN
Race Juan Manuel Fangio
Pole Stirling Moss
Fastest lap Stirling Moss

ROUND 7 – GERMANY
Race Juan Manuel Fangio
Pole Juan Manuel Fangio
Fastest lap Juan Manuel Fangio

ROUND 8 – ITALY
Race Stirling Moss
Pole Juan Manuel Fangio
Fastest lap Stirling Moss

prevented Hawthorn and Tony Brooks from starting the race.

Moss, starting on the front row of the grid alongside former Mercedes team-mate Fangio and Castellotti, raced into the lead and was five seconds in front at the end of the first lap. Fangio made a mistake at Ste Devoté on the second lap and his spin caused Vanwall driver Harry Schell and Musso to go off and out of the race. Fangio rejoined and moved up to fourth following the retirement of Castellotti because of a clutch problem, and he gained third place when he overtook Behra. Team orders crept in when Collins allowed Fangio past to attempt to overhaul Moss's advantage in the race but the Argentine driver hit a wall and eventually pitted, handing his car to Castellotti.

Ferrari opted to bring Collins into the pits midway through the race and Fangio returned to the track in his place. He had regained his composure but had just 30 laps to catch leader Moss, who had a 45-second advantage. With 15 laps remaining, Moss was almost shunted out of the race in bizarre circumstances when his team-mate Cesare Perdisa, who was being lapped, suffered brake failure at the moment Moss went him past him. The two cars collided, one of the catches on Moss' bonnet was damaged and it lifted up slightly during some of the high-speed corners. But the Maserati driver kept his cool to take the chequered flag by six seconds from Fangio.

Former World Champion Giuseppe Farina, who finished his Formula One career in 1955, intended to race a Ferrari in the Indianapolis 500 but failed to compete after he missed the only dry session of qualifying and could not post a time. No Championship regular took part as American pole-sitter Pat Flaherty avoided a number of accidents in his John Zink Special to win ahead of Sam Hanks.

Victory for Collins

The fourth event of the calendar was the Belgian Grand Prix at Spa-Francorchamps, and it was to be significant for Briton Collins as he secured his maiden race victory with a faultless drive. The Ferrari driver ended almost one minute ahead of local driver Paul Frere, in a Ferrari, as Fangio was once again hampered by problems.

Fangio, as ever at the head of the grid with rival Moss and Collins, made a slow start in wet conditions and Moss guided his Maserati to the head of the field ahead of Castellotti. But Fangio quickly moved back into second by the end of lap three and then took the lead by the fifth lap.

Moss's challenge received a blow when he lost a wheel on the hill after Eau Rouge, but he managed to get the car back to the pits and take over from Perdisa. He was soon in sixth place when Castellotti retired with mechanical problems and at two-thirds race distance Fangio was forced out when he suffered transmission failure. Moss settled for third while Collins, who was handed the lead when Fangio exited the race, held off the challenge of Frere to

1956 DRIVERS' CHAMPIONSHIP

DRIVER	TEAM	POINTS
Juan Manuel Fangio	Lancia-Ferrari	30
Stirling Moss	Maserati	27
Peter Collins	Lancia-Ferrari	25
Jean Behra	Maserati	22
Pat Flaherty	Watson	8
Eugenio Castellotti	Lancia-Ferrari	7.5
Paul Frere	Lancia-Ferrari	6
Sam Hanks	Kurtis-Kraft	6
Francesco Godia	Maserati	6
Jack Fairman	Connaught	5
Luigi Musso	Lancia-Ferrari	4
Mike Hawthorn	Maserati	4
Ron Flockhart	Connaught	4
Don Freeland	Phillips	4
Cesare Perdisa	Maserati	3
Harry Schell	Vanwall	3
Alfonso de Portago	Lancia-Ferrari	3
Johnnie Parsons	Kuzma	3
Olivier Gendebien	Lancia-Ferrari	2
Hernando da Silva Ramos	Gordoni	2
Luigi Villoresi	Maserati	2
Horace Gould	Maserati	2
Louis Rosier	Maserati	2

claim his first-ever win. The victory made Collins the third Briton to win in as many years.

Collins in the frame

The emergence of the talented Collins would continue when he won again in the French Grand Prix a month later to move to the head of the Championship standings. With the BRMs missing from the grid for a second successive race in Reims, Hawthorn appeared in place of Trintignant in a Vanwall, while Trintignant debuted for the new Bugatti team.

The Maseratis failed to show their true pace and Ferrari dominated qualifying. Fangio, Castellotti and Collins held the front row of the grid and Moss was on the third row with his team-mate Behra. The race proved to be no different as Ferrari once again dominated proceedings.

Harry Schell and Moss both retired early, but both replaced team-mates in Vanwalls and Maseratis respectively and it was American Schell who impressed most with a fine display of sheer speed. In fact, he was so quick he caught Castellotti and Collins unaware and went past them, only for the Ferrari duo to hit back and join Fangio ahead of him.

But a fuel pump problem cost Schell valuable time and a leaking fuel line forced Fangio down to fourth. He would end fourth as Collins held off Castellotti's challenge to claim back-to-back wins.

Fangio got himself back into the Championship picture when a number of retirements allowed him to take the the British Grand Prix at Silverstone, which witnessed the return of the BRMs.

With Hawthorn and Brooks back behind the wheel of the British marque, they impressed in their home event. Hawthorn qualified on the first row along with Moss and Fangio and then made an instant impression on the race when he led during the early stages. Brooks also made a good start and ran second in the early stages.

Brooks exchanged places twice with Fangio, who was in third, before Moss's Maserati moved up to second on lap 11. Five laps later Moss challenged Hawthorn, pressurising him to sacrifice the lead while Brooks slowly went backwards.

Hawthorn lost another place when Maserati's Roy Salvadori overtook him and he retired minutes later after his car lost power and faded. Brooks' BRM stopped and lost time while it was repaired, but minutes after he returned to the track the young British driver was thrown out of the cockpit of his burnt-out car after a crash.

With Moss still leading, Fangio and Collins closed the gap when second-placed Salvadori was hampered by a fuel-line problem and Moss' advantage was reduced when he pitted after he ran low on oil. Collins retired but immediately took over from the Marquis de Portago and Salvadori's problems forced him to quit the race.

Moss was next to suffer problems and was forced to pit again when his engine lost power and the stop gave the lead to Fangio. Moss's Maserati was fixed, but another problem forced him to pit for a third time and he eventually called it a day when his

Peter Collins at the start of the Belgian Grand Prix.

Juan Manuel Fangio and Peter Collins battle it out at the Italian Grand Prix.

axle broke. Fangio ended one lap ahead of Collins, who finished second with the ever-consistent Behra once again third.

No duel in Germany

At the Nurburgring Fangio, Collins and Castellotti were all on the front row as expected and were joined by Moss. It was Collins who was quickest off the grid but Fangio had soon raced into the ascendancy. But with the two drivers seemingly on course for another duel, Collins' car began to produce fumes in the cockpit and he had to retire when his team discovered that the cause of the problem was a split in the fuel-line.

Fangio was out on his own as Moss attempted to reduce the gap. Collins returned to the track in De Portago's car and targeted Behra, who was running in third position. Frenchman Behra had to stop when a strap broke on his car, but Collins, who had moved up to third, made a mistake and spun off and subsequently retired.

Fangio increased his lead to eventually finish 45 seconds ahead of Moss, who in turn ended more than seven minutes ahead of Behra.

The final race of the season in Italy presented three drivers, Fangio, Behra, and Collins, with the chance of World Championship glory and it was to end with a third title for Fangio, albeit in strange circumstances.

Fangio held an eight-point lead over Collins and Behra and the only way he could lose the title battle was if he failed to finish and one of the challengers won the race and posted the fastest lap.

That scenario remained plausible when he was forced to retire with a broken steering-arm. When Behra also retired it was expected that Luigi Musso, who was due to pit, would hand over the controls to Fangio but he remained inside the cockpit and it was not until Collins made one of the most sporting gestures that Fangio's hopes of a fourth World Championship were finally secured.

Collins could have won a first title but sensationally handed over to Fangio, who eventually finished second, to hand him the Championship. Leader Moss ran out of fuel with five laps to go as he aimed to coast to victory and had to rely on team-mate Luigi Piotti to push him into the pits for a refuel. Fortunately for Moss, Musso, who had overtaken him during the stop, suffered steering problems and Moss came home six seconds ahead of the field. But the year was Fangio's and it was all thanks to the sportsmanship of Collins.

SHORTS

The legendary Brickyard track, host to the Indianapolis 500, was given a face-lift in 1956, with the whole circuit resurfaced in response to the disastrous '55 race in which Manuel Ayulo was involved in a crash in qualifying and later died from his injuries, and reigning champion Bill Vukovich was killed when his car burst into flames. The changes were a success – at least for this year – and the race passed without incident.

Mike Hawthorn

MIKE HAWTHORN, Britain's first World Champion, was the embodiment of national post-war aspirations. His reputation for wild partying off-track belied the commitment he showed behind the wheel.

CAREER DETAILS

1929 Born 10 April in Mexborough, Yorkshire
1950 Moves from motorcycle scrambles to four-wheeled competition at the Brighton Speed Trials
1952 Graduates to single-seaters and won first time out in a Formula Two Cooper at Goodwood, beating Fangio later in the day. GP début follows with fourth place in Belgian GP behind the Ferraris. Third at British GP, finish ing season fourth overall
1953 Accepts Enzo Ferrari's offer of a works drive. Wins French GP from Fangio by a second. Finishes season fourth overall
1954 Finishes season in third place
1955 Quits racing, following death of his father, to run family's garage business. Later rejoined Ferrari
1956 Mixed-up season swapping between Maserati, BRM and Vanwall chassis
1957 Bounces back with Ferrari
1958 Wins World Championship to become Britain's first World Champion. Wins only one GP compared to Moss's four GP wins, but consistent scoring secured him title
1959 Killed in road accident on 22 January on Guildford by-pass, Surrey

FORMULA ONE RECORD

Year	Team	Wins	Poles	Fast laps	Pts
1952	Cooper	0	0	0	10
1953	Ferrari	1	0	0	19
1954	Ferrari	1	0	1	24.5
1955	Vanwall	0	0	0	–
	Ferrari	0	0	0	–
1956	Maserati	0	0	0	–
	BRM	0	0	0	–
	Vanwall	0	0	0	–
1957	Ferrari	0	0	0	4
1958	Ferrari	1	4	5	42

Mike Hawthorn fulfilled a Boy's Own image of a racing driver – the flying neck scarf, the bow-tie, the pipe and battered cap, the practical jokes. To everyone he was a hero, the tall blond who enjoyed life and did motor-racing as a diversion, the encapsulation of post-war British spirit. "While Mike was quite likely to be seen in the bar on the eve of a race, I was more likely to be tucked up in bed," recalled rival Stirling Moss.

Hawthorn's father Leslie, a keen motorcycle racer, bought a partnership in the TT Garage business in Farnham, Surrey, idyllically close to Brooklands racetrack, when his son was just two years old. Young Hawthorn's love of speed found first expression in motorcycle scrambles and trials while he was a schoolboy. He transferred to four wheels at the 1950 Brighton Speed Trials. By 1952 he had graduated to single-seaters and won first time out in a Formula Two at Goodwood. Later in the day he sensationally beat a similarly-equipped Fangio – a demonstration that was the making of his reputation.

Hawthorn rose to international prominence on the same wave of British passion for motor-racing that propelled Moss, Peter Collins and Tony Brooks to public acclaim in the 1950s. "As British as the Royal Family and roast beef," was how he was once described. "He was always laughing and sticking two fingers up, very much alive," said British racer Roy Salvadori. He had a similar air of boyish gaucheness as his great friend Collins, but Hawthorn was also a formidable competitor – although inconsistently so. There were days when he seemed to suffer from a maddening lack of interest. In the mood, however, he was difficult to beat and made his mark when, hired by Ferrari at the start of the 1953 season, he won the French Grand Prix at Reims, beating Fangio to the chequered flag by just one second.

"We would go screaming down the straight side by side absolutely flat-out, grinning at each other, with me crouching down in the cockpit, trying to save every ounce of wind resistance. We were only inches apart and I could clearly see the rev counter in Fangio's cockpit," recalled Hawthorn of the duel.

He finished 1953 ranked fourth overall, with the nation hailing its own world-class Grand Prix driver. It was not a happy time for Hawthorn, however. He hit headlines for allegedly dodging National Service but a combination of a kidney condition and the after-effects of burns sustained in the 1954 Syracuse Grand Prix would have almost certainly rendered him ineligible on medical grounds.

In that year, he finished third in the Championship table behind Fangio and José Froilan

Mike Hawthorn drives the Ferrari D246 in 1958, the year he won the World Championship.

> "If you take away the normal hazards of motor-racing, you take away the reasons for going motor-racing."

Hawthorn on the danger inherent in his sport

Gonzalez. The death of his father saw him quit Ferrari temporarily to run the family's garage business. He rejoined the *scuderia* but by then the mighty Mercedes team were winning everything. He would also drive the Jaguar D-Types in long-distance sports car races, winning the Sebring 12-Hours. He also won the Le Mans 24 Hours sharing a Jaguar D-Type with Ivor Bueb, but his race was spoiled when he was involved in the accident that resulted in Pierre Levegh's Mercedes flying into the crowd, killing more than 80 spectators.

The 1956 season was a mix-up as he jumped between Maserati, BRM and Vanwall chassis but in 1957 he bounced back as a front-runner with Ferrari and was paired with close friend Collins in the Ferrari team. 1958 turned out to be a season-long battle between Moss and Hawthorn – and British domination of Formula One.

At a Stewards' Enquiry following the Portuguese Grand Prix, at Oporto, Moss famously testified that Hawthorn had not actually driven illegally, against the flow of traffic on the circuit, so Hawthorn's second place was allowed to stand. Moss's sportsmanlike gesture ultimately cost him the world title and gave the title to his arch-rival Hawthorn.

The plateau of happy competitive racing ended for Hawthorn with the tragic death of Collins in the 1958 German Grand Prix. Given the number two before the Championship-settling Moroccan Grand Prix at Casablanca soon afterwards, a superstitious Hawthorn changed it to number six instead. "No doubt it was partly due to nerves, but as Peter [Collins] and Luigi [Musso] had both been killed with the number two on their car, I asked to have it altered." He finished second to win the World Championship – Britain's first Formula One World Champion – but immediately announced his retirement. He was set to consolidate a career in business when he crashed his Jaguar saloon on the 'Hogs-Back' Guildford by-pass early in 1959.

Mike Hawthorn, a formidable competitor who was always laughing... very much alive.

1957
Fifth title for amazing Fangio

Fangio wins in his home race in Buenos Aires.

TALKING POINT
THE END OF AN ERA

The 1957 season signalled the end of an era in motor racing history when Argentine Juan Manuel Fangio announced he would bow out of the sport after his fifth Championship success.

Fangio won his fifth title, and a fourth successive Championship, with Maserati but both driver and manufacturer officially left Formula One at the end of the season.

Maserati cited a lack of funds for their withdrawal but Fangio did return briefly after 1957 to compete in just two more races – in Argentina, where he won, and in France when he was fourth. But the sport had lost a true great from its regular list of drivers.

Despite guiding a Ferrari to World Championship success for his fourth title, Juan Manuel Fangio opted to switch to rival manufacturer Maserati for the 1957 season and his decision was rewarded when he landed his fifth, and final, title and more importantly the fourth successive Championship that would not be equalled again this century. The win also marked the withdrawal of Maserati, who blamed a lack of funds on their failure to return to the sport to defend the Championship.

Argentine Fangio replaced Stirling Moss in the latest 250F model, with the British driver moving to Vanwall, while the talented Mike Hawthorn rejoined Ferrari for a third time from BRM. He teamed up with close friend Peter Collins and Eugenio Castellotti but the Italian marque was to endure a nightmare year in which they failed to win a race.

Fangio comfortable at home

It was the irrepressible Fangio who once again triumphed in his home race in Argentina, despite Moss, who raced in a Maserati for the last time before his move to Vanwall, outpacing him in qualifying. But it was Frenchman Jean Behra who led the race early on after he had started alongside Moss and Fangio at the head of the grid.

Moss had been forced to pit at the end of the first lap after his slow start had been caused by damage to the throttle mechanism, and Behra remained in front after exchanging the lead with Castellotti. Collins was soon in front, however, but a clutch problem forced him into the pits for repairs.

Fangio soon moved into the ascendancy when he overtook Behra while the leader of the chasing pack, Castellotti, spun and allowed Hawthorn into third. But Ferrari's problems began to mount when both Hawthorn and Musso retired with the same clutch problem that had put Collins in the pits.

With Fangio and Behra coasting to first and second, Castellotti's attempts to secure third failed when a wheel fell off with 24 laps remaining. He retired, and it would be his last Grand Prix before he was killed in a crash in testing two months later.

The drivers had to wait four months for the next Championship event, the Monaco Grand Prix, and by the time it came around Moss was with Vanwall and Fangio was now the undisputed number one at Maserati. Maurice Trintignant was the replacement for Castellotti. Once again, the dominant Fangio and Moss occupied the front row of the grid with Collins alongside them.

Moss and Collins exchanged the lead in the opening laps but the two crashed out on lap four. Moss, leading at the time, left the track at the chicane, and when Collins attempted to avoid a collision he hit the wall. Fangio steered clear of trouble to lead but Tony Brooks braked hard and was hit from behind by Hawthorn, although Brooks remained in the race. Brooks chased Fangio home to record an impressive second, with the only excitement in the race coming in the battle for third place with American Masten Gregory claiming a podium finish in his Maserati. Jack Brabham, in a Cooper Climax, arrived into the fray but a fuel pump failure cost him and he ended sixth.

Test driver dies

Once again, Giuseppe Farina planned to run in the Indianapolis 500 but this time he was prevented from doing so after Keith Andrews crashed the car in testing. He was killed in the incident and the car was destroyed and Farina, the only European on the driver entry list, did not race.

The event remained on the world calendar despite none of the Championship entrants competing and Sam Hanks, who had raced every year since 1940, finally won in a Belond Exhaust Special. The American driver promptly retired from motor-racing after the success.

The drivers returned to competitive action in the French Grand Prix, the fourth round of the Championship at the Rouen-les-Essarts circuit after the Belgian and Dutch Grand Prix's had been cancelled. The two races, scheduled in June, failed to take place after race organizers disputed funding.

Moss and Brooks missed the French event for Vanwall through a sinus infection and a crash in Le Mans, respectively, and were replaced by Roy Salvadori and Stuart Lewis-Evans. Luigi Musso was back with Ferrari. Moss's absence meant Fangio had little opposition and he earned pole position and won his third race of the season. Fangio made a slow start but was in front by lap four as Musso handed the lead to the Argentine driver. BRM driver Ron Flockhart seriously damaged his car in a crash but escaped unhurt. Musso held on to second and when Behra dropped down to fourth when Collins went past him the top three remained unchanged at the chequered flag. Behra lost a further place to Hawthorn as Ferrari added respectability to their season with a two-three-four finish.

Moss and Brooks both returned to the cockpit of their Vanwalls in the British Grand Prix, which was held at Aintree, and it looked as if they had not been away as they qualified first and third respectively. Fangio, for a change, was fourth.

Behra, who had qualified second, was quickest off the startline but Moss, with the home crowd behind him, ended the opening lap in front. He built up a lead but was forced to pit when his car got problems and Behra extended his own lead.

Brooks, regarded as the second driver to Moss, was called into the pits and he handed over his Vanwall to his senior team-mate. Moss rejoined in ninth – Brooks was in second when he came into the pit-lane – but quickly emerged through the field and moved up to fifth. Hawthorn went in pursuit of Behra as Fangio and Collins fell by the wayside with mechanical problems and Moss caught up with the third-placed Lewis-Evans, also in a Vanwall. But the race changed on lap 69 when Behra's clutch exploded and subsequently Hawthorn suffered a puncture after running over the debris left on the track.

Lewis-Evans, narrowly ahead of Moss, was a shock leader but Moss went past and into the lead for a dream win in his home event. The dream one-two for British manufacturer Vanwall was denied when a broken throttle linkage forced Lewis-Evans

RACE BY RACE DETAILS

ROUND 1 – ARGENTINA
Race Juan Manuel Fangio
Pole Stirling Moss
Fastest lap Stirling Moss

ROUND 2 – MONACO
Race Juan Manuel Fangio
Pole Juan Manuel Fangio
Fastest lap Juan Manuel Fangio

ROUND 3 – UNITED STATES
Race Sam Hanks
Pole Pat O'Connor
Fastest lap Jim Rathman

ROUND 4 – FRANCE
Race Juan Manuel Fangio
Pole Juan Manuel Fangio
Fastest lap Luigi Musso

ROUND 5 – BRITAIN
Race Stirling Moss
Pole Stirling Moss
Fastest lap Stirling Moss

ROUND 6 – GERMANY
Race Juan Manuel Fangio
Pole Juan Manuel Fangio
Fastest lap Juan Manuel Fangio

ROUND 7 – PESCARA
Race Stirling Moss
Pole Juan Manuel Fangio
Fastest lap Stirling Moss

ROUND 8 – ITALY
Race Stirling Moss
Pole Stuart Lewis-Evans
Fastest lap Tony Brooks

Jack Brabham pushes his Cooper back to the pits after a fuel pump problem put him out of the Monaco Grand Prix.

Stirling Moss takes the flag at Aintree after a dream win in the British Grand Prix.

out of the race. But Moss's victory marked a historic day for British motor-racing with the first-ever win for a British marque.

Vanwall make an impression

Vanwall's impressive rise to prominence put the Maseratis and Ferraris on edge for a thrilling 22-lap encounter at the Nurburgring for the German Grand Prix, but it was Fangio who left his mark on the history of motor-racing to win one of the all-time classic races with some of the most spectacular driving the sport has seen, as he guaranteed a fifth title two races before the end of the season.

He claimed pole for the race, which featured three Porsches for the first time, but it was Ferrari duo Collins and Hawthorn who battled for supremacy. Fangio eventually took over at the head of the field and gradually increased his advantage as the two chased him.

A slow pit-stop in mid-race cost Fangio the lead but he produced one of the best drives of his career to overtake Collins and Hawthorn on the penultimate lap and the display crowned a magnificent season for the Argentine as he landed a fifth title.

The Pescara Grand Prix had been held since 1924, but it made a debut appearance on the World Championship calendar following the cancellation of the Belgian and Dutch Grands Prix at Spa-Francorchamps and Zandvoort. The race itself was only scheduled to last 18 laps because of the mammoth 16-mile length of the road circuit.

But Ferrari chief Enzo Ferrari refused to send cars for Hawthorn and Collins to compete in, because Fangio had sewn up the Championship in the German Grand Prix. The Italian also did not give the British drivers a car in protest at the Italian government's decision to ban road-racing following the accident which killed Ferrari driver Alfonso de Portago in the Mille Miglia.

Musso competed in a Ferrari, but only as a privateer, and he qualified in third, but the race was a shoot-out between the Maserati of Fangio and the Vanwall of Moss. Musso led as the race started but the opening was marred when Maserati privateer Horaco Gould hit a mechanic who had been slow in leaving the grid. Vanwall's Brooks retired with mechanical problems on the opening lap, which proved to be one of the most dramatic of the season.

Moss overtook Musso and Fangio ran in third before a number of casualties succumbed due to the extensive heat on the August day. Overheating tyres cost Lewis-Evans as he suffered two punctures and Behra was troubled by engine failure.

With just six laps remaining, Musso exited the race when his engine blew and the oil he leaked on to the track sent Fangio into a spin. The spin result-

SHORTS

The 1957 Championship race was again dominated by two names, Fangio and Moss, as the great rivals battled head-to-head throughout the season. The Brit and the Argentine accounted for six of eight pole positions, recorded five fastest laps and finished as winners in seven of the eight Championship races. Unfortunately for Moss, Fangio would again prevail while he was forced to play bridesmaid for the second year in succession.

ed in a damaged wheel for the Maserati driver and by the time his problem had been rectified Moss had roared into an unassailable lead. In fact, Moss's advantage was so big he had time to stop for a drink and to have his oil topped up and beat second-placed Fangio by over three minutes as he added a second race win to Vanwall's record.

Finale in Italy

Ferrari returned to action in the season finale in Italy, but the Monza circuit featured no banking for the first time. The track had been distinguished by the banking but it featured a circuit not too dissimilar to the current design.

With Ferrari back in the fold, the race was set to be a three-way battle with the Maseratis and Vanwalls and it was the emerging Lewis-Evans who claimed pole position for the race. The British marque was in such good shape Vanwalls occupied the head of the grid, with Moss and Brooks joining him.

The three Vanwalls were quick off the grid but by the end of the first lap Behra was up to second with Moss in front of him. Fangio joined the leading quartet and the five left the rest behind. The traditional slipstreaming of Monza allowed the five to constantly change places, with Moss and Behra exchanging the lead on several occasions.

Fangio challenged Moss' lead but ended behind the three Vanwalls again. Fangio moved back into second when first Brooks pitted and then Lewis-Evans has problems and had to pit. Moss led Fangio home but the real battle was for third with the impressive von Trips winning the tussle after Behra (new tyres), Harry Schell (an oil leak on his Maserati), Collins (engine trouble) and Hawthorn (split fuel pipe) all lost the chance of a podium finish.

Fangio's remarkable achievement of five championships was undoubtedly the act of one of the greatest drivers in the history of the sport. But 1957 would be his last full year in the sport and the title-winning season signalled the exit of Maserati.

Ferrari had endured a nightmare year after lifting the Championship with Juan Manuel Fangio the previous year. The disastrous deaths of Eugenio Castellotti and Alfonso de Portago, who were both killed in action, marred the season. It was one of the bleakest periods in the short history of Enzo Ferrari's team. They did not win a single race and the bitter pill would only be made easier to swallow with the withdrawal of Maserati after Fangio's fifth success.

1957 DRIVERS' CHAMPIONSHIP

DRIVER	TEAM	POINTS
Juan Manuel Fangio	Maserati	40
Stirling Moss	Maserati/Vanwall	25
Luigi Musso	Lancia-Ferrari	16
Mike Hawthorn	Lancia-Ferrari	13
Tony Brooks	Vanwall	11
Masten Gregory	Maserati	10
Harry Schell	Maserati	8
Sam Hanks	Epperly	8
Peter Collins	Lancia-Ferrari	8
Jean Behra	Maserati	8
Jim Rathmann	Epperly	7
Stuart Lewis-Evans	Connaught/Vanwall	5
Maurice Trintignant	Lancia-Ferrari	5
Wolfgang von Trips	Lancia-Ferrari	4
Carlos Menditeguy	Maserati	4
Jimmy Bryan	Kuzma	4
Paul Russo	Kurtis-Kraft	3
Roy Salvadori	Cooper-Climax	2
Andy Linden	Kurtis-Kraft	2
Giorgio Scarlatti	Maserati	1
José Froilan Gonzalez	Lancia-Ferrari	1
Alfonso de Portago	Lancia-Ferrari	1

Juan Fangio takes victory in Germany where he also confirmed his fifth title.

1958
Britain's first Formula One title

TALKING POINT
TRIUMPH AND TRAGEDY FOR BRITAIN

Formula One may have been dominated by Juan Manuel Fangio during the first decade of the World Championship but 1958 was to be Britain's year, with Ferrari driver Mike Hawthorn benefiting from the retirement of the legendary Argentinian.

Hawthorn narrowly ended a titanic season-long battle with compatriot Stirling Moss as champion to replace Fangio at the top of Formula One, but his success was overshadowed by the death of team-mate and close friend Peter Collins in the German Grand Prix and another Ferrari driver, Luigi Musso, in the French Grand Prix.

The tragedy prompted champion Hawthorn to quit the sport at the end of the season, but he too would lose his life, along with his two children, at the start of 1959.

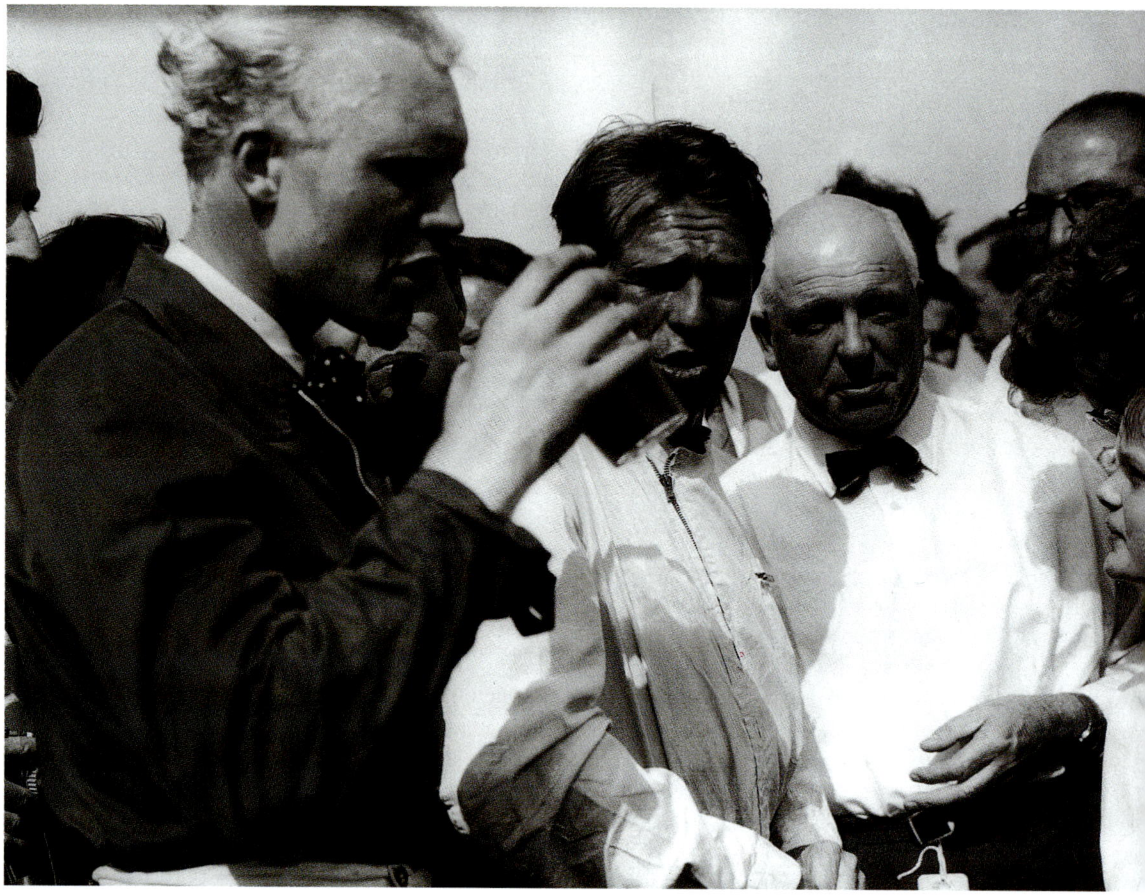

Mike Hawthorn and Peter Collins enjoy a drink after the British Grand Prix at Silverstone.

With reigning Champion Juan Manuel Fangio withdrawing from Formula One, apart from his occasional entry as a privateer, and the Maserati team he powered to the title joining him on the sidelines, Ferrari undoubtedly had the perfect opportunity to return to the top of the sport. They took it with open arms.

By the end of the year, Ferrari driver Mike Hawthorn had overcome rival Stirling Moss, once again in a Maserati, to put himself into the Formula One history books as Britain's first World Champion.

This year, Ferrari opted to replace the old Lancia chassis with the new Dino 246 and had Hawthorn, Peter Collins and Luigi Musso as their Championship contenders. Vanwall kept their 1957 line-up – Moss, Tony Brooks and Stuart Lewis-Evans – and were the only real pretenders to what threatened to be a Ferrari monopoly.

Fangio competed in his home event, the Argentinian Grand Prix, which once again opened the season, behind the wheel of a Ferrari 250, while a number of other drivers found themselves in privateer Ferraris. With Vanwall and fellow-British manufacturer BRM not competing in the South American event, Moss was cleared to race in Rob Walker's Cooper-Climax 43.

Just 10 cars competed and, despite retiring from the World Championship, it was Fangio who was quickest in qualifying going to the head of the grid alongside Ferrari team-mates Hawthorn and Collins.

Moss win in Argentina

It was Frenchman Jean Behra, however, competing as a privateer in a Ferrari, who was quickest at the start of the race as Collins was forced to retire with driveshaft failure. Hawthorn and Fangio moved ahead of Behra by the end of the second lap. By lap 10 it was Fangio, rather than Hawthorn, who was in the ascendancy, but his long-standing rival Moss had grabbed most attention with his speed in the Cooper-Climax as he moved into second. Fangio pitted and sacrificed the lead, but worse was to follow.

Behra's chances of catching Moss were reduced

when he spun, but Fangio's were dashed completely when his engine began to misfire. Musso and Hawthorn chased Moss but, expecting the leader to make a pit-stop, failed to push hard enough.

Moss did not stop and the tiny Cooper-Climax coasted to victory. It was the first for the British manufacturer in the World Championship and would start a revolution of rear-engine machines.

Four months after Moss' win in Argentina, the World Championship resumed in Monaco. Prospects looked bright for Ferrari after they had triumphed in the non-championship Syracuse Grand Prix and the International Trophy. But in fact, the event turned out to be a British monopoly of sorts.

Enter Team Lotus

Monaco marked the introduction of Team Lotus into the World Championship with Cliff Allison and Graham Hill, and the Connaughts also had a revival after Bernie Ecclestone had purchased the cars. But he and fellow-drivers Bruce Kessler and Paul Emery all failed to qualify.

Brooks' Vanwall topped qualifying, and Behra and Jack Brabham followed him; but it was Salvadori, in a factory Cooper, who went into the lead at the start. However, he had to pit after he collided with a fellow-competitor and bent his suspension.

Behra led from Brooks, but a misfire forced the latter to retire on lap 22 of the 100 scheduled laps, and when Behra had to pit because of brake trouble it was Hawthorn in front, but with Moss breathing down his neck. Moss soon moved into the lead but engine failure forced him out.

When a broken fuel pump cost Hawthorn his place, it was Trintignant who led in the same Cooper. His 40-second advantage allowed him to ease to victory as Musso and Behra, recovered from his problem, followed him home.

The third round, the Dutch Grand Prix, followed a week after Monaco and the field almost replicated Monte Carlo. Both Vanwall and Ferrari ran with the same line-up, while Rob Walker had Brabham and Salvadori behind the wheel. He also provided a private car for Trintignant. Vanwall drivers Lewis-Evans, Brooks and Moss dominated qualifying and held the front row of the grid with the BRM of Behra and Brabham behind them alongside Hawthorn.

A large crowd watched the race, held on a Monday morning, and witnessed Moss run in front early. Brooks, who had begun at the front, was hit from behind and had to pit for repairs two laps. Moss extended his advantage and eventually won to end Cooper's hopes of a third victory.

The USA beamed at the prospect of Fangio competing in the Indianapolis 500, again included on the World Championship calendar despite lack of interest from the regular drivers. Fangio, however, opted not to qualify despite taking part in initial practice. The Argentine deemed his car too slow and unreliable and the race turned into an all-American affair once again. Jimmy Bryan won in a Belond AP Special, but 1958 turned into another year The Brickyard would care to forget.

The field passed through the opening corners without incident but at turn three disaster struck. Ed Elisian lost control, went into the wall and collected Dick Rathmann on the way. Jimmy Reece spun and was hit by Bob Veith and Pat O'Connor. O'Connor flipped and died from his injuries, and Jerry Unser crashed over a wall and dislocated his shoulder.

The regulars were back in action at Spa-Francorchamps in June, as Formula One returned to the Belgian track after a two-year absence. The circuit featured adjustments, the average speed had been increased and Ferrari finally returned to form.

Hawthorn claimed pole with Musso second and

RACE BY RACE DETAILS

ROUND 1 – ARGENTINA
Race Stirling Moss
Pole Juan Manuel Fangio
Fastest lap Juan Manuel Fangio

ROUND 2 – MONACO
Race Maurice Trintignant
Pole Tony Brooks
Fastest lap Mike Hawthorn

ROUND 3 – HOLLAND
Race Stirling Moss
Pole Stuart Lewis-Evans
Fastest lap Stirling Moss

ROUND 4 – UNITED STATES
Race Jimmy Bryan
Pole Jim Rathmann
Fastest lap Tony Bettenhausen

ROUND 5 – BELGIUM
Race Tony Brooks
Pole Mike Hawthorn
Fastest lap Mike Hawthorn

ROUND 6 – FRANCE
Race Mike Hawthorn
Pole Mike Hawthorn
Fastest lap Mike Hawthorn

ROUND 7 – BRITAIN
Race Peter Collins
Pole Stirling Moss
Fastest lap Mike Hawthorn

ROUND 8 – GERMANY
Race Tony Brooks
Pole Mike Hawthorn
Fastest lap Stirling Moss

Round 9 – PORTUGAL
Race Stirling Moss
Pole Stirling Moss
Fastest lap Mike Hawthorn

ROUND 10 – ITALY
Race Tony Brooks
Pole Stirling Moss
Fastest lap Phil Hill

ROUND 11 – MOROCCO
Race Stirling Moss
Pole Mike Hawthorn
Fastest lap Stirling Moss

The first woman to compete in the World Championship, Theresa de Filipis, competed in the Belgian Grand Prix.

Luigi Musso gets into his Ferrari before the start of the French Grand Prix during which he lost control of his car and went into a ditch. He died later in hospital.

Brooks fourth. Moss split the trio in third, but missed a gear when leading on the first lap up the hill after Eau Rouge and blew his engine.

Collins challenged new leader Brooks, but his engine, which was not right on the grid, failed. He was followed out by team-mate Musso, who crashed after tyre failure. Brooks coasted to take the flag ahead of Hawthorn with Lewis-Evans third.

First woman in Formula One

The event added another chapter to the history of the sport when Theresa de Fillipis became the first woman to start a World Championship race. The 37-year-old was over half a minute slower than pole-sitter Hawthorn and ended two laps down on winner Brooks in 10th.

Ferrari's search for a first win of the season ended at the French Grand Prix in Reims. Hawthorn claimed a victory, but Musso's death marred the day.

Fangio competed in the Maserati 250F development car "Piccolo" and put it eighth on the grid. The BRM of Schell led the race in its early stages but Hawthorn soon emerged in front as Collins dropped back on the fifth lap when something became lodged under his brake pedal. On lap 10, however, tragedy struck. Musso arrived into the Muizon Corner at 150 mph attempting to close the gap on Hawthorn, who was leading, but lost control and ended in the ditch. His machine somersaulted and the Italian was thrown from the cockpit. He died in hospital.

The race also signalled the end for Fangio. The 47-year-old would never race in Grand Prix again.

Collins, whose relationship with Enzo Ferrari had became increasingly strained, proved his worth when he won the British Grand Prix to ensure the revival continued.

The event had threatened to be one of the most open races of the season – one car each from Ferrari, Vanwall, BRM and Cooper were on the front row of the grid. It turned out to be Ferrari's race with Hawthorn following Collins home.

Collins made an immediate impact as he burst into the lead from the second row of the grid and extended his lead lap by lap, while Hawthorn and Moss broke away from the pack. When Moss's Vanwall blew up on lap 26, the result was beyond doubt. Hawthorn pitted to have his oil topped up but emerged ahead of Salvadori, who had overcame Lewis-Evans in their battle for third place.

The victory would be Collins' last in Formula One. Two weeks later the Briton died from injuries he received in a spectacular crash in the German Grand Prix.

Crash in Germany kills Collins

Collins lost the lead to Brooks towards the end of the race at the Nurburgring, and in trying to catch the Vanwall driver went wide at Pflanzgarten, caught a wheel in the ditch and was thrown from the cockpit into a tree.

Moss had exited the race after four laps because of a broken magneto and Hawthorn would retire within minutes of Collins' accident, citing clutch failure. Brooks duly won ahead of Salvadori with

SHORTS

Despite his retirement, Fangio still managed to send shockwaves of anticipation throughout the sport as a privateer. At his home GP in Argentina he took pole and led before retiring and drove the French GP in a Maserati development car. US fans beamed with excitement at the prospect of Fangio competing in the Indy 500, but he opted not to qualify despite taking part in the initial stages of practice, deeming his car too slow.

Trintignant third.

It had been the first time Formula One and Formula Two cars had competed in the same race – 26 cars ran – and the Formula Two contingent included Bruce McLaren, a future star of the sport.

After losing Musso and Collins in the space of three races, Enzo Ferrari opted to run just two cars in the Portuguese Grand Prix in Porto. The street track featured cobbles, tramlines and posts, but the Vanwall coped admirably.

Moss, who started at the front with Lewis-Evans and Hawthorn, was quickest at the beginning and after exchanging places with Hawthorn temporarily led the field home with Hawthorn in tow.

In the penultimate round at Monza, Ferrari debutante Phil Hill made an immediate impact on as he briefly led Moss and Hawthorn before the latter took over at the front. Further back, von Trips suffered a broken leg when he clashed with Schell and was thrown from his car as it landed after flying through the air. Schell, whose car had also been airborne, was unhurt.

The titanic battle between Hawthorn and Moss, who could both win the title, continued at Monza and the result was seemingly decided when Moss dropped out through gearbox problems. But Moss' team-mate Brooks ensured the tussle would carry on in the Moroccan Grand Prix when he slipstreamed Hawthorn to take the win in Italy. Debutante Hill finished a creditable third.

Morocco's debut on the international motor-racing scene came with the season-ending race, on the Ain Diab circuit near Casablanca, and the race, like the film, was fit for any screen as the Championship was decided in true style, with newly-crowned King Mohammed V watching.

Moss had to win, set the fastest lap time and hope Hawthorn ended third at best if he was to stand a chance of the Championship. Moss made the best start and after an error by Hill, Hawthorn waved the rookie through to challenge the leader.

Brooks, out to help Moss's cause, overtook Hawthorn to set up a thrilling finale. But Moss dented his car and his own hopes when he ran into the back of Wolfgang Seidel before setting a new lap record, which handed him the extra point needed.

When Brooks' engine blew, Hawthorn was set for a maiden title and Hill was ordered to let him past into second place. Lewis-Evans, another of Moss' team-mates, attempted to close the gap on Hawthorn but his engine blew up.

With oil spilling on to the track, Lewis-Evans's car caught fire and he jumped out with his overalls alight. The blaze was extinguished and he was flown back to Britain for treatment. He died six days later in a specialist burns unit in East Grinstead.

Moss eased to victory but it was not enough to land the Championship. The only consolation for Vanwall, both for the title defeat and the Lewis-Evans tragedy, lay in their success in the inaugural Constructors' Championship.

Hawthorn entered the record-books as Britain's first title-winner but days later the 29-year-old announced his retirement. Three months later he, too, would lose his life when racing his Jaguar road car with Rob Walker's Mercedes on the Guildford by-pass. Hawthorn had overcome the adversity of watching two team-mates die in action to become World Champion, but his impending retirement and then death left its mark on British motor-racing.

1958 DRIVERS' CHAMPIONSHIP

DRIVER	TEAM	POINTS
Mike Hawthorn	Ferrari	42
Stirling Moss	Cooper-Climax/Vanwall	41
Tony Brooks	Vanwall	24
Roy Salvadori	Cooper-Climax	15
Peter Collins	Ferrari	14
Harry Schell	BRM	14
Maurice Trintignant	Cooper-Climax	12
Luigi Musso	Ferrari	12
Stuart Lewis-Evans	Vanwall	11
Phil Hill	Ferrari	9
Wolfgang von Trips	Ferrari	9
Jean Behra	BRM	9
Jimmy Bryan	Epperly	8
Juan Manuel Fangio	Maserati	7
George Amick	Epperly	6
Johnny Boyd	Kurtis-Kraft	4
Tony Bettenhausen	Epperly	4
Jack Brabham	Cooper-Climax	3
Cliff Allison	Lotus-Climax	3
Jo Bonnier	BRM	3
Jim Rathmann	Epperly	2

Ferrari cars in a one-two lead in the German Grand Prix.

Stirling Moss

CAREER DETAILS

1929	Born 17 September
1949	Progresses to racing from hill climbs and racks up Formula Three wins
1950	Signs to drive the HWM Formula Two car
1951-3	Career progress hindered because English cars were no match for Italian Alfa Romeos and Maseratis. Tried hand at rallying to further himself and came second in the 1952 Monte Carlo Rally
1955	Signs to drive for Mercedes, alongside Fangio. Finishes season runner-up to his World Champion team-mate
1956	After Mercedes' withdrawal, moves to Maserati. Again finishes year runner-up to Fangio, who had moved to Ferrari
1957	Drives a Vanwall, winning three races, but still finishes behind Fangio
1958	Wins four GPs with Vanwall, including the "deciding" Moroccan GP, but is runner-up for fourth year in succession, after title rival Mike Hawthorn scrabbles past Ferrari team-mate Phil Hill to secure point and pip Moss
1959	Drives assorted cars. Won two races
1960	Drives assorted cars, including a Lotus, and gives marque its maiden win at Monaco. Sustains leg and back injuries when thrown out of car during qualifying at Spa
1962	Retires following crash into an earth bank at non-championship race at Goodwood
1970s	Forays with touring cars, followed by increasing number of sorties in historic racing
2000	Knighted for services to motorsport

FORMULA ONE RECORD

Year	Team	Wins	Poles	Fast laps	Pts
1951	HWM	0	0	0	0
1952	HWM	0	0	0	0
	ERA	0	0	0	0
	Connaught	0	0	0	0
1953	Connaught	0	0	0	0
	Cooper	0	0	0	0
1954	Maserati	0	0	1	4
1955	Mercedes	1	1	2	23
1956	Maserati	2	1	3	27
1957	Maserati	0	1	1	–
	Vanwall	3	1	2	25
1958	Cooper Cl	1	0	0	–
	Vanwall	3	3	3	41
1959	Cooper Cl	2	4	2	–
	BRM	0	0	2	25.5
1960	Cooper Cl	0	1	1	–
	Lotus Cl	2	3	1	19
1961	Lotus Cl	2	1	2	21

STIRLING MOSS WON RACES GALORE, but never the title. If he had put reason before passion, said Enzo Ferrari, he would have been World Champion. He was more than deserving of it.

Stirling Moss driving in a 100-mile road race in 1961.

Born into a family steeped in motorsport, Stirling Moss developed his trademark racing skills – speed, adaptability and a certain wiliness – on local hill climbs.

In 1949 he moved to racing, racking up Formula Three wins, then signed to drive the HWM Formula Two car a year later, as well as participating in every sports car race he was offered a ride in. Even rallying was considered in a quest to further his career. The fact that he finished second in the Monte Carlo Rally of 1952 is largely forgotten.

Later in life, he has always been quick to separate drivers who lived for motor-racing and those who competed without that total love of their sport. "I never raced for fun, although it was fun to race," he said.

His Grand Prix outings between 1951 and 1953 may have been doomed, since his British cars were no match for the superior Italian Alfa Romeos and Maseratis, but he demonstrated a fighting instinct and an uncanny ability to get the best out of any car he stepped into.

To some, however, he was always too hard on his equipment. According to Jack Brabham, Moss was the quickest guy around but didn't know how to save a car. If the car lasted the course, he generally won. "There ought to be someone who can build a car capable of taking all he can give it," mused Phil Hill in 1960.

In 1954 Moss approached Alfred Neubauer, the boss of the Mercedes team, who suggested Moss should spend the year showing what he could do in a competitive car, so a Maserati was bought and privately entered. First time out Moss finished on the podium, in third place, at the Belgian Grand Prix, and Neubauer signed him to drive alongside Juan Manuel Fangio in the Mercedes in 1955.

Stirling Moss took his first World Championship win when Fangio seemed to let him pass in the British Grand Prix at Aintree. They ended the year with Fangio the World Champion and Moss the runner-up.

Moss finished runner-up for the next three seasons, making four in succession. In 1956, driving for Maserati, he won twice, securing only one less Grand Prix win than Fangio.

In 1957, patriotism saw him combine forces with Vanwall for whom he won three races. Remaining loyal to Vanwall in 1958 he won four times – in Argentina, The Netherlands, Portugal and Morocco – but was runner-up to Mike Hawthorn, who had won only once but had been a consistent points-scorer (his tally boosted crucially, as it turned out, by Moss's sporting evidence to a Stewards' Enquiry at the Portuguese Grand Prix in Oporto enabling Hawthorn's second place to stand).

The Championship went down to the wire at the Moroccan Grand Prix on the outskirts of Casablanca. Moss led all the way, and set fastest

> "I would rather lose a race driving fast enough to win it than win one driving slow enough to lose it."

Stirling Moss expressing his principle of racing.

lap, but Hawthorn scrambled into second place when Tony Brooks blew up and Phil Hill let him through to take the crown on points.

It was a devastating blow for Moss and Vanwall (who had the consolation of winning the inaugural constructors' title), and was made even worse when team-mate Stuart Lewis-Evans, who had crashed heavily, succumbed to his severe burns.

"I was really very upset. I really reckoned that I deserved to win it. To lose to a guy you are sure you can beat is obviously pretty disturbing," said Moss.

For the next two years he drove assorted cars, but was predominantly seen in a Cooper, winning twice in 1959. He raced a Lotus, and gave the marque its maiden win at the Monaco Grand Prix of 1960. He won again later that year after recovering from back and leg injuries which he had sustained when he was thrown out of his car during qualifying for the Belgian Grand Prix.

In 1961, regulations changed radically, with 2.5-litre engines being replaced by 1.5-litre engines. Ferrari, who were well-prepared, were almost unbeatable. But even though Moss raced with a less-powerful Coventry Climax engine in his Lotus, he still managed to win twice on circuits where skill held a premium.

He was always the yardstick by which his peers were judged, yet his career came to an end when he crashed into an earth bank in a non-championship race at Goodwood in 1962, incurring serious head injuries. He came back too soon and quit too early, he later complained.

In the late 1970s he dabbled with touring cars and has since become a regular in historic racing series. In 2000 he was knighted for services to motor sport.

"Being the name of a chap who won the title a certain year is less important to me than being the chap who many say should have won it but never did – it gives me a sort of uniqueness," he said.

Moss takes first place in the British Grand Prix at Aintree.

1959
Battle of the Britons

TALKING POINT

THE REAR-ENGINED REVOLUTION

The year signalled a major turning point in the design of the Formula One car. Cooper had trialled their rear-engined concept in Formula Three and Formula Two and in 1958 it had begun to enter and win Grand Prix.

With a 2.5 litre engine to power the nimble chassis, the team got it spot-on. They secured five wins to clinch the Constructors' Championship, and give New Zealander Bruce McLaren the world drivers' title.

It was the beginning of the end for the front-engined Formula One car, and by the end of the following year BRM, Lotus and giants Ferrari had bowed down to the Cooper concept.

After newly-crowned World Champion Mike Hawthorn's death in a road accident, Vanwall pulled out of racing, citing ill-health as the cause, although the rate of fatalities in the 1958 season is thought to have been the true reason. This left Ferrari as the only team on the grid ever to have won a Grand Prix – but there was a surprise in store for the Italian team.

Coventry-Climax had created a new 2.5-litre engine to fit in the back of the Cooper, and so began the rear-engined revolution. BRM followed suit and, despite having the best drivers of the day, Ferrari could only muster two victories during the year.

Coopers show class

Monte Carlo in May saw the start of the World Championship season, and immediately the Coopers took the fight to Ferrari, taking both pole position and a race win in the glamorous harbour-side setting.

The Ferraris had expected to dominate, but the new Cooper was flying and pushed Tony Brooks and Phil Hill on to the second row of the grid in the famous scarlet cars. It was the Rob Walker-entered Cooper-Climax of Stirling Moss which pipped Jean Behra's Ferrari to pole position, with the works Cooper of Australian Jack Brabham filling the remaining spot on the front row.

As the field headed into St. Devote at the start it was Behra who came through the middle of the Coopers to take the lead and he managed to hold it until lap 22 when Moss finally got past. The circuit is notoriously difficult to overtake on, but soon after Moss passed the Ferrari, Brabham pushed Behra down to third. When he suffered engine failure on the very next lap, the reason for the Ferrari driver's demise was revealed.

Phil Hill was now the top Ferrari in third, but he was struggling to get to grips with the twisty circuit and spun an amazing four times. Despite this he was still able to finish fourth.

Leader Moss, however, was not so lucky. His Cooper developed engine problems, and on lap 81 of 100 he could continue no more. This left Brabham to cruise to his first World Championship victory, 20 seconds ahead of Brooks' Ferrari.

Once again, no European entries made it across the Atlantic for the Indy 500 at the end of May – the reason perhaps being that another round of the World Championship, the Dutch Grand Prix, was to take place just one day after the American event!

Indy 500 fatalities

The race was won by Rodger Ward, but was marred by two fatalities in the two qualifying weekends. Jerry Unser, a member of the great American racing family, had survived a massive crash one year earlier, but this time the circuit was to claim him when he died from serious burns. In a separate incident, Bob Cortner hit the turn three wall head-on and died instantly.

But the race went ahead, and it was Johnny

The new Cooper-Climax in action at the Monaco Grand Prix.

Stirling Moss in his Cooper-Climax at the Monaco Grand Prix which was won by his title rival Jack Brabham.

Thompson's Lesovski on pole ahead of Eddie Sachs and Jim Rathmann. Sachs was no match for his front-row counterparts and faded into the distance at the start, leaving a battle up front between Thompson, Pat Flaherty and the two Watson Roadsters of Rathmann and Ward. As the race developed, it became a battle between the Watsons as both Flaherty and Thompson fell out, and Ward came through to win by 23 seconds.

Barely 24 hours after Indianapolis, the "real" Formula One racers were back in action on the Dutch circuit of Zandvoort, and it was to be another new name on the winners' list, Swede Jo Bonnier in the BRM.

Stirling Moss had spent time testing for the team at the track in the week prior to the event and the work he did helped put Bonnier on the top spot for the race, but Moss, back in the Cooper, could only manage third on the grid.

There were only 15 cars on the grid for the start of the race, and it was a good start for the Swede, but with Moss slipping back into a midfield battle it was Masten Gregory's works Cooper that took the race to the BRM. He took the lead on lap two but, suffering gearbox maladies, Bonnier was able to squeeze by to regain it on lap 12.

Brabham then passed Gregory as he dropped back into the chasing pack of Behra and Moss, and together they caught the leaders. It was drama at the front when Moss took the lead and Behra spun, but when Moss retired it was back to square one, and Bonnier was left to take the victory 15 seconds ahead of Brabham's Cooper.

Ferrari's first victory of the year

Ferrari had been beaten in every race they had entered so far in 1959, and something had to be done. The team sent five works cars to the Reims circuit in France for the fourth round of the World Championship, and they were rewarded with their first victory of the season in a race that Tony Brooks dominated from start to finish.

The Englishman lined up on pole, with team-mate Phil Hill joining him on the front row, split by the ever-competitive Cooper of Jack Brabham. Brooks got off the line well and was followed into the first corner by Moss, who had stormed up from the second row as Behra's Ferrari sat motionless on the grid.

Early on in the race the track at the Thillois hairpin began to break up due to the heat and Gregory, who was running third, suffered a cut face from a flying stone and retired from "driver exhaustion".

Brooks escaped problems, and behind him there were endless battles with Trintignant, Brabham and Hill all having stints in second. Moss also ran well before his clutch failed, and it was Hill who followed Brooks home to take a Ferrari one-two.

It was truly a Battle of Britain when the Championship moved to the Silverstone circuit in mid-July. Ferrari was hit by strikes in Italy and, unable to make it, they left the British teams BRM, Aston Martin, Cooper and Lotus to fight it out for the honours.

Aston Martin sprang a surprise by putting their uncompetitive DBR4 on the front row, but it was Brabham's Cooper which secured pole. Ferrari had

RACE BY RACE DETAILS

ROUND 1 – MONACO
Race Jack Brabham
Pole Stirling Moss
Fastest lap Jack Brabham

ROUND 2 – INDIANAPOLIS
Race Rodger Ward
Pole Johnny Thompson
Fastest lap Johnny Thompson

ROUND 3 – HOLLAND
Race Jo Bonnier
Pole Jo Bonnier
Fastest lap Stirling Moss

ROUND 4 – FRANCE
Race Tony Brooks
Pole Tony Brooks
Fastest lap Stirling Moss

ROUND 5 – BRITAIN
Race Jack Brabham
Pole Jack Brabham
Fastest lap Stirling Moss/ Bruce McLaren

ROUND 6 – GERMANY
Race Tony Brooks
Pole Tony Brooks
Fastest lap Tony Brooks

ROUND 7 – PORTUGAL
Race Stirling Moss
Pole Stirling Moss
Fastest lap Stirling Moss

ROUND 8 – ITALY
Race Stirling Moss
Pole Stirling Moss
Fastest lap Phil Hill

Round 9 – UNITED STATES
Race Bruce McLaren
Pole Stirling Moss
Fastest lap Maurice Trintignant

Jo Bonnier with the victor's laurels after the Dutch Grand Prix.

released the French Grand Prix winner Tony Brooks for the race and he took a drive in the Vanwall, but the machinery was not at all competitive and he lined up 17th on the grid and retired on lap 13 with a misfiring engine.

After a good start Brabham was never threatened, but behind him there was a battle as Moss moved up through the field from his lowly third-row grid slot before an unscheduled pit-stop allowed McLaren to take second.

Brabham was an uncatchable 22 seconds in the lead, but Moss wanted to take second from McLaren and came back to catch the New Zealander. The crowd enjoyed watching a massive battle which saw the pair race side by side on the last lap, and they crossed the line with Moss heading McLaren by just 0.2 seconds.

Grand Prix in two parts

The German Grand Prix changed venues to Berlin in 1959, but the length of the straights on the new track caused problems for the cars, and meant the introduction of the first-ever two-part Grand Prix.

Before the race even began tragedy struck the German circuit when long-time Grand Prix star Jean Behra was killed in a supporting sports-car race as he was thrown from his car into a flagpole.

Still mourning his death, the Grand Prix stars lined up for the first heat of the F1 race the following day, and it was Brooks' Ferrari on pole with Moss, Gurney and Brabham alongside. It was mixed fortunes for Championship rivals Moss and Brooks at the start which saw the Ferrari driver fly into the lead and Moss end his race with transmission failure.

Brooks battled with Gurney and Gregory, but eventually came through to win the heat and so lined up in pole for the next race. A bad start saw him slip back to fourth behind McLaren, Hill and Bonnier, but

SHORTS

The 1959 US Grand Prix proved unique for several reasons. Not only was it the first Grand Prix to be held in the US, it was also the only Formula One event ever to be staged at Florida's famous Sebring airfield track. The race also produced another moment for the record-books when the chequered flag was taken by Bruce McLaren who, at 22, became the youngest-ever winner of a Grand Prix – a record that still stands today.

the Briton soon battled back to take victory and when the aggregate times were calculated it was a Ferrari 1-2-3, putting the Italian team right back in the Championship race.

If everyone thought the Ferrari domination of the German Grand Prix was a prelude to the rest of the season, they were forced to think again when the Championship arrived at Monsanto Park in Portugal.

There was not an Italian car in sight as the Coopers claimed the top four places on the grid and Ferrari struggled, with Tony Brooks, winner of the previous race, languishing down in 10th position. Moss led from pole and lapped the entire field on his way to victory, but the race was not without incident.

Phil Hill was forced to pit when he spun his Ferrari on lap five, and the unfortunate American was hit by the spinning Lotus of Graham Hill when he returned to the track! Brabham, who was going well in second, was also involved in an incident when his Cooper flew off the circuit and hit a telegraph pole, throwing the Australian into the middle of the track. Gregory was next on the scene, and fortunately for Brabham his team-mate managed to avoid hitting him. With all that going on behind him, Moss kept his cool to record his first victory of the year as Gregory held on to second place.

On the seesaw of fortunes between the two top teams it was Ferrari's turn to make a comeback, and they piled all their might into a five-strong squad, hoping to help Brooks in his fight for the Championship. But all the assistance of his team-mates could not prevent failure for Brooks, and he watched his Championship challenge slip further away as an early retirement allowed another Cooper win for Moss, to leave the title race wide open.

The three Championship contenders were alongside each other on the grid, and it was Moss who took the lead as Phil Hill's Ferrari slid in ahead of Brabham. Hill, Gurney and Moss battled it out up front, and Hill eventually settled into a comfortable top spot – but the race was lost by Ferrari when a tactical error handed victory to Moss.

At half-distance, all the Italian cars were called into the pits for new tyres, and they expected the Coopers to follow. But they didn't, and Moss won by almost 50 seconds. Hill made up time to catch and pass Brabham, but there was nothing he could do to prevent Moss taking his second win in succession.

Brabham clinches title in US

It was still anyone's year, with Brabham, Moss, and Brooks all in with a chance of taking the title as the teams went to America for the first-ever United States Grand Prix. The race location tempted the Indy 500 winner to fight the Europeans for the first time, but Rodger Ward was 43 seconds off the pace!

Tensions were high, and at the end of practice Cooper had the upper hand. Moss was ahead of Brabham, and the Ecurie Blue-run Cooper of Harry Schell knocked Brooks down to row two. Ferrari protested, but their complaints were ignored and the grid stood.

Brabham took the lead, but Moss got past before the end of the opening lap and began to pull away. It looked good for the Briton, but on lap five disaster struck and Moss was out, his Championship hopes blown away with yet another transmission failure. Brabham was well ahead of Brooks and the title looked to be his – but on the final lap he ran out of fuel. McLaren ducked out from behind the New Zealander and took the win. Trintignant passed Brabham for second and Brooks took third, but it was not enough. Brabham pushed his machine over the line to take fourth, but it didn't matter – he'd already won the Championship.

1959 DRIVERS' CHAMPIONSHIP

DRIVER	TEAM	POINTS
Jack Brabham	Cooper Climax	31
Tony Brooks	Ferrari	27
Stirling Moss	Cooper Climax/BRM	25.5
Phil Hill	Ferrari	20
Maurice Trintignant	Cooper Climax	19
Bruce McLaren	Cooper Climax	16.5
Dan Gurney	Ferrari	13
Jo Bonnier	BRM	10
Masten Gregory	Cooper Climax	10
Rodger Ward	Watson	8
Jim Rathmann	Watson	6
Harry Schell	BRM	5
Innes Ireland	Lotus Climax	5
Johnny Thomson	Lesovsky	5
Olivier Gendebien	Ferrari	3
Tony Bettenhausen	Epperly	3
Cliff Allison	Ferrari	2
Jean Behra	Ferrari	2
Paul Goldsmith	Epperly	2

Jack Brabham wins the British Grand Prix.

1960
Brabham secures second title

TALKING POINT

BRITISH BOYCOTT ITALIAN GP

For the first time since the early 1950's when the World Championship was run to Formula Two regulations, the lesser category joined the hierarchical Grand Prix scene. With the series already sewn up by Jack Brabham in his Cooper-Climax and the Italian racing authorities opting to run the Italian Grand Prix on a combined road and oval circuit, the big British teams decided to boycott the event.

The boycott left Ferrari on their own at the head of the grid, along with some privateers. Therefore, to boost numbers in the field, the FIA invited Formula Two cars to compete in the event. Porsche took up the option and ran two Formula Two 718 cars for Hans Herrmann and Edgar Barth. All of the Formula Two cars were included in qualifying and in overall classification at the end of the season.

Another rule change to affect the season was the abolition of awarding a point to the driver who gained the fastest lap in the race. Instead, the point went to the driver who finished sixth, and the rule still stands today.

Colin Chapman (left) with his Lotus team drivers, Jim Clark and Alan Stacey (centre) at the Dutch Grand Prix.

The decade of the Swingin' Sixties began where the last decade had ended as Australian Jack Brabham secured his second consecutive world drivers' title for Cooper as rear-engined machines dominated the series. By retaining his crown, Brabham provided the perfect response to critics who suggested his 1959 success had been achieved as a direct result of Stirling Moss's constant bad luck. Brabham's uncanny knack of being able to guide his machine to victory was in stark contrast to Moss' all-out attacking approach and helped team owner John Cooper celebrate a clean sweep of the titles on offer for a second successive year.

But though Cooper held off the challenge of Lotus to claim the Constructors' Cup, it was the emergence of Colin Chapman's team and the Lotus 18 that helped Formula One move into a new era and set new standards for others to follow. As the opportunities to gain commercial rewards snowballed, the whole ethos of Grand Prix racing was changing from its playboy image in the 1950s to a more commercialized, business approach.

The Lotus 18 was designed as a multi-formula car and raced in events as diverse as the one-litre Formula Junior and the Grand Prix formula. A spaceframe chassis clad in aluminium and glass-fibre panels was complemented by independent front and rear suspension, with wishbones, coil-spring damper units, transverse links and radius arms. Chapman's rear set-up was a new design, and one that would be copied by other designers in the following years. Each wheel was mounted on a light-alloy hub carrier to which was mounted a bottom wishbone parallel to the half-shaft and with its base to the wheel. It was located by radius arms at the top, the half-shaft acting as the upper wishbone. The big disadvantage of the system was that the wheel was unsupported in the event of an axle or structural break.

While the British teams dominated, Ferrari chose to retain its front-engined D246 with a strong line-up of American Phil Hill, fellow-countryman Richie Ginther, the German Count Wolfgang Berghe von Trips, Cliff Allison of England and popular Belgian Willy Mairesse. Cooper had Brabham and New Zealander Bruce McLaren at the wheel once again, ably supported by a number of others driving cars run by private stables.

Brabham suffers from slow start

The season-opening race was in Buenos Aires, Argentina, in February – slightly later than usual – and Brabham got off to the worst possible start as Cooper team-mate McLaren took the chequered flag.

Brabham had qualified badly and started 10th on the grid, with Moss in pole position. But McLaren started from 13th and was fortunate to benefit from the retirement of several top drivers.

Moss seemed the early favourite after leading for two separate spells, but the suspension on his Cooper failed exactly halfway through the 80-lap race.

Two laps later, Brabham retired with gearbox failure and that paved the way for McLaren to power through to victory. Cliff Allison was second for Ferrari, while Moss took over Maurice's Trintignant's car to take third.

In the second race of the season, at the enigmatic Monaco Grand Prix, Brabham's luck did not change as he was disqualified for receiving a push start after a spin 40 laps into the 100-lap race.

Before the start Moss had switched from the Cooper team to Lotus and he celebrated his debut race for his new outfit with victory in the winding streets of the principality.

Moss had taken pole position for the race and for the first 67 laps swapped the lead with Jo Bonnier's BRM and Brabham, until the latter's disqualification.

The turning-point came when the rain fell and several drivers crashed or broke down in the changing conditions. Several crossed the line with damaged cars in a bid to gain Championship points, but apart from a slight problem with his spark plugs Moss steered clear of problems and took his first win of the season ahead of McLaren and Phil Hill's Ferrari.

Once again the third round of the Championship went to Indianapolis for the Indy 500 and, like the years preceding it, European teams and drivers ignored the event.

The event, held in May, produced a similar battle to the previous year as Jim Rathmann, Rodger Ward and Johnny Thompson battled to take the win at the famous "Brickyard" circuit.

Ward and Rathmann pulled away from Thompson in the final stages and after Ward suffered tyre problems Rathmann took victory in the 200-lap race. The Ken Paul Special driver was not to know but he went down in history as the last driver to win the Indianapolis 500 as part of the World Championship.

Europe's top drivers returned for the fourth round as Zandvoort hosted the Dutch Grand Prix. The event began with controversy as teams disputed the prize money available and several drivers withdrew before the race.

Moss took pole position for the 75-lap race, but alongside him were Brabham and Innes Ireland in a Lotus. Ireland seemed to get the best start, but was beaten into the first corner by Brabham, who led the field after a sluggish start from Moss.

The race, however, was marred after just 11 laps as Dan Gurney crashed his BRM after brake failure at a chicane. As his car spun it struck and killed a spectator, who was in a prohibited area by the edge

RACE BY RACE DETAILS

ROUND 1 – ARGENTINA
Race Bruce McLaren
Pole Stirling Moss
Fastest lap Stirling Moss

ROUND 2 – MONACO
Race Stirling Moss
Pole Stirling Moss
Fastest lap Bruce McLaren

ROUND 3 – INDIANAPOLIS
Race Jim Rathmann
Pole Eddie Sachs
Fastest lap n/a

ROUND 4 – HOLLAND
Race Jack Brabham
Pole Stirling Moss
Fastest lap Stirling Moss

ROUND 5 – BELGIUM
Race Jack Brabham
Pole Jack Brabham
Fastest lap Jack Brabham

ROUND 6 – FRANCE
Race Jack Brabham
Pole Jack Brabham
Fastest lap Jack Brabham

ROUND 7 – BRITAIN
Race Jack Brabham
Pole Jack Brabham
Fastest lap Graham Hill

ROUND 8 – PORTUGAL
Race Jack Brabham
Pole John Surtees
Fastest lap John Surtees

ROUND 9 – ITALY
Race Phil Hill
Pole Phil Hill
Fastest lap Phil Hill

ROUND 10 – UNITED STATES
Race Stirling Moss
Pole Stirling Moss
Fastest lap Jack Brabham

Jack Brabham in his Cooper

John Surtees

CAREER DETAILS

1934	Born 11 February, near Westerham, Kent
1956	Wins the 500cc motorcycle World Championship
1958	Motorcycle World Champion
1959	Motorcycle World Champion. Tests himself for Vanwall and Aston Martin
1960	Motorcycle World Champion in 350cc and 500cc. Switched full-time to cars F1 debut for Lotus at Monaco, second place at Silverstone and pole position in Portugal
1961	Victory in non-Championship Glover Trophy race
1962	Second in British and German Grands Prix
1963	Moves to Ferrari. First Grand Prix win at Nurburgring
1964	Formula One World Champion, after securing two more wins in the German and Italian Grands Prix
1965	Badly injured when his CanAm Lola T70 crashed at Mosport Park in Canada
1966	Leaves Ferrari mid-season after fall-out with team manager
1967	Last lap victory for Honda in Italian Grand Prix
1969	Signs for BRM. Dismal year
1970	Sets up own team

FORMULA ONE RECORD

Year	Team	Wins	Poles	Fast laps	Pts
1960	Lotus Climax	0	1	1	6
1961	Cooper Climax	0	0	0	4
1962	Lola Climax	0	1	0	19
1963	Ferrari	1	1	3	22
1964	Ferrari	2	2	2	40
1965	Ferrari	0	0	0	17
1966	Ferrari	1	1	1	–
	Cooper Mas	1	1	2	28
1967	Honda	1	0	0	20
1968	Honda	0	1	1	12
1969	BRM	0	0	0	6
1970	McLaren Ford	0	0	1	–
	Surtees Ford	0	0	0	3
1971	Surtees Ford	0	0	0	3
1972	Surtees Ford	0	0	0	0

EQUALLY RESILIENT ON TWO WHEELS and four, John Surtees achieved the unparalleled feat of winning World Championships on motorcycles and in cars by the age of 30.

John Surtees was born near Westerham, Kent on 11 February, 1934, with motorbikes in his genes. As a teenager he rode passenger in his garage-owning father Jack's racing combination. After school, he became an apprentice at the Vincent motorcycle company whose 1000cc Black Shadow achieved contemporary cult status. Surtees built his own 500cc racing machine, known as the Grey Shadow, and won at his home circuit of Brands Hatch in his first year as a solo rider. Between 1956 and 1960, Surtees – now a member of the Italian MV Agusta team – won seven different world motorcycle Championships.

In 1959, having won universal respect for his prowess on a motorcycle, Surtees tried out an Aston Martin at Goodwood for Reg Parnell. His racing debut came in a Formula Junior Cooper BMC in March 1960. Victory at Goodwood – his maiden race on four wheels – saw Lotus boss Colin Chapman invite him to drive for his Grand Prix team whenever the races did not clash with his motorcycle commitments.

Surtees made his Formula One debut for Lotus at Monaco. One race later he finished second at Silverstone in the British Grand Prix before taking pole position in Portugal, a race he dominated until damaging a radiator against straw bales.

Despite prodigious show of speed, this was a period in which Colin Chapman was forging his deep alliance with Jim Clark, and Surtees decided against being number two to the Scot. A certain take-it-or-leave-it demeanour did not instantly endear him to the four-wheeled racing scene, as fellow-biker-turned-Formula One driver Mike Hailwood later testified. "He had a really hard time breaking into the car world. I think many of the established stars of Formula One resented someone coming in from what they felt was an inferior sport and showing them the way."

He left Lotus just as the British team began to assert themselves and raced a Yeoman Credit Racing Team Cooper, managing just a pair of fifth place finishes plus fastest lap in the non-championship Glover Trophy Race (it was the popular

John Surtees takes the flag in the Italian Grand Prix in 1967.

> "I sparked off some quite prickly feelings among some members of the Grand Prix fraternity."

John Surtees in 1964 – many resented his move from motorcyling to Grand Prix racing.

belief that Moss was trying to match his time when he crashed into the earth bank, effectively ending his Formula One career).

Things improved the following season, 1962, when the team fielded a pair of Lolas under the Bowmaker Racing banner, and he was second in the British and German Grands Prix. In 1963 Surtees took up Enzo Ferrari's repeated offer of a works drive. It was to prove the launching pad to success, not least because the fanatical fans already admired him from his bike career with the Italian MV Agusta outfit. Surtees took his first win at the Nurburgring – a race that demonstrated his class.

In 1964 he won the World Championship for Ferrari in a dramatic Mexican Grand Prix in which the title first slipped from Clark's hands, then from Graham Hill's, before falling to Surtees.

His 1965 season was disrupted after a heavy crash in a Lola CanAm T70 at Mosport Park in Canada, but he astonished doctors with the speed of his recovery and returned to Ferrari for 1966. A courageous racer, he excelled on classic road circuits and took a superb victory at Spa-Francorchamps after an intense battle with Jochen Rindt, but quit the Italian team midway through the 1966 season after falling out with team manager Eugenio Dragoni – thus leaving Jack Brabham a clear run at the title. He drove for Cooper until the end of the season winning the final race, the Mexican Grand Prix.

For the next few years he concentrated on developing Honda's challenge, which included a last-lap victory in the 1967 Italian Grand Prix. In 1969 he signed for BRM but after a dismal season, exacerbated by medical complications which were the legacy of his CanAm crash, he left to set up his own team for 1970, just as BRM started winning again.

The impetus behind setting up his own team was that he would never again need to compromise his ideas on the technical approach to racing. Surtees distinguished himself from his peers in his obsessive interest in the workings of his machines, but it was a recurrent criticism that he became bogged down in the quest for technical perfection and should have got on solely with racing.

His team was not a success. In 1973, Mike Hailwood said of the Surtees TS14A: "The car rarely held together for more than five minutes at a time."

The verdict of Alan Jones, the plain-talking Australian who drove for him in 1976, was not favourable either. "He thought he knew everything there was to know about racing. Former drivers always think they know best – their driver is just a surrogate for themselves. His ego got in the way of the team." Surtees retired from the cockpit in 1972. His team ceased competing in 1978.

1961
Hill's title proves bittersweet

TALKING POINT

HILL TITLE OVERSHADOWED BY TRAGEDY

American Phil Hill's maiden, and only, World Championship success was overshadowed by the tragic death of his Ferrari teammate Wolfgang von Trips – the only man who could take the title from him. Going into the penultimate race of the season in Italy, Hill and von Trips were set for a titanic battle, but Hill was crowned Champion after the first lap when von Trips' race ended in tragedy. The German tangled with Jim Clark and was killed, along with 12 spectators. Hill went on to become Champion almost unnoticed following the accident, and Ferrari boycotted the final round of the season in the United States because of the tragedy.

Stirling Moss crosses the finishing line at the Monaco Grand Prix.

It was time for the face of Formula One to change and Ferrari were best-placed to take advantage of the 1.5-litre era. The Italian marque had effectively taken the previous year out to develop their contender – dubbed "sharknose" – which boasted a V6 engine and the British manufacturers were slow to respond to the changes in rules.

The season, which did not start until May, was much like a merry-go-round in drivers' line-ups. Only Cooper and Ferrari retained their drivers from the previous year – Jack Brabham and Bruce McLaren remained with Cooper while Ferrari had Ritchie Ginther, Phil Hill and Wolfgang von Trips – with Jo Bonnier and Dan Gurney switching from BRM to newcomers Porsche, who had been a success in Formula Two, to partner Hans Herrman. Tony Brooks moved to BRM from BRP and Olivier Gendebien joined the new Equipe Nationale Belge team in a series of changes. John Surtees was another driver on the move, as he opted to drive a Reg Parnell Racing Cooper instead of driving for Lotus.

The opening race in Monaco was a disaster for

Giancarlo Baghetti in his Ferrari.

Lotus, as Jim Clark only just made the race after crashing heavily at Ste Devoté during practice and Innes Ireland broke his leg and destroyed his car in an accident in the tunnel. Stirling Moss was on pole in his Lotus while amazingly Clark was on the front row thanks to a lap time posted before his crash.

Ferrari's Ginther was quickest off the grid and Clark was forced to pit with fuel-pump problems before Moss raced into the ascendancy with Hill, who had overtaken Ginther and Bonnier, on his tail. But despite the threat posed by his challengers, Moss produced one of the performances of his career to win in Monaco.

The British driver fought off Hill and then Ginther, overcoming the disadvantage in power to take the chequered flag. Von Trips was classified fourth behind his two Ferrari team-mates despite crashing on the last lap of the race.

No stopping von Trips

The second race of the season was the Dutch Grand Prix at Zandvoort and coming just a week after Monaco, Lotus were forced to replace the injured Ireland with Trevor Taylor.

It was an all-Ferrari front row with Hill the quicker, while Moss put his underpowered Lotus on the second row. Von Trips raced into the lead with BRM's Graham Hill and Phil Hill chasing him. Clark, who had started on the fourth row, stormed into fourth and battled with Phil Hill as Graham Hill dropped out of contention.

Graham Hill had to fight with Moss and Ginther for fourth and it was Moss who came out on top after Ginther was hampered when his throttle stuck open. The win was von Trips' first in the World Championship as his title challenge gathered momentum.

Moss returned to Spa-Francorchamps, where he had broken his leg the previous year, but could only finish eighth. Ireland was back in action after recovering from the broken leg sustained in Monaco as Grand Prix racing returned to Belgium, despite the tragic race in 1960 in which British drivers Chris Bristow and Alan Stacey were killed.

BRP had only one Lotus 18 and Cliff Allison and Henry Taylor battled for the drive in the race by sharing it in qualifying. But as a direct result of the one-on-one shoot-out, Allison crashed heavily and rolled the car. He was forced to end his motor racing career after he suffered severe leg injuries.

Phil Hill was on pole again and took the lead in the race, but the American was soon overtaken by local driver Gendebien, who was competing in a fourth Ferrari, painted in Belgian yellow and run by the Equipe Nationale Belge team. Von Trips and Ginther also featured at the head of the race and the four Ferrari drivers exchanged the lead numerous times. Hill emerged on top and was followed home by von Trips, Ginther and then Gendebien as Ferrari claimed the top four spots.

The French Grand Prix produced an historic result that has yet to be repeated as Giancarlo Baghetti, in a privately-entered Ferrari, raced to victory on his World Championship debut. The Italian had never before tasted defeat after winning every non-championship Grand Prix he had competed in.

Von Trips and Ginther chased pole-sitter Hill but Moss moved into third when Ginther spun before

RACE BY RACE DETAILS

ROUND 1 – MONACO
Race Stirling Moss
Pole Stirling Moss
Fastest lap Richie Ginther

ROUND 2 – HOLLAND
Race Wolfgang von Trips
Pole Phil Hill
Fastest lap Jim Clark

ROUND 3 – BELGIUM
Race Phil Hill
Pole Phil Hill
Fastest lap Richie Ginther

ROUND 4 – FRANCE
Race Giancarlo Baghetti
Pole Phil Hill
Fastest lap Phil Hill

ROUND 5 – BRITAIN
Race Wolfgang von Trips
Pole Phil Hill
Fastest lap Tony Brooks

ROUND 6 – GERMANY
Race Stirling Moss
Pole Phil Hill
Fastest lap Phil Hill

ROUND 7 – ITALY
Race Phil Hill
Pole Wolfgang von Trips
Fastest lap Giancarlo Baghetti

ROUND 8 – UNITED STATES
Race Innes Ireland
Pole Jack Brabham
Fastest lap Stirling Moss

Graham Hill

CAREER DETAILS

1929	Born 15 February, Hampstead, London
1950	Wins Henley Regatta's Grand Challenge Cup
1956	Almost wins Autosport club racing series but for mechanical failure in final round.
1958	Makes GP debut for Lotus at Monaco
1962	World Champion with BRM
1963	Runner-up to Jim Clark, first Monaco win
1964	Runner-up to John Surtees, second Monaco win
1965	Runner-up to Jim Clark, third Monaco win
1966	Wins the Indianapolis 500
1968	Wins second title, in Lotus, from former team-mate Jackie Stewart, fourth Monaco win
1969	Fifth Monaco win, smashes both legs at US GP at Watkins Glen
1970	Scores point on return at South African GP at Kyalami
1972	Wins Le Mans with Henri Pescarolo, becoming first driver to win the triple crown of F1, Indy 500 and Le Mans.
1973	Sets up his own F1 team
1975	Killed when his plane crashed on to Arkley Golf Course on 29 November

FORMULA ONE RECORD

Year	Team	Wins	Poles	Fast laps	Pts
1958	Lotus Climax	0	0	0	–
	Lotus F2	0	0	0	0
1959	Lotus Climax	0	0	0	0
1960	BRM	0	0	1	4
1961	BRM	0	0	0	3
1962	BRM	4	1	3	42
1963	BRM	2	2	0	29
1964	BRM	2	1	1	39
1965	BRM	2	4	3	40
1966	BRM	0	0	0	17
1967	Lotus BRM	0	0	0	–
	Lotus Ford	0	3	2	15
1968	Lotus Ford	3	2	0	48
1969	Lotus Ford	1	0	0	19
1970	Lotus Ford	0	0	0	7
1971	Br Ford	0	0	0	2
1972	Br Ford	0	0	0	4
1973	Shad Ford	0	0	0	0
1974	Lola Ford		0	0	1
1975	Lola Ford	0	0	0	0

FIVE TIMES A WINNER at Monaco and the life and soul of any party, Graham Hill was the only driver to have won the F1 World Championship, the Indianapolis 500 and Le Mans and epitomized racing glamour.

Graham Hill, the son of a successful stockbroker, had been taken on as an apprentice at Smith's Instruments at Cricklewood after schooling at Hendon Tech. He spent his spare time at the London Rowing Club, whose white flashes would soon decorate his – and later his son Damon's – crash helmet. In 1950, as stroke in the LRC's Eight, he won Henley Regatta's Grand Challenge Cup.

It was not until three years later that he bought his first car. He did not pass his driving test until he was 24, but became addicted to racing facing forwards (as opposed to rowing) after attending the racing school at Brands Hatch. He gave up his job to work as a mechanic there, competing in one of the school cars in lieu of payment. He talked his way into a job at the emergent Lotus team after hitching a ride back from the Kent circuit with Colin Chapman and Mike Costin – each assumed he was a friend of the other, but Hill, the consummate opportunist, knew neither.

"Hill was never short of what some would have called 'brass neck' or 'bull', and others, more politely, charisma," as one GP sage later wrote.

Hill built his own Lotus XI for 1956 and would have been victor of the Autosport club racing series but for a mechanical failure in the final round. The epitome of charm – with his slicked-back hair, clipped moustache and debonair wit – he talked his way into drives in Cooper and Lotus sportscars in the late Fifties. When Chapman took Lotus into F1 Hill was one of his drivers. He made his GP debut at Monaco, running fourth until a wheel fell off.

Disenchanted with the fragility of Lotus, he left for BRM at the end of 1959. "Drivers such as Fangio, Moss, Clark and Stewart were natural drivers. I've never been described as this. I had to work at it," Hill later said of his pragmatically determined approach to climbing the ladder of success. As Tony Brooks recalled, "He was one of the first guys who breathed, ate and slept motor-racing and he spent a lot of time at the BRM factory. He put an awful lot of effort into the technical side."

By 1962, he was equipped with a new V8 ready to storm the World Championship. He won the Dutch, German and Italian GPs to set up a South African finale with Jim Clark. The Scot led, but when the Lotus broke, Hill snatched victory and the title. He was runner-up to Clark, John Surtees and Clark again in 1963, 1964 and 1965. He was dismayed by the defeat by Surtees as he had scored more points than the former motorcyclist, but lost out by a point on a technicality, when dropped scores were taken into consideration.

In 1966 Hill won the Indianapolis 500. In 1967 he

Graham Hill on the streets of Monaco.

Graham Hill chats with Jim Clark in 1964.

"If the worst ever happens, then it means simply that I have been asked to pay the bill for the happiness of my life."

was lured back to Lotus as team-mate to Jim Clark, who had narrowly missed out on the title to Denny Hulme. However, the Lotus 49 with new Ford Cosworth DFV engine had been a sensation when introduced mid-season and everything looked promising for the dream-team line-up in 1968. Clark won the season-opening South African GP but was killed in a Formula Two race. His death devastated Chapman, leaving Hill laudably to lead Lotus back from the abyss, winning the Spanish GP and going on to take the title against strong opposition from Jackie Stewart's Matra and Hulme's McLaren.

"I was terribly upset over Jimmy's death but, as a racing driver, I couldn't allow my emotions to come through. If I did, I would have been lost and unable to cope – and I'm sure all racing drivers feel the same," he said.

In 1969 Hill was outpaced by new team-mate Jochen Rindt. Then at Watkins Glen he spun and popped his seatbelt. Unable to refasten it, he resumed but had a puncture, crashed and was thrown out breaking his legs. He returned in 1971 with Brabham but was never the same driver. After racing a Shadow, a Lola and finally a Hill for his own Embassy Racing team, he vacated the cockpit in 1975 for the up-and-coming Tony Brise.

In 1972 he had won the Le Mans 24 Hours with Henri Pescarolo, becoming the first – and to date, only – driver to win the F1 World Championship, the Indianapolis 500 and Le Mans. After 176 Grand Prix starts, and 14 victories, he finally hung up his helmet, intending to concentrate on management. Piloting his plane back from testing at Paul Ricard, he hit a tree on the approach to Elstree. Brise also died in the crash, along with the team manager, designer and two mechanics.

1962
Hill heads British dominance

TALKING POINT

THE HILL-CLARK ERA

The season marked the beginning of an intense rivalry between two of Britain's best-ever racers. With their British-built machines, Jim Clark and Graham Hill had both finally reached the pinnacle of the sport, and they had done it at the same point in time.

The BRM was more powerful than the revolutionary monocoque Lotus, and Hill managed to secure his first World Championship, but it was simply a prelude to the long-running battles ahead as the two teams developed and the England-Scotland rivalry took over Formula One.

The new year saw big changes as the sport lost some of its biggest names, and drivers and teams swapped allegiances. Just one month before the season began, Stirling Moss crashed heavily at Goodwood and although he survived, the incident brought his racing career to an end.

Jack Brabham left the Cooper team to form his own eponymous squad, whilst Lotus made history by running the first monocoque chassis in Formula 1, the Lotus 25. However, it could not do anything to stop Graham Hill and the BRM team from taking the title as the V8 engine made a resurgence and the British teams began to dominate once again.

The Lotus monocoque chassis.

Hill triumphs as Brits dominate grid

Reigning World Champions Ferrari could only manage a best place of ninth on the grid as the season began at Zandvoort. Instead of Italian dominance, an all-British line-up of John Surtees, Hill and Jim Clark sat on the front row, and through an incident-packed race it was Hill who was left out in front to cruise to victory.

Clark and Hill beat Surtees into turn one while behind them, Dan Gurney got off to a flier and dragged his Porsche up to third from eighth on the grid. His race was to end eventually with a gear lever problem, but his presence served as a warning for the future.

Behind the leaders, Ricardo Rodriguez spun and, when Brabham could do nothing to avoid hitting the Ferrari, it was the end of the race for both of them. Third-placed Surtees then had a big accident on lap 8, and he was lucky to escape injury after wishbone failure on his Lola.

Clark dropped back when clutch trouble hit his Lotus and Hill cruised by to take the victory from Trevor Taylor's Lotus. Ferrari restored some pride with third and fourth, but it was not the start the title-holders were hoping for.

The field moved to Monaco in June for a classic. The weather was not ideal, and the exciting race was full of incidents, accidents, mechanical failures and

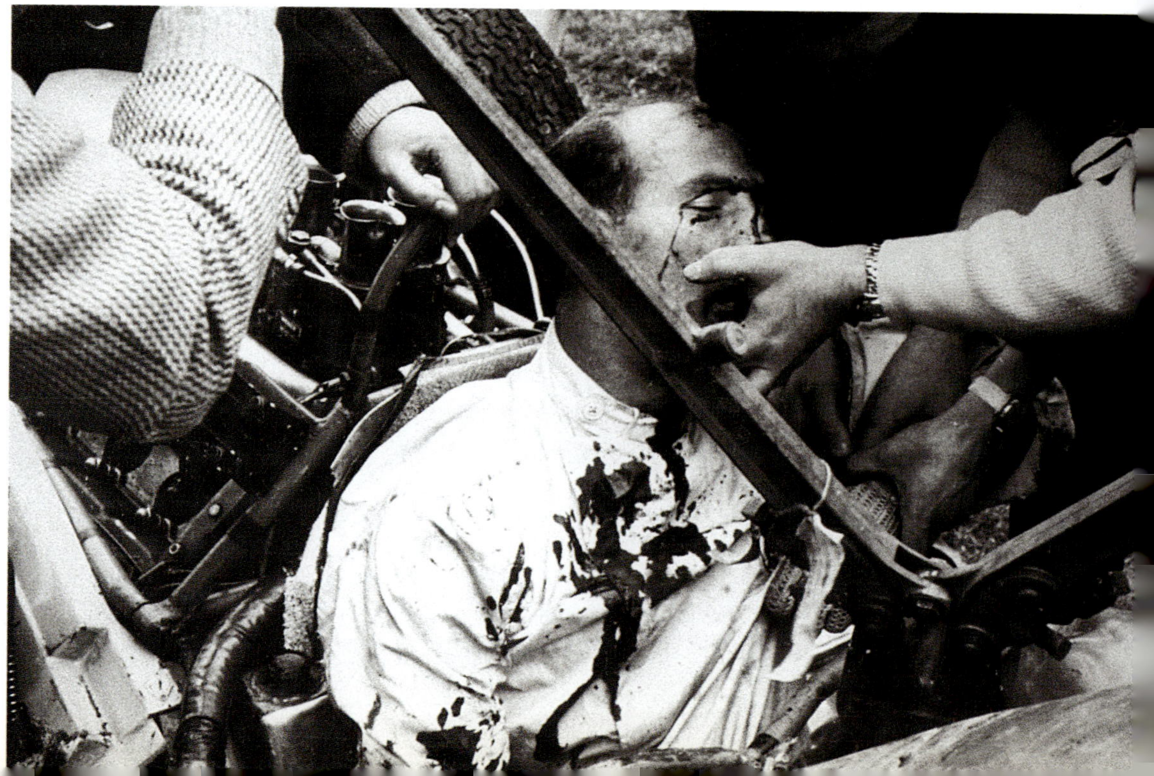

Officials help Stirling Moss after his crash at Goodwood which ended his career.

Graham Hill, Jim Clark and Phil Hill on the podium at the Belgian Grand Prix.

plenty of lead changes. Through all the muddle, it was Bruce McLaren who came home victorious when Graham Hill's BRM failed him just seven laps from the flag.

Practice was dogged by rain, but it was the usual suspects who lined up on row one with Jim Clark on pole ahead of Graham Hill and McLaren. However, that didn't seem to matter to Willy Mairesse, who stormed through the trio to be first into St Devoté. But on a damp track, and struggling to keep control, the Ferrari allowed Hill and McLaren to slip by, and when Mairesse spun at the Station Hairpin his race was effectively over.

There was more incident in the midfield as Richie Ginther's BRM ploughed into the Lotuses of Maurice Trintignant and Innes Ireland. Ireland kept going, but Ginther and Trintignant were joined by Dan Gurney's Porsche as early retirements. When the frantic first lap was over, with McLaren ahead of Hill, they began a tough 10-lap battle for the lead before Hill began to get away. Behind them, Clark was scything through the field and having passed Phil Hill, Brabham and McLaren, he was up to the back of the leader. But it was all in vain, and he went out on lap 55 when his clutch failed him once again.

It looked like Hill's race, but the Briton's BRM began giving fatal smoke signals, and on lap 93 McLaren passed him, soon followed by Phil Hill and Bandini who gave Ferrari a two-three finish.

Clark wins Belgian thriller

Two weeks after the incident-packed Monaco race, the third round of the World Championship at Spa Francorchamps did not disappoint, with a fabulous five-car slipstreaming battle in the early stages which eventually left Clark in front to take victory.

Gurney's Porsche team were on strike, but he was not without a car in Belgium. However, the Lotus-BRM he took over was not fast enough and he withdrew after qualifying. How fortunes would change just one race later.

Clark also struggled when his engine failed early on in the practice session and he could only manage 12th on the grid as his rivals Graham Hill and McLaren sat in prime position on row one. The Scot, however, rocketed through the midfield pack to claim fourth by the end of lap one and joined Hill, Taylor, McLaren and Mairesse in a high-speed power battle for the lead. By lap nine Clark had completed his rise to the top and began to pull away.

Behind the Scot, Mairesse closed on Taylor's second-placed Lotus and on lap 26 they came together in a dramatic accident. The Lotus hit a telegraph pole, while Mairesse's Ferrari overturned and burst into flames.

Miraculously they suffered only minor injuries, and with those two out Clark was left with a huge lead over Graham Hill's struggling BRM, which claimed runners-up spot.

The French Grand Prix in July was Ferrari's turn to miss a race through a strike, as Porsche returned to do battle with the Britons in Rouen. As their rivals went out one by one, the German team stormed to their first World Championship win.

Gurney's Porsche was back on the third row at the start, and both Hill and Surtees beat Clark off the line, followed by McLaren and Brabham. The latter became the first of the leaders to suffer mechanical problems with suspension failure on lap 10, when McLaren also dropped from the pack after a

RACE BY RACE DETAILS

ROUND 1 – HOLLAND
Race Graham Hill
Pole John Surtees
Fastest Lap Bruce McLaren

ROUND 2 – MONACO
Race Bruce McLaren
Pole Jim Clark
Fastest Lap Jim Clark

ROUND 3 – BELGIUM
Race Jim Clark
Pole Graham Hill
Fastest Lap Jim Clark

ROUND 4 – FRANCE
Race Dan Gurney
Pole Jim Clark
Fastest Lap Graham Hill

ROUND 5 – BRITAIN
Race Jim Clark
Pole Jim Clark
Fastest Lap Jim Clark

ROUND 6 – GERMANY
Race Graham Hill
Pole Dan Gurney
Fastest Lap Graham Hill

ROUND 7 – ITALY
Race Graham Hill
Pole Jim Clark
Fastest Lap Graham Hill

ROUND 8 – UNITED STATES
Race Jim Clark
Pole Jim Clark
Fastest Lap Jim Clark

ROUND 9 – SOUTH AFRICA
Race Graham Hill
Pole Jim Clark
Fastest Lap Jim Clark

1962 DRIVERS' CHAMPIONSHIP

DRIVER	TEAM	POINTS
Graham Hill	BRM	42
Jim Clark	Lotus Climax	30
Bruce McLaren	Cooper Climax	27
John Surtees	Lola Climax	19
Dan Gurney	Porsche	15
Phil Hill	Ferrari	14
Tony Maggs	Cooper Climax	13
Richie Ginther	BRM	10
Jack Brabham	Lotus Cli/Brabham Cli	9
Trevor Taylor	Lotus Climax	6
Giancarlo Baghetti	Ferrari	5
Lorenzo Bandini	Ferrari	4
Ricardo Rodriguez	Ferrari	4
Willy Mairesse	Ferrari	3
Jo Bonnier	Porsche	3
Innes Ireland	Lotus Climax	2
Carel Godin de Beaufort	Porsche	2
Masten Gregory	Lotus BRM	1
Neville Lederle	Lotus Climax	1

gear selection problem.

Surtees was out of the running three laps later with fuel-feed problems, and Gregory and Bonnier, who had caught up with the lead pack, were also let down by mechanical problems.

Hill was safely in the lead, but he lost his advantage to Clark when backmarker Jack Lewis suffered brake failure and careered into the BRM on lap 30.

Hill was back in front when the Scot stopped with front suspension problems, and once again he looked odds-on for the win. However, as was becoming the norm towards the end of a race, his BRM began to misfire, and Gurney was able to reel him in to secure Porsche win number one a whole lap ahead of the Cooper of Tony Maggs.

Brits dominate on home soil

Aintree was the venue for the British round of the World Championship, but the crowd were not treated to the drama they had come to expect after the thrills of the previous rounds, and although it was a popular win for Clark, his runaway flag-to-flag victory failed to provide much excitement during the 75-lap race.

Clark led into turn one and continued to lap faster than anyone as he dominated the event and built up a massive lead over second-placed Surtees. McLaren, Hill and Brabham followed Surtees to the finish in a race which saw just five retirements.

Torrential rain at the Nurburgring provided the main challenge for the Grand Prix runners as the Championship moved on to round six. After an accident-marred qualifying session, race day dawned with a cloud-covered sky, and when the rain-delayed race finally got underway the promised battle never developed, leaving Graham Hill to take a close but unchallenged victory for BRM.

At the start, Clark's Lotus failed to get away from the front row, and it transpired that the Scot had failed to switch on his fuel-pumps. That left Gurney to lead from pole, followed by Graham Hill, who had qualified well despite being hit in practice by a falling on-board television camera.

Ferrari loses power struggle to BRM

Ferrari were back to full strength after entering just one car in the previous race, but despite a great start from Phil Hill, who shot his Ferrari up to third from a disappointing 12th on the grid, they could do nothing to prevent BRM taking the win.

Hill took the lead on lap three, and although Gurney rallied once he had fixed the battery problem, he could only climb back to third. Nobody could pass the BRM man, and he finished the race just 2.5 seconds ahead of Surtees to develop a good lead in the Championship.

Ferrari were going through a lean period and once again their V6 engine couldn't match the power of the BRM unit, and the British team helped themselves to a dominant one-two finish. With Hill the only Championship contender to claim points, the drivers' title now looked all but over. Hill's team-mate Ginther followed him home 30 seconds adrift.

Jim Clark was desperate for victory as the teams crossed the Atlantic for the penultimate round of the Championship at Watkins Glen. With all their drivers out of the running, Ferrari had given up early and did not bother to go to America, so even more than ever the battle for honours was fought between Lotus and BRM.

Hill had won the previous two races, but it was not to be this time as Clark's Lotus took the spoils in a straight fight between the two Britons, and in doing so not only kept his Championship hopes alive, but

Dan Gurney got his first win in the French Grand Prix.

Jim Clark signals his victory in the United States Grand Prix accompanied by Colin Chapman.

1962 CONSTRUCTORS' CUP

TEAM (Engine)	POINTS
BRM	42
LOTUS CLIMAX	36
COOPER CLIMAX	29
LOLA CLIMAX	19
FERRARI	18
PORSCHE	18
BRABHAM CLIMAX	6
LOTUS BRM	1

turned a first title for the Scot into a very realistic proposition.

Clark was always on the pace at Watkins Glen, and he took the lead from pole with Hill getting ahead of team-mate Ginther who had qualified ahead of him. After a close battle, Hill finally passed Clark for the lead on lap 12, but the Lotus man eventually won out when he regained it on lap 19.

Behind the leaders, Gurney and Ginther battled it out for third before the BRM hit engine trouble. Luckily for Hill, his car did not suffer a similar fate, but he could not compete with Clark, and with the pair having lapped the rest of the field Hill ended the race nine seconds adrift of his Championship rival, with McLaren the best of the rest in third.

Hill crowned Champion as Clark falters

The world was made to wait three months before the Championship could be decided at the final race of the season in South Africa at the end of December. A massive crowd gathered at the East London track to watch the title finale. Hill still had the upper hand, and Clark's challenge was simple: win and he would become World Champion. Anything less simply wouldn't do.

The Scot took pole and, sure enough, his Championship rival sat alongside him as the cars waited on the grid. When the race began Clark shot into the lead and Hill brought up the rear, but could not stay in touch. It looked like things were slipping away for the Londoner. With Clark getting away, Hill was left on his own in second, able to stay out of the tremendous battle between McLaren, Surtees and Tony Maggs' Cooper raging behind him. Then, 25 laps away from the world crown, disaster struck the leader as his engine began to smoke.

Clark was forced into the pits with an oil leak on lap 61, and it was all over. The Coopers of McLaren and Maggs remained out of contention, and an unchallenged Hill was left to win the race and in doing so take his first World Championship title by a comfortable 12 points from Clark.

SHORTS

Jim Clark's victory at Watkins Glen was the beginning of a very successful run in America. for the Scot. He went on to win two more U.S. Grand Prix races, all at the Watkins Glen circuit, and then turned his attention to the Indianapolis 500 where, in 1965, he became the first non-American to capture the title. His exploits in the U.S. earned him a place in the Motorsports Hall of Fame of America.

Denny Hulme

CAREER DETAILS

1936	Born 18 June, Nelson, New Zealand
1956	Starts racing
1960	Moves to Europe to race in Formula Junior
1961	Works as mechanic in Jack Brabham's garage
1962	Begins season in one of Tyrrell's Cooper Formula Juniors, moved to a Brabham
1963	Wins seven times in Formula Junior in works Brabham
1964	Stars for Brabham in Tasman series, Hulme finished runner-up in Formula Two Championship
1965	Finishes runner-up behind Brabham in Formula Two title. Joins Brabham's Formula One team. GP debut at Monaco
1967	Wins World Championship ahead of boss Jack Brabham and Jim Clark
1968	Joins Bruce McLaren's team for seven years and six wins
1968-70	Also races with great success in CanAm sports cars, winning series in 1968 and 1970.
1975	Retires
1992	Awarded OBE. Dies 4 October of a heart attack while competing in Australia's famous touring car race

FORMULA ONE RECORD

Year	Team	Wins	Poles	Fast laps	Pts
1965	Brabham Cl	0	0	0	5
1966	Brabham Cl	0	0	0	–
	Brabham Rep	0	0	1	18
1967	Brabham Rep	2	0	2	51
1968	McLaren BRM	0	0	0	–
	McLaren Ford	2	0	0	33
1969	McLaren Ford	1	0	0	20
1970	McLaren Ford	0	0	0	27
1971	McLaren Ford	0	0	1	9
1972	McLaren Ford	1	0	1	39
1973	McLaren Ford	1	1	3	26
1974	McLaren Ford	1	0	1	20

DENNY HULME, the first New Zealander to win the World Championship, remained loyal to fellow-Antipodean team-owners Jack Brabham and Bruce McLaren and raced simply because he loved it.

Denis Hulme during the Monaco Grand Prix in 1967.

Denis Hulme (pronounced "Hulm", not Hume – "you can't knock the 'ell out of Hulme," he used to say) spent much of his youth on his grandparents' tobacco farm on the South Island. In the late 1940s his family moved to Te Puke where his father, Clive, started a haulage business. A mechanic in a local garage, young Denny maintained his father's trucks and tractors, and earned extra money delivering equipment and materials to farms.

Having saved up enough to buy a brand-new MG TF by the age of 20, he started racing in 1956, first of all in hill climbs, before taking his car to the circuits. Success followed, and after spending 1959 campaigning in a single-seater he won a place on the "Driver to Europe" scheme, sponsored by the New Zealand International Grand Prix Association.

Hulme's father Clive had been awarded the Victoria Cross for his valour during World War II action in Crete and it was often noted his son inherited the same qualities of single-mindedness and resoluteness when it came to his motor-racing career. In many ways, Hulme – nicknamed "the Bear" for his taciturn manner and occasional grouchiness – was the least likely of World Champions. He went racing because he loved the sport, not for any form of self-aggrandizement. (He was later to become a public relations nightmare – "I know the people I really have to know – which is about three – but I don't like smalltalk and I haven't time for people who just sit down and talk about nothing, putting on as big a front as they can," he said in 1968.)

He quickly acquired experience racing his Cooper-BMC in Formula Junior all over Europe. However, his friend George Lawton, also on the "Driver to Europe" scheme, was killed and Hulme returned home. Having overcome his despondency, he returned to Britain in 1961 to work as a mechanic at Jack Brabham's garage, which funded more competition in Formula Junior and marked the start of a long relationship with his fellow-Antipodean.

Having begun the 1962 season in one of Ken Tyrrell's Cooper Formula Juniors, he moved over to a Brabham and continued with the works Brabham outfit in 1963, winning seven times out of 14 starts.

"Beneath a rugged exterior is a quietly-spoken, dedicated man. There is nothing subtle about him. He is completely genuine."

Denis Hulme officially retired at the end of 1974 but carried on racing in Australia.

In 1964, after starring for Brabham in the Tasman series, he joined the boss's F2 team and was runner-up in the European F2 Championship. Hulme earned his first drives at non-championship F1 events in the Brabham F1 team during this year. In 1965, Brabham and Hulme cleaned up in the F2 Championship again, and Hulme made his GP debut at Monaco, standing in for Dan Gurney. A prolific sports car racer, too, he won the Tourist Trophy in a Brabham BT8.

Two solid seasons followed, racing alongside his boss who won the Championship in 1966, the first ever by a driver in a car of his own construction. In Hulme's best year, 1967, he won the Monaco and German Grands Prix and claimed the World Championship in the Brabham BT20-Repco V8 ahead of his team-mate, boss and mentor, and also Jim Clark.

His maiden victory at Monaco that year was overshadowed by the horrendous fire that engulfed the inverted Ferrari of Lorenzo Baldini, who had been running second behind Hulme. The Italian died of his burns within a week. It was a strange victory all round, with Hulme the garlanded victor being asked his name by the elderly Clerk of the Course Louis Chiron at the post-race presentation.

In 1968 Hulme joined the team of compatriot Bruce McLaren, for whom he had been competing in the CanAm series between Grands Prix (winning the title in 1968 and 1970). To the rugged, easy-going Kiwi, the relaxed atmosphere of the sports racers was preferable to the preening environment of F1. Their domination of this North American series attained such a status it was known as "The Bruce and Denny Show". Hulme remained with McLaren for seven years until he retired, scoring six more F1 GP wins along the way.

Although he officially retired from F1 at the end of the 1974 season, Hulme found it hard to withdraw from the motorsport scene, racing various classes of cars and trucks. In 1992 he was competing in the Bathurst 1000km in Australia when spectators saw his BMW M3 suddenly pull off the track and park neatly by the Armco barrier. When marshals arrived at the scene they found Hulme dead from a massive heart attack, still strapped into his seat.

1963
Clark wins title in style

TALKING POINT
DRIVERS TAKE IT TO THE MEX

For the first time in the World Championship, a race was held in Mexico as Grand Prix fever stretched to another country outside Europe.

The Autodromo Hermanos Rodriguez was the venue for the Mexican Grand Prix and after its debut the circuit went on to host races until 1970. After a 16-year absence it returned to the calendar to run from 1986 to 1992.

Jim Clark, Nigel Mansell and Alain Prost are all masters of the circuit, having each won two of the 15 races held in Mexico. The circuit, situated in the Eastern suburbs of Mexico City, is tough on the stamina and fitness of any competing driver.

In the early days, the circuit was 3.107 miles per lap in length, and, combined with the searing heat, tested the endurance of the drivers. In 1970, the circuit was reduced to 2.747 miles per lap length, but it still provided a stiff challenge throughout the years.

Graham Hill in first place at Monaco.

Jim Clark and his trusty Lotus car were the undeniable highlight of the season as the Scottish driver won seven of the 10 rounds to secure his first Championship in stylish fashion. It was a devastating display of driving ability from Clark and propelled him to the higher echelons of motor-racing.

Before Clark ran away with the title, the preseason provided plenty of action and was dominated by the withdrawal of Porsche from the mainstream World Championship series. The exit of the German marque forced American racer Dan Gurney to look elsewhere for a drive, and he found one with Jack Brabham's own team.

Bowmaker/Lola also withdrew, forcing John Surtees to take a drive with the Ferrari team at one of its lowest ebbs. Ferrari had been rocked by the departure of many of its engineering and driving staff, who formed a new ATS team. Surtees was joined by Willy Mairesse at Ferrari, while Phil Hill and Giancarlo Baghetti jumped ship from Ferrari to join ATS. Hill and Baghetti would regret that decision, as they would end the season without a point.

The season began late as Monaco hosted the opening round in May on a warm, dry and bright day. Clark seemed to be starting the season well as he claimed pole position for the 100-lap race.

But on race day, Clark's luck ran out. Graham Hill, driving for BRM, took the lead from the start as his rival dropped to third behind Hill's team-mate Richie Ginther. Clark started to show his talent as he first reeled in Ginther and then on lap 18 overtook Hill to take the lead.

For a few laps Hill pressured Clark for the lead, but the latter soon pulled away with a series of quick laps. But Clark's glory was only to last until the 78th lap, as a gearbox failure forced him out of the race. That left Hill to re-take the lead and win the race. Ginther had maintained second place while Bruce McLaren finished third in a Cooper.

Clark claims dramatic victory

For the second round in Belgium in June, three new teams graced the Championship. BRP, spearheaded by Innes Ireland, ATS with Phil Hill and Baghetti and Scirocco, represented by Tony Settember and Ian Burgess, all arrived on the scene.

However, none of the teams provided a threat to Lotus and BRM at the front, as Graham Hill claimed pole position for the race. Clark did struggle in qualifying and was left down in eighth on the grid.

But Clark redeemed himself with an extraordinary start as he claimed the lead after overtaking seven cars. The early stages of the race were marred by an incident on the fifth lap as Trevor Taylor crashed his Lotus heavily, but came out of it unscathed.

In damp conditions, many drivers fell foul of the weather, and as Clark pulled away from the rest of the field no less than 12 drivers failed to finish the race. Graham Hill was an early retirement on lap 17 of the 32 as his BRM suffered a gearbox problem.

Tony Maggs suddenly became a contender to challenge Clark as retirements promoted him up the field. Brabham's car had electronic problems, while Surtees dropped back with a fuel-injector fault.

Maggs was third, behind Gurney and Clark, before a spin five laps from the finish ended his race and promoted Ginther to third. A late charge from Bruce McLaren in a Cooper earned him second and dropped Gurney and Ginther back a place each, but the race was already over as Clark claimed his maiden win of the season.

The Zandvoort circuit hosted the third round of the series and the only notable driver change before the event involved Ferrari, as they replaced Mairesse with Ludovico Scarfiotti. BRM and ATS also produced new cars for the event, but the latter once again failed to make an impression.

Clark took pole position for the race and again

Jim Clark heads the field in the Mexican Grand Prix.

RACE BY RACE DETAILS

ROUND 1 – MONACO
Race Graham Hill
Pole Jim Clark
Fastest lap John Surtees

ROUND 2 – BELGIUM
Race Jim Clark
Pole Graham Hill
Fastest lap Jim Clark

ROUND 3 – HOLLAND
Race Jim Clark
Pole Jim Clark
Fastest lap Jim Clark

ROUND 4 – FRANCE
Race Jim Clark
Pole Jim Clark
Fastest lap Jim Clark

ROUND 5 – BRITAIN
Race Jim Clark
Pole Jim Clark
Fastest lap John Surtees

ROUND 6 – GERMANY
Race John Surtees
Pole Jim Clark
Fastest lap John Surtees

ROUND 7 – ITALY
Race Jim Clark
Pole John Surtees
Fastest lap Jim Clark

ROUND 8 – UNITED STATES
Race Graham Hill
Pole Graham Hill
Fastest lap Jim Clark

ROUND 9 – MEXICO
Race Jim Clark
Pole Jim Clark
Fastest lap Jim Clark

ROUND 10 – SOUTH AFRICA
Race Jim Clark
Pole Jim Clark
Fastest lap Dan Gurney

produced an immaculate display to dominate proceedings. He led from start to finish to take his second successive victory of the season and stamp his authority on the campaign for the first time.

McLaren, who started third on the grid, suffered gearbox failure and was the first big name to drop out after just five laps. He was soon followed by the two ATS cars of Phil Hill and Baghetti.

As Clark pulled away in the lead, Graham Hill and Brabham battled for second place and the latter had the better of it until he was forced to retire with a throttle problem on lap 55 of the 80-lap race. Hill then ran into problems himself as his car overheated. He was overtaken by Gurney and eventually pulled out of the race on lap 69.

That left a processional finish as Clark claimed

1963 DRIVERS' CHAMPIONSHIP

DRIVER	TEAM	POINTS
Jim Clark	Lotus Climax	54
Graham Hill	BRM	29
Richie Ginther	BRM	29
John Surtees	Ferrari	22
Dan Gurney	Brabham Climax	19
Bruce McLaren	Cooper Climax	17
Jack Brabham	Brabham Climax	14
Tony Maggs	Cooper Climax	9
Innes Ireland	BRP BRM	6
Lorenzo Bandini	BRM/Ferrari	6
Jo Bonnier	Cooper Climax	6
Gerhard Mitter	Porsche	3
Jim Hall	Lotus BRM	3
Carel Godin de Beaufort	Porsche	2
Trevor Taylor	Lotus Climax	1
Ludovico Scarfiotti	Ferrari	1
Jo Siffert	Lotus BRM	1

Jim Clark gives boss Colin Chapman a lift as they celebrate Clark's first World Championship.

his second win of the season with Gurney a clear second and Surtees third.

Clark takes control of Championship

By now, Clark was in full flow and for the next round in France, back at the Reims circuit after a year at the Rouen track, he continued to dominate the action as his Lotus left the field in his exhaust-fumes.

Clark claimed pole position for the 53-lap race, fractionally ahead of the new BRM 1.6 of Graham Hill. ATS were missing from the start-line as they worked on their cars after a disastrous introduction to top-level motorsport.

The race itself provided even more action – and controversy – as French race officials seemed to create their own rules. Hill stalled his BRM on the grid, a common problem with the British driver, but instead of being forced to start at the back at the re-start, as the rules dictate, Hill was allowed to re-start from his qualifying position of second on the grid.

Clark took his third consecutive victory of the season and Graham Hill looked set to take second place but was cruelly denied that by Tony Maggs on the penultimate lap as his throttle slipped. After an investigation into the start-line fiasco, Hill was allowed to keep his third-place classification, but was not awarded any points for the finish.

Silverstone made a return to the series as it hosted the British Grand Prix once again. Aintree, in Liverpool, had hosted the race for the previous two years, but it now returned to its spiritual home.

Several local drivers joined the usual field, including Mike Hailwood, Reg Parnell and Bob Anderson. Hailwood was the best privateer finisher as he brought his Lotus 24 home in eighth place.

Once again the other drivers were overshadowed as Clark claimed a convincing victory, his fourth successive win. Clark started badly from pole position, but it took him just four laps to reel in leader Brabham and take charge.

Clark led for the remainder of the 82-lap race and demonstrated to the large crowd how to drive a Grand Prix car. Graham Hill then ran second and was cruelly denied runner-up spot when, on the final lap, his BRM ran out of fuel and allowed the Ferrari of Surtees to pass with the finish line in sight.

Surtees ends Clark's streak

Surtees' good fortune continued two weeks after the British Grand Prix as he ended Clark's dominance and winning streak in the World Championship with victory in the action-packed German Grand Prix at the Nurburgring.

Clark claimed pole position for the race, which provided no less than six accidents in the opening five laps. Lorenzo Bandini crashed his BRM P57 car before completing a lap, while Innes Ireland crashed out on the first lap in his Lotus 24. Mairesse suffered the worst crash of the race on the same lap as he lost control of his Ferrari at Flugplatz. A medic was killed after being hit by the out-of-control car, while Mairesse suffered such severe arm injuries that he never raced in a Grand Prix again.

Chris Amon crashed out in his Lola on lap three, while Tony Settember had an accident in his Scirocco on lap five. Sandwiched between those two incidents, McLaren had a big shunt in his Cooper. McLaren was knocked unconscious and suffered a serious knee injury.

At the front, the leaders had fortunately steered

clear of all the shunts and Ginther, Surtees and Clark swapped the lead in the opening four laps. On lap five, however, Surtees took charge as Clark's Lotus and Ginther's BRM both suffered engine troubles. Surtees pulled away and secured Ferrari's first World Championship win for two years.

Fresh from their triumph in Germany, Ferrari returned to their homeland for the next round of the Championship as Monza hosted the Italian Grand Prix in September. Unfortunately for the *scuderia* their home race was not to be their happiest.

Bandini had joined Ferrari from Scuderia Centro Sud to replace the injured Mairesse, but both he and Surtees failed to finish the 86-lap race, along with all other Ferrari-powered competitors.

The race, which was originally planned to run on the longer road and oval circuit at Monza, was run on the shorter circuit and was marred immediately by a heavy crash involving Amon. The Lola driver suffered a shunt in practice and sustained serious injuries, forcing him out for the weekend.

Lotus had a new driver for the race as Mike Spence came in to team up with Clark after Taylor had suffered injury in a non-championship event, the Mediterranean Grand Prix. Surtees had offered optimism to Ferrari by claiming pole for the race, but he was soon overshadowed by Graham Hill, Clark and Gurney. The lead changed hands no fewer than 28 times in the first 56 laps between the four drivers. Surtees was leading before engine trouble ended his race on lap 16.

Clark takes chequered flag and world title

Clark started to dominate the race from lap 56 and was helped by the retirements of Hill on lap 59 and Gurney five laps later. Ginther was promoted to second and McLaren to third, but by the finish both drivers were over 90 seconds behind winner Clark, who had re-stamped his authority on the series.

Clark's win sealed the World Championship with events in the United States, Mexico and South Africa still to unfold. He was in good spirits when he arrived at Watkins Glen, but that soon changed as a battery problem left him on the grid at the start of the 110-lap race.

Hill had taken pole for the race and he went on to claim his first win of the season. Clark again produced a faultless display from his enforced start at the back of the field to eventually finish third behind second-placed Ginther.

Clark returned to winning ways three weeks later when the Championship arrived in Mexico for the first time, as he claimed pole position and led from the start in the 45-lap race. Brabham was second and Ginther third, but the record-books were on the verge of being rewritten as Clark equalled Juan Manuel Fangio's record of six wins in a season.

With the Championship in the bag, Clark's only concern for the final round in South Africa was to try and beat Fangio's record.

Clark boosted his confidence by claiming pole position for the 85-lap race and in the end won by more than a minute from Gurney as he put the finishing touches to a remarkable season with his name in the record-books. His seventh win of the season was never in doubt and the record was just reward for a dominant season from the Scot.

SHORTS

The French Grand Prix, held at the Reims track, was full of incident, much of it created by the inept French officials. The Graham Hill re-start debacle was not the only peculiarity of the day. Amazingly, the race officials started the race with a red flag, which normally signifies the race is stopped. However, despite the confusion all the drivers got away safely and normal order was restored as Jim Clark sped away into the lead.

1963 CONSTRUCTORS' CUP

TEAM (Engine)	POINTS
LOTUS CLIMAX	54
BRM	36
BRABHAM CLIMAX	28
FERRARI	26
COOPER CLIMAX	25
BRP BRM	6
PORSCHE	5
LOTUS BRM	4

Jim Clark leading in the French Grand Prix.

Phil Hill

CAREER DETAILS

1927 Born 20 April, in Miami, Florida
1950 Begins racing in US West Coast sports car series
1954 Comes to Europe to race in the Le Mans 24 Hours
1955 Wins National Sports Car Championship in USA in privately-entered Ferrari. Subsequently offered works Ferrari drive at Le Mans
1958 Promoted to Ferrari Formula One team midway through season. Partnered Olivier Gendebien to victory at Le Mans. Helped team-mate Mike Hawthorn win World Championship
1959 Finishes second in French and Italian Grands Prix
1960 Produces first of three Grand Prix wins, triumphing at Monza
1961 Best Formula One season. World Champion in Ferrari, with two wins. Title won after death of team-mate Wolfgang von Trips in penultimate race at Monza. Another Le Mans win with Gendebien
1962 Third Le Mans win with Gendebien. Last year at Ferrari
1963 No success with ATS and Cooper, returned to sports cars
1967 Ill health prompts retirement

FORMULA ONE RECORD

Year	Team	Wins	Poles	Fast laps	Pts
1958	Maserati	0	0	0	–
	Ferrari F2	0	0	0	–
	Ferrari	0	0	1	9
1959	Ferrari	0	0	1	20
1960	Ferrari	1	1	2	–
	Cooper	0	0	0	16
1961	Ferrari	2	5	2	34
1962	Ferrari	0	0	0	14
1963	ATS	0	0	0	–
	Lotus BRM	0	0	0	0
1964	Cooper Climax	0	0	0	1

PHIL HILL, master of Le Mans and the first American to make an impression in Formula One, won the 1961 World Championship in his "Sharknose" Ferrari after the death of team-mate Wolfgang von Trips.

Phil Hill in the distinctive red of Ferrari in 1962.

Phil Hill took his first drive in a family friend's brand-new 1936 Oldsmobile at the age of nine. Hill was sitting in the car pretending to drive when the owner asked if he knew how to. The future World Champion replied "Sure!" To the horror of all onlookers, the Olds owner got into the passenger seat and let Hill drive around the block. "That started my ultra-interest in cars," recalled Hill.

By 1961 Hill had become the first American to win the Formula One world drivers' Championship. Mario Andretti followed 17 years later, but Hill remains the only American-born F1 Champion.

Born in Miami, Florida, but raised in Santa Monica, California, Hill's childhood coincided with the rise of southern Californian sports car-racing. As a teenager, he became one of the first members of the California Sportscar Club in 1946. He majored in business administration at the University of Southern California but quit to work on Offenhauser-powered midgets.

Hill went to Great Britain in 1949 to study maintenance at the Jaguar factory as part of his job with a new dealership. When he returned to California, he brought with him an XK120. After winning the initial road race of the United States at Pebble Beach in 1950, Hill kept driving – in endurance races, the Mexican Road Race and countless other events. By 1955, he had "retired" twice, but in that year, he won at the Nassau Speed Week and that led to a factory ride in sports car-racing.

For two years, Hill continued to win races. With Oliver Gendebien, he won in the torrential rain at Le Mans in 1958, a race he would always nominate his favourite. Sitting on a tool bag to see over the windscreen and soaked to the skin from the start, Hill recalled the impossibility of seeing in the dark.

"I drove down the Mulsanne straight at top speed and waited to hear the resonance of exhaust in front of me. As soon as I could sense the location of a car in the blackness, it was a flash of light, the bare outline of car and driver and then back into the darkness, peering ahead for the next one...While my winning the 1961 Formula One Championship was the biggest event of my career, the 1958 Le Mans remains the most rewarding to me."

He waited for an offer to drive in Formula One from Enzo Ferrari. On 7 September 1958, he got it and made his debut at Monza. Hill played a key role

> "He was a brilliant driver, especially in sports cars. But I don't think he had anything like the same virtuosity in a Grand Prix car."
>
> *John Cooper*

Phil Hill in 1961.

in winning Mike Hawthorn's World Championship, waving his British colleague through in the Moroccan Grand Prix decider, enabling Hawthorn to finish second behind Moss and win the title on points.

With third-place finishes in the Italian and Moroccan Grands Prix, he had impressed enough to be granted a full season with Ferrari in 1959. He finished the year with two second places – at the French and Italian Grands Prix. The following season was a struggle with the outmoded front-engined Ferrari but Hill produced his maiden Grand Prix win at Monza.

In 1961 Ferrari were well-prepared for the first year of the new 1.5-litre F1 regulations. The World Championship was the result of one of the toughest season-long battles in Grand Prix history. In their new mid-engine Ferraris, Hill and team-mate Wolfgang von Trips swapped the title lead from race to race.

There were personal triumphs, like Hill driving the first-ever sub-nine-minute lap at the difficult Nurburgring, but it was not until the penultimate race of the year, the Italian Grand Prix, that the title was settled, and only when von Trips was killed in a first-lap accident. Hill, though shaken, won by a single point. Ferrari decided not to participate in the year's last Grand Prix out of deference to the Monza disaster. Thus the newly-crowned world driver's Champion did not compete in his home Grand Prix at Watkins Glen.

Other highlights in his illustrious career include winning Le Mans three times, the 12 hours of Sebring three times and the Argentine 1000 km three times. He won the first and last races of his driving career, the final victory being the BOAC 500 at Brands Hatch in England in 1967.

Within Formula One, his title never accorded him superstar status. "At times, when the mood took him, he was a brilliant driver, especially in sports cars. But I don't think he had anything like the same virtuosity in a Grand Prix car. I don't think Phil would have won the 1961 World Championship had von Trips not been killed in the Monza accident," observed John Cooper.

Hill remained at Ferrari in 1962, coming close to a second drivers' title. He was released and moved on to less glittering times at ATS and Cooper before retreating to sports car-racing. He had won two further Le Mans victories with Gendebien in 1961 and 1962. In 1967 ill health forced him to retire and he returned to California to run a classic car restoration business.

1964
Single point decides title race

TALKING POINT
CLIMAX BLOWS IT FOR CLARK

In all honesty, the year should have seen Jim Clark retain the world drivers' title, but he was let down by disastrous reliability from the Climax engine. Clark only made it to the end in three of the 10 races, but he won those three and if it were not for regular early exits, he would have cruised to the world crown.

His engine let him down an incredible six times, robbing him of much-needed points in his quest for the Championship, and often in the dying moments of the race. During the season he led a total of 322 laps, more than double his nearest challenger, while eventual World Champion John Surtees managed just 89, but had the reliability to take him through.

A late Ferrari resurgence helped former motorcycle World Champion John Surtees become the first man to win World Championships on both two and four wheels, but it was a close-run thing and, quite literally, the title race went right down to the line.

Four races into the season, Surtees had just six points to his name, and the Ferrari looked anything but a title-winning car. However, it was the reliability problems that plagued many of the other runners that would help the Italian team to victory, and a strong end to the season, coupled with Graham Hill's stuttering form and Clark's engine problems, hauled Surtees up in the points standings to take the Championship by a single point.

After a busy run of non-championship races, the real business began at Monaco in early May. Innes Ireland, Jim Clark, John Surtees and Jack Brabham had all taken encouraging victories in the pre-season events, but when it mattered it was Graham Hill and the BRM team who moved back on top.

Ireland had a bad start to the season when he was involved in a car accident on the way to the race, injuring his knee. A further crash during practice kept him sidelined for two races.

Hill wins opener at Monaco

At the start in Monte Carlo, Hill slipped down to fourth as Clark, Brabham and Gurney led off the line, but the lead Lotus, which was dragging an anti-roll bar, was called into the pits on lap 36 to avoid disqualification and dropped to third.

The Scot battled back up through the field while Brabham went the other way, suffering from engine troubles. By lap 53 Gurney, suffering from a fuel leak, had slowed Hill enough to allow Clark to catch up, and the three were close together in a tight bunch.

Finally, Hill found a way past the American to take the lead, and sailed away to victory. Both Gurney and Clark stopped before the end of the race to leave Hill a lap clear of the field, with team-mate Richie Ginther best of the rest.

With three manufacturers on the front row of the grid for round two at Zandvoort, it was anybody's race, but in the end nobody could catch reigning World Champion Clark as he powered his Lotus 25 to a dominant victory.

Although he was pipped to pole by the Brabham of American Gurney, Clark led from start to finish, eventually taking the flag nearly a minute ahead of the improving Ferrari of Surtees. It was the first top three placing for the Italian marque since Surtees' victory in Germany six races previously, and it was a warning shot to the British teams that Ferrari were on the way back.

Clark had made it into the first corner narrowly ahead of Hill with Gurney and Peter Arundell chas-

John Surtees claimed the World Championship for himself and Ferrari.

Dan Gurney in the Brabham Rover car.

ing fast. However, it was Surtees who was attacking, and by lap 22 he was up to second place, but he just couldn't get close to Clark's pace, and had to settle for the runner-up's spot, nearly 50 seconds behind.

Hill dropped back with a misfiring engine and struggled to fourth place behind Arundell, who finished an entire lap adrift of the leaders.

Lotus gave Clark a new car for round three of the Championship at the Belgian Grand Prix, but its debut netted a disappointing sixth place on the grid. In a race of ever-changing leaders, his grid position was immaterial, and Clark was the lucky one who took the win in a dramatic run to the finish.

The initial leader was Arundell, who shot up from the second row, with Hill suffering a particularly poor start and slipping down to fifth. But Arundell's glory was not to last and Gurney, Surtees, Clark and Hill all made it past by the end of lap two.

Now it was Surtees' turn for a brief lead, but his was to last only as long as Arundell's and on lap three his Ferrari engine gave up the ghost. Gurney was back in front, and began to pull away as Hill and Clark became embroiled in a race for second place – but a curse was to hit the leader once again when the American's Brabham ran out of fuel, leaving Hill to take up the mantle.

But luck was not on the leader's side, and it was Hill's turn to have his lead taken away when his BRM came to a halt with a fuel-pump problem. This handed the lead to Bruce McLaren's Cooper but, unbelieveably, there was one more twist of fate to hit the unlucky leader in a race nobody seemed destined to win. When McLaren's stuttering engine gave up, a flying Clark made it past the New Zealander to take the win on the line, and this time there was no time for fate to steal it away – but the Lotus did run out of fuel on the running-down lap!

Gurney leads Brabham to maiden victory

In a fairly uneventful fourth race of the season, Clark was robbed of victory by an engine failure, and while Brabham was engaged in a tight battle with Graham Hill for second it was left to Gurney to take the French Grand Prix win and cruise to a first World Championship victory for the Brabham team.

Gurney qualified in second position on the grid, but it was Clark who took the early lead, with Surtees in third before he hit reliability problems again and a split oil-pipe ended his race. Both Hill and McLaren had spins which sent them down the field, but the former was able to climb back up to challenge and take Brabham for second.

By this time, however, Gurney was now leading, and well ahead of the rest. Although Brabham stayed with the flying Hill, there was nothing he could do to get past and secure a one-two for his own team, and he had to be content with watching his team-mate take their debut win.

It was three-up for Clark and Lotus when the field moved to the new British Grand Prix circuit of Brands Hatch for the fifth race of the season, and the reigning World Champion was looking in good form. He took another flag-to-flag victory in a close race, with Graham Hill second.

RACE BY RACE DETAILS

ROUND 1 – MONACO
Race Graham Hill
Pole Jim Clark
Fastest Lap Graham Hill

Round 2 – HOLLAND
Race Jim Clark
Pole Dan Gurney
Fastest Lap Jim Clark

Round 3 – BELGIUM
Race Jim Clark
Pole Dan Gurney
Fastest Lap Dan Gurney

ROUND 4 – FRANCE
Race Dan Gurney
Pole Jim Clark
Fastest Lap Jack Brabham

ROUND 5 – BRITAIN
Race Jim Clark
Pole Jim Clark
Fastest Lap Jim Clark

ROUND 6 – GERMANY
Race John Surtees
Pole John Surtees
Fastest Lap John Surtees

ROUND 7 – AUSTRIA
Race Lorenzo Bandini
Pole Graham Hill
Fastest Lap Dan Gurney

ROUND 8 – ITALY
Race John Surtees
Pole John Surtees
Fastest Lap John Surtees

ROUND 9 – UNITED STATES
Race Graham Hill
Pole Jim Clark
Fastest Lap Jim Clark

ROUND 10 – MEXICO
Race Dan Gurney
Pole Jim Clark
Fastest Lap Jim Clark

1964 DRIVERS' CHAMPIONSHIP

DRIVER	TEAM	POINTS
John Surtees	Ferrari	40
Graham Hill	BRM	39
Jim Clark	Lotus Climax	32
Lorenzo Bandini	Ferrari	23
Richie Ginther	BRM	23
Dan Gurney	Brabham Climax	19
Bruce McLaren	Cooper Climax	13
Jack Brabham	Brabham Climax	11
Peter Arundell	Lotus Climax	11
Jo Siffert	Brabham Climax	7
Bob Anderson	Brabham Climax	5
Tony Maggs	BRM	4
Mike Spence	Lotus Climax	4
Innes Ireland	BRP BRM	4
Jo Bonnier	Cooper Cli/Brab Cli	3
Chris Amon	Lotus BRM	2
Walt Hansgen	Lotus Climax	2
Maurice Trintignant	BRM	2
Trevor Taylor	BRP BRM	1
Mike Hailwood	Lotus BRM	1
Phil Hill	Cooper Climax	1
Pedro Rodriguez	Ferrari	1

The Honda team makes its debut in Germany.

Clark got a flier at the start and Gurney managed to out-drag Hill into second place off the line, but the American was soon out with ignition problems. That left Hill to close on Clark and although the two ran in formation for many laps, the BRM could never get past Clark's Lotus, and Hill finished the race just under three seconds behind.

John Surtees was the only other man on the lead lap, but he was more than a minute behind the top two. However, he notched up some important points by finishing third, and the Briton's finish began a run of results that was to take him to the World Championship.

An engine problem for Clark's Lotus in Germany was enough to give a lifeline to Ferrari, and Surtees didn't have to be asked twice to grab his first win of the season, dominating the race and crossing the line 80 seconds ahead of Graham Hill.

Practice ended with two Ferraris sandwiching Clark and Gurney on the front row, but the result was overshadowed by an accident involving Carel Godin de Beaufort, who suffered serious injuries when his old Porsche flew off the circuit and hit a tree. Tragically, he died two days later.

Lorenzo Bandini took the lead at the start of the 15-lap race on the long Nurburgring circuit, but Clark soon got past the Italian and began to pull away. However, Surtees was setting a storming pace, and he plucked off Gurney and Clark to claim a lead that was never challenged. The two men he had overtaken were both hit by mechanical troubles, and when Brabham's eponymous car also hit trouble, Hill found himself handed a surprise second place ahead of Bandini.

The race was also notable as Honda's first Formula One. However, it wasn't the success they had hoped, and after lining up last on the grid Ronnie Bucknam spun out of the race on lap 11 to end a rather inauspicious Grand Prix debut for the Japanese motoring giant.

Cars suffer on new track

The bumpy Zeltweg track was the venue for the next race, in Austria, included in the Championship calender for the first time. All the teams had trouble with the uneven surface, and practice was plagued with suspension failures. The bumps also took their toll on many cars in the race, and it was Bandini who came through without problems to take his only Grand Prix victory.

The start saw both Clark and Graham Hill left on the line, and Brabham straight into the pits with a fuel-feed problem, so Gurney took up the lead until Surtees snatched it from him on lap two. Bandini was running a solid race, and moved up to second when team-mate Surtees went out with suspension failure. Clark managed to take it from him, but soon after the Lotus retired with driveshaft failure, and Bandini

SHORTS

Ferrari's red machines have been synonymous with auto-racing for decades but in 1964 the team would appear very different when they arrived in America for the ninth round of the 1964 Championship. Team owner Enzo Ferrari was in a dispute with the Italian racing authorities, and in a stunning move, he ditched the famous Ferrari red in favour of the white and blue colour scheme of the North American Racing Team.

was back in second.

Gurney, though, was a long way clear, but when his Brabham succumbed to the bumps with suspension failure, Bandini found himself in the lead. There was drama when Phil Hill's Cooper crashed and burned, but that did not affect the result and the Ferrari made it home six seconds ahead of Ginther, and three laps in front of third-placed Bob Anderson's private Brabham.

As usual, the Italian Grand Prix was all about slipstreaming, but after an early straight-line battle between Gurney and Surtees it was the Ferrari man who took the win in front of their fans at Imola, and in doing so put himself in serious contention for the World Championship.

At the start, McLaren shot up from the second row to take the lead as Hill suffered clutch problems and never left the grid. However the New Zealander was soon back in third as Surtees and Gurney began their long battle. They regularly swapped the lead until Gurney suffered engine problems and let McLaren back in to claim second.

Clark had run well but again engine failure was to blame for his early demise, and in the closing moments Bandini pulled his Ferrari across the line to claim third by just 0.1 seconds from Ginther.

The Ferrari team was on a high going into the American Grand Prix after winning on home soil, but it was Graham Hill who raced to his second victory of the season to put himself in prime spot for the drivers' title.

Surtees did make a good start, but Hill managed to work his way up the field into second. Clark got past him, however, and chased Surtees down to claim the lead, but yet again his engine let him down, leaving Surtees and Hill in a battle for victory that eventually went to the BRM man.

The race all but finished Clark's chances of retaining the title, and left Surtees and Hill to battle it out in the last round.

Three weeks after his American victory, Hill arrived in Mexico for the final race with a five-point Championship lead. However, he had already counted six races, the maximum allowed, and any points he scored would have to replace his lowest score of three points.

Nail-biting finale sees Surtees crowned Champion

Surtees had a good chance of taking the title, and even Clark could still take it if his rivals failed to finish. It was the Lotus driver who looked in the best form as the race began, having taken pole by posting a lap time one second faster than anybody else.

Clark took the lead and it looked like it wasn't going to be Hill's day when the elastic on his goggles broke and he dropped back – such a simple thing, but it would effectively cost the Briton his second World Championship.

With Hill in 10th place and Surtees even further back with a misfiring engine, the title looked possible for Clark. But Surtees' engine miraculously fixed itself and both of Clark's rivals were able to rise up the field.

By lap 12, Hill had made it to third and, as things stood, he would become World Champion. But it wasn't over yet, and Hill was out of the running when he spun and damaged his exhaust. Surtees dropped to fourth when team-mate Bandini got past him, and the Briton knew he would fail in his title bid if he remained outside the top three.

But just as Clark looked on the verge of Championship number two, his superb race came to an end on the very last lap when his engine seized and Gurney went on to win. Surtees was now at the mercy of Bandini, who had to move over if the Briton was to win the Championship. He duly did, and in one of the most exciting title finales ever, Surtees had done it.

1964 CONSTRUCTORS' CUP

TEAM (Engine)	POINTS
FERRARI	45
BRM	42
LOTUS CLIMAX	37
BRABHAM CLIMAX	30
COOPER CLIMAX	16
BRABHAM BRM	7
BRP-BRM	5
LOTUS BRM	3

Jim Clark is consoled after his engine breaks down.

Jochen Rindt

THE ONLY POSTHUMOUS World Champion, Jochen Rindt, king of Formula Two racing, would undoubtedly have ranked among the Formula One greats. His premature death gave momentum to the push for increased driver safety.

CAREER DETAILS

1942	Born 18 April, in Mainz-am-Rhein, Germany
1943	Orphaned during wartime raid and moved to maternal grandparents in Graz, Austria
1959	Sent to England
1960	Starts competing in hill-climbs
1963	Formula Junior
1964	Bursts on to Formula Two scene beating Graham Hill at Crystal Palace. Makes Grand Prix debut Austrian Grand Prix
1965	Formula One with Cooper. Won Le Mans with Masten Gregory
1967	Wins nine Formula Two races
1968	Moves to Brabham
1969	Joins Lotus. Took first win at United States Grand Prix
1970	Wins at Monaco and took four consecutive victories in new Lotus 72. Dies on 5 September in practice at Monza. Awarded World Championship posthumously

FORMULA ONE RECORD

Year	Team	Wins	Poles	Fast laps	Pts
1964	Brab BRM	0	0	0	–
1965	Cooper Cli	0	0	0	4
1966	Cooper Mas	0	0	0	22
1967	Cooper Mas	0	0	0	6
1968	Brab Repco	0	2	0	8
1969	Lotus Ford	1	5	2	22
1970	Lotus Ford	5	3	1	45

Jochen Rindt with Roberto Rodriguez and Salvadore

"If only" is the unsung refrain of Karl Jochen Rindt's career. If only he had found a drive worthy of his talents sooner than his move to Lotus in 1969, he would surely have accumulated many more than his six Grand Prix wins. If only he had heeded his nagging fears about the fragility of his Lotus, he might have retired – as he had been considering following the deaths of close friends Piers Courage and Bruce McLaren – when the car failed during practice at Monza, killing him at the age of only 28.

Rindt committed 100 per cent to his racing career on all fronts. Born in Germany (he would later consider himself Austrian) to wealthy parents – his father owned a spice mill, his mother was a lawyer – he was orphaned during a bombing raid on Hamburg in 1943 and brought up by his maternal grandparents in Austria. In 1964 he would sell the family spice mill (and all his cars) to get into Formula Two and establish himself.

In every outing on the track he gave his all. "As a driver I thought Jochen was the sort of person who tended to drive at ten-tenths most of the time. Not that I was worried about him from the point of view of flying off the road. But he was always driving that near the edge that something was liable to happen to him through no real fault of his own," remarked Jack Brabham.

Rindt started competing in hill climbs in 1960 with a Simca Montlhery, bought for him by his grandfather as an 18th birthday present, a year after first witnessing a race at Goodwood while enrolled as a student in England. In 1962 he progressed to racing an Alfa Romeo Giulietta – bought by his widowed grandmother – and tried Formula Junior the following season.

In 1964 he made his Grand Prix debut, driving a Rob Walker Racing Brabham in the Austrian Grand Prix, but his reputation was forged when he burst on to the Formula Two scene at Crystal Palace, beating Graham Hill, Jim Clark and Denny Hulme, and gave a devastating display of raw speed and mesmerising

> "A lot of people think I'm braver than Dick Tracy, but I can be just as scared as anybody."

car control. Motor Sport observed he hardly put a wheel wrong throughout the race.

He would always be king of Formula Two, capable of matching the likes of Jim Clark and Jackie Stewart, but his Formula One career stalled in a succession of poor cars. In 1965 he returned to Formula One with a Cooper, but he was only to finish in the points twice. His hunger for victory, however, was boosted by a surprise win in the Le Mans 24 Hours partnering Masten Gregory in a privately-entered Ferrari.

For two seasons Rindt had largely unsuccessful campaigns in a works Cooper-Maserati, with two second places in the Belgian and US Grands Prix in 1966 the high-point. He then won nine Formula Two races in 1967 in a Roy Winkelmann Brabham.

In 1968 Rindt moved to the Brabham team, which had outclassed the field consistently for two years, but its new Repco engine was a failure. Thwarted again, with just two third places to show for two years in the team, Rindt by now craved a competitive car. Lured by big money from Colin Chapman, he joined Lotus in 1969, but was wary of the engineering standards.

A broken rear wing when he was on course for his first victory at Silverstone did little to boost his confidence or cement his relationship with Chapman, who held up his hands and exclaimed: "What am I going to do with this bloke? He has lightning reflexes, is bloody quick, but keeps telling me how to design my cars."

The relationship did eventually gel, and Rindt took his first win at the United States Grand Prix at the end of 1969. He had another win in the Lotus 49 at Monaco in 1970 before streaming to four consecutive victories in the sleek new Lotus 72. "A monkey could have won in this car today. Thank you!" he beamed in gratitude to Chapman after seizing victory from Jacky Ickx in the German Grand Prix at Hockenheim. It was to be his last ever Grand Prix win.

He was clearly heading towards a World Championship crown, but the deaths of his friends Piers Courage and Bruce McLaren increased his trepidation. Sadly his fears were realized when, during practice for the Italian Grand Prix at Monza, Rindt was killed after crashing under-braking for the Parabolica, thus becoming motor-racing's only posthumous World Champion.

"He drove so hard and put his car through so much there was always a chance that one day he wouldn't be able to put it all back together again," said Graham Hill.

Jochen Rindt in his Cooper-Maserati.

1965
Clark cruises to Championship

TALKING POINT

INDY CONQUERED

Although no longer part of the World Championship, the Indy 500 remained a great race that many Formula One drivers dreamed of winning. In 1965 it was inconveniently scheduled to coincide with the Monaco Grand Prix, but Jim Clark was so keen to win it, he sacrificed a round of the World Championship to travel to the United States and compete.

The Scotsman's absence from the Monaco race handed victory on a plate to his main rival Graham Hill, but to Clark it didn't matter. In his rear-engined Lotus, revolutionary in America, he became the first 'real' Grand Prix driver to win the Indy 500 – and with maximum points scored in the Formula One series, his absence in Monaco became an irrelevancy.

Fantastic form at the start of the year saw Jim Clark clock up a winning points tally without a challenge. He won six of the first seven races to take an unassailable points score, and it mattered little that he failed to finish the last three.

He had won the Championship incredibly early and the Lotus, although still suffering slight reliability problems, was much-improved in that area from the constantly-failing machine of the previous year. Graham Hill was the best of the rest, but he could only manage two wins during the year, and although he finished all but the last race of the season he struggled with consistency and simply couldn't match the dominant Clark.

Clark hints at dominance to come

There was little change on both the driver and car front when the teams arrived in South Africa for the first race of the year.

On New Year's Day, just five weeks after the finale of the previous season, the Ferrari team were back in red after running in American blue and white at the end of 1964, and John Surtees' machine sported the coveted number one.

However, it was Clark who proved that, despite losing the Championship the year before, he was still the form man. He not only took pole by almost a second, but took a flag-to-flag victory to give Lotus a great start to the season.

It would have been a perfect one-two finish for the British team were it not for new World Champion Surtees, who stole second when he pressured Clark's team-mate Mike Spence into a spin.

The BRM of Graham Hill cruised into third, and most notably, his team-mate Jackie Stewart completed a fantastic Formula One debut by taking a point for sixth.

Although the new season began right at the start of the year it was five months before the teams met again, this time in the glamorous setting of Monaco.

The race was on the same weekend as the Indianapolis 500 in America, and Clark's decision to race in the States was not greeted with much admiration by the event's organizers. The disagreement between the Automobile Club de Monaco and Team Lotus ended with the team's withdrawal, and left Hill free to claim his third consecutive victory at the circuit.

The day began well for BRM when Stewart followed Hill into turn one, and it was going well until Hill came across Bob Anderson's Brabham, which had slowed dramatically. The former World Champion had to go up an escape road to avoid him, and that dropped him to fifth place.

Stewart spun out of the lead four laps later, leaving Brabham ahead, only for his engine to give up soon afterwards. That left Bandini's Ferrari in the lead, but Hill was going well and managed to pass him and take the victory.

There was drama at the end when Paul Hawkins spun his Lotus into the harbour, but he escaped unhurt and the headlines went to triple-winner Hill.

Jackie Stewart makes his debut in the South African Grand Prix.

Graham Hill is followed by Lorenzo Bandini in the Monaco Grand Prix.

After his excellent Monaco victory, Hill struggled in the wet and the returning Clark dominated when the teams arrived in Belgium for the third round.

There was some controversy on the Friday when the organising body decided to pay appearance money only to the top six teams. That left just four places on the grid for the remaining teams, and they refused to take part in practice.

However, a compromise was eventually reached, and 20 cars roared on to the grid. The front row comprised Hill, Clark, and Stewart, and it was the pole man who got the best start.

However, Hill struggled with the handling of the BRM in wet conditions, and rapidly dropped down the field. Clark passed the Englishman and pulled into an insurmountable lead and Surtees, Bruce McLaren and Jack Brabham all took places from Hill before the end of the race.

In the second dramatic incident in two races, Richard Attwood came out unscathed when he spun into a telegraph pole and his Lotus burst into flames.

When the title contenders resumed battle in France, it was a dominant flag-to-flag victory for Clark, with nobody else able to run him close. He took pole, led off the line and immediately pulled away from Stewart, who had moved into second.

The two Scots then extended their lead from the rest of the field, with Surtees more than a minute behind as best of the rest in his Ferrari.

The order changed very little during the whole race, and it was Denny Hulme who took fourth, having replaced Brabham at the Australian's team before the start of the round.

Hill, meanwhile, slowly made his way up through the field and managed to secure fifth place by the end of the race. For the BRM driver, it was a disappointment made worse by his rival's dominant form.

Clark continues awesome form

The World Championship returned to Silverstone after a brief foray at Brands Hatch the previous year, and round five saw another classic Clark win. Hill gave the Scot a fright when he closed towards the end, but Clark managed to keep ahead and take his third win in a row.

Richie Ginther slipped his Honda into the lead at the start, but he was soon down to fourth as Clark, Hill and Surtees all made it past the American. The leading trio then spread out and drove their own races, and Clark looked unstoppable.

However, Clark's Lotus began to misfire in the last few laps and Hill began to see a sight of glory. He chased hard and closed right up on the ailing machine of his rival, but it was to no avail, and Clark stayed ahead to take his fourth consecutive British Grand Prix victory.

Behind the lead pair, Surtees was pressured by Clark's team-mate Mike Spence, but he kept his Ferrari ahead to score four Championship points. With the dominance of Clark, however, the reigning Champion could already see his title slipping away.

One week after the race in Britain, Honda improved on their front row position to take pole for round six in Holland. However, when it came to the race it was a different matter, and the Lotus and BRM cars swamped Ginther's Japanese machine. Once again, it was Clark who came out ahead of Hill in the battle of the Britons.

RACE BY RACE DETAILS

ROUND 1 – SOUTH AFRICA
Race Jim Clark
Pole Jim Clark
Fastest Lap Jim Clark

ROUND 2 – MONACO
Race Graham Hill
Pole Graham Hill
Fastest Lap Graham Hill

ROUND 3 – BELGIUM
Race Jim Clark
Pole Graham Hill
Fastest Lap Jim Clark

ROUND 4 – FRANCE
Race Jim Clark
Pole Jim Clark
Fastest Lap Jim Clark

ROUND 5 – BRITAIN
Race Jim Clark
Pole Jim Clark
Fastest Lap Graham Hill

ROUND 6 – HOLLAND
Race Jim Clark
Pole Graham Hill
Fastest Lap Jim Clark

ROUND 7 – GERMANY
Race Jim Clark
Pole Jim Clark
Fastest Lap Jim Clark

ROUND 8 – ITALY
Race Jackie Stewart
Pole Jim Clark
Fastest Lap Jim Clark

ROUND 9 UNITED STATES
Race Graham Hill
Pole Graham Hill
Fastest Lap Graham Hill

ROUND 10 – MEXICO
Race Richie Ginther
Pole Jim Clark
Fastest Lap Dan Gurney

1965 DRIVERS' CHAMPIONSHIP

DRIVER	TEAM	POINTS
Jim Clark	Lotus Climax	54
Graham Hill	BRM	40
Jackie Stewart	BRM	33
Dan Gurney	Brabham Climax	25
John Surtees	Ferrari	17
Lorenzo Bandini	Ferrari	13
Richie Ginther	Honda	11
Mike Spence	Lotus Climax	10
Bruce McLaren	Cooper Climax	10
Jack Brabham	Brabham Climax	9
Denny Hulme	Brabham Climax	5
Jo Siffert	Brabham Climax	5
Jochen Rindt	Cooper Climax	4
Pedro Rodriguez	Ferrari	2
Ron Bucknum	Honda	2
Dickie Attwood	Lotus BRM	2

Ginther got away well, but it only took Hill two laps to get past. It was another two laps before Clark made it into second, but once he had, he soon caught the BRM.

Clark was past by the end of lap five, and the flying Scot disappeared into the distance as Hill struggled with his pace. It was a difficult race for the Englishman, and he dropped back into the clutches of Gurney and Stewart who both made it past before the end.

Stewart eventually made it past the Honda man, but there was nothing he could do to catch Clark, who had now all but secured the Championship.

Clark was having an unbelievable season, and he arrived in Germany with the prospect of winning the World Championship after just seven of the 10 rounds. With a dominant performance, he took a sixth win of the season and secured an unbeatable points tally.

Championship decided in record time

The scale of Clark's monopoly at the head of the grid was displayed in qualifying when he lapped the circuit three seconds faster than his nearest rival. He shared the front row with Stewart and Hill's BRMs, and the Ferrari of Surtees.

If practice was not a clear enough sign that Clark was a worthy World Champion, then it was definitely confirmed in the race. A perfect start sent him into the first corner ahead of the rest, and he repeatedly broke the lap record on the way to a 16-second victory.

Hill managed to claim second, but there was nothing he could do to prevent Clark taking the title. The Scot had chalked up maximum points, and it was now impossible for him to be caught. He was the new World Champion.

The next race, in Monza, took place more than a month later, and it saw a surprise debut win for future World Champion Jackie Stewart.

In a fast-moving slipstreaming battle it was BRM's Graham Hill who looked like taking the win, but an uncharacteristic mistake right at the end saw his team-mate slip by to steal the victory.

Clark flew in practice to take the pole by 0.2 seconds from Hill, with Stewart completing the front row. Hill was behind them alongside Bandini on the second row. And it was this group who set off at a pace in a frantic battle for the early lead. Surtees dropped back off the line but he soon returned to join the battle despite driving without a clutch.

Surtees battled through to the lead but his failing car worsened, and he eventually dropped back down the field and into retirement on lap 34.

The race turned into a battle between the two BRMs and Clark but he went out with 13 laps remaining when he suffered a fuel-pump problem, leaving Hill and Stewart to fight it out.

Although Stewart was close, it looked to be in the bag for Hill. But on lap 75 of 76 he made a costly mistake at the Parabolica and Stewart didn't need to be asked a second time. He was through to win from Hill, with Gurney's Brabham a distant third.

Formula One moved to the United States for

Jim Clark on the podium at the German Grand Prix.

Graham Hill and Jackie Stewart race at Monza.

the next round at Watkins Glen, and Hill made up for his mistake in the last race by securing a confident victory in difficult conditions as Clark and Stewart disappeared. Surtees had not even made it to the race, after a terrible crash at Mosport Park saw him seriously injured, including a badly-broken leg.

Without him in America, the front row comprised Hill and Clark, with the second filled by Ginther and the Lotus of Spence, who was still recovering after a somersaulting crash in the non-championship Mediterranean Grand Prix saw him end up in a lake.

Hill got the better of Clark at the start but the Scot chased and caught him by the second lap. Behind them, Stewart had a fine first lap to move into third position. Stewart soon faded and retired with a throttle problem while in the battle for the lead Hill moved ahead once more. He was never to be caught as his nearest rival fell out of the race with engine problems on lap 12.

Gurney and Brabham battled for second and it was the American who took the place 12 seconds behind Hill.

Champion Clarke limps home

It was fortunate for Clark that he had sealed the Championship back in August because he posted yet another retirement with engine problems as Ginther took an historic first Grand Prix victory not only for himself but for both Honda and tyre manufacturer Goodyear.

Qualifying started dramatically when Tim Parnell fired Innes Ireland for being late to the circuit. The on-track action, though, was slightly more predictable than the Lotus boss, and it was Clark on pole with Gurney's Brabham alongside.

It was Ginther's Honda that took the early lead with a fantastic start and Stewart also got past the front row men into second. Clark was out early, and Stewart soon slipped down the field.

Gurney eventually moved up to second and began his chase of the leading Honda. But he was unable to close in on the leader and Ginther made it to the top of the podium with a three-second winning margin. He led home Gurney and Spence after Hill's engine failed at the last, but it was an inconspicuous end to the season for the new World Champion, who had failed to finish the last three races. But the results didn't bother Clark, who finished the year with maximum points after his early-season form.

SHORTS

Californian Richie Ginther, who grew up in Los Angeles racing hot-rods, is not just remembered for his one and only Grand Prix victory at the 1965 race in Mexico City. Ginther, an accomplished mechanic, is widely credited with introducing the rear spoiler into auto-racing during his time as a development driver for Ferrari, who, suitably impressed, added it to their sports cars.

1965 CONSTRUCTORS' CUP

TEAM (Engine)	POINTS
LOTUS-CLIMAX	54
BRM	45
BRABHAM-CLIMAX	27
FERRARI	26
COOPER-CLIMAX	14
HONDA	11
BRABHAM-BRM	5
LOTUS-BRM	2

Jackie Stewart

CAREER DETAILS

1939	Born 11 June, in Dumbarton
1960	Narrowly fails to qualify for British Olympic clay pigeon-shooting team
1962	Makes his mark on club scene
1964	Drives Ecurie Ecosse stock. Impresses in one-off Formula Three drive and declines offer to drive in Formula One in a Cooper. Formula One debut at Rand GP in South Africa
1965	Joins BRM as No. 2 to Graham Hill. Finishes year third. First Formula One victory in non-championship Daily Express Trophy at Silverstone. Wins Italian Grand Prix. Tasman series Champion
1966	Wins at Monaco
1968	Signs with Tyrrell. Wins Dutch Grand Prix. Family moved to Switzerland
1969	Wins six races and world title, accruing highest number of points ever scored
1971	Wins six times. World Champion
1972	Wins four races
1973	Wins five races. Equals Jim Clark's record of 25 Grand Prix wins. Retires as World Champion after 100th Grand Prix at Watkins Glen
1997	With elder son Paul forms Stewart Grand Prix
1999	Johnny Herbert brings team its maiden victory at European Grand Prix
2000	Team, taken over by Ford, renamed Jaguar Racing
2001	Knighted for services to motor racing

FORMULA ONE RECORD

Year	Team	Wins	Poles	Fast laps	Pts
1965	BRM	1	0	0	33
1966	BRM	1	0	0	14
1967	BRM	0	0	0	10
1968	Matra Ford	3	0	2	36
1969	Matra Ford	6	2	5	63
1970	March Ford	1	3	0	–
	Tyrrell Ford	0	1	0	25
1971	Tyrrell Ford	6	6	3	62
1972	Tyrrell Ford	4	2	4	45
1973	Tyrrell Ford	5	3	1	71

JACKIE STEWART, three times World Champion and charismatic ambassador for F1, transformed the status of drivers from sportsmen to celebrities, and pushed for sweeping changes in safety standards.

Jackie Stewart during the French Grand Prix in 1969.

There are few images that encapsulate sport in the 1960s so much as Jackie Stewart with long Beatle-inspired hair, sideburns, black corduroy cap and big dark glasses – in Monaco, of course. Stewart was a man of his time. As shrewd off the track as he was on it, he was the first driver to embrace the cult of sportsman as celebrity.

His subsequent role as ambassador for his sport has somewhat eclipsed the memory of his phenomenal skill behind the wheel. His speed was apparent to all around him, yet some questioned his courage because of his campaign for greater driver safety. Self-discipline and diligent physical preparation backed up an astute mental approach. His driving style was marked by almost machine-like consistency. He deserves respect for knowing when to retire. He could so easily have been tempted to continue and set even more records.

Born John Young Stewart in Dumbarton in 1939, Jackie Stewart was a natural sportsman, especially in disciplines demanding good eye-hand co-ordination. His father Robert, who had raced motorcycles as an amateur, owned a garage selling Jaguars. Jackie's brother Jimmy, eight years his senior, had a growing reputation as a talented racer. Jimmy drove for Ecurie Ecosse and competed in the British Grand Prix of 1953 (going off at Copse in the wet). Soon afterwards he was seriously injured in an accident at Le Mans, and retired. His parents strongly discouraged Jackie from even considering motor-racing as a career. Instead, Jackie Stewart turned to his second love – shooting. He excelled at this activity, representing his country several times, and his name had already been pencilled in for the 1960 Olympic team. However, he performed poorly at the final trials and was omitted from the squad.

In 1963, Barry Filer, a customer of the family dealership, offered Stewart a car to race at Oulton Park. In front of Ken Tyrrell, Stewart nonchalantly outpaced the likes of Bruce McLaren and Tyrrell immediately offered him a place in his Formula Three team, which Jackie gladly accepted. It was the start of a partnership that would see them one day at the pinnacle of the sport.

After two years spent gaining experience, Stewart joined Graham Hill at BRM in 1965 (Tyrrell did not yet have an F1 team). He scored his first Championship point in his debut race in South Africa and won his first Grand Prix, at Monza, in the same year. At the end of his rookie season he finished third in the World Drivers' Championship.

The next season was coloured by an incident that would affect Stewart's outlook for ever. At the Belgian Grand Prix at Spa, he crashed and overturned, fracturing his collarbone and soaking himself in petrol.

"I lay trapped in the car for twenty-five minutes, unable to be moved," he said. "Graham [Hill] and Bob Bondurant got me out using the spanners from a spectator's toolkit. There were no doctors and there was nowhere to put me. Eventually an ambulance took me to a first aid spot near the control tower and I was left on a stretcher, on the floor, surrounded by cigarette ends.

"I realized that if this was the best we had there was something sadly wrong: things wrong with the racetrack, the cars, the medical side, the fire-fighting and the emergency crews. There were also grass banks that were launch-pads, things you went straight into, trees that were unprotected and so on. It was ridiculous.

"If I have any legacy to leave the sport, I hope it will be seen to be in an area of safety, because when I arrived in Grand Prix racing so-called precautions and safety measures were diabolical." From that day on he would have a spanner taped to the BRM's steering-wheel.

Returning to racing in 1967, Stewart found himself in the virtually-undriveable BRM car and still finished second in the World Championship. That year saw possibly his greatest race, at the winding Nurburgring in Germany, when he won in the driving rain, competing with a broken wrist.

A year later he renewed his partnership with Tyrrell, who had moved up in class to Formula One. In 1969 he accrued six Grand Prix wins at the wheel of a Matra-Ford and won the World Championship. His 1970 season was spoilt by chassis problems, but he won the drivers' title again in 1971 after the car had undergone major revision.

Stomach ulcers affected Stewart in 1972 but in 1973 he was hailed World Champion for a third time. He now held the record for most GP wins (27) and, as his 100th Grand Prix start was beckoning at Watkins Glen, he announced his imminent retirement. Tragically, his team-mate and protégé, François Cevert was killed in qualifying for that race, the team pulled out and the Scotsman's career as a driver was over.

In 1997, however, he returned as chairman of Stewart Racing in partnership with his son Paul and Ford. Selling out to Ford, the team was re-named Jaguar Racing for the 2000 season. Jackie Stewart was knighted in 2001.

"I reckoned that as a driver I was being paid for my skill. I wasn't being paid to risk my life."

Jackie Stewart's priority was always safety.

1966
New engines; 'old' Champion

TALKING POINT

TEAMS REV UP FOR ENGINE CHANGES

The World Championship experienced a big change as three-litre engines were introduced and all the teams faced a race over the winter break to prepare their cars for the new regulations.

As the cars became more powerful and different to drive, the increased capacity of all the power units turned Formula One on its head as nobody dared predict who would win the World Championship.

Many drivers had used a Climax engine in previous years, but when they failed to produce a suitable unit for the start of the 1966 Championship they had to find their own solutions.

Jack Brabham set up his own team and the new V8 engine from the Australian Repco company gave him a new lease of life. The Cooper team opted for a V12 Maserati engine, while Bruce McLaren also set up a new team and used Ford engines.

Ferrari used V12 engines of their own brand, while BRM and Lotus were forced to use two-litre versions of their V8 Climax engines. All the different types and sizes of engines provided a fascinating Championship as each performed to different levels on different circuits.

Engineers work on the Honda U12 engine.

A burst of four race wins in the middle of the season was enough to secure Jack Brabham a third World Championship as the change in engine capacity otherwise produced sporadic race winners.

Brabham, driving for his own team, was unstoppable from France to Germany as his lightweight engine from Repco proved the one to beat. Brabham was, therefore, challenged for the Championship by a series of drivers – namely John Surtees and Lorenzo Bandini of Ferrari, Jackie Stewart of BRM and Jim Clark of Lotus.

Many of the top teams kept their driver line-ups the same, as Lotus retained Jim Clark and Peter Arundell returned, having recovered from his injuries of the previous season.

Surtees was back in action for Ferrari although

Jack Brabham toasts his World Championship title.

he was still suffering from some of the injuries he sustained the previous year in a CanAm crash. Bandini remained his team-mate.

With Dan Gurney doing his own thing, Brabham promoted Denny Hulme to be his number two. Cooper recruited Richie Ginther to partner Jochen Rindt, while BRM retained Graham Hill and Jackie Stewart.

Firestone also joined the tyre war with Goodyear and Dunlop as the Championship threw together the most varied cars in its history, with vast numbers of combinations of chassis, tyres, engines and, of course, drivers.

Stewart makes perfect start

The first action of the season went with the form book as reigning Champion Clark took pole position for the season-opening Monaco Grand Prix in May.

At the start of the 100-lap race, unpredictability prevailed as Clark suffered problems with his gearbox and Surtees took the lead with the two BRMs of Hill and Stewart close behind.

Surtees' lead lasted for just 14 laps until a transmission problem forced him to retire.

After Surtees' Ferrari had dropped out it gifted the lead to Stewart, who did not look back and powered to his second race win of what would turn out to be an illustrious career. Second place went to Bandini, while Hill was third and Bob Bondurant fourth, to complete the only classified drivers in the race. Clark retired 40 laps from the finish with a suspension problem.

Gurney was a new addition to the field for the next round of the Championship in Belgium. The Spa-Francorchamps circuit provided the debut for Gurney's Climax-engined Eagle car. Later in the season he was to use Weslake V12 engines, but in Belgium they were not yet ready.

The first new Lotus-BRM 43 appeared in the hands of Arundell but Clark stayed with his two-litre Lotus-Climax from the previous year. As most teams struggled with technical problems in qualifying for the 28-lap race Surtees took pole, closely followed by Austrian Rindt, Bandini and Brabham.

Chaos reigns in Belgium

Race-day provided even more action as remarkable scenes marred the opening lap of the race. Eight drivers had accidents on the first lap as heavy rain soaked the circuit and sent them skidding off the track, including Stewart, Hill, Clark, Bondurant and Hulme.

Most cars went off at the Masta Kink part of the circuit and Bondurant was fortunate to avoid serious injury when he overturned his car. Stewart was not so lucky and he suffered a broken shoulder, a cracked rib and internal bruising after rolling his BRM.

Stewart was also covered in petrol and trapped upside-down in the car. His team-mate Hill, who had

RACE BY RACE DETAILS

ROUND 1 – MONACO
Race Jackie Stewart
Pole: Jim Clark
Fastest lap Lorenzo Bandini

ROUND 2 – BELGIUM
Race John Surtees
Pole John Surtees
Fastest lap John Surtees

ROUND 3 – FRANCE
Race Jack Brabham
Pole Lorenzo Bandini
Fastest lap Lorenzo Bandini

ROUND 4 – BRITAIN
Race Jack Brabham
Pole Jack Brabham
Fastest lap Jack Brabham

ROUND 5 – HOLLAND
Race Jack Brabham
Pole Jack Brabham
Fastest lap Denny Hulme

ROUND 6 – GERMANY
Race Jack Brabham
Pole Jim Clark
Fastest lap John Surtees

ROUND 7 – ITALY
Race Ludovico Scarfiotti
Pole Mike Parkes
Fastest lap Ludovico Scarfiotti

ROUND 8 – UNITED STATES
Race Jim Clark
Pole Jack Brabham
Fastest lap John Surtees

ROUND 9 – MEXICO
Race John Surtees
Pole John Surtees
Fastest lap Richie Ginther

Jim Clark

CAREER DETAILS

1936	Born 4 March
1960	Signs for Lotus. GP debut in the Dutch GP
1961	Full-time GP driver with Lotus. Involved in the accident at Monza which killed Wolfgang von Trips and 13 spectators
1962	Scores first GP win at Spa-Francorchamps. Runner-up to Graham Hill
1963	World Champion, second on debut in Indianapolis 500
1964	Finishes third behind Surtees and Hill
1965	World Champion, and winner of the Indianapolis 500
1968	Dies 7 April, at Hockenheim

FORMULA ONE RECORD

Year	Team	Wins	Poles	Fast laps	Pts
1960	Lotus Cl	0	0	0	8
1961	Lotus Cl	0	0	1	11
1962	Lotus Cl	3	6	5	30
1963	Lotus Cl	7	7	6	54
1964	Lotus Cl	3	5	4	32
1965	Lotus Cl	6	6	6	54
1966	Lotus Cl	0	2	0	–
	Lotus BRM	1	0	0	16
1967	Lotus BRM	0	0	0	–
	Lotus Cl	0	0	1	–
	Lotus Ford	4	6	4	41
1968	Lotus Ford	1	1	1	9

JIM CLARK, the mild-mannered farmer from the Scottish borders, won two World Championships and the unequivocal admiration of all who witnessed his virtuoso performances.

Jim Clark had every weapon in a driver's armoury: speed, courage, judgement, brilliant reflexes and an innate ability to get the maximum out of any car he drove. Colin Chapman maintained he only used nine-tenths of his talent, "which makes the gulf between him and other drivers even bigger".

He won 25 of his 72 Grands Prix and his victory in the 1965 Indianapolis 500 crushed the American racing psyche. From 1962, he was the best wherever he lined up and his peers knew it. "He could jump in darn near anything and drive the wheels off it," said Dan Gurney, the only driver Clark considered a threat. To many, he remains the greatest racing driver in history.

The tragedy of his early death at the age of 32 is that he was becoming more relaxed with the cosmopolitan appreciation of his virtuoso talent. Part of his mystique stemmed from his gentle, unassuming character. He was a private – some said "unreadable" man – who loved whizzing up the A1 in his Elan to the tranquillity of his family farm in Duns, just over the border in Scotland.

"His nails were bitten almost to the core. He was the coolest, calmest, most calculating racing driver in the world, and he continually bit his nails and chewed his fingers with nervousness. If there was anybody who was going to have an ulcer it would have been Jim Clark. In a way he was a terribly highly-tensed man and yet...the moment he slipped into a racing car he changed," noted Jackie Stewart.

The son of a Berwickshire farmer, Clark started racing in a friend's car, initially without the knowledge of his parents. After a few local rallies, close friend Ian Scott-Watson lent him a DKW for his first race in 1956. A Porsche followed, and for 1958 local garage-owner Jock McBain re-formed the Border Reivers team and bought a Jaguar D Type with which Clark won 12 races from 20 starts.

Scott-Watson then bought a Lotus Elite for Clark to drive. He also won races in a Lister Jaguar, which underlined his ability. When a drive with Aston Martin's Grand Prix team collapsed with the project in 1960, he signed for Formula Two and Formula Junior with Colin Chapman's embryonic Lotus set-up. Clark's bond with Chapman would prove to be the most remarkable owner/driver team-up in history. There was something almost telepathic about their relationship which transcended mere friendship. They fed off each other's brilliance.

Jim Clark waits while adjustments are made to his car.

> "If he had his way he would creep away into obscurity until the next race. He's not interested in the glamour or the frills."
>
> *John Cooper*

Clark considered farming to be his real occupation.

Clark started winning immediately. He made his debut at the Dutch Grand Prix, running fifth before retiring. In 1961 he became a full-time GP driver, but his season was marred by his involvement in the accident at Monza that killed Wolfgang von Trips and 11 spectators. In 1962 he scored his first GP win at Spa-Francorchamps and fought with Graham Hill for the title, which he lost in the final race in South Africa when his Lotus broke while he was leading.

In 1963 Clark was invincible, winning seven races out of 10 started. He also came second on his debut in the Indianapolis 500 – a race that saw local hero Parnelli Jones controversially allowed to continue to victory in a car that was leaking oil. Even with such fulfilment of his talent, he shrank from the spotlight. "I'm just beginning to wonder if I want to be World Champion," he mused mid-season. "There will be so much fuss and drama. Farming is really my occupation, and racing just a hobby."

In 1964 he finished third behind John Surtees and Hill. In 1965 he captured a second world title with wins in the South African, Belgian, French, British, Dutch and German Grands Prix, along with victory in the Indianapolis 500.

Clark drove exclusively in F1 for the innovative Chapman, and the impact of their success shocked the establishment – the days of the traditional, front-engined machines were numbered. In 1962 Clark benefited from the first proper monocoque F1 car, the Lotus 25, and again, after a lull in 1966, from the power of the Ford Cosworth DFV V8 in 1967.

But Chapman's elegant creations were infuriatingly fragile. Clark lost both the 1962 and 1964 World Championships in the final races through mechanical failure. Had the 49 been more reliable he would have triumphed in 1967 too.

He bounced back in mid-1967 with Cosworth power, gave the engine a debut win at Zandwoort and pushed Denny Hulme hard for the title. He started 1968 by winning the South African Grand Prix to break Fangio's record of 24 Grand Prix victories. Then, driving in a Formula Two race at Hockenheim, he crashed following a sudden rear tyre failure on 7 April, when his Lotus slid off the track at high speed into a tree. Even at a time when driver fatalities were common, his accident rocked the racing world. As Chris Amon put it, "If this can happen to Jimmy, what chance do the rest of us have?"

1967
Hulme pips boss to title

Smoke rises from the crash during the Monaco Grand Prix which killed Lorenzo Bandini.

TALKING POINT
COSWORTH COME TO THE FORE

Cosworth came to the fore as the Ford-owned engine company developed a new engine and joined forces with Lotus to start a new era in the sport.

After an indifferent season the previous year, the Lotus 49 was boosted by the new power unit from Cosworth, which was labelled the DFV. Colin Chapman had persuaded Ford to finance the deal for the new engine and in the years to come it moved into a class of its own.

The DFV, or Double Four Valve engine, was a V8 and was used at first exclusively by Lotus, who also added Graham Hill to their driver line-up to join up with Jim Clark. Several top teams adopted the DFV system with their engines in the following years and it became an essential part of the make-up of a power unit if it was to be competitive at the highest level.

Less than three months after winning the World Championship Jack Brabham joined the other competitors as they returned to action at the all-new Kyalami circuit in South Africa, which hosted the first race on the second day of the year.

Brabham was again joined in his own Brabham-Repco team by Denny Hulme, and it was the New Zealand racer who continued the team's solid form with a second successive title for the outfit.

Brabham were one of the few teams to maintain their driver line-up from the previous year and before the maiden race in South Africa many drivers swapped teams. One of the most notable was Graham Hill's move from BRM to Lotus, who had the new and revolutionary DFV Cosworth engines and driver Jim Clark.

Hill replaced the dropped Peter Arundell and BRM brought in Mike Spence to replace Hill. John Surtees left the Cooper-Maserati team to drive for the new Honda outfit and he was replaced by Pedro Rodriguez, who partnered Jochen Rindt.

Dan Gurney recruited Honda reject Richie Ginther for his Eagle-Weslake team and Bruce McLaren let Chris Amon leave to join Lorenzo Bandini at the Ferrari team. The drivers all got used to their new surroundings for the first race of the season, which was at high altitude.

Brabham and Hulme started the season where they had left off as they claimed the top two spots in qualifying for the 80-lap race. At the start of the race Hulme led, but Brabham spun and was forced back to fourth.

Surtees chased Hulme hard along with local privateer John Love in a Cooper-Climax and Hulme held them off until the brakes on his car started to falter and he was forced to drop back.

Amazingly, Love led for 12 laps, but he was hunted down by Rodriguez, who had started from fourth on the grid and stayed in contention. Rodriguez eventually overtook Love with just seven laps remaining to take the first win of the season. Love finished a creditable second, while Surtees was third and Hulme fourth.

Ferrari's Bandini dies

The second round of the Championship was five months after the South African opener and the May event was marred by the death of talented Ferrari racer Bandini, who rolled his car at a chicane 81 laps into the 100-lap race. The car caught fire with Bandini trapped upside-down in the cockpit and he died of his injuries three days after the race.

Brabham had taken pole for the race but his engine blew up at the start and he spun into the middle of the chasing pack. No other cars were forced to retire and Hulme took the lead after starting from fourth on the grid, but he was overtaken by Jackie Stewart on lap six.

Stewart, however, was at the front for just nine laps as transmission failure forced him to retire, handing the lead back to Hulme, who maintained his advantage to the chequered flag to take his first win of the season.

Three weeks after Bandini's death, Ferrari named Mike Parkes as his replacement and Zandvoort hosted the next round of the Championship. Hill started to show the potential of the new DFV Cosworth engine as he claimed pole position for the 90-lap race.

At the start, a race official was slow leaving the track and held up Hulme as he stood in the middle of the second row. Hill was quick off the line and he led for the opening 10 laps before a gearbox fault ended his race and handed the lead to Brabham.

Brabham was pushed hard by Clark, Hulme and Amon and it was Lotus driver Clark who made the breakthrough and overtook Brabham to claim the lead on the 16th lap. Once in front, Clark never looked like being beaten as he raced to victory.

Belgium hosted the next round of the Championship in June at the Spa-Francorchamps circuit. Clark took pole for the race, closely followed by Dan Gurney, who had won the Le Mans 24-Hour race a week earlier.

Hill was third on the grid, but his race was ruined almost before a wheel turned on race-day as the battery failed on his car, forcing him to start from the pits and way back from the rest of the field. Gurney also ruined his hard work in qualifying by losing several places after failing to put his car in gear at the start.

Clark led from pole position on the first lap, but behind him Parkes was lucky to survive a high-speed accident as he crashed at Blanchimont. He suffered serious leg injuries, a broken wrist and a head injury, and he never raced again – although he did stay on at Ferrari as an engineer.

Leader Clark was caught by Stewart, who overtook on lap 13. He led for seven laps but was thwarted by a faulty gearbox.

On lap 20 Gurney took the lead and he went on to win by more than a minute. It would be Eagle's first and last Grand Prix victory. Stewart finished second with Amon third.

Brabham wins in France

The next round of the Championship was a damp and dour affair as only 20,000 spectators turned out to watch the French Grand Prix at the Bugatti circuit, which was new to the Championship.

The decision by the Automobile Club de France to move the race away from the more traditional Reims or Rouen circuits did not prove popular, as the Bugatti circuit, which incorporated the Le Mans 24-Hour track and a twisty in-section, hosted the 80-lap race.

Hill took pole and was closely followed by Brabham and Gurney on the grid. The Englishman took the lead at the start of the race with Gurney, Brabham, Clark and Amon chasing him but in the course of the second lap Brabham went ahead and a lap later Gurney slipped behind Clark as well, leaving the two Lotus drivers to chase Brabham.

It was not long before Clark worked his way past Hill and he took the lead on the fifth lap. Hill also overtook Brabham and everything was looking good for Team Lotus. Hill took the lead from Clark on lap 11 but stopped with a transmission failure soon afterwards.

Nine laps later Clark stopped with the same problem and so Brabham went back into the lead with Gurney behind him and Amon third, although it was not long before the Ferrari was overtaken by Hulme.

Brabham maintained his lead and secured his first win as reigning Champion. He was the fifth different winner from the first five races of the season as the Championship remained up for grabs, although Hulme had a distinct advantage after claiming more top-six finishes than anybody else.

RACE BY RACE DETAILS

ROUND 1 – SOUTH AFRICA
Race Pedro Rodriguez
Pole Jack Brabham
Fastest lap Denny Hulme

ROUND 2 – MONACO
Race Denny Hulme
Pole Jack Brabham
Fastest lap Jim Clark

ROUND 3 – HOLLAND
Race Jim Clark
Pole Graham Hill
Fastest lap Jim Clark

ROUND 4 – BELGIUM
Race Dan Gurney
Pole Jim Clark
Fastest lap Dan Gurney

ROUND 5 – FRANCE
Race Jack Brabham
Pole Graham Hill
Fastest lap Graham Hill

ROUND 6 – BRITAIN
Race Jim Clark
Pole Jim Clark
Fastest lap Denny Hulme

ROUND 7 – GERMANY
Race Denny Hulme
Pole Jim Clark
Fastest lap Dan Gurney

ROUND 8 – CANADA
Race Jack Brabham
Pole Jim Clark
Fastest lap Jim Clark

ROUND 9 – ITALY
Race John Surtees
Pole Jim Clark
Fastest lap Jim Clark

ROUND 10 – UNITED STATES
Race Jim Clark
Pole Graham Hill
Fastest lap Graham Hill

ROUND 11–MEXICO
Race Jim Clark
Pole Jim Clark
Fastest lap Jim Clark

Jim Clark winning his debut race with Lotus.

Dan Gurney after winning the Belgium Grand Prix at Spa Francorchamps in 1967.

1967 DRIVERS' CHAMPIONSHIP

DRIVER	TEAM	POINTS
Denny Hulme	Brabham Repco	51
Jack Brabham	Brabham Repco	46
Jim Clark	Lotus Ford	41
John Surtees	Honda	20
Chris Amon	Ferrari	20
Pedro Rodriguez	Cooper Maserati	15
Graham Hill	Lotus Ford	15
Dan Gurney	Eagle Weslake	13
Jackie Stewart	BRM	10
Mike Spence	BRM	9
John Love	Cooper Climax	6
Jochen Rindt	Cooper Maserati	6
Jo Siffert	Cooper Maserati	6
Bruce McLaren	McLaren BRM	3
Jo Bonnier	Cooper Maserati	3
Chris Irwin	BRM	2
Mike Parkes	Ferrari	2
Bob Anderson	Brabham Climax	2
Guy Ligier	Brabham Repco	1
Ludovico Scarfiotti	Ferrari	1
Jacky Ickx	Cooper Maserati	1

The sixth round of the Championship was held at Silverstone and all of the British contingent were keen to do well in their home race. Scottish driver Clark claimed pole while Londoner Hill was second on the grid, after recovering from a broken suspension in practice.

Clark had a new Lotus built up overnight and took the lead from team-mate Hill at the start of the race – a lead he maintained until lap 25, when Hill battled back to take top spot.

Hill led until lap 54, when a rear suspension problem dropped him back. But his progress was ended for good 10 laps later when an engine problem forced him out. Clark regained the lead and did not look back as he powered to victory, his second of the season, from Hulme, Amon and Brabham.

Like the previous year, the field at the next round in Germany contained Formula Two cars but the Nurburgring circuit had attempted to be better-prepared for their inclusion, as it developed its pit area to slow the cars as they approached.

Clark, buoyed by his win in Britain, claimed pole position in Germany – nearly 10 seconds ahead of the rest of the field. Rising Belgian star Jacky Ickx was an amazing third on the grid in his Formula Two car. Hill crashed in practice for the race and was down in 13th on the grid.

Clark led from the start for the first three laps before a suspension fault ended his race and handed the lead to Gurney, with Hulme second and Brabham third. Gurney led until lap 13 when a driveshaft failure forced him to retire and left Hulme to claim his second win of the season. Ickx had been on course for a podium finish, but a suspension problem also ended his race two laps from the finish.

Canada awarded Grand Prix

As Canada celebrated its centenary year, the FIA awarded the nation a Grand Prix after repeated applications and the Mosport Park track hosted the Canadian Grand Prix in August.

The formidable qualifying duo of Clark and Hill were once again at the front of the grid. Hulme, who still led the World Championship, was alongside them on row one.

Rain fell at the start of the race and Clark took the lead, with Hulme and Brabham close behind. As the track began to dry Clark and Brabham excelled until the former went out with an ignition problem on lap 69 of the 90-lap race.

That left Brabham to take the lead, closely followed by the consistent Hulme. The two Brabham-Repco drivers maintained their one-two positions for the remaining 21 laps and Gurney finished a distant third.

As the Championship moved to Italy and Monza for the ninth round, Cooper-Maserati gave the ever-

Denis Hulme in his Brabham BT19 car at the German Grand Prix.

SHORTS

Lotus-Ford showcased their new Cosworth DFV system at the third race of the season at Zandvoort. It proved a dream start as Jim Clark claimed pole and then won the race with relative ease. The V8 engine sparkled for the entirety of the year with Clark winning three more races – at Silverstone, Watkins Glen and Mexico City – and capturing five poles in his bid for the World Championship.

improving Ickx a drive alongside Rindt. Clark once again took pole position in qualifying as he defied reliability problems to take top spot. Brabham was also on the front row with McLaren.

Clark was desperate for victory to catch Hulme and Brabham in the drivers' standings but he suffered an unfortunate break as he recovered from a flat tyre to lead the race, only to be denied victory on the last lap.

Brabham and Hill had started the race well and Clark suffered his flat tyre early in the race. Hill led until lap 58 before an engine failure, while Clark battled back through the field and fought with Brabham for the lead.

Clark had made up a complete lap to catch Brabham and he had just taken the lead on the last lap when a fuel-pump failure forced him to retire. That allowed Brabham and Surtees, who had battled his way up to the front from ninth on the grid, to come through and it was Surtees who took the chequered flag to earn a maiden win for Honda.

Brabham's second place earned his Brabham-Repco team a second consecutive Constructors' Cup, despite Hulme's retirement on lap 30 when his car overheated. Now only he and Hulme could mathematically win the title.

Hulme pips team-boss to world title

Hulme was three points ahead of Brabham heading into the penultimate round of the Championship at Watkins Glen. Hill took pole for the 108-lap race while Brabham and Hulme looked nervous in fifth and sixth respectively on the grid.

Hill led for the first 40 laps of the race before he was overtaken by Clark, who went on to take the chequered flag for his third win of the season despite a buckled suspension, but all eyes were on Hulme and Brabham.

Hulme had got the better of his team boss and was running fourth when Brabham got a puncture and dropped further back. Hulme eventually took third in the race, but Brabham battled for a brave fifth-place finish as the Championship went to the last race of the season in Mexico, with Hulme's lead now five points.

All Hulme needed to do when the teams arrived in Mexico was keep Brabham in sight, and the two drivers once again qualified sixth and fifth respectively as Clark took pole.

Hill led the race for the first two laps before Clark took over to power to victory – his fourth of the season and the most for any other driver.

Hulme drove a sensible race and took no risks as he allowed Brabham to finish second, safe in the knowledge that his third-placed result was enough to claim his first World Championship.

1967 CONSTRUCTORS' CUP

TEAM (Engine)	POINTS
BRABHAM REPCO	63
LOTUS FORD	44
COOPER MASERATI	28
HONDA	20
FERRARI	20
BRM	17
EAGLE WESLAKE	13
COOPER CLIMAX	6
LOTUS BRM	6
McLAREN BRM	3
BRABHAM CLIMAX	2

1968
Hill and Lotus crowned

TALKING POINT

SPONSORSHIP AND WINGS ARRIVE

Formula One took on a new look with the arrival of wings and, perhaps more significantly, sponsorship. The commercialisation of the sport offered a new outlook with several teams changing the colour of their machines after signing deals. The green and yellow Lotus team became red, white and gold after penning a deal with Gold Leaf cigarettes. In the process, national colours became a thing of the past and British racing green was assigned to the Grand Prix scrapbook. At the same time, front and rear wings offered added speed to the cars and had a positive effect on Grands Prix, with Lotus pioneering the newly-discovered aerodynamics of Formula One cars.

Bruce McLaren celebrating his first win at the Belgium Grand Prix.

Reigning Champion Denny Hulme opted to switch from Brabham to the McLaren-BRM team, but the New Zealander failed to match his exploits of the previous year. Instead, the season belonged to Graham Hill as he powered Lotus to the title.

Hill and Jim Clark kept faith with Lotus as the British marque kept an unchanged driver line-up, but there were changes elsewhere. Jochen Rindt took over from Hulme with Brabham, who kept the same car despite Repco working on a new V8 engine. Chris Amon remained with Ferrari and was joined by Belgian Jacky Ickx, while BRM, with a completely new car, kept Mike Spence and signed Cooper's Pedro Rodriguez to replace Jackie Stewart.

Stewart had opted to join the all-new Matra International team run by Ken Tyrrell. The car consisted of a Matra chassis and Cosworth engines and Matra Sports entered a second car with a V12 engine for Frenchman Jean-Pierre Beltoise.

After Rindt and Rodriguez's departure from

Jacky Ickx after his win in the French Grand Prix.

Cooper, Lodovico Scarfiotti and Brian Redman landed drives and Rob Walker went into the partnership with Jack Durlacher to run a Cooper-Maserati for Joseph Siffert.

Lotus secures one-two at season opener

The opening race of the season, the South African Grand Prix at Kyalami, was run on New Year's Day and Clark stormed to pole position ahead of teammate Hill. Stewart made an impressive start to his Matra spell as he joined the Lotus duo on the first row of the grid.

Stewart took the lead when the race got underway ahead of Clark as Hill dropped back to seventh. By the end of lap two, Clark had overtaken Stewart and ran at the head of the field.

Brabham, who was running in third, dropped back when engine trouble affected him. Rindt moved up to third, but was passed by Hill on lap 13 and then Hill passed Stewart to take second 14 laps later. Stewart's impressive performance in the Matra ended on lap 47 when he retired with connecting-rod failure. Rindt benefited from Stewart's exit as he moved up to third and the order remained the same to the chequered flag.

The result was a dominant one-two for Lotus, but the victory would be Clark's last in a World Championship event. The British driver was killed in a Formula Two race at Hockenheim in April, before the start of the European season, when he crashed into a tree during the Deutschland Trophae race.

The European season started five months after the South African race, when the Spanish Grand Prix was held at the new Jarama in late May. The gap between the races saw Bruce McLaren take the Race of Champions in the McLaren M7A in March, while Hulme won the International Trophy three weeks later.

Stewart was ruled out of action for a month in March when he damaged ligaments in his wrist following a crash in a Formula Two race at Jarama, and Lotus' problems deepened when Spence died as a wheel struck him in his cockpit after he crashed in turn one at Indianapolis.

The Jarama race, naturally, was a subdued event following the tragedies. It was the first Spanish Grand Prix in 14 years, but Lotus and BRM opted to run only one car each. Ferrari's Amon qualified on pole with Rodriguez, the only BRM driver, second ahead of Hulme.

The two enjoyed a titanic battle at the head of the race before Rodriguez crashed on lap 28, and Amon was denied victory when his fuel-pump failed on lap 58. Lotus' Hill secured a second victory of the season for the team, who ran in the colours of Gold Leaf for the first time, ahead of Hulme.

Safety question looms over Monaco

The Monaco Grand Prix was held in late May but was reduced by 20 laps after Lorenzo Bandini's crash the previous year. The chicane had been tightened to avoid a repeat of the incident, but Ferrari turned their back on the event due to their concern over the safety standards of the circuit.

Lotus, with front and rear wings on their car for the first time, introduced Jackie Oliver as the replacement for the late Clark, while Matra ran debutant Johnny Servoz-Gavin with Stewart still ruled out of action because of his wrist injury. Servoz-Gavin immediately impressed as he qualified second behind Spanish Grand Prix winner Hill.

Servoz-Gavin raced into the lead in the race, but suffered driveshaft failure and crashed. Hill led the field home from there on. With a number of accidents in the opening laps, only five cars were left in the race by lap 16 and, despite all five drivers finishing the race, it had been an anti-climax. Cooper's Scarfiotti ended fourth in his last race before he died during a hill-climbing event.

The fourth round of the Championship was held in Belgium and Ferrari returned to competitive action. Lotus' introduction of front and rear wings had sparked a trend as a number of teams opted to mimic the wings. Stewart made a welcome return for Matra and Gurney and Hulme were back on the scene after finishing second and fourth, respectively, in the Indianapolis 500.

Amon was quickest off the grid, but his lead lasted just two laps before Surtees went ahead. Brian Redman, of Cooper-BRM, went out of the race on lap seven when his suspension failed and he crashed over a concrete barrier and into a parked car.

RACE BY RACE DETAILS

ROUND 1 – SOUTH AFRICA
Race Jim Clark
Pole Jim Clark
Fastest lap Jim Clark

ROUND 2 – SPAIN
Race Graham Hill
Pole Chris Amon
Fastest lap Jean-Pierre Beltoise

ROUND 3 – MONACO
Race Graham Hill
Pole Graham Hill
Fastest lap Richard Attwood

ROUND 4 – BELGIUM
Race Bruce McLaren
Pole Chris Amon
Fastest lap John Surtees

ROUND 5 – HOLLAND
Race Jackie Stewart
Pole Chris Amon
Fastest lap Jean-Pierre Beltoise

ROUND 6 – FRANCE
Race Jacky Ickx
Pole Jochen Rindt
Fastest lap Pedro Rodriguez

ROUND 7 – BRITAIN
Race Joseph Siffert
Pole Graham Hill
Fastest lap Joseph Siffert

ROUND 8 – GERMANY
Race Jackie Stewart
Pole Jacky Ickx
Fastest lap Jackie Stewart

ROUND 9 – ITALY
Race Denny Hulme
Pole John Surtees
Fastest lap Jackie Oliver

ROUND 10 – CANADA
Race Denny Hulme
Pole Jochen Rindt
Fastest lap Joseph Siffert

ROUND 11 – UNITED STATES
Race Jackie Stewart
Pole Mario Andretti
Fastest lap Jackie Stewart

ROUND 12 – MEXICO
Race Graham Hill
Pole Joseph Siffert
Fastest lap Joseph Siffert

1968 DRIVERS' CHAMPIONSHIP

DRIVER	TEAM	POINTS
Graham Hill	Lotus Ford	48
Jackie Stewart	Matra Ford	36
Denny Hulme	McL BRM/McL Ford	33
Jacky Ickx	Ferrari	27
Bruce McLaren	McLaren Ford	22
Pedro Rodriguez	BRM	18
Jo Siffert	Lotus Ford	12
John Surtees	Honda	12
Jean-Pierre Beltoise	Matra/Matra Ford	11
Chris Amon	Ferrari	10
Jim Clark	Lotus Ford	9
Jochen Rindt	Brabham Repco	8
Dickie Attwood	BRM	6
Johnny Servoz-Gavin	Matra Ford	6
Jackie Oliver	Lotus Ford	6
Ludovico Scarfiotti	Cooper BRM	6
Lucien Bianchi	Cooper BRM	5
Vic Elford	Cooper BRM	5
Brian Redman	Cooper BRM	4
Piers Courage	BRM	4
Dan Gurney	McLaren Ford	3
Jo Bonnier	McLaren BRM/Honda	3
Silvio Moser	Brabham Repco	2
Jack Brabham	Brabham Repco	2

Luckily, he escaped with a broken right arm and minor burns after his spectacular accident.

Leader Surtees retired when his suspension failed just one lap after Amon had quit the race with a radiator problem. Hulme was left in the lead but, after exchanging position with Stewart a number of times, the Ferrari driver slowed down because of mechanical difficulties.

Stewart was left with a lead of more than 30 seconds, but Matra were denied a victory when he ran out of petrol on the penultimate lap. He ended fourth as McLaren landed his team's first-ever Grand Prix win.

But Stewart was not to be denied, as he took victory in the Dutch Grand Prix at Zandvoort two weeks later. The British driver led Matra to a one-two with Beltoise trailing him.

Tragedy strikes French race – again

The French Grand Prix returned to Rouen-les-Essarts in early July, and the race resulted in a fifth different winner of the season with youngster Ickx handing Ferrari their only win that year. The event, however, cost a fourth driver his life as veteran Jo Schlesser died.

Schlesser was involved in the race after Surtees refused to compete in the Honda RA302 chassis he had tested, but he was killed on lap three when he lost control of the car. It overturned and burst into flames and with the magnesium chassis and full fuel tank on fire Schlesser could not be saved.

During qualifying, Lotus' Oliver somehow escaped injury after a 125 mph crash but the damage sustained to his car meant he would not compete in the race. Rindt was quickest ahead of Stewart's Matra.

Light rain hit the circuit at the start of the race, and only Ickx opted to run on full wet tyres. The Belgian benefited as he raced into the lead prior to Schlesser's accident.

On lap 19, Ickx made a mistake and lost the lead to Rodriguez, but the talented Ferrari driver was back ahead within two laps and stayed there for the rest of the race.

With Hill boasting a healthy lead in the Championship standings, a vociferous crowd turned out to support him in the British Grand Prix at Brands Hatch but, despite qualifying on pole, the Englishman's title bid was hampered by retirement.

The Lotus driver was alongside team-mate Oliver at the head of the grid and led the rain-affected race after smoke had poured out of Oliver's car. Despite the problem Oliver continued, and when Hill retired on lap 27 with rear suspension problems he was back in front.

But Oliver stopped on the track when his transmission failed midway through the race. Siffert, in a Rob Walker Lotus, held on to his lead to give Walker his first win in seven years.

In Germany, BMW entered the Lola-BMW Formula Two car as they assessed the state of Formula One. The field otherwise remained unchanged and Ickx qualified on pole ahead of Ferrari team-mate Amon by more than 10 seconds.

Once again in wet conditions, Stewart opened up a significant gap from the third row of the grid and by the end of the second lap he was 34 seconds in front. He eventually won the race by more than four minutes as Hill trailed him home.

Andretti makes FI debut

The Italian Grand Prix signalled the arrival of American Mario Andretti in a third Lotus and Servoz-Gavin landed a seat as the second Matra International driver following Tyrrell's decision to expand the team. Ferrari offered a drive to Briton Derek Bell, while David Hobbs ran in a second Honda RA301.

Andretti and his fellow-American Bobby Unser

Jackie Stewart wins in the wet at the German Grand Prix.

Mario Andretti leads from pole position in the United States Grand Prix.

1968 CONSTRUCTORS' CUP

TEAM (Engine)	POINTS
LOTUS FORD	62
McLAREN FORD	49
MATRA FORD	45
FERRARI	32
BRM	28
COOPER BRM	14
HONDA	14
BRABHAM REPCO	10
MATRA	8
McLAREN BRM	3

both set early times in qualifying before they flew back to the United States for a race at Indianapolis. But they were warned that they faced a ban from the Monza race if they ran in the American event and subsequently neither returned for the Italian Grand Prix.

McLaren, who had qualified second behind Surtees, led the race in its infancy but was passed by Surtees on lap seven. One lap later, McLaren was back in front as third-placed Amon crashed and Surtees hit a wall trying to avoid the Ferrari driver. A four-way battle for the lead ensued between McLaren, Stewart, Siffert and Hulme.

McLaren dropped out of the battle on lap 35 after an oil leak and Stewart followed eight laps later. On lap 59, rear suspension failure ended Siffert's challenge and Hulme coasted to the chequered flag. The impressive Servoz-Gavin underlined his growing reputation as he won the battle for second.

Hulme added another victory in Canada but he had luck on his side again as Amon was denied a win when his transmission failed 17 laps from the end.

The race was switched from Mosport Park to Mont-Tremblant in Quebec as the World Championship season ended with three races in the Americas. Ickx, who was one of four drivers with a chance of the title, suffered a broken leg after a qualifying crash.

As a result of his second successive victory, Hulme moved level on points with Hill at the top of the standings.

Hill cruises to second Championship

Andretti and Unser competed in the United States Grand Prix at Watkins Glen and the former produced a major shock by putting his Lotus on pole position. But Stewart, who had been second on the grid, led after the first lap.

Andretti then dropped to the back when he pitted after part of his car trailed on the floor, and eventually retired with clutch problems. Stewart and Hill were left to finish first and second to set up a shoot-out in the final race of the season in Mexico.

Hulme's title aspirations suffered a major setback when he spun on an oil patch on the track and damaged his brakes. The pit-stop cost him valuable time and, in his bid to get back into a points-scoring position, he crashed in the closing stages.

With three drivers – Hill, Stewart and Hulme – all in with a chance of becoming World Champion, the final round in Mexico City was a tense affair. Siffert was on pole, but Hill led by the end of the opening lap. The tension increased as Hill and Stewart exchanged the lead several times, while Hulme ran behind them in third. Hulme retired on lap 11, however, when he hit a guardrail after he suffered rear suspension failure.

Pole-sitter Siffert took the lead on lap 22 but pitted as Hill and Stewart battled at the front again. But Stewart dropped away because of handling problems and ended the race in seventh. Hill eased to a second World Championship as he won the race ahead of McLaren.

SHORTS

Already mourning the loss of Jim Clark, Formula One suffered again when Jo Schlesser was killed at Rouen-les-Essarts. Schlesser was involved in the race after John Surtees refused to compete in the Honda RA302 chassis he had tested and was killed on lap three when he lost control of the car, after it overturned and burst into flames with a full fuel tank.

1969
Stewart no longer bridesmaid

TALKING POINT

A WING AND A PRAYER

The FIA were forced to ban the use of high rear wings after Lotus drivers Graham Hill and Jochen Rindt experienced the dangers of such aids at first hand. First Hill and then Rindt crashed out of the Spanish Grand Prix at Montjuich Park after rear wing failure sent their cars out of control. Both incidents occurred in the same uphill section of the circuit and Rindt overturned after he hit Hill's abandoned car. Rindt suffered a broken nose and missed the Monaco Grand Prix, but he returned, as did the rear wings in a much less extreme format. They later became part of the bodywork of the car and were much safer.

The big discovery of the season was four-wheel drive cars but Matra, McLaren and Lotus all tried it out and opted against introducing it. It did not suit the sport at the time and development was put on hold temporarily.

First Lotus and Matra tried the new invention out at the Dutch Grand Prix and two pairs of four-wheel drive cars appeared in the British Grand Prix. But they were a major flop, as the two-wheel drive models proved sufficient.

Jackie Stewart, runner-up to Graham Hill the previous year, handled the two-wheel drive in his usual manner as he dominated proceedings as he marched to a maiden title. The British driver was still with Ken Tyrrell and remained behind the wheel of his Ford-powered car despite the withdrawal of designers Matra International from Formula One.

The usual merry-go-round of driver changes was again evident when the teams took to the grid for the season-opening South African Grand Prix in March. Jean-Pierre Beltoise was employed to partner Stewart and the impressive Johnny Servoz-Gavin in Tyrrell's squad.

Jochen Rindt jumped at the chance to link up with Graham Hill at Lotus, while Jacky Ickx left Ferrari to replace the Austrian at Brabham, who had decided to run DFV power-units rather than the Repco V8s. In addition John Surtees, who was on the market following Honda's withdrawal from the sport, joined former Lotus driver Jackie Oliver at BRM.

Jack Brabham, with the new Cosworth engine on board, set the pace in qualifying at Kyalami but Stewart began the season as he meant to go on by leading the race from start to finish. He emerged ahead of Brabham at the end of the first lap and never relinquished the lead again.

Brabham's rear wing failed on lap seven and cost him time while Andretti, competing in a third Lotus, exited the race after 31 laps when his transmission failed. Stewart won the race by 18 seconds ahead of second-placed Hill.

Ferrari stutters; Stewart capitalizes

The second round of the Championship took place two months later at Montjuich Park in Barcelona. The track had been used in the 1930s and the Spanish government decided to alternate the Spanish Grand Prix between the Madrid circuit of Jarama and the Catalunya track.

The event was the first World Championship race in which Piers Courage competed as he ran in a Frank Williams Brabham, but it was Rindt who was quickest in qualifying.

The Austrian roared into a commanding lead, but on lap nine his Lotus team-mate Hill was thwarted with rear wing problems and emerged unscathed after a heavy crash. Then, just 11 laps later, exactly the same thing happened to Rindt, but despite overturning as he ran into Hill's stationary car, the Austrian suffered only a broken nose.

Ferrari driver Amon was left at the head of the field but Stewart was handed a second successive victory when the new V12 Ferrari seized on the leaders. Ickx, the only man close enough to challenge for the lead after Brabham and Jo Siffert retired, also suffered rear wing failure to give Stewart a 100 per cent start to the season.

High-wings caused crashes for Jochen Rindt and Graham Hill at the Spanish Grand Prix.

Graham Hill in his Lotus car at the Monaco Grand Prix in 1969.

The injured Rindt missed the Monaco Grand Prix because of his broken nose and Lotus replaced him with Richard Attwood. After several further incidents involving rear wing failure in the first practice session, the FIA imposed an immediate ban on the aerodynamic aids. The times from the session were cancelled, despite teams expressing their discontent at the move.

In the end, the in-form Stewart grabbed pole ahead of Amon. Stewart's early-season dominance continued as he led the field from the off and the Briton was clear by lap 10. At the same time, Surtees suffered gearbox failure and Brabham ran into the back of him in the tunnel. Both escaped injury.

Amon went out of the race on lap 16 and Beltoise, who was fourth, followed him after his driveshaft failed. When Stewart retired because of the same problem as Beltoise, Hill was left to claim a fifth Monaco win. Courage, in only his second World Championship event, landed an impressive second place after Ickx retired with rear suspension failure.

After the Belgian Grand Prix was cancelled because of a dispute between race organizers and the Grand Prix Drivers' Association over the safety of the Spa-Francorchamps circuit, there was a five-week break until the next event.

Safety issues prompt changes

Instead, the circus arrived at Zandvoort for the Dutch Grand Prix and, with the high rear wings banned, Lotus and Matra opted to run four-wheel-drive cars in an attempt to increase grip. Hill and Stewart both ran the new evolution of the cars.

But the duo opted to run in their original machines in qualifying after the four-wheel drives flopped. Stewart qualified second while Hill was third as Rindt claimed pole position.

Hill was quickest off the grid as Rindt and Stewart chased him, but both drivers had passed him and the Englishman's Lotus was down to third. Rindt extended his lead but retired on lap 17 as Stewart was left in front on his own. The Scotsman led Siffert home as Hill ended down the field after handling problems hindered his challenge.

More significantly, the Dutch Grand Prix weekend was marked by the announcement that Ferrari had agreed to go into collaboration with fellow-Italian manufacturer Fiat. The deal was not to have an immediate effect but the funds made available by Fiat would have a lasting effect on Ferrari's status and competitiveness in future years.

The venue for the French Grand Prix once again changed, with the race returning to Clermont-Ferrand after a four-year absence. The field boasted just 13 cars with BRM absent and Brabham out of action after he broke his ankle in a testing crash at Silverstone.

Stewart, with three wins out of four, was again dominant as he powered to pole position by more than two seconds. The British driver was similarly dominant in the race as he led from start to finish.

Beltoise, in Tyrrell's second Matra, claimed a one-two for the team after first Hulme, with a damaged front roll bar, and Ickx, who made a mistake on the penultimate lap, sacrificed the chance of vital Championship points. McLaren claimed fourth in bizarre circumstances after Rindt retired because the twisting circuit had made him feel ill.

Stewart completes fifth win

In the British Grand Prix at Silverstone, Hill returned to the cockpit of Lotus' four-wheel-drive but

RACE BY RACE DETAILS

ROUND 1 – SOUTH AFRICA
Race Jackie Stewart
Pole Jack Brabham
Fastest lap Jackie Stewart

ROUND 2 – SPAIN
Race Jackie Stewart
Pole Jochen Rindt
Fastest lap Jochen Rindt

ROUND 3 – MONACO
Race Graham Hill
Pole Jackie Stewart
Fastest lap Jackie Stewart

ROUND 4 – HOLLAND
Race Jackie Stewart
Pole Jochen Rindt
Fastest lap Jackie Stewart

ROUND 5 – FRANCE
Race Jackie Stewart
Pole Jackie Stewart
Fastest lap Jackie Stewart

ROUND 6 – BRITAIN
Race Jackie Stewart
Pole Jochen Rindt
Fastest lap Jackie Stewart

ROUND 7 – GERMANY
Race Jacky Ickx
Pole Jacky Ickx
Fastest lap Jacky Ickx

ROUND 8 – ITALY
Race Jackie Stewart
Pole Jochen Rindt
Fastest lap Jean-Pierre Beltoise

ROUND 9 – CANADA
Race Jacky Ickx
Pole Jacky Ickx
Fastest lap Jacky Ickx

ROUND 10 – UNITED STATES
Race Jochen Rindt
Pole Jochen Rindt
Fastest lap Jochen Rindt

ROUND 11 – MEXICO
Race Denny Hulme
Pole Jack Brabham
Fastest lap Jacky Ickx

1969 DRIVERS' CHAMPIONSHIP

DRIVER	TEAM	POINTS
Jackie Stewart	Matra Ford	63
Jacky Ickx	Brabham Ford	37
Bruce McLaren	McLaren Ford	26
Jochen Rindt	Lotus Ford	22
Jean-Pierre Beltoise	Matra Ford	21
Denny Hulme	McLaren Ford	20
Graham Hill	Lotus Ford	19
Piers Courage	Brabham Ford	16
Jo Siffert	Lotus Ford	15
Jack Brabham	Brabham Ford	14
John Surtees	BRM	6
Chris Amon	Ferrari	4
Dickie Attwood	Lotus Ford	3
Pedro Rodriguez	Ferrari	3
Vic Elford	McLaren Ford	3
Johnny Servoz-Gavin	Matra Ford	1
Silvio Moser	Brabham Ford	1
Jackie Oliver	BRM	1

Stewart, still competing in his usual two-wheel-drive car, landed a fifth win of the season.

BRM were back on the grid after the future of the team had been resolved. Tim Parnell was the new team manager, with Reg Parnell Racing now closed. Brabham was still missing because of his broken ankle.

Stewart crashed heavily in practice on Saturday and forced Beltoise to run in the four-wheel-drive after taking over his car. He failed to settle in the new car and ended second on the grid as Rindt landed pole position.

Rindt and Stewart enjoyed a titanic battle throughout the race as the latter chased the race leader. In the end, the new rear wing design on Rindt's Lotus came loose and the Austrian had to pit. Stewart had a 30-second advantage and the title favourite eased home, as he opened up a gap and gained victory by a lap.

In Germany two weeks later, Ferrari did not compete after a last-minute decision, and a number of Formula Two competitors withdrew after BMW's Gerhard Mitter was killed in an accident during Friday's practice. The idea of running Formula One and Formula Two cars in the same race remained but Mitter's death left just eight runners from the lower category.

Ickx beat Stewart to pole position and the Belgian driver finally ended Stewart's stranglehold as he won the race to take Brabham's first victory for two years.

Ickx made a slow start to the race as Stewart led, but the opening exchanges were marred when Andretti, once again in a third Lotus, crashed and Vic Elford, competing in a privateer McLaren, ran into a stray wheel and flipped upside-down in the trees. Andretti helped him from the wreckage but he had suffered three breaks of the arm.

Stewart held off Ickx's challenge for the lead until lap seven when he was finally passed and the Brabham driver went on to win by over a minute after gearbox problems slowed down Stewart, who still finished second.

Champion crowned at Monza

There was a month-long wait for the next race in Italy. In the gap between the two Championship races Ickx had continued his upward trend by winning the Oulton Park Gold Cup. For their home event at Monza, Ferrari surprisingly entered only one car, for Pedro Rodriguez. Despite Ferrari's lack of interest a big crowd still attended the Italian Grand Prix.

Once again Rindt demonstrated his potential by setting the fastest time in qualifying and an epic race ensued during which eight drivers battled for, and held, the lead.

Rindt, Stewart, Hulme, Courage, Hill, McLaren, Beltoise and Siffert all held the lead as the drivers put on an exhibition of slipstreaming. Hulme and Courage disappeared from the frame with 11 laps to go and Hill also retired with five laps remaining. Rindt moved ahead of leader Stewart on the last lap to set himself up for his first win of the year. But Stewart returned to the lead, then Beltoise moved ahead of the duo before he went wide at Parabolica and ended third as Stewart sealed his first World Championship success with his sixth win of the season.

Stewart's race win was an amazing feat with the top four finishers being separated by less than 0.2

Jackie Stewart and his wife on the podium at Monza after winning the Italian Grand Prix.

Jochen Rindt on the podium.

seconds, and his subsequent title glory arrived with three races left to run.

The Canadian Grand Prix switched back to Mosport Park and the usual Championship racers were again in action. The in-form Ickx qualified on pole with newly-crowned Champion Stewart on the second row.

Rindt led the race in the early stages but Stewart was in front by lap six. Ickx, who had passed Rindt, then exchanged the lead with Stewart. But the duo collided as Ickx tried to overtake Stewart and the latter was unable to re-start his car. Ickx eased to victory with Brabham second ahead of Rindt.

Rindt wins – finally!

Rindt finally ended his search for a win in America, but the race was marred by a crash involving Hill, who broke both his legs. Rindt was on pole for the Watkins Glen race and he led British pair Stewart and Hill during the opening laps of the race.

Stewart passed the Austrian on lap 12, after Hulme had retired, but Rindt returned to the front nine laps later. By lap 36 Stewart had retired with smoke billowing out of the back of his car and as a result Rindt broke his seasonal duck.

But Hill's accident left its mark on the event. The Englishman had spun in mid-race and had to push-start his Lotus, but could not fasten the seat belts after leaving the cockpit. When he crashed on lap 91, Hill was thrown from his overturned car and broke both legs on impact.

In the final race of the season in Mexico City, Lotus opted not to replace Hill following his accident. Brabham and Ickx, in a pair of Brabhams, topped the times in qualifying.

Stewart made the best start and was chased by Brabham and Ickx, and on lap six Ickx's pressure forced Stewart to allow him past. Hulme, who looked to be back to his best, moved up to second ahead of Stewart, who was also passed by Brabham.

The top four positions remained the same to the finish line as the season ended in an anti-climax following Stewart's early dominance of the year. Hill recovered from his injuries, but did not appear in another race for the rest of the year.

SHORTS

The Dutch Grand Prix at Zandvoort proved a significant weekend for one of auto-racing's most storied teams. The event was marked by an announcement that Ferrari had agreed to go into collaboration with fellow-Italian manufacturer Fiat. The deal was not to have an immediate effect but the funds made available by Fiat would have a lasting effect on Ferrari's competitiveness in future years.

1969 CONSTRUCTORS' CUP

TEAM (Engine)	POINTS
LOTUS FORD	59
FERRARI	52
MATRA FORD	48
BRABHAM FORD	35
McLAREN FORD	35
MATRA SIMCA	23
BRM	23
SURTEES FORD	3

1970
Rindt claims posthumous title

Jochen Rindt in action. He died following a crash at Monza, but was posthumously crowned Formula One champion.

TALKING POINT

A SAD END TO A TRAGIC YEAR

Jochen Rindt won the Championship at the American Grand Prix, but unfortunately he was not there to see it. At the time, Formula One was still reeling from his death in the previous race. The Austrian had become the first, and only, posthumous World Champion in a year which saw an astonishing three Grand Prix drivers die in action. Rindt had taken just one victory during his six seasons in Formula One before his move to Lotus for the 1970 season, and the new car finally gave him the machinery to show his potential. Although he only finished in five races, he won every one of them and was undoubtedly a star of the future. But his life was tragically cut short at the age of 28.

It was a tragic year as three drivers lost their lives during the course of the season. Bruce McLaren and Piers Courage died within 19 days of each other in the middle of the year, and Jochen Rindt's terrible crash at Monza added to the agony in a sad season for Formula One.

Ferrari enjoyed a resurgence in form towards the end of the season but could not scale the points tally Rindt had clocked up through the five victories before his death, and Formula One ended the season without its World Champion.

The new decade began with major changes to the Formula One line-up. Perhaps the most significant was the introduction of the March name to Formula One and the arrival of Max Mosley on the Grand Prix scene.

And it was the March of Jackie Stewart on pole position when the teams lined up on the grid for the opening race of the season in South Africa. He got off the line well and led for the first 19 laps as a spin caused havoc behind him. A fast-starting Rindt collided with Chris Amon and then hit Jack Brabham, dropping the Australian down to sixth.

Brabham moved up through the field and by lap 20 was in the lead. Stewart slowly slipped back to end the race in third after the McLaren of Denny Hulme moved ahead of him.

Six weeks later the teams arrived in Spain for round two, and only 18 starters lined up on the grid after controversy over appearance money. Brabham continued his impressive form to claim pole. Stewart took the lead at the start and he was never caught. All his challengers faded away and left the Scot to take the first victory for the March chassis (see Shorts).

The next round at Monaco was another filled with mechanical retirements, but the race went down to the last lap as leader Brabham flew into the straw bales to gift Rindt the victory.

Tragedy strikes McLaren

The teams arrived in Belgium for the next event of the series after a four-week break. That break had been filled with tragedy for the McLaren team. Just two days after Hulme burned his hands at the Indianapolis 500, the New Zealand-born team owner McLaren was killed testing one of his CanAm cars at Goodwood.

The team was absent from Spa, as was Johnny Servoz-Gavin who had retired with eyesight problems after being hit by a branch in a winter off-road event.

At the front, it was business as usual with Jackie Stewart on pole, closely followed by Rindt and Jacky Ickx. The three were involved in a tight battle at the start and all of them led during lap one. After that, Amon and Stewart battled as Pedro Rodriguez slipped ahead of Rindt and into third.

Mexican Rodriguez was flying and passed both Amon and Stewart to take the lead and pull away by lap five. Stewart dropped back into the clutches of Brabham, but again the Australian left the track, this time when his feet became tangled up with a rag in his cockpit.

It did not set him back too much and he was soon back up the field, only to suffer clutch failure and sacrifice third to Jean-Pierre Beltoise. But there was no stopping Rodriguez, who took the chequered flag ahead of Amon to become the fourth different winner in as many races.

At the Dutch Grand Prix, tragedy was to strike yet again as Formula One claimed its second life in two-and-a-half weeks. Brabham and Rodriguez had escaped injury after rolling their cars in qualifying, but during the race Piers Courage was not so lucky. He rolled his De Tomaso on lap 23 and it caught fire. Trapped underneath, there was nothing he could do to escape.

After the accident, the race seemed irrelevant, but it did continue and it was Rindt who eventually took the chequered flag.

The Austrian claimed his second successive victory at the French Grand Prix and made it four in a row in Britain and Germany.

Rindt's excursion to Brands Hatch, however, was not all plain-sailing and there was a dramatic finish to the seventh race of the season.

A bad start from pole position dropped Rindt behind Brabham and the Ferrari of Ickx and the pair were embroiled in a direct fight during the early laps. Ickx passed Brabham after some wheel-to-wheel action on lap one and he stayed ahead despite being hounded all the way.

It was all over for the Ferrari man by lap seven when a faulty differential put Ickx out of he race. It was Rindt, not Brabham, who assumed the lead after he passed the Australian at the same moment Ickx went out.

Brabham challenged Rindt for the remainder of the race and took the opportunity to move in front when the Austrian missed a gear on lap 69. Brabham was able to pull out a 13-second lead, but it was not enough as he was forced to coast home and allow Rindt through to win on the flag.

The venue for the German Grand Prix was switched to Hockenheim because safety work had not been done at the Nuburgring.

It was the first Formula One race to be held at the circuit and a dramatic five-car battle ensued, with Rindt taking what proved to be his last Grand Prix win.

Austrian disappointment for Rindt

An ever-improving Ferrari team secured first and third on the grid, but race favourite Rindt planted his Lotus on the front row. It was Ickx, however, who took the lead at the start with Rindt second and Jo Siffert, Clay Regazzoni and Amon all in close pursuit.

The multi-car battle eventually became a duel between Rindt and Ickx when Siffert lacked pace and the others suffered engine failures. There was no let-up all the way to the finish. Rindt nosed home just 0.7 seconds ahead of the Ferrari. Meanwhile, a young Emerson Fittipaldi scored his first Formula One point by bringing his works Lotus 49 home in fourth.

The expected local victory for Rindt did not materialize when the field moved to the Osterreichring for the Austrian Grand Prix two weeks later. The massive, partisan crowd were sent home disappointed after mechanical failure forced Rindt out early and left Ferrari to sweep home and take a dominant one-two finish.

Rindt topped the times in practice and had

RACE BY RACE DETAILS

ROUND 1 – SOUTH AFRICA
Race Jack Brabham
Pole Jackie Stewart
Fastest lap John Surtees/Jack Brabham

ROUND 2 – SPAIN
Race Jackie Stewart
Pole Jack Brabham
Fastest lap Jack Brabham

ROUND 3 – MONACO
Race Jochen Rindt
Pole Jackie Stewart
Fastest lap Jochen Rindt

ROUND 4 – BELGIUM
Race Pedro Rodriguez
Pole Jackie Stewart
Fastest lap Chris Amon

ROUND 5 – NETHERLANDS
Race Jochen Rindt
Pole Jochen Rindt
Fastest lap Jacky Ickx

ROUND 6 – FRANCE
Race Jochen Rindt
Pole Jacky Ickx
Fastest lap Jack Brabham

ROUND 7 – BRITAIN
Race Jochen Rindt
Pole Jochen Rindt
Fastest lap Jack Brabham

ROUND 8 – GERMANY
Race Jochen Rindt
Pole Jacky Ickx
Fastest lap Jacky Ickx

ROUND 9 – AUSTRIA
Race Jacky Ickx
Pole Jochen Rindt
Fastest lap Jacky Ickx/Clay Regazzoni

ROUND 10 – ITALY
Race Clay Regazzoni
Pole Jacky Ickx
Fastest lap Clay Regazzoni

ROUND 11 – CANADA
Race Jacky Ickx
Pole Jackie Stewart
Fastest lap Clay Regazzoni

ROUND 12 – UNITED STATES
Race Emerson Fittipaldi
Pole Jacky Ickx
Fastest lap Jacky Ickx

ROUND 13 – MEXICO
Race Jacky Ickx
Pole Clay Regazzoni
Fastest lap Jacky Ickx

Jack Brabham won the opening race of the 1970 season in South Africa.

1970 DRIVERS' CHAMPIONSHIP

DRIVER	TEAM	POINTS
Jochen Rindt	Lotus Ford	45
Jacky Ickx	Ferrari	40
Clay Regazzoni	Ferrari	33
Denny Hulme	McLaren Ford	27
Jack Brabham	Brabham Ford	25
Jackie Stewart	March Ford	25
Pedro Rodriguez	BRM	23
Chris Amon	March Ford	23
Jean-Pierre Beltoise	Matra Simca	16
Emerson Fittipaldi	Lotus Ford	12
Rolf Stommelen	Brabham Ford	10
Henri Pescarolo	Matra Simca	8
Graham Hill	Lotus Ford	7
Bruce McLaren	McLaren Ford	6
Mario Andretti	March Ford	4
Reine Weisell	Lotus Ford	4
Ignazio Giunti	Ferrari	3
John Surtees	McLaren Ford/Surtees Ford	3
John Miles	Lotus Ford	2
Johnny Servoz-Gavin	March Ford	2
Jackie Oliver	BRM	2
Dan Gurney	McLaren Ford	1
François Cevert	March Ford	1
Peter Gethin	McLaren Ford	1
Derek Bell	Surtees Ford	1

Jackie Ickx crashes out of the British Grand Prix at Brands Hatch, handing Jochen Rindt victory.

Regazzoni alongside him on row one, the promising Swiss driver having out-qualified his Ferrari team-mate Ickx. Graham Hill and Ronnie Peterson, meanwhile, were both pre-race casualties. Disgruntled with his uncompetitive Lotus 49, Briton Hill did not turn up, while Peterson's Antique Automobiles team had run out of engines.

Ferrari were fast, and the Italian cars passed Rindt off the line. Regazzoni waved his team-mate Ickx past with just one lap gone and that was the end of the race as a spectacle. The pair were unstoppable and Rindt's challenge finally ended when his engine failed at one-third distance.

Death of a champion

The next race at Monza saw tragedy strike Formula One yet again when Championship leader Rindt was killed. The Austrian died in Saturday practice when his Lotus speared off the track under braking and smashed heavily into the barriers at the Parabolica. His Lotus was wrecked, and so was Formula One. Rindt was taken to hospital, but he was pronounced dead on arrival.

It was the second major crash of the weekend, and Fittipaldi was given a reality check by the Saturday events after his dramatic moment one day earlier when he went off in the same place. His Lotus crashed over an earth bank and came to rest in the trackside trees. Fortunately he did not hit any.

Qualifying went on after Rindt's accident, and Ferrari's Ickx ended the session on pole and converted it into a race lead the following day. For four laps he was in front, but Rodriguez and Stewart made it past and, battling together, were both overtaken by the flying Regazzoni, who grabbed the lead on lap 10.

The three cars slipstreamed each other, switching the lead on several occasions until Rodriguez dropped out with engine failure. Jackie Oliver and Ickx joined the battle for the lead, but both eventually retired to leave Regazzoni to take his first win ahead of Stewart with Frenchman Beltoise third. The result was, however, overshadowed by Rindt's death.

Ferrari showed their might in the next round of the season at the Canadian circuit of Mont-Tremblant. With Lotus still absent after the Monza tragedy, Ferrari were left to dominate and take their second one-two finish of the season.

Stewart set the pace in qualifying in the new Tyrrell, seemingly overcoming his frustration at not competing at Monza after he suffered reliability problems during the practice sessions. With the problems ironed out, Stewart was able to take pole ahead of the Ferrari of Ickx.

He took the lead at the start, and all was looking good for Stewart until he dropped out of the race with an axle failure. Ickx had led the chase ahead of Rodriguez, who made the best start to the race when he moved up to third from seventh.

SHORTS

March Engineering entered Formula One after testing a Formula Three car the year before. Major backing from oil treatment company STP allowed the British company to make a rapid move up the motor-racing ladder. At the season-opener in South Africa, March had five DFV-powered cars in the race, including the Tyrrells of Jackie Stewart and Johnny Servoz-Gavin who were running March chassis. Stewart gave March their first win as he took the chequered flag at Jarama, only the second race of the Championship.

Ickx took the lead when Stewart went out on lap 32, and he was nearly 30 seconds ahead of team-mate Regazzoni who had moved past Rodriguez, François Cevert and John Surtees. Amon eventually moved up to take third at the finish, but the Ferraris were too far ahead to catch.

The victory moved Ickx up to second in the Championship, but Rindt was so far ahead that the Ferrari man had to win the final two rounds to overhaul him. Ickx, therefore, had to take victory in the following round in America two weeks later.

But a pole position was not converted into the win required as a fuel leak robbed him of his hopes at Watkins Glen and the Championship was awarded posthumously to Rindt.

Lotus had returned with Emerson Fittipaldi as their team leader, hoping to defend Rindt's points lead by stealing some from the late driver's Ferrari rival Ickx.

Tyrrell continued to impress with their new 001 car, and Stewart was the man who took the lead at the start of the race. Both he and Rodriguez were quicker than pole-sitter Ickx while Fittipaldi did his team no favours with a disappointing opening which sent him down from the second row to eighth place.

Surtees and Oliver soon dropped out of the lead pack as Rodriguez was passed by both Ickx and Regazzoni as the Ferraris went in chase of Stewart. Regazzoni left his team-mate out on his own when forced to stop for a tyre change, but on lap 57 Ickx coasted into the pits, his Championship challenge ended by a fuel leak.

The demise of the Ferrari left Stewart clear, but just as it looked all clear for the new chassis' first win, he was forced out of the race with an oil leak. Rodriguez moved up into first place but it was Fittipaldi who became the third youngest Formula One winner after the leader dropped to second when he ran out of fuel.

End of a difficult year

Although the Championship was over by the time the final race of the season in Mexico arrived, the Formula One circus still drew in an estimated 200,000 fans. The circuit was not built to cope with such a massive crowd and safety barriers were pulled down in the quest for more space.

Organizers considered cancelling the race but fearing a riot if they called it off, the start was delayed for an hour as spectators were moved off the grass verges on the edge of the circuit.

This accomplished, Regazzoni led from pole with Stewart and Ickx in hot pursuit, but the Swiss driver was soon bumped down to third and dropped back. Stewart dropped out of second when forced to pit with steering column failure to leave the Ferraris up front on their own once again.

Brabham settled into third, but the Australian's last Formula One race was ended with an engine failure on lap 53.

That left Hulme to follow the Ferraris home in third as the crowd broke ranks once again and invaded the track right at the end. It was Ferrari's third one-two of the season, and Formula One was pleased to see the end of what had been a truly tragic year left to the memory of Austrian Rindt.

1970 CONSTRUCTORS' CUP

TEAM (Engine)	POINTS
LOTUS FORD	59
FERRARI	52
MATRA FORD	48
BRABHAM FORD	35
McLAREN FORD	35
MATRA SIMCA	23
BRM	23
SURTEES FORD	3

Piers Courage and his De Tomaso. The Englishman was killed during the Dutch Grand Prix.

Emerson Fittipaldi

CAREER DETAILS

1946	Born 12 December in São Paolo, Brazil
1965	Progresses to cars from motorbikes and karts
1967	Turns to single-seaters. Brazilian Formula Zee Champion
1969	Moves to Europe. Wins the Lombank F3 title in Jim Russell's Lotus
1970	Signs for Lotus F2 team, making F1 debut mid-season
1972	Youngest ever World Champion in Lotus
1973	Runner-up to Jackie Stewart
1974	World Champion in McLaren
1975	Runner-up to Niki Lauda
1976	Leaves to join Copersucar-backed team
1981	Retires from F1
1989	Indy Car Champion for Patrick Racing, wins Indianapolis 500
1993	Wins Indianapolis 500
1996	Injures back in crash at Michigan
1997	Further injures back in aircraft accident. Retires.

FORMULA ONE RECORD

Year	Team	Wins	Poles	Fast laps	Pts
1970	Lotus	1	0	0	12
1971	Lotus	0	0	0	16
1972	Lotus	5	3	0	61
1973	Lotus	3	1	5	55
1974	McLaren	3	2	0	55
1975	McLaren	2	0	1	45
1976	Ferrari	0	0	0	3
1977	Copersucar	0	0	0	11
1978	Copersucar	0	0	0	17
1979	Copersucar	0	0	0	1
1980	Fittipaldi	0	0	0	5

EMERSON FITTIPALDI, the youngest World Champion at the age of 25, became the elder statesman of the CART circuit and ignited passion in fellow-Brazilians Nelson Piquet and Ayrton Senna.

Emerson Fittipaldi enjoyed a film-script rise to prominence, but the youngest Formula One Champion dashed his reputation for shrewdness with one rash decision when, in 1976, he chose to drive his own underfunded Copersucar instead of going for what could have been a third World Championship. The project bankrupted him, but he re-launched himself and became the respected elder statesman of the CART circuit, with two Indy 500 victories to his credit.

The son of well-known Brazilian motorsport journalist Wilson Fittipaldi, Emerson started racing on 50cc motorbikes, following older brother Wilson Junior into karts. Both progressed to cars in 1965, racing a Renault Gordoni. In 1967 he turned to single-seaters and was crowned Brazilian Formula Vee Champion.

Having trounced the opposition in Brazil, he moved to Europe in 1969. He bought a Formula Ford car and was simply invincible. Legendary racing school owner Jim Russell spotted his talent and signed Fittipaldi to race his Lotus Formula Three car.

He duly won the Lombank Formula Three title that year, displaying the smooth and controlled style that would remain his trademark. *Flying On The Ground* is the apt name of his autobiography.

Lotus signed him for its Formula Two team for 1970 and in mid-season Colin Chapman hurried him on to the biggest stage, partly to prevent Formula One rivals from poaching him. In May he became the third team member after Jochen Rindt and John Miles. He made his debut at Brands Hatch driving an old Lotus 49 in which he finished eighth.

His second race in Germany saw him score his first Championship points (for fourth place). Then after the death of Rindt, Fittipaldi took over the number one drive and won the United States Grand Prix at Watkins Glen – only his fifth time out – clinching the World Championship for his fallen team-mate and rescuing his devastated team.

Fittipaldi's 1971 season was interrupted by a road accident which contributed to a downturn in form. The following year, however, the fairytale was realized. At Monza, he claimed the drivers' title, becoming the youngest World Champion.

His victory in the ageing Lotus 72D with five wins, one second and a fourth in 11 races, was the last of a decade in which the fabled Lotus team won five world titles.

"I was happy. Everybody was happy. It was like a love story film," he said. "I don't think many people understand just how competitive Formula One real-

Emerson Fittipaldi enjoyed the best and the worst of times after being crowned the youngest Formula One World Champion.

> “The cockpit of a racing car is one of the most relaxing places in the world.”

ly is. To find that last half-second which puts you ahead of the rest of the field is really very difficult."

He started 1973 well, winning both the Argentinian and Brazilian Grands Prix, but the season became strained due to the brilliance of his new team-mate Ronnie Peterson. The burden of developing the car, only to be out-qualified by Peterson, soon frustrated Fittipaldi. He finished the year runner-up to Jackie Stewart.

Fittipaldi must also have mused that Lotus was entering a down period after the superb Lotus 72 had reached the end of its life in the fastest lane. A move to McLaren brought him three wins, numerous points-scoring finishes and ultimately his second World Championship in 1974.

The next year was one of turmoil which included a half-hearted Brands Hatch Race of Champions and a walkout at the Spanish Grand Prix. Disgusted with the political machinations of Formula One, he turned inward.

Helped by sponsorship from the Brazilian state-run sugar cartel, Copersucar, he formed his own team with brother Wilson Junior, but they could not reproduce the magic and he was at the blunt end of the grid.

"It was the biggest mistake I ever made in my life," said Fittipaldi. "I had offers from Ferrari, from Frank [Williams]... It was extremely demoralising for me, having won the Championship twice. Sometimes I didn't even qualify. It was terrible."

The Fittipaldi team closed down in 1982. A few years later, he went to America and drove with the WIT Indycar team. Mid-season he replaced the injured Chip Ganassi at Patrick Racing and stayed with the team throughout the late 1980s and early 1990s, winning the Indianapolis 500 in 1989 and 1993 and the CART Championship in 1989.

In 1990 he joined Penske and continued to be a big draw until 1996 when he injured his back after crashing at Michigan.

A year later he compounded the injury in a light aircraft accident which prompted him to retire. He moved on to manage Brazil's young racing talent. Nelson Piquet declared: "Emerson created the sport of motor racing in Brazil."

Emerson Fittipaldi inspired a new generation of Brazilian drivers such as Nelson Piquet and Ayrton Senna.

1971

Stewart enjoys the early finish

TALKING POINT

BELTOISE BAN

Frenchman Jean-Pierre Beltoise was banned for a total of four races in the Formula One season after killing Ferrari driver Ignazio Giunti in an accident in a pre-season sports car race.

Matra Simca driver Beltoise accidentally hit Giunti as he was pushing his Ferrari back to the pits during the Buenos Aires 1000 sports car race in January. Some say he should never have been allowed to race at all in the season as a mark of respect to Giunti.

Beltoise missed the season-opening Grand Prix in South Africa and despite returning for the second round in Spain his race ban was reinforced for the races in Germany, Austria and Italy later in the season.

After Giunti's death, just two months before the start of the season, Ferrari were forced to search for a third driver and opted to recruit Mario Andretti, who failed to last the season as he went to race in America mid-way through the Formula One campaign.

This season belonged to the ever-impressive Jackie Stewart as he dominated from the outset in his Tyrrell Ford and had all but wrapped up the Championship after seven of the 11 races.

Stewart was joined in the Tyrrell Ford team by François Cevert, who pushed him hard. Behind Stewart, the field was equally spread and, in the five races of the season the Scot did not win, five different drivers took the chequered flag.

There were not many moves in the driver market before the season started in South Africa. Ferrari brought in Mario Andretti to team-up with Jacky Ickx and Clay Regazzoni in the new 312B/2 car. The Frank Williams' Racing team was represented by Henri Pescarolo and for one race in France with Jean Max.

Team Lotus developed their 1970 car further for Emerson Fittipaldi and Reine Wisell. March lost both drivers in pre-season. Chris Amon joined Matra Simca with Jean-Pierre Beltoise and Jo Siffert joining BRM, with Denny Hulme and Peter Gethin.

March relied on the lesser-known Alex Soler-Reig, Pescarolo, Andrea de Adamich and Ronnie Peterson. Graham Hill joined Brabham Ford, owned by the now-retired Jack Brabham, who had Tim Schenken as his other driver.

Andretti's South African success

The season was also dominated by a tyre war as Goodyear and Dunlop went head-to-head and drivers were forced to choose in a season when the sport needed to recover from the death of Jochen Rindt the previous year.

The opening round was at Kyalami in South Africa and Andretti celebrated inclusion in the Ferrari team with victory in the 79-lap race.

Regazzoni took the lead at the start of the race, pushed hard by Fittipaldi and Ickx, who had started from the third row. Denny Hulme, Pedro Rodriguez and Andretti were also in close proximity as Stewart dropped to seventh.

Regazzoni led for the first 16 laps until Hulme, who had already passed Ickx and Fittipaldi, moved in to first place on lap 17. Jo Siffert and Rodriguez went out on laps 31 and 33 respectively as their cars overheated.

Stewart's team-mate Cevert suffered an accident on lap 45 and went out while Fittipaldi's race ended on lap 58 when his engine failed.

But on lap 75, just four from the chequered flag, Hulme's luck ran out. He needed to pit to repair a suspension problem and and the race was lost as Andretti, who had crept up to second, inherited first place and held his nerve to take the win.

Stewart, meanwhile, recovered from his dismal start and overtook Regazzoni in the latter stages to take second place with the Italian driver third.

On 18 April the Championship resumed at Montjuich Park in Spain. Belgian star Ickx took pole for the 75-lap race with a dominant display in qualifying and was joined on the front row by team-mate Regazzoni and the Matra of Amon.

Stewart was on the second row with the BRM of Rodriguez while Beltoise was on the third row of the grid for his first race after regaining his licence for his part in the accident which killed Ferrari's Ignazio Giunti in pre-season.

Stewart had obviously not been satisfied with his lacklustre start in South Africa as he powered into second place. The Scot immediately piled the pressure on Ickx, who had retained first place off pole

Jean-Pierre Beltoise missed four races of the 1971 Formula One season because of a ban.

Ronnie Peterson finished runner-up to Jackie Stewart in the 1971 Formula One drivers' Championship.

position and took the lead from the Belgian driver on lap six. Even the fastest lap of the day from Ickx could not reel in Stewart, who won his first race of the season.

Ickx took second place, while Regazzoni's race had ended on lap 13 with an engine problem. He was soon followed out by South Africa winner Andretti, who had a fuel pump problem on lap 50, and Fittipaldi, whose suspension went on lap 54.

When the Formula One contingent arrived in Monaco for the third round in May they learned that 18 cars would be allowed to start rather than the previous top-16 qualifiers on the demanding street circuit.

Andretti, whose season had started so well in South Africa, suffered another setback as he failed to qualify despite the extended field. Rain wiped out Thursday's qualification and he was thwarted by a mechanical problem the following day.

In contrast, Stewart was unstoppable as he topped the times in qualifying and shared the front row with Ickx. Siffert and Amon were on the second row and the BRMs of Pedro Rodriguez and Hulme lined up on the third.

With an important start essential at the tight circuit, where overtaking is limited, Stewart did not disappoint and got away well.

Hill, usually a master of Monaco, was the first casualty as he crashed out after a mistake on the opening lap. Peter Gethin also had an accident on lap 22 and two laps later Regazzoni also crashed out after starting from a lowly 11th.

Stewart, meanwhile, steered clear of trouble and went on to win his second consecutive race. Ronnie Peterson in a March Ford, however, almost stole his thunder progressing from eighth on the grid to finish second with Ickx third.

The season was constantly criticized for its stop-start calendar and the mood of the competitors was not improved when the Belgian Grand Prix was cancelled due to safety concerns with Spa-Francorchamps.

The cancellation meant the next round did not take place until mid-June when Zandvoort hosted the Dutch Grand Prix. One driver missing was Fittipaldi, injured in a road accident and replaced by South African racer Dave Charlton.

Stewart, for once, was not at the front for qualifying as Ickx took pole position for the 70-lap race, with Pedro Rodriguez second and the Scot down in third. Stewart paid the price when the rain started to fall on race day.

Rodriguez was holding his own until lap 32, when Ickx overtook as he mastered the damp conditions. Ickx took the chequered flag and Rodriguez held on for second place with Regazzoni third. Stewart failed to recover from his spin and finished down in 11th after being lapped five times.

After his first win of the season, Ickx went to the new Paul Ricard circuit in France in confident mood for the next round in July.

Stewart still strong

Fittipaldi sported a bandaged arm after his road crash while Stewart reminded Ickx and company who was leading the Championship. Stewart took pole position for the 55-lap race with Regazzoni second, fractionally ahead of his Ferrari team-mate.

In the race, the weekend went from bad to worse for Ickx when he went out on lap four with engine problems. Sixteen laps later Ferrari's second racer went out as Regazzoni, who had been pushing Stewart, crashed after spinning on oil dropped by the blown engine of Ronnie Peterson's Alfa Romeo.

Graham Hill, who had started from fourth on the grid, also slipped on the oil, but was able to get

RACE BY RACE DETAILS

ROUND 1 – SOUTH AFRICA
Race Mario Andretti
Pole Jackie Stewart
Fastest lap Mario Andretti

ROUND 2 – SPAIN
Race Jackie Stewart
Pole Jacky Ickx
Fastest lap Jacky Ickx

ROUND 3 – MONACO
Race Jackie Stewart
Pole Jackie Stewart
Fastest lap Jackie Stewart

ROUND 4 – HOLLAND
Race Jacky Ickx
Pole Jacky Ickx
Fastest lap Jacky Ickx

ROUND 5 – FRANCE
Race Jackie Stewart
Pole Jackie Stewart
Fastest lap Jackie Stewart

ROUND 6 – BRITAIN
Race Jackie Stewart
Pole Clay Regazzoni
Fastest lap Jackie Stewart

ROUND 7 – GERMANY
Race Jackie Stewart
Pole Jackie Stewart
Fastest lap François Cevert

ROUND 8 – AUSTRIA
Race Jo Siffert
Pole Jo Siffert
Fastest lap Jo Siffert

ROUND 9 – ITALY
Race Peter Gethin
Pole Chris Amon
Fastest lap Henri Pescarolo

ROUND 10 – CANADA
Race Jackie Stewart
Pole Jackie Stewart
Fastest lap Denny Hulme

ROUND 11 – UNITED STATES
Race François Cevert
Pole Jackie Stewart
Fastest lap Jacky Ickx

1971 DRIVERS' CHAMPIONSHIP

DRIVER	TEAM	POINTS
Jackie Stewart	Tyrrell Ford	62
Ronnie Peterson	March Ford	33
François Cevert	Tyrrell Ford	26
Jacky Ickx	Ferrari	19
Jo Siffert	BRM	19
Emerson Fittipaldi	Lotus Ford	16
Clay Regazzoni	Ferrari	13
Mario Andretti	Ferrari	12
Peter Gethin	BRM	9
Pedro Rodriguez	BRM	9
Chris Amon	Matra Simca	9
Reine Wisell	Lotus Ford	9
Denny Hulme	McLaren Ford	9
Tim Schenken	Brabham Ford	5
Howden Ganley	BRM	5
Henri Pescarolo	March Ford	4
Mark Donohue	McLaren Ford	4
Mike Hailwood	Surtees Ford	3
Rolf Stommelen	Surtees Ford	3
John Surtees	Surtees Ford	3
Graham Hill	Brabham Ford	2
Jean-Pierre Beltoise	Matra Simca	1

to the pits for repairs. Stewart steered clear of trouble to keep his lead but all the action let Rodriguez in to second place before his ignition failed on lap 27 and forced him out.

While Stewart powered away for his third win of the season, team-mate Cevert had crept up to third and was promoted to second after Rodriguez's retirement to give Tyrrell a one-two finish. Fittipaldi marked his return with an impressive third place.

As the drivers arrived at Silverstone for the British Grand Prix they were mourning the death of Rodriguez in a non-Championship event. The Mexican driver crashed a Ferrari sports car in an Interserie race at the Norisring. Trapped in his burning vehicle, he died in hospital a few hours later.

BRM did not to replace him as Siffert and Howden Ganley ran their only two cars at Silverstone. McLaren ran a third car for Jack Oliver and Surtees ran Derek Bell alongside himself and Rolf Stommelen in his private team.

In qualifying, Regazzoni secured pole with Stewart and Siffert also on the front row. Fittipaldi and Peterson were on the second row. Ickx, Hulme and Schenken were on the third.

At the start there was an immediate incident as Oliver, in his first race, ran into the back of Hill and forced both out of the race. Ickx made a tremendous start and as the field settled was second behind Regazzoni, with Stewart third.

Stewart was not behind long and overtook Ickx on the second lap before catching Regazzoni on lap four to take a lead he never surrendered.

The next race of the Championship was at the Nurburgring as the German Grand Prix returned after a year at Hockenheim. In its absence in 1970, Nurburgring officials had taken the opportunity to renovate the circuit, resurfacing the track, adding

Pedro Rodriguez was killed when his Ferrari sports car crashed in an Interserie race at the Norisring.

SHORTS

The 1971 season was dominated by Jackie Stewart. The Tyrrell-Ford driver wrapped the title up early, eventually finishing a commanding 29 points clear of his nearest rival, Ronnie Peterson, thanks to six victories from the scheduled 11 races. The Scot also chalked up six poles and three fastest laps on his way to the second of his three World Championships.

run-off areas and putting in new fencing.

Two driver line-ups changed before the race as Beltoise was suspended again and was not replaced, while Andretti returned for Ferrari.

Stewart secured pole position for the German event and he took his third consecutive win to maintain his stranglehold on the Championship.

As the Championship moved to Austria for the eighth round, Stewart knew that a win or the failure of Ickx to finish the race would secure him the World Championship.

BRM brought in Peter Gethin to replace the late Rodriguez, and Oliver took Gethin's vacated seat at McLaren. And the race also marked the introduction of an unknown Austrian on his home track as Niki Lauda competed in a March factory car. It was the first race of what turned out to be an illustrious career for Lauda.

Finish imperfect

Qualifying produced a scintillating battle between Stewart and Siffert, who took pole from the Championship leader, and Siffert was obviously boosted by the pole position as he held off Stewart at the start of the 54-lap race.

Regazzoni, who had started from fourth on the grid, was the first big-name casualty of the race as he went out on lap eight with engine trouble. Lauda retired on lap 20 with handling problems and as Siffert sped away at the front of the field the most significant action of the race occurred.

Ickx, pushing hard in the knowledge that he needed a win to keep the pressure on Stewart, went out of the race when the ignition went on his car on lap 31– so the Championship went to Stewart.

Stewart was unable to celebrate in the best fashion and made an early exit five laps later after losing a wheel.

That left the way clear for Siffert to take his first win of the season, despite a deflated tyre as Fittipaldi finished second and Schenken third.

Controversy marred the next round of the Championship in Italy as Lotus refused to enter any cars for Fittipaldi and Wisell. The death of their driver Jochen Rindt at Monza a year earlier had left the

1971 CONSTRUCTORS' CUP

TEAM (Engine)	POINTS
TYRRELL FORD	73
BRM	36
FERRARI	33
MARCH FORD	33
LOTUS FORD	21
McLAREN FORD	10
MATRA SIMCA	9
SURTEES FORD	8
BRABHAM FORD	5

Jackie Stewart with the drivers' Championship trophy at the German Grand Prix.

team embroiled in legal problems with the Italian circuit.

On the track McLaren were missing Hulme, who was competing in America, and Beltoise, who was still suspended. Surtees brought in an extra car for Mike Hailwood, who went on to have a race to remember.

Stewart arrived at Monza on the crest of a wave after securing the World Championship, but he was sadly out-powered by his competitors at the twisty circuit.

Amon took pole position for the 55-lap race in his Matra, but neither Stewart, Ickx or Regazzoni were among the five divers that were to battle it out at the finish.

Peter Gethin in a BRM, Ronnie Petersen in a March, Cevert in a Tyrrell, Hailwood in a Surtees and Ganley in a BRM were all separated by just 0.61 seconds. In the end, Gethin took the win after starting from 11th on the grid as he passed the chequered flag just 0.01 seconds ahead of Petersen.

It was the closest finish in the history of Formula One as Cevert finished third, Hailwood fourth in his first race for Surtees and Ganley fifth.

After the extraordinary scenes in Italy the season moved back across the Atlantic for the final two races. The Mosport Park circuit in Canada and the Watkins Glen circuit in the United States hosted the last two races with Stewart already crowned Champion.

In Canada, Stewart added the gloss to a triumphant season as he won his sixth race of the season

Two weeks later, it was the turn of team-mate Cevert to take the chequered flag and win the first World Championship point of his career.

1972
Fittipaldi's Brazilian magic

TALKING POINT

FITTIPALDI BECOMES THE YOUNGEST CHAMPION

The emergence of talented young Brazilian Emerson Fittipaldi had not gone unnoticed in his first two seasons in Formula One with Lotus in 1970 and 1971, but it was 1972 that would be the making of him.

His one race victory in America in 1970 was added with another five race wins as he entered the record-books to become the youngest World Champion. He landed the title after winning in Italy in September.

At just 25 years, eight months and 29 days, Fittipaldi secured a maiden Championship as his rivals failed to match his inspired performances. He dominated proceedings in the aptly-named Lotus 72.

Fittipaldi also made history when he and brother Wilson became the first siblings to compete in the same race when they lined up for the Spanish Grand Prix at Jarama.

Emerson Fittipaldi on the podium after winning the Austrian Grand Prix.

After the death of Jo Siffert at the end of 1971, important changes marked the arrival of the 1972 season. Siffert perished when his car overturned and burst into flames after a high-speed crash in the World Championship victory race at Brands Hatch. BRM swooped to sign Jean-Pierre Beltoise on loan to partner Peter Gethin and Howden Ganley.

More significantly, BRM gained the backing of Marlboro after sponsors Yardley offered their assistance to McLaren, who retained former Champion Denny Hulme and added American driver Peter Revson.

Tyrrell kept their line-up of reigning Champion Jackie Stewart and François Cevert, while Ferrari remained unchanged with Jacky Ickx, Clay Regazzoni and Mario Andretti.

Dave Walker, who replaced Reine Wisell, joined Emerson Fittipaldi at Lotus, who secured a sponsorship deal with John Player Special. There was also a change at Brabham when Bernie Ecclestone bought the team from Ron Tauranac and drafted in rising Argentine talent Carlos Reutemann to partner the experienced Graham Hill.

Austrian Niki Lauda bought a drive with March Engineering through money borrowed from an Austrian bank, while Matra, who loaned Beltoise to BRM, ran just one car. John Surtees allowed Mike Hailwood and Brabham's Tim Schenken to drive the Brooke Bond Oxo cars.

The year also saw the arrival of the Martini-sponsored Tecno team with Derek Bell and Nanni Galli as drivers of the flat 12-engined cars. Former Vanwall manager David Yorke was given the task of bringing the best out of the team. Frank Williams also had plans to enter a car of his own and former Brabham owner Tauranac built him a chassis named Politoys, after the project sponsor.

Ecclestone's decision to hand Reutemann his chance in Formula One prompted enough interest for Argentina to warrant a date on the calendar and the Buenos Aires race opened the World Championship. In a sensational twist, the 29-year-old debutant outpaced World Champion Stewart in qualifying and grabbed pole position for his home event.

Stewart, however, led the race in its

infancy and got the defence of his title off to the best possible start by taking the chequered flag ahead of Denny Hulme and Ickx.

The Formula One circus had a six-week gap before the second round of the Championship at Kyalami in South Africa. Beltoise ran for the first time in a BRM and Williams ran up-and-coming Brazilian Carlos Pace for his debut.

Despite the break in action, Stewart carried on from where he left off in Argentina by powering to pole position, narrowly quicker than Ferrari's Regazzoni and Fittipaldi.

Stewart lost the lead briefly at the start of the race as Hulme emerged the quickest off the grid, but the World Champion managed to build up a significant lead as the battle for second place heated up with Hulme, Fittipaldi and the impressive Hailwood now clear of the remainder of the field.

Hulme dropped back when his car overheated before Hailwood overtook the Brazilian to go in to second. Soon both British drivers were forced to retire, leaving a struggling Fittipaldi to sacrifice the lead, and the win, to the now-recovered Hulme.

Two months later in Spain, Fittipaldi entered the record books when he and sibling Wilson, who replaced Brabham driver Reutemann, became the first brothers to compete in a World Championship event.

Hulme was quickest off the grid ahead of Stewart and Regazzoni, who had started from the third row. But after three laps, Hulme was down to fifth with gearbox problems and Stewart led Ickx and Fittipaldi.

The talented Fittipaldi swept past Ickx and then raced into the lead. Ferrari's Ickx moved ahead of Stewart into second before Hulme retired on lap 48 with engine failure when running in fourth. But 20 laps from the end of the 90-lap race, Stewart made a mistake and spun into the barriers as Regazzoni coasted home behind Fittipaldi and Ickx.

Fittipaldi claimed pole two weeks later in Monaco. The race conditions were treacherous and Beltoise, who began quickest, had a major advantage.

The Frenchman, driving for BRM, opened up a lead and Regazzoni, closest to him, helped him further when he went on to the escape route at the chicane and collected Fittipaldi and Ickx in doing so. All returned to the track but the result was set.

Fittipaldi dominant

Ickx ended second and Fittipaldi third after winning the battle with Stewart and Regazzoni, but the race provided Beltoise with his first, and only, Grand Prix victory.

Formula One returned to Belgium in early June at the newly-built Nivelles circuit near Brussels. Andretti was still absent for Ferrari, but Revson made a return for McLaren and Reutemann was also back in action for Brabham.

Fittipaldi was quickest in qualifying and started ahead of Regazzoni, while Stewart missed the race on advice of doctors because of a stomach ulcer. Regazzoni made the best start and led Fittipaldi and Ickx during the opening stages.

Fittipaldi took the lead on lap nine before a throttle problem ended Ickx's race on lap 26. Tyrrell's François Cevert moved into second ahead of Regazzoni, who later crashed out when he made a mistake as he lapped Galli.

Regazzoni's retirement handed Chris Amon the

RACE BY RACE DETAILS

ROUND 1 – ARGENTINA
Race Jackie Stewart
Pole Carlos Reutemann
Fastest lap Jackie Stewart

ROUND 2 – SOUTH AFRICA
Race Denny Hulme
Pole Jackie Stewart
Fastest lap Mike Hailwood

ROUND 3 – SPAIN
Race Emerson Fittipaldi
Pole Jacky Ickx
Fastest lap Jacky Ickx

ROUND 4 – MONACO
Race Jean-Pierre Beltoise
Pole Emerson Fittipaldi
Fastest lap Jean-Pierre Beltoise

ROUND 5 – BELGIUM
Race Emerson Fittipaldi
Pole Emerson Fittipaldi
Fastest lap Chris Amon

ROUND 6 – FRANCE
Race Jackie Stewart
Pole Chris Amon
Fastest lap Chris Amon

ROUND 7 – BRITAIN
Race Emerson Fittipaldi
Pole Jacky Ickx
Fastest lap Jackie Stewart

ROUND 8 – GERMANY
Race Jacky Ickx
Pole Jacky Ickx
Fastest lap Jacky Ickx

ROUND 9 – AUSTRIA
Race Emerson Fittipaldi
Pole Emerson Fittipaldi
Fastest lap Denny Hulme

ROUND 10 – ITALY
Race Emerson Fittipaldi
Pole Jacky Ickx
Fastest lap Jacky Ickx

ROUND 11 – CANADA
Race Jackie Stewart
Pole Peter Revson
Fastest lap Jackie Stewart

ROUND 12 – UNITED STATES
Race Jackie Stewart
Pole Jackie Stewart
Fastest lap Jackie Stewart

Jackie Stewart (left) and François Cevert enjoy a light moment at the Brazilian Grand Prix.

1972 DRIVERS' CHAMPIONSHIP

DRIVER	TEAM	POINTS
Emerson Fittipaldi	Lotus Ford	61
Jackie Stewart	Tyrrell Ford	45
Denny Hulme	McLaren Ford	39
Jacky Ickx	Ferrari	27
Peter Revson	McLaren Ford	23
François Cevert	Tyrrell Ford	15
Clay Regazzoni	Ferrari	15
Mike Hailwood	Surtees Ford	13
Chris Amon	Matra Ford	12
Ronnie Peterson	March Ford	12
Jean-Pierre Beltoise	BRM	9
Mario Andretti	Ferrari	4
Brian Redman	McLaren Ford/BRM	4
Graham Hill	Brabham Ford	4
Howard Ganley	BRM	4
Andrea de Adamich	Surtees Ford	3
Carlos Reutemann	Brabham Ford	3
Carlos Pace	March Ford	3
Tim Schenken	Surtees Ford	2
Peter Gethin	BRM	1
Arturo Merzario	Ferrari	1

chance of a place on the podium, but the New Zealander had to pit for fuel after a leak and he ended sixth. Hulme recovered to take third as Fittipaldi and Cevert dominated the race.

The cancellation of the Dutch Grand Prix because of safety concerns left a one-month gap between the Belgian event and the French Grand Prix at Clermont-Ferrand.

Amon qualified on pole in the new version of the Matra and he led the race from the outset. Helmut Marko of BRM exited the last race of his career in bizarre circumstances when on lap nine he was hit in the left eye by a stone thrown up by Fittipaldi's Lotus. He lost the sight in the eye and never raced again.

Ferrari's long wait ends

Stewart moved up to second when he overtook Hulme on lap 17 and then inherited the lead when flying stones punctured one of Amon's tyres. When Hulme pitted for a routine tyre change, Ickx was second, but he had to pit and it was Fittipaldi who trailed Stewart home.

Ferrari's wait for a race victory was seemingly set to end when Ickx dominated the British Grand Prix at Brands Hatch, but after luck deserted the Belgian driver it was Fittipaldi who claimed the win and stamped his authority on the Championship battle.

Fittipaldi's victory handed him a 16-point lead over Stewart in the Championship standings, but Ickx upset the formbook in the German Grand Prix and Ferrari finally came home in first place. Once again, Ickx qualified quickest and led the race during its infancy. His case received a major boost after a collision between Stewart and Ronnie Peterson's March. Peterson spun on lap nine and ended behind Stewart as Fittipaldi moved up to challenge Ickx. But two laps later Fittipaldi retired and Regazzoni was now in second and remained there to secure a one-two for Ferrari.

Two weeks later, an unchanged field competed in the Austrian Grand Prix at the Osterreichring and Fittipaldi made up for his disappointment in the German race by landing pole position. But it was Stewart starting on the second row who raced into the lead and opened up an advantage as second-placed Regazzoni held up Fittipaldi for four laps suffering with fuel-feed problems. Regazzoni eventually pitted and Fittipaldi soon closed the gap on Stewart.

On lap 24, Fittipaldi moved into the lead and three laps later Stewart lost a further place when Hulme overtook him for second. Stewart lost more places to Peterson and Revson as Fittipaldi held off the challenge of Hulme by just one second to open up a 25-point lead in the Championship.

With two Grands Prix remaining, a win in the tenth round of the series in Italy sealed the Championship for Fittipaldi in just his third season in Formula One. On this occasion, however, it was luck rather than judgement that landed victory for the Brazilian.

SHORTS

BRM's partnership with Marlboro wasn't the only interesting team news in 1972. The year also brought the arrival of the Martini-sponsored Tecno team with Derek Bell and Nanni Galli named as the drivers. Former Vanwall manager David Yorke was given the task of bringing the best out of the team. Frank Williams also had plans to enter a car of his own and former Brabham owner Tauranac built him a chassis named Politoys, after the sponsor behind the project.

Emerson Fittipaldi finds himself in a familiar position – out in the lead with his Lotus Ford.

Jackie Stewart lost his world Championship crown to Emerson Fittipaldi in 1971.

Fittipaldi benefited from the exit of Stewart at the start of the race as well as Regazzoni, who retired with rear suspension damage after he ran into backmarker Carlos Pace. Amon and Ickx also dropped out to hand Fittipadli the Monza race. In doing so, he booked a place in the sports record books as the youngest World Champion.

Anti-climax in the United States

Monza had featured key safety changes with two new chicanes in a bid to reduce speeds and break up the traditional slipstreaming at the circuit. The first chicane was put just before the pit-lane while the second was implemented on the back straight. Emphasis on slipstreaming was almost a thing of the past for drivers at Monza with braking the biggest challenge.

The penultimate round of the Championship, the Canadian Grand Prix, remained at Mosport Park for a second year after Mont-Tremblant, which had been scheduled to host the event, was closed down because of disputes with the local racing authorities.

Lotus opted to replace Dave Walker with Reine Wisell, while the latter's drive with BRM went to local driver Bill Brack. It was McLaren's Revson and Hulme who dominated qualifying and monopolized the front row of the grid.

Peterson, who started from third, made an immediate impact on the field but lost his lead on lap four when he made a mistake and allowed Stewart to move ahead. Peterson remained second until lap 54 when he collided with Graham Hill, who he was attempting to lap, and suffered a bent steering arm. His car came to a stop close to the pit lane and the Swedish driver pushed it in to the garages and then rejoined the race only to be disqualified. A collision for Fittipaldi ruled him out of the chase to catch runaway leader Stewart as Revson and Hulme won the battle for a place on the podium alongside the Tyrrell driver.

The final race of the season once again proved to be an anti-climax as Fittipaldi had already wrapped-up the title. It was held at Watkins Glen and boasted a field of 31 cars. Significantly, it signalled the arrival of future World Champion Jody Scheckter in a third McLaren, while Tyrrell ran a third car for Patrick Depailler.

Qualifying for the race ended with the same result that had finished the Canadian Grand Prix with Stewart, Revson and Hulme leading the field. South African Scheckter made an immediate impact as he rolled onto the third row of the grid. Matra's Amon suffered problems on Sunday morning and started the race from the back.

Fittipaldi leaves his mark

Regazzoni ran into Reutemann and Revson as the trio vied for position at the start of the race and Stewart eased ahead of Hulme with Fittipaldi and a fast-starting Scheckter the key chasers. By lap five, Reutemann, Revson and Fittipaldi had all pitted for repairs on their cars.

Cevert charged through the field to hand Tyrrell a one-two as Hulme finished third, but Scheckter was denied a points finish on his Formula One debut when he spun in the rain and dropped down to ninth, one lap down on winner Stewart.

Regardless of Stewart's victories in the final two races of the season, the emerging Fittipaldi had left his mark on the sport. He dominated throughout the middle section of the season as his more illustrious team-mates failed to match his raw talent to lift a maiden title and become the youngest driver to win the coveted world crown.

1972 CONSTRUCTORS' CUP

TEAM (Engine)	POINTS
LOTUS FORD	61
TYRRELL FORD	51
McLAREN FORD	47
FERRARI	33
SURTEES FORD	18
MARCH FORD	15
BRM	14
MATRA FORD	12
BRABHAM FORD	7

Niki Lauda

HE CAME BACK FROM THE DEAD to secure three World Championships. Niki Lauda's guile, self-confidence and pathological decisiveness meant he could never be underestimated.

CAREER DETAILS

1949	Born 22 February
1964	Buys his first VW Cabriolet. Completes apprenticeship as mechanic while studying for A-levels
1968	First race with Mini Cooper S, 2nd place
1971	First F1 season with March Ford
1974	Signs with Ferrari
1975	F1 World Champion in Ferrari
1976	Serious accident at Nurburgring on 1 August. Returns to cockpit 30 days later
1977	F1 World Champion for second time in Ferrari
1979	Founds Lauda Air. Retires from F1
1979-82	Expansion of Lauda Air fails due to monopoly of national carrier Austrian Airlines.
1982	Returns to F1 with McLaren
1984	F1 World Champion for third time in McLaren
1985	Retires from racing
1992-97	Consultant to Ferrari
2001	Consultant to Jaguar

FORMULA ONE RECORD

Year	Team	Wins	Poles	Fast laps	Pts
1971	March	0	0	0	0
1972	March	0	0	0	0
1973	BRM	0	0	0	2
1974	Ferrari	2	9	4	38
1975	Ferrari	5	9	2	64
1976	Ferrari	5	3	4	68
1977	Ferrari	3	2	3	72
1978	Brabham	2	1	4	44
1979	Brabham	0	0	0	4
1982	McLaren	2	0	1	30
1983	McLaren	0	0	1	12
1984	McLaren	5	0	5	72
1985	McLaren	1	0	1	14

Niki Lauda's success has been ascribed to the sort of self-confidence usually reserved for megalomaniacs, minus the psychosis. Seldom faster than the best of his rivals, he avoided risks he considered unnecessary. His mental approach – to everything – was unsparingly straight: "After the accident I am looking worse than some people are born – but at least I can say it was an accident," was his view on his facial disfigurement.

Lauda was the antithesis of the *tifosi* persona at Ferrari, but never captured hearts the way Gilles Villeneuve did. Critics say he had superior machinery, yet he had talented team-mates whom he outshone in the same cars. The buck-toothed Austrian became a *bona fide* legend in his own style.

Lauda was born into a family of wealthy Viennese industrialists. From an early age it was clear he was going to challenge his family's expectations. He showed an instinctive interest in motor mechanics. As a boy, visiting relatives let him park their cars. In his teens he bought a 1949 Volkswagen Beetle convertible and charged around a relative's estate.

In 1968 Lauda entered his first race, a hill climb, in a Cooper and finished second. Despite his father's resistance, he competed in hill climbs and later Formula Vee. He did his stint hauling a Formula Three car on a trailer around Europe. In 1971 he abandoned that, having managed to secure a loan to buy a season at March partnering Ronnie Peterson. He finished 10th and made an inauspicious Formula One debut in the Austrian Grand Prix. In 1972 he took out a further loan to continue at March. He won the British John Player Formula Two title, but failed to impress in Europe.

Niki Lauda, pictured in 1974, collects the plaudits on the podium.

Niki Lauda prepares for the British Grand Prix in 1978.

"He had no right to be driving there because he was nowhere near healed. It was the most courageous thing I have ever witnessed in sport."

Jackie Stewart on Lauda's come-back at Monza in 1976

Despite running up debts that would have disgraced a banana republic, he persuaded Louis Stanley at BRM to sell him a seat. His abilities were at last noticed. He got the call from Ferrari just before his finances collapsed.

In 1974, Lauda finished fourth in the Championship. The next season Lauda described as the "unbelievable year" as he took the 1975 Championship in a car technically superior to any of the competition. His maiden Formula One victory was at Monaco and he finished with five Grand Prix wins.

Lauda is known most for the Championship he did not win following severe injuries suffered in the 1976 German Grand Prix at the Nurburgring. His Ferrari swerved off, hit an embankment, bounced back across the track, was collected by Brett Lunger and burst into flames. Several drivers including Lunger, Guy Edwards and a fearless Arturo Merzario managed to drag him clear. Toxic gases damaged his lungs; he had severe burns and lapsed into a coma.

Miraculously he rallied. In a show of courage that is difficult to overstate, Lauda was back in a Ferrari cockpit 30 days after being read the last rites. He later said of his comeback: "At Monza I was rigid with fear. Terrified. Diarrhoea. Heart pounding. Throwing up."

His absence had seen James Hunt close up. Lauda's return produced an amazing fourth place and three points. Hunt scored wins in both North American races which pulled him to within three points of Lauda with only Fuji left on the calendar.

The race started in a torrential downpour. After two laps Lauda pulled up, saying it was crazy to drive in such conditions. The rain soon slackened, and Hunt finished third, collecting four points to take the title.

In 1977 Lauda cruised to his second Championship but abruptly walked out on Ferrari in Canada and took up with Bernie Ecclestone and Gordon Murray at Brabham. It was not the success that might have been expected from the trio. The Alfa 12-cylinder was not up to the task while Ecclestone was busy running the business end of Formula One.

In Canada in 1979, exactly two years after abandoning Ferrari, Lauda decided in the middle of practice that he wanted to retire there and then.

"I no longer want to drive racing cars round and round in circles," he said succinctly.

For two seasons he devoted himself to his airline business but returned to racing in 1982 for financial reasons, signing with McLaren to partner John Watson.

Lauda's comeback became tangled up in the FISA–FOCA war about superlicences, a dispute eventually settled in the drivers' favour. It did not take long for Lauda to reacquaint himself with winning again. At Long Beach he won in only his third race back and also triumphed at Brands Hatch. While 1983 was a no-win year as the TAG Turbo was shaken down, 1984 ended with Lauda back at the pinnacle of his sport. He won the Championship by a mere half-point but had the measure of his faster rival and new team-mate, Alain Prost.

Lauda did not hang around. His second and final departure from Formula One, at Adelaide in 1985, was typically announced with scarcely a glance over the shoulder – so many of his actions were clinically precipitous.

1973
Stewart claims hat-trick of titles

Emerson Fittipaldi flies the flag for Brazil after his victory at Interlagos.

TALKING POINT

HAILWOOD HAILED AS HERO

Mike Hailwood emerged as a hero in the South African Grand Prix, but ultimately it was not for victory, nor for a Championship success. The British driver was at the centre of a huge crash on lap three of the race when local competitor Dave Charlton crashed and caused a major accident as Clay Regazzoni's BRM hit Hailwood's Surtees. The Swiss driver's car immediately burst into flames, but Hailwood dragged an unconscious Regazzoni out of the cockpit and was awarded the George Medal for his bravery. Regazzoni, for the record, escaped with minor burns while Charlton and Jacky Ickx, who was also involved in the collision, were unhurt.

After Emerson Fittipaldi's first Championship success in Formula One, Lotus' notion of dominance of the sport failed to materialize despite the capture of the talented Ronnie Peterson from March.

That ideal dominance was destroyed as Tyrrell's Jackie Stewart landed his third world title. It would be the British driver's last year in Formula One, but the season would prove that Chapman's decision to run two "top" drivers hampered his team's chances.

Stewart remained in an unchanged Tyrrell line-up with François Cevert as his team-mate, but Peterson's switch to Lotus was one of a number of changes. Graham Hill was dropped by Brabham boss Bernie Ecclestone and the former World Champion promptly set up his own team, Embassy Racing. Clay Regazzoni moved to BRM and Ferrari opted for Arturo Merzario as his replacement.

Niki Lauda joined Jean-Pierre Beltoise and Regazzoni at BRM, while March ran one factory car for youngster Jean-Pierre Jarier. Howard Ganley left BRM in favour of Williams, and Tecno's Nanni Galli joined him at the Marlboro-backed team. Chris Amon was left with Tecno as his only choice after Matra's decision to withdraw from the sport.

The season saw the arrival of two new teams. American outfit Shadow joined the grid with Jackie Oliver and US veteran George Follmer behind the wheel of the all-black challenger and Mo Nunn created the first Ensign Formula One car for Rikki von Opel. Briton Hill struck a deal with Shadow to run a car in his Embassy colours.

In the opening race in Argentina, Cevert avoided a collision to lead at the first corner but Regazzoni, on his first outing in the BRM, moved ahead on the second lap of the race. It was not until lap 29 that Frenchman Cevert moved back in front as Regazzoni pitted for a tyre change. Behind the leader Stewart, Fittipaldi and Peterson battled before the latter pitted with an engine problem.

Stewart dropped behind Fittipaldi and the Brazilian Champion took the lead 10 laps from home to begin the defence of his title in perfect fashion.

Fittipaldi's title success in 1972 had sparked calls for a Championship race for Brazil – the country had hosted a non-Championship race during Fittipaldi's victorious year – and Interlagos was chosen to hold the event.

It was, however, Peterson who landed pole position. Fittipaldi, the race favourite, swiftly moved into the lead at the start and Pace, another Brazilian, made an immediate impact from the third row of the grid to move up to second.

On lap six, pole-sitter Peterson crashed heavily and Pace soon joined him on the retirement list. Fittipaldi secured his second win of the season ahead of Stewart, with Denny Hulme claiming third.

The third round of the Championship was held in South Africa in early March and the Kyalami race was significant for the Shadow team, who began their first Grand Prix.

Hulme demonstrated the potential of the new McLaren M23 in qualifying as he outpaced the in-form Fittipaldi, while Jody Scheckter underlined his own ability as he joined the duo on the front row.

But on lap three a horrifying incident left its mark on the large crowd in South Africa. Local competitor Dave Charlton challenged Carlos Reutemann but lost control of his Lucky Strike Lotus and crashed into Mike Hailwood's Surtees. Regazzoni then ran into Hailwood and his BRM burst into flames with the Swiss driver unconscious inside. Without hesitation, Hailwood exited his car and pulled Regazzoni clear of the inferno. Hailwood was later awarded the George Medal for his bravery while Regazzoni suffered no more than minor burns.

Hulme's hopes of a dream debut in the new McLaren were destroyed when he suffered a puncture. Stewart took the lead from Scheckter on lap seven and he remained at the head of the field for the remainder of the 79-lap race.

Scheckter, who had lost places to Revson and Fittipaldi because of a tyre change, was denied a memorable fourth-place finish in front of his home fans when his engine blew three laps from the end.

Seven weeks later in Spain, Fittipaldi's impressive start to the season continued. Cevert ended second with Shadow driver Follmer, in only his second Grand Prix, in third.

The Belgian event was hit with problems before the race got underway as the Grand Prix Drivers' Association threatened to cancel the race after the track at Zolder, which had been resurfaced late because of a dispute, broke up following testing. The row between the organizers and the teams ran into the Saturday but, when it became evident the asphalt was good enough to race, qualifying burst into life with Peterson on pole.

After stretching out an early lead over Peterson, Cevert spun off and handed the advantage to Fittipaldi. Five laps later Stewart emerged in front as fuel pressure problems hampered the Brazilian. Cevert recovered and passed Fittipaldi, who struggled home for third, to give Tyrrell a one-two.

Stewart went on to get his third win of the season in Monaco as a straight battle with Fittipaldi gathered pace.

Hulme excels in Sweden

Sweden hosted a round of the Championship for the first time in mid June after Peterson's elevation to Lotus prompted its inclusion. The Scandinavian Raceway in Anderstorp hosted the race and home driver Peterson handed the crowd what they wanted when he put his car on pole position.

Hulme, however, produced the drive of his life in the new M23 to land a long-awaited victory. He overtook Fittipaldi, who suffered gearbox failure, and then went into second when Stewart retired with rear brake failure with three laps remaining, and then saved his best moment for the penultimate lap when he denied Peterson a win in his homeland.

The French Grand Prix at the Circuit Paul Ricard followed and the field was increased in number as Ferrari brought a second car back for Merzario.

James Hunt makes his debut in Monaco on 31 May 1973.

RACE BY RACE DETAILS

ROUND 1 – ARGENTINA
Race Emerson Fittipaldi
Pole Clay Regazzoni
Fastest lap Emerson Fittipaldi

ROUND 2 – BRAZIL
Race Emerson Fittipaldi
Pole Ronnie Peterson
Fastest lap Emerson Fittipaldi

ROUND 3 – SOUTH AFRICA
Race Jackie Stewart
Pole Denny Hulme
Fastest lap Emerson Fittipaldi

ROUND 4 – SPAIN
Race Emerson Fittipaldi
Pole Ronnie Peterson
Fastest lap Ronnie Peterson

ROUND 5 – BELGIUM
Race Jackie Stewart
Pole Ronnie Peterson
Fastest lap François Cevert

ROUND 6 – MONACO
Race Jackie Stewart
Pole Jackie Stewart
Fastest lap Emerson Fittipaldi

ROUND 7 – SWEDEN
Race Denny Hulme
Pole Ronnie Peterson
Fastest lap Denny Hulme

ROUND 8 – FRANCE
Race Ronnie Peterson
Pole Jackie Stewart
Fastest lap Denny Hulme

ROUND 9 – BRITAIN
Race Peter Revson
Pole Ronnie Peterson
Fastest lap James Hunt

ROUND 10 – HOLLAND
Race Jackie Stewart
Pole Ronnie Peterson
Fastest lap Ronnie Peterson

ROUND 11 – GERMANY
Race Jackie Stewart
Pole Jackie Stewart
Fastest lap Carlos Pace

ROUND 12 – AUSTRIA
Race Ronnie Peterson
Pole Emerson Fittipaldi
Fastest lap Carlos Pace

ROUND 13 – ITALY
Race Ronnie Peterson
Pole Ronnie Peterson
Fastest lap Jackie Stewart

ROUND 14 – CANADA
Race Peter Revson
Pole Ronnie Peterson
Fastest lap Emerson Fittipaldi

ROUND 15 – UNITED STATES
Race Ronnie Peterson
Pole Ronnie Peterson
Fastest lap James Hunt

1973 DRIVERS' CHAMPIONSHIP

DRIVER	TEAM	POINTS
Jackie Stewart	Tyrrell Ford	71
Emerson Fittipaldi	Lotus Ford	55
Ronnie Peterson	Lotus Ford	52
François Cevert	Tyrrell Ford	47
Peter Revson	McLaren Ford	38
Denny Hulme	McLaren Ford	26
Carlos Reutemann	Brabham Ford	16
James Hunt	March Ford	14
Jacky Ickx	Ferrari	12
Jean-Pierre Beltoise	BRM	9
Carlos Pace	Surtees Ford	7
Arturo Merzario	Ferrari	6
George Follmer	Shadow Ford	5
Jackie Oliver	Shadow Ford	4
Andrea de Adamich	Surtees Ford/Brabham Ford	3
Wilson Fittipaldi	Brabham Ford	3
Clay Regazzoni	BRM	2
Niki Lauda	BRM	2
Chris Amon	Tecno/Tyrrell Ford	1
Gijs van Lennep	ISO Ford	1
Howden Ganley	ISO Ford	1

Jody Scheckter spins on the first lap of the British Grand Prix and causes an eight-car crash.

Scheckter, who had qualified second behind Stewart, burst into the lead ahead of Peterson. Stewart, who was third, disappeared from the picture with a tyre problem and Peterson promptly waved team-mate Fittipaldi through to challenge Scheckter.

South African Scheckter refused to allow the World Champion through and the two collided on lap 42, and both had to retire as Peterson went on to claim his first Grand Prix victory. Stewart recovered and finished fourth which gave him the lead in the Championship.

New faces at Brands Hatch

Several new drivers made their debuts in the British Grand Prix with Roger Williamson joining March in place of the disillusioned Jean-Pierre Jarier and John Watson making his debut with Brabham. Williams handed a second car to New Zealander Graham McRae.

At the end of the first lap, Scheckter caused a major accident when his McLaren spun across the gravel and into the pitwall before coming to rest in the middle of the circuit. Eight cars arrived at the scene and collided.

SHORTS

The 1973 season brought about the arrival of two new Formula one teams. American outfit Shadow joined the grid with Jackie Oliver and US veteran George Follmer behind the wheel of the all-black challenger and Mo Nunn created the first Ensign Formula One car for Rikki von Opel. Briton Graham Hill struck a deal with Shadow to run a car in his Embassy colours.

Brabham's Andrea da Adamich suffered a broken ankle. Race officials took 30 minutes to free Da Adamich from his wreckage and more than one hour to restart the race.

Once underway, it was a direct fight between Peterson and McLaren's Peter Revson. The American took the lead on lap 39 and that landed the win – his first Grand Prix.

Tragedy marred the Dutch Grand Prix at Zandvoort in late July when Roger Williamson was killed. His car overturned and burst into flames by the side of the track. David Purley tried to rescue him from the wreckage but his efforts were in vain.

Peterson led from the off, but dropped to third nine laps from the end after suffering gearbox problems as Tyrrell secured a one-two with Stewart leading Cevert home.

With only a week separating the Dutch and the German Grands Prix, a number of teams decided to miss the Nurburgring event. March withdrew following Williamson's death while Ferrari, Ensign, Tecno and Hesketh did not compete.

Ferrari allowed Ickx to drive a McLaren while Fittipaldi, still troubled by an ankle injury suffered in practice at Zandvoort, could only qualify in 14th. Stewart eased to the chequered flag ahead of Cevert to land his 27th career victory as the Frenchman moved ahead of Fittipaldi into second in the Championship standings.

Ferrari returned to action in Austria, but Ickx did not compete and Merzario ran in the team's only entry. Lauda was another non-starter after he had broken his wrist in Germany, while Ensign and Tecno were back in action with modifications to their cars.

Peterson was again the quicker starter but Revson's McLaren failed to get off the grid and a collision with Mike Beuttler caused the March to spill oil onto the track. Fittipaldi moved up to second and his team-mate waved him into the lead in an attempt to close the gap on Stewart in the Championship.

He remained in front until lap 49 when his fuel pipe split and Stewart gained second behind Peterson. The Tyrrell driver's second place opened his lead in the series to 24 points with only three races remaining.

Ickx returned to Ferrari on a temporary contract and Lauda was sufficiently recovered from his broken wrist to return for BRM. Peterson, on pole yet again, raced into the lead ahead of Fittipaldi and Revson in third following pit-stops for Merzario, Stewart and Hulme.

The top three remained unchanged as Stewart produced an impressive drive to finish fourth. The points were enough to guarantee him a third world title as Peterson won to give Lotus their first one-two result for five years.

Lotus take on Tyrrell

In the penultimate race of the season in Canada, the focus of attention turned from the drivers' Championship to the manufacturers' crown, which was finely balanced between Lotus and Tyrrell. Chris Amon drove a third Tyrrell, Ickx had once again left Ferrari and McLaren's Scheckter appeared for the first time since causing the multiple pile-up at Silverstone.

In an almost expected move, Peterson led from pole but Lauda moved into the lead on lap three. Peterson crashed out on lap 17 as Fittipaldi moved up to second before taking the lead when Lauda pitted for a tyre change.

Confusion was caused when the safety car came out following a collision between Cevert and Scheckter. The leader was not the man behind the pace car and back-markers gained almost a lap as Shadow's Oliver was classified as being in front of Revson.

Revson, in the competitive McLaren, moved into the lead and coasted home as Fittipaldi charged through the field to grab second. The confusion over the result continued after the race but Revson was confirmed as the winner thanks to a stroke of luck.

The final race of the season in New York would be Stewart's 100th and last Grand Prix, but he did not go out in winning fashion. Having already been crowned Champion, the main focus of attention was on Stewart's team-mate Cevert's battle with Fittipaldi for second place in the overall standings.

Peterson topped the times on Friday despite a heavy accident, but on Saturday Cevert was killed after a high-speed crash into the Watkins Glen barriers. Tyrrell withdrew – giving up the chance of winning the manufacturers' title.

The race was an anti-climax as Peterson and Hunt in the Hesketh challenged for the win. Eventually, the Swedish Lotus driver won by six-tenths of a second as he denied Hunt a maiden Grand Prix victory.

The season belonged to Stewart for a remarkable drive with an underpowered car as he dominated the quick but unreliable Lotus. The Scot bowed out in style with a third Championship, but he was denied the chance to end with a win following the death of his team-mate Cevert.

1973 CONSTRUCTORS' CUP

TEAM (Engine)	POINTS
LOTUS FORD	92
TYRRELL FORD	82
McLAREN FORD	58
BRABHAM FORD	22
MARCH FORD	14
BRM	12
FERRARI	12
SHADOW FORD	9
SURTEES FORD	7
ISO FORD	2
TECNO	1

The pace car causes confusion during the Canadian Grand Prix.

James Hunt

WITH HIS transformation from "Hunt the Shunt" to playboy World Champion to acerbic TV commentator, James Hunt was – and remains posthumously – the personification of F1 charisma.

CAREER DETAILS

1947	Born 29 August, Belmont, Surrey
1972	F2 with Hesketh
1973	Finishes eighth in World Championship; March
1974	March (Argentina and Brazil GPs only); then Hesketh, again finishes eighth
1975	Finishes fourth with Hesketh
1976	World Champion with McLaren
1977	Finishes fifth with McLaren
1978	Finishes 13th with McLaren
1979	Signs for Wolf. No Championship points
1993	Dies 15 June, Wimbledon

FORMULA ONE RECORD

Year	Team	Wins	Poles	Fast laps	Pts
1973	March	0	0	2	14
1974	March	0	0	0	15
1974	Hesketh	0	0	0	–
1975	Hesketh	1	0	1	33
1976	McLaren	6	8	2	69
1977	McLaren	3	6	3	40
1978	Wolf	0	0	0	8

James Hunt liked to live life in the fast lane but also had a serious side.

James Hunt had a tempestuous talent, backed up by maverick charm, dry wit and a lovable casualness. He partied as hard as he drove, but also had a serious side which left him ambivalent about the fame which followed his title victory in 1976.

"Image-making is a risk," he said. "I've questioned myself about it and I've tried to be an ostrich and ignore other people's glamorous, distorted view of me as much as I can. Limelight's a danger and so is wealth. It's like giving a dog a big juicy bone. When he didn't have one he could live without it, but once he's tasted one, he hangs on like grim death."

Hunt's background was middle class. His father was a London stockbroker who gave his son a public-school education – Cheam and Wellington. Hunt played at Junior Wimbledon and considered medicine as a career.

"The one thing that never entered my head was

becoming a racing driver," he later recalled. "Then, exactly on my 18th birthday, a friend took me to Silverstone. I went back to my parents that night and announced that all their anxieties about my fecklessness were over. I was going to become a World Champion driver. Not just any old driver but World Champion."

Having cut his teeth in Formula Ford 1600 in the late 1960s, he moved into Formula Three and earned the soubriquet "Hunt the Shunt". Lord Hesketh lifted him into Formula Two at the wheel of a second-hand March 712M and then plunged him into Formula One.

Hunt said: "His attitude was that we were doing pretty badly in Formula Two and for very little additional cost we could do badly in Formula One."

His first outing in a Grand Prix car had come at the Brands Hatch Race of Champions where he finished third in a rented Surtees TS9B. The team then switched to a March 731 and he made his Championship debut at Monaco. Engine trouble prevented a points finish.

But he was soon on a roll and in 1973, he finished fourth in the British Grand Prix, third at Zandvoort and second in the United States.

Hunt won his first Grand Prix the following year in Holland. By the end of 1975, however, the cost of running a Formula One team had become prohibitive and Hesketh withdrew.

Hunt was unemployed, but within weeks he was signed up to drive for McLaren along with Jochen Mass following, Emerson Fittipaldi's departure to Copersucar. He went on to win the Spanish Grand Prix but only after appealing against disqualification.

His battle with arch-rival and close friend Niki Lauda proved the core of the season's competition. Hunt's Championship chances were enhanced when Lauda was badly burned in an accident at the Nurburgring, but within six weeks the Austrian had forced himself back to resume battle.

Hunt had to overcome a deficit of 17 points in the last three races if he was going to overhaul Lauda. He won both North American races and when Lauda pulled out of the rain-washed Japanese Grand Prix at Fuji, Hunt clinched the title with his third-place finish.

In 1977 the competitive punch of the McLaren M23 was undermined by the new generation of Lotus ground-effect machines. Despite three race victories he finished fifth in the World Championship and then slumped to a lowly thirteenth place the following season.

Seeking rejuvenation, he switched to the Wolf team for 1979, but felt ground-effect chassis technology reduced the driver's contribution to the point where he was no longer interested. He quit after the Monaco Grand Prix.

In retirement Hunt busied himself with various business ventures and shared the BBC commentary booth with Murray Walker. The motor racing community was shocked when he died at his Wimbledon home of a heart-attack aged just 45.

"I can talk to James about women and backgammon, tennis, taxes, Spain, food, childhood, but I can't get him to talk to me about cars."

Teddy Mayer, McLaren boss, 1978

1974
Consistency is key for Fittipaldi

Carlos Reutemann celebrates on the podium following his victory in the South African Grand Prix.

TALKING POINT

CONSISTENCY AND RELIABILITY WINS

Emerson Fittipaldi won just two races on his way to the Championship in 1974, and was certainly not used to running up at the front. He scored points in all but five of the races, and took seven podium finishes. However, the Brazilian led just 77 of the 979 laps in the season to become only the sixth most regular leader of the year. That accolade went to Niki Lauda, who led over one-third of the laps but was let down by the reliability of his Ferrari and only finished in the points six times. Peterson won the most races, but his inability to pick up regular points saw him end down in fifth place to prove that reliability is king.

The Formula One Championship faced cancellation as the global fuel crisis took hold, but after getting the go-ahead, it proved to be a thriller.

There were seven different race winners and the Championship was taken down to the wire with three drivers still in with a chance at the final race. Eventually it was Emerson Fittipaldi who took his second World Championship with a consistent performance that saw him finish in the points in all but five of the 15 races.

With reigning World Champion Jackie Stewart retiring at the end of the previous season, it was all shuffle within the teams when they arrived in Buenos Aires for the Argentinian Grand Prix.

Stewart's former team, Tyrrell, had a completely new driver line-up with the arrival of Patrick Depailler and young South African Jody Scheckter. But it was McLaren's Denny Hulme who went on to win the season-opener and take the upper hand in a battle with Ferrari.

Fittipaldi dominated the weekend when the teams moved up the South American continent to Brazil and the Interlagos circuit for round two. It took a bit of luck but as the leaders faded, Fittipaldi made up for a poor start to claim the victory.

Two months separated the Brazilian race from the season's next event in Kyalami, but once again tragedy was to strike Formula One. Peter Revson was killed in a head-on crash with the barriers after his Shadow suffered a suspension failure. His death played heavily on the drivers' minds during the race weekend, but the event went ahead and Reutemann became the third different winner in three races.

When the Grand Prix circus arrived in Spain a month later, Shadow were back in action after the loss of Revson and there were plenty of new cars on the grid. But nothing could stop the might of Ferrari with Lauda and Regazzoni taking a one-two finish after qualifying first and third.

The wet conditions slowed the cars significantly and the race was ended when it reached its time limit of two hours. Fittipaldi claimed third when he passed Hans Stuck, but the race was remembered for Ferrari's dominance and Lauda's first Grand Prix win.

Round five saw Fittipaldi lead more than half the laps at the Belgian track of Nivelles as he went on to finish first ahead of Ferrari's Lauda to take his second victory of the season.

Ferrari scored an all-red front row for the sixth

round of the Championship in the glamorous setting of Monte Carlo, but a mistake from Regazzoni and ignition problems for Lauda allowed Peterson through to take the victory for Lotus as just nine cars made it to the end.

The Ferraris got off to a good start and moved into an unchallenged lead. Jean-Pierre Jarier was the closest runner, and behind him Hulme and Jean-Pierre Beltoise crashed causing a melée of mangled cars including Merzario, Carlos Pace, Brian Redman, Vittorio Brambilla, Vern Schuppan and Tim Schencken.

The field was a bare skeleton of the starting 25 with just 12 laps gone, but the action continued as leader Regazzoni spun out of the lead. Peterson was on a charge and overtook Jarier before setting off in chase of Lauda.

But there was no need for the chase as Lauda retired and Peterson went on to win from South African Scheckter.

Two weeks after the Monaco Grand Prix, the field moved to Sweden and it was Tyrrell who had the upper hand, taking a one-two in qualifying to set up a similar result in the race.

With 14 laps left, Hunt found himself behind the Tyrells of Scheckter and Depailler in third. He closed to within three seconds of the pair, who were nose-to-tail at the front, but he could not pass and the race was Scheckter's – his first Grand Prix victory.

Championship still open

Formula One entered the following race, the Dutch Grand Prix, in one of the most unpredictable states since the World Championship had begun. There had been six different winners in the past seven races and the Championship was still wide open.

For the second successive race it was the top two on the grid that went on to take victory in the race with Lauda heading a one-two victory for Ferrari to score his second win of the season.

The Surrey-based Trojan team caused some controversy before the event when they protested their third exclusion in three races. They were allowed in, but failed to qualify.

Next up was the French race in Dijon-Prenois, and this time it was Peterson's turn to take a second victory of the season – although it was Lauda who would take the lead in the Championship standings with second place in the race.

Peterson lined up alongside pole man Lauda on the grid and the latter assumed the lead on lap 17. He quickly pulled away from Lauda's Ferrari, which had been holding him up after developing a vibration problem, and Fittipaldi was looking good to challenge for the lead before retiring with engine failure.

Scheckter closed on Regazzoni towards the end, but the South African could not take the final spot

Jody Scheckter leads Patrick Depailler at the Swedish Grand Prix on 30 March 1974.

on the podium and the pair were too far away from Peterson and Lauda to challenge for the lead.

The next Grand Prix in Britain saw a field of 34 cars fighting for 25 places, and among the most notable of the non-qualifiers was Italian female driver Lella Lombardi, brought in by Bernie Ecclestone's Brabham team.

Lauda took his third pole in a row and had Peterson alongside him on the same qualifying time. Other Championship challengers Fittipaldi and Regazzoni were on row four, but it was Scheckter who eventually took the victory from third on the grid.

Lauda led off the line and stayed there for 69 laps. Reutemann spun and Peterson and Regazzoni both fell by the wayside with punctures to leave Scheckter and Lauda clear in front.

But Lauda was also hit with a puncture and before he could make it to the pits his tyre disintegrated to allow Fittipaldi through into second and Ickx third, with Scheckter a clear 15 seconds ahead.

There was another large entry list for the German Grand Prix two weeks later. Amid crashes and controversy, it was Regazzoni who took a start-to-flag victory in the 14-lap race around the massive 14-mile Nurburgring circuit.

Regazzoni's team-mate Lauda was on pole again but made a terrible start and his race ended when he tried to climb back up the field and spun into retirement after touching Scheckter. There was another

RACE BY RACE DETAILS

ROUND 1 – ARGENTINA
Race Denny Hulme
Pole Ronnie Peterson
Fastest lap Clay Regazzoni

ROUND 2 – BRAZIL
Race Emerson Fittipaldi
Pole Emerson Fittipaldi
Fastest lap Clay Regazzoni

ROUND 3 – SOUTH AFRICA
Race Carlos Reutemann
Pole Niki Lauda
Fastest lap Carlos Reutemann

ROUND 4 – SPAIN
Race Niki Lauda
Pole Niki Lauda
Fastest lap Niki Lauda

ROUND 5 – BELGIUM
Race Emerson Fittipaldi
Pole Clay Regazzoni
Fastest lap Denny Hulme

ROUND 6 – MONACO
Race Ronnie Peterson
Pole Niki Lauda
Fastest lap Ronnie Peterson

ROUND 7 – SWEDEN
Race: Jody Scheckter
Pole: Patrick Depallier
Fastest lap: Patrick Depallier

ROUND 8 – NETHERLANDS
Race Niki Lauda
Pole Niki Lauda
Fastest lap Ronnie Peterson

ROUND 9 – ITALY
Race Ronnie Peterson
Pole Niki Lauda
Fastest lap Jody Scheckter

ROUND 10 – BRITAIN
Race Jody Scheckter
Pole Niki Lauda
Fastest lap Niki Lauda

ROUND 11 – GERMANY
Race Clay Regazzoni
Pole Niki Lauda
Fastest lap Jody Scheckter

ROUND 12 – AUSTRIA
Race Carlos Reutemann
Pole Niki Lauda
Fastest lap Clay Regazzoni

ROUND 13 – ITALY
Race Ronnie Peterson
Pole Niki Lauda
Fastest lap Carlos Pace

ROUND 14 – CANADA
Race Emerson Fittipaldi
Pole Emerson Fittipaldi
Fastest lap Niki Lauda

ROUND 15 – UNITED STATES
Race Carlos Reutemann
Pole Carlos Reutemann
Fastest lap Carlos Pace

1974 DRIVERS' CHAMPIONSHIP

DRIVER	TEAM	POINTS
Emerson Fittipaldi	McLaren Ford	55
Clay Regazzoni	Ferrari	52
Jody Scheckter	Tyrrell Ford	45
Niki Lauda	Ferrari	38
Ronnie Peterson	Lotus Ford	35
Carlos Reutemann	Brabham Ford	32
Denny Hulme	McLaren Ford	20
James Hunt	Hesketh Ford	15
Patrick Depailler	Tyrrell Ford	14
Jacky Ickx	Lotus Ford	12
Mike Hailwood	McLaren Ford	12
Carlos Pace	Surtees Ford/Brabham	11
Jean-Pierre Beltoise	BRM	10
Jean-Pierre Jarier	Shadow Ford	6
John Watson	Brabham Ford	6
Hanz-Joachim Stuck	March Ford	5
Arturo Merzario	Williams Ford	4
Vittorio Brambilla	March Ford	1
Graham Hill	Lola Ford	1
Tom Pryce	Shadow Ford	1

clash on the grid and both McLarens went out when Fittipaldi was hit by team-mate Hulme after a slow getaway.

Hailwood had a major accident when his McLaren took to the air over a jump on the circuit and crashed heavily on the final lap, breaking the Briton's leg and ending his seven-year Grand Prix career. The race result left the Championship with four drivers still in the hunt – Regazzoni, Scheckter, Lauda and Fittipaldi.

But none of the Championship contenders were to take a win at the next round in Austria. In fact, none of them got within the top four as all but fifth-place finisher Regazzoni went out with engine problems to leave Reutemann out in front for an unexpected victory.

Lauda's hope

Lauda boosted the crowd's hope of a home win and a Championship challenge by placing his Ferrari on pole with Reutemann second. Fittipaldi also looked good for points, but the day did not go so well for Scheckter who managed only fifth.

Reutemann jumped Lauda at the start to take a lead he would never relinquish while Championship leader Regazzoni climbed to fourth from eighth on the grid. He then went one better when he passed Pace for third before Scheckter went out with engine problems on lap eight.

Soon after, Lauda's Ferrari began to misfire and he dropped out of second and then out of the race on lap 17. Fittipaldi was the next top man out on lap 38 and Regazzoni, who was now up to second, suffered a puncture. Pace assumed second but soon went out with a fuel pipe problem and Peterson joined him after suffering transmission problems to leave Hulme to take second ahead of Hunt.

Peterson's Italian job

Regazzoni was still ahead in the Championship when the field moved to Monza for the Italian race. This time, however, it was his turn to drop out of the proceedings along with Ferrari team-mate Lauda as his rivals scored valuable points. But once again, it was a non-Championship contender who took the spoils as Peterson took his third win of the season for Lotus.

Lauda excited the *tifosi* when he took his sixth pole in a row, but it was not to be a race victory for the Italian crowd despite things looking perfect for the Scuderia.

Regazzoni was in second just a few laps into the race after moving past Pace and Reutemann. John Watson, Reutemann and Pace all went out of the lead pack to leave the Ferraris comfortably ahead of Peterson with Fittipaldi fourth.

On lap 30, Lauda's Ferrari started to smoke and he was out two laps later. It was not a good sign for the Italian team and their concerns were realized when Regazzoni also retired while leading.

Peterson and Fittipaldi were left to fight for 12 laps and the Swede finally won by less than a second with Scheckter third.

The Championship was incredibly tight and just

Niki Lauda on board his Ferrari.

The crowd celebrations quickly get underway as Emerson Fittipaldi claims his second world title.

1974 CONSTRUCTORS' CUP

TEAM (Engine)	POINTS
McLAREN FORD	73
FERRARI	65
TYRRELL FORD	52
LOTUS FORD	42
BRABHAM FORD	35
HESKETH FORD	15
BRM	10
SHADOW FORD	7
MARCH FORD	6
WILLIAMS FORD	4
SURTEES FORD	3
LOLA FORD	1

four points covered the top three drivers with Lauda still in with an outside chance as the teams crossed the Atlantic for the final two races in North America.

Canada was the first stop, but the Championship was not to be concluded at Mosport Park. Fittipaldi, third in the series, took the win to set himself up for the title while Scheckter's retirement all but ended his bid.

Lauda remained in contention but Fittipaldi just stopped the Austrian taking a seventh successive pole. This did not prevent Lauda from taking the lead at the start ahead of Fittipaldi, Regazzoni and Scheckter as the four Championship contenders filled the four top positions.

Scheckter moved up to third and chased the lead pair and the order remained the same until over half-distance when the South African's brakes failed and he crashed out on lap 48.

SHORTS

Arguably the most talented Grand Prix driver never to have won a World Championship race, New Zealander Chris Amon debuted his own car – the Amon F101 – at the 1974 Spanish Grand Prix. Developed with the backing of John Dalton, the car proved problematic from the start, with Amon routinely missing races due to mechanical difficulties. He eventually disbanded the team with the 1974 season still underway.

Lauda looked set for the win but 10 laps from the end he crashed out of the lead after hitting debris. Fittipaldi moved up to take the victory ahead of the closely battling pair of Regazzoni in second and Peterson third.

Title showdown

And so the Championship went down to the wire in the United States Grand Prix at Watkins Glen.

The title battle was down to three but in reality it was down to a straight fight between McLaren and Ferrari with Fittipaldi and Regazzoni on equal points.

Pre-race testing had not gone well for Regazzoni who crashed heavily and needed a new chassis from Italy. He was also suffering with a bruised leg. Neither contender qualified well and Lauda glimpsed title hope by leading the pair off the grid in fourth.

Reutemann, Hunt and Pace were the top three into the first corner after poor qualifying from the Championship rivals left Fittipaldi down in sixth with Regazzoni seventh and dropping back with an ill-handling Ferrari.

With the Swiss driver out of the running, Fittipaldi concentrated on Scheckter who was eight points behind him.

A terrible accident almost halted the race when Helmuth Koinigg went straight into the crash barriers on lap 10, and died instantly.

The race was not stopped and on lap 45 it was all over anyway. Scheckter retired with a fuel leak and although Fittipaldi only managed fourth in the race behind the top three of Reutemann, Pace, and Hunt, it was his day and his Championship.

Ronnie Peterson

RONNIE PETERSON showed commitment and mesmerising car control. Sweden's greatest driver was the fastest in his day but tragically did not live to fulfil his talent.

CAREER DETAILS

1944	Born 14 February in Orebro, Sweden
1966	Progresses to Formula Three from karts
1968	Swedish Formula Three Champion in a Tecno
1969	Works driver with Tecno, won at Monaco
1970	Makes GP debut with March
1971	Elevated to works March F1 team. Ends season runner-up to Jackie Stewart
1973	Moves to Lotus. Finished third behind Stewart and team-mate Emerson Fittipaldi
1974	Three more victories in ageing Lotus
1976	Signs for March
1977	Disastrous season in Tyrrell
1978	Returns to Lotus as No. 2 to Mario Andretti. They dominated season, with Peterson fulfilling contract not to race his team-mate. Dies on 11 September following a starting grid accident at Monza. Posthumously declared runner-up in World Championship

FORMULA ONE RECORD

Year	Team	Wins	Poles	Fast laps	Pts
1970	March	0	0	0	0
1971	March	0	0	0	33
1972	March	0	0	0	12
1973	Lotus	4	9	2	5
1974	Lotus	3	1	2	35
1975	Lotus	0	0	0	6
1976	Lotus	0	0	0	0
1976	March	1	1	1	10
1977	Tyrrell	0	0	1	7
1978	Lotus	2	3	3	51

Ronnie Peterson puts his Lotus through its paces at the French Grand Prix.

Plumes of tyre smoke and an armful of opposite lock characterized the spectacle, commitment and extraordinary car control for which Ronnie Peterson is hailed. One of the most dynamic talents of his era, the gentle Swedish driver won 10 Grands Prix, but his potential was sadly never to be fulfilled. He died from complications following a start-line shunt at Monza in 1978 – the same race in which team-mate Mario Andretti secured the World Championship unchallenged by his graciously sportsmanlike Number Two.

Peterson acquired his seat-of-the-pants style in the early 1960s European karting scene, picking up a string of Swedish titles. He stormed into Formula Three in 1966 but it was not until he bought a Tecno in 1968 that his talent was appreciated. Propelled into Tecno's works outfit, he eventually won notice by winning a sensational battle for victory in the shop-window 1969 Monaco Grand Prix supporting race, beating his compatriot Reine Wisell after a wheel-to-wheel battle.

In 1970 he graduated into Formula One, signing a three-year contract with the fledgling March team. Elevated to the works March Formula One team in 1971 he scored five second places, ending the season runner-up to Jackie Stewart in the World Championship.

"He was considered *the* talent, pure and simple," commented Niki Lauda on Peterson's 1971 season in Formula Two.

He had a gift of driving cars which were handling badly and of driving flat out in all circumstances.

> "Ronnie was every man's dream of a racer. He just breathed, walked and talked motor racing the whole time."
>
> **Peter Warr**, *Lotus team manager*

Ronnie Peterson did not live to realize his promise.

The March team was run on a shoestring budget and it was not until Peterson left for Lotus in 1973 that he won his first race at the French Grand Prix. He also won Austrian, Italian and US East Grands Prix to finish third in the Championship. Paired with Emerson Fittipaldi, the reigning World Champion, the Swede's brilliance unnerved the Brazilian, who soon left for McLaren.

Peterson continued with Lotus as team leader in 1973 and 1974 but the ageing Lotus 72 had seen its day. In 1976 he returned to March but had limited success before 1977 brought an offer to drive the complex six-wheel Tyrrell – not a gift horse for a driver acknowledged to have a lack of mechanical sympathy.

In 1978 Peterson returned to Lotus as a number two to Mario Andretti. As an indication of his character, Peterson accepted this position without malice and re-discovered his love of racing.

"This car gave me back my inspiration," he said simply of the Lotus 79.

Colin Chapman's dream team dominated with Peterson scoring a pair of spectacular wins. With admirable integrity, he acted the loyal Number Two but there were times when his superiority could not be disguised, such as when he outqualified his teammate at Brands Hatch even though he had half a tank of fuel and was using hard compound tyres, rather than the qualifiers which were held for Andretti.

After his victory at Zeltweg in Austria he trailed Andretti by only nine points with four races remaining. It was already known that he was to leave Lotus at the end of the season and some suggested that he should just go for the Championship with nothing to lose. Nothing except his word.

"I'm going to McLaren next year," he said. "It's not announced yet, but Mario knows. Some of these people who say I should forget our agreement now...I don't understand them. I had open eyes when I signed the contract, and I also gave my word. If I break it now, who will ever trust me again?"

At the next race Andretti's car broke an exhaust and lost power, yet Peterson followed him over the line – he felt his time would come next year when he would have been team leader at McLaren. Cruelly this most popular of drivers never realized that promise. A multiple start-line shunt at Monza left him with serious leg injuries. He died from a resultant embolism, leaving his peers in mourning.

Andretti was disconsolate: "I wanted that title so badly but I did not want to win it like this. What the hell shall I do with it now? I don't feel anything for it."

1975
Lauda drives to deserved win

TALKING POINT

CROWD TRAGEDY AND THE DEATH OF A CHAMPION

The 1975 season was tinged with sadness, as five spectators were killed during the Spanish Grand Prix and the world of Formula One lost one of its greatest drivers when Graham Hill perished in a plane crash little more than a month after the last race of the season in November.

The Spanish Grand Prix at Montjuich Park circuit courted controversy early on as the Grand Prix Drivers' Association was unhappy with the barriers at the track and went on strike until they were improved.

Jacky Ickx, in a Lotus, was the only major driver to venture out in practice on Friday as work was carried out on the barriers throughout the day and into Saturday.

The drivers were still not happy by qualifying on Saturday afternoon and the session was not run at full speed as Emerson Fittipaldi, the most unhappy of the drivers, completed the minimum three laps to qualify – at slow speed.

On the morning of the event Fittipaldi refused to race and went home, joined by Wilson Fittipaldi and Arturo Merzario, who retired after a lap.

Their worst fears turned into reality on lap 26 when the rear wing of Rolf Stommelen's Hill–Ford came off and forced it into the barriers. They failed to prevent the car going over and into the crowd, killing five people and seriously injuring Stommelen.

The organizers panicked and failed to stop the race for a further four laps. When it was aborted the drivers in the top six were all given half points.

Hill's death came after he crashed his light aeroplane in November while returning from a test session at the Paul Ricard circuit.

Niki Lauda was the man to beat as he secured Ferrari's first title for 11 years. John Surtees had been the last man to win the World Championship for the Maranello-based team until the enigmatic Austrian Lauda ended their exile from top spot.

Lauda won five of the 14 races in a season that had started many changes to the Grand Prix squads. The Yardley team had withdrawn, so McLaren concentrated their efforts on a single two-car team for Emerson Fittipaldi and Jochen Mass, who had replaced the retired Denny Hulme.

Tyrrell, Lotus, Ferrari, Brabham, Shadow, Hesketh and Hill all retained their driver line-ups while Frank Williams raced a team under his name for the first time with drivers Arturo Merzario and Jacques Laffitte.

March provided a car for Vittorio Brambilla. Penske and Parnelli both turned into full-time teams, and Wilson Fittipaldi started to promote the Fittipaldi chassis. A tyre war was also averted as Firestone withdrew, allowing Goodyear a rubber monopoly.

Fittipaldi off to a flyer

Jean-Pierre Jarier took pole position for the opening 53-lap Argentinian Grand Prix in his Shadow DN5, beating the Brabham of Carlos Pace into second place on the grid.

Jarier's transmission failed on the formation lap and he was not able to make the grid. This allowed Carlos Reutemann in a Brabham to beat team-mate Pace off the line. James Hunt took the lead from Reutemann on lap 26 and Fittipaldi, in a McLaren, also overtook the Brabham driver. By lap 35 Fittipaldi had taken Hunt, and as Pace retired with engine trouble on lap 46, the Brazilian driver maintained his lead to take the first win of the season.

The Championship moved on to the Brazilian circuit of Interlagos two weeks later and Jarier took his second successive pole position for the 40-lap race, closely followed by Fittipaldi and Pace.

Fittipaldi was beaten to the first corner by Reutemann and fell further behind when the Ferraris of Clay Regazzoni and Lauda, and the Tyrrell of Scheckter passed him on the first lap.

Jarier, meanwhile, also dropped a place as Reutemann led for the first four laps, but he soon fought back and by lap five was the leader. By lap 32, however, he was out with engine failure.

It was left to Pace who took his first Grand Prix victory ahead of home driver Fittipaldi and third-placed Mass.

Graham Hill was killed in a plane crash on 29 November 1975.

A month passed before the third round of the Championship in South Africa at the Kyalami circuit. Brabham completed a one-two on the grid as Pace took pole ahead of his team-mate Reutemann.

Scheckter had qualified third for the race and after Pace held his lead at the start for the opening two laps, sparked a euphoric reaction from his home crowd as he took top spot on lap three.

Once in front, Scheckter was not going to relinquish the chance to win in front of his supporters and sped away from the rest of the field to claim the victory.

Disaster in Spain

The Spanish Grand Prix that followed was surrounded by controversy. It was remembered for safety fears that surrounded the race after several drivers threatened to boycott the event because of concerns over safety barriers. Five spectators died after Rolf Stommelen's car lost a rear wing and ploughed into the crowd.

The Fittipaldis refused to compete after Lauda took pole for the 29-lap race and it did not take long to see why. Brambilla attempted to pass Mario

Andretti's Parnelli off the line and the two cars touched. Andretti was shunted into Lauda who then crashed into his Ferrari team-mate Regazzoni, forcing both drivers out.

Stommelen was leading when his tragic accident occurred. In the four laps it took the stewards to abort the race, Mass inherited the lead with Jacky Ickx creeping into second and Reutemann third. Pace had been taken out by Stommelen's crash and that left Jarier in fourth, Brambilla fifth and Lombardi sixth.

The top six drivers were awarded half points because the race was stopped early, making Lombardi the first woman to score World Championship points. The Formula One authorities were left to investigate their decision to allow the race to go ahead amid such fierce safety concerns.

Lauda holds on

As the sport reeled from the safety failures at the Spanish Grand Prix, the organizers of the next race in Monaco allowed just 18 cars to qualify.

Hill returned for the race but failed to make it on to the grid, along with Wilson Fittipaldi, Lombardi and five other drivers. But Lauda at last fulfilled his potential and took pole position for the 75-lap race, with the Shadows of Tom Pryce and Jarier second and third on the grid.

Lauda came under Fittipaldi's challenge, who pushed the Austrian all the way to the flag. But Lauda held out for his first win of the season and Pace, who had powered from eighth on the grid, came third behind the Brazilian.

Lauda and the rest of the field lined up for the Belgian Grand Prix at the Zolder circuit two weeks later and he wasted no time in continuing his good form with pole position for the 70-lap race.

The first two laps were eventful as Lauda lost first place to Pace and Mass crashed out on the opening lap, closely followed by rookie Jones who had an accident on the second lap. Pace's lead lasted just four laps as Brambilla took top spot.

Lauda, however, had kept in touch with the front-runners and he took Brambilla on lap six. Jarier spun out of the race on lap 13 as Lauda extended his lead at the front and went on to take his second successive win.

Sweden hosted the next race at the Anderstorp circuit and Andretti returned from America for the event. Frank Williams also brought in two new drivers, Damien Magee and Ian Scheckter, to replace Merzario and Lafitte. Hill also replaced François Migault with Vern Schuppen.

Brambilla forgot his misery in Belgium and took pole position for the 80-lap race in his March as Lauda could only manage to claim fifth place on the grid behind Jarier, Reutemann and Depailler.

At the start of the race, Brambilla held his lead as the top six remained unchanged for the opening laps. Reutemann was the earliest mover when he overtook Jarier but on lap 15 Brambilla dropped down the order with an overheating car.

Commanding form

That gifted the lead to Reutemann who sped away with Lauda, Regazzoni and Andretti in close attendance. The Brabham started to develop understeer problems and Lauda, sensing his chance to complete a hat-trick of wins, began a charge which netted second place after Pace's exit and brought him closer to the suffering Reutemann.

The Austrian kept his cool in the final laps and took his third straight win with Reutemann clinging on for second place from Regazzoni in third and Andretti in fourth.

Lauda was in commanding form and had taken the lead in the drivers' Championship, but his dominance was ended by ever-improving Briton Hunt in Holland as the Zandvoort circuit hosted the next round.

Lauda had taken pole position for the race with Hunt third on the grid, and these positions were maintained for the first 12 laps as the rain fell and all the drivers were on wet tyres.

As the weather conditions improved and the track started to dry out, Hunt was the first driver to come in for slick tyres. The effect was immediate and he took the lead from Regazzoni on lap 15 after

The aftermath of the Spanish Grand Prix when five spectators were killed.

RACE BY RACE DETAILS

ROUND 1 – ARGENTINA
Race Emerson Fittipaldi
Pole Jean-Pierre Jarier
Fastest lap James Hunt

ROUND 2 – BRAZIL
Race Carlos Pace
Pole Jean-Pierre Jarier
Fastest lap Jean-Pierre Jarier

ROUND 3 – SOUTH AFRICA
Race Jody Scheckter
Pole Carlos Pace
Fastest lap Carlos Pace

ROUND 4 – SPAIN
Race Jochen Mass
Pole Niki Lauda
Fastest lap Mario Andretti

ROUND 5 – MONACO
Race Niki Lauda
Pole Niki Lauda
Fastest lap Patrick Depailler

ROUND 6 – BELGIUM
Race Niki Lauda
Pole Niki Lauda
Fastest lap Clay Regazzoni

ROUND 7 – SWEDEN
Race Niki Lauda
Pole Vittorio Brambilla
Fastest lap Niki Lauda

ROUND 8 – HOLLAND
Race James Hunt
Pole Niki Lauda
Fastest lap Niki Lauda

ROUND 9 – FRANCE
Race Niki Lauda
Pole Niki Lauda
Fastest lap Jochen Mass

ROUND 10 – BRITAIN
Race Emerson Fittipaldi
Pole Tom Pryce
Fastest lap Clay Regazzoni

ROUND 11 – GERMANY
Race Carlos Reutemann
Pole Niki Lauda
Fastest lap Clay Regazzoni

ROUND 12 – AUSTRIA
Race Vittorio Brambilla
Pole Niki Lauda
Fastest lap Vittorio Brambilla

ROUND 13 – ITALY
Race Clay Regazzoni
Pole Niki Lauda
Fastest lap Clay Regazzoni

ROUND 14 – UNITED STATES
Race Niki Lauda
Pole Niki Lauda
Fastest lap Emerson Fittipaldi

1975 DRIVERS' CHAMPIONSHIP

DRIVER	TEAM	POINTS
Niki Lauda	Ferrari	64.5
Emerson Fittipaldi	McLaren Ford	45
Carlos Reutemann	Brabham Ford	37
James Hunt	Hesketh Ford	33
Clay Regazzoni	Ferrari	25
Carlos Pace	Brabham Ford	24
Jody Scheckter	Tyrrell Ford	20
Jochen Mass	McLaren Ford	20
Patrick Depailler	Tyrrell Ford	12
Tom Pryce	Shadow Ford	8
Vittorio Brambilla	March Ford	6.5
Jacques Laffitte	Williams Ford	6
Ronnie Peterson	Lotus Ford	6
Mario Andretti	Parnelli Ford	5
Mark Donohue	Penske Ford/March Ford	5
Jacky Ickx	Lotus Ford	3
Alan Jones	Hill Ford	2
Jean-Pierre Jarier	Shadow Ford	1.5
Tony Brise	Hill Ford	1
Gijs van Lennep	Ensign Ford	1
Lella Lombardi	March Ford	0.5

Niki Lauda (right) toasts his first Grand Prix victory, in Sweden.

the Ferrari driver had led for one lap when Lauda was in for a pit-stop.

Hunt and Lauda battled it out at the front for the remainder of the race. The British racer held on for 60 laps to beat Lauda and claim his first Grand Prix win and the only victory in Hesketh's history.

Lauda regained his composure and re-stamped his authority on the Championship by claiming pole position for the 54-lap French Grand Prix.

Lauda was in no mood to accept another defeat and led from lights to flag for his fourth win in five races, with Hunt second and Mass third.

Silverstone smash

Lauda's victory at the Ricard circuit left him once again in command at the top of the Championship as the season moved to Silverstone for what was one of the most accident-filled races in history.

SHORTS

The South African Grand Prix, held at the Kyalami circuit, saw Lella Lombardi become the first women since 1958 to qualify for a Grand Prix, as she put her March in 26th place on the grid. The Italian earned her chance at the big time by proving her critics wrong with a fourth place finish in the 1974 Formula 5000 Championship.

Pryce claimed pole for the 56-lap race at the renovated Northamptonshire circuit. A huge field of competitors gathered for the event with the exception of Ickx, who had grown disillusioned at Lotus and decided to quit the sport. Pryce was followed on the grid by Pace and Lauda as a big crowd arrived on race day.

All the drivers started the race on slick tyres and the lead changed hands three times between Pace, Regazzoni and Pryce before the latter crashed out on lap 20 as the rain started to fall.

The weather was changeable and the rain was on and off as Jim Crawford crashed out on lap 28, followed by Hans-Joachim Stuck on lap 45 – but there was more to come.

As the rain returned by lap 50, 14 drivers crashed out in the next six laps. Jarier went at Woodcote and he was followed by Tony Brise, Pace, Scheckter, Hunt, Brian Henton, John Nicholson, David Morgan and Wilson Fittipaldi, who all went off at Club while Depailler, Mark Donohue and John Watson exited at Stowe.

Lauda and Mass also went off in the wet conditions and the race was aborted with Emerson Fittipaldi in the lead. Half points were awarded to the top six drivers at the start of lap 56, so Pace was classified in second, Scheckter third, Hunt fourth, Donohue fifth and Brambilla sixth. Lauda only managed eighth in a race where the spectators certainly got their money's worth.

The teams had their work cut out to repair their damaged cars for the next round in Germany, two weeks after the British race, and Surtees could not manage it in time so Watson was loaned to Lotus for the 14-lap race on the long Nurburgring circuit.

Williams brought in Ian Ashley to race alongside Lafitte, but Ashley failed to start the race as he suffered a big crash in practice and seriously injured his ankles. Lauda took pole position ahead of Pace and Scheckter.

Lauda maintained his lead when the race began but Scheckter had a terrible start and dropped to the back of the field. Scheckter had battled back through the field by lap seven but his car careered into a barrier after a puncture to one of his tyres.

On lap 10, Hunt went out with a rear hub problem and Reutemann reeled Lauda in to take the lead from the Austrian driver. The stuttering Lauda was also overtaken by Lafitte in the latter stages and settled for third place as Reutemann took victory with Lafitte second.

Donohue death

Lauda arrived at his home track, the Osterreichring, with a strong lead in the Championship despite his failure to win in Germany. Proceedings in Austria were to be overshadowed, however, by the death of Donohue in the warm-up. He suffered a tyre failure and his March crashed over a barrier, also killing a marshal.

Wilson Fittipaldi was forced to withdraw when he broke two bones in his hand in a qualifying session accident and Lauda once again took pole in front of his home crowd for the 29-lap race.

Lauda led for the first 14 laps of the race and seemed to be cruising to victory and the Championship on home soil, but the rest of the field stayed close and Hunt took the lead on lap 15.

Brambilla soon moved to challenge at the front of the field and as Lauda dropped to sixth, he took Hunt for the lead 10 laps from the finish.

Brambilla performed well to fend off the challenge of Hunt and claim March's first victory. In his excitement he crashed embarrassingly on the victory lap and was left to complete his lap of honour in a severely damaged car.

Two weeks later, Lauda arrived at Monza for the Italian Grand Prix knowing that just half a point would be enough for him to win the title as the United States Grand Prix was now the last race. The Canadian event had been cancelled because of financial reasons.

Lauda took pole for the 52-lap race at Monza but was beaten off the line by Ferrari's Regazzoni, who was in no mood to relinquish first place on his team's home circuit and led to the chequered flag to deny Lauda victory.

But Lauda was able to stay close to the front-runners and as Emerson Fittipaldi claimed second place, Lauda finished third and won the World Championship in front of his Ferrari team's army of passionate and vociferous fans.

Lauda celebrated his title victory with a dominant performance in the final race of the season in America when he claimed his ninth pole of the campaign for the 59-lap race and then led from lights to flag.

Fittipaldi finished second and Mass was third, but Lauda's victory added the finishing touches to a fine season for the Ferrari driver.

1975 CONSTRUCTORS' CUP

TEAM (Engine)	POINTS
FERRARI	72.5
BRABHAM FORD	54
McLAREN FORD	53
HESKETH FORD	33
TYRRELL FORD	25
SHADOW FORD	9.5
LOTUS FORD	9
MARCH FORD	7.5
WILLIAMS FORD	6
PARNELLI FORD	5
HILL FORD	3
PENSKE FORD	2
ENSIGN FORD	1

The British Grand Prix of 1975 proved to be one of the most accident-filled races in the history of Formula One.

Mario Andretti

MARIO ANDRETTI is the sport's greatest all-rounder, the only man to have won the Formula One World Championship, the Daytona 500 Nascar race and the Indianapolis 500.

CAREER DETAILS

1940	Born 28 February in Montana, Italy
1955	Emigrates with family to Nazareth, Pennsylvania
1964	Graduates to IndyCar racing
1965	Competes in the Indianapolis 500 for the first time and wins IndyCar title
1966	Wins second IndyCar title
1967	Wins Daytona 500
1968	Makes F1 debut for Lotus at end of season
1969	Wins Indianapolis 500 and third IndyCar title
1978	Drives sensational Lotus 79 to F1 world Championship title
1982	Last F1 outings
1984	Wins fourth IndyCar title
1993	Wins last Champcar race aged 53 in Phoenix, Arizona
1994	Retires

FORMULA ONE RECORD

Year	Team	Wins	Poles	Fast laps	Pts
1968	Lotus	0	1	0	0
1969	Lotus	0	0	0	0
1970	March	0	0	0	4
1971	Ferrari	1	0	1	12
1972	Ferrari	0	0	0	4
1973		–	–	–	–
1974	Parnelli	0	0	0	0
1975	Parnelli	0	0	1	5
1976	Lotus	1	1	1	22
1976	Parnelli	0	0	0	0
1977	Lotus	4	7	4	47
1978	Lotus	6	8	3	64
1979	Lotus	0	0	0	14
1980	Lotus	0	0	0	1
1981	Alfa Romeo	0	0	0	3
1982	Williams	0	0	0	4
1982	Ferrari	0	1	0	0

Mario Andretti's reputation among his peers was not one of great virtuosity, but of great determination.

Mario Andretti embodies the "American Dream". Born in Montana, near Trieste, during the Second World War, he spent the first seven years of his life with his family escaping Communism in a displaced person's camp in Lucca, before emigrating to the United States in 1955. As a child he had been so desperate to see Alberto Ascari race a Ferrari, he scrambled under a fence at Monza. His passion for racing – still evident at the age of 60 when he angled for a drive at Le Mans 2000 – was fuelled by memories of Ascari and the Mille Miglia.

"When I was about fourteen I got my first race – on a motorbike – because I had this priest who was a really good friend," Andretti recalled. "He knew this burning desire I had to race and so he fixed it. One time I got a broken kneecap flopping a bike and I made him lie to my parents. I said, "You tell them I fell down the marble steps serving Mass or you lose an altar boy!"

In 1959, Mario and twin brother Aldo competed at the local speedway and were equally successful.

"I don't think we ever came second," he said. "We either won or crashed. That's how aggressive we were."

Aldo retired after fracturing his skull but Mario drove midget racers on dirt ovals, gradually moving up the scale of cars and prize money.

Nicknamed Super Wop, he won the American title and graduated to IndyCar racing in 1964. He amazed the establishment by winning the title the following year. Proving his skills to be effortlessly versatile, he also starred in NASCAR stock cars, winning the Daytona 500 in 1967.

He won two more IndyCar titles in 1966 and 1969, and stunned European racing sages by qualifying his Lotus on pole in his F1 debut at Watkins Glen late in the 1968 season.

Andretti was already a Daytona 500 winner, Sebring winner, two-times USAC Champion and four-times Indianapolis 500 competitor when he entered his first Formula One race. He had earned all the money he could ever need, but those memories of Ascari lured him to the challenge of the Formula One World Championship.

His reputation among his fellow-drivers was not one of great virtuosity, but of great determination. A Concorde commuter, dividing his time between IndyCar, sports car racing and Formula One

Mario Andretti in action during the Spanish Grand Prix on 8 May 1977.

"I figure I was put on the earth to drive race cars."

between 1969 and 1974, Andretti had mixed Formula One success with Lotus, March and Ferrari – for whom he won the 1971 South African Grand Prix.

In 1975 he committed to Formula One full-time with the American Parnelli team. The outfit soon folded and Andretti was back at Lotus for 1976. Victory in the season-ending Japanese Grand Prix showed progress had been made followed by a year of consolidation 1977. Then came 1978 and the spectacular ground-effect Lotus 79. So dominant was Lotus that Andretti's major competition for the title was his team-mate Ronnie Peterson.

Andretti came to Monza leading Peterson by 12 points. At the start, James Hunt was punted into Peterson by another car. Peterson's car in turn hit the Armco heavily and burst into flames. The race was red-flagged as Hunt, Patrick Depailler, Clay Regazzoni and race marshals worked bravely to free the stricken Peterson.

The race restarted after a two-hour delay and Andretti's sixth-place finish was enough to clinch the title.

"It could have been the happiest day of my life, instead it has turned out to be the saddest," Andretti said, unwilling to celebrate after hearing Peterson had died of complications from the multiple leg injuries he suffered in the start-line shunt.

Andretti competed for four more seasons, two with Lotus, one with Alfa Romeo, and three races in 1982 with Williams and, once again, Ferrari. At Monza that year, his next to last Formula One race, he authoritatively put his Ferrari on the pole to the delight of his kindred spirits, the *tifosi*.

The thrill of Formula One had gone and he crossed the Atlantic again. In 1984 he won a fourth IndyCar title and was consistently at the sharp end of the field until his final few seasons when he raced alongside Nigel Mansell for the Newman/Haas team in the early 1990s.

1976
The Hunt(er) gets his prey

TALKING POINT
TYRRELL'S SIX-WHEELER

British team Tyrrell produced one of Formula One's most unique sights in the 1976 season when they created a six-wheeled car which brought the paddock to a standstill in wonder.

The P34 car made its debut in the Spanish Grand Prix and was used for the rest of the season with Patrick Depailler and Jody Scheckter at the wheel for the remaining 13 races.

The cars used six small wheels and worked under the theory that the more rubber on the track the more stable the car would be in different downforce situations at the varying circuits.

The P34 was relatively consistent as Scheckter and Depailler challenged near the front throughout the season. The drivers even completed a one-two finish in the Swedish Grand Prix at Anderstorp as Scheckter took his only win of the season.

The team scored a total of 71 points over the season and only just lost the battle for second place in the Constructor's Championship to McLaren, but by 1977 the team deemed the six-wheeler uncompetitive and reverted to the more conventional four wheels.

The season started in sombre mood following the death of Graham Hill two months prior to the start of the season in January. Hill crashed his light plane on the way back from a testing session in France, and in an inadvertent tribute the Formula One world provided a remarkable season from start to finish.

Before the start of the season Lord Hesketh decided to disband his team, leaving James Hunt without a drive. However, just a few days after that decision Emerson Fittipaldi opted to leave McLaren for his brother Wilson's eponymous team, and that left the way open for Hunt to take the Brazilian's McLaren seat.

Elsewhere, Shadow lost their sponsorship with Universal Oil and their resources were severely affected. Frank Williams went into partnership with Walter Wolf and hired Jacky Ickx and Renzo Zorzi as his drivers, and Jacques Laffitte joined the newly-created Ligier team. Lotus had a new 77 car for drivers Mario Andretti and Ronnie Peterson, and Ferrari retained their driver line-up of Clay Regazzoni and Niki Lauder.

Hunt and Lauda head to head

The field headed for Interlagos and the first race of the season in Brazil. It was the first of 16 races which would enthral the sporting world as Hunt and Lauda went head to head, with the latter surviving an horrific accident midway through the season.

Hunt took pole for the 40-lap Brazilian race, with Lauda second and Jean-Pierre Jarier third or a race which set a new precedent, as it was started, for the first time, by a set of lights rather than a flag.

Regazzoni, who had started from fourth, took the lead as the lights went green but Lauda kept in touch as Hunt dropped back after a slow start. Lauda maintained his lead as Hunt went out seven laps from the finish when he spun with a stuck throttle. Patrick Depailler was promoted to second behind winner Lauda.

Before the second round in South Africa, Peterson left Lotus for the March team as female racer Lombardi quit the sport, Surtees came back with driver Brett Lunger, Williams signed up Michel Leclerc to partner Ickx and Ensign returned with Chris Amon at the wheel.

Hunt took pole position for the race, with Lauda close behind in second place on the grid. It took Lauda until the first corner to amend the positions in his favour as he beat Hunt off the line and raced into the lead, pulling away from Hunt and the rest of the field. He led for the entire 78-lap race to claim his second win of the season.

For the third round, the Championship moved to Long Beach and the United States West Grand Prix and for once Lauda or Hunt were not on the front row for the 80-lap race. Lauda's team-mate Clay Regazzoni took pole position with Hunt third and Lauda fourth on the grid.

Regazzoni got a good start and never looked back as the rest of the field battled it out. Reutemann and Brambilla crashed out at the start and three laps later Hunt's race was over as he also spun off. Championship leader Lauda finished second to complete a Ferrari one-two, while Depailler was third.

The six-wheel Tyrrell car on display at the Swedish Grand Prix.

James Hunt flies off at the British Grand Prix.

Hunt's authority turns to gloom

Controversy reigned in the fourth round in Spain as Hunt started to stamp his authority on the Championship.

Hunt took pole at the Jarama circuit, with Lauda second on the grid for the 75-lap race. The British driver, however, had a bad start and Lauda led the race for the first 31 laps before Hunt reeled in the Ferrari driver and took top spot, which he held for the remainder of the race. However, he was disqualified as the race stewards deemed his McLaren was too wide. The win was gifted to Lauda, with second place going to Gunnar Nilsson and third to Reutemann. Hunt and his team would appeal and find out their fate later in the season.

Despondent after his Spanish problems, Hunt was a shadow of himself as the teams arrived at Zolder for the Belgian Grand Prix. Lauda took pole for the race, fractionally ahead of his team-mate Regazzoni. Hunt was left to settle for third on the grid.

At the start of the 70-lap race, the two Ferraris sped away, and as Hunt attempted to keep up with Lauda and Regazzoni he went out of the race on lap 35 with transmission problems. That left the way clear for Lauda to claim his third win of the season with Regazzoni completing the Ferrari one-two.

Lauda was now in a dominant position in the Championship as he still had the Spanish Grand Prix win to his credit when the teams arrived in Monaco for the next round in May. Hunt was a favourite with the British fans, but he had failed to make a big impact so far and his season was about to get worse in the principality. Hunt could only manage to qualify 14th for the 78-lap race as Lauda took pole ahead of Regazzoni.

On race day, Lauda produced a faultless performance to lead from start to finish, while Hunt dropped to the back after a spin and was then forced to retire on lap 25 with an engine problem.

Hunt's morale was hit hard, and he had little time to recover as just two weeks later the next round took place in North Sweden at Anderstorp.

Scheckter claimed a remarkable pole position for the race in his six-wheeled Tyrrell as Lauda and Hunt were left down the grid in fourth and seventh respectively. Andretti also displayed the potential of the new Lotus 77 as he qualified second for the 72-lap race.

Andretti then started and took the lead on the first lap – but he started too well, and was penalized one minute for jumping the start and on lap 45 his engine blew, Scheckter had the lead and an amazing win.

Lauda and Hunt, meanwhile, had failed to make an impression on the lead and finished third and fifth respectively.

Hunt's fifth place in Sweden had not made much of an impact on the drivers' standings as Lauda had finished third in the same race, but the British driver took a moral victory in qualifying for the next race in France at the start of July by taking pole position ahead of Lauda.

Hunt must have thought each start was an

RACE BY RACE DETAILS

ROUND 1 – BRAZIL
Race Niki Lauda
Pole James Hunt
Fastest lap Jean-Pierre Jarier

ROUND 2 – SOUTH AFRICA
Race Niki Lauda
Pole James Hunt
Fastest lap Niki Lauda

ROUND 3 – UNITED STATES WEST
Race Clay Regazzoni
Pole Clay Regazzoni
Fastest lap Clay Regazzoni

ROUND 4 – SPAIN
Race James Hunt
Pole James Hunt
Fastest lap Jochen Mass

ROUND 5 – BELGIUM
Race Niki Lauda
Pole Niki Lauda
Fastest lap Niki Lauda

ROUND 6 – MONACO
Race Niki Lauda
Pole Niki Lauda
Fastest lap Clay Regazzoni

ROUND 7 – SWEDEN
Race Ronnie Peterson
Pole Jody Scheckter
Fastest lap Mario Andretti

ROUND 8 – FRANCE
Race James Hunt
Pole James Hunt
Fastest lap Niki Lauda

ROUND 9 – BRITAIN
Race Niki Lauda
Pole Niki Lauda
Fastest lap Niki Lauda

ROUND 10 – GERMANY
Race James Hunt
Pole James Hunt
Fastest lap Jody Scheckter

ROUND 11 – AUSTRIA
Race James Hunt
Pole James Hunt
Fastest lap James Hunt

ROUND 12 – HOLLAND
Race James Hunt
Pole Ronnie Peterson
Fastest lap Clay Regazzoni

ROUND 13 – ITALY
Race Ronnie Peterson
Pole Jacques Laffitte
Fastest lap Ronnie Peterson

ROUND 14 – CANADA
Race James Hunt
Pole James Hunt
Fastest lap Patrick Depailler

ROUND 15 – UNITED STATES EAST
Race James Hunt
Pole James Hunt
Fastest lap James Hunt

ROUND 16 – JAPAN
Race Mario Andretti
Pole Mario Andretti
Fastest lap Masahiro Hasemi

1976 DRIVERS' CHAMPIONSHIP

DRIVER	TEAM	POINTS
James Hunt	McLaren Ford	69
Niki Lauda	Ferrari	68
Jody Scheckter	Tyrrell Ford	49
Patrick Depailler	Tyrrell Ford	39
Clay Regazzoni	Ferrari	31
Mario Andretti	Parnelli Ford/Lotus Ford	22
John Watson	Penske Ford	20
Jacques Lafitte	Ligier Matra	20
Jochen Mass	McLaren Ford	19
Gunnar Nilsson	Lotsu Ford	11
Ronnie Peterson	March Ford	10
Tom Pryce	Shadow Ford	10
Hans-Joachim Stuck	March Ford	8
Carlos Pace	Brabham Alfa Romeo	7
Alan Jones	Surtees Ford	7
Carlos Reutemann	Brabham Alfa Romeo	3
Emerson Fittipaldi	Fittipaldi Ford	3
Chris Amon	Ensign Ford	2
Rolf Stommelen	Brabham Alfa Romeo	1
Vittorio Brambilla	March Ford	1

Hunt celebrates his win at the Dutch Grand Prix in Zandvoort.

action replay as he was once again beaten off the line by Lauda, but the Briton's luck changed at last when the Ferrari driver retired on lap eight with a crankshaft fault.

Hunt inherited the lead and he powered away to take his second win of the season, although at the time it was the only one that counted.

Hunt's Spanish title reinstated

That was soon to change, however, as the FIA reinstated the Briton as the winner of the Spanish Grand Prix before the next round in his homeland on 18 July. The decision boosted Hunt, especially after his win in France, and it would have a remarkable effect on the McLaren driver for the remainder of the season.

Hunt was still 26 points behind Lauda in Championship terms, but his attention was focused on an event-filled British Grand Prix at Brands Hatch, which hosted the race after improvements to the circuit.

Lauda took pole position for the 76-lap race, with Hunt second on the grid, and the Austrian maintained his lead at the start of the race. Regazzoni powered past Hunt to challenge his team-mate on the first lap, but pushed too hard and the two Ferraris touched at the Paddock Hill bend. Regazzoni spun into the path of Hunt, who in taking evasive action clipped the Ferrari and launched through the air, landing heavily. Laffitte also smashed into Regazzoni, damaging both cars.

The race was stopped, the organizers deciding there was too much debris on the track. The teams argued whether Laffitte, Hunt and Regazzoni could join the restart, but McLaren repaired Hunt's car and the other two jumped into their spare cars and started for a second time. Lauda again took the lead and maintained his first place until lap 45, when a gearbox problem slowed him down and Hunt came back. Hunt quickly took the lead and went on to win the race in front of an ecstatic crowd.

Lauda held on for second place and Ferrari appealed against Hunt's inclusion in the restart to set up another long-running inquiry, which this time left the British driver's victory in doubt.

The next race at the Nurburgring in Germany provided further controversy as the title race took another traumatic twist in the 14-lap German Grand Prix.

Ickx had been sacked by the Williams team after a series of unimpressive results and was missing from the field as Hunt took pole position, with Lauda once again close behind in second place on the grid.

Disaster for Lauda

Suddenly disaster struck for Lauda as he lost control of his Ferrari just after a pit stop, ploughed through a fence and into a mound of earth. The car burst into flames, bounced back on to the track and was hit by the oncoming cars of Harald Etrl and Brett Lunger. Guy Edwards was also quickly on the scene

SHORTS

The South African Grand Prix, held at the Kyalami circuit, saw Lella Lombardi become the first women since 1958 to qualify for a Grand Prix, as she put her March in 26th place on the grid. The Italian earned her chance at the big time by proving her critics wrong with a fourth place finish in the 1974 Formula 5000 Championship.

and all three drivers tried to get Lauda out of the burning wreckage. The Austrian was rescued but had to be rushed to hospital with serious burns.

Chris Amon and Stuck withdrew before the restart, which was completed in dry conditions and saw Hunt win with Scheckter second, Mass third, Pace fourth, Gunnar Nilsson fifth and Rolf Stommelen sixth. But all thoughts were with Lauda, who was fighting for his life.

Two weeks after the race in Germany, the Championship rolled on to Austria for a race which was almost cancelled after Ferrari announced their withdrawal from the sport because of the reinstatement of Hunt's Spanish win. Lauda was still in a critical condition in hospital.

But the 54-lap race at the Osterreichring went ahead and Hunt claimed pole position, with John Watson an impressive second on the grid in his Penske and Peterson third.

Hunt started badly and dropped back as Watson took the lead and battled at the front of the field with Peterson. Scheckter joined the battle by lap 10 but retired when he spun out four laps later. Peterson also dropped back as his car developed mechanical problems, and that left the way clear for Watson to claim his first win of the season, with Hunt finishing way down in fourth.

Before the next race in Holland at the end of August, Lauda made an incredible recovery and proposed to come back for the Italian Grand Prix in early September. Lauda was still 23 points ahead in the Championship, but the lead was dramatically reduced at the Zandvoort circuit as Hunt came from second place on the grid to pass pole-sitter Peterson and win the race ahead of Regazzoni.

Austrian Lauda then announced the unbelievable when he confirmed his return for the Italian round of the series despite being scarred badly after his horror crash in Germany. Ferrari were forced to run three cars for their home Grand Prix after previously employing Reutemann to replace Lauda.

The rain-hit qualifying session allowed Laffitte to take pole with Lauda fifth and Hunt a disastrous 27th on the grid. Scheckter started second on the grid and he took the lead at the start, but it was Peterson who charged through the field from eighth to take the lead by lap 11. On the same lap Hunt spun out as Championship rival Lauda maintained his position near the front of the field.

Regazzoni charged to challenge at the front but Peterson kept his nerve to win the race with Regazzoni second, Scheckter third and Lauda fourth.

After the Italian race there was further disappointment for Hunt, who learned that Ferrari's appeal against his British Grand Prix win had been successful and the winning points were transferred to Lauda's account. That decision left Hunt in need of a miracle performance in the last three races of the season in Canada, United States East and Japan to claim the world title.

Niki Lauda made a remarkable recovery after his crash at the Nurburgring.

He duly obliged. Hunt took pole position for the 80-lap Canadian Grand Prix in October and after trailing Peterson for eight laps he took the lead and did not look back as he won at the Mosport Park circuit. Lauda finished out of the points in eighth.

Championship title race tightens

The gap was now down to eight points and Hunt took pole again at Watkins Glen for the United States East Grand Prix with Scheckter second on the grid and Lauda in fifth. The British driver came out on top just 13 laps from the finish of the 59-lap race.

The results in America meant the fascinating Championship battle would go down to the last race of the season at the Fuji circuit in Japan. The gap at the top was down to just three points and Japan provided another unforgettable and controversial race.

Hunt out-qualified Lauda and took the lead from the start. Lauda struggled to find any pace and by lap two he came into the pits to withdraw sensationally.

For the next 59 laps Hunt led and seemed to be speeding to the World Championship, but as the track dried he struggled and started to drop back as Depailler and then Andretti came through.

Hunt then faced a nightmare scenario as one of his rear tyres started to deflate. He was forced to come into the pits and dropped down to fifth, knowing that he needed at least a fourth-placed finish to beat Lauda to the title. Hunt had less than 10 laps to catch Regazzoni and Jones, but he did it and overtook both in the latter stages to finish third, behind Depailler and winner Andretti. The podium finish was enough to give Hunt the world title in what is regarded as one of the most eventful seasons in Formula One.

1976 CONSTRUCTORS' CUP

TEAM (ENGINE)	POINTS
FERRARI	83
McLAREN FORD	74
TYRRELL FORD	71
LOTUS FORD	29
LIGIER MATRA	20
PENSKE FORD	20
MARCH FORD	19
SHADOW FORD	10
BRABHAM ALFA ROMEO	9
SURTEES FORD	7
FITTIPALDI FORD	3
ENSIGN FORD	2
PARNELLI FORD	1

Jody Scheckter

He burst on to the scene as a headstrong prodigy, but Jody Scheckter won the World Championship for Ferrari in 1979 in conservative style and retired as a wry elder statesman.

CAREER DETAILS

1950	Born 29 January, East London, South Africa
1971	Comes to Britain on Driver to Europe scholarship
1972	Earns place with McLaren
1973	Triggers massive accident at British GP
1974	Joins Tyrrell
1977	Joins Wolf, finishes runner-up behind Niki Lauda
1979	Joins Ferrari. Wins World Championship
1980	Retires and sets up business in the United States

FORMULA ONE RECORD

Year	Team	Wins	Poles	Fast laps	Pts
1972	McLaren	0	0	0	0
1973	McLaren	0	0	0	0
1974	Tyrrell	2	0	2	45
1975	Tyrrell	1	0	0	20
1976	Tyrrell	1	1	1	49
1977	Wolf	3	1	2	55
1978	Wolf	0	0	0	24
1979	Ferrari	3	1	1	51
1980	Ferrari	0	0	0	2

"At the beginning I thought I was the fastest driver in the world. At the end I thought I was the cleverest driver." Formula One was the university of life for Jody Scheckter. Ever his own man, he began his career with a reputation for rough-edged, headstrong, somewhat foolhardy driving and left, seven full seasons later, as a droll elder statesman insistent on improving circuit safety.

Scheckter was born in East London, where the South African Grand Prix had been staged. His father had a Renault dealership – in which young Jody served an apprenticeship – and also built karts. Jody ran a go-kart at the age of 12 before trying motorbikes and, at the age of 18, saloon cars. After obligatory National Service, Scheckter returned to racing and was the star of the Team Lawson sports car team. Having won the national Formula Ford title in his Lola T200 Formula Ford, he won South Africa's Driver to Europe scholarship and made a huge impact on his arrival in 1971. "Spin or win" were the headlines of a brief Formula Ford career.

He stepped up to Formula Three and proved himself a race winner by the end of the season. McLaren signed him to race for their Formula Two team in 1972. He was a front runner in Formula Two and bagged one win – the Greater London Trophy at Crystal Palace. McLaren gave him his Grand Prix debut at Watkins Glen, where he finished a solid ninth.

"Spin or win" was again the theme of 1973. He made dazzling progress, leading the French Grand Prix, only his third race, but caused a multiple pile-up at the start of the British Grand Prix which not only halted the race but took out half the field. While he heard calls for him to be banned on this side of the Atlantic, he also raced for Sid Taylor in America, winning the L and M F5000 series completely without mishap.

In 1974 he moved to Tyrrell to replace the retiring Jackie Stewart and the deceased François Cevert. Still a relative rookie, Scheckter won an impressive two races and finished third in the World Championship. In 1975, just one race victory in front of the home crowds cheered up an unsuccessful year. In 1976 he made the bizarre six-wheel P34 launched by Tyrrell a serious threat, winning the Swedish Grand Prix. Again he finished third in the title race behind James Hunt and Niki Lauda.

Jody Scheckter appreciates his reception after achieving his debut win in Argentina in 1977.

"Jody has probably got the greatest innate talent we shall ever see in motor-racing."

Jackie Stewart, 1974

Scheckter risked much in his move to Wolf in 1977 but it paid off with a brilliant winning debut in Argentina – working up the field from 11th on the grid, taking the lead with just five laps to go, staying cool when car after car expired under the hottest of southern suns. It was followed by victories in Monaco and Canada to end the season as runner-up to Lauda.

After a poor season in 1978 with a troublesome new Wolf chassis, Scheckter moved to Ferrari with the stated intention of becoming World Champion. With an almost conservative approach far removed from his wild early days, he shrugged off the shock of being beaten by teammate Gilles Villeneuve in the new 312T4's first two races. In fact he forged a close friendship with the French-Canadian and knuckled down to a season of consistency and reliability, eventually securing the Championship through dependable points-scoring. He was crowned at Monza, with Villeneuve dutifully trailing him.

"I felt the year's pressure fall from my shoulders. It hadn't been like a race's pressure; it was a year's pressure. It was tremendous pressure," he said. Soon he had relaxed enough to quip: "The first time I really appreciated that I'd won the World Championship was when I got home to Monaco a few days after Monza. I found that my laundry was returned in two days rather than four!"

The following year was the worst of his career – the lowest point being his failure to qualify at Montreal. Bemused by the twist of fate, and demoralized, Scheckter retired and set up a firearms training enterprise in the United States. "I won't hang on too long once I've stopped enjoying things. It's too dangerous not to require 100 per cent effort," he had said in his Championship-winning year.

Selling out lucratively in the late 1990s, he settled in Britain to oversee the racing careers of his sons Tomas and Toby.

Scheckter put his wild early days behind him to achieve consistency and reliability.

Gilles Villeneuve

DRIVING LIKE AN INSPIRED GENIUS or a hooligan (opinions remain divided), Gilles Villeneuve liked nothing more than an honest, fearless, wheel-to-wheel battle.

CAREER DETAILS

1950	Born 18 January, in Saint-Jean-sur-Richelieu, Quebec
1973	Success in Formula Ford
1976	Noticed by James Hunt at a race at Trois Rivières
1977	Makes GP debut with McLaren at Silverstone. Signs for Ferrari
1978	Maiden GP victory at Canadian GP
1979	Three more GP wins at Kyalami, Long Beach and Watkins Glen. Runner-up in World Championship to team-mate Jody Scheckter
1981	Wins Monaco and Spanish GPs
1982	Dies in practice at Zolder on 8 May

FORMULA ONE RECORD

Year	Team	Wins	Poles	Fast laps	Pts
1977	McLaren	0	0	0	–
1977	Ferrari	0	0	0	–
1978	Ferrari	1	0	1	17
1979	Ferrari	3	1	5	47
1980	Ferrari	0	0	0	6
1981	Ferrari	2	1	1	25
1982	Ferrari	0	0	0	6

To many, the combination of Gilles Villeneuve and Ferrari was simply what motor racing "should be all about", The point is to charge all the time, unless you are first. That's the whole point of "racing", the little French-Canadian said with his endearing boy-racer innocence.

From 67 Grand Prix starts he won only six races, but his deceptively cavalier attitude and astonishingly uninhibited talent thrilled spectators while earning the respect of his peers. "I know that no human being can perform miracles, but Gilles makes you wonder sometimes," said Jacques Lafitte.

"The way I remember it, Gilles always cultivated the image of a daredevil," recalled Ferrari team-mate Jody Scheckter. "He would always have the wheels spinning in the pit-lane, changing gear without the clutch. I suppose it gave me a certain confidence, because I figured that's where I would get the advantage in the end, by being gentler with the machinery."

His son Jacques – the 1997 World Champion – maintains the showmanship was completely instinctive. "He was always crazy, like with snowmobiles, helicopters, four-by-four jeeps or whatever. He would go out there and kill the thing, then repair it in his garage, then go out and kill it again. In his skiing he was always trying to jump this and jump that. He wasn't a very good skier, but he still skied like a madman," he recalled.

Gilles Villeneuve started racing snowmobiles and tried drag-racing before turning to Formula Ford in 1973. He won seven out of 10 races, a success which prompted a move into Formula Atlantic to challenge his skills. Despite being sidelined by a fractured leg, he was quick to make an impression. After a race at Trois Rivières in 1976, in which he soundly thrashed James Hunt, he got the call-up from McLaren (Hunt having advised them to sign Villeneuve as soon as possible).

He had just one race with McLaren, the 1977 British Grand Prix at Silverstone, which saw Villeneuve in one spin after another. Some said he looked completely out of his depth. Others saw he was finding the limits in a Grand Prix car, taking the McLaren to the limits of its adhesion and beyond. McLaren passed up the chance of signing him. However, Ferrari snapped him up to replace Niki Lauda, who had suddenly decided to retire after

"The crowds loved him because he, of all the men out there, was so clearly working without a net."

Nigel Roebuck

clinching the 1977 Championship.

In Villeneuve's second race for the Italians, at Fuji, he ran into Ronnie Peterson's Tyrrell and the Ferrari somersaulted wildly into a spectator area, killing two. His first full season did not start much better. Villeneuve was involved in a series of accidents, not all of his own making. But his raw speed was obvious. At Monza he enjoyed an awesome battle with Mario Andretti, only for both drivers to be penalized for jumping the start. His maiden Grand Prix win came in Canada in the last race of 1978, but Villeneuve – typically for the racer he was at heart – felt he had not won on merit. His triumph was sealed only after Jean-Pierre Jarier's Lotus retired because of an oil leak.

In 1979 Scheckter won the Championship with three Grand Prix wins – the same tally as Villeneuve, who was honourable about team orders. While the South African won through conservative points-scoring, Villeneuve produced the more flamboyant moments. There was his duel with Alan Jones at Zandvoort (tyre, wheel and underside of gearbox all trashed and beamed worldwide via TV), a brilliant battle with René Arnoux at Dijon and an amazing qualifying performance at Watkins Glen in the rain when he was 11 seconds quicker than Scheckter.

The 1980 Ferrari was awful. Not even Villeneuve could steer it to a podium finish. The turbo-powered 1981 car brought him back to equal terms with the Brabhams and Williams and to two successive race wins. At Monaco he got the better of Alan Jones; at Jarama he drove superbly from seventh on the grid to keep the pack behind him.

Then came the year the legend was forged. In 1982, the Ferraris were in a strong position. At Imola, Villeneuve scorched to an emotional pole position in front of the jubilant *tifosi*. He had the race under control until, on the last lap, his unemotional and determined team-mate Didier Pironi reneged on an agreement and "stole" the victory from him. Villeneuve – as honest as he was fearless – was consumed with shock and outrage.

Two weeks later at Zolder for the Belgian Grand Prix, Villeneuve – still not speaking to Pironi – stormed out to practice, still furious over his team-mate's treachery – and never came back. His Ferrari, touching Jochen Mass's March, cart-wheeled with sickening violence, throwing the hapless driver from the car. There was no chance of survival. To this day, the *tifosi* paint a maple leaf on pole at Imola to commemorate their brave hero's antics.

Above: *Many acclaimed Gilles Villeneuve as a genius.*

Previous page: *Villeneuve driving for Ferrari at the South African Grand Prix in 1979.*

1978
American holds crown

> **TALKING POINT**
>
> **FAN POWER**
>
> Brabham turned to its fans for a bit of success when the team installed massive air blowers in the rear of their cars for the Swedish Grand Prix. They claimed the fans were used to cool the engines, but in fact they pulled air from underneath the car to create suction which pulled the car down towards the track and created astonishing grip. Rival teams protested, but Gordon Murray's cars were allowed to race and, more importantly, win. But just one race later the legality decision had been overturned and Brabham were left frantically returning their cars to the original specifications after the fans were banned.

In a year which saw tremendous dominance from the revolutionary Lotus 79, Mario Andretti became only the second American driver to hold the world crown, but his title victory was soured by the death of his nearest challenger and close team-mate Ronnie Peterson in a controversial incident for which Riccardo Patrese was blamed.

The Argentinian Grand Prix season-opener was a true prelude to the year ahead with a dominant victory for Andretti and Lotus, despite the team not yet running their revolutionary Lotus 79.

World Champion driver Niki Lauda had switched camps from Ferrari to Brabham after being lured by Bernie Ecclestone and the promise of a revolutionary new car. But Ferrari were still on the pace though Carlos Reutemann could only manage second on the grid as Andretti secured pole and steamed away into the distance when the race got underway.

Rio carnival's rival

The next race saw the introduction of a new circuit to the calendar as the Brazilian Grand Prix moved from Interlagos to the Jacarepagua circuit, just outside the glamorous city of Rio de Janeiro.

Grand Prix racing proved a worthy entertainment rival to the Rio carnival as Reutemann became the second driver to win from lights to flag in as many races.

Ronnie Peterson claimed pole for Lotus ahead of James Hunt, Andretti, and Reutemann, while the new Arrows team arrived but did not make an impression on the grid, with Riccardo Patrese only able to steer the FA1 into 18th place on the grid.

Reutemann got away best of all and Hunt led the chase, but it was to no avail as he dropped down after a pit-stop, and Andretti also fell out of second place when his gearbox remained jammed in fourth.

That let Fittipaldi and Lauda through to take second and third. A six-week gap between races left enough time for teams to complete new cars, and there were 30 entrants for the 300th World Championship race at the South African circuit of Kyalami.

Ferrari had their new machines available but neither Lotus nor Brabham had finished their revolutionary new cars. Despite this, Lauda put his Brabham on pole ahead of the old Lotus 78 of Andretti as the Ferraris struggled.

Lauda muddles the group

Lauda confused the grid when he made a last-minute decision to line up on a different side of the grid than originally planned, and several rows started in reverse order!

Both Andretti and Scheckter pulled ahead of the confused Lauda at the start, with Hunt moving into third. But by lap five, the Englishman had to retire with engine problems as Patrese made the early moves up the field.

But an engine blow put the Italian driver out of the race just as victory looked to be his. Depallier assumed the lead, but his Cosworth engine began to smoke, and in an intense battle to the line on the final lap, Peterson passed him to take the victory.

The World Championship finally arrived in Europe for round five of the series, the Monaco Grand Prix, at the start of May, and an exciting race ended in the first of only three victories that year not to go to Ferrari or McLaren.

Only 20 starters were allowed on the tight and twisty circuit and Watson was first into Sainte

Niki Lauda driving the new fan car in the Swedish Grand Prix.

Riccardo Patrese had victory in the South African Grand Prix snatched away when his car's engine blew.

Devote after passing Reutemann off the line. Depallier was a fast starter in his Tyrrell and moved up to second from the third row.

The situation became messy as the field piled into the chicane on the first lap. Lauda hit Reutemann as they battled for third, and Hunt took avoiding action but hit the wall instead. The Austrian raced on unscathed, but the other two had to pit for repairs.

On lap 38 Watson took to an escape road and lost the lead to Depallier, who went on to take his first Grand Prix victory.

Debut of Lotus 79

The next race was the Belgian Grand Prix, and Lotus finally debuted the revolutionary 79 ground-effect car to stunning effect. In the hands of Mario Andretti, the new car took its first win straight out of the box. The American showed his car's dominance by taking pole position in qualifying by nearly 0.8 seconds from Reutemann's Ferrari, and soared into the distance at the start.

Behind him there was chaos as Reutemann missed a gear and the pack tried to avoid him. Villeneuve made it past to take second, but Lauda and Scheckter collided and Patrese and Hunt also clashed. The crashes put Lauda and Hunt out immediately, and Fittipaldi also ended his race without completing a lap.

The race settled down with Andretti ahead of Villeneuve, but the Ferrari drive was forced to pit with a blown tyre leaving the Lotus 79 ahead of Peterson's 78, and not even a stop for new tyres could keep the Swede from second place as he battled back past Reutemann and Lafitte. Then they collided and Lafitte was sent spinning out, which let Villeneuve up to fourth.

When the teams arrived in Spain Lotus had two 79s, but more importantly the team had stolen sponsorship from Hesketh, which went to the wall because of the loss of money. And Lotus truly dominated the event, with a one-two in both qualifying and the race itself.

Andretti secured pole, a second faster than Lotus' nearest competitor, the Ferrari of Carlos Reutemann. Fourth-placed Hunt got off the line best in his McLaren to head the field into the first corner but once Andretti was past Hunt on lap six, there was no catching him, as the superior road-holding of the Lotus showed through.

Fan dance!

After two wins in a row, Lotus were blitzed by the arrival of Brabham's controversial fan car in the next race at the Swedish track of Anderstorp. Despite protests after qualifying, the cars were permitted to race, and Lauda won the ground-effect battle to give the BT46B its only victory.

Initial signs were good for the Lotus squad when Andretti once again put his car on pole, but the Brabhams sat ominously in second and third. Andretti duly took the lead and Lauda led the Brabham chase as Patrese and Watson provided the other challenge. The lead pair battled hard, and after leading for 38 laps Andretti made a mistake, which let Lauda through. Andretti was comfortable in second

RACE BY RACE DETAILS

ROUND 1 – ARGENTINA
Race Mario Andretti
Pole Mario Andretti
Fastest lap Gilles Villeneuve

ROUND 2 – BRAZIL
Race Carlos Reutemann
Pole Ronnie Peterson
Fastest lap Carlos Reutemann

ROUND 3 – SOUTH AFRICA
Race Ronnie Peterson
Pole Niki Lauda
Fastest lap Mario Andretti

ROUND 4 – UNITED STATES WEST
Race Carlos Reutemann
Pole Carlos Reutemann
Fastest lap Alan Jones

ROUND 5 – MONACO
Race Patrick Depallier
Pole Carlos Reutemann
Fastest lap Niki Lauda

ROUND 6 – BELGIUM
Race Mario Andretti
Pole Mario Andretti
Fastest lap Ronnie Peterson

ROUND 7 – SPAIN
Race Mario Andretti
Pole Mario Andretti
Fastest lap Mario Andretti

ROUND 8 – SWEDEN
Race Niki Lauda
Pole Mario Andretti
Fastest lap Niki Lauda

ROUND 9 – FRANCE
Race Mario Andretti
Pole John Watson
Fastest lap Carlos Reutemann

ROUND 10 – BRITAIN
Race Carlos Reutemann
Pole Ronnie Peterson
Fastest lap Niki Lauda

ROUND 11 – GERMANY
Race Mario Andretti
Pole Mario Andretti
Fastest lap Ronnie Peterson

ROUND 12 – AUSTRIA
Race Ronnie Peterson
Pole Ronnie Peterson
Fastest lap Ronnie Peterson

ROUND 13 – NETHERLANDS
Race Mario Andretti
Pole Mario Andretti
Fastest lap Niki Lauda

ROUND 14 – ITALY
Race Niki Lauda
Pole Mario Andretti
Fastest lap Mario Andretti

ROUND 15 – UNITED STATES EAST
Race Carlos Reutemann
Pole Mario Andretti
Fastest lap Jean-Pierre Jarier

ROUND 16 – CANADA
Race Gilles Villeneuve
Pole Jean-Pierre Jarier
Fastest lap Alan Jones

1978 DRIVERS' CHAMPIONSHIP

DRIVER	TEAM	POINTS
Mario Andretti	Lotus Ford	64
Ronnie Peterson	Lotus Ford	51
Carlos Reutemann	Ferrari	48
Niki Lauda	Brabham Alfa-Romeo	44
Patrick Depallier	Tyrrell Ford	34
John Watson	Brabham Alfa-Romeo	25
Jody Scheckter	Wolf Ford	24
Jacques Laffitte	Ligier Matra	19
Gilles Villeneuve	Ferrari	17
Emerson Fittipaldi	Fittipaldi Ford	17
Alan Jones	Williams Ford	11
Riccardo Patrese	Arrows Ford	11
James Hunt	McLaren Ford	8
Patrick Tambay	McLaren Ford	8
Didier Pironi	Tyrrell Ford	7
Clay Regazzoni	Shadow Ford	4
Jean-Pierre Jabouille	Renault	3
Hans-Joachim Stuck	Shadow Ford	2
Hector Rebaque	Lotus Ford	1
Vittorio Brambilla	Surtees Ford	1
Derek Daly	Ensign Ford	1

place but he went out with piston failure on lap 46.

When the Grand Prix teams reconvened in France two weeks later, the fan car was gone, banned by the authorities for using an illegal aerodynamic device, and Brabham had its work cut out to return its cars to their original specifications.

Despite the missing fans Brabham still performed well, and Watson took pole position from Andretti by the smallest of margins.

However, Andretti was ahead of Watson before the end of the first lap and then led all the way to the finish as the Lotus 79 returned to dominance after a brief Brabham beating.

Surprise for Reutemann

Brands Hatch was the venue for the next race, and Reutemann was a surprise winner of the British Grand Prix after both Lotuses dropped out of the race. The pair of 79s had taken another one-two grid position for Lotus, but race day was a different story as unreliability caused a temporary halt to the team's dominance of the sport.

Things seemingly returned to normality for the next race at the German track of Hockenheim with yet another all-Lotus front row, and one more victory for Andretti.

Young debutant Nelson Piquet arrived at Ensign but lined up 21st on the grid, yet was still ahead of Scheckter by the end of the opening lap because the South African dropped right down the field with fuel-feed problems.

Up front, Peterson got ahead of Andretti and Jones moved ahead of Lauda to take third. Lauda was soon out of the race when his Alfa-Romeo engine blew; then on lap four Peterson let Lotus Number One Andretti through as the pair dominated.

The competition just could not keep up, and many of them fell out of the race. Hunt was out with a puncture on lap 20; then Jones fell out of third 11 laps later.

But the expected Lotus one-two failed to materialize when Peterson's gearbox failed, to leave Andretti to win by more than 15 seconds from second-placed Scheckter, with Laffitte third.

SHORTS

When Mario Andretti clinched the 1978 Formula one World Championship in Colin Chapman's Lotus 79 he became just the second American, after Phil Hill in 1961, to win the drivers' title. Andretti also joined another exclusive club, becoming its sole member, as the only driver in history to have won the Daytona 500, the Indianapolis 500 and the F1 World Championship.

Mario Andretti is chased by Ronnie Peterson in the Dutch Grand Prix.

The Grand Prix field moved to Austria for round 12, with the Lotus of Andretti now moving clear in the Championship. But his race at the Osterreichring did not last long, and he was out before a lap was completed.

The two weeks preceding the race had seen a court case charge Arrows with copyright infringement after the team had blatantly copied parts directly from designs for the Shadow car.

The FA1 was banned, but the ruling did not prevent the Arrows team turning up with a brand-new A1 car, which they had been building in secret as they expected the ruling to go against them.

The high altitude made Renault's turbocharged car more competitive than ever, and it was Jean-Pierre Jabouille who was best of the rest in qualifying, as the Lotus cars filled the front row for the third time in succession.

Andretti had a poor start as Peterson was quickest off the line, and when the American tried to regain second place from Reutemann later in the lap, the pair touched and Andretti's ambitious move put him straight out of the race.

Rain soon arrived, and on lap four Scheckter was caught out and went spinning into Andretti's parked Lotus to bring out the red flags. The race was re-started with the new grid being based on the positions before Scheckter's crash, which put

Peterson on pole with Depallier second.

Third-placed Watson stalled on the line and the field was scattered by the parked Brabham. Patrese and Harald Ertl put each other out at the restart, and Jones and Hunt also went out. Peterson held on in front as the track dried and the front-runners began to come in for new tyres, and Depallier made it into second by the end, with Villeneuve's Ferrari in third.

It was another one-two for Lotus in the Dutch Grand Prix, and Andretti moved further ahead in the title chase as he beat his team-mate Peterson by nine World Championship points.

Once again a second separated pole-sitter Andretti from his team's nearest challenger who this time was Lauda's Brabham, with the Ferrari pair right behind.

Andretti led from Peterson off the start line and it remained that way for the whole race, and that was that. Although the Championship was not over, Peterson was a clear number two at the Lotus team and he was virtually out of the running.

There was some drama in the race, however, when Didier Pironi and Patrese collided at turn two. The Arrows was still in the road as the field came round for the second lap, but somehow all of the drivers managed to avoid the stationary car. Other than a couple of positional changes, the leaders remained the same, and it was the Brabhams of Lauda and Watson that came home in third and fourth.

Five weeks separated the Dutch race from the penultimate round in the United States, but the sport was steeped in controversy after Peterson had perished in the non-Championship Italian race, and the drivers blamed Patrese for his death. The Italian was refused entry by the organizers of the American event and so tried to get the race cancelled. He failed and had to sit it out.

With his team-mate gone Andretti was crowned World Champion and was a second clear of the rest of the field after qualifying on pole with Reutemann's Ferrari his closest challenger. But Andretti's race morning did not go well and he had a dramatic accident in the warm-up. He took to the grid in new team-mate Jarier's car and led from the off.

But the Lotuses were not running well and Andretti dropped behind Reutemann, Villeneuve and Jones before retiring with an engine problem. Villeneuve also had a problem with his Ferrari to leave Reutemann to take the win from Jones with Scheckter promoted to third when Jarier ran out of fuel.

The final race of the season took place on a newly-created circuit on the Ile de Nôtre Dame in Montreal. The title race was now well and truly over, and Villeneuve took the opportunity to take his first-ever Grand Prix win in front of his home crowd.

Andretti was in an unusual ninth on the grid, and it was his team-mate Jarier who took advantage of a competitive Lotus to take pole ahead of Scheckter and Villeneuve.

Villeneuve dropped into fourth behind Jones, but Jarier was clear in the lead by the end of the opening lap. Unused to his position at the rear of the top six, Andretti was fighting hard with Watson and the pair spun down the field after a collision on lap six.

On lap 18 Villeneuve moved past Jones, who dropped back with a slow puncture, and soon overtook Scheckter to take second. He was 30 seconds behind Jarier, but the Frenchman had to retire with brake problems to leave Villeneuve a popular winner. Scheckter was more than 13 seconds behind in second with Reutemann's Ferrari in third.

But for the new World Champion, there was little to celebrate on the day with 10th place. His title victory was further soured by the death of his friend Ronnie Peterson.

1978 CONSTRUCTORS' CUP

TEAM (ENGINE)	WINS
LOTUS FORD	86
FERRARI	58
BRABHAM ALFA-ROMEO	53
TYRRELL FORD	38
WOLF FORD	24
LIGIER MATRA	19
FITTIPALDI FORD	17
McLAREN FORD	15
WILLIAMS FORD	11
ARROWS FORD	11
SHADOW FORD	6
RENAULT	3
SURTEES FORD	1
ENSIGN FORD	1

It was a sad day for Formula One when Ronnie Peterson died during the Italian Grand Prix after crashing.

Jacky Ickx

AS MERCURIAL IN A SPORTS CAR as in Formula One, Jacky Ickx overflowed with natural talent, but his prodigious skills became diluted in a succession of uncompetitive cars.

CAREER DETAILS

1945	Born 1 January in Ixelles, Belgium
1965	Wins his national saloon car Championship
1966	F2 debut at 21
1968	Signs for Ferrari. First GP win. Finishes 4th in World Championship.
1969	Joins Brabham. Runner-up in World Championship.
1970	Rejoins Ferrari in F1 and sports car events. Runner-up in World Championship.
1973	Quits Ferrari mid-season. Drives freelance for McLaren and Williams.
1974	Signs for Lotus. Decline of F1 career begins.
1979	Returns to F1 with Ligier.
1992	Retires from all racing.

FORMULA ONE RECORD

Year	Team	Wins	Poles	Fast laps	Pts
1966	Matra (F2)	0	0	0	–
1967	Matra (F2)	0	0	0	–
1967	Cooper	0	0	0	1
1968	Ferrari	1	1	0	27
1969	Brabham	2	2	3	37
1970	Ferrari	3	4	5	40
1971	Ferrari	1	2	3	19
1972	Ferrari	1	4	3	27
1973	Ferrari	0	0	0	12
1973	McLaren	0	0	0	–
1973	ISO	0	0	0	–
1974	Lotus	0	0	0	12
1975	Lotus	0	0	0	3
1976	Williams	0	0	0	–
1976	Ensign	0	0	0	–
1977	Ensign	0	0	0	–
1978	Ensign	0	0	0	–
1979	Ligier	0	0	3	15

Jacky Ickx won his first Grand Prix race in front of his home crowd at Spa-Francorchamps.

Jacques-Bernard Ickx, the son of a well-known Belgian motor-racing journalist, was three times national motorcycle trials Champion when he was barely out of nappies. He switched to cars in his teens, winning the Belgian saloon car Championship in his Lotus Cortina at the age of 20.

Under the wing of Ken Tyrrell, this prodigy made an immediate impact in Formula Two culminating in a qualifying sensation at the Nurburgring in 1966. Third fastest in practice – with only Formula One drivers Denny Hulme and Jim Clark quicker – he had to start with the other Formula Two cars at the back of the grid, but, in the course of four laps, carved his way through the field to fourth place before his suspension broke, forcing his retirement after 12 laps. The buzz of the Formula One paddock, he guest-drove for Cooper at Monza to score his first Championship point, and signed for Ferrari in 1968.

Ickx did not wait long for his first Grand Prix victory. He had retired from his first two Grands Prix, started from the front row and finished third at his home Grand Prix at Spa-Francorchamps, picked up a point at Zandvoort, and in the pouring rain at Rouen-les-Essarts he took his first win. Consistent points-scoring at Brands Hatch, the Nurburgring and Monza gave him an outside Championship chance in his debut season, but a crash in Canada – breaking his left leg – ended his season prematurely.

In 1969 contractual considerations prompted Ickx to switch to Brabham in order to continue driving for the JW Gulf sportscar operation. He duly won Le Mans in one of the closest finishes ever. The Brabham team was focused on triple Champion owner Jack Brabham. At first, Ickx's results were poor, but he inherited the number one car when Brabham broke his foot and things immediately improved. Jacky finished third in France, second in England and won the Grands Prix of Canada and Germany. In Mexico Ickx finished second and ended the season runner-up.

Unwilling to continue as Number Two, Ickx left Brabham for Ferrari in 1970. Again, he began the season weakly. During the Spanish Grand Prix he crashed, his car bursting into flames. Unable to escape for 20 seconds, he was hospitalized with severe burns, but remained philosophical about the inherent danger of his sport. "There isn't a single driver who hasn't left his hotel room in the morning well aware that he may well not return," he said.

By Monaco, 17 days later, he was back in the cockpit for the Monaco Grand Prix, but his Ferrari was no match for Jochen Rindt's Lotus. The car started to improve and at Hockenheim he battled with Rindt, but finished second. Ickx won the Austrian Grand Prix but at Monza Rindt tragically lost his life during free practice, leaving Ickx the only driver mathematically able to take the Championship from him. Ickx won in Canada but finished only fourth in the United States Grand Prix, thus relinquishing his Championship dreams.

"What I felt was a sense of release," he said. "I was saying to myself: 'You're not going to win this race any more: you're not going to be Champion.' If I had won, it would have given me no satisfaction – no satisfaction at all."

In 1971 Ickx and Ferrari started as favourites, but the Championship went to the other Jackie, Stewart, and Tyrrell. Ickx won at Zandvoort, but otherwise suffered multiple retirements, while Stewart took one win after the other. The Scot and Belgian not only fought on the track but also off the track: Stewart constantly fought for more safety measures, while Ickx thought the challenge of racing was being compromised.

In 1972 Ickx's Ferrari finished second in Spain and Monaco, but otherwise the Ferrari was notable only for its retirements – except at the Nurburgring, where Ickx gave his great rival Stewart no chance at all.

"Ickx is first and foremost a fighter. He is forever giving his all, whatever the car. He is a conqueror – a very brave man and very, very clever," said François Cevert.

In 1973 the Ferrari proved to be fundamentally uncompetitive. Ickx managed one fourth place before leaving halfway through the season on bad terms. In a McLaren for the next Grand Prix, he raced to a resolute third place. In 1974 Ickx signed for Lotus but the successor to the dominant Lotus 72 was not competitive and Ickx managed only one podium finish in Brazil. The following year was even more disastrous and Ickx left the team midway through the season, even though he managed a second place in the chaotic Grand Prix of Spain. His determination flickering, he raced only intermittently after Lotus, with Williams, Ensign and Ligier until the end of 1979.

He was lured back to competition in the 1980s to drive for the Rothmans Porsche sportscar team, and won the World Championship twice and added a further two wins to his total at Le Mans, ending his career with a record six victories in the French classic. Typically of this true racer, he began competing in rally raids with Rothmans Porsche machinery and went on to win the classic Paris-Dakar in 1983. He also served as clerk of the course for the Monaco Grand Prix. He finally retired from racing in 1992.

"There is something passionate about fighting a car gone mad."

Jacky Ickx making an impression in a high-wing car at the Spanish Grand Prix in 1969

1979
Scheckter consistency pays

> **TALKING POINT**
>
> **TURBO BREAKTHROUGH**
>
> Renault finally scored the first victory of the Turbo era two years after debuting their revolutionary engine. The team had a poor start to the season, then suffered a real low in Monaco when they had a disastrous time qualifying at the back of the grid and finishing the race in last place. But how fortunes turned just one race later. Jean-Pierre Jabouille converted pole at the Dijon-Prenois track into a race win as the French team finally took a victory on home soil and it kick-started a roll for the team. Although they did not win another race during the season, the team scored four pole positions in a row, and although poor reliability and several accidents hampered their race success, the pace of the car was enough to convince Formula One teams to think about a turbo future.

All the teams started the 1979 season in Argentina with cars based on the same principle as the Lotus 79, and although Lotus did not field a new car immediately, they did have a new look.

John Player Special had quit the sport and the Norfolk-based team had secured a deal with Martini and Tissot to turn their cars from all-black to white. Meanwhile, there were personnel changes in virtually every team on the grid. Jody Scheckter replaced Carlos Reutemann at Ferrari, John Watson was in at McLaren, James Hunt had been lured to Wolf and Brazilian youngster Nelson Piquet made his debut.

Ligier victim

French teams Ligier and Renault both became two-car teams, and it was the former which surprised the paddock by taking a stunning victory in the season-opener in Argentina, as they left Lotus trailing in their wake.

The Ligiers had taken up their all-too-familiar one-two grid positions for the race, but it was stopped on the opening lap after a pile-up. Scheckter and Watson collided and collected Didier Pironi, Patrick Tambay, Piquet and Arturo Merzario, leaving all but Watson unable to take the restart.

As Depailler led the restart, Reutemann's Lotus climbed up the field and took the misfiring Ligier of Depailler on lap 44. Watson also passed the struggling Ligier before the end to claim second.

The next round took place at the Interlagos circuit in Brazil, which was back on the calendar after a one-year break for resurfacing. The drivers were still complaining about the bumps, but once again the track suited the Ligiers and their two French drivers stormed to a dominant one-two finish.

The teams lined up row-by-row on the grid with the Ligier pair on row one, a still shocked Lotus squad on row two and the Ferrari pair behind them. Laffitte took the lead at the start and never gave it up.

His team-mate Depailler did not get off the line well, however, and Reutemann sneaked his Lotus into second. Having none of it, Depailler was soon back past and followed Laffitte for the entire 40-lap race to complete an all-French one-two finish.

Andretti had to retire his Lotus on lap two with a misfire and that promoted his team-mate Reutemann to third, which he held for the rest of the race to claim his second podium finish of the year.

Fittipaldi battled to climb up the top six, but his race ended when he had to pit with a loose wheel, leaving the Ferraris of Villeneuve and Scheckter to claim fifth and sixth, with Pironi's Tyrrell getting the better of them in fourth.

New car for Ferrari

The Ligier stranglehold was broken in the next round when the teams moved continents for the South African Grand Prix at Kyalami. Ferrari turned up with their new 312T4 and turned the competition on its head by taking a one-two victory as the Ligiers dropped out after accidents.

Jean-Pierre Jabouille's old Renault RS01 had been a surprise pole-sitter, but a downpour halted the race.

The race was restarted with an emerging Villeneuve in pole, and he took full advantage of his position to build an impressive lead in the wet. Some drivers had gambled on slick tyres, and when the track dried out it left Villeneuve in difficulties. When he pitted for slicks, his team-mate Scheckter took the lead. Villeneuve was left in second after his stop but he chased and caught the South African, eventually taking the lead when home favourite Scheckter had to pit.

Another continent change saw the teams move to the United States for a west coast race at Long Beach. Once again the Ferraris were a dominant force, and took their second win of the season as Ligier continued to struggle to find past form.

Incredibly, just one race afterclaiming pole position, neither Renault qualified for the race, and it was Ferrari on pole once again. But grid positions were to mean nothing after the chaos of the start.

Villeneuve overshot his position as he led the field around, so he decided to take them round

Jody Scheckter's move to Ferrari obviously paid dividends.

Jacques Laffitte climbed through the field to win the first race of the season in Argentina.

RACE BY RACE DETAILS

ROUND 1 – ARGENTINA
Race Jacques Laffitte
Pole Jacques Laffitte
Fastest lap Jacques Laffitte

ROUND 2 – BRAZIL
Race Jacques Laffitte
Pole Jacques Laffitte
Fastest lap Jacques Laffitte

ROUND 3 – SOUTH AFRICA
Race Gilles Villeneuve
Pole Jean-Pierre Jabouille
Fastest lap Gilles Villeneuve

ROUND 4 – UNITED STATES WEST
Race Gilles Villeneuve
Pole Gilles Villeneuve
Fastest lap Gilles Villeneuve

ROUND 5 – SPAIN
Race Patrick Depallier
Pole Jacques Laffitte
Fastest lap Gilles Villeneuve

ROUND 6 – BELGIUM
Race Jody Scheckter
Pole Jacques Laffitte
Fastest lap Gilles Villeneuve

ROUND 7 – MONACO
Race Jody Scheckter
Pole Jody Scheckter
Fastest lap Patrick Depallier

ROUND 8 – FRANCE
Race Jean-Pierre Jabouille
Pole Jean-Pierre Jabouille
Fastest lap René Arnoux

ROUND 9 – BRITAIN
Race Clay Regazzoni
Pole Alan Jones
Fastest lap Clay Regazzoni

ROUND 10 – GERMANY
Race Alan Jones
Pole Jean-Pierre Jabouille
Fastest lap Gilles Villeneuve

ROUND 11 – AUSTRIA
Race Alan Jones
Pole René Arnoux
Fastest lap René Arnoux

ROUND 12 – NETHERLANDS
Race Alan Jones
Pole René Arnoux
Fastest lap Gilles Villeneuve

ROUND 13 – ITALY
Race Jody Scheckter
Pole Jean-Pierre Jabouille
Fastest lap Clay Regazzoni

ROUND 14 – CANADA
Race Alan Jones
Pole Alan Jones
Fastest lap Alan Jones

ROUND 15 – UNITED STATES EAST
Race Gilles Villeneuve
Pole Alan Jones
Fastest lap Nelson Piquet

again. When they returned to the grid, however, Laffitte's fifth-placed Ligier went sideways and Villeneuve led the field round for a third time. But officials stopped half the grid, and when the other half returned they were forced to weave through to pick up their grid positions.

Once the race finally began, Villeneuve led as Depailler moved his Ligier from fourth to second but Scheckter damaged his front wing in an effort to pass the Frenchman. In a more dramatic crash behind them, Patrick Tambay flew into the air after hitting Jan Lammer's Shadow and landed on top of Piquet's Brabham.

Scheckter moved back up to second on lap 27 and the Ferraris pulled away to leave a frantic battle for third which finished with Alan Jones bringing his Williams home third, more than 30 seconds behind.

Lotus 80

The new Lotus 80 finally debuted at the next round, the Spanish Grand Prix in Jarama. But it did not bring success to the marque, as it was even beaten by the old car in the race in which top honours went to Depailler's Ligier.

The French team showed a clear return to form in qualifying by taking their expected front row positions, but an engine failure for Laffitte on lap 15 left Depailler to fly the flag alone. Depailler had, in fact, taken the lead at the start, and in his desperation to get ahead of his team-mate Laffitte blew his engine up when he missed a gear. Reutemann had moved from eighth to third on the first lap, and took and held second once Laffitte was out. But Depailler stayed out in front to score his first and Ligier's third win of the season.

The teams arrived in Belgium with a works Alfa Romeo back in Grand Prix racing for the first time since 1951. But the car could not mimic the team's former glories, and driver Bruno Giacomelli languished in 14th place before crashing out.

After qualifying it looked as if another Ligier domination was on the cards, as they lined up at the front of the grid again. But it was not to be, and Scheckter put in a superb performance to take the win after starting in seventh place.

Laffitte dropped to fourth as the unexpectedly fast Jones and Piquet followed Depailler off the line. But he eventually passed the pair in front as well as his team-mate to claim the lead by lap19.

Jones passed Depailler too, and took the lead himself on lap 24. Andretti, who had ditched the new Lotus 80 in preference to the old car for the race, went out with brake failure on lap 27, but more importantly for the race, the leading Williams dropped out on lap 40 with electrical failure.

Depailler passed his team-mate, then crashed out of the lead soon after regaining it to leave compatriot Laffitte with an advantage. But he was chased down by Scheckter, who had recovered from a second-lap incident, and the Ferrari man eventually pulled out ahead of Laffitte to claim the win as Pironi made a late pass to claim third from Reutemann.

The title battle between Ferrari and Ligier was heating up when the Championship moved to

1980
A two-horse race

TALKING POINT

WHAT A DIFFERENCE A YEAR MAKES

When South African Jody Scheckter was crowned World Champion for Ferrari in 1979 he could have been forgiven for thinking he would continue his form into the new decade.

But Ferrari went the route of developing a turbo engine rather than concentrating on the all-conquering ground-effect designs, and as others improved around them, they had a terrible season.

Scheckter consistently qualified towards the back of the grid and scored just a single points finish in the entire season.

His team-mate Gilles Villeneuve fared little better and, after clocking up 113 points the previous year, the Italian marque netted just eight this time around: definitely a season to forget for the men from Maranello.

Williams were on a roll and clearly had the best chassis in the field at the start of 1980. Their Australian driver Alan Jones, who had won four of the last six races the previous year, started as clear favourite and ended as World Champion – but not without a challenge. Carlos Reutemann joined Jones at the team as Clay Regazzoni moved to Ensign. Ferrari retained their drivers and were already working on a turbo engine after taking the hint from Renault's success. But it was not ready and the flat-12 they were forced to use compromised their chassis.

Ligier improved the JS11 and took on Didier Pironi to replace Alfa Romeo-bound Patrick Depailler, while the Brabham team remained the same except for a colour change from red to blue and white. But perhaps the most significant change to the Grand Prix grid for 1980 was the arrival of future World Champion Alain Prost at McLaren, who partnered and regularly out-performed the experienced John Watson.

The new season dawned in predictable style with Jones on pole for the Argentinian Grand Prix, winning a comfortable race victory. It was a clear pointer that Williams were on the way up and that Ferrari were heading in the opposite direction.

Early setback for Jones

Two weeks later, and Jones saw the other side of the coin as he qualified a terrible 12th for the Brazilian Grand Prix. There was nothing he could do from there, even with the dominant Williams, and it was left to René Arnoux to capitalize on his Renault turbo engine's liking of the Interlagos circuit and claim the victory.

Arnoux's team-mate Jean-Pierre Jabouille had planted his Renault on pole, and Pironi lined up alongside him on the grid. But it was Villeneuve who got off to a flier and shot up from third to enter the first corner ahead.

Reutemann's immediate retirement with driveshaft failure added to Williams' qualifying disappointment, but Jones was out to make amends and began to climb up the field. By lap three it was an all-French top four, with Jabouille leading Ligier pair Pironi and Laffitte and team-mate Arnoux after all four went past Villeneuve. The Canadian was dropping like a stone and after losing two more places chose to go for new tyres in an attempt to halt the slide.

Laffitte dropped out and Pironi pitted to leave the Renaults out in front. But the turbo let go on Jabouille's car with 26 laps gone to leave Arnoux clear to take his first Championship victory. De Angelis was a distant second, a disappointed Jones third, followed by Pironi and Prost, who picked up two more Championship points for fifth.

Prost's debut season took a dive in round three when he crashed heavily during an accident-marred qualifying session for the South African Grand Prix.

In the first of two major crashes during the session, a suspension failure sent the Frenchman flying into the barriers and he suffered a broken wrist. Marc Surer, however, was dealt another blow when his ATS went straight on into the barriers and severely damaged his legs.

Alan Jones leading in the penultimate Grand Prix of the season in Canada. His victory there secured the World Championship.

Nigel Mansell takes time out with team-mate Elio de Angelis before his debut at the Austrian Grand Prix.

Piquet makes up ground

Jones, low on the grid, made a stunning start from row four to shoot past four drivers and close right up on the Renaults into the first corner. Laffitte got him back, but it was not long before Jones fell out of fourth with a gearbox failure. Just as it looked like a one-two for Renault, Jabouille's tyre failed and Arnoux was left to take his second win in a row ahead of the Ligier pair, Laffitte and Pironi, with Piquet scoring more points in fourth.

Prost was still out of action when the teams headed to Long Beach for the American Grand Prix which saw the start of Piquet's Championship challenge, as he took the first win of what would be a long and successful career. Jones continued his disappointing form in fifth.

Lammers went out immediately at the first corner with a driveshaft failure. Piquet increased his lead ahead of Jones, but sensationally, on lap 42, Jones collided with backmarker Giacomelli, who was having a difficult day having caused a number of crashes earlier, and the second-placed man was out.

It left Piquet to win well ahead of Patrese, with Ferrari taking their first points of the season in fifth. Regazzoni was closing on Arnoux for third when the brakes failed on his Ensign and he crashed into an abandoned car and flew into a concrete barrier. Spinal injuries left him paralysed, as his racing career came to a premature end.

Mayhem in Monaco

More than a month passed before the Formula One cars raced again, when the field returned to Europe for the Belgian Grand Prix at Zolder. And the race saw yet another new man step on to the top of the podium as Pironi took his debut win.

Jones was back on form and qualified in pole position, but Pironi was in a threatening position alongside him and shot into the lead at the start. He did not relinquish it in an uneventful race which saw the pair finish in the same positions, followed by Reutemann in the second Williams.

The field arrived in Monaco two weeks later and produced a crash spectacular when a mammoth first-lap accident was followed by the departure of the leader into the famous Monaco Armco midway through the race.

Pironi planted his Ligier on pole ahead of the Williams pair of Reutemann and Jones. The three got off the line in grid order and were followed through Sainte Devoté by Laffitte, Depailler and Piquet. But behind them Daly was literally flying after smashing into the rear of Giacomelli's Alfa, spinning into Prost as a result, and launching off the ground to eventually land on top of Jarier's Tyrrell.

After that the race seemed quite uneventful as, other than Jones' exit with differential failure, little changed in the lead order. That was until the rain began to fall and, with a stuttering gearbox, Pironi lost his luck in Casino Square and hit the barriers. So Reutemann was left to win, while Laffitte scored an uneventful second with Piquet third.

Jones makes it count

As a political war took over Formula One, the teams moved to Spain, but several had boycotted the race. Alan Jones' win was scratched from the record books and did not count in the points table.

RACE BY RACE DETAILS

ROUND 1 – ARGENTINA
Race Alan Jones
Pole Alan Jones
Fastest lap Alan Jones

ROUND 2 – BRAZIL
Race René Arnoux
Pole Jean-Pierre Jabouille
Fastest lap René Arnoux

ROUND 3 – SOUTH AFRICA
Race René Arnoux
Pole Jean-Pierre Jabouille
Fastest lap René Arnoux

ROUND 4 – UNITED STATES (WEST)
Race Nelson Piquet
Pole Nelson Piquet
Fastest lap Nelson Piquet

ROUND 5 – BELGIUM
Race Didier Pironi
Pole Alan Jones
Fastest lap Jacques Laffitte

ROUND 6 – MONACO
Race Carlos Reutemann
Pole Didier Pironi
Fastest lap Carlos Reutemann

ROUND 7 – FRANCE
Race Alan Jones
Pole Jacques Laffitte
Fastest lap Alan Jones

ROUND 8 – BRITAIN
Race Alan Jones
Pole Didier Pironi
Fastest lap Didier Pironi

ROUND 9 – GERMANY
Race Jacques Laffitte
Pole Alan Jones
Fastest lap Alan Jones

ROUND 10 – AUSTRIA
Race Jean-Pierre Jabouille
Pole René Arnoux
Fastest lap René Arnoux

ROUND 11 – NETHERLANDS
Race Nelson Piquet
Pole René Arnoux
Fastest lap René Arnoux

ROUND 12 – ITALY
Race Nelson Piquet
Pole René Arnoux
Fastest lap Alan Jones

ROUND 13 – CANADA
Race Alan Jones
Pole Nelson Piquet
Fastest lap Didier Pironi

ROUND 14 – UNITED STATES (EAST)
Race Alan Jones
Pole Bruno Giacomelli
Fastest lap Alan Jones

1980 DRIVERS' CHAMPIONSHIP

DRIVER	TEAM	POINTS
Alan Jones	Williams Ford	67
Nelson Piquet	Brabham Ford	54
Carlos Reutemann	Williams Ford	42
Jacques Laffitte	Ligier Ford	34
Didier Pironi	Ligier Ford	32
René Arnoux	Renault	29
Elio de Angelis	Lotus Ford	13
Jean-Pierre Jabouille	Renault	9
Riccardo Patrese	Arrows Ford	7
Keke Rosberg	Fittipaldi Ford	6
Derek Daly	Tyrrell Ford	6
John Watson	McLaren Ford	6
Jean Pierre Jarier	Tyrrell Ford	6
Gilles Villeneuve	Ferrari	6
Emmerson Fittipaldi	Fittipaldi Ford	5
Alain Prost	McLaren Ford	5
Jochen Mass	Arrows Ford	4
Bruno Giacomelli	Alfa Romeo	4
Jody Scheckter	Ferrari	2
Hector Rebaque	Brabham Ford	1
Mario Andretti	Lotus Ford	1

And so it was on to France. With an agreement reached between the warring factions, all the teams were back in action and Jones was to make this one count as the top Frenchmen all suffered home blues.

Pironi moved ahead of his team-mate, Jacques Laffitte, before the end to claim second. Piquet finished fourth behind the Ligiers and a slowing Arnoux, and the second Williams of Reutemann filled out the top six.

The next round was held at Brands Hatch as the British Grand Prix returned to the Kent circuit after a two-year hiatus. Pironi shot into the lead and pulled out a comfortable gap as Laffitte held off Jones for second. Then on lap 19 the leader coasted into the pits with a flat tyre and rejoined in last place.

Laffitte then fell foul to a similar problem, but for him the conclusion was much more spectacular. His tyre blew and he shot off the circuit and into the catch fencing. Leader number two accounted for: and that left Jones.

The Australian won, 11 seconds ahead of Piquet, with Reutemann third, Daly and Jarier taking fourth and fifth for Tyrrell and Prost scoring a point for McLaren in sixth.

Tragedy at Hockenheim

In the month prior to the German Grand Prix, Depailler was killed in a tragic testing accident at Hockenheim. With the catch fencing inexplicably missing, the Frenchman flew straight into the barriers and had no chance. It was a subdued field of drivers who arrived at the circuit for the German race as Formula One tried to carry on.

Alfa Romeo fielded just one car, for Giacomelli, as a mark of respect to Depailler, but the RAM team appeared with Rupert Keegan in the driving seat.

Clay Regazzoni (no 14) heads for third position at Long Beach before the crash which left him with spine injuries that paralysed him.

A dispute between FISA and FOCA led to a depleted field at the Spanish Grand Prix and no official result.

Jabouille, capitalizing on the turbo engine's liking of the circuit, scorched into the lead halfway through the opening lap and never looked back. But his race was ended a lap after his team-mate's as both Renaults went out with valve spring troubles.

Jones led, but he needed new tyres and his pit-stop dropped him to third behind his second-placed Williams team-mate Reutemann and eventual winner Laffitte. Jones had to settle for third ahead of Piquet, Giacomelli and Villeneuve, who scored a much-needed point for Ferrari.

One week later at the Austrian Grand Prix, there was one notable addition who would eventually leave his mark on the sport. Nigel Mansell made his debut in an Essex Lotus, running well until an engine failure 14 laps from the finish.

SHORTS

Frenchman Patrick Depailler, killed in a testing accident at Hockenheim in 1980, grew up inspired by the example of his compatriot Jean Behra. He was a loyal member of the Tyrrell line-up for five years and won the Monaco Grand Prix in 1978. In the year before his death, he sustained serious injuries in a hang-gliding accident and, after struggling back to fitness, joined Alfa Romeo. He died just eight days short of his 36th birthday.

Down to the wire

Jones led the Championship by 11 points when the teams moved to the Netherlands for round 10, but he finished out of the points, allowing race winner Piquet to close the gap.

The Italian Grand Prix was moved to Imola after the huge pile-up at Monza two years previously, and there was more drama when six laps into the race, Villeneuve's Ferrari speared off the circuit after a tyre blow-out and went straight into the barriers. Miraculously, Villeneuve was unhurt.

But the race did bring about a change in the World Championship lead with Piquet leading Jones home by 30 seconds.

There was now just one point in it with two races to go, and the field left Europe for Montreal and a Canadian Grand Prix which would see the crowning of a new World Champion.

Jones closes in on title

Appropriately the first two places on the grid went to Championship order, as struggling reigning World Champion Scheckter failed to qualify his Ferrari.

The lead pair both started well but Piquet refused to let Jones past and they collided, sending Piquet out of the race as Jones continued. The crash devastated the field with eight cars put out in the ensuing mêlée.

The race was stopped, and Piquet jumped in his spare car to take the restart. He claimed the lead after dropping to third at the start, but on lap 24 his engine gave up and he was out of the race. Jones was left at the head of the field.

Jabouille suffered a horrific crash and had to be cut out of his wrecked Renault, suffering bad leg injuries, but up front it was Pironi who was challenging Jones.

The second-placed man, however, had jumped the start and was given a 60-second time penalty. Jones let him through, but it did not matter. With the time penalty added Pironi dropped to third. Jones won, and was World Champion.

One week later the Grand Prix season concluded in America, and Jones crowned his World Championship victory with a final race win.

Giacomelli led from Piquet and Reutemann at the start as Jones, Andrea de Cesaris and Arnoux all took to the gravel at turn one. A disappointed Piquet soon spun off as Jones began his fightback, and the Australian was into second by lap 30, chasing Giacomelli. Suddenly, two laps later, the Alfa ground to a halt with electrical failure and gifted the lead to Jones who won from Reutemann and Pironi.

And so Jones ended his season as he had begun it – on top of the rostrum. Only this time, it was as World Champion.

1980 CONSTRUCTORS' CUP

TEAM (Engine)	POINTS
WILLIAMS FORD	120
LIGIER FORD	66
BRABHAM FORD	55
RENAULT	38
LOTUS FORD	14
TYRRELL FORD	12
ARROWS FORD	11
FITTIPALDI FORD	11
McLAREN FORD	11
FERRARI	8
ALFA ROMEO	4

Alan Jones

CAREER DETAILS

1946	Born 2 November, in Melbourne, Victoria
1963	National karting Champion
1967	Comes to England but finds cost of racing prohibitive
1970	Returns to England with fellow Aussie Brian McGuire and runs F3 Brabhams
1973	Finishes second in British series
1974	Runs in Formula Atlantic
1975	F1 debut with Stiller's Hesketh. Subs for Graham Hill's Embassy team
1976	Storms to second place behind James Hunt in Race of Champions in a Surtees
1977	Maiden GP victory in Austria
1978	Moves to Williams
1979	Wins four GPs in Patrick Head's ground-effect FW07. Finishes third behind Scheckter and Villeneuve
1980	Wins first World Championship for Williams with five victories
1981	Retires at end of season
1983	Brief return with Arrows
1985–6	Returns to Haas Lola team. Retires.

FORMULA ONE RECORD

Year	Team	Wins	Poles	Fast laps	Pts
1974	Hesketh	0	0	0	2
1975	Lola	0	0	0	–
1976	Surtees	0	0	0	7
1977	Shadow	1	0	0	22
1978	Williams	0	0	2	11
1979	Williams	4	3	1	40
1980	Williams	5	3	5	67
1981	Williams	2	0	0	46
1983	Arrows	0	0	0	0
1985	Lola	0	0	0	0
1986	Lola	0	0	0	4

A TOUGH AND RUTHLESS COMBATANT, Alan Jones won the 1980 Drivers' crown in the superb ground-effect FW07, helping Williams to their first Constructors' Cup victory.

The son of Stan Jones, who had won the non-Championship Australian Grand Prix in 1959, young Alan left school to gain experience in his father's Holden dealership. National karting Champion at the age of 16, he switched to cars, first racing a Mini and then an old Cooper before coming to England in 1967 dreaming of becoming World Champion.

With no money to fund himself he was soon back in Melbourne, but returned three years later to race in Formula Three full of the fire, determination and gutsy racing pragmatism which would become his trademark (and the benchmark for drivers subsequently employed by Frank Williams and Patrick Head). Scraping together cash by dealing in second-hand cars, he and his wife Beverley lived a frugal life until Jones's break came when Harry Stiller ran him in Formula Atlantic.

In 1975, Jones stepped up to Formula One with Stiller's Hesketh, but managed only three Grands Prix before its owner moved abroad for tax reasons. At the invitation of Graham Hill, Jones subbed for the injured Rolf Stommelen in the Embassy team. He finished fifth at the Nurburgring before the German was declared fit to resume racing duties.

A brilliant drive in the 1976 Race of Champions at the wheel of a Surtees, where he finished second behind James Hunt, earned him a contract for the season. He ended the season fourth, but a frostiness in relations with Surtees left him without the prospect of a Grand Prix drive.

"He thought he knew everything there was to know about racing," Jones said of his former World Champion team boss. "Former drivers always think they know best – their driver is just a surrogate for themselves. His ego got in the way of the team."

When, in 1977, Tom Pryce was killed in South Africa, Jones succeeded him in the Shadow team and showed his skill by winning in Austria and charging to several points finishes with some hard-bitten aggressive drives – duly attracting the attention of Frank Williams, who signed him for 1978. The chemistry between the three was the catalyst for the emergence of Jones the racer and Williams the top Formula One outfit.

"He passed car after car. I remember turning to Patrick [Head] and saying 'I don't mind if we don't finish; I've had my money's worth, because he's not just a good driver, he's an exciting driver, and I hadn't been excited by a driver's performance in many years," said Williams, recalling Jones's prowess in the 1978 United States West Grand Prix at Long Beach.

It was his inspirational qualities which impressed

Alan Jones racing in the Argentinian Grand Prix in Buenos Aires in 1980, the year he went on to become World Champion.

> "I wouldn't say he's the quickest driver around but he has a very good understanding of racing and a first-class tactical brain."
>
> *James Hunt* on Alan Jones in 1981

Celebrating his win at the British Grand Prix in 1980.

Patrick Head: "The great thing about Alan was his ability to lift everybody's morale when things were going badly. That is not a quality displayed by many drivers."

The no-nonsense Aussie perfectly suited Head's no-nonsense machine. He made several outstanding showings, often dogging the omnipotent Lotus 79s. He also took the Can-Am title in the Haas/Hall Lola T333. But for early-season unreliability in the new ground-effect Williams FW07, the 1979 season could have been his as he notched up four wins from five starts in the second half of the Championship. He finished third behind the Ferraris of Jody Scheckter and Gilles Villeneuve, but he had set out his stall. He stormed to the 1980 title with swaggering dominance. He was less happy with team-mate Carlos Reutemann to fight, but might well have retained the crown in 1981 but for poor reliability. He ended his career at Williams with a typical lights-to-flag victory at Caesar's Palace, racing into self-imposed retirement with the same ferocity with which he had started his career.

"There are pressures that derive from the extreme competitiveness of the sport," he said explaining his motivation to race. "I am constitutionally incapable of getting into a car and being jovial and relaxed. I cannot take it easy or say it doesn't matter that there are a dozen things wrong with the car. Perhaps my ego won't allow me to do that. I have to be the quickest, I have to be the best. If I'm not, I blow my cool."

Many fans were to wish that he had accepted retirement, but after racing Porsches in Australia, he was lured back to race briefly for Arrows in 1983. "I thought I could go back to Australia and race just for fun; but you don't race just for fun. It's work and if I'm going to work, I might as well be back making the money for it," he mused.

Two years later he could not resist an offer from Haas Lola, but the car was a fiasco – "about as useful as an ashtray on a motorcycle," was his disgruntled verdict and he pottered through the 1986 season in obscurity. He has since raced touring cars and worked as a commentator on Australian television.

1981
Piquet squeezes in first

TALKING POINT

SIX CENTIMETRES IS ENOUGH

To many, six centimetres may seem a minor distance, but to Brabham it was the distance which helped them back to the top of Formula One. The six centimetres in this instance was the minimum legal distance a Formula car could be from the ground. Of course, cars could only be measured when they were stationary and on the ground, but Brabham masterminded a hydro-pneumatic suspension which lowered the car on the track and, despite the ongoing debate over its legality, Nelson Piquet steered the car to Championship success.

Alan Jones wins the United States (West) Grand Prix at Long Beach.

The disappointment of losing out to Alan Jones the previous year prompted the perfect response from Brabham's Nelson Piquet as he powered to his maiden World Championship success in style to land the first title for the marque since Bernie Ecclestone took over the reins.

But the season was marred by off-track disputes, which were evident from the opening stages of the season. The South African Grand Prix, expected to kick-start the year into life, turned into a non-event when a host of disagreements between FISA and FOCA resulted in only cars associated with the latter competing at Kyalami. That race was won by Carlos Reutemann in the Williams FW07B but it did not count for points in the World Championship. What the race did signal was the first full Michelin grid following Goodyear's decision to withdraw from the sport.

Long Beach was the destination for the season-opener in the Championship and the Formula One paddock featured a number of driver changes. Williams were unchanged with Reutemann and Champion Jones, Brabham held on to Piquet and Hector Rebaque, but Alain Prost quit McLaren in favour of a move to Renault despite signing a two-year contract.

Ron Dennis was in the process of taking over McLaren and brought in Andrea de Cesaris to partner John Watson. The duo were provided with a new all-carbon fibre chassis, which had been designed by John Barnard, for the United States Grand Prix.

Mansell in, Fittipaldi out

Ligier, now called Talbot-Ligier with Matra V12 engines, were still without Jean-Pierre Jabouille following his crash in Canada in 1980 and had Jean-Pierre Jarier alongside Jacques Laffitte, while Ferrari, who replaced the retiring Jody Scheckter with Didier Pironi, introduced the new turbocharged V6 engine.

Mario Andretti opted to join Alfa Romeo from Lotus, who introduced the controversial "twin-chassis" for the Long Beach race where Briton Nigel Mansell was employed to partner Elio de Angelis. Former Champion Emerson Fittipaldi finally decided to hang up his helmet and hired Chico Serra to drive with Keke Rosberg.

In the opening race, Gilles Villeneuve made a superb start from fifth on the grid, but failed to stop at the first turn and lost ground as Patrese led Williams pair Jones and Reutemann. Prost endured a nightmare debut with Renault after a collision with

***Opposite**: Riccardo Patrese had pole position at Long Beach but failed to capitalize on it.*

de Cesaris' McLaren forced both out of the race.

Reutemann moved in front on the second lap before Villeneuve's race ended on lap 18 through driveshaft failure. Jones, however, was back in front soon after when Reutemann ran wide as he lapped Ensign's Marc Surer, and pole-sitter Piquet ended third in his Brabham.

The banning of sliding skirts was questioned in the second race of the season in Brazil when Brabham used a new hydro-pneumatic suspension that allowed the car to be closer to the ground on the track than it was off it.

Prost made a bad start in his Renault and as a result of his lack of speed Andretti ran over the top of Villeneuve's Ferrari, while behind them René Arnoux, of Renault, Eddie Cheever, Stohr and Serra all became involved in the incident. At the front, Surer handed a dream result to his Ensign team when he finished an impressive fourth.

But Reutemann caused controversy by winning the race, despite calls from his Williams team to allow World Champion Jones through for victory, leaving a split in the Williams team when they arrived in Reutemann's homeland for the Argentinian Grand Prix two weeks later.

Brabham under scrutiny

The new Lotus 88 was again banned, as it had been in Brazil, and team boss Colin Chapman left the Buenos Aires circuit before the start of practice. Piquet took pole and the victory for Brabham as the hydro-pneumatic suspension came under intense scrutiny. By the time the first European race of the season got underway at Imola in early May, the controversy surrounding Brabham's hydro-pneumatic suspension had gone and all of the teams were running the system. Lotus, however, opted to miss the race as they tested a new 87 chassis with the "twin-chassis" 88 still banned.

The Imola event was named the San Marino Grand Prix, after the independent state some 50 miles away from the circuit, following the decision to hand the Italian Grand Prix back to Monza.

The race signalled the arrival of the new Toleman team although drivers Brian Henton and Derek Warwick failed to qualify. The car had a Brian Hart turbo engine and ran on Pirelli tyres, but failed to make the race. Rising star Michele Alboreto brought much-needed backing to Tyrrell and was given his Formula One debut.

In wet conditions, Villeneuve and Pironi powered away from the rest of the field and Reutemann was left in third after his acrimonious relationship with team-mate Jones worsened when they collided on the opening lap. Reutemann lost third place when he made a mistake at the final chicane and the improving Patrese finished on the podium for Arrows.

Danger in the pit-lanes

The controversy over hydro-pneumatic suspension returned prior to the Belgian Grand Prix, but the arguments paled into insignificance during Friday's practice when Osella mechanic Giovanni Amedeo was killed in a bizarre incident. Reutemann ran into Amedeo when he fell from the pit-lane and the mechanic died in hospital. The accident brought calls from drivers that pit-lanes were too congested and, fearful their opinions were not being considered, they organized a strike before the race.

However, on the second formation lap, Patrese stalled and mechanic Dave Luckett leapt from the pit-lane to attempt to re-start the stricken vehicle. But Patrese was then hit by Arrows team-mate Stohr and the collision pushed Patrese's car into Luckett. Fortunately, Luckett was not seriously injured.

At the restart, Pironi took the lead ahead of Reutemann and Piquet. Williams' Jones soon passed

RACE BY RACE DETAILS

ROUND 1 – UNITED STATES (WEST)
Race Alan Jones
Pole Riccardo Patrese
Fastest lap Alan Jones

ROUND 2 – BRAZIL
Race Carlos Reutemann
Pole Nelson Piquet
Fastest lap Marc Surer

ROUND 3 – ARGENTINA
Race Nelson Piquet
Pole Nelson Piquet
Fastest lap Nelson Piquet

ROUND 4 – SAN MARINO
Race Nelson Piquet
Pole Gilles Villeneuve
Fastest lap Gilles Villeneuve

ROUND 5 – BELGIUM
Race Carlos Reutemann
Pole Carlos Reutemann
Fastest lap Carlos Reutemann

ROUND 6 – MONACO
Race Gilles Villeneuve
Pole Nelson Piquet
Fastest lap Alan Jones

ROUND 7 – SPAIN
Race Gilles Villeneuve
Pole Jacques Laffitte
Fastest lap Alan Jones

ROUND 8 – FRANCE
Race Alain Prost
Pole René Arnoux
Fastest lap Alain Prost

ROUND 9 – BRITAIN
Race John Watson
Pole René Arnoux
Fastest lap René Arnoux

ROUND 10 – GERMANY
Race Nelson Piquet
Pole Alain Prost
Fastest lap Alan Jones

ROUND 11 – AUSTRIA
Race Jacques Laffitte
Pole René Arnoux
Fastest lap Jacques Laffitte

ROUND 12 – HOLLAND
Race Alain Prost
Pole Alain Prost
Fastest lap Alan Jones

ROUND 13 – ITALY
Race Alain Prost
Pole René Arnoux
Fastest lap Carlos Reutemann

ROUND 14 – CANADA
Race Jacques Laffitte
Pole Nelson Piquet
Fastest lap John Watson

ROUND 15 – UNITED STATES (EAST)
Race Alan Jones
Pole Carlos Reutemann
Fastest lap Didier Pironi

1981 DRIVERS' CHAMPIONSHIP

DRIVER	TEAM	POINTS
Nelson Piquet	Brabham	50
Carlos Reutemann	Williams	49
Alan Jones	Williams	46
Jacques Laffitte	Ligier	44
Alain Prost	Renault	43
John Watson	McLaren	27
Gilles Villeneuve	Ferrari	25
Elio de Angelis	Lotus	14
René Arnoux	Renault	11
Hector Rebaque	Brabham	11
Eddie Cheever	Tyrrell	10
Riccardo Patrese	Arrows	10
Didier Pironi	Ferrari	9
Nigel Mansell	Lotus	9
Bruno Giacomelli	Alfa Romeo	7
Marc Surer	Theodore/Ensign	4
Mario Andretti	Alfa Romeo	3
Slim Borgudd	ATS	1
Andrea de Cesaris	McLaren	1
Patrick Tambay	Theodore	1
Eliseo Salazar	Ensign	1

Nelson Piquet comes home in fifth place in the United States (East) Grand Prix giving him the Championship.

Reutemann and then a collision with Piquet left the one-time leader's Brabham in the safety fencing. By lap 12 the Australian was in front but eight laps later his car jumped out of gear and he crashed into the barriers. He destroyed his radiator and scalded his leg. Pironi had dropped back so Reutemann was the new leader and he held off the challenge from Laffitte and Mansell to take the chequered flag.

Return of Goodyear

Villeneuve secured back-to-back wins with victories in Monaco and Spain. Admittedly, he benefited from Jones' misfortune at Jarama after the Williams driver had surprisingly crashed out when dominating at the head of the field.

Laffitte had landed pole, but the Ligier driver made a slow start and was overtaken by Jones, Reutemann and Villeneuve. By the end of the first lap, Villeneuve's Ferrari was up to second as Jones built up a healthy lead until his demise on lap 14.

Villeneuve and Reutemann duelled before the latter dropped down the field with gearbox problems. The race ended with five cars – Villeneuve, Laffitte, Watson, Reutemann and Elio de Angelis—separated by just 1.24 seconds, with the Ferrari's horsepower giving Villeneuve sufficient speed on the straights to hold off his rivals.

Tambay replaced the retiring Jabouille at Ligier-Talbot and his drive with Theodore was taken by Surer, who did not compete in the race at Jarama after being replaced at Ensign by Salazar. Tambay made his debut in the French Grand Prix at Dijon and that race saw the return to Formula One of Goodyear with Williams and Brabham sporting the American suppliers tyres.

Piquet led Watson and Prost from the off as the race became a procession. But on lap 58 of the race, a torrential downpour brought the event alive as officials stopped the drivers. Prost benefited from the restart and Piquet dropped down to fifth. Prost remained in front for the remainder of the race to record his maiden win.

SHORTS

Alan Jones, who retired at the end of 1981, simply could not leave racing alone. Within two years he announced he was returning to Formula One with Arrows, but the move was later aborted. Afterwards, he was a regular feature in Australian touring cars before going into broadcasting as a commentator.

Entanglements at Zandvoort

Lotus were back in action in two 87s in Germany two weeks later and running on Goodyear tyres. Third-placed Reutemann was quicker off the grid than Arnoux and challenged Prost for the lead on the opening lap of the race. Reutemann's team-mate Jones pushed for supremacy after he overtook Piquet and the Argentinian on lap 21 and finally moved ahead of Prost and Piquet. But then Jones' car suffered engine problems and Piquet eased home for the win.

Renault held the front row again with Prost ahead of Arnoux on the grid for the Dutch Grand Prix at Zandvoort. As the pair made steady starts, chaos ensued behind as six drivers collided on the opening lap.

Villeneuve tried to squeeze into a gap between Patrese and Giacomelli, only to be sent airborne after colliding with the latter's Alfa Romeo. Jones

Gilles Villeneuve overcomes car problems to take first position in the Monaco Grand Prix.

soon moved ahead of Arnoux and then began to challenge Prost for the lead, but tyre problems prevented him from passing Prost and he dropped back behind Piquet as the Renault driver eased home for the win. The second-place finish drew Piquet level with Reutemann in the Championship standings.

The Italian Grand Prix was back at Monza, its spiritual home, after a year's absence and the title race was hotting up, with many tipping the impressive Prost for honours.

Prost, Reutemann and Arnoux led the field, although Pironi entered the top three briefly, as Villeneuve retired. Laffitte joined him as he slid off following the arrival of rain and Arnoux also went off in the wet to leave Prost out on his own.

Piquet ran in third after a gearbox jam forced Giacomelli to pit, but he was denied the points which would have put him clear in the World Championship as he finished sixth after an engine blow. Prost secured the win with Jones second and Reutemann ending third.

End of an era

Before the Canadian Grand Prix, Jones announced that he would retire at the end of the season, while Andretti was also rumoured to be quitting Formula One. Siegfried Stohr would also not run again in the sport. For the Canadian race, Gilles Villeneuve's brother Jacques partnered Patrese at Arrows.

Piquet and Reutemann held the front row positions in Montreal, but Jones took the lead at the start of a wet race. Ferrari's Villeneuve, meanwhile, crashed into Arnoux and sent him into a spin as the Canadian's team-mate Pironi was also wiped out.

Jones spun in the conditions and Prost led Laffitte, only for the order to change on lap 13 when the Ligier-Talbot driver took the lead and his ensuing win gave Laffitte an outside chance of the title.

Reutemann and Piquet headed into the final race of the season, which was held in a car park in Las Vegas, separated by just one point at the head of the standings. Laffitte's win in Canada had left him just six points behind the Argentinian.

Laffitte made a quick start to move up to seventh, but Piquet lost ground and was eighth. Jones was never caught as the battle for points raged behind him. Laffitte moved into the points in fifth, but Piquet was behind Reutemann with both outside the points. On lap 17, Piquet finally overtook the Argentinian and five laps later moved into the top six after getting past Watson. He was fifth briefly when Villeneuve had a fuel problem, but Andretti overtook him and demoted him to sixth again. Giacomelli retired from fourth leaving Piquet and Reutemann in fifth and sixth, and on level points in the series. When broken rear suspension forced Andretti out, the title was Piquet's for the taking.

Prost pitted, but he moved back up to second in his recovery. Reutemann's afternoon proved fruitless as he went backwards and ended outside the points. Piquet's fifth-place finish was enough to crown him Champion and hand him his first title.

1981 CONSTRUCTORS' CUP

TEAM (Engine)	POINTS
WILLIAMS FORD	95
BRABHAM FORD	61
RENAULT	54
TALBOT LIGIER	44
FERRARI	34
McLAREN FORD	28
LOTUS FORD	22
ALFA ROMEO	10
ARROWS FORD	10
TYRRELL FORD	10
ENSIGN FORD	5
ATS FORD	1
THEODOR FORD	1

Keke Rosberg

KEKE ROSBERG BECAME THE UNHERALDED 1982 World Champion amid a season of tragic incidents. The Finn's performances, as turbo-charged as his 1982 Williams, won him acclaim as a great entertainer.

CAREER DETAILS

1948	Born 6 December in Stockholm, Sweden
1973	Former Finnish karting Champion switches to cars in Formula Vee series
1974	European Formula Super Vee Champion
1977	Wins the Tasman Formula Pacific title
1978	Wins Tasman title again. Made F1 debut. Wins international trophy at Silverstone.
1979	F1 campaign with Wolf
1980	Moves to Fittipaldi team
1982	Joins Williams. Wins one GP (Swiss) and becomes World Champion
1983	Brilliant win at Monaco
1986	Joins McLaren and retires.

FORMULA ONE RECORD

Year	Team	Wins	Poles	Fast laps	Pts
1978	Theodore	0	0	0	–
1978	ATS	0	0	0	–
1978	Wolf	0	0	0	–
1979	Wolf	0	0	0	–
1980	Fittipaldi	0	0	0	6
1981	Fittipaldi	0	0	0	–
1982	Williams	1	1	0	44
1983	Williams	1	1	0	27
1984	Williams	1	0	0	20
1985	Williams	2	2	1	40
1986	McLaren	1	1	0	22

Keke Rosberg driving for Williams in 1982, his first year with the team.

"You can only do one thing well in life. This is all I care about. I don't have the time or the inclination to be interested in anything else," said Keke Rosberg.

Born Keijo Rosberg in Sweden of Finnish parents, Rosberg's single-mindedness saw him crowned three times as national karting Champion before he switched to car racing at the age of 24 in the European and Scandinavian Formula Vee series. Progressing to Formula Super Vee, he became European Champion in 1975 before embarking on a disappointing run in Formula Two.

At the end of 1976, however, the ambitious Finn travelled to New Zealand and won the 1977 Tasman Formula Pacific title. This gave him the impetus to commute between Formula Two (in which he was classified sixth overall) and the North American Formula Atlantic Championship. In 1978 he effectively duplicated that year, winning the Tasman title again, progressing to fifth overall in Formula Two and ending runner-up in Formula Atlantic.

It was a gruelling schedule, rewarded when the Formula One team owners marked him in their notebooks after a stunning Formula One debut for the new Theodore team which saw the Finn win the International Trophy in exacting, rain-drenched conditions at Silverstone. In World Championship races, he failed to make an impression in three makes of uncompetitive car (Theodore, ATS and the Wolf).

Nineteen seventy-nine was another campaign for Wolf which ended without a Championship point. "I was ashamed. Imagine the despair when all you can do is sit in the car and watch the other cars go by," he later recalled. Wolf amalgamated with the Fittipaldi team, with Rosberg part of the package. He scored Championship points on his first outing in Buenos Aires, but the team did not have the technical resources to render the car competitive. Rosberg floundered until 1982, when Frank Williams signed him to replace Alan Jones.

"Long blond hair, Gucci briefcase, Rolex gold identity bracelet...Frank, I think he is very quick," was Carlos Reutemann's verdict when asked by Williams what he made of his new team-mate. With top-rate equipment, Rosberg proved a bold team leader after Reutemann walked away two races in, though his technique did not please purists.

The Williams break was a fantastic opportunity

"He had charisma. He'd be drinking schnapps or smoking cigarettes, but he'd also do a race distance at a street circuit in boiling hot temperatures and not collapse."

Gerhard Berger

Keke Rosberg – a bold team leader.

which he determined to maximize. He won only one race, the Swiss Grand Prix at Dijon, but his consistency during the era of dominant but fragile turbos brought him the world title after Ferrari lost both Gilles Villeneuve and Didier Pironi.

In 1983 the normally-aspirated Williams was left wanting by the turbo cars but Rosberg won spectacularly at Monaco driving on slicks throughout a wet/dry race. He had a similar cameo win in 1984 when, in a season of developing the Honda turbo engines, Rosberg's brilliance shone through again in Dallas, where he won a remarkable race in 100-degree heat. "Driving an F1 car is painful. For me it is sheer physical strain. I can think of no other sport in the world which is so punishing. But I love to push myself to the extreme. I love to see how far I can push my body, how much it will take," he said.

Forced to fulfill his contract at Williams, he competed with determination against Nigel Mansell for supremacy within the team in 1985 – winning three races to Mansell's two. "The human being I can get along with; the professional person I'm not so sure about," he said of his team-mate.

Relations with Williams were not cordial. Long before the Williams became the dominant force at the end of the season he signed a lucrative deal to join McLaren as Niki Lauda's replacement, but there was already a sense that he had lost the edge on his combative spirit. "I'm sorry, I'm nearly 37 and I don't have the balls to bang wheels at 170mph. What I need is a month in Formula Three, I guess, to learn how to race him," he said after battling with Ayrton Senna at the 1985 European Grand Prix. He stayed only one season, honest enough to acknowledge that Alain Prost was faster. "I thought I was the fastest driver in the world until I went to McLaren with Alain Prost," he said. His bid to retire in style, however, was ruined when a tyre failed while he was leading his final race in Adelaide.

Rosberg is still involved in Formula One through managing the business affairs of Mika Hakkinen and Olivier Panis.

1982
Tragedy in Belgium

TALKING POINT

A TRAGIC SEASON

The 1982 season will be remembered for many reasons, but unfortunately it is also marked as the year that Grand Prix racing lost one of its most enigmatic and talented drivers, Gilles Villeneuve.

Canadian Villeneuve had captured the hearts of Ferrari fans with his impressive, on-the-limit driving, and his death in qualifying for the Belgian Grand Prix at Zolder shocked the *tifosi* and the entire motor-racing world.

Villeneuve was pushing hard to out-qualify his Ferrari team-mate Didier Pironi when he hit the back of Jochen Mass' March and was launched into an aerial spin.

The impact was at high speed and propelled Villeneuve out of his car. He never stood a chance and died of his injuries. Ferrari, as a mark of respect, withdrew Pironi from the race as the team mourned the loss of one of their most entertaining drivers.

Canada also showed its respect for its most successful racing driver of the time in the name of its Montreal track. The venue was known as the Gilles Villeneuve Circuit by the time the season reached Canada later in 1982, and the circuit still hosts a race in the Championship to this day.

Keke Rosberg celebrates his World Championship in Las Vegas, despite only coming fifth in the race.

The 1982 season was one of the most incident-filled in the history of the sport as strikes, drivers' deaths, crashes and internal team wrangles occurred throughout the Championship. The incidents diverted attention from the fact that Finnish driver Keke Rosberg claimed his only World Championship despite winning just one race in his Williams. His consistency was the secret of his success.

At the start of the season, several big guns lined up and all had the potential to win the title. Niki Lauda returned after a two-year absence at McLaren. Rosberg joined Williams and teamed up with Carlos Reutemann, while Brabham employed Riccardo Patrese to partner Nelson Piquet. Andrea de Cesaris had moved across to Alfa Romeo to partner Bruno Giacomelli. Renault retained Frenchman Alain Prost and René Arnoux while Ferrari continued with Gilles Villeneuve and Didier Pironi. The Ligier team hired Eddie Cheever to partner Jacques Laffitte and Lotus continued with Elio de Angelis and Nigel Mansell. March also returned to the grid with Jochen Mass and Raul Boesel.

Early problems

All the teams headed for Kyalami in South Africa for the season-opening race, but it was clouded in controversy when drivers called a strike over the issue of superlicences. Qualifying was restricted to just one day and Arnoux claimed pole for Renault.

Arnoux started the race well and led until lap 13, when he encountered traffic and his Renault team-mate Prost, who had started from fifth on the grid, was able to slip past and into first place. He powered to the first win of the season.

The Argentinian Grand Prix was cancelled due to reported financial problems, so there was a two-month gap until the field reconvened in Brazil for the second round race at the Jacarepagua circuit.

Villeneuve took the lead from Prost at the start. The top six remained unchanged until lap 21 when Reutemann and Arnoux both crashed out, and a lap later Lauda also spun out. Villeneuve still had the lead as Prost dropped back behind Piquet and Rosberg, but on lap 30 the leader spun out and Piquet took over to lead for the remainder of the race as he took the win, with Rosberg second and Prost third. However, opposing teams protested that Piquet's Brabham and Rosberg's Williams were illegally lightweight. The race stewards agreed and disqualified both drivers, awarding Prost the victory.

Quick fix for Williams

In the two weeks before the next round, the United States West, Reutemann announced his retirement and came up with Mario Andretti as a replacement. He was installed by the time they reached the Long Beach circuit for the next race. De Cesaris caused a surprise in qualifying for the 75-lap race as he took pole position in his Alfa Romeo.

The race was accident-filled, with 12 drivers crashing out; Winkelhock, Prost, Arnoux, Pironi, Andretti and Piquet were among the victims. The way was left clear for Lauda to power to his first win of the season. Rosberg had driven a steady race to finish second, while Villeneuve was third but was later disqualified for what the authorities deemed as an illegal rear wing. That left Patrese classified third, Alboreto fourth, de Angelis fifth and Watson sixth.

The row over Piquet and Rosberg's disqualifications in Brazil had rumbled on as the teams went to San Marino for the next round and after the FIA ruled the exclusions should stand Brabham, Williams, March, Lotus, McLaren, Arrows and Ligier all boycotted the race which was won by Pironi, much to the anger of Villeneuve whom he had outbraked on the Tosa Corner. Villeneuve finished second and was furious with his team-mate as the teams headed to the ill-fated Belgian Grand Prix.

Disaster in Belgium

The boycotting teams returned to action at Zolder after reaching a compromise with the FIA and Williams had taken the time out to employ Derek Daly to replace Andretti.

Villeneuve was disgruntled and had sworn never to speak to Pironi again after the San Marino incident. His competitive nature meant he wanted to beat Pironi in qualifying and as the session came to an end he was pushing hard to make up the small deficit on his team-mate. Tragically, Villeneuve ploughed into the back of Mass' March and became airborne, landing nose-first on an earth bank. The car was obliterated and Villeneuve died later the same day in hospital. The Ferrari team immediately withdrew from the event.

The race was won by John Watson with Rosberg second. But Villeneuve's death had cast a shadow over the sport as the teams headed to Monaco for the next round. Ferrari took one car to the principality for Pironi and he was fifth in qualifying for the 76-lap race as Arnoux again took pole, in front of Patrese, Giacomelli and Prost.

Fortune smiles on Patrese

Arnoux led from pole at the start of the race until he spun off on lap 14 and his Renault team-mate Prost inherited first place as he led from Patrese and the other big guns. Prost looked comfortable in the lead until the rain started to fall in the latter stages. Watson, Piquet, Lauda and Rosberg had all retired with mechanical problems before Prost succumbed to the wet conditions three laps from the finish and spun out of the race.

Patrese and Pironi battled in the final three laps and they provided plenty of action. Patrese held the lead after Prost went out, but he spun and Pironi went through. Pironi started to slow down and his Ferrari ran out of fuel on the last lap and de Cesaris, who was running third, also stopped short with his Alfa Romeo out of fuel. The marshals, meanwhile, had pushed Patrese, as his car was in a dangerous position and this acted as a bump-start. Patrese

Niki Lauda enjoys his win with McLaren in the United States West Grand Prix.

RACE BY RACE DETAILS

ROUND 1 – SOUTH AFRICA
Race Alain Prost
Pole René Arnoux
Fastest lap Alain Prost

ROUND 2 – BRAZIL
Race Alain Prost
Pole Alain Prost
Fastest lap Alain Prost

ROUND 3 – UNITED STATES (WEST)
Race Niki Lauda
Pole Andrea de Cesaris
Fastest lap Niki Lauda

ROUND 4 – SAN MARINO
Race Didier Pironi
Pole René Arnoux
Fastest lap Didier Pironi

ROUND 5 – BELGIUM
Race John Watson
Pole Alain Prost
Fastest lap John Watson

ROUND 6 – MONACO
Race Riccardo Patrese
Pole René Arnoux
Fastest lap Riccardo Patrese

ROUND 7 – UNITED STATES (EAST)
Race John Watson
Poll Alain Prost
Fastest lap Alain Prost

ROUND 8 – CANADA
Race Nelson Piquet
Pole Didier Pironi
Fastest lap Didier Pironi

ROUND 9 – HOLLAND
Race Didier Pironi
Pole René Arnoux
Fastest lap Derek Warwick

ROUND 10 – BRITAIN
Race Niki Lauda
Pole Keke Rosberg
Fastest lap Brian Henton

ROUND 11 – FRANCE
Race René Arnoux
Pole René Arnoux
Fastest lap Riccardo Patrese

ROUND 12 – GERMANY
Race Patrick Tambay
Pole Didier Pironi
Fastest lap Nelson Piquet

ROUND 13 – AUSTRIA
Race Elio de Angelis
Pole Nelson Piquet
Fastest lap Nelson Piquet

ROUND 14 – SWITZERLAND
Race Keke Rosberg
Pole Alain Prost
Fastest lap Alain Prost

ROUND 15 – ITALY
Race René Arnoux
Pole Mario Andretti
Fastest lap René Arnoux

ROUND 16 – CAESARS PALACE
Race Michele Alboreto
Pole Alain Prost
Fastest lap Michele Alboreto

1982 DRIVERS' CHAMPIONSHIP

DRIVER	TEAM	POINTS
Keke Rosberg	Williams Ford	44
John Watson	McLaren Ford	39
Didier Pironi	Ferrari	39
Alain Prost	Renault	34
Niki Lauda	McLaren Ford	30
René Arnoux	Renault	28
Michele Alboreto	Tyrrell Ford	25
Patrick Tambay	Ferrari	25
Elio de Angelis	Lotus Ford	23
Riccardo Patrese	Brab Ford/Brab BMW	21
Nelson Piquet	Brabham BMW	20
Eddie Cheever	Talbot Matra	15
Derek Daly	Williams Ford	8
Nigel Mansell	Lotus Ford	7
Carlos Reutemann	Williams Ford	6
Gilles Villeneuve	Ferrari	6
Andrea de Cesaris	Alfa Romeo	5
Jacques Laffitte	Talbot Matra	5
Mario Andretti	Ferrari	4
Jean-Pierre Jarier	Osella Ford	3
Marc Surer	Arrows Ford	3
Manfred Winkelhock	ATS Ford	2
Eliseo Salazar	ATS Ford	2
Bruno Giacomelli	Alfa Romeo	2
Mauro Baldi	Arrows Ford	2
Chico Serra	Fittipaldi Ford	1

Pironi and Villeneuve battle it out at the San Marino Grand Prix, which left Villeneuve fuming at his team-mate.

cruised through to victory and Pironi was classified second with de Cesaris third.

After Patrese's amazing win in Monaco, Ferrari confirmed that Patrick Tambay would replace Villeneuve after the next round in America, held at the Detroit circuit. Ferrari again ran just one car for Pironi at the event which was again won by Watson.

Second tragedy

One week after the race in Detroit, the teams re-grouped for the next round in Montreal. It was the mid-point of the season and the Championship race was wide open as five different drivers had won the first seven races.

Pironi, still the lone Ferrari representative, responded to his team's hard work on the test track by securing pole position for the 70-lap race, with the Renaults of Arnoux and Prost second and third on the grid respectively, but the start was marred by a crash involving several drivers as Pironi stalled on the grid and was hit by Boesl's March. Riccardo Palleti then also hit the Ferrari of Pironi, who was pushed across the track in his car and into the path of Geoff Less' Theodore.

Paletti was trapped in his car and, as it caught fire, Pironi and several marshals helped him out. But his injuries were so severe that he died in hospital.

The race was not restarted until six in the evening and Pironi, in the Ferrari spare car, was immediately overtaken on the first lap by Arnoux, followed soon after by Prost, Piquet, Watson and Rosberg as Pironi dropped back. Mansell also collided with Giacomelli and broke his wrist as Arnoux attempted to hold off the challenge of Piquet at the front. By lap nine Piquet had taken the lead from Arnoux and he went on to dominate the race.

SHORTS

Didier Pironi is one of Formula One's most inspired figures, but, like his Ferrari team-mate Gilles Villeneuve, his life was to end in tragic circumstances. The 1982 Formula One Championship seemed his for the taking until he broke both of his legs during a test for the East German Grand Prix. He never raced in Formula One again but, needing to fulfil his competitive edge, he turned to powerboat racing and was killed in an accident off the coast at Southampton, in England, in 1987.

Pironi holds his nerve

Tambay arrived on the scene for Ferrari as the teams reached Zandvoort, but he only managed sixth place in a qualifying session which saw the Renaults back at the front of the grid. Arnoux took pole ahead of Prost.

Prost took his team-mate at the start and led for four laps before Pironi charged through to take first place. Arnoux crashed out of the race on lap 22 and Prost followed three laps later with engine problems. Pironi, meanwhile, stayed cool as he was chased by Piquet, Rosberg, Lauda and Daly to take his second win of the season.

Two weeks after the Dutch race, the Championship arrived in England for the British Grand Prix and the event attracted a large crowd as Irishman Watson led the title race from Pironi and Rosberg. Mansell also returned for his home event now his wrist had healed.

On race day there was immediate action as Rosberg (in pole position) stalled before the start of the formation lap and was forced to start from the back of the grid. That left Patrese in pole, but he also failed to get away and was hit from behind by Arnoux, taking both cars out of the race. That left Piquet in the lead and Pironi second as Rosberg drove a quick first lap to pass eight drivers. On the second lap, Chico Serra's Fittipaldi collided with Jean-Pierre Jarier's Osella and flew through the air and backwards into a barrier. Serra emerged unscathed but the incident also forced Watson to spin and he went out of the race.

Piquet's lead lasted just nine laps as he was forced to retire with a fuel pump problem and that allowed Lauda, who had overtaken Pironi, to come through and take the lead.

Another blow for Ferrari

There were just seven days before the next round in France, and Mansell decided to withdraw from the event. He was replaced by Lees.

Arnoux held his lead at the start, but the Brabhams looked strong as Patrese and Piquet moved up to second and third respectively. Patrese, however, retired on lap eight with an engine fault after briefly taking the lead off Arnoux for four laps.

On lap 11 Mass was involved in a spectacular accident as he hit Mauro Baldi's Arrows and ploughed into a spectator area. The car caught light, but Mass got out in time and neither the driver nor any of the crowd was seriously injured.

Piquet had acquired the lead after Patrese's departure but also suffered an engine problem and retired on lap 23, leaving the way clear for Arnoux to charge through and claim the win.

As the teams arrived at Hockenheim for the German Grand Prix, Mansell returned and Mass, missing after his big crash in France, was replaced by Rupert Keegan.

Won by Tambay, who was now Ferrari's only driver, the race will also be remembered for a remarkable incident involving Piquet and Chilean driver Salazar, driving an ATS. Piquet was running well near the front of the field when he clashed with Salazar and both drivers crashed out. An irate Piquet proceeded to attack the ATS driver.

Rosberg's consistency counts

Rosberg sensed his chance of the title and he subsequently upped his challenge as the Swiss Grand Prix took place for the first time since 1954. As motor racing was banned in Switzerland the race was held at the Dijon-Prenois circuit in France.

Prost took pole for the 80-lap race in front of his home crowd, and he led for 78 of those 80, seemingly heading for another win, but Rosberg had stayed close and took the Frenchman on the penultimate lap. It was his first (and only) win of the season. All of a sudden he was the Championship leader.

After a win for Arnoux in the Italian Grand Prix, the title battle went to the last race in Las Vegas Rosberg just needed to hope that Watson did not win to claim the world title. Prost took pole for the 75-lap race as Rosberg and Watson both battled at the front of the field. Prost was overtaken by Alboreto on the lap 52 and he went on to win with Watson second, Cheever third and Prost fourth. But Rosberg had kept in touch with the front four and finished fifth to ensure that the World Championship was his, despite the fact he had won just one race in the entire season.

1982 CONSTRUCTORS' CUP

TEAM (Engine)	POINTS
FERRARI	74
McLAREN FORD	69
RENAULT	62
WILLIAMS FORD	58
LOTUS FORD	30
TYRRELL FORD	25
BRABHAM BMW	22
TALBOT MATRA	20
BRABHAM FORD	19
ALFA ROMEO	7
ARROWS FORD	5
ATS FORD	4
OSELLA FORD	3
FITTIPALDI FORD	1

Officials and emergency staff deal with the aftermath of Gilles Villeneuve's crash at the Belgian Grand Prix at Zolder.

Didier Pironi

CAREER DETAILS

1952	Born 26 March in Villecresnes, France
1974	French Formule Renault Champion
1975	Competes in Formule Super Renault
1976	Formule Super Renault Champion
1977	Promoted to Elf Martini Formula 2 squad
1978	F1 debut as Tyrrell driver. Le Mans winner
1980	Moves to Ligier. First GP win at Zolder
1981	Joins Gilles Villeneuve at Ferrari
1982	Imola incident. Crash at Hockenheim
1987	Dies in powerboat crash

FORMULA ONE RECORD

Year	Team	Wins	Poles	Fast laps	Pts
1978	Tyrrell	0	0	0	7
1979	Tyrrell	0	0	0	14
1980	Ligier	1	2	3	32
1981	Ferrari	0	0	1	9
1982	Ferrari	2	2	2	39

MOTIVATED BY A DESPERATE AMBITION to become France's first World Champion, Didier Pironi never achieved that goal in a career marred by controversy and tragedy.

Didier Pironi could well have been crowned World Champion in 1982 had he not crashed, unsighted by driving rain, into Alain Prost's Renault in practice for the German Grand Prix at Hockenheim. His feet and ankles were miraculously saved but never recovered enough to allow him back to the cockpit. His cool, ruthless approach had been calculated towards becoming France's first World Champion, but his fate was to watch his younger compatriot Prost develop into his nation's hero.

The accident occurred just eight races after the San Marino Grand Prix, when Pironi, aiming to prove he was the equal of team-mate Gilles Villeneuve, "stole" the win from the French-Canadian on the last lap against team orders. The two never spoke again. Two weeks later Villeneuve, still livid at the betrayal, crashed in practice at Zolder. His many friends put the blame for his state of mind firmly on Pironi.

Contemporary observers affirm that ruthlessness drove Pironi's talent. In 1980 he had said, "The only thing that interests me in F1 is the World Championship. If I began to think I couldn't win it, I would stop. I don't want to spend my life in F1 for the sake of it."

Two years later he dressed it up more poetically. "When I met Enzo Ferrari, I discovered what it is to have a real passion in life," he said. "It is something noble. Once you find that out, you know that any singular passion – even collecting butterflies – is worthy of one's total devotion. Now I have no doubt. This is my life."

Of his relationship with Villeneuve, the only team-mate whom he had struggled to match, he would only hint at the intensity of his view of their personal competition. "In Formula One you are part of a racing stable and the number one driver is the stud and he's the one you're always compared with, every race. What they do is praise one and forget the other one. You feel wounded and resentful, so between two men with the same team, ironically you get more – a lot more – rivalry."

Pironi was introduced to motor sport by his cousin José Dolhem. In 1972 he won a scholarship drive in the French Formule Renault series after attending the Winfield racing school. After two

Pironi takes the winner's flag at the San Marino Grand Prix in 1982, a race which left him in bitter dispute with his team-mate Gilles Villeneuve.

"There are one or two drivers who never give up. Pironi's one of them. You think you've lost him, you ease up, look in your mirror and there he is again."

Alan Jones 1981

A reflective Didier Pironi.

years of dedicated learning he emerged as the 1974 Champion. Two years of racing in the Formule Super Renault series, initially supporting René Arnoux, earned him another Championship title.

Pironi took a calculated route to gaining the attention required to secure a Formula One drive. Promoted to the Elf Martini Formula Two squad in 1977, he gambled on a one-off Formula Three entry in the showcase race at Monaco. With extra confidence from that showing, he took his first Formula Two win at Estoril and was duly signed by the Tyrrell Grand Prix team. "Driving is more a state of mind than the use of intelligence," he said. "The driver's problems are moral and psychological rather than intellectual."

His Formula One career was promising at the outset: he completed four of his first six races in the points, but finished 15th as the end of the season was coloured by too many shunts. He also won at Le Mans. He was then kept to his contract by Tyrrell for an inconsequential 1979 season before moving to Ligier. And in the true blue French Equipe Ligier Gitanes outfit, Pironi outperformed Jacques Laffitte to take his maiden Grand Prix win at Zolder.

The departure of Jody Scheckter from Ferrari gave the Frenchman, classified a respectable fifth in the 1980 Championship, a coveted drive. Villeneuve had the measure of the unrefined new turbo cars and Pironi was frustrated not to do better than race to a single fourth place in the course of the year. With typical intensity, he resolved 1982 would be his year.

It started badly with 18th in Kyalami, sixth in Brazil and an off at Long Beach. Then, at Imola, came the controversial saga in which Pironi was said to have reneged on a gentleman's agreement as he stole certain victory from his team-mate on the last lap. Recriminations were bitter when the aggrieved Villeneuve fatally crashed in practice for the following race at Zolder. Pironi, now team leader, produced a run of admirable performances. But his crash at Hockenheim finished his career as a driver, and Keke Rosberg sneaked away with his title by five points.

Pironi turned to powerboat racing but was killed in an accident off the Isle of Wight in August 1987.

1983
New engines show class

TALKING POINT

MOSS RETURNS

Prior to the German Grand Prix in August, Brabham ran a test at the Brands Hatch circuit in Kent for a host of drivers as they aimed to develop their car after the introduction of flat-bottomed cars.

That might not seem too unusual, but one of the drivers to don his overalls and climb into the cockpit of a Brabham was none other than British hero and racer of the past, Stirling Moss.

Moss was 53 at the time of the test, but he rejoined the racing fraternity to help his former Cooper-Climax team-mate from the 1950s, Jack Brabham, and his ever-changing team.

Brabham and Moss had been not only team-mates, but also rivals throughout the 1950s and early 1960s in Formula One and the test is arguably one of the most bizarre in the history of the sport.

Also testing before the German Grand Prix for the Williams team was a young Brazilian driver, whom Frank Williams believed had a future in the sport, even if he did not have the sponsors at the time to make it big straight away. The name of the young man in the Williams? Ayrton Senna.

After the trials and tribulations of the previous season, the Grand Prix paddock returned to action in 1983 with several different faces in the teams and cars which had a distinct difference from their predecessors – with turbo-charged engines under the chassis and new flat-bottomed regulations.

Lotus, who were rocked by the death of their team founder Colin Chapman in the close season, kept their driver line-up the same, with Nigel Mansell partnering Elio de Angelis in the Renault-powered cars. Reigning Champion Keke Rosberg had a new partner at Williams, who were still supplied by Cosworth engines, in Jacques Lafitte. The Benetton clothing company also entered the sport, sponsoring the Tyrrell team, who retained Michele Alboreto and signed Danny Sullivan. Brabham kept Riccardo Patrese and Nelson Piquet, but had a new BMW-powered car which would ultimately make a massive impression on the season. BMW also supplied a power-unit to the one-car ATS team for Manfred Winkelhock.

John Watson and Niki Lauda continued with McLaren, while Alain Prost was joined by Eddie Cheever at Renault. Ligier employed Raul Boesel and Jean-Pierre Jarier, Alfa Romeo had Andrea de Cesaris and Mauro Baldi, and Derek Warwick and Bruno Giacomelli represented Toleman. Arrows, with drivers Marc Surer and Chico Serra, Theodore, with drivers Roberto Guerrero, and Osella with drivers Corrado Fabi and Piercarlo Ghinzani made up the main runners, but the Fittipaldi team was missing after it had ceased to exist in the close season.

Opening success for Piquet

Rosberg claimed pole position for the 63-lap Brazilian Grand Prix, with Prost, Tambay, Piquet, Warwick and Arnoux behind him on the grid at the Jacarepagua Circuit.

At the start of the race Rosberg led from pole with Prost in close proximity, but Piquet also started well and on lap seven he overtook both Prost and Rosberg to take the lead and eventually win the first race of the season. Rosberg, who had come second, was disqualified after the race for receiving a push-start but none of the drivers below him were promoted a place, so the points for third to sixth place stood.

For the second round of the Championship the field arrived in Long Beach, California and a familiar face was back on the track as Arrows lured Alan Jones out of retirement. But while Tambay took pole position for the 75-lap race with his Ferrari team-mate Arnoux alongside him on the front row, it was John Watson who ended up the winner with Lauda second.

Italian joy

As the teams headed back across the Atlantic for the French Grand Prix, Jones was missing for Arrows having cut short his comeback, Serra was back in his place. In qualifying for the 54-lap race, Prost secured pole in his Renault with team-mate Cheever on the front row.

In the race, Prost maintained his lead at the start as United States West Grand Prix winner Watson

Patrick Tambay leading from Keke Rosberg at the San Marino Grand Prix at Imola.

Alain Prost winning the British Grand Prix in his Renault car.

retired on the third lap with a throttle problem. Prost was being chased hard by Piquet and on lap 30 Piquet took the lead from the French driver but held it for just two laps as Prost came back to take top spot. Prost held his lead to the chequered flag to take his first win of the season, as Piquet was left to settle for second.

Imola hosted the next round of the championship and, with the fanatical Italian fans in attendance, the Ferrari of Arnoux cruised to pole position for the 60-lap race, with Piquet second on the grid and Arnoux's team-mate Tambay third.

To the delight of the Italian fans Piquet suffered a disastrous start in the race as he stalled on the grid allowing Arnoux to speed away in the lead with Tambay second.

By lap 12 Arnoux had also lost his lead to Patrese, who had moved up from fifth on the grid. Tambay was also in close contention and he took Patrese for the race lead on lap 34. Arnoux, by now, was third but was boosted to second when Patrese went out on lap 54. Prost, however, crept past Arnoux before the finish, but the Ferrari fans saw a "home" winner as Tambay steered his scarlet car over the line first.

The attractive Principality of Monaco hosted the next round and qualifying for the 76-lap race produced some surprises as McLaren duo Lauda and Watson were among eight drivers who failed to qualify for the reduced-field grid on the Monte Carlo streets. Prost took pole position for the race from Arnoux, Cheever, Tambay and Rosberg.

Prost makes Pole his own

On the first lap of the race, Prost maintained his lead but behind him Mansell and Alboreto both crashed out. By the second lap Rosberg took the lead from Prost, while Winkelhock, Boesel and Arnoux all became casualties. Rosberg, however, was flying and he held off the challenge of Prost and Piquet, as Warwick, Surer and Laffitte all crashed in the latter stages, to win with Piquet sneaking second place away from Prost.

The Formula One bandwagon rolled across Europe to Belgium for the sixth round at the redeveloped, and shorter, Spa-Francorchamps circuit.

The start of the race was marred by confusion as the starter deemed that cars were not lined up properly. Some of the drivers did not realize it had been aborted and sped away. The cars should have immediately lined up and restarted but instead returned to the grid and team mechanics were allowed out to tweak the cars and in some cases add more fuel.

As the race restarted, de Cesaris beat Prost off the line and led for the first 18 laps before experiencing problems with his car and being forced into a long pit-stop. Prost inherited the lead and over the next five laps battled with Patrese. He regained the lead on lap 24 and held it for the remainder of the race as de Cesaris dropped out with engine trouble on lap 25.

Arnoux holds on for win

The next round was at the Detroit circuit, where Tambay stalled on the grid and Michele Alboreto had a surprise win, after Arnoux and Piquet made a battle of the race but were both beaten by engine failure and a puncture respectively.

A week after the Detroit race, the field moved north for the Canadian Grand Prix at the Montreal circuit and it was business as usual for Arnoux as he took pole position again for the 70-lap race. Prost was second on the grid.

RACE BY RACE DETAILS

ROUND 1 – BRAZIL
Race Nelson Piquet
Pole Keke Rosberg
Fastest lap Nelson Piquet

ROUND 2 – UNITED STATES (WEST)
Race John Watson
Pole Patrick Tambay
Fastest lap Niki Lauda

ROUND 3 – FRANCE
Race Alain Prost
Pole Alain Prost
Fastest lap Alain Prost

ROUND 4 – SAN MARINO
Race Patrick Tambay
Pole René Arnoux
Fastest lap Riccardo Patrese

ROUND 5 – MONACO
Race Keke Rosberg
Pole Alain Prost
Fastest lap Nelson Piquet

ROUND 6 – BELGIUM
Race Alain Prost
Pole Alain Prost
Fastest lap Andrea de Cesaris

ROUND 7 – UNITED STATES (EAST)
Race Michele Alboreto
Pole René Arnoux
Fastest lap John Watson

ROUND 8 – CANADA
Race René Arnoux
Pole René Arnoux
Fastest lap Patrick Tambay

ROUND 9 – BRITAIN
Race Alain Prost
Pole René Arnoux
Fastest lap Alain Prost

ROUND 10 – GERMANY
Race René Arnoux
Pole Patrick Tambay
Fastest lap René Arnoux

ROUND 11 – AUSTRIA
Race Alain Prost
Pole Patrick Tambay
Fastest lap Alain Prost

ROUND 12 – HOLLAND
Race René Arnoux
Pole Nelson Piquet
Fastest lap René Arnoux

ROUND 13 – ITALY
Race Nelson Piquet
Pole Riccardo Patrese
Fastest lap Nelson Piquet

ROUND 14 – EUROPE (BRITAIN)
Race Nelson Piquet
Pole Elio de Angelis
Fastest lap Nigel Mansell

ROUND 15 – SOUTH AFRICA
Race Riccardo Patrese
Pole Patrick Tambay
Fastest lap Nelson Piquet

1983 DRIVERS' CHAMPIONSHIP

DRIVER	TEAM	POINTS
Nelson Piquet	Brabham	59
Alain Prost	Renault	57
René Arnoux	Ferrari	49
Patrick Tambay	Ferrari	40
Keke Rosberg	Williams	27
John Watson	McLaren	22
Eddie Cheever	Renault	22
Andrea de Cesaris	Alfa Romeo	15
Riccardo Patrese	Brabham	13
Niki Lauda	McLaren	12
Jacques Laffitte	Williams	11
Michele Alboreto	Tyrrell	10
Nigel Mansell	Lotus	10
Derek Warwick	Toleman	9
Marc Surer	Arrows	4
Mauro Baldi	Alfa Romeo	3
Elio de Angelis	Lotus	2
Danny Sullivan	Tyrrell	2
Johnny Cecotto	Theodore	1
Bruno Giacomelli	Toleman	1

Arnoux this time made a good start and led for the first half of the race, but on lap 36 Patrese, who had closely followed Arnoux, took the leader with a fine overtaking manoeuvre, but his lead lasted just two laps before the Ferrari driver came back to take top spot. Arnoux sensed his chance and after Patrese dropped out on lap 56 with a gearbox problem he held on for victory from Cheever, Tambay, Rosberg, Prost and Watson.

Prior to the United States race in Detroit, Lotus had employed the services of designer Gérard Ducarouge and he designed two new cars for de Angelis and Mansell which were ready for action at the British Grand Prix. The two Ferraris got a quick start but it was Tambay who led after the first lap, ahead of his team-mate Arnoux, Prost, Patrese, Cheever and de Angelis. And Tambay held his lead until lap 19 when Prost powered past as Arnoux dropped back behind the Renault and the advancing Piquet. Prost and Piquet then took over as the Ferraris struggled to keep pace. Piquet took the lead on lap 37, but Prost came back four laps later and regained the advantage. Prost held on to claim the win with Piquet second, Tambay third and Mansell fourth after he overtook Arnoux late in the race.

Turbos relish thin air

Three weeks after the British race the Championship rolled on to Germany and the Hockenheim circuit, where Tambay claimed pole position despite rumours that he would be dropped by Ferrari at the end of the season. Arnoux made it a Ferrari one-two on the front row with de Cesaris third, Piquet fourth and Prost fifth.

In the race, Tambay led for the first lap but was overtaken soon after by Arnoux on the second lap as Mansell went out with engine trouble. On lap four Alboreto retired with a water pump fault and on laps 10 and 11 de Angelis and Tambay respectively went out of the race. Arnoux only briefly surrendered the lead to Piquet before claiming victory.

As the field arrived at the high-altitude Osterreichring in Austria, it was clear that the cars with turbo engines would work better in the thinner air, and so it proved in qualifying. Ferrari dominated again as Tambay took pole from Arnoux. Mansell was third in a Lotus from Piquet, Prost and Patrese. Local hero Lauda, however, did not have a turbo engine in his McLaren and started in 14th place.

The front four on the grid also displayed their superiority in the race as they sped away unaware of the carnage behind them. De Angelis had lost control of his Lotus and hit Giacomelli's Toleman, putting both drivers out. Further back, Ghinzani hit Laffitte, who in turn crashed into Surer. Surer then went into a spin and crashed into Fabi, who was clipped from behind by Watson.

At the front, Tambay held his lead until lap 22 when he was taken by team-mate Arnoux, who in the next 25 laps battled with Patrese for the lead as Tambay dropped out on lap 30 with an engine fault.

Prost, however, lingered in the background with intent and on lap 48 of the 53 he took Arnoux and Patrese for the lead and did not look back as he took the chequered flag from the two rivals.

SHORTS

René Arnoux, who so delighted the Italian fans by driving to pole-position at Imola and eventually winning, was always considered an outsider to the world of Formula One. He lacked the connections of other drivers, but that did not stop him winning several Grands Prix. He continued racing at the highest level until 1989.

Alain Prost celebrates his win at the Austrian Grand Prix at the Osterreichring.

Nelson Piquet wears the World Champion's laurels at the South African Grand Prix, although he finished third.

1983 CONSTRUCTORS' CUP

TEAM (Engine)	POINTS
FERRARI	89
RENAULT	79
BRABHAM BMW	72
WILLIAMS FORD/HONDA	38
McLAREN FORD/PORSCHE	34
ALFA ROMEO	18
TYRRELL FORD	12
LOTUS FORD/RENAULT	12
TOLEMAN HART	10
ARROWS FORD	4
THEODORE FORD	1

Prost and Piquet battle it out

Two weeks after the Austrian race the next round took place at the Zandvoort circuit in Holland and McLaren brought out their new MP4/1E car for Lauda. However, it did not help the Austrian as he qualified 19th, while Championship challenger Piquet took pole from Tambay, de Angelis and fellow title hunter Prost.

Piquet took the lead at the start as Tambay was slow off the line. On lap 41, as Prost challenged for the lead, he clashed with Piquet and the two drivers collided. Piquet went out and Prost only continued for half a lap before he went out with a broken wing. That left Arnoux to inherit the lead and he held it for the remainder of the race.

Prior to the Italian Grand Prix the talk of the paddock was Championship challengers Prost and Piquet's clash in Holland. However, it was Patrese who took pole position.

At the start, Patrese led from Piquet but his race was over three laps later as he retired with an engine blowout. That allowed Piquet to take the lead, which he kept for the remainder of the race with Arnoux in hot pursuit.

Brands Hatch decides crown

The penultimate round of the Championship was hosted at Brands Hatch and called the European Grand Prix after the cancellation of a round in New York. Arnoux was still in with a shout of the Championship after his second place in Italy, but Prost and Piquet were the favourites.

Qualifying for the 76-lap race produced a surprise as de Angelis took top spot on the grid ahead of Patrese, Mansell, Piquet, Arnoux, Tambay, Cheever and Prost. Patrese took the lead at the start as de Angelis dropped back. On lap 10 de Angelis came back and challenged Patrese for the lead, but the two drivers clashed and spun, gifting the lead to Piquet.

Patrese recovered and stayed ahead of Prost but a spin late in the race let Prost through into second as Piquet sped away for the win. Prost secured second place ahead of Mansell.

As the teams gathered in South Africa for the final round, Prost led the Championship by two points from Piquet while Arnoux was six points further back as the last race promised to provide a spectacular finale at the Kyalami circuit.

Tambay took pole position for the 77-lap race ahead of Piquet, who was second with Prost in fifth. Piquet got off to the perfect start as he took the lead from Tambay off the line and powered into a commanding lead. Arnoux's race and Championship hopes went up in smoke after nine laps as his engine blew and on lap 35 Prost's worst nightmare came true as he retired with a fault on his turbo. That left the way clear for Piquet to win the Championship if he could finish fourth or better. Once he learned of his rivals' retirements he began to coast around the circuit and Patrese took the lead on lap 60, soon followed by de Cesaris.

As the chequered flag came down on Patrese for the win, de Cesaris finished second and Piquet claimed third place and snatched the Championship from Prost's grasp by just two points. The defeat was all too much for Prost and he split with the Renault team soon after in acrimonious circumstances.

Nelson Piquet

CAREER DETAILS

1952	Born 17 August, in Rio de Janeiro
1971	Brazilian karting Champion
1977	Races in European Formula Three series
1978	F1 debut with Ensign
1979	Signs for Brabham
1981	World Champion
1983	World Champion
1986	Joins Williams
1987	World Champion
1988	Joins Lotus
1990	Joins Benetton
1991	Retires from F1 at end of season
1992	Crashes at Indianapolis
1993	Returns to Indianapolis

FORMULA ONE RECORD

Year	Team	Wins	Poles	Fast laps	Pts
1978	Ensign	0	0	0	–
1978	McLaren	0	0	0	–
1978	Brabham	0	0	0	–
1979	Brabham	0	0	1	3
1980	Brabham	3	2	1	54
1981	Brabham	3	4	1	50
1982	Brabham	1	1	2	20
1983	Brabham	3	1	4	59
1984	Brabham	2	9	3	29
1985	Brabham	1	1	0	21
1986	Williams	4	2	7	69
1987	Williams	3	4	4	73
1988	Lotus	0	0	0	22
1989	Lotus	0	0	0	12
1990	Benetton	2	0	0	43
1991	Benetton	1	0	0	26

A SHEER LOVE OF RACING characterized the charismatic Brazilian's three world titles, but his critics say Nelson Piquet never competed with the demeanour of a true Champion.

It is hard to believe that, despite winning three World Championships and 23 Grands Prix, Nelson Piquet's reputation has been overshadowed by the colossal Eighties rivalry of Alain Prost and Ayrton Senna. A racer of immense talent, Piquet was also wily, cunning and doubly shrewd in playing down his ambitions. He was in this game for his irreverent self, and did not care what impression he made.

He put his success down to consistency – and the statistics prove his point. From 203 Grand Prix starts, he had 24 pole positions and 23 fastest laps to add to his 23 victories. "It is very easy to do a good year and be World Champion. Well, not easy, but not so difficult. If you are in Formula One, you have the talent already. So if you have the right team and the right car, you win. To win three times; that means I am very, very consistent."

Piquet, born in Rio de Janeiro, began racing in karts. In 1971 he landed the Brazilian national title and turned to car racing in Formula Super Vee and sports cars.

By 1977 he was ready for the European Formula Three series, winning two rounds. In 1978 he tackled Formula Three in Britain, beating not only his much-touted compatriot Chico Serra but also Derek Warwick. His Formula One opportunity came swiftly. He made his debut with Ensign in the German Grand Prix, then had three outings in a BS Fabrications McLaren. After a stunning practice performance in the third Brabham-Alfa at Montreal, Bernie Ecclestone signed him as team-mate to Niki Lauda for 1979.

On the pace immediately, but with few results to show for it, Piquet nevertheless became team leader when Lauda retired at the end of the season. In 1980 he took three victories and challenged Alan Jones for the title, which he secured the following year by shrewdly edging out Carlos Reutemann in the final race at Las Vegas. The 1982 season suffered from unreliability, but in 1983 Piquet battled against Prost, steadily whittling away his lead before overhauling him in the last round at Kyalami.

The Brazilian probably remained too loyal to the close-knit Brabham outfit. He took three wins over the course of two seasons before signing for assured front-running (and a big pay packet) at Williams.

Therein began the nasty Piquet-Mansell rivalry which spiralled from a professional bitterness over team orders – Piquet was not amused by Williams' refusal to ask Mansell to give way to him, a situation he felt had allowed Prost to snatch the title – into a

"Nelson had an unbelievable natural talent but he didn't really have respect for other people, and this I never liked."

Gerhard Berger

puerile spat on a personal level.

"It was a successful year as far as results were concerned, but it was painful. The loudest noise in the motorhome after a race we'd won would be the complaints of our guy who finished second," said Williams' technical director Patrick Head.

After a big accident early in the 1987 season, Piquet, who had worked out how to out-psyche Mansell, was relaxed. "You wouldn't think he had a care in the world. He sleeps before a race, relaxes and tells silly jokes all the time in shocking English," said Frank Williams. Piquet duly went on to win his third title.

There followed a disastrous two seasons at Lotus which lowered his stock to the extent that observers thought Flavio Briatore mad when he offered the Brazilian a performance-related contract.

His retainer was minimal but supplemented by $100,000 per Championship point – and he went on to score 44. His position at Benetton was jeopardized by the arrival of Michael Schumacher and Tom Walkinshaw who came with a commitment to Martin Brundle for 1992.

With a final flourish Piquet showed his spirit when, out-qualified consistently by Schumacher, he determined to turn the tables in the last race in Adelaide. He achieved his goal – and went on to finish fourth in his final Grand Prix.

With no seat in Formula One, he decided to try the challenge of the Indianapolis 500. A huge crash in practice left him with appallingly crushed feet and legs. The prognosis was depressing but he vowed to get back in the cockpit. A year later he qualified for the Indianapolis 500, and has since raced in touring cars and made a couple of visits to Le Mans.

Above: *Nelson Piquet, a great competitor.*
Previous page: *Piquet in action in the Argentina Grand Prix of 1981.*

1984
Senna makes an impact

TALKING POINT
PIQUET GETS HIS FEET BURNED

The reliability of his Brabham cost Nelson Piquet a chance to challenge McLaren's Niki Lauda and Alain Prost for the title. But more importantly, any attempts to increase the performance of the car ensured that Piquet would remember the season for some strange reasons. Brabham introduced an oil cooler system in the front of the car for the Canadian Grand Prix, which was intended to help weight distribution. It helped the performance as Piquet led the race from start to finish, but it did nothing to cool the Brazilian, as it burned his feet!

The Formula One paddock was barely recognizable from that which had ended the 1983 season, with a number of key changes. New regulations were imposed on the cars, with a maximum of 220 litres of fuel permitted per race and refuelling was banned. Driver changes were also common with the most significant change coming in the form of Frenchman Alain Prost, who quit Renault and joined McLaren to partner Niki Lauda.

Riccardo Patrese left Brabham in favour of Benetton-backed Alfa Romeo and was joined by Eddie Cheever, while Renault employed Patrick Tambay and Derek Warwick to spearhead their Championship challenge. Michele Alboreto replaced Tambay at Ferrari and Tyrrell, the only team without turbo-charged engines, opted to blood youngsters Martin Brundle and Stefan Bellof. Ligier secured a supply of Renault engines and had two new drivers in the form of Andrea de Cesaris and rising French star François Hesnault, while Toleman had Johnny Cecotto and young Brazilian Ayrton Senna forming their challenge. Arrows, meanwhile, landed a supply of BMW power units and kept Marc Surer and Thierry Boutsen. Lotus, Williams and ATS retained their 1983 line-ups, but Osella decided to run just one car for the season.

Lotus' Elio de Angelis claimed the first pole position of the year for the Brazilian Grand Prix in Rio, but Alboreto, who was second on the grid, made the best start. Alboreto led Warwick, who tangled with Lauda, before brake problems sent his Ferrari into a spin.

Warwick's dream denied

Lauda assumed the lead after passing Warwick and McLaren held a one-two until Lauda pitted for his routine stop, only to require work on an electrical problem. During the pit-stop period, Mansell had crashed out, René Arnoux's Ferrari had blown up and Brabham's Nelson Piquet had also retired. Warwick was denied a dream start to the season when he suffered suspension damage after a collision with Lauda and spun off. Prost was left to win the race.

The second round was held at Kyalami in South Africa, the second time the Championship had visited the country in six months after the event was moved to the start of the season. Twenty-seven cars were entered, but only 26 were permitted to race and Boutsen missed out as Piquet qualified on pole.

The Sunday morning warm-up provided the biggest incident of the weekend. Osella's Jean-Pierre Jarier went off at the Jukskei Sweep and the car was torn in half with the monocoque hurtling down the track. The leaking fuel from the car caught fire and Piercarlo Ghinzani suffered burns to his right hand as he tried to avoid the flames and exit his cockpit. The injury left him unable to race and Boutsen was given a reprieve.

Prost's McLaren did not start ahead of the race and the Frenchman jumped into the spare. He was meant to start from the pit-lane but drove out of the pits and initially took up an illegal position at the back of the grid. But after Mansell stalled, the cars completed another formation lap and Prost took up his correct position and began from the pit-lane.

The McLaren duo of Alain Prost and Niki Lauda competing in the Austrian Grand Prix which Lauda went on to win.

Alain Prost celebrates his win in Monaco.

Changes and disputes

Mansell took the lead as the race got underway at the second attempt, but problems for him, Rosberg and Piquet allowed Niki Lauda to go out in front for an easy win, while Ayrton Senna scored his first World Championship point for Toleman when he finished sixth.

The European season started with the Belgian Grand Prix at Zolder and the event marked the arrival of the Spirit team with former Alfa Romeo driver Mauro Baldi behind the challenge. In the only other change to the field, Boutsen was behind the wheel of Arrows' new A7 chassis. After Ferrari duo Alboreto and Arnoux, both on Goodyear tyres, got the upper hand in qualifying and held the front row positions, it became a race between Alboreto and Warwick with Alboreto securing his first win in a Ferrari.

A one-week break was all that separated the Belgian race and the fourth round of the season, the San Marino Grand Prix at Imola. Marc Surer replaced Boutsen in the Arrows A7 in the only change to the Zolder field, but Senna failed to qualify for the race after a dispute between his Toleman team and Pirelli, in addition to a misfire, denied him track time.

Prost was an easy winner as clutch difficulties hampered Lauda, while Tambay and Cheever collided to put the Renault driver out of the race and Piquet encountered turbo problems.

Senna grows in stature

Senna's failure to qualify at Imola resulted in the appearance of Toleman's new TG184 chassis in the French Grand Prix at Dijon-Prenois, and the Arrows A7 was back at the hands of Boutsen. But the Monaco Grand Prix underlined the growing reputation of Brazilian Senna, who was denied a potential maiden win when the race was red-flagged in the principality to hand Prost a fortunate victory in a rain-hit race.

Relief for Prost

Senna was furious at the decision, while Prost was relieved. The story of the race, however, came in the form of Stefan Bellof, who steered his Tyrrell from the back of the grid to an impressive third place with Arnoux ending fourth.

Piquet's poor run of form ended with a dominant display in Montreal as he won the Canadian Grand Prix from pole position.

In the race, Renault had opted to run just Warwick with broken leg victim Tambay ruled out, while Corrado Fabi stood in for brother Teo at Brabham for the second race in succession.

Piquet's return to form continued in the first of back-to-back United States Grands Prix in Detroit as he won from pole position again. The win, however, was fortunate for the Brazilian after he made a slow start and lost a wheel at the start of the race only for a restart to be ordered as a result of the carnage. Tambay was back in action for Renault after recovering from his broken leg, and Jonathan Palmer was back in action after missing the Canadian race in favour of an appearance in the Le Mans 24-Hour sportscar race.

Prost made the better start, but Mansell, third on the grid, attempted to squeeze into a gap

RACE BY RACE DETAILS

ROUND 1 – BRAZIL
Race Alain Prost
Pole Elio de Angelis
Fastest lap Alain Prost

ROUND 2 – SOUTH AFRICA
Race Niki Lauda
Pole Nelson Piquet
Fastest lap Patrick Tambay

ROUND 3 – BELGIUM
Race Michele Alboreto
Pole Michele Alboreto
Fastest lap René Arnoux

ROUND 4 – SAN MARINO
Race Alain Prost
Pole Nelson Piquet
Fastest lap Nelson Piquet

ROUND 5 – FRANCE
Race Niki Lauda
Pole Patrick Tambay
Fastest lap Alain Prost

ROUND 6 – MONACO
Race Alain Prost
Pole Alain Prost
Fastest lap Ayrton Senna

ROUND 7 – CANADA
Race Nelson Piquet
Pole Nelson Piquet
Fastest lap Nelson Piquet

ROUND 8 – UNITED STATES (EAST)
Race Nelson Piquet
Pole Nelson Piquet
Fastest lap Derek Warwick

ROUND 9 – UNITED STATES (WEST)
Race Keke Rosberg
Pole Nigel Mansell
Fastest lap Niki Lauda

ROUND 10 – BRITAIN
Race Niki Lauda
Pole Nelson Piquet
Fastest lap Niki Lauda

ROUND 11 – GERMANY
Race Alain Prost
Pole Alain Prost
Fastest lap Alain Prost

ROUND 12 – AUSTRIA
Race Niki Lauda
Pole Nelson Piquet
Fastest lap Niki Lauda

ROUND 13 – HOLLAND
Race Alain Prost
Pole Alain Prost
Fastest lap René Arnoux

ROUND 14 – ITALY
Race Niki Lauda
Pole Nelson Piquet
Fastest lap Niki Lauda

ROUND 15 – EUROPE
Race Alain Prost
Pole Nelson Piquet
Fastest lap Nelson Piquet

ROUND 16 – PORTUGAL
Race Alain Prost
Pole Nelson Piquet
Fastest lap Niki Lauda

1984 DRIVERS' CHAMPIONSHIP

DRIVER	TEAM	POINTS
Niki Lauda	McLaren	72
Alain Prost	McLaren	71.5
Elio de Angelis	Lotus	34
Michele Alboreto	Ferrari	30.5
Nelson Piquet	Brabham	29
René Arnoux	Ferrari	27
Derek Warwick	Renault	23
Keke Rosberg	Williams	20.5
Nigel Mansell	Lotus	13
Ayrton Senna	Toleman	13
Patrick Tambay	Renault	11
Teo Fabi	Brabham	9
Riccardo Patrese	Alfa Romeo	8
Thierry Boutsen	Arrows	5
Jacques Laffitte	Williams	5
Andrea de Cesaris	Ligier	3
Eddie Cheever	Alfa Romeo	3
Stefan Johansson	Tyrrell	3
Piercarlo Ghinzani	Osella	2
Marc Surer	Arrows	1

The crowd at Detroit looks on as race officials deal with the cars affected by the collision between Mansell and Piquet and Surer and Senna.

between the Frenchman's McLaren and Piquet. Mansell nudged Piquet into the wall and Arrows driver Surer collided with the Brazilian, with Senna's suspension being damaged by a flying tyre from the wreckage of the Brabham. Officials were left with no choice but to stop the race because of the debris on the track and Piquet and Senna jumped into their spare cars. Piquet went on to lead the remainder of the restarted race as he secured victory, but Surer did not compete because there was no T-car available.

While Piquet dominated the race, the star was Martin Brundle as he powered his Tyrrell to second from 11th on the grid. The Englishman was up to sixth at the mid-race pit-stops and benefited from the retirements of Alboreto and Warwick to finish behind Piquet.

Mishaps in Dallas

The second race in America was held in a car park in Dallas two weeks after the Detroit race, and despite Piquet's form, Mansell grabbed pole for Lotus, whose cars were best suited to the warm conditions. He made a good start and had team-mate de Angelis and Warwick behind him. Senna, who was running fourth, hit a wall on the second lap and lost ground on the leaders when he had to pit for repairs.

On lap 36, Rosberg got back ahead of Prost for second and then moved into the lead as he outmanoeuvred Mansell. The track, however, was beginning to break up because of the heat, and Prost became another casualty of the track when he crashed out on lap 57. Arnoux, who started from the back of the grid after his car failed to fire up at the start of the formation lap, chased Rosberg home and finished an impressive second. Mansell finished sixth after he pushed his car over the finish line having run out of fuel. He collapsed with exhaustion after passing the line.

Order was restored in the British Grand Prix in mid-July but Brundle missed his home race after his accident in Dallas. Stefan Johansson replaced him at Tyrrell, but the team received bad news after they were banned over the use of lead balls in the water ballast on their cars. All the points scored during the season were taken away, despite an appeal against the decision.

The race also marked the introduction of a new Italian team, Minardi, but an incident in practice

SHORTS

Mauro Baldi, who spearheaded Alfa Romeo's Championship challenge in 1983, did not enjoy a successful career in Formula One. He lost his drive a year later, but then went on to drive sportscars for Lancia, Porsche, Sauber and Peugeot, winning the Sports Car World Championship in 1990. Four years later, he took the chequered flag at the Le Mans 24 Hours.

Alain Prost, Niki Lauda and Ayrton Senna celebrate on the podium after the Portuguese Grand Prix at Estoril.

1984 CONSTRUCTORS' CUP

TEAM (Engine)	POINTS
McLAREN PORSCHE	143.5
FERRARI	57.5
LOTUS RENAULT	47
BRABHAM BMW	38
RENAULT	34
WILLIAMS HONDA	25.5
TOLEMAN HART	16
ALFA ROMEO BENETTON	11
ARROWS FORD	6
OSELLA ALFA	4
LIGIER RENAULT	3
ATS BMW	1

marred the event almost before it had begun. Cecotto crashed heavily at the Westfield Corner and suffered leg injuries that would end his career.

Another near-miss

Another sickening incident was to follow at the start of the race. Riccardo Patrese attempted to overtake Laffitte at Bottom bend but spun, forcing Cheever and Johansson, who was racing under Tyrrell's appeal, to lift off. RAM's Philippe Alliot failed to slow and flew over Johansson and onto Cheever's car.

The race was not stopped and Piquet led Prost and Lauda until lap 12 when the Frenchman forced his way through into the lead. But by the end of that lap Palmer crashed heavily and his car ended alongside the edge of the track after rebounding off the barriers. This time the race was stopped and the restart grid was based on the order on the 11th lap so Piquet was on pole. Prost took the lead but when he disappeared with gearbox failure Lauda was left in front and he finished ahead of Warwick.

Toleman decided against replacing the injured Cecotto for the German Grand Prix at Hockenheim two weeks later, which saw the McLaren duo ease to another one-two. Then, prior to the Austrian Grand Prix, rumours linked the improving Senna with a move to Lotus despite him having another year to run on his contract with Toleman. The race itself witnessed the arrival of Gerhard Berger, who was given his chance by ATS.

Senna moves to Lotus

In fact Senna's move was not announced until the morning of the Dutch Grand Prix at Zandvoort. The news left Mansell and de Angelis wondering if they had a future with Lotus and Toleman later suspended Senna for the Monza race over his decision to join Lotus. The rumour mill suggested that Mansell was Williams-bound with Laffitte set to return to Ligier.

The penultimate round of the Championship, the European Grand Prix, was held at the new Nurburgring for the first time, but drivers complained the German circuit was not demanding enough. In the gap between races, Zakspeed unveiled a Formula One car, Michelin announced their exit from the sport, while McLaren defected to Goodyear and Brabham to Pirelli. Carl Haas stated his plans for his team to enter the Championship in 1986 and BMW told ATS that they would not be supplying engines for the new season.

Lauda success

Senna was back for Toleman but retired at the first corner after he caused a six-car collision. Prost led all of the way to win ahead of Alboreto and Piquet, who both ran out of fuel. Lauda finished fourth to keep him four-and-a-half points ahead of team-mate Prost, meaning second place in Portugal would be enough to hand him another world crown. He did exactly that to beat Prost by the narrowest margin in the history of the sport—half a point.

The event, held in Estoril, was the first in 24 years in Portugal and Prost qualified second while Lauda was a distant 11th. But by lap 28, Lauda was into the points and five laps later he was ahead of Senna and running third. Brake trouble on Mansell's Lotus allowed the Austrian up to second on lap 52 after the Englishman spun and he remained there to land the world title.

Nigel Mansell

CAREER DETAILS

1953	Born 8 August in Baughton, Worcestershire
1980	Formula One debut with Lotus
1985	Moves to Williams. Maiden GP win at Brands Hatch
1989	Signs for Ferrari
1991	Returns to Williams
1992	World Champion
1993	Wins the Indycar title
1994	Few drives at Williams after Senna's death
1995	Farcical alliance with McLaren

FORMULA ONE RECORD

Year	Team	Wins	Poles	Fast laps	Pts
1980	Lotus	0	0	0	0
1981	Lotus	0	0	0	8
1982	Lotus	0	0	0	7
1983	Lotus	0	0	1	10
1984	Lotus	0	1	0	13
1985	Williams	2	1	1	31
1986	Williams	5	2	4	70
1987	Williams	6	8	3	61
1988	Williams	0	0	1	12
1989	Ferrari	2	0	3	38
1990	Ferrari	1	3	3	37
1991	Williams	5	2	6	72
1992	Williams	9	14	8	108
1994	Williams	1	1	0	13
1995	McLaren	0	0	0	0

HIS HARD CLIMB to the pinnacle of Formula One made him a prickly character, but Nigel Mansell is undoubtedly one of the bravest and most entertaining drivers of his age.

After stunning early success in karting and Formula Ford, Nigel Mansell failed to make an impression in Formula Three and Formula Two. However, his fire and commitment were recognized by Lotus boss Colin Chapman, who placed him as test driver and then gave him his Formula One break in the 1980 Austrian Grand Prix at the Osterreichring. In extreme discomfort as fuel leaking into the cockpit burnt his skin, Mansell battled on until the engine failed. It was the first display of that trademark bulldog spirit.

"It's no use denying it, the similarities are there. Even at this stage I instinctively know I've got a boy who is going to go all the way to the top. I can already feel he and I are developing the kind of relationship Jimmy and I shared," Chapman said, comparing Mansell to Jim Clark.

Mansell earned a full-time drive at Lotus in 1981, but the next four seasons were fruitless. When Chapman died suddenly of a heart attack in December 1982, Mansell lost his prime backer and mentor. When he threw away the lead of the Monaco Grand Prix in 1984, slithering into the Armco, many doubted if he would ever win a race, let alone a World Championship.

"He's unfit to be a Formula One driver," said Keke Rosberg, his new Williams team-mate. Mansell's lucky move to Williams for the 1985 season was greeted with universal consternation. "I couldn't understand what Frank Williams was up to when he took on Nigel," said Ken Tyrrell. "He used to go off and make mistakes. Then he won the Grand Prix of Europe at Brands Hatch and it was like turning a switch. All of a sudden he became a racing driver."

Mansell soon got the measure of Rosberg and won his maiden Grand Prix at Brands Hatch. The following season he irritated new team leader Nelson Piquet by launching his own title bid. With five wins, the Championship could have been his, but for a failure to get the car in gear in the penultimate race in Mexico and a tyre failure in the last round at Adelaide.

He and Piquet had a straight fight for the 1987 crown. Twelve points behind the Brazilian with two races to go, another drama – a crash in qualifying which seriously injured his back – gave Piquet his third World Championship. After a dud 1988 sea-

Nigel Mansell comes in 0to take the flag at the British Grand Prix at Silverstone.

"The one thing you absolutely knew about Nigel is that he always gives 100 per cent when he is in the cockpit."

Williams technical director ***Patrick Head.***

son, powered by Judd engines, Mansell accepted a lucrative move to Ferrari.

"It was like a command from the Pope: how could I refuse?" he said, while Frank Williams mused, "I'll miss him as a driver, not as a bloke."

What a start. The man who would be called *Il Leone* by the *tifosi* won on his first time out for the *Scuderia*. He finished fourth overall that 1989 season, with a captivating drive in Hungary to his credit. A skirmish with Senna in Portugal led to his suspension from the Spanish Grand Prix a week later, but worse was to come the following season when Alain Prost became his team-mate. Four early-season wins had the Maranello men focused on the politically savvy Frenchman and Mansell announced his retirement.

In 1991 he was back at Williams. He won five Grands Prix but his Championship challenge disappeared after a pit-stop fiasco in Portugal. In the FW14B, however, Mansell had magic machinery and scorched away with the 1992 Championship with a brio that caught the public imagination. Victory at Silverstone saw him mobbed. "I actually ran one person over, but I was only going a few miles an hour and he loved it," he marvelled.

Relations with Williams had deteriorated. Unable to reach terms, and with Prost imminent as a Williams driver, Mansell headed off to race in Indycars with the Newman-Haas team. Amazingly, he scooped the title, and relished an environment in which he was universally admired.

"He has a very strong persecution complex, thinks that everybody is trying to shaft him at all times. On a day-to-day basis that became extremely wearing," Patrick Head said of him, before Mansell came back for a few races after Senna's death. He won a satisfying victory in Adelaide, but Williams decided to invest in the future for 1995 and chose David Coulthard to partner Damon Hill.

In an ill-advised gesture, Mansell forged a brief alliance with Ron Dennis, only for them to fall out when the Briton failed to fit the car.

"When you've won 31 Grands Prix, and two world titles, your tolerance threshold is that bit lower. You know straightaway when you're in a bad car and you have a pretty good idea how much work needs to be done to make it competitive. I realized it was a bad car the first day I drove it in testing," he said. The tit-for-tat accusations of arrogance were a tawdry end to the bullish Mansell story.

Nigel Mansell celebrates his win at the Brazilian Grand Prix in 1989.

1985
Honours are shared out

TALKING POINT

ADELAIDE ALIVE

Formula One had never seen anything like it before. The Championship may have been long finished but the racing-mad Aussies did not care. The Grand Prix was coming to town and they were going to have a party. The bumpy, twisty streets of quiet, church-filled Adelaide came alive with the sound of roaring racing cars and the event would prove to be Formula One's favourite for years to come.

The third of November saw race day dawn with the expected Australian sun burning down on the circuit, and 107,500 fans turned up to experience the spectacle they had heard about in jingles and advertisements throughout the city. There were endless street parties and the relaxed Australian atmosphere flooded from the grandstands to the teams themselves.

It had very much an end-of-term feel to it, with the drivers lining up for a photograph on the grid before the start, and the result seemed to matter little. Keke Rosberg crossed the line within inches of flamboyant flag-waver Glen Dix to win the inaugural race and afterwards praised the organizers for simply the best job in the world. They were to continue doing so until the race's demise in 1995.

In a season which saw eight different Grand Prix winners from five different teams it was consistency that reigned supreme in 1985. Alain Prost was the man who finished most races in the points, and with every one of those 11 results a podium position he was the man who took the Championship. His closest challenger, Michele Alboreto, finish 20 points behind for Ferrari.

The season began with a mostly unchanged line-up in the top teams as McLaren, Renault, Ferrari and Alfa Romeo all stuck with their 1984 drivers. But perhaps the most significant move was that of Briton Nigel Mansell, who left Lotus to begin a long and successful association with the Williams team. Toleman were forced to miss the first three races after a disagreement with tyre suppliers, and ATS had closed down completely, forcing Gerhard Berger to move to join Thierry Boutsen at Arrows. Minardi made its full debut in 1985, as did Zakspeed.

Senna off the mark

Alboreto, fourth in the 1984 Championship, began the new season on a high with pole position in the season-opening Brazilian Grand Prix. But Williams' Keke Rosberg moved clear ahead at the start and Alboreto only managed to come in third.

Soon after the first race of the season, Ferrari sacked Frenchman René Arnoux because of his physical condition, and Stefan Johansson was brought in by the Italian marque for the second race of the season, the Portuguese Grand Prix.

Senna claimed his first-ever pole position, and it was to be a race to remember for the young Brazilian. In pouring rain, he took the lead at the start and was never challenged as he put in a masterful display to claim his first Grand Prix victory.

Senna continued his form in the San Marino Grand Prix by taking pole position ahead of Rosberg.

Mansell not slick enough

The Brazilian star took the lead as a slow-off-the-line Rosberg dropped behind Senna's team-mate de Angelis, the Ferrari of Alboreto, and Prost's McLaren. Lauda also moved ahead of Rosberg on lap six.

Alboreto dropped out with electronics problems on lap 30 to leave the McLaren pair Senna's only challengers, but Lauda was put into a spin by faulty electronics and Senna looked to be in the clear for his second win in a row. But he ran out of fuel with two laps to go, as did Johansson who had claimed the lead when Senna retired. That left Prost up front, also struggling with fuel reserves, and after a slow final lap he stopped just after he had crossed the line to claim victory. However, after scrutineering, his McLaren was deemed underweight and de Angelis was awarded his second and last win.

The next race in Monaco saw the return of the Toleman team, who had secured the now-defunct Spirit's tyre supply and also acquired the Benetton sponsorship and Teo Fabi from Alfa Romeo. Senna claimed his third pole position in a row ahead of the Williams of Mansell, and the pair got away in grid order at the start. But behind them and in the middle of the pack, Gerhard Berger's engine died and he was hit by Tambay and Johansson to put all three out of the race.

Ayrton Senna heads the field during the Portuguese Grand Prix.

The spectators become a blur as Keke Rosberg zooms past during the British Grand Prix at Silverstone.

Mansell shot down the order as he struggled on the twisty streets of the principality, and when Senna's engine failed on lap 14, Alboreto assumed the lead.

This was to last just five laps, however, before he slid wide on oil left at Sainte Devoté after a fiery accident between Patrese and Piquet. He dropped further back with a punctured tyre, but fought back to claim second by the end, seven seconds behind winner Prost.

The next race was due to be the Belgian Grand Prix, but after qualifying the track had been torn up so badly by all the cars the race was cancelled. That meant the Canadian Grand Prix was next on the agenda, but after a Senna hat-trick, it was a different Lotus on pole when de Angelis clocked fastest time in qualifying.

See-saw season

Senna made it an all-black front row, but in the race it was all red as Ferrari claimed their first victory of the season with a one-two finish.

There was just one week's break before the American Grand Prix at Detroit, and once again it was a Lotus on pole after Senna claimed the honours in qualifying. But it was to be row-three starter Rosberg who ended the victor.

In the opening lap Rosberg passed Mansell, Prost and Alboreto to move into second, and after eight laps he was in the lead as Senna, struggling with tyre difficulties, pulled into the pits and fell down the pack.

Rosberg had to stop to clear his radiators, but he soon moved ahead of the field once more to win from Johansson and Alboreto, who had moved up a position when Senna crashed out.

The French Grand Prix was next on the agenda, and it was to produce the fifth different winner of the season when Piquet took the spoils for Brabham. Rosberg, fresh from his American victory, broke the Lotus stranglehold in qualifying by claiming pole position for Williams, but Senna was alongside him on the front row. Piquet was in fifth.

Mansell was sidelined by a massive qualifying crash when a burst tyre sent him into the catch fencing and he was hit on the head by a pole.

Senna v Prost

When the field arrived at Silverstone for the British Grand Prix, Rosberg was back on top in qualifying and made the first 160-mph average speed on the high-speed track. But in the race, it was the battle between Senna and Prost which wowed the crowd.

Senna made a superb start to move from fourth to first off the line, but behind them confusion reigned. Johansson hit a sideways Tambay and as a result Piercarlo Ghinzani and Philippe Alliot also collided. With Rosberg, Mansell and de Cesaris all out of the running Prost closed on Senna and they fought nose-to-tail until Senna's engine began to falter and Prost made it past on lap 58.

Senna briefly regained the lead, but eventually ran out of fuel and Prost was shown the chequered flag first, with Alboreto second and Laffitte third. The flag, however, was waved one lap early but although Piquet would have taken the final podium spot when Laffitte ran out of fuel, the result was not altered after the race.

The German Grand Prix found a new home at the Nurburgring, and the Toleman team found a new lease of life as a much improved car and engine allowed Fabi to plant it on pole, a massive 1.2 seconds ahead of the rest of the field. But the Italian made a poor start and he dropped back as Johansson, Rosberg and Senna battled for the lead. Senna made it through on the inside and as Alboreto

RACE BY RACE DETAILS

ROUND 1 – BRAZIL
Race Alain Prost
Pole Michele Alboreto
Fastest lap Alain Prost

ROUND 2 – PORTUGAL
Race Ayrton Senna
Pole Ayrton Senna
Fastest lap Ayrton Senna

ROUND 3 – SAN MARINO
Race Alain Prost
Pole Ayrton Senna
Fastest lap Michele Alboreto

ROUND 4 – MONACO
Race Alain Prost
Pole Ayrton Senna
Fastest lap Michele Alboreto

ROUND 5 – CANADA
Race Michele Alboreto
Pole Elio de Angelis
Fastest lap Ayrton Senna

ROUND 6 – UNITED STATES
Race Keke Rosberg
Pole Ayrton Senna
Fastest lap Ayrton Senna

ROUND 7 – FRANCE
Race Nelson Piquet
Pole Keke Rosberg
Fastest lap Keke Rosberg

ROUND 8 – BRITAIN
Race Alain Prost
Pole Keke Rosberg
Fastest lap Alain Prost

ROUND 9 – GERMANY
Race Michele Alboreto
Pole Teo Fabi
Fastest lap Niki Lauda

ROUND 10 – AUSTRIA
Race Alain Prost
Pole Alain Prost
Fastest lap Alain Prost

ROUND 11 – NETHERLANDS
Race Niki Lauda
Pole Nelson Piquet
Fastest lap Alain Prost

ROUND 12 – ITALY
Race Alain Prost
Pole Ayrton Senna
Fastest lap Nigel Mansell

ROUND 13 – BELGIUM
Race Ayrton Senna
Pole Alain Prost
Fastest lap Alain Prost

ROUND 14 – EUROPE
Race Nigel Mansell
Pole Ayrton Senna
Fastest lap Jacques Laffitte

ROUND 15 – SOUTH AFRICA
Race Nigel Mansell
Pole Nigel Mansell
Fastest lap Keke Rosberg

ROUND 16 – AUSTRALIA
Race Keke Rosberg
Pole Ayrton Senna
Fastest lap Keke Rosberg

1985 DRIVERS' CHAMPIONSHIP

DRIVER	TEAM	POINTS
Alain Prost	McLaren TAG	73
Michele Alboreto	Ferrari	53
Keke Rosberg	Williams Honda	40
Ayrton Senna	Lotus Renault	38
Elio de Angelis	Lotus Renault	33
Nigel Mansell	Williams Honda	31
Stefan Johansson	Ferrari	26
Nelson Piquet	Brabham BMW	21
Jacques Laffitte	Ligier Renault	16
Niki Lauda	McLaren TAG	14
Patrick Tambay	Renault	11
Thierry Boutsen	Arrows BMW	11
Derek Warwick	Renault	5
Marc Surer	Brabham BMW	5
Philippe Streiff	Ligier Renault	4
Stefan Bellof	Tyrrell Ford	4
René Arnoux	Ferrari	3
Andrea de Cesaris	Ligier Renault	3
Gerhard Berger	Arrows BMW	3
Ivan Capelli	Tyrrell Renault	3

followed him through he hit his own team-mate Johansson and punctured his tyre.

Rosberg was soon in the lead, while Senna's race ended on lap 27 with transmission problems. Fabi's disappointing performance ended in retirement two laps later by which time Rosberg was struggling. Once again tyres were his downfall and when he pitted for a change he lost the lead to Alboreto. Prost had a quiet race to follow the Ferrari home in second, and Laffitte managed third.

Before the Austrian Grand Prix Formula One lost a driver when RAM's Manfred Winkelhock died in a sportscar race in Canada. He was replaced by Briton Kenny Acheson.

Lauda bows out

Niki Lauda's end-of-season retirement decision began a spate of paddock announcements as Rosberg decided to replace him at McLaren for 1986. Piquet would shift to fill the vacant seat at Williams, and de Angelis decided to start the following season with Brabham.

All the talk seemed to make the racing irrelevant, but as soon as the race began it was all-action as the grid became a mass of confusion: Fabi did not move and Mansell was slow off the line and the race was red-flagged.

At the restart Rosberg led from Prost but retired four laps in with engine failure to leave the McLarens in a one-two position. De Cesaris escaped unhurt with a massive accident on lap 14 when he dramatically rolled his Ligier, but he was punished when team-boss Guy Ligier gave him the sack on his return to the pits.

Lauda looked to have sealed the race until lap 40 when the turbo on his McLaren failed and Prost retook the lead. Both Piquet and Mansell dropped out of the race to leave Senna in second with the Ferraris of Alboreto and Johansson third and fourth.

Just one week later came the Dutch Grand Prix, which saw Lauda claim victory after a dramatically close finish with Prost, and the debut of the Beatrice Lola team with Alan Jones at the wheel, but it was Piquet's Brabham on pole sitting alongside Rosberg when the field lined up for the race.

Bellof death rocks F1

In the weekend between the Dutch and Italian Grand Prix, a sportscar race in Belgium hit Formula One hard when Tyrrell driver Stefan Bellof, racing a Porsche, was killed at Eau Rouge and Zakspeed's Jonathan Palmer broke his leg in a crash driving a similar car. Neither team replaced their drivers for the Italian race, but de Cesaris' departure from Ligier allowed Philippe Streiff to make a return to Formula One. The race was won by Prost after a battle between him and Rosberg.

The Belgian Grand Prix had been re-scheduled for the week after Italy, and once again rain-master Senna proved his skills by taking a comfortable victory as others struggled. Although Prost claimed pole position, nothing could bother Senna, who sailed away to victory almost half a minute clear of

SHORTS

Stefan Bellof was one of the most promising talents to emerge in Formula One during the early 1980s. Having won two major Formula Two races and joined Tyrrell, he was seen as a future candidate for the World Championship. His death in 1985 at the Spa-Francorchamps circuit in Belgium once again cast a shadow over motorsport.

Nigel Mansell overcame duels with both team-mate Keke Rosberg and Ayrton Senna to claim his first Grand Prix – the European – at Brands Hatch.

Two winners: Nigel Mansell celebrates his first race win while Alain Prost delights in becoming World Champion.

1985 CONSTRUCTORS' CUP

TEAM (Engine)	POINTS
McLAREN TAG	90
FERRARI	82
WILLIAMS HONDA	71
LOTUS RENAULT	71
BRABHAM BMW	26
LIGIER RENAULT	23
RENAULT	16
ARROWS BMW	14
TYRRELL FORD	4
TYRRELL RENAULT	3

second-placed Mansell. Prost was third almost a minute behind, with Rosberg recovering to claim fourth ahead of Piquet and Warwick.

When the teams turned up at Brands Hatch for the European Grand Prix three weeks later the field had lost Niki Lauda with a wrist problem and McLaren replaced him with John Watson.

Mansell's the best of British

Senna claimed pole for Lotus and Piquet sat alongside him on the grid with the Williams pair filling the second row, Mansell getting the better of his team-mate Rosberg.

Rosberg was slow away and forced Prost onto the grass, but suddenly he got going and flew into second place behind Senna. The lead pair clashed on lap 7 and third man Piquet hit the spinning Rosberg, sending them both out of the running. Senna continued, but Mansell gave chase and when his team-mate Rosberg, one lap down, blocked the leading Brazilian, Mansell capitalized and went into first place for his first win.

Prost had needed fifth place to clinch the World Championship and he sealed it with fourth, becoming the first-ever Frenchman to take the title.

Just two weeks after his maiden victory Mansell did it again at the South African Grand Prix when he beat his team-mate Rosberg in a Williams one-two. Though not all the usual competition had turned up to the Kyalami circuit. Political problems had scared away the two French teams Ligier and Renault, RAM was out of money and Zakspeed also failed to attend. Beatrice withdrew before the race when Jones became unwell and the field was down to 20 cars.

Prost is king

Rosberg soon cut through the pack and, after Piquet's Brabham dropped out, the Finn chased and caught team-mate Mansell. Then came the action-packed lap 8 which saw Rosberg take the lead and lose it almost immediately as he went off on spilt oil.

Prost took the final podium position with Johansson claiming points for Ferrari in fourth and the Arrows pair of Berger and Boutsen taking the final points.

And so to Australia and the final race of the season at the new Adelaide street circuit which was to become a Formula One favourite.

In a relaxed atmosphere Senna claimed pole position ahead of Mansell, but after the Briton took the lead at the start the pair collided midway through the first lap and Mansell was out.

Rosberg capitalized on the incident to grab the lead from Senna and the pair battled hard for much of the race. Rosberg decided to pit for tyres and as he slowed to enter the pits Senna hit the back of the Williams and damaged his front wing. He tried to struggle on with handling problems but was forced to pit.

Rosberg led again but made a second stop as the Adelaide asphalt took its toll on tyres, so Senna was back in front of Lauda, who then ended his last Grand Prix in the wall. Rosberg closed again on Senna and when the Lotus driver's engine began to smoke Rosberg was through.

But the action was not over: the Ligier pair collided, leaving Streiff without a right front wheel. Still, he drove it the remaining lap to the finish and amazingly managed to hold onto third position.

It was a dramatic end to an exciting season.

Alain Prost

Alain Prost won the World Championship four times, maximizing his innate skill with detailed analysis. Undramatic as his race wins tended to be, he is undoubtedly one of the absolute greats.

CAREER DETAILS

1955	Born 24 February in Lorette, France
1973	World Karting Champion
1980	Formula One debut in Argentina
1981	Joins Renault. Maiden victory in French GP
1983	Runner-up in World Championship
1984	Runner-up again
1985	World Champion with McLaren
1986	World Champion with McLaren
1989	World Champion with McLaren
1991	Retires after two seasons with Ferrari
1993	Returns with Williams. World Champion

FORMULA ONE RECORD

Year	Team	Wins	Poles	Fast laps	Pts
1980	McLaren	0	0	0	5
1981	Renault	3	2	1	43
1982	Renault	2	5	4	34
1983	Renault	4	3	3	57
1984	McLaren	7	3	3	71
1985	McLaren	5	2	5	73
1986	McLaren	4	1	2	72
1987	McLaren	3	0	2	46
1988	McLaren	7	2	7	87
1989	McLaren	4	2	5	76
1990	Ferrari	5	0	2	71
1991	Ferrari	0	0	1	34
1993	Williams	7	13	6	99

Alain Prost drives for McLaren during the Grand Prix at Monaco in 1984.

Alain Prost, aka "The Professor", is Formula One's most efficiently successful competitor ever. Four World Championships, a total of 51 Grand Prix wins and 798.5 points from 199 starts (an average of almost four points per race, the equivalent of finishing in third place every time he raced) rendered him an inexorable challenger.

His period of dominance coincided with the emergence of Ayrton Senna – who was in many ways his opposite, being Latin and a natural risk-taker. The Brazilian was an ace qualifier and nerve-less racer; the Frenchman accrued fastest laps and undramatic race wins. The result was an intense, captivating and aggressive rivalry which brought the best, and the worst, out of both men.

"He is the most complete driver there is," said Stirling Moss. "You could say that Senna is the fastest, but that is only one aspect of driving in F1. Alain's knowledge is phenomenal, in terms of setting up a car, motivating the pits, race tactics and psychology. Senna is the racer, but Prost is the racing driver."

Prost was born on 24 February, in Lorette, Saint-Chamond, close to St Etienne. His racing career was never anything other than brilliant. He won the world karting title in 1973, then turned to cars and a course at the Winfield school. He dominated Formule Renault, Formule Super Renault and in 1978 Formula Three, including a noteworthy win at Monaco. McLaren immediately signed him.

He made his Grand Prix debut in Argentina, out-pacing team-mate John Watson to finish in the points with the effortlessly smooth driving style which was his trademark. "The mark of his brilliance is that the faster he drives, the smoother he looks. You just cannot tell when he is on the limit," was Frank Williams' appraisal of his skill.

After breaking a wrist at Kyalami, the rest of the 1980 season did not amount to much, except that Renault secured his services for the following year. Fittingly Prost's maiden win was the French Grand Prix at Dijon-Prenois. He also won the Dutch and Italian rounds, finishing the year fifth and in the mood to fulfil his ambitions.

"Winning your first Grand Prix is a passport to the future," he mused. "Once you have won, you are free from all the inhibitions and complexes that have held you back. You know that you are every bit as good as those around you, and Formula One takes on an entirely new aspect. You have climbed a

"He bites his finger nails so deeply...He's just concentrating on his job all the time."

Patrick Tambay

"The Professor" celebrates one of his many wins at Monaco.

mountain which, only the night before, appeared insurmountable."

In 1982 he finished fourth and in 1983 he lost the Championship to Nelson Piquet by just two points.

Both Renault and the French press blamed Prost for allowing Piquet to snatch the glory, and the Frenchman shuttled back to McLaren. In 1984 he lost out to Niki Lauda by just half a point, but finally succeeded in becoming the first French World Champion in 1985. Remarkably he defended his title against the superior Williams-Hondas in 1986, clinching the title in the famous three-way shoot-out in Adelaide which Mansell lost with a rear-tyre blow-out.

Three more years at McLaren brought him fourth overall in 1987, runner-up to team-mate Senna in 1988 and the world crown again in 1989. The title was decided when Prost subtly chopped the Brazilian at Suzuka after he had criticized Senna's attitude. "The problem with Ayrton is that he cannot accept not to win and he can't accept that someone might resist one of his overtaking moves. He will not accept that he has been overtaken or that he cannot overtake another car. He thinks he can't kill himself because he believes in God and I think that's very dangerous for the other drivers."

The last two years of their McLaren partnership had seen a steady, bitter deterioration in the drivers' relationship which opened out after Prost had moved to Ferrari. The 1990 Championship was decided in Senna's favour when he reciprocated and drove into the back of Prost's Ferrari at the start, erasing a season of purposeful work.

"What [Senna] did was more than unsporting, it was disgusting. If everybody wants to drive in this way, then the sport is finished," he ranted.

The 1991 Ferrari was a disappointment and Prost, embroiled in off-track politics, was sacked for his outspoken criticism. He took a year's sabbatical and returned to race for Williams in 1993. Mansell's fury, and subsequent departure, left his fourth World Championship little more than a formality with 13 pole positions and seven wins. The prospect of Senna joining him as team-mate in 1994 was an inducement to announce his retirement.

His attitude only intensified his reputation for selfishness. Bernie Ecclestone expressed annoyance at the way Prost had "used" Formula One. "He retired once to suit himself and he came back to suit himself," he said. "Now he has retired again and let's hope this time it is on a permanent basis. I think he must walk down the pit-lane and think he sees a sign saying Public Convenience."

After Senna's death in 1994 he declared he would never race again. "The only driver I respected...with his death, half my career has gone," Prost lamented. He tested for McLaren and later took over the Ligier team, renaming it Prost for 1997.

1986
A four-horse race

Ayrton Senna driving for Lotus heads the field at the Spanish Grand Prix.

TALKING POINT

FRANK WILLIAMS' YEAR OF HEAVEN AND HELL

Team manager Frank Williams had been in Formula One for years before disaster struck and he suffered a car crash from which many would have struggled to return.

Just before the season started he was paralysed from the neck down and laid up in hospital for half a year.

But still his team battled on, under his guidance and led through his right-hand man Patrick Head, to take the Constructors' Championship and nearly claim the drivers' crown.

Williams faced life in a wheelchair, but returned to Formula One for the first time since his accident at the Brands Hatch paddock in mid July to watch his ever-improving Honda-powered cars battle each other for their fifth victory of the season.

Mansell had the edge in that race and, although the Briton's battles with team-mate Nelson Piquet would eventually lose Williams the drivers' title, the year was a success and he returned to lead the team once more.

After winning his first World Championship title the previous year, Alain Prost was looking for number two. But he had some tough competition. The Williams-Hondas were now a real force and Ayrton Senna, with his genius for qualifying, was in with a shout for Lotus.

For most of the season it was a four-horse race but the Williams pair of Nigel Mansell and Nelson Piquet suffered from internal battles and often stole points from each other. It was "Le Professeur" Prost who capitalized on consistency and a fair share of luck to take the title after an unbelievable final race of the season.

It was all change at the top for 1986, with Keke Rosberg's move to McLaren setting off a chain of transfers. Piquet took his place at Williams, Elio de Angelis filled his seat at Brabham and was replaced at Lotus by Johnny Dumfries after Senna had blocked Derek Warwick's move to the team. Meanwhile Benetton had taken over the reins of the Toleman team, which hired Gerhard Berger to partner Teo Fabi, and Renault was gone. Many of their staff moved to strengthen the Ligier-Renault team which held on to Jacques Laffitte and brought in René Arnoux, sacked by Ferrari after the first race of the previous year.

But not long before the season began, Frank Williams was seriously injured in a car crash. Paralysed from the neck down, he was forced to spend most of the year in a hospital bed.

The season itself got off to a dramatic start as Mansell and Senna began their ever-hardening rivalry with a battle at the first corner of the first race in Brazil. Senna was on pole with Piquet alongside him on the front row and Mansell right behind him, but Senna was swamped by the Williams-Hondas as the season got under way and Mansell challenged him for the lead.

Battle of the giants

Senna was having none of it, and Mansell ended the first race in the barriers without even completing a lap. But Senna still had to battle with the other Williams of Piquet, and he lost the lead on lap three and dropped back at a rate of one second per lap. Prost cruised through the field from a lowly ninth on the grid and claimed third after the pit-stops, but went out with engine failure. That left Arnoux in third, but Ligier team-mate Laffitte passed him before the end to claim the final podium spot behind Piquet and second-placed Senna.

Round two saw the return of the Spanish Grand Prix after a five-year absence. Held at the newly-built Jerez circuit, it produced a classic.

Opposite: *The mass pile-up which occurred on lap one of the British Grand Prix at Brands Hatch.*

The Senna-Mansell rivalry continued with a race-long battle concluding with the second-closest finish in Formula One history as they crossed the line 0.014 seconds apart.

Spain was a hard act to follow and, although the San Marino Grand Prix two weeks later had its share of drama, it could not compete for excitement.

The top three on the grid had not changed since the season began, but this time Piquet stopped Senna converting his customary pole into a race lead as Mansell dropped back with engine trouble.

Bearing failure hits Senna

On lap four Senna was passed by McLaren's Prost and Rosberg, who switched positions soon after, Rosberg assuming the lead on lap 11 when Senna suffered a wheel-bearing failure. But Prost stole the lead from his team-mate during the pit-stops and held on to the end. Piquet eventually claimed second and Berger took the final podium spot

Prost finally broke Senna's stranglehold on pole position at the next race in Monaco, and controlled the race to take a comfortable victory.

The most dramatic incident came on lap 67 when Martin Brundle and Patrick Tambay survived a collision unhurt, Tambay flying through the air and somersaulting into the barriers. De Angelis, however, was not so lucky. In testing at Paul Ricard for the Belgian Grand Prix, his Brabham's rear wing failed. It rolled over the barriers, landed upside-down and burst into flames. Pulled from the wreckage, he died from his injuries in a Marseilles hospital.

Subdued, Grand Prix racing soldiered on and Brabham fielded only one car at Spa. Berger took a surprise front-row place after qualifying behind Piquet, but his glory proved fleeting.

McLaren and Benetton in a tangle

As Piquet stormed away, the Benetton driver was slow off the line. Berger tangled with Prost at the first corner hairpin, causing mayhem in the midfield. Fortunately most survived unscathed and Senna was left in second place, soon taking the lead when Piquet went out on lap 16 with a turbo control fault. Mansell had dropped behind Senna after spinning, but claimed the lead after the pit-stops and eventually won by 20 seconds.

Canada was next and, as Warwick replaced de Angelis at Brabham, Arrows lost Surer, seriously hurt in a rallying accident. Tambay was also missing from the grid after crashing in morning warm-up and injuring his feet. Mansell led the race from pole position and took a healthy lead as Senna held up the rest of the pack. Rosberg and Prost mounted a challenge which saw the Finn as leader briefly but in the end Mansell emerged the winner.

Prost's comeback

After a difficult pit-stop Prost had climbed back to claim second with Piquet third, and a fuel-conserving Rosberg fourth.

The United States was the next fixture, and after normal service resumed in qualifying Senna claimed his second win of the season. But despite taking the lead from pole it was not an easy ride for the Brazilian in a race which saw five leaders.

Senna had the fastest stop of the leaders, came out in front and was never challenged. Behind him was a comedy of errors, as Arnoux hit a crashed Piquet and then reversed into Boutsen's Arrows. Laffitte passed Prost's misfiring McLaren in the dying stages to claim second and Alboreto earned points for Ferrari with a fourth place.

After de Angelis' death the teams were faced with a much-modified Circuit Paul Ricard for the French Grand Prix at the start of July. The high-speed esses where he crashed had gone and the circuit had been dramatically shortened.

RACE BY RACE DETAILS

ROUND 1 – BRAZIL
Race Nelson Piquet
Pole Ayrton Senna
Fastest lap Nelson Piquet

ROUND 2 – SPAIN
Race Ayrton Senna
Pole Ayrton Senna
Fastest lap Nigel Mansell

ROUND 3 – SAN MARINO
Race Alain Prost
Pole Ayrton Senna
Fastest lap Nelson Piquet

ROUND 4 – MONACO
Race Alain Prost
Pole Alain Prost
Fastest lap Alain Prost

ROUND 5 – BELGIUM
Race Nigel Mansell
Pole Nelson Piquet
Fastest lap Alain Prost

ROUND 6 – CANADA
Race Nigel Mansell
Pole Nigel Mansell
Fastest lap Nelson Piquet

ROUND 7 – UNITED STATES
Race Ayrton Senna
Pole Ayrton Senna
Fastest lap Nelson Piquet

ROUND 8 – FRANCE
Race Nigel Mansell
Pole Ayrton Senna
Fastest lap Nigel Mansell

ROUND 9 – BRITAIN
Race Nigel Mansell
Pole Nelson Piquet
Fastest lap Nigel Mansell

ROUND 10 – GERMANY
Race Nelson Piquet
Pole Keke Rosberg
Fastest lap Gerhard Berger

ROUND 11 – HUNGARY
Race Nelson Piquet
Pole Ayrton Senna
Fastest lap Nelson Piquet

ROUND 12 – AUSTRIA
Race Alain Prost
Pole Teo Fabi
Fastest lap Gerhard Berger

ROUND 13 – ITALY
Race Nelson Piquet
Pole Teo Fabi
Fastest lap Teo Fabi

ROUND 14 – PORTUGAL
Race Nigel Mansell
Pole Ayrton Senna
Fastest lap Nigel Mansell

ROUND 15 – MEXICO
Race Gerhard Berger
Pole Ayrton Senna
Fastest lap Nelson Piquet

ROUND 16 – AUSTRALIA
Race Alain Prost
Pole Nigel Mansell
Fastest lap Nelson Piquet

1986 DRIVERS' CHAMPIONSHIP

DRIVER	TEAM	POINTS
Alain Prost	McLaren TAG	72
Nigel Mansell	Williams Honda	70
Nelson Piquet	Williams Honda	69
Ayrton Senna	Lotus Renault	55
Stefan Johansson	Ferrari	23
Keke Rosberg	McLaren TAG	22
Gerhard Berger	Benetton BMW	17
Michele Alboreto	Ferrari	14
René Arnoux	Ligier Renault	14
Jacques Laffitte	Ligier Renault	14
Martin Brundle	Tyrrell Renault	8
Alan Jones	Lola Ford	4
Johnny Dumfries	Lotus Renault	3
Philippe Streiff	Tyrrell Renault	3
Teo Fabi	Benetton BMW	2
Patrick Tambay	Lola Ford	2
Riccardo Patrese	Brabham BMW	2
Christian Danner	Arrows BMW	1
Philippe Alliot	Ligier Renault	1

Genius of a designer

The race saw the arrival of a man who would revolutionize the Formula One machine: genius designer Adrian Newey, making a low-key entrance with Haas-Lola.

Yet again it was Senna, followed by the Williams pair, in qualifying, as the Brazilian continued to demonstrate his mastery of the late flying lap. Senna lost the lead to Mansell off the line as Alboreto stalled, but worse was to come when on lap five he spun off on oil left by the blown engine of Andrea de Cesaris' Minardi. That left Mansell clear ahead of Arnoux and Berger, but they were soon picked off by the McLarens of Prost and Rosberg. However, there was no catching the Brit, who won by 17 seconds from Prost.

Career ends for Laffitte

One week later the teams crossed the Channel to arrive at Brands Hatch in Kent for the British Grand Prix, which provided drama with a mass pile-up on the opening lap. On the first corner Boutsen lost control in the middle of the pack and as Johansson swerved to avoid him Laffitte, who had equalled Graham Hill's record of Grand Prix starts, had nowhere to go but head-on into the barriers. The nine-car crash severely damaged his legs, ending his career.

Ninety minutes later the race was restarted and Mansell – saved by the restart after car failure – followed team-mate Piquet into the first corner. Mansell took the lead when Piquet missed a gear on lap 23. Piquet hounded him for the ensuing 53 laps but could never find a way past, and the delighted crowd witnessed another Mansell victory.

Hockenheim in Germany was the next venue, and with plenty of lead changes it was certainly a dramatic affair.

Senna took the lead at the start, Berger passed Rosberg for second and Piquet claimed third from Prost. Before long Rosberg and Piquet found themselves battling at the front. Piquet took the lead on lap six and after all the differently-timed pit-stops shuffled the pack they ended up back in the same order, with Piquet unchallenged for victory and the McLarens seemingly certain of second and third.

Then disaster struck: both ran out of fuel on the final lap, leaving Senna in second, Mansell third, Arnoux fourth and the McLarens the final two points scorers.

Behind the Iron Curtain

Two weeks later the World Championship circus moved to Hungary, going behind the Iron Curtain for the first time. The Hungaroring circuit outside Budapest was twisty, making overtaking difficult. With pole position secured Senna looked well-placed to win. But he was challenged by his fellow Brazilian, Piquet, who held Senna off to win.

Just 11 points covered the top four as the teams headed to the Osterreichring for the Austrian Grand Prix, but the leading quartet were missing from the top two positions after the developing Benetton team put in a superb performance in qualifying to lock out the front row. However, it was Prost who found himself taking the chequered flag ahead of Ferrari pair Alboreto and Johansson.

The Italian Grand Prix followed three weeks later, with *tifosi*-favourite Alboreto struggling after injuring his shoulder falling off a motorbike and Piquet emerging as a winner ahead of Mansell.

At the Portuguese Grand Prix, Senna's bid for a

Amazingly Nigel Mansell survived the blow-out of his rear tyre during the Australian Grand Prix.

Alain Prost wields the trophy from the Australian Grand Prix and celebrates his second World Championship.

1986 CONSTRUCTORS' CUP

TEAM (Engine)	POINTS
WILLIAMS HONDA	141
McLAREN TAG	96
LOTUS RENAULT	58
FERRARI	37
LIGIER RENAULT	29
BENETTON BMW	19
TYRRELL RENAULT	11
LOLA FORD	6
BRABHAM BMW	2
ARROWS BMW	1

SHORTS

Elio de Angelis was lucky enough to have family backing to help him when he entered the competitive world of Formula One, but it was a natural ability which saw him contend for the major prizes. The former karting Champion and Formula Three star made his debut with Shadow in 1979 and narrowly missed out on points in his first race in Argentina where he came seventh. His first win was at the Austrian Grand Prix where he beat the would-be Champion Keke Rosberg.

second victory in as many years started well when he took pole position for the 70-lap race.

But Mansell sat threateningly alongside him and moved ahead off the line to claim a lead he would never lose as he set the fastest lap and dominated the day. Senna ran second for much of a dull race with few changes in the field, dropping to fourth when his tank ran dry on the last lap and leaving Prost to finish second ahead of Piquet, allowing them all to move clear of the unfortunate Senna in the Championship.

The Mexican Grand Prix was the first for 16 years and, although the Mexico City track had been completely rebuilt, it was still bumpy and difficult for both car and driver. Senna once again took pole with the Williams of Piquet and Mansell next and final Championship contender Prost back in sixth.

Left behind at the start, Mansell dropped to the back as Piquet passed Senna off the line. Mansell fought through the backmarkers only to have to pit for new tyres and do it all again. Berger decided not to change tyres but the other frontrunners did, struggling with the heat blistering their Goodyear rubber. Berger, on Pirellis, assumed the lead and held it to take his maiden Grand Prix win.

Epic finale

Senna's third place put him out of contention, but Prost in second, Piquet fourth and Mansell fifth all had a chance of the title with one race to go. That race, the Australian Grand Prix, witnessed some of the greatest drama in Grand Prix history.

Mansell had a clear advantage in the three-way battle, taking a seven-point lead to Adelaide, and confidently took pole ahead of team-mate Piquet with Senna shading Prost for third. Senna shot into the lead on the first lap as Mansell fell behind Piquet and a fast-starting Rosberg. Rosberg was the first man to make a break at the front on lap seven.

Piquet spun after pressure from Prost but charged back to pass Mansell for second on lap 44 after Prost suffered a puncture. He too battled back to attack the Williams pair: Rosberg lost the lead with a burst tyre and with 25 laps to go it was anybody's race – the title was still up for grabs. But on lap 63 came heartbreak for Mansell and his British fans when his left rear tyre exploded at 180 mph. Miraculously he controlled the car, but his chances were shot. It was down to two.

Williams called Piquet in to change tyres, fearing Rosberg's and Mansell's fate could befall him too. Prost stayed out, and although Piquet chased back to within four seconds it was too late: the title was Prost's.

1987
Piquet claims his prize

TALKING POINT

TURBO CHALLENGE

Turbo engines had come into the sport and turned it on its head in recent years as cars got quicker and quicker, and technology, some said, was taking away the skill of the driver.

As a result of ill-feeling in the paddock and, to a degree, uncertainty at where the turbo era would lead, the sport's governing body – the FIA – ruled that turbo engines would be banned from 1989 and replaced completely by atmospheric engines in 1989. The "atmo" engines, as they were known, would be reverted to, but with a larger 3.5-litre capacity. Hence, in 1987, the FIA introduced separate World Championships for drivers and constructors using the new atmo engines, as an incentive to others to revert to the alternative of turbo early.

The Jim Clark Trophy was awarded to the winning driver of the Championship for the atmo engine-powered car, while the Colin Chapman Trophy was awarded to the best constructor of the season in the same category.

The drivers of atmo-engined cars were still classified in the conventional World Championship which was, as usual, dominated by the big-name drivers who stuck with the teams equipped with turbo-powered cars.

As Nelson Piquet, Nigel Mansell, Alain Prost, Ayrton Senna and Gerhard Berger battled it out for the World Championship, Jonathan Palmer won the Jim Clark Trophy over the season in his Tyrrell car. Tyrrell in turn won the Colin Chapman Trophy.

Above: *Nigel Mansell injured his back in Japan.* ***Below opposite:*** *Ayrton Senna during the Monaco Grand Prix.*

This season proved one of the most exciting in the sport's history as several "big-gun" drivers battled for the Championship. Nelson Piquet stayed with the Honda-powered Williams team, partnered by another title favourite, Nigel Mansell.

Alain Prost was also fancied in pre-season as he remained with the TAG Porsche-powered McLaren team. Prost was joined by Stefan Johansson, who had left Ferrari.

Gerhard Berger from Benetton teamed up with Michele Alboreto at Ferrari, replacing Johansson. The two could not be written off as nobody knew what to expect from the Italian outfit.

Benetton were boosted by an engine deal with Ford and lined up Thierry Boutsen and Teo Fabi. Lotus were also dark horses, securing an engine deal with Honda and Japanese driver Satoru Nakajima as part of the package, joining Ayrton Senna.

The money men

Sponsors also came to the fore as Marlboro linked up with McLaren, Canon with Williams and Camel with Lotus. It had all the makings of a spectacular season, and so it turned out to be.

It opened with the Brazilian Grand Prix at the Jacarepagua circuit, and qualifying for the 61-lap race brought all the big names to the front of the grid as Mansell took pole position from Piquet, Senna, Fabi and Prost.

Piquet started well and beat Mansell off the line to lead. Fabi was the first retirement on lap nine as his Benetton's engine blew, and by lap seven Senna had overtaken Piquet.

Senna, however, was followed through by Prost who took the lead himself four laps later. He, in turn, was ahead for just three laps before Piquet regained first position on lap 17 – only to see Prost pass him again on lap 20.

On lap 50 Senna went out with a blown engine and Prost claimed the season's first win. Piquet finished second, Johansson third, Berger fourth, Boutsen fifth and pole-sitter Mansell sixth.

Piquet write-off

Three weeks later, the San Marino Grand Prix brought the field back to Europe. Senna took pole position at Imola for the 59-lap race but pre-race activity was marred by a crash involving Piquet, who wrote off his Williams and, concussed, was barred from racing. Another non-starter was René Arnoux, a casualty of suspension failure on his Ligier-Megatron.

Senna started badly and Mansell, second on the grid, beat him off the line. Prost retired on lap 14 with alternator failure and faulty electrics also put Berger's Ferrari out two laps later.

Mansell, meanwhile, hounded by Senna and Alboreto, lost his lead to the latter on lap 22. Alboreto, however, led for just two laps before Senna came back, but Mansell was still in the background and regained first place a lap later.

Mansell held off his challengers for the rest of the race and after Alex Caffi, on lap 54, and Derek Warwick, on lap 55, had retired after running out of fuel, Mansell took the chequered flag from Senna, Alboreto, Johansson, Martin Brundle and Nakajima.

Next was the 43-lap Belgian Grand Prix, and Mansell took pole at Spa-Francorchamps from Piquet, Senna, Berger, Alboreto and Prost.

Disaster for Palmer and Senna

In a spectacularly disastrous start, Palmer crashed his Tyrrell and Senna his Lotus, forcing a restart. Piquet took first place, holding off the quick-starting Prost, as Mansell dropped back. Berger went out on lap two with turbo failure and Patrese's clutch went on lap five.

Alboreto's Ferrari retired on lap nine when a wheel-bearing disintegrated and a lap later Piquet lost the lead to Prost. Yet worse was to come on lap 11 when turbo trouble forced him to retire.

Mansell pushed hard to catch Prost, only to crash out on lap 17, allowing Prost to claim his second win of the season from McLaren team-mate Johansson and Andrea de Cesaris, classified third despite his Brabham running out of fuel a lap behind the winner.

Mansell recovered from his Belgian setback by claiming pole position for the 78-lap Monaco Grand Prix from Senna, Piquet, Prost and Alboreto. Christian Danner in a Zakspeed was excluded from the start as punishment for dangerous driving in a clash with Alboreto. Adrian Campos, injured after crashing his Minardi in qualifying, also did not start.

Mansell's misery

As the lights went out Mansell got away smartly and led for 29 laps until a troublesome turbocharger ended his race, gifting the lead to Senna, who held off the challenge of Mansell's Williams team-mate Piquet to take his first win in the principality. Piquet finished second from Alboreto, Berger, Palmer and Ivan Capelli in a March. Prost, who retired three laps from the finish with a faulty engine, was still classified ninth.

Mansell's luck did not improve when the field travelled to Detroit for the US Grand Prix. He started the weekend well, taking pole for the 63-lap race, and sped into the lead from the start, with Senna and Piquet close behind. But on lap 33 the Briton started to experience cramp and dropped back, allowing Senna, Prost, Piquet and Berger through to take first, second, third and fourth. Mansell – in excruciating pain – eventually finished fifth, ahead of Arrows' Eddie Cheever, who ran out of fuel three laps from home.

In France two weeks later Mansell's fortunes took a turn for the better: he again claimed pole, but this time turned that into points and a victory in the 80-lap race at Paul Ricard.

Cheever was the first retirement on the opening lap as his ignition failed. Mansell briefly lost his lead to team-mate Piquet, but took it back on lap 45 and held on for his second win of the season. Piquet was second, Prost third, Senna fourth, Fabi fifth and Streiff sixth. The timing was perfect for Mansell's home race, the British Grand Prix at Silverstone. Piquet beat him to pole position but Mansell was second on the grid from Senna and Prost.

Ghinzani banned

Piercarlo Ghinzani was banned after his mechanics refuelled and push-started his Ligier on the circuit after it broke down. In Friday practice, Ghinzani also

RACE BY RACE DETAILS

ROUND 1 – BRAZIL
Race Alain Prost
Pole Nigel Mansell
Fastest lap Nelson Piquet

ROUND 2 – SAN MARINO
Race Nigel Mansell
Pole Ayrton Senna
Fastest lap Teo Fabi

ROUND 3 – BELGIUM
Race Alain Prost
Pole Nigel Mansell
Fastest lap Alain Prost

ROUND 4 – MONACO
Race Ayrton Senna
Pole Nigel Mansell
Fastest lap Ayrton Senna

ROUND 5 – UNITED STATES
Race Ayrton Senna
Pole Nigel Mansell
Fastest lap Ayrton Senna

ROUND 6 – FRANCE
Race Nigel Mansell
Pole Nigel Mansell
Fastest lap Nelson Piquet

ROUND 7 – BRITAIN
Race Nigel Mansell
Pole Nelson Piquet
Fastest lap Nigel Mansell

ROUND 8 – GERMANY
Race Nelson Piquet
Pole Nigel Mansell
Fastest lap Nigel Mansell

ROUND 9 – HUNGARY
Race Nelson Piquet
Pole Nigel Mansell
Fastest lap Nelson Piquet

ROUND 10 – AUSTRIA
Race Nigel Mansell
Pole Nelson Piquet
Fastest lap Nigel Mansell

ROUND 11 – ITALY
Race Nelson Piquet
Pole Nelson Piquet
Fastest lap Ayrton Senna

ROUND 12 – PORTUGAL
Race Alain Prost
Pole Gerhard Berger
Fastest lap Gerhard Berger

ROUND 13 – SPAIN
Race Nigel Mansell
Pole Nelson Piquet
Fastest lap Gerhard Berger

ROUND 14 – MEXICO
Race Nigel Mansell
Pole Nigel Mansell
Fastest lap Nelson Piquet

ROUND 15 – JAPAN
Race Gerhard Berger
Pole Gerhard Berger
Fastest lap Alain Prost

ROUND 16 – AUSTRALIA
Race Gerhard Berger
Pole Gerhard Berger
Fastest lap Gerhard Berger

1987 DRIVERS' CHAMPIONSHIP

DRIVER	TEAM	POINTS
Nelson Piquet	Williams	73
Nigel Mansell	Williams	61
Ayrton Senna	Lotus	57
Alain Prost	McLaren	46
Gerhard Berger	Ferrari	36
Stefan Johansson	McLaren	30
Michele Alboreto	Ferrari	17
Thierry Boutsen	Benetton	16
Teo Fabi	Benetton	12
Eddie Cheever	Arrows	8
Saturo Nakajima	Lotus	7
Jonathan Palmer	Tyrrell	7
Riccardo Patrese	Brabham	6
Andrea de Cesaris	Brabham	4
Philippe Streiff	Tyrrell	4
Derek Warwick	Arrows	3
Philippe Alliot	Lola	3
Martin Brundle	Zakspeed	2
René Arnoux	Ligier	1
Ivan Capelli	March	1
Roberto Moreno	AGS	1

completed two laps after the chequered flag to infuriate the stewards.

At the start, Piquet sped into the lead from Mansell, opening a battle which would live long in the memory.

Berger, Johansson, Patrese, Cheever, Alboreto and Prost all went out with mechanical problems before the 62nd lap of 65 when Mansell pulled off a remarkable overtaking manoeuvre on Piquet going into the Stowe corner. It was brave and spectacular but, most importantly, eventually gave Mansell a win from Piquet, Senna, Nakajima, Warwick and Fabi.

Hockenheim in Germany, with its long, fast straights, hosted the next round. Mansell, brimming with confidence, took pole for the 44-lap race from Senna, Prost and Piquet. Briefly losing the lead to Senna at the start, he recovered by the second lap, the top four remaining extremely close. Patrese's Brabham retired on lap five with engine problems, and on lap seven Prost overtook Mansell to gain the lead.

De Cesaris blows up

Alboreto retired on lap 10 with turbo problems and de Cesaris's Brabham blew its engine two laps later. On lap 18 Mansell overhauled Prost but led for just three laps before the Frenchman came back.

Mansell then retired on lap 25 when his engine blew, but worse was to follow for Prost 14 laps later – and just five laps from victory – as his McLaren's alternator failed, forcing him out and clearing the way for the patient and consistent Piquet to take the lead and the victory, from Johansson – who finished with a flat tyre – Senna, Streiff, Palmer and Philippe Alliot in a Larrousse.

For the next round, 76 laps at Hungary's Hungaroring, Mansell once again took pole from Berger, Piquet, Prost, Alboreto and Senna.

Mansell led from pole with Piquet in close proximity. Berger went out on lap 13 with a mechanical fault and Johansson a lap later with a blown gearbox.

SHORTS

As the teams headed to Spain, Mansell was trailing Piquet in the Championship and needed something special. He took second place on the grid to Piquet but Mansell was in no mood to give up, seized the lead at the start and held it to the chequered flag. The win bred confidence and Mansell went into the next round in Mexico City knowing another would put him back into the title race.

A jubilant Nigel Mansell lifts the trophy at the British Grand Prix.

All for the lack of a wheel nut

Mansell's Williams seemed suited to the Hungarian circuit but disaster struck just six laps from the finish as a wheel nut fell off. It was a bitter pill to swallow as Mansell watched Piquet power through for another fortuitous victory. Senna finished second from Prost, Boutsen, Patrese and Warwick, but the title race had swung back in Piquet's favour thanks to Mansell's uncertain fortunes.

The Briton bounced back in an eventful Austrian Grand Prix. This time Piquet took pole position from Mansell, Berger, Boutsen, Fabi and Alboreto.

On race day, two massive crashes on the pit straight forced two restarts. Fortunately, no drivers were injured, but Streiff failed to start again as his Tyrrell was too badly damaged.

Piquet led from the restart but second-placed Mansell kept him under intense pressure. Turbo trouble put Berger out early again on lap five with a turbo problem and 15 laps later Mansell made his move and took Piquet for the lead. For all his might Piquet could not catch the resurgent Mansell, who powered to victory. Piquet was second, from Fabi, Boutsen, Senna and Prost. Martin Brundle, 14th in his Zakspeed, was disqualified for a wing illegality.

In Monza for the 50-lap Italian Grand Prix, Piquet took pole from Mansell, Prost and Senna. Nicola Larini in a Coloni and Pascal Fabre in an AGS failed to qualify.

Piquet much-needed win

Piquet led from pole from Senna and Mansell, losing the lead to Senna on lap 23 but battling back seven laps from the finish to clinch a much-needed win. Senna finished second from Mansell, Berger, Boutsen and Johansson in a rather processional race.

For once, there was a different pole-sitter for the 70-lap Portuguese Grand Prix, Berger heading the Estoril grid from Mansell, Prost and Piquet.

The race was stopped after Danner, who qualified 16th, spun into a barrier on the first lap. Though uninjured, he failed to make the restart.

Berger lost his lead in the restart and Mansell powered through, but the German came back a lap later and found himself in the unusual position of first place. Mansell, meanwhile, retired on lap 13 with faulty electronics.

Prost pressure

Berger led until lap 33 when Ferrari team-mate Alboreto took over, only to lose out to the resurgent Berger, sensing his first win of the season. He was on course for a memorable victory, but you could never count out Prost, who put Berger under increasing pressure, took the lead three laps from the finish and won the race. A dejected Berger was in second place from Piquet, Fabi, Johansson and Cheever. Senna was seventh.

As the teams headed to Spain, Mansell was now trailing Piquet in the Championship and needed something special as the campaign entered its latter stages. He took second place on the grid in Jerez to Piquet on pole, but Mansell was in no mood to give up, seized the lead at the start of the 72-lap race and held it to the chequered flag. Prost finished second, from Johansson, Piquet, Senna and Alliot.

The win bred confidence and Mansell went into the next round in Mexico City knowing another would put him back into the title race with Piquet.

Mansell took pole position for the 63-lap race from Berger, Piquet, Boutsen and Prost, but lost top spot to Berger at the start, the German speeding away as accidents littered the opening lap. Prost, Danner, Nakajima and Brundle all went out in accidents on lap one and Berger, meanwhile, was taken on lap two by Boutsen, now leading a Grand Prix for the first time in the season.

Boutsen cruelly denied

Boutsen was cruelly denied a longer spell at the front as his Benetton's electronics failed on lap 15, giving Berger back the lead, but Mansell had made up ground and reclaimed first place on lap 21. However, his victory quest hit a setback nine laps later when Warwick lost control of his Arrows and was involved in a massive shunt.

Saturo Nakajima looks pleased after winning his first point in Formula One with Lotus and a Honda engine.

Remarkably, he emerged unscathed, but the race was stopped and restarted for a distance of 31 laps. It did not faze Mansell and he led from the restart to the finish to get himself back in the game. Piquet was second, retaining his advantage, but Mansell looked favourite for the title as the season went into its last two races in Japan and Australia.

The season had seen many ups and downs, but nobody could have predicted the anti-climax which would end it.

A back injury before the Japanese Grand Prix weekend forced Mansell out of the last two races, effectively gifting the Championship to Piquet, who went to Japan not knowing Mansell would not make Australia.

Ironically, Piquet failed to finish either race, thanks to engine failure in Japan and a brake problem in Australia, but it did not matter. Berger won both races to end his personal season on a high, but Piquet claimed a remarkable Championship – when nobody knew what was around the next corner.

1987 CONSTRUCTORS' CUP

TEAM (Engine)	POINTS
WILLIAMS HONDA	137
McLAREN PORSCHE	76
LOTUS HONDA	64
FERRARI	53
BENETTON FORD	28
ARROWS MEGATRON BMW	11
TYRRELL FORD	11
BRABHAM BMW	10
LOLA FORD	3
ZAKSPEED	2
LIGIER MEGATRON	1
MARCH FORD	1
AGS FORD	1

Carlos Reutemann

A HEAVYWEIGHT PRESENCE with a lightweight record, Carlos Reutemann remained an enigma. His ability to pull off occasional dazzling wins was matched by performances of numbing mediocrity.

CAREER DETAILS

1942	Born 12 April, in Santa Fe, Argentina
1970	Comes to Europe to compete in F2 with Brabham
1972	F1 debut with Brabham
1974	Maiden F1 victory at Kyalami
1976	Signs for Ferrari
1979	Signs for Lotus
1980	Signs for Williams
1981	Finishes runner up – career-best ranking.
1982	Retires

FORMULA ONE RECORD

Year	Team	Wins	Poles	Fast laps	Pts
1972	Brabham	0	1	0	3
1973	Brabham	0	0	0	16
1974	Brabham	3	1	0	32
1975	Brabham	1	0	0	37
1976	Brabham	0	0	0	3
1976	Ferrari	0	0	0	-
1977	Ferrari	1	0	0	42
1978	Ferrari	4	2	2	48
1979	Lotus	0	0	0	20
1980	Williams	1	0	0	42
1981	Williams	2	2	2	49
1982	Williams	0	0	0	6

On his day, Carlos Reutemann was simply inspirational, but his career suffered from an inferiority complex rarely found in racing drivers. "Carlos had a problem," explained Brabham designer Gordon Murray. "He lived in a kind of box. The box consisted of a few drivers and himself and inside that box, for some reason, there was always someone ahead of Carlos. 'Oh,' he'd say, 'Hulme is quicker than I am. Emerson is quicker than I am. I think I am number four.'"

"He needed psychological support more than other drivers," concurred Frank Williams. "He needed to be aware that everyone in the team was wearing a Reutemann lapel badge and an Argentine scarf."

The serious-minded perfectionist, the son of a cattle rancher from Santa Fe, had a season in Europe sponsored by Automobil Club Argentino racing a Brabham BT30. Two years later, in 1970, he returned to the European scene as a member of the Argentinian-backed Formula Two team and nearly pipped Ronnie Peterson in the final standings.

Signed by Bernie Ecclestone for Brabham in 1972, Reutemann qualified on pole position for his first Grand Prix outing in front of his home crowd at Buenos Aires. He finished seventh – and, disappointingly, was never to win in Argentina. He won the non-title Brazilian Grand Prix to emphasize his promise, but a bad crash at Thruxton in Formula

Reutemann in action during the South African Grand Prix for Brabham.

Celebrating his first win in the South African Grand Prix of 1974.

"When his head's in the right place, he's a fantastic driver."

James Hunt 1981

Two knocked his confidence.

It was not until 1974 that Brabham designer Gordon Murray produced a machine, the BT44, with which Reutemann could express his talent. Either on flying form or mysteriously lacklustre, he chalked up victories in the South African, Austrian and United States Grands Prix. The following year he would win the German Grand Prix at the Nurburgring in the Brabham BT44B derivative, but when the team concluded a deal to use the Alfa Romeo flat-12 engine for 1976, Reutemann seemed to lose his motivation.

Frustrated by the new cars, he negotiated a release and signed with Ferrari. He raced only once for the new team, at Monza, but lined up alongside Niki Lauda for the 1977 season. The two men did not hit it off together, with the Austrian delighting in humiliating his team-mate. Reutemann's prospects improved in 1978 once Lauda moved to Brabham. Leading the Ferrari challenge, the Argentine won the Brazilian, Long Beach, British and United States Grands Prix in fine style, but failed to capitalize on a potential Championship-winning situation.

"To win a Championship, you have to have a driver who wants to win," said Enzo Ferrari pointedly in 1978. Three years later Reutemann himself mused: "At Ferrari I was always made to think that though I was capable of winning races, it wasn't in my temperament to be a winner."

An unproductive season at Team Lotus in 1979 was followed by a move to Williams where he was recruited as team-mate to Alan Jones. Once more, Reutemann was paired alongside someone with whom he had little in common. Jones was bullishly extrovert, Reutemann was introverted and supersensitive. In 1980 he scored a solitary victory at Monaco, only after Jones and Didier Pironi's Ligier retired ahead of him, but in 1981 he would mount the strongest Championship challenge of his career.

He started the season by winning the Brazilian Grand Prix against team orders, ignoring pit signals to drop back behind Jones. He was penalized financially, but Carlos could not have cared less. In his view, he was a racer, and racers do not throw away victories. After a succession of good performances, including another victory in Belgium, he arrived at Las Vegas for the final race of the season on the threshold of the Championship. With a blindingly quick qualifying lap to snatch pole position, he set himself up inspirationally, but when the starting lights went green, Reutemann unaccountably seemed to capitulate. A handling problem undermined his confidence and he faded to eighth place, the title going by one point to Nelson Piquet who finished semi-conscious in fifth place.

He returned in 1982, finished a brilliant second in the opening race and then quit after the next. He never went back on that spontaneous decision, although he subsequently acknowledged that he had given up prematurely. His reasons remain an enigma. In 1991 Reutemann was elected Governor of Argentina's Santa Fe province when there was also much talk of him as a future president of his country. "Whatever happens, life will stay the same afterwards. The sun will come up from the east and go down in the west. There are more things than just motor racing and World Championships," he had said midway through his racing career.

1988
First places count

TALKING POINT

POINTS DON'T MAKE PRIZES

The famous saying that points make prizes could not have been further from the truth in the 1988 season. McLaren team-mates Alain Prost and Ayrton Senna had a season-long battle for the Championship and the latter was crowned Champion, despite scoring fewer points. Prost ended with 112 points to Senna's 102, but the Brazilian was awarded the Championship thanks to his eight wins to Prost's seven. The decision to count a driver's best 11 results benefited Senna and he duly landed the title.

The season will be remembered for the tumultuous battle between McLaren team-mates Senna and Prost but, more significantly, the year brought the turbo era to an end as the FIA introduced new rulings on specification for the following season.

Prost and Senna's duel saw the latter crowned Champion, despite scoring fewer points than his team-mate, thanks to a decision to reward the most consistent driver with the title, based on each man's best 11 results from the season's 16 races. With eight wins, Senna was thus at the head of the standings.

The season kicked off in Senna's homeland, Brazil, with the local favourite landing pole position, but the race at Jacarepagua did not turn out as he planned. Lying second on lap 31, he was disqualified after starting the race from the pit-lane in the spare car when his race chassis developed a problem on the parade lap.

Overheating engines

Before Senna's exit, Williams' Riccardo Patrese and Nigel Mansell had both retired with their Judd engines overheating, a disappointing start for the British team.

Prost, second on the grid, led Ferrari's Gerhard Berger home by 10 seconds, while Piquet gave the Brazilians something to cheer about despite Senna's disqualification, guiding his Lotus home in third ahead of Derek Warwick's Arrows.

In the San Marino Grand Prix at Imola, Senna's exit in Brazil prompted the perfect response from him as he grabbed pole ahead of Prost. Senna led from the off, Prost on his tail, and the McLaren pair banked a one-two, lapping the entire field with less than three seconds between them at the chequered flag.

Monaco hosted the third round and again Senna dominated proceedings, although a rare and surprising error gifted a second win to his team-mate Prost.

Lotus' Satoru Nakajima surprisingly failed to qualify and only 10 drivers survived the gruelling 78-lap race. Piquet and Mansell crashed – Piquet on the opening lap – both Ligiers suffered electrical problems and a needless accident forced Senna to retire. Leading his team-mate by almost one minute, a lapse in concentration allowed his front left wheel to collide with the barriers on the street circuit and the resulting damage ended his race 12 laps from the end.

Prost's victory

Senna hit back immediately, however, landing pole position for the Mexican Grand Prix. But the Brazilian's plans for the Mexico City race suffered a setback as Prost stormed to his third win of the season.

At the front, Prost led from Senna for the entire

Champion Ayrton Senna and team-mate Alain Prost enjoy the champagne at the Australian Grand Prix.

Ayrton Senna was forced to retire from the Monaco Grand Prix after he collided with the barriers.

race after a quicker start, and only third-placed Berger finished on the same lap as the McLarens, ahead of team-mate Alboreto, with Arrows duo Warwick and Eddie Cheever holding the final points positions. Lotus' Piquet was denied a top-six finish when problems with his Honda engine took him out with nine laps remaining.

The circus headed north for the Canadian Grand Prix, and Senna got his Championship challenge back on course with a win from pole on the grid. Prost made the better start but Senna assumed the lead on lap 19 and never looked back.

Too hot

Tyrrell's Bailey was an opening-lap casualty and ignition problems in the heat of Montreal put Berger's Ferrari out on lap 22 as McLaren's Senna and Prost left the rest trailing in their wake. Williams pair Mansell and Patrese went out within four laps of each other thanks to the problematic Judd engine (Mansell's 28th-lap exit was his fifth in as many races) and Arrows' Cheever retired on lap 31. Alboreto's engine sent him to join Berger in the Ferrari garage on lap 33, and Senna and Prost remained untouched with only Benetton's Boutsen on the same lap at the finish.

Inspired, Senna dominated again in the heat of Detroit seven days later, finishing almost 40 seconds ahead of Prost, the only man on the same lap at the end of the 63-lap race.

Mansell's miserable season continued as electrical troubles put him out. Arrows' Warwick crashed on lap 24, Piquet's Lotus two laps later, and Patrese joined team-mate Mansell when his Judd engine's electrics also failed.

Ghinzani excluded

In the French Grand Prix at Paul Ricard, Prost claimed his first pole position of the season in his homeland. Senna, who had started from the front of the grid in the opening six races, was second.

Zakspeed's Ghinzani, who qualified 22nd, was excluded after missing his weight check and Prost was quickest off the grid, chased by Senna and Ferrari duo Berger and Alboreto. Senna's pressure on Prost paid off when he overhauled him during the pit-stop period to take the lead and the race order remained stable until gearbox problems for Senna resulted in slower lap times.

Prost took the lead on lap 61 and won, sending the home fans crazy, while Senna had sufficient advantage to remain ahead of Alboreto, who led team-mate Berger home. Piquet ended fifth and Nannini picked up a point for Benetton.

Wet and wild

The British Grand Prix at Silverstone in July was the first rain-affected race of the season. Ferrari finally bettered McLaren in qualifying, with Berger and Alboreto on the front row, but Prost quit after 24 laps complaining the wet conditions were hazardous.

Berger led Senna off the line and stayed there until lap 14, when the Brazilian got in front and stayed there for his fourth win of the campaign ahead of Williams' Mansell, finishing for the first time that season. Benetton's Nannini was third for his first-ever podium, while Mauricio Gugelmin ended fourth after an impressive performance for Leyton House.

The Championship's ninth round, the German

RACE BY RACE DETAILS

ROUND 1 – BRAZIL
Race Alain Prost
Pole Ayrton Senna
Fastest lap Gerhard Berger

ROUND 2 – SAN MARINO
Race Ayrton Senna
Pole Ayrton Senna
Fastest lap Alain Prost

ROUND 3 – MONACO
Race Alain Prost
Pole Ayrton Senna
Fastest lap Ayrton Senna

ROUND 4 – MEXICO
Race Alain Prost
Pole Ayrton Senna
Fastest lap Alain Prost

ROUND 5 – CANADA
Race Ayrton Senna
Pole Ayrton Senna
Fastest lap Ayrton Senna

ROUND 6 – UNITED STATES
Race Ayrton Senna
Pole Ayrton Senna
Fastest lap Ayrton Senna

ROUND 7 – FRANCE
Race Alain Prost
Pole Alain Prost
Fastest lap Alain Prost

ROUND 8 – BRITAIN
Race Ayrton Senna
Pole Gerhard Berger
Fastest lap Nigel Mansell

ROUND 9 – GERMANY
Race Ayrton Senna
Pole Ayrton Senna
Fastest lap Alessandro Nannini

ROUND 10 – HUNGARY
Race Ayrton Senna
Pole Ayrton Senna
Fastest lap Alain Prost

ROUND 11 – BELGIUM
Race Ayrton Senna
Pole Ayrton Senna
Fastest lap Gerhard Berger

ROUND 12 – ITALY
Race Gerhard Berger
Pole Ayrton Senna
Fastest lap Michele Alboreto

ROUND 13 – PORTUGAL
Race Alain Prost
Pole Alain Prost
Fastest lap Gerhard Berger

ROUND 14 – SPAIN
Race Alain Prost
Pole Ayrton Senna
Fastest lap Alain Prost

ROUND 15 – JAPAN
Race Ayrton Senna
Pole Ayrton Senna
Fastest lap Ayrton Senna

ROUND 16 – AUSTRALIA
Race Alain Prost
Pole Ayrton Senna
Fastest lap Alain Prost

1988 DRIVERS' CHAMPIONSHIP

DRIVER	TEAM	POINTS
Ayrton Senna	McLaren	90
Alain Prost	McLaren	87
Gerhard Berger	Ferrari	41
Thierry Boutsen	Benetton Ford	27
Michele Alboreto	Ferrari	24
Nelson Piquet	Lotus Honda	22
Ivan Capelli	March	17
Derek Warwick	Arrows	17
Alessandro Nannini	Benetton Ford	12
Nigel Mansell	Williams	12
Riccardo Patrese	Williams	8
Eddie Cheever	Arrows	6
Mauricio Gugelmin	March	5
Jonathan Palmer	Tyrrell	5
Andrea de Cesaris	Rial-Ford	3
Pierluigi Martini	Minardi	1
Satoru Nakajima	Lotus-Honda	1

Grand Prix, was at Hockenheim, and Senna won from pole to move within two points of Prost in the standings. Again it was raining, but this time Prost continued, trailing Senna home for second place ahead of Berger and Alboreto. Leyton House's run of form continued, Capelli finishing fifth ahead of Boutsen.

Crashes for Mansell and Piquet

Mansell failed to build on his performance at Silverstone, crashing on lap 16, and team-mate Patrese exited after a 34th-lap accident. Piquet crashed out on the opening lap.

Senna's third straight win came two weeks later when he led all the way at the Hungaroring. Quicker off the grid than Mansell, who qualified second, Senna held a big advantage for much of the race.

Mansell retired yet again on lap 60 due to the heat. Prost ended the race less than 0.6 seconds down on Senna, with Boutsen third and Berger fourth. Gugelmin, in fifth, kept Leyton House's impressive season going and sixth-placed Patrese scored only his second point of the year.

Dominant Senna

Senna's dominance continued in Belgium, leading Prost home for his fourth straight win. Mansell, out with a viral infection, was replaced by compatriot Martin Brundle.

Senna qualified on pole ahead of Prost, immediately took the lead and stayed there throughout the opening stages as Berger, third in his Ferrari, disappeared with electrical problems. Engine failure forced Patrese out on lap 30 and Ferrari's challenge ended five laps later when a similar problem struck Alboreto, lying third behind the McLarens.

Senna won by half a minute from Prost, with Benetton duo Boutsen and Nannini third and fourth. Post-race scrutineering saw the Benettons disqualified for fuel irregularities and Capelli was classified third ahead of Piquet, Warwick and Cheever. Brundle finished seventh, but Frank Williams decided to hand Mansell's drive to Frenchman Jean-Louis Schlesser for the Italian Grand Prix.

Senna and Prost held the front row ahead of Berger and Alboreto and the Brazilian led at the start from his McLaren team-mate. Piquet retired on lap 11 when his Lotus spun off while he was in the points.

Prost's problems

The race order remained static until lap 34 when a rare problem with the Honda engine forced Prost, lying second, to retire. Senna was seemingly heading for a fifth straight win, with Berger and Alboreto out of sight. But on lap 49, just two from the end, he attempted to overtake backmarker Schlesser but tangled with the Williams driver. They touched at the chicane and the collision sent Senna spinning out, although he was classified 10th.

Berger led Alboreto home by half a second for a memorable Ferrari one-two on their home circuit which ended McLaren's winning run.

Senna and Prost's title tussle became more evident in Portugal in September, and it was the

SHORTS

It was a disappointing year for Nigel Mansell who was forced to drop out of numerous races due to problems which included electrical faults, overheating, heat exhaustion and general mechanical failure. Then, he went down with a viral infection just before the Belgian Grand Prix and was out for both that race and the Italian Grand Prix. In Belgium his place was taken by Martin Brundle and then by Jean-Louis Schlesser.

Nigel Mansell achieved second place at the British Grand Prix after a poor start to the season.

Gerhard Berger and Michele Alboreto managed to break the stranglehold of Senna and Prost at Monza.

1988 CONSTRUCTORS' CUP

TEAM (Engine)	POINTS
McLAREN HONDA	199
FERRARI	65
BENETTON FORD	39
LOTUS HONDA	23
ARROWS MEGATRON	23
MARCH JUDD	22
WILLIAMS JUDD	20
TYRRELL FORD	5
RIAL FORD	3
MINARDI FORD	1

Frenchman who boosted his chances of taking a third world title.

The Estoril race had to be restarted and Prost was on pole, with Senna also on the front row. Senna made the better start and led the opening lap. The Brazilian swerved at Prost as he pulled alongside, but Prost remained focused and took the lead as Senna's move pushed him down the field.

Capelli challenge

Capelli was Prost's nearest challenger, qualifying third in his Leyton House, and pushed the McLaren driver hard early on. Meanwhile Cheever of Arrows retired with turbo problems. Patrese's race was ended by a radiator leak on lap 29 and Piquet followed him five laps later with a clutch problem.

Prost held off the challenge of Capelli to win, with Boutsen third, Warwick staying ahead of Alboreto to claim fourth for Arrows and Senna picking up a point for sixth after the retirement of Nannini, hit by the heat, and Mansell, who had crashed out.

Senna banked pole position for the Spanish Grand Prix a week later, but lost out to Prost heading for the first corner and never got back into contention.

Glitch

A McLaren one-two was on the cards until bizarre computer data produced confusing fuel consumption readings for Senna's car, causing the Brazilian to drop back to fourth behind Mansell and Nannini. Patrese completed a welcome weekend for Williams with fifth and Berger was sixth.

Senna secured the title in Japan with his eighth win, qualifying on pole ahead of Prost and Berger for the penultimate race of the season, but dropping to 14th when he stalled on the grid.

Prost assumed the lead as his team-mate restarted his engine and once again the impressive Capelli was on his tail. By lap 16, the pressure had told and Capelli was leading, albeit for only a lap before Prost moved ahead again. But his electrics failed on lap 19 and Mansell crashed out five laps later. Senna was back up to second, took the lead on lap 28 and never looked back, powering to the title as rain fell on Suzuka.

Piquet, feeling ill, retired on lap 34 and Cheever's turbo went a lap later. Boutsen finished third behind Senna and Prost: Berger, Nannini and Patrese completed the top six.

The Australian final round proved an anti-climax. Prost cruised to victory in Adelaide, sacrificing the lead only once to Berger, but it was a little too late for the Frenchman.

Senna was on pole, but lost out to Prost entering the first corner. Prost led for 13 laps before Berger overhauled him, while Mansell, Piquet and Patrese competed with Senna for third.

Berger spun off on lap 25 under pressure from Prost and the McLaren was left to win from his team-mate as Piquet got the better of Patrese, Boutsen and Capelli in the battle for third place. Mansell spun off on lap 65 when in the points.

The victory was Prost's seventh of the season, but with only the best 11 results counting towards the Championship he lost out to Senna, with eight wins to his name.

Riccardo Patrese

FORMULA ONE'S MOST ENDURING CAMPAIGNER with an amazing 256 Grand Prix starts, Riccardo Patrese matured from a controversial "enfant terrible" into an amiable elder statesman.

CAREER DETAILS

1954	Born 17 April in Padua, Italy
1972	Italian kart Champion
1974	Wins world kart title
1975	Switches to cars, finishing runner-up in Formula Italia
1976	Wins Italian and European Formula Three series
1977	Makes F1 debut for the Shadow team
1978	Blamed for triggering accident at Italian GP in which Ronnie Peterson dies
1982	Joins Brabham and won maiden GP at Monaco
1988	Joins Williams
1993	Joins Benetton and retires from F1

FORMULA ONE RECORD

Year	Team	Wins	Poles	Fast laps	Pts
1977	Shadow	0	0	0	1
1978	Arrows	0	0	0	11
1979	Arrows	0	0	0	2
1980	Arrows	0	0	0	7
1981	Arrows	0	1	0	10
1982	Brabham	1	0	2	21
1983	Brabham	1	1	1	13
1984	Alfa Romeo	-	0	0	8
1985	Alfa Romeo	0	0	0	–
1986	Brabham	0	0	0	2
1987	Brabham	0	0	0	6
1987	Williams	0	0	0	–
1988	Williams	0	0	0	8
1989	Williams	0	1	1	40
1990	Williams	1	0	4	23
1991	Williams	2	4	2	53
1992	Williams	1	1	3	56
1993	Benetton	0	0	0	20

Patrese on his way to first place in the San Marino Grand Prix of 1990.

It is hard to believe that Riccardo Patrese, the mellow, confident Williams driver of the late Eighties, was the same wild and assured *arriviste* driver whose rough-edged reputation earned him the blame (subsequently cleared) for triggering the accident at Monza in 1978 that resulted in the death of Ronnie Peterson.

As a child the Italian, born in Padua, was a sensation in karts. National Champion in 1972, he took the world title two years later before moving into car racing in Formula Italia. He consolidated his whizz-kid reputation by finishing runner-up to Bruno Giacomelli in the 1975 Championship. The following year he won the Italian Formula Three title and, after an embittered battle with Conny Andersson, he also took the European crown in the final round.

He made the natural progression to Formula Two in 1976, enjoying a successful season in a Chevron, before being propelled into Formula One when the Shadow team dropped Renzo Zorzi after five races. Keen to make his mark, he immediately proved his talent with his first points finish at the Japanese Grand Prix, even if his off-track attitude caused some consternation.

At the start of 1978 he showed staggering speed and led the South African Grand Prix – his new Arrows team's second race – until engine failure ruined the show. Still showing signs of unruliness in his driving, he found the Formula One world quick to blame him for causing the first-lap multiple crash at Monza that resulted in the death of the popular Ronnie Peterson. Until he was cleared almost four years later, he endured an emotional pressure that would have reduced a weaker man.

"For four years I had to ask myself the same question: am I a killer? All the time I knew I was not, but it was almost too much to bear. None of the drivers ever had the guts to tell me, but for many I was the killer of Ronnie Peterson," he said later.

From 1979 to 1981 he remained obdurately loyal to Arrows with few results to show for his undoubted skill. He would taste success only with a

"I don't play politics and maybe that is one of my problems, because in Formula One sometimes you win with politics. I play my cards on the table not under the table."

A happy Riccardo on the podium at Imola in 1990.

move to the competitive Brabham team in 1982 when in an otherwise grey year he won his first Grand Prix at Monaco. The following season was also ruined by inconsistency: he threw away a certain victory at Imola but ended the year sweeping away the opposition at Kyalami.

In 1984 and 1985 his career took a downward plunge as he wrestled the Benetton-sponsored Alfa to little avail before returning to Brabham. Frank Williams offered him the second Williams drive and the faith he and Patrick Head put in him revitalized the unfulfilled Italian. If 1988 was his bedding-in year, the following season saw the start of a relaxed and profitable relationship with technical director Head that provided the basic development work from which the great period of Williams' glory sprang. Nigel Mansell had gone to Ferrari, Renault had replaced Judd, and Patrese responded to the responsibility.

"You'll call Riccardo up, ask him to test at a moment's notice, and he'll say: 'Fine, no problem, I'll be there.' He's not a selfish man, which is quite rare as a driver. His ego is under control, too...which is also quite rare," said Head in praise of the experienced campaigner.

In 1990 he won an emotional victory at Imola, but the following season – with wins in Mexico and Portugal – was probably his most fulfilling as a racer. He made a superb start to the season, giving Mansell, who had returned from Ferrari, a run for his money. "We had a bit of a problem on one of the bends but at the end of the race we looked each other in the eye and decided that it was every man for himself on the track," the Italian said after the United States Grand Prix at Phoenix.

His best Championship finish, runner-up to Mansell in 1992, paradoxically saw him outperformed by his rampant Williams team-mate. A move to Benetton as 39-year-old team-mate to the *wunderkind* Michael Schumacher confirmed his loss of pace and deep-seated motivation in Formula One. After an unspectacular, though lucrative, drive in German Super Touring behind the wheel of a Ford Mondeo, and a one-off outing at Le Mans in 1997, Patrese slipped into retirement. Ever popular, he can now be seen annually at Monaco as he revisits the scene of his 1982 triumph.

1989
Another McLaren battle

> **TALKING POINT**
>
> **THE FEUD**
>
> San Marino, 1 May: a date and a place which would have ironic – and tragic – repercussions in the life of Ayrton Senna. In 1989, on the very day and the very track which witnessed his death five years later, the Brazilian began a feud which to this day remains a mystery in his enigmatic life.
>
> Gerhard Berger had just survived a dramatic, fiery crash at the very corner which claimed Senna five years later, and Senna made a pact with team-mate Alain Prost not to pass on the first lap. But when Prost claimed the lead Senna's competitive instinct forced him past at Tosa on lap one. The feud grew and grew until, it is believed, only minutes before the tragic events of 1 May 1994.
>
> For the rest of the 1989 season their relationship was full of needle and Prost left at the end of the year, but the bitter and intriguing rivalry born that day endured.

Johnny Herbert looking ready to go on his debut for Benetton at the Brazilian Grand Prix.

The 1989 season began a new era, with turbochargers outlawed and normally-aspirated engines given a new lease of life, and a new tyre war was brewing between newcomers Pirelli and leaders Goodyear. But one thing which did not change was the fortunes of the top teams: McLaren, so dominant in 1988, once again saw their great pairing of Prost and Senna battle for top honours.

In the big pre-season move, Nigel Mansell went to Ferrari alongside Gerhard Berger, but the V12-engined car had struggled in testing with its revolutionary but problematic semi-automatic gearbox.

To partner Alessandro Nannini, Benetton signed Britain's Johnny Herbert, still recovering from a shattering F3000 crash the previous year, while March kept Ivan Capelli and Mauricio Gugelmin and Judd engines. Lamborghini made their Formula One bow with Larrousse, though without team partner Didier Camels, under arrest for shooting his wife in a domestic argument; and Brabham returned after being sold by Bernie Ecclestone.

Paralysed

The season started on a grim note when, before the first race in Brazil, Philippe Streiff rolled his AGS in testing and was partially paralysed when a roll-hoop failed. But with the growing popularity of Formula One the Brazilian race saw a massive entry of 38 cars, and pre-qualifying was necessary to reduce the field to 30 for practice sessions.

Senna had taken 13 out of 16 possible poles in 1988 so it was no surprise to see him heading the 26-strong field for the season opener, but the home favourite was slow away and Berger and Patrese came up on either side. The inevitable happened: Senna and Berger spun off, leaving the Williams in the lead with team-mate Thierry Boutsen second. Mansell passed Boutsen and, on lap 15, made a stunning move to take the lead which bolstered his reputation as *Il Leone*. Once the pit-stop shuffling concluded he was in front and went on to win.

Narrow escape

But Ferrari came back down to earth with a bang at San Marino's Imola, their second home. Not only did McLaren claim a one-two finish to get their Championship challenge back on the rails, but Berger's Ferrari suffered a spectacular fourth-lap crash at the Tamburello corner which could have claimed his life. He escaped with a broken rib and second-degree burns to his hands and, amazingly, was racing again within five weeks..

The race, which had been stopped, resumed. Prost claimed the lead at the restart, only to lose it to Senna who took the victory, well ahead of the infuriated Prost.

A McLaren one-two

Monaco was next, and although the slow, twisty circuit was the opposite of Imola it saw another one-two for McLaren. Ferrari ran just one car and Mansell could only manage fifth on the grid and eventually retired with gearbox problems.

Next came Mexico and Berger was back. Still with bandaged hands, he qualified on the third row but only lasted 16 laps before his car failed him. Once again, the race seemed not a question of which team would win, but which McLaren driver would take the spoils. After an initial stoppage following a four-car crash at the end of the first lap, the race got under way with Senna leading Prost into turn one. But the Frenchman was struggling with his tyres and never recovered from a pit-stop.

Mansell climbed through the field, only to drop out after two-thirds of the distance. Patrese was there to claim second ahead of Alboreto's reliable Tyrrell. Prost settled for a disappointing fifth behind Nannini's Benetton.

Sweltering heat in Phoenix, Arizona kept the crowds away for the US Grand Prix, and the race did little to enthuse America about Formula One. But two weeks later a dramatically wet Canadian Grand Prix in Montreal saw the first non-McLaren victory since Mansell in the season opener.

Variable conditions saw Mansell, Nannini and Luis Sala pit after the parade lap to take a gamble on slick tyres. Thinking the race had started when it hadn't, they powered out of the pits and found themselves out in front, but were soon black-flagged, leaving true leader Prost ahead of Senna and Patrese.

Prost swapped to slicks on lap one but then retired with suspension failure, and there was another black flag, this time for Stefan Johansson whose Onyx had trailed a tyre hammer and associated hoses and metal gantries out of the pit lane. But then came the rain, and the slick tyre gamblers were forced in leaving Patrese with a healthy lead, Warwick second and Nicola Larini's Osella third.

Senna so close

When the latter pair retired and Patrese was forced to pit with fading wet tyres, a freshly-shod Senna cruised into the lead, only for engine failure to snatch victory away three laps from the end. As Patrese struggled with a loose undertray, Boutsen moved past to lead a one-two for the Williams Renault squad, de Cesaris taking the final podium place for Dallara.

The teams arriving in France for the seventh round showed many changes. Emanuele Piro replaced Herbert at Benetton amid internal political wranglings. Yannick Dalmas, suffering from Legionnaires' Disease, was dropped for Eric Bernard, Derek Warwick, injured in a karting accident, was replaced by Martin Donnelly and Michele

Thierry Boutsen celebrates his win at the Canadian Grand Prix in fine style.

RACE BY RACE DETAILS

ROUND 1 – BRAZIL
Race Nigel Mansell
Pole Ayrton Senna
Fastest lap Riccardo Patrese

ROUND 2 – SAN MARINO
Race Ayrton Senna
Pole Ayrton Senna
Fastest lap Alain Prost

ROUND 3 – MONACO
Race Ayrton Senna
Pole Ayrton Senna
Fastest lap Alain Prost

ROUND 4 – MEXICO
Race Ayrton Senna
Pole Ayrton Senna
Fastest lap Nigel Mansell

ROUND 5 – UNITED STATES
Race Alain Prost
Pole Ayrton Senna
Fastest lap Ayrton Senna

ROUND 6 – CANADA
Race Thierry Boutsen
Pole Alain Prost
Fastest lap Jonathan Palmer

ROUND 7 – FRANCE
Race Alain Prost
Pole Alain Prost
Fastest lap Mauricio Gugelmin

ROUND 8 – BRITAIN
Race Alain Prost
Pole Ayrton Senna
Fastest lap Nigel Mansell

ROUND 9 – GERMANY
Race Ayrton Senna
Pole Ayrton Senna
Fastest lap Ayrton Senna

ROUND 10 – HUNGARY
Race Nigel Mansell
Pole Riccardo Patrese
Fastest lap Nigel Mansell

ROUND 11 – BELGIUM
Race Ayrton Senna
Pole Ayrton Senna
Fastest lap Alain Prost

ROUND 12 – ITALY
Race Alain Prost
Pole Ayrton Senna
Fastest lap Alain Prost

ROUND 13 – PORTUGAL
Race Gerhard Berger
Pole Ayrton Senna
Fastest lap Gerhard Berger

ROUND 14 – SPAIN
Race Ayrton Senna
Pole Ayrton Senna
Fastest lap Ayrton Senna

ROUND 15 – JAPAN
Race Ayrton Senna
Pole Ayrton Senna
Fastest lap Alain Prost

ROUND 16 – AUSTRALIA
Race Thierry Boutsen
Pole Ayrton Senna
Fastest lap Satoru Nakajima

1989 DRIVERS' CHAMPIONSHIP

DRIVER	TEAM	POINTS
Alain Prost	McLaren Honda	76
Ayrton Senna	McLaren Honda	60
Riccardo Patrese	Williams Renault	40
Nigel Mansell	Ferrari	38
Thierry Boutsen	Williams Renault	37
Alessandro Nannini	Benetton Ford	32
Gerhard Berger	Ferrari	21
Nelson Piquet	Lotus Judd	12
Jean Alesi	Tyrrell Ford	8
Derek Warwick	Arrows Ford	7
Stefan Johansson	Onyx Ford	6
Michele Alboreto	Tyrrell Ford	6
Eddie Cheever	Arrows Ford	6
Johnny Herbert	Benetton Ford	5
Pierluigi Martini	Minardi Ford	5
Andrea de Cesaris	Dallara Ford	4
Mauricio Gugelmin	March Judd	4
Stefano Modena	Brabham Judd	4
Alex Caffi	Dallara Ford	4
Martin Brundle	Brabham Judd	4
Christian Danner	Rial Ford	3
Satoru Nakajima	Lotus Judd	3
René Arnoux	Ligier Ford	2
Emanuele Pirro	Benetton Ford	2
Jonathan Palmer	Tyrrell Ford	2
Gabriele Tarquini	AGS Ford	1
Philippe Alliot	Lola Lamborghini	1
Olivier Grouillard	Ligier Ford	1

Alboreto left Tyrrell, making way for youngster Jean Alesi, when they secured Camel sponsorship.

These new faces must have wondered what they were getting into when the race began with one of Grand Prix's most memorable start-line accidents.

Collision

As Senna and Prost moved comfortably into position at the front, Mauricio Gugelmin's Leyton House car collided with Boutsen and Mansell, flew into the air, flipped over and landed in the escape road. Senna's transmission failed at the restart to leave local hero Prost in the clear for a popular victory.

In the end Mansell was second, Patrese third, Alesi an impressive fourth on his debut, Johansson fifth and Ligier's Olivier Grouillard sixth.

When Formula One moved to Silverstone, Prost's lead was strengthened by another mixed day for McLaren. Senna forced his way past Prost into Copse Corner at the start, but on lap 12 the Brazilian spun out to leave Prost leading again.

Mansell second

Home favourite Mansell finished second, almost 20 seconds adrift, with Nannini third for Benetton after Boutsen suffered a puncture. Piquet was fourth for Lotus and Minardi, fifth and sixth, claimed enough points to move away from the back-marking teams, which were required to battle it out for a place in the qualifying sessions.

Major managerial changes at Lotus before the next round in Germany did little to affect the placings, as Senna and Prost scored a McLaren one-two.

A long stop lost Senna the lead to Prost, but when the Frenchman encountered gearbox trouble Senna moved up and sped to victory. Prost held second, more than a minute ahead of Mansell, with Patrese, Piquet and Warwick the final points scorers.

SHORTS

Still desperate to win in case of an overturned decision, Senna claimed pole position and led for much of the final race in Australia. But, in ridiculously wet conditions, Senna ploughed into the back of Brundle's Brabham and retired his three-wheeled car. Piquet did the same to Ghinzani's Osella, and the new World Champion Prost had not even bothered to take part, withdrawing before the race. Conditions had been extremely dangerous and it was left to Boutsen to claim the last victory of the season.

Career highlight

Hungary was next and the McLaren stranglehold was broken again after a superb, reactive overtaking move by Mansell in one of the drives of his career.

Patrese was on pole and stayed ahead of Senna at the start. Mansell was down in 12th place after a disastrous qualifying session but ploughed through the field to lie second and begin pursuing Senna. On lap 58 they came up on Johansson's Onyx. For once Senna was slightly unaware of the traffic ahead and, as the McLaren slowed, Mansell jerked out and shot into the lead, winning by almost half a minute.

Talk was more of politics than racing when the circus arrived in Belgium. Brabham's future was in doubt after owner Joachim Luhti's arrest, while Benetton had a new boss, Flavio Briatore. Alesi, off challenging for the F3000 title, was replaced by

Ayrton Senna (foreground) and Alain Prost prepare for the Japanese Grand Prix.

1989 CONSTRUCTORS' CUP

TEAM (Engine)	POINTS
McLAREN HONDA	141
WILLIAMS RENAULT	77
FERRARI	59
BENETTON FORD	39
TYRRELL FORD	16
LOTUS JUDD	15
ARROWS FORD	13
DALLARA FORD	8
BRABHAM JUDD	8
ONYX FORD	6
MINARDI FORD	6
MARCH JUDD	4
LIGIER FORD	3
RIAL FORD	3
AGS FORD	3
LOLA LAMBORGHINI	1

Benetton-exile Johnny Herbert, while Lotus plumbed the depths as both Satoru Nakajima and three-times World Champion Piquet failed to qualify.

Business as usual

However, it was business as usual up the grid with Senna ahead of Prost again, and that's how it stayed from start to finish.

In Italy two weeks later the action was again mostly in the paddock rather than on the track. Signings for the 1990 season were gathering pace, as were the Ferraris. Buoyed up by home support they ran second and third behind Senna for the early part of the race before Prost moved ahead of them, benefiting from Senna's misfortune when the Brazilian's engine failed. Mansell dropped out with 12 laps to go, but Berger upheld Ferrari honour with second.

Thriller

Four races remained, and the Portuguese Grand Prix in Estoril was a thriller. The leaders lined up in the same order as at Monza but this time Berger pulled ahead of Senna. Mansell passed the Brazilian for second on lap eight and for once the McLarens no longer looked invincible. Then, disastrously, Mansell overshot his pit and reversed back into it. The illegal move resulted in a black flag, but the Briton ignored it. He then collided with Senna while fighting for second place and the incident, which put both out of the race, earned Mansell a one-race ban.

Berger cruised to victory, Prost gained on his title rival Senna with second and Mansell threatened to retire over his ban but the FIA were adamant and he missed the Spanish Grand Prix.

Still hoping

Senna's title bid looked to be over, but he was on pole in Jerez and led from lights-to-flag to keep his hopes alive. After 14 races, Senna had to take victory in both the remaining events to stand a chance of retaining his title. In the Japanese Grand Prix, three weeks after his Portuguese victory, he blew it.

Prost beat pole-sitter Senna at the start and built up a slender lead, but Senna closed the gap and they ran nose-to-tail for six laps before the Brazilian made a desperate move on lap 46. Coming into the chicane Senna lunged to the inside, Prost turned, the McLarens locked and the Championship was over. But Senna thought otherwise: after seeing Prost climb out of his stricken McLaren, Senna demanded a push-start from the marshals and made it back on track.

After pitting for a new nosecone, Senna caught and passed Nannini to cross the line first. But in parc-fermé he was met by FIA officials, and it was Nannini who claimed the top spot.

Senna had been disqualified not for receiving marshal help but for cutting out the chicane. Prost was the new World Champion. Senna accused FIA president Jean-Marie Balestre of favouring his compatriot Prost and fixing the World Championship, but his cries could not alter the result.

Still desperate to win in case of an overturned decision, Senna claimed pole position and led for much of the final race in Australia. But the Championship was settled without the need for arguments when, in ridiculously wet conditions, Senna had to retire, while new World Champion Prost had not even bothered to take part.

Previous page: *Mauricio Gugelmin's stunning accident at the beginning of the French Grand Prix.*

1990
It all comes down to Japan

TALKING POINT

TURNING NOSES UP

Formula One turned its nose up at tradition during the 1990 season with the introduction by Tyrrell of the high-nose concept, which would revolutionize the look of the Formula One car. The concept was devised by Harvey Postlethwaite and allowed better airflow underneath the floor of the car, which in turn allowed better and more efficient aerodynamics in that area of the car.

But because the wing works best closer to the ground, it could not be moved up with the nose, so it was mounted on a bizarre 'handlebar moustache'-style arrangement, and for Tyrrell it was a huge success.

Clearly, it was the future of Formula One. Several teams copied the idea with similar designs during the season, even more converting to it the following year; the concept was to form an important design criterion for more than a decade afterwards.

Riccardo Patrese salutes the crowd after his win at the San Marino Grand Prix.

The Prost and Senna era continued, and although they were now in different teams, the two were almost inseparable at the head of the Championship table again. The title decider was to come down to a dramatic crash in the penultimate race, which this time left Senna with the Championship crown.

The McLaren "dream team" had turned into a nightmare situation for boss Ron Dennis, after internal wranglings left 1989 Champion Alain Prost and runner-up Ayrton Senna not on speaking terms; the pair split for the 1990 season, with Prost moving to join Nigel Mansell at Ferrari. Gerhard Berger switched the other way and began what was to become a close friendship and an impressive partnership with Senna.

The Williams team remained with Boutsen and Patrese, while Benetton signed Nelson Piquet to partner Alessandro Nannini. Lotus brought in Martin Donnelly to partner Derek Warwick, while both the Tyrrell and March teams had varied success throughout the year.

Opposite: *Ivan Capelli is delighted with his second place at the French Grand Prix which signalled a huge improvement in form for the Leyton House team.*

New boy Alesi takes on Senna

The Tyrrell squad had a good start when in the first race of the year, in Phoenix, Arizona, a new kid on the block put in a stern challenge to an old favourite as Jean Alesi showed his talent on the bumpy street circuit. The French-Sicilian grabbed the lead for Tyrrell from pole-man Gerhard Berger at the start. Alesi ran clear in the lead ahead of Berger but Senna was right behind, and when Berger spun and had to pit the way was left clear for Senna.

The Brazilian closed on Alesi and passed him, only to be sensationally passed himself as the young charger refused to let status get in the way of racing. However, Senna challenged again a few laps later, and this time he was too good for Alesi and held the lead.

The McLaren pair occupied the front row of the grid for round two in Brazil, but Senna once again failed to win on his home soil. Prost took his first win for the team – his sixth victory in Brazil – with Berger beating his team-mate Senna to second.

Mansell came fourth, and the good result for Ferrari boosted the crowd for the San Marino Grand Prix three weeks later, but the result would not please the Italian supporters.

Patrese stole the lead from a struggling Berger, and went on to score his third Grand Prix win five seconds ahead of the McLaren man. Nannini claimed Benetton's first podium of the year, and Prost, Piquet and Alesi rounded off the points finishers.

First-lap Monaco carnage

Monaco was at its best for the fourth race of the season, and local resident Ayrton Senna secured his 45th pole position to line up ahead of rival Prost. It was a clean start, but at Mirabeau third-placed Alesi dived for the inside and passed Prost, who was then hit by Berger as the McLaren man tried to follow Alesi through. The sideways Ferrari created a huge traffic jam as the field funnelled and shuffled past, and the race was stopped.

Both Berger and Prost joined the restart, and it was the same positions at the front with Senna pulling away to leave Prost fighting off Alesi's challenge. Prost retired with battery failure, and that left Alesi, driving the radical new high-nosed Tyrrell, under pressure from Berger for the rest of the race, and as they battled they closed on Senna. But they could not pass him, and the race ended with victory for the Brazilian.

Round five of the season in Canada began with controversy as Ferrari launched a technologically advanced boat to take part in the annual mechanics' boat race. They could perhaps have done with it for the race itself, when the heavens opened to create a slippery, wet circuit. Senna won despite a spate of rain-related accidents.

Sunny Mexico City was the venue for round six of the Championship, and the heat was on for McLaren as Prost and Mansell dominated for Ferrari. Berger held pole position, but Patrese moved ahead on the long run into the first corner and Senna followed him through into second.

His lead was to last only a lap, however, as Senna hassled and eventually moved into the lead. Prost closed on Senna to fight for the lead. The Brazilian's pace had been slowed by a puncture, and Prost took the lead nine laps from the end when Senna's tyre finally blew and forced him into the pits.

Leyton House surprise

The Formula One circus moved to France and the Paul Ricard circuit for round seven, and there was a surprise jump in performance for the Leyton House team. Just one race after both Adrian Newey-designed cars had failed to qualify, a new underside on the car allowed Ivan Capelli sensationally to lead the race until being overhauled by Senna three laps from the end.

When Berger and Senna both messed up their pit-stops and dropped down the field, Prost found himself behind Capelli, but just as it looked as if Capelli would hold on until the end, Prost sneaked past to claim a home win.

A hop across the English Channel brought many of the teams on to home ground for the British Grand Prix, but it would not be a glory day for home hero Mansell at sunny Silverstone. The British star claimed pole position and, although Senna got the better start to move into the lead, Mansell was having none of it and pushed Senna to the limit.

The crowd were loving it, and cheered wildly when Mansell got past and Senna almost immediately spun. Berger took up the McLaren charge on the front man when Senna pitted for new tyres, and when Mansell's gearbox momentarily malfunctioned on Hangar Straight he was past. Mansell reclaimed the lead from Berger but, with just nine laps to run, his gearbox finally gave up and he pulled off at Copse Corner, throwing his gloves into the crowd and later emotionally announcing his decision to retire at the end of the year.

Meanwhile, Prost caught and passed Berger for the lead, and went on to claim his first hat-trick of victories, with Boutsen second ahead of a lucky Senna. Prost's run of form had moved him two points ahead of Senna in the Championship race, and the pair were beginning to pull away as the teams

RACE BY RACE DETAILS

ROUND 1 – UNITED STATES
Race Ayrton Senna
Pole Gerhard Berger
Fastest lap Gerhard Berger

ROUND 2 – BRAZIL
Race Alain Prost
Pole Ayrton Senna
Fastest lap Gerhard Berger

ROUND 3 – SAN MARINO
Race Riccardo Patrese
Pole Ayrton Senna
Fastest lap Alessandro Nannini

ROUND 4 – MONACO
Race Ayrton Senna
Pole Ayrton Senna
Fastest lap Ayrton Senna

ROUND 5 – CANADA
Race Ayrton Senna
Pole Ayrton Senna
Fastest lap Gerhard Berger

ROUND 6 – MEXICO
Race Alain Prost
Pole Gerhard Berger
Fastest lap Alain Prost

ROUND 7 – FRANCE
Race Alain Prost
Pole Nigel Mansell
Fastest lap Nigel Mansell

ROUND 8 – BRITAIN
Race Alain Prost
Pole Nigel Mansell
Fastest lap Nigel Mansell

ROUND 9 – GERMANY
Race Ayrton Senna
Pole Ayrton Senna
Fastest lap Thierry Boutsen

ROUND 10 – HUNGARY
Race Thierry Boutsen
Pole Thierry Boutsen
Fastest lap Riccardo Patrese

ROUND 11 – BELGIUM
Race Ayrton Senna
Pole Ayrton Senna
Fastest lap Alain Prost

ROUND 12 – ITALY
Race Ayrton Senna
Pole Ayrton Senna
Fastest lap Ayrton Senna

ROUND 13 – PORTUGAL
Race Nigel Mansell
Pole Nigel Mansell
Fastest lap Riccardo Patrese

ROUND 14 – SPAIN
Race Alain Prost
Pole Ayrton Senna
Fastest lap Riccardo Patrese

ROUND 15 – JAPAN
Race Nelson Piquet
Pole Ayrton Senna
Fastest lap Riccardo Patrese

ROUND 16 – AUSTRALIA
Race Nelson Piquet
Pole Ayrton Senna
Fastest lap Nigel Mansell

1990 DRIVERS' CHAMPIONSHIP

DRIVER	TEAM	POINTS
Ayrton Senna	McLaren Honda	78
Alain Prost	Ferrari	71
Nelson Piquet	Benetton Ford	43
Gerhard Berger	McLaren Honda	43
Nigel Mansell	Ferrari	37
Thierry Boutsen	Williams Renault	34
Riccardo Patrese	Williams Renault	23
Alessandro Nannini	Benetton Ford	21
Jean Alesi	Tyrrell Ford	13
Roberto Moreno	Benetton Ford	6
Ivan Capelli	Leyton House Judd	6
Aguri Suzuki	Lola Lamborghini	6
Eric Bernard	Lola Lamborghini	5
Derek Warwick	Lotus Lamborghini	3
Satoru Nakajima	Tyrrell Ford	3
Alex Caffi	Arrows Ford	2
Stefano Modena	Brabham Judd	2
Mauricio Gugelmin	Leyton House Judd	1

Martin Donnelly was lucky to survive this horrific crash before the Spanish Grand Prix, but it ended his career.

moved to Germany for round nine. It was an all-McLaren front row at the Hockenheim circuit but Senna eventually went on to win.

Boutsen's premier pole

In Hungary, Thierry Boutsen secured his first ever pole position and held the lead from the start to take a deserved victory.

Senna made an early pit stop for tyres which, although a rear right tyre stuck and cost him time, proved to be a good decision as he moved through the field to challenge Boutsen by the end.

However, Senna's climb was not entirely fair as he punted Nannini out to claim second place, and his team-mate did exactly the same thing to Mansell a few laps later. But not even Senna could make it past a determined Boutsen, and he had to follow him home ahead of Piquet, Patrese, Watson and Bernard.

A (for once) sunny Spa-Francorchamps was the next venue for the World Championship, and Senna returned to the front when he claimed the upper hand in qualifying, but the race was to require three starts before it got going fully.

The first incident saw Mansell punted into the barriers before the first corner, but a more serious accident involving Minardi's Paolo Barilla caused a second stoppage when his heavy crash created a hole in the metal trackside barriers.

Thankfully, Barilla survived, and when the race finally began it was Senna who claimed the early lead and was never headed. The Brazilian even pitted without losing the lead – but only just – as he shot out in front of Nannini who had stayed out to take a chance on worn tyres.

But Nannini's tyres faded, and he dropped back into the clutches of Prost, who got past at the bus-stop chicane, and Berger, who stole third after a long battle with the Italian. Nannini ended the race in fourth, with team-mate Piquet in fifth and Gugelmin sixth for March.

Italy was next on the agenda, and Prost pleased the fanatical *tifosi* by putting the Ferrari on the front row, albeit alongside the confident Senna's McLaren. Prost dropped back at the start, but he was given a second chance when Warwick went off at the Parabolica in his Lotus, hit the barrier, and came to rest upside down in the centre of the track.

Amazingly, Warwick was unhurt, and climbed out of the upturned car to run back to the pits and jump in the spare in time for the restart.

Once again the McLaren pair took the lead at the start, with Senna leading Berger into the first corner as Alesi, pushing for a drive with Ferrari for 1991, put in an impressive performance. But it was to end prematurely for Alesi, when he spun out after hitting the kerbs in the first chicane on lap five.

Senna was never challenged as he stormed to victory ahead of Prost, and claimed the race to be his most successful of the year; he later admitted it

SHORTS

Far from being an anti-climax, the final race of the season in Australia was a true party event, as it represented the 500th ever World Championship race, with past greats such as Juan Manuel Fangio, Jack Brabham, Jackie Stewart and Stirling Moss all present for the celebrations.

was the most decisive moment of his Championship challenge. Berger made it onto the podium in third and Mansell, Patrese and Nakajima claimed the remaining points positions.

Senna was now looking good for the Championship, remaining 16 points ahead of his rival Prost in the title battle as the field moved to Estoril in Portugal. There was a Ferrari resurgence at this race, as the Italian team filled the front row with Mansell claiming pole for the important race. But Mansell fluffed his start, and when he moved across on team-mate Prost it allowed the two McLarens through.

Senna led Berger as the top four battled closely, and after the pit-stops the Brazilian was still ahead, although Mansell had now moved to second. The Briton was on a charge, and after hounding Senna for 14 laps he ducked out of the Brazilian's slip-stream and took the lead into the first corner.

Prost began to challenge Senna for second, but an accident between Suzuki and Alex Caffi – in which the latter injured his ankle and was unable to be removed easily from the car – stopped the race early.

So Mansell won, scoring a record-equalling 16th victory for a British driver, and after Prost finished behind Senna to allow the title gap to open, the Frenchman blasted the Ferrari management for not backing his efforts.

Disaster for Donnelly

One week later, Formula One was rocked by the biggest accident it had witnessed in years when Martin Donnelly crashed heavily during practice for the Spanish Grand Prix. The Irishman was thrown from his car into the middle of the track at Jerez and lay motionless as rescue teams rushed to help him, and although he survived, the accident was to end his career.

In qualifying, it was a 50th pole position for Senna, and he converted it into a race lead at the start. Prost moved into second place and trailed the McLaren for 25 laps, unable to get past but carefully plotting his pit-stop tactics.

And it worked. Mansell went in early and Prost came out just behind him, but essentially when Senna went in one lap later he was slightly slower than the Ferrari team, and as he exited the pits Mansell pulled over to allow Prost through then blocked Senna to allow the Frenchman to build a lead.

Senna was almost immediately past and hounding Prost, but Piquet was still in front after refusing to stop. His tactics failed, however, and when he ran wide Prost took the lead; Senna was soon out with a water leak. The Brazilian was left to watch his rival claim his fourth victory as he led Mansell to a Ferrari one-two with Nannini, Boutsen, Patrese and Suzuki.

Season showdown

It all came down to the penultimate race of the season in Japan, and the showdown everyone was expecting came – but not in the way they had hoped. The title rivals lined up on the front row, with Senna on pole but not happy at starting on what he deemed to be the wrong side of the track.

Sure enough, Prost moved in to claim the first corner, but Senna had nothing to lose and would not give in. He put his car's nose inside at the first corner and it was all over. The pair clashed and the title battle was decided in a cloud of dust as Senna climbed out of his car as Champion.

1990 CONSTRUCTORS' CUP

TEAM (Engine)	POINTS
McLAREN HONDA	121
FERRARI	110
BENETTON FORD	71
WILLIAMS RENAULT	57
TYRRELL FORD	16
LEYTON HOUSE JUDD	7
LOTUS LAMBORGHINI	3
BRABHAM LAMBORGHINI	2
ARROWS JUDD	2

It was not quite the kind of Championship win that Senna would have liked when this crash at the Japanese Grand Prix between him and Alain Prost decided the destination of the title.

Ayrton Senna

CAREER DETAILS

1960	Born 21 March, in São Paolo
1973-81	Races karts in Brazil
1981	Formula Ford
1982	British and European Formula Ford champion
1983	Formula Three champion
1984	Signs for Toleman
1985	Switches to Lotus. Maiden GP win in Portugal
1987	First of record six Monaco GP wins
1988	Joins McLaren. World champion
1989	Runner-up behind Prost
1990	World Champion
1991	World Champion
1994	Moves to Williams. Dies 1 May at Imola

FORMULA ONE RECORD

Year	Team	Wins	Poles	Fast laps	Pts
1984	Toleman	0	0	1	13
1985	Lotus	2	7	3	38
1986	Lotus	2	8	0	55
1987	Lotus	2	1	3	57
1988	McLaren	8	13	3	90
1989	McLaren	6	13	3	60
1990	McLaren	6	10	2	78
1991	McLaren	7	8	2	96
1992	McLaren	3	1	1	50
1993	McLaren	5	1	1	73
1994	Williams	0	3	0	-

WITH AWESOME INTENSITY, Ayrton Senna's phenomenal talent and mystique extended beyond the bounds of his three World Championships. The sport lost its greatest driver on 1 May, 1994.

"He's an enigma, he's not something that anybody is going to handle or understand," said Ayrton Senna's first boss in Formula One, Alex Hawkridge of Toleman, in 1984. Ten years – and three World Championships, 41 Grands Prix wins, a record 65 pole positions and several controversies later – the mesmerising genius died at the age of 34 when his Williams mysteriously veered off into the concrete wall at Tamburello.

The previous day Senna had wept for Roland Ratzenberger, who had been killed in qualifying. The Brazilian had planned to wave the Austrian flag as a tribute to the popular Ratzenberger in the event of his victory at Imola. That compassionate nobility – subsequently revealed further in unpublicized charity work – compounded regard for him. Shy, private, a driven solitary, Senna radiated a star quality which went beyond his ability to maximize the potential of any car. His racing philosophy and obsession with learning and dissecting could be applied to life itself.

"The harder I push, the more I find within myself," he said. "I am always looking for the next step, a different world to go into, areas where I have not been before. It's lonely driving a Grand Prix car, but very absorbing. I have experienced new sensations and I want more. That is my excitement, my motivation."

Ayrton Senna da Silva, born into a wealthy São Paolo family, raced karts from an early age. He narrowly missed winning the karting World Championship, a failure which is said to have rankled deeply. In 1981 he came to Britain to make his Formula Ford debut. He won the series with 12 wins, and returned the following year to dominate the 2000 series with a tally of 21 wins from 27 starts. In 1983 his Formula Three endeavours saw him pitted against Martin Brundle. A suicidal mid-season run threatened to jeopardize his chances but his refusal to give up carried him through to eventual victory.

He tested for McLaren and Williams but it was Toleman who gave him his Formula One debut. When it became clear that the team could not provide the ambitious Brazilian with competitive machinery, he ruthlessly wriggled out of his contract and joined Lotus. He soon won his first Grand Prix around a rain-soaked Estoril circuit. Over the next three seasons he won only six races, due to the unreliability of the Lotus. Realizing he needed a Honda engine and a strong chassis, he manoeuvred himself to McLaren to partner Alain Prost for 1988.

By the end of the year he was World Champion, scoring eight wins (to Prost's seven) in a dominant

Ayrton Senna thrills the crowds during the Monaco Grand Prix in 1987.

manner which ruffled the Frenchman. The relationship between Prost and Senna was never anything but uneasy, and in 1989 open hostilities broke out as paranoia fuelled their rivalry. This time Prost came off better as he subtly took out the Brazilian at the Suzuka chicane. The rivalry deepened as the Frenchman moved to Ferrari, and in an inspiring campaign saw his season's endeavour nearly culminate in a defence of his title at Suzuka, only for all to be wasted as Senna drove into the back of him at the first corner.

With his friend Gerhard Berger as team-mate, Senna took his second World Championship in 1991 by beating the re-emerging Williams. In the following season Nigel Mansell was impossible to beat in the glorious Williams FW14B. Senna showed his guile and commitment with wins in Monaco, Hungary and Monza, but became frustrated at the prospect of McLaren's loss of Honda power and his inability to gain the coveted Williams drive alongside Prost in 1993 (the Frenchman had a clause in his contract forbidding him as a team-mate).

Much to his chagrin, his fears proved correct. He could not match Prost in the '93 Williams. His five wins that year in the Ford-powered McLaren are testimony to his brilliance. Few will forget his opening lap in the wet in the Grand Prix of Europe at Donington Park. In Monaco he passed Graham Hill's record with his sixth victory. In Adelaide, his last Grand Prix for McLaren, and a race he knew to be the last of Prost's career, he determined to win. It was his last experience on the top of the podium.

In 1994 he secured his dream, a drive in the Williams which had dominated in recent years. Alas, the FW16 was troublesome at the start. Senna struggled to match Michael Schumacher in the Benetton. After two races he had no points to the German's 20. Then at Imola came disaster.

"He was no ordinary person. He was very clever, shrewd, focused, tough – all the things I admired. He was actually a greater man out of the car than in it," Frank Williams said in tribute, as the sport tried to come to terms with the loss of its most influential protagonist. "When Ayrton lost his life, it was like losing your own child," said Ron Dennis. Brazil went into formal mourning as people tried to take comfort in the mystic statements he had often made about the nature of his vocation: "The start of a race is a totally unreal moment. It is like a dream, like entering another world."

> "Senna is a genius. I define genius as just the right side of imbalance. He is highly-developed to the point where he is almost over the edge. It's a close call."
>
> *Martin Brundle*

Senna – as inspirational off the track as he was on it.

1991
New kids on the block

TALKING POINT

JORDAN'S BIGGEST BATTLE

Jordan was a new kid on the block, but it was making waves. The Irish battlers soon moved out of the pre-qualifying lottery which was forced upon all newcomers, and they were regularly scoring points when driver Bertrand Gachot was hit with a jail sentence for assault. the result was that in came a driver by the name of Michael Schumacher.

The German *wunderkind* was another of talent-spotting team boss Eddie Jordan's classic finds, and as far as the enigmatic Irishman was concerned Schumacher was his.

Not so. In a bitter contractual wrangle, which still hurts Eddie Jordan to this day, Benetton chiefs Tom Walkinshaw and Flavio Briatore, with the help of Grand Prix organizer Bernie Ecclestone, stole the young talent from under Jordan's nose and made him a Benetton driver for four years.

Jordan was, and still is, bitter about it. He had lost the man who, with such clear talent, could have been a key influence in the rapid development of the team into a major force.

Instead, Jordan lost out and the team's debut year became simply a good memory which hopefully would help them through the tough times ahead.

Nigel Mansell rues the mistake which shut down his engine and cost him first place in the Canadian Grand Prix.

Confidence was low at McLaren before the start of the season. World Champion Ayrton Senna had spent little time testing the new car, but neither he nor Gerhard Berger believed its Honda engine was powerful enough to beat the Ferraris. Alain Prost was joined at the Italian *scuderia* by Jean Alesi.

But waiting in the wings was Williams. Red Five was back, and Nigel Mansell helped the team blossom into true title contenders. The 1990 season had been all about Prost versus Senna, but this year would see Williams come to the fore and Mansell take up the challenge.

Meanwhile, there was a new face on the scene, Eddie Jordan bringing his Irish charm to Formula One with his little eponymous team and perhaps the best-looking car on the grid, in the shape of the Irish-green Gary Anderson-designed Jordan 191. The team had to face the rigours of pre-qualifying in the early part of the season, but not even Jordan quite foresaw the impact his team would make in its debut season.

When the teams arrived at Phoenix for the opening American Grand Prix, however, it seemed to take up where it had left off the year before, with Senna sitting next to Prost on the front row of the grid. And it was Senna who went into the lead at the first corner.

Senna's McLaren was ultra-competitive and built up a commanding lead which could never be closed.

Senna triumphs at São Paolo

Two weeks later, the field moved south to Senna's home town of São Paolo for the Brazilian Grand Prix, and after eight attempts he finally won it – and how he won. Once again, he was dominant with the on-form McLaren in difficult wet conditions, but the race was exhausting and he overcame the intense pain of muscular spasms to come out victorious at the end of the race. Patrese claimed second, with Senna's team-mate Berger third followed by Prost, Piquet and Alesi, while Mansell was still left with no points to his name.

The teams returned to Europe and Imola for the San Marino Grand Prix, and Senna sealed another dominant weekend by taking his third victory in a row as Ferrari had a disaster in front of their devoted fans on a very rainy race day.

Mansell's Williams out of gear

The Briton's Williams once again had problems with the gearbox, and when he was nudged into a spin at the end of the first lap Mansell was left to walk back to the pits to have an angry word in the ear of his engineers.

The sun returned to Formula One when the Championship moved on to the glamorous setting of Monte Carlo for round four, and Senna proved that come rain or shine he was a tough man to beat.

On the Saturday there was a huge accident at the swimming-pool complex when Alex Caffi collid-

Opposite: *Alain Prost ahead of the field in the French Grand Prix held for the first time at Magny Cours. The Frenchman eventually finished second behind Nigel Mansell.*

ed with the barriers, splitting his car in two but escaping unhurt.

In the race itself, with Senna in a commanding lead, Prost was hounded by former team-mate Mansell for second place, and the Briton executed a perfect manoeuvre into the chicane to overtake him before Prost lost time when he got a wheelnut stuck under the rear of the car during a pit-stop but nobody could touch Senna out in front, and he finished a comfortable 18 seconds ahead of a relieved Mansell, whose gearbox finally held out to the end of the race, with Alesi maintaining Ferrari honour in third.

The dominant Senna was already 29 points ahead of his rivals when the teams left Europe again for the Canadian city of Montreal, but his relentless run of victories finally came to an end. The chink in Senna's armour was already showing after qualifying as the Williams pair of Mansell on pole and Patrese, having recovered after an earlier accident, occupied the front row of the grid with the Brazilian down in third.

Never count your chickens...

Suzuki's Lola went up in flames when a fuel line broke on the third lap as Senna chased the leading Williams pair, only to retire on lap 25 with a misfiring engine. It was not McLaren's day. Mansell looked set for victory but on the very last lap, waving to the crowd, he accidentally knocked his ignition switch; his engine cut out within sight of the flag, and Piquet won for Benetton ahead of Modena's Tyrrell and Mansell's team-mate Patrese.

Mexico was next and Senna, who had cut his head open in a jet-ski accident, had more bad luck as he went too fast into the Peraltada corner in Friday qualifying and rolled his McLaren in the gravel. He climbed out, but the cracks were there and Senna was weakening.

Patrese was suffering with a stomach bug but still managed to claim pole position ahead of Mansell, as Williams filled the front row for the second race in succession. But in the race Mansell was quickest off the line as the pack shuffled on the opening lap, and Senna came off best to slot into second as his team-mate Berger retired almost immediately with a blown engine. Alesi also had a go at Mansell, but came off worst and spun to leave the Williams pair nose to tail in victory with Senna almost a minute behind, clearly beaten at last.

It was back to home comforts when the Championship moved to France for round seven at the new, purpose-built circuit of Magny Cours, where finally it was success for Mansell. With Prost second and Senna third, he went on to clock up his 17th victory and break the record for the most wins ever by an English driver.

It was perfect timing to boost the crowds to bursting point for the British Grand Prix at a newly-modified Silverstone circuit just one week later. Behind the scenes, businessman Tom Walkinshaw had taken a 33-percent stake in the Benetton team, but all that mattered for the crowd was Mansell taking pole position. And, in a classic qualifying session, he did just that. However, with the sun blazing down on race day, Mansell did not get away well and it was Senna, who had earlier declared the Williams cars to be better than his McLaren, who shot into the lead.

Senna thumbs a lift

However, Mansell was victorious, driven home by crowd power and waving both hands excitedly as he crossed the line. He was even more delighted when he saw Senna stationary at the side of the track, out of fuel and out of second place. Mansell, ever the gentleman, picked him up and provided the photo

RACE BY RACE DETAILS

ROUND 1 – UNITED STATES
Race Ayrton Senna
Pole Ayrton Senna
Fastest lap Jean Alesi

ROUND 2 – BRAZIL
Race Ayrton Senna
Pole Ayrton Senna
Fastest lap Nigel Mansell

ROUND 3 – SAN MARINO
Race Ayrton Senna
Pole Ayrton Senna
Fastest lap Gerhard Berger

ROUND 4 – MONACO
Race Ayrton Senna
Pole Ayrton Senna
Fastest lap Alain Prost

ROUND 5 – CANADA
Race Nelson Piquet
Pole Riccardo Patrese
Fastest lap Nigel Mansell

ROUND 6 – MEXICO
Race Riccardo Patrese
Pole Riccardo Patrese
Fastest lap Nigel Mansell

ROUND 7 – FRANCE
Race Nigel Mansell
Pole Riccardo Patrese
Fastest lap Nigel Mansell

ROUND 8 – BRITAIN
Race Nigel Mansell
Pole Nigel Mansell
Fastest lap Nigel Mansell

ROUND 9 – GERMANY
Race Nigel Mansell
Pole Nigel Mansell
Fastest lap Riccardo Patrese

ROUND 10 – HUNGARY
Race Ayrton Senna
Pole Ayrton Senna
Fastest lap Bertrand Gachot

ROUND 11 – BELGIUM
Race Ayrton Senna
Pole Ayrton Senna
Fastest lap Roberto Moreno

ROUND 12 – ITALY
Race Nigel Mansell
Pole Ayrton Senna
Fastest lap Ayrton Senna

ROUND 13 – PORTUGAL
Race Riccardo Patrese
Pole Riccardo Patrese
Fastest lap Nigel Mansell

ROUND 14 – SPAIN
Race Nigel Mansell
Pole Gerhard Berger
Fastest lap Riccardo Patrese

ROUND 15 – JAPAN
Race Gerhard Berger
Pole Gerhard Berger
Fastest lap Ayrton Senna

ROUND 16 – AUSTRALIA
Race Ayrton Senna
Pole Ayrton Senna
Fastest lap Gerhard Berger

1991 DRIVERS' CHAMPIONSHIP

DRIVER	TEAM	POINTS
Ayrton Senna	McLaren Honda	96
Nigel Mansell	Williams Renault	72
Riccardo Patrese	Williams Renault	53
Gerhard Berger	McLaren Honda	43
Alain Prost	Ferrari	34
Nelson Piquet	Benetton Ford	26.5
Jean Alesi	Ferrari	21
Stefano Modena	Tyrrell Honda	10
Andrea De Cesaris	Jordan Ford	9
Roberto Moreno	Benetton Ford	8
Pierluigi Martini	Minardi Ferrari	6
JJ Lehto	Dallara Ford	4
Bertrand Gachot	Jordan Ford	4
Michael Schumacher	Benetton Ford	4
Mika Hakkinen	Lotus Judd	2
Martin Brundle	Brabham Yamaha	2
Satoru Nakajima	Tyrrell Honda	2
Julian Bailey	Lotus Judd	1
Eric Bernard	Lola Ford	1
Ivan Capelli	Leyton House Ilmor	1
Aguri Suzuki	Lola Ford	1
Emanuele Pirro	Dallara Judd	1
Mark Blundell	Brabham Yamaha	1
Gianni Morbidelli	Ferrari	1

opportunity of the season as Senna rode home on his rival's sidepod.

Berger picked up the points for second place and Prost finished a minute down in third. Senna, by virtue of lapping the rest of the field, was classified fourth one lap down, and Piquet and Gachot picked up the final points.

The Championship moved on to the power circuit of Hockenheim in Germany for the next round, and once again Mansell's Renault-engined Williams looked favourite.

On race day, Mansell made the perfect start from pole, and when he blocked Senna from making a move the Brazilian was slowed, allowing his team-mate Berger up to second. Senna, Patrese and Prost battled hard for third as Mansell pulled away and, after a successful pit stop, the Briton held the lead to come home ahead of team-mate Patrese; Senna, for the second time in the season, had run out of fuel on the final lap.

Things had gone Mansell's way at Hockenheim, and after Senna's failure to finish there Mansell was just eight points behind the Brazilian going into the next round in Hungary.

Kiss and make up

On the track, Senna claimed the all-important pole position and, knowing the race could be won or lost in the first corner, made sure he got off the line well to lead ahead of Patrese and Mansell at the start. Mansell shook his fist at his team-mate, demanding to be let through. Patrese obliged, and Mansell set off in pursuit of Senna as Prost continued his disappointing season at Ferrari with another retirement.

But Senna had chosen a clever mix of soft and ultra-soft tyres which, with a bit of careful driving, allowed him comfortably to stay ahead of the rest to take his first win since Monaco six races previously. Mansell was second, having had to watch the Championship gap lengthen again, and Patrese played second fiddle at Williams to take third. Berger, Alesi and Capelli rounded out the top six.

Spa was next, for the Belgian Grand Prix, and with Senna having won four of the last seven races there and Honda giving him some important improvements to the engine, he was confident of another.

Bertrand Gachot had been jailed for assault using CS gas on a London taxi driver, and Eddie Jordan – ever the talent-spotter – drafted in Mercedes sportscar driver Michael Schumacher. He immediately impressed, setting the eighth-fastest time in the opening session, but Senna underlined his own success at the front with pole position as Mansell was beaten to the front row by Prost.

But the luck was all Senna's towards the end of the race, as Mansell went out with electrical problems and Alesi lost the lead when his engine failed. The Jordan of de Cesaris was going well and

SHORTS

New boy Mika Hakkinen made a dramatic entry to Formula One at Phoenix for the wrong reasons, after knocking his steering-wheel release and coming to a tyre-smoking halt on the straight before re-attaching the wheel, only to retire later.

In the meantime, Nigel Mansell acquired some extra horsepower before the Hungarian Grand Prix when he was presented with a horse for his birthday.

No one could have guessed at the success to come for Michael Schumacher when he made his debut for Jordan at the Belgian Grand Prix.

By now driving for Benetton, Michael Schumacher went on to show his potential in the Italian Grand Prix.

1991 CONSTRUCTORS' CUP

TEAM (Engine)	POINTS
McLAREN HONDA	139
WILLIAMS RENAULT	125
FERRARI	55.5
BENETTON FORD	38.5
JORDAN FORD	13
TYRRELL HONDA	12
MINARDI FERRARI	6
DALLARA JUDD	5
BRABHAM YAMAHA	3
LOTUS JUDD	3
LOLA FORD	2
LEYTON HOUSE ILMOR	1

catching Senna, now in the lead, but it was not to last and the team was distraught to see an almost certain podium place disappear when the engine failed. So, Senna won again, with Berger making it a McLaren one-two.

Belgium had seen another major twist in the Championship and with Mansell's failure to finish, this time it was Senna who regained a big advantage. But behind the scenes Schumacher had sensationally moved to Benetton after a battle between the mighty Italian team and British minnows Jordan.

The Championship challenge continued in Italy as the top four made a break at the start of the Monza race, with Senna making a fast start as Patrese led the chase and soon made it past, only to spin out a lap later with a gearbox problem. But Mansell did it on his own, passing Senna on lap 24, and although Senna stopped for new tyres and shot back, Mansell had beaten him fair and square to take a little chunk out of his Championship lead.

The gods desert Mansell

Portugal was next, and it was the Championship understudies on the front row, with Patrese and Berger ahead of team-mates Mansell and Senna. Mansell went round the outside of Senna at the first corner to hold onto third, then slipped down the inside of Berger at the very next corner for second. He claimed the lead on lap 17, but disaster struck when his right rear wheelnut was not fixed properly in his tyre stop and, as he left his pit, the wheel came off to leave Mansell stranded in the fast lane, his tyre bouncing down the pit-lane. A distraught Mansell could only sit and weep as his team worked to put on a new wheel, but he was disqualified soon after for incorrect procedures in the pit-lane.

Patrese held on to win, stealing four important points from Senna, but Mansell's title chances were fading. Alesi claimed the final podium spot, and Schumacher clocked up his first point for sixth.

The teams moved to the new Circuit de Catalunya facility just outside Barcelona for the next race, and things did not go well for Mansell even before the start when he injured his left ankle in a charity football match.

It was spitting with rain when the race began, and pole-sitter Berger made a good start to lead his team-mate Senna into the first corner with Mansell third. Mansell passed Senna in a classic wheel-to-wheel battle on the pit straight as the Williams and McLaren wheels came closer and closer to clashing.

But Senna reclaimed the lead when the pair came into the pits together and the Williams crew – still wary of events in the last race – were slow to perform. Mansell hounded Senna into an uncharacteristic mistake which spun him down the field, but Berger, who had earlier been waved through by the Brazilian, was still ahead.

Mansell made short work of him, however, and after Schumacher had spun off challenging Berger, the Austrian retired to leave Prost second and Patrese third, with Senna fifth. So the Championship remained up for grabs, and it meant Mansell had to win at all costs in the penultimate race in Japan.

For the race, it was an all-McLaren front row, but as Berger led, Mansell challenged Senna on lap 10 only to run wide into turn one and end his title challenge in the gravel, to leave Senna as Champion.

Berger conceded the lead to the new winner of the drivers' title, but before the end Senna returned the compliment as thanks for the help he had received throughout the season. Berger went on to lead home a McLaren one-two with Patrese third and Prost fourth.

1992
Mansell magic does the trick

TALKING POINT

"MANSELL-MANIA"

The British Grand Prix saw a new high in adoration for Britain's moustachioed megastar Nigel Mansell, as the British public rode a wave of enthusiasm which crashed on to the Silverstone circuit after the Birmingham-born hero's greatest victory.

Cheers and wildly-waved Union Jacks greeted the Williams driver on every corner of the 59-lap race, but as he came across the line to take the chequered flag he was personally greeted by one crazed fan running across the track in front of him. That man had pre-empted a fan-attack on the circuit which prevented Mansell from making it to the pits on his victory lap. He was stopped three-quarters of the way around as wave after wave of fans swarmed his car and forced it to a standstill, but not before he had run over one man's foot in the quest to get back.

The pit straight was packed as the crowds jostled and pushed, waiting to catch a glimpse of their hero as he stepped on to the winner's podium, and waiting to taste the victory champagne. Yes, it was dangerous, and Silverstone was given a knuckle-rap by the sport's governing body, but it was pure sport-driven emotion which overflowed that day – Mansell-mania at its maddest.

Opposite: *Riccardo Patrese led Nigel Mansell in the French Grand Prix but waved his team-mate through for his sixth win of the season.*

Despite Mansell's stunning form in 1992, Ayrton Senna still managed to show who was boss at the Monaco Grand Prix.

Reigning champion Ayrton Senna was in a far from confident mood when the year began – and rightly so. He had taken the title in 1991 mostly as a result of his early form, and Williams had shown by the end of the year that they were the team to beat. Their FW14 would provide Nigel Mansell with victory after victory in the season ahead as he, along with the Renault-engined squad, proved dominant and unstoppable.

Briton Martin Brundle found himself with a plum drive at Benetton, but he would struggle to wrestle his home fan base from their hero Mansell, while it was all change at Jordan after the success of the previous year, with a Yamaha engine which would be their downfall. Giovanna Amati became the first woman in Formula One for 15 years, but there was an important man missing, Alain Prost taking a sabbatical after being sacked by Ferrari at the end of 1991 and deciding the Ligier he had tested in the close season was not competitive enough for him.

The new season dawned with the series making a return to South Africa for the first time since 1985, and the victor of that race became the winner again on the newly-modified circuit of Kyalami. Mansell began the season in dominant form, and scorched to his 18th pole position after qualifying 0.8 seconds ahead of his nearest rival, Senna.

Despite a trademark Senna charge at the start, it was the Williams pair who made it to the first corner ahead, as Mansell took up a lead which he would not relinquish for the rest of the race.

Ferrari had a dismal start to the season, as both Ivan Capelli and Jean Alesi dropped out early on with engine failures, Mansell leading Patrese home for a Williams one-two and Senna opening his Championship account with third. Schumacher put in an impressive run to claim fourth for Benetton, while Johnny Herbert scored his best result in three years with a sixth place.

A continent swap saw the teams move to Mexico, but the bumpy track was causing problems for everyone – none more so than Senna, who had a big "off" in Friday practice and was stuck in the car in immense pain after injuring his leg. He recovered to qualify in sixth, but once again it was the Williams cars at the front of the pack, with Schumacher, increasing in confidence with every lap, lining up in third.

Mansell was clear at the start, as Ferrari's woes continued when Capelli was punted into the wall by Karl Wendlinger's Leyton House. The Williams man led from start to finish to lead home the second successive Williams one-two ahead of Schumacher as the lead cars remained in their grid order. Gerhard Berger and Martin Brundle had a battle for fourth after Senna went out with transmission failure and Alesi's engine expired again, but the Briton's Benetton failed 20 laps from the finish to leave

Berger fourth, Andrea De Cesaris fifth and Mika Hakkinen sixth.

McLaren means business

In a bid to break down Williams' domination, McLaren took six cars to the next race in Brazil, but it was Williams who needed the spare chassis after an incident between Senna and Mansell in qualifying. Mansell was on a quick lap and thought Senna would move over for him, but he second-guessed the Brazilian's move incorrectly and, having gone the wrong side of him, was left with nowhere to go but the hard concrete wall.

Mansell, who described it as "just one of those things", suffered minor injuries, but still managed to put in the most dominant qualifying performance in years as he finished more than a second faster than his team-mate and more than two seconds faster than third-placed Senna.

But at the start it was Patrese who made the better getaway and shot into the lead as the Williams cars once again did not give Senna a look-in. Senna was struggling in his home race, however, and after holding up Schumacher – much to the dissatisfaction of the German – he retired with electronics failure.

Mansell could not pass Patrese on the track, but a faster pit-stop got him out ahead of his Italian team-mate and it was three out of three for Mansell. Schumacher cruised home to take his second podium in a row and, after a battle for fourth between Alesi and Brundle ended at turn one, Alesi claimed the position to take Ferrari's first finish of the year, with team-mate Capelli right behind and Alboreto taking the final point for Footwork.

The field moved to Europe for round four, but the rain in Spain which welcomed the teams home would not stem the consistent dominance of the Williams team as Mansell cruised home to continue his perfect score. Mansell led from pole, but Schumacher could not hold on to second after claiming his first front-row grid spot, and dropped behind Patrese.

Alesi made a superb start from the fourth row to climb up to the front before he spun while challenging Berger, and an anger-induced tyre-smoking return to the right direction ruined his tyres. He pitted for a new set halfway through the race, and so followed a superb drive which saw him push through the field to eventual third place behind the Benetton of Schumacher, who had assumed second when Patrese spun out.

Dominant Williams

So it may not have been a fourth successive Williams one-two, but their dominance was still clear for all to see, and when the field headed to San Marino they all knew nobody else stood a chance. How right they were. Once again Williams dominated, Mansell recording a record-breaking start to the season with his fifth pole position and his fifth victory of the year.

Cheered on by the *tifosi*, *Il Leone* – still supported by many in Italy as a former Ferrari hero – put in another lights-to-flag victory as Patrese made it the fourth Williams one-two of the season. The Williams pair were clear from the start, but Ferrari hearts were broken when Alesi, who ran as high as third, went out after clattering the McLaren of Gerhard Berger, and when Ivan Capelli's Ferrari also failed it was home time for many of the Italian fans.

Senna finished a distant third, but there were only two men spraying champagne on the podium because a shattered Senna, suffering from severe cramp and shoulder pain, could not make it out of his car until some time after the end of the race.

The pain for the Brazilian also showed in the Championship table. He was now 30 points behind in the title race, but Monaco was a different story. It was his patch. Senna was the master of Monaco, and once again he would prove it.

RACE BY RACE DETAILS

ROUND 1 – SOUTH AFRICA
Race Nigel Mansell
Pole Nigel Mansell
Fastest lap Nigel Mansell

ROUND 2 – MEXICO
Race Nigel Mansell
Pole Nigel Mansell
Fastest lap Gerhard Berger

ROUND 3 – BRAZIL
Race Nigel Mansell
Pole Nigel Mansell
Fastest lap Riccardo Patrese

ROUND 4 – SPAIN
Race Nigel Mansell
Pole Nigel Mansell
Fastest lap Nigel Mansell

ROUND 5 – SAN MARINO
Race Nigel Mansell
Pole Nigel Mansell
Fastest lap Riccardo Patrese

ROUND 6 – MONACO
Race Ayrton Senna
Pole Nigel Mansell
Fastest lap Nigel Mansell

ROUND 7 – CANADA
Race Gerhard Berger
Pole Ayrton Senna
Fastest lap Gerhard Berger

ROUND 8 – FRANCE
Race Nigel Mansell
Pole Nigel Mansell
Fastest lap Nigel Mansell

ROUND 9 – BRITAIN
Race Nigel Mansell
Pole Nigel Mansell
Fastest lap Nigel Mansell

ROUND 10 – GERMANY
Race Nigel Mansell
Pole Nigel Mansell
Fastest lap Riccardo Patrese

ROUND 11 – HUNGARY
Race Ayrton Senna
Pole Riccardo Patrese
Fastest lap Nigel Mansell

ROUND 12 – BELGIUM
Race Michael Schumacher
Pole Nigel Mansell
Fastest lap Michael Schumacher

ROUND 13 – ITALY
Race Ayrton Senna
Pole Nigel Mansell
Fastest lap Nigel Mansell

ROUND 14 – PORTUGAL
Race Nigel Mansell
Pole Nigel Mansell
Fastest lap Ayrton Senna

ROUND 15 – JAPAN
Race Riccardo Patrese
Pole Nigel Mansell
Fastest lap Nigel Mansell

ROUND 16 – AUSTRALIA
Race Gerhard Berger
Pole Nigel Mansell
Fastest lap Michael Schumacher

1992 DRIVERS' CHAMPIONSHIP

DRIVER	TEAM	POINTS
Nigel Mansell	Williams Renault	108
Riccardo Patrese	Williams Renault	56
Michael Schumacher	Benetton Ford	53
Ayrton Senna	McLaren Honda	50
Gerhard Berger	McLaren Honda	49
Martin Brundle	Benetton Ford	38
Jean Alesi	Ferrari	18
Mika Hakkinen	McLaren Honda	11
Andrea De Cesaris	Tyrrell Ilmor	8
Michele Alboreto	Footwork Mugen	6
Eric Comas	Ligier Renault	4
Karl Wendlinger	Sauber Ilmor	3
Ivan Capelli	Ferrari	3
Thierry Boutsen	Ligier Renault	2
Pierluigi Martini	Dallara Ferrari	2
Johnny Herbert	Lotus Ford	2a
Bertrand Gachot	Lola Lamborghini	1
Christian Fittipaldi	Minardi Lamborghini	1
Stefano Modena	Andrea Moda Judd	1

Mansell, helped by the active suspension on his ultra-advanced Williams, dominated around the bumpy streets in qualifying and led the field into Sainte Devoté at the start of the race. Behind him a resurgent Senna slipped past Patrese to claim second, but Mansell was soon clear and had the race in the bag until eight laps from the end when, after Capelli ended his race by placing his Ferrari on top of the barriers at La Rascasse, Mansell pitted with a suspected puncture.

When he came out he was behind Senna, and the man who had lost only once in five years at the Monaco track made his car as big as possible around the already-tight Armco barriers. He held off Mansell, despite relentless pressure, to end the Briton's run and score his own landmark win with his fifth victory, equalling Graham Hill's record around the streets of the principality.

Patrese was the final man on the podium, with the Benetton pairing of Schumacher and Brundle next on the results sheet, and Gachot scoring his first point since returning from his jail sentence the previous year.

Senna was on a roll, and when the Championship headed back across the Atlantic to the Circuit Gilles Villeneuve in Canada, he was the fastest man on the track. The Brazilian displaced Mansell on pole for the first time in the season, and led the Williams driver into the first corner at the start.

Once again Senna was hard to pass, and when Mansell tried to go by into the chicane at the end of lap 14, he hit the dusty inside line and went straight over the gravel to end his race on the pit straight, gesticulating furiously at Senna when he came past on the next lap.

SHORTS

Mansell claimed that crowd support was worth one second per lap, and he proved as much at the British Grand Prix by putting in his most dominant qualifying performance of the season to take pole by more than two seconds from team-mate Patrese, and three seconds faster than his closest non-Williams rival Senna.

But Senna's chance of claiming 10 points over his rival ended when his electronics failed. Patrese was out soon after and Capelli smashed into the wall in the Ferrari. That left Senna's team-mate, Berger, who was nursing a gearbox problem, to bring his car home and claim the second successive win for McLaren, with Schumacher second and Alesi third.

But Williams was not about to let its dominance falter – not on the home soil of its French engine supplier Renault – and the next race, at Magny Cours, witnessed a dramatic return to form.

Mansell took his seventh pole of the season, but Patrese led the Williams one-two into the first corner where, one lap later, Schumacher took Senna out of the race. Berger joined his team-mate Senna

Nigel Mansell and Michael Schumacher enjoy the celebrations at the Belgian Grand Prix.

Nigel Mansell celebrates his win in Portugal already assured of the Championship and on his way to a record nine wins.

1992 CONSTRUCTORS' CUP

TEAM (Engine)	WINS
WILLIAMS RENAULT	164
McLAREN HONDA	99
BENETTON FORD	91
FERRARI	21
LOTUS FORD	13
TYRRELL ILMOR	8
FOOTWORK MUGEN	6
LIGIER RENAULT	6
MARCH ILMOR	3
DALLARA FERRARI	2
LARROUSSE VENTURI LAMBORGHINI	1
MINARDI LAMBORGHINI	1
JORDAN YAMAHA	1

in the viewing stands 10 laps later to witness another domination by the Williams pair, before sudden rain caused the race to be stopped.

It proved to be only a quick shower, however, and when the race was restarted it was dry again, and Patrese cruised into the lead ahead of Mansell. The rain soon returned and saw car after car peel off into the pits, but Alesi stayed out and put in a dramatic display of skilful car control to move up the field before being forced out with an engine problem.

That left Patrese to wave Mansell through for his sixth victory of the season and another Williams one-two ahead of Brundle – who made his debut on the podium – Hakkinen and Comas, who both scored their best-ever results up until that point. Mansell's form had excited the British public, and there was a massive crowd cheering him on for the British Grand Prix at Silverstone one week later.

Patrese made the better start and led into Copse, but that was the only corner at which Mansell would trail anyone. He went past Patrese approaching the second bend, and nobody came close for the rest of the race. Mansell could even afford to make a 12-second pit stop without losing the lead as he headed another Williams one-two, with Brundle making it two Britons on the podium by finishing ahead of his team-mate Schumacher.

Debut for Damon

Damon Hill drove his Brabham to 16th place, but the Grand Prix debut of a man who would replace Mansell in the crowd's hearts in the future went relatively unnoticed as the fans raided the track in celebration of the achievements of their current hero.

The Williams steamroller next moved on to Hockenheim for the German Grand Prix, and once again it crushed the opposition with yet another fine display. It was the usual top three on the grid, and although Patrese again made the better start to beat Mansell to the first corner, the Briton was through into the lead by the second corner just as in Britain two weeks before.

The Williams cars moved clear but Senna, who decided to try to go through without a pit-stop, gained the lead when the leading pair pitted for tyres. Mansell soon caught him but, as had happened in Monaco, Senna made it difficult to pass and there was a classic fight, with Mansell cutting across a chicane when a move went wrong. Eventually, he made it past and soon afterwards Patrese caught the Brazilian, but he could not pass him; as Mansell slowed, Patrese went for a last-gasp effort but spun into retirement to leave Senna trailing Mansell, and Schumacher picking up a fortunate third place.

Mansell now had a massive 86 Championship points to Patrese's 40 and, incredibly, in only the 11th race and almost three months before the end of the season, Mansell had the chance to secure the title. But Patrese was the man on pole when the field lined up at the Hungaroring, and although Mansell had a terrible start and dropped down to fourth, he was soon back past the two McLarens and hounding Patrese for the lead.

When Patrese spun and retired with a blown engine, all Mansell needed to do was finish third to claim the Championship – and now he was in the lead. But a puncture forced him into a pit-stop, and when he returned to the track he had to fight back from sixth; although it seemed a tough task, Mansell did it. He fought his way through to second ahead of Berger, and although he finished behind the victorious Senna, he had finally achieved his lifetime ambition of becoming World Champion.

Gerhard Berger

CAREER DETAILS

1959	Born 27 August, in Worgl, nr Innsbruck
1984	F1 debut with ATS
1985	Moves to Arrows-BMW
1986	Moves to Benetton. Maiden F1 win.
1987	Joins Ferrari
1989	Accident at Tamburello
1990	Joins McLaren
1993	Returns to Ferrari
1996	Joins Benetton
1997	Retires

FORMULA ONE RECORD

Year	Team	Wins	Poles	Fast laps	Pts
1984	ATS	0	0	0	-
1985	Arrows	0	0	0	3
1986	Benetton	1	0	2	17
1987	Ferrari	2	3	3	36
1988	Ferrari	1	1	3	41
1989	Ferrari	1	0	1	21
1990	McLaren	0	2	3	43
1991	McLaren	1	2	2	43
1992	McLaren	2	0	2	49
1993	Ferrari	0	0	0	12
1994	Ferrari	1	2	0	41
1995	Ferrari	0	1	2	31
1996	Benetton	0	0	1	21
1997	Benetton	1	1	2	27

GERHARD BERGER'S CAREER coincided with the prime of Prost, Piquet, Senna, Mansell and Schumacher. Third three times in the World Championship, he was one of Formula One's last cavaliers

In a 14-year career Gerhard Berger won 10 Grands Prix (one gifted him by McLaren team-mate Ayrton Senna) from 210 starts. Some argue that this statistic proved his ability in different kinds of car, while others are of the opinion that, having started 190 of those races in a Ferrari, McLaren or a Benetton, the tall, ebullient Austrian with the aggressive driving style should have done much better.

Berger had limited early racing experience, first in Alfas, then in the German and European Formula Three series. In 1984 he made his Formula One debut with ATS in his home Grand Prix at the Osterreichring. Sixth place at Monza confirmed his promise and he duly lined up in the Arrows-BMW team as Thierry Boutsen's team-mate at the start of the following season. He retired from five of the first seven races of 1985, but found some consistency in the second half of the season.

His connections with BMW (he was a member of their Touring car squad in the early 1980s) saw him move to Benetton, now powered by the German company. Despite a mid-season string of retirements, he produced some spellbinding drives including his maiden Grand Prix win in Mexico and ended the season clutching a contract with Ferrari for 1987. "I didn't speak the language, but you know he liked to speak about girls, I liked to speak about girls, so it went well," he said of his meeting with the legendary Enzo Ferrari.

He always looked sharp and never finished lower than fourth – when he finished. That was the problem. In nine out of 16 races, his car failed to finish. He ended the season well with consecutive wins at Suzuka and Adelaide. McLaren dominated the 1988 season to such an extent that Berger's strong performances in the Ferrari were to no avail. Ironically, it was probably his strongest year.

In 1989 he finished just three races (winner in Estoril, second in Monza and Jerez), but his season was coloured by an horrendous accident at the Tamburello corner at Imola which later claimed the life of his great friend Ayrton Senna. "Something snapped at the front of the car and it went completely out of control. I tried to brake a little. I was heading straight for the wall. I thought, 'My God, this is going to be the big one,'" he later recalled.

The switch to McLaren on a three-year contract as replacement for Alain Prost was brave, considering it brought with it Ayrton Senna as team-mate. Berger, who had been psychologically overwhelmed by Mansell at Ferrari, struggled to keep up with his brilliant team-mate, but he resolved to learn from the Brazilian's obsessive application. The pair became good foils for each other. "He

Gerhard Berger in action for Ferrari at the Italian Grand Prix.

It was unfortunate that Berger's consistency never gave him the World Championship.

> "He has pace, courage and lots of aggression. He likes a fight and isn't afraid to bang wheels from time to time."
>
> *Nigel Mansell*

taught me a lot about racing. I taught him how to laugh," Berger said.

He headed back to Ferrari in 1993, lured by a massive retainer, but the *scuderia* was in bad shape. Berger struggled to adapt to active suspension and ended the season a dismal eighth. The following season was far worse. In the third race at Imola, his close friend and compatriot Roland Ratzenberger lost his life during qualifying, followed 24 hours later by Senna's fatal accident. He withdrew from the restarted race and spent a week soul-searching about whether to continue his career.

"After the race at Imola, I went to the hospital because I wanted to see Ayrton again. I did see him, and then Monday morning back home was very, very difficult, a strange day. Very empty. I felt nothing. I felt very far away from myself," he revealed.

"I have always raced with my heart. I lived for it. Racing is what I've done for my whole life. However, if my feelings tell me that I am unable to take the risks required, then I will quit. My big problem at the moment is that I have lost faith in technology. I have had so many accidents in which technical failure was the cause that I have lost confidence."

Berger decided to carry on and ended up third, for the third time, in the World Championship. He had one more year at Maranello and proved himself a valuable team player under the aegis of new team boss Jean Todt. Six third-place finishes showed the restructuring of the team was working, but Berger did not stay to benefit when Michael Schumacher arrived in 1996, switching to the empty berth at Benetton.

Again, he had difficulty adapting to the new team environs, as he explained in his inimitable way: "The older you get, the more you get used to somebody and the more difficult it is to change. If you are a young boy and you get a new girlfriend, it is easy to adapt; you stay together and you feel fine. But if you get to 40 or 45 and you start something new, it is so hard to get used to it."

His final two years were testing. His last win at Hockenheim in 1997 was a triumphant way to remind everyone of his talent, but he had lost his motivation. "On particular occasions I wasn't driving the same way as before. If you had a wet race and you couldn't see anything, I was starting to lift off and think about what could go wrong. I needed a season off – a season to relax. But you don't get that luxury in Formula One. It was time to stop."

He now attends races as head of motor sport with BMW.

1993
Senna and Prost resume rivalry

TALKING POINT
ZERO HERO

The number one disappeared from Formula One for the start of 1993 after reigning World Champion Nigel Mansell defected to America's IndyCar racing circuit, his place in the Williams team being taken by Alain Prost.

But it was Damon Hill who was given the dubious honour of becoming the first ever number zero in Formula One as Williams, now without the driver who actually won the right to carry the number one the previous year, were forced to lose their Championship-winning number.

Hill had been promoted from the Williams test team to join triple World Champion Prost, and was given the chance of a lifetime to prove he was no number zero. With three wins and third place in the Championship, he did just that.

But, incredibly, Williams seemed unable to hold on to their champions, and as Prost sat on the verge of becoming the 1993 winner, he too announced his plans to leave the series after taking the title.

Once again, Williams were left in the lurch as Grand Prix champions – but without the car number to prove it – and Hill had to be their zero hero once again in 1994.

Ayrton Senna was unsure about racing in 1993, and had tested a Penske IndyCar as he considered joining reigning Grand Prix Champion Nigel Mansell on the other side of the Atlantic. McLaren, he thought, could not provide him with a good enough car, but he joined them with a sceptical attitude on a race-by-race basis, and eventually stayed for the year.

Damon Hill joined the returning Alain Prost at Williams after promotion from the test team, Riccardo Patrese switched to join Michael Schumacher at Benetton, and Michael Andretti made the opposite move to that of Mansell by leaving IndyCar racing to join McLaren.

But when the season began in South Africa, Senna and Prost resumed their career-long rivalry after Prost's year away, as the pair lined up alongside each other on the grid at Kyalami.

Senna left the line best to claim the first corner as three cars, including that of Senna's new American team-mate Andretti, stalled on the grid. Hill was up to second as Prost made a dismal start, but the Briton's impressive debut was not to last long, and he spun unchallenged to drop down the field and ultimately crash out after colliding with Alex Zanardi.

Up front, it was back to Senna versus Prost for the lead, but Senna was unable to keep Prost behind, and after dropping behind Schumacher he pitted for new tyres.

Senna challenged back through the field to second, but not even a late rainstorm could prevent Prost from taking an expected victory on his Williams debut, with Blundell delighted to take a podium place for Ligier after Warwick spun three laps from the finish.

Fun formula

In Brazil, Williams had another major sponsor, having captured the much-coveted Sega contract so placing Sonic the Hedgehog's legs on the side of the car. But McLaren, which had been vying for the contract, hit back during the season by sticking a squashed hedgehog logo on the car for every victory. Yes, fun was still very much a part of Formula One.

On the racetrack it was business as usual for Williams, with Hill joining his team-mate on the front row of the grid ahead of Senna and Schumacher. Prost shot away at the start as Senna passed Hill for second, but behind them Andretti had another disastrous start when he cut across Berger, sending the Ferrari off, and cartwheeling his own McLaren through the gravel trap. Hill was past Senna before the lap was over, before a sudden downpour created even more action.

An inspired early switch to dry tyres jumped Senna above Hill, and the Brazilian held on to win his second race in his homeland, delighted to receive the trophy from past master Juan Manuel Fangio.

The field moved to Europe after just two events for an Easter weekend race at Donington Park in England, and the circuit's first ever World Championship Grand Prix. Williams underlined the competitiveness of their car by taking pole position ahead through Hill, with Schumacher the best of the rest some 1.5 seconds back, but race day saw April showers create a spectacular if confusing race, with Senna revelling in the conditions. He was fourth on the grid, but in what has often been termed his best-ever lap – perhaps his best-ever race – he was up to first when the field began lap two.

Despite driving the fastest lap, Damon Hill's fortunes were fated at the British Grand Prix at Silverstone.

Christian Fittipaldi somersaults over Minardi team-mate Pierluigi Martini after clipping his car at Monza.

Williams had got their set-up drastically wrong and Prost struggled in the race, lapped by both runaway winner Senna and team-mate Hill, who himself was more than a minute adrift of the Brazilian by the end.

Imola was next on the agenda for round four, and after a crash-filled qualifying session for McLaren, it was Prost and Hill on the front row again. But Prost was bogged down at the start, and this allowed Hill through to lead as Senna also powered through to claim second. Senna tried for the lead but slid wide as Hill blocked the challenge, but Hill went straight on at the chicane and Senna was through. The Brazilian would not last long before hydraulic problems ended his race, and this allowed Prost to move into an unchallenged lead after Hill had earlier spun out of the race.

But it was Prost on pole again when the cars lined up on the grid for the Spanish Grand Prix at the Circuit de Catalunya, and although he lost the early lead to Hill, an engine failure for the Briton left Prost clear to win again. He was never challenged, and finished comfortably ahead of Senna, who had soaked up pressure from Schumacher before the German slid wide on oil left from Zanardi's blown engine.

Next stop on the Championship tour was the glamorous harbourside track of Monaco, and with five wins in six years it took a brave man to bet against another Senna victory: brave, and stupid. Senna may have had difficulties in practice, crashing twice, but come race day he claimed win number six in glitzy Monte Carlo.

There was a surprise in the paddock at the next race in Canada, when the sport's governing body announced that the active suspension systems being used did not comply with the regulations. That did not prevent Prost claiming his seventh consecutive pole position and turning it into win number four for the season on race day.

The Championship reached its midway point when it moved to France, and on their home ground things looked good for Renault, with the top four grid spots filled by cars powered by their engines.

Premier pole for Hill

Hill claimed his first-ever pole position, and led Prost away at the start as the Ligier pair slotted in behind, before Blundell put himself out.

Hill led into the pit-stops, but Prost took advantage when the Briton was held up as he came out behind Andretti, and was almost hit by a Sauber in the pits. A fast stop moved Prost ahead, and there he stayed as Hill followed behind to claim Williams' first one-two of the season.

Senna was now 13 points behind in the Championship race, and he needed a good result the following week when the teams headed to Silverstone for the British Grand Prix.

A dramatic qualifying session saw Prost take pole position away from home hero Hill right at the last minute, but the Briton got his revenge at the start of the race itself to storm into the lead. Hill was clearly ahead by the time Prost made it past Senna, who had also passed Prost at the start. But when Badoer stopped, the safety car came out and Hill's lead was gone. He stayed ahead when racing resumed, but a plume of smoke billowing out of the back of his Williams signalled the end of his day.

So Prost went on to win with Schumacher sec-

RACE BY RACE DETAILS

ROUND 1 – SOUTH AFRICA
Race Alain Prost
Pole Alain Prost
Fastest lap Alain Prost

ROUND 2 – BRAZIL
Race Ayrton Senna
Pole Alain Prost
Fastest lap Michael Schumacher

ROUND 3 – EUROPE
Race Ayrton Senna
Pole Alain Prost
Fastest lap Ayrton Senna

ROUND 4 – SAN MARINO
Race Alain Prost
Pole Alain Prost
Fastest lap Alain Prost

ROUND 5 – SPAIN
Race Alain Prost
Pole Alain Prost
Fastest lap Michael Schumacher

ROUND 6 – MONACO
Race Ayrton Senna
Pole Alain Prost
Fastest lap Alain Prost

ROUND 7 – CANADA
Race Alain Prost
Pole Alain Prost
Fastest lap Michael Schumacher

ROUND 8 – FRANCE
Race Alain Prost
Pole Damon Hill
Fastest lap Michael Schumacher

ROUND 9 – BRITAIN
Race Alain Prost
Pole Alain Prost
Fastest lap Damon Hill

ROUND 10 – GERMANY
Race Alain Prost
Pole Alain Prost
Fastest lap Michael Schumacher

ROUND 11 – HUNGARY
Race Damon Hill
Pole Alain Prost
Fastest lap Alain Prost

ROUND 12 – BELGIUM
Race Damon Hill
Pole Alain Prost
Fastest lap Alain Prost

ROUND 13 – ITALY
Race Damon Hill
Pole Alain Prost
Fastest lap Damon Hill

ROUND 14 – PORTUGAL
Race Michael Schumacher
Pole Damon Hill
Fastest lap Damon Hill

ROUND 15 – JAPAN
Race Ayrton Senna
Pole Alain Prost
Fastest lap Alain Prost

ROUND 16 – AUSTRALIA
Race Ayrton Senna
Pole Ayrton Senna
Fastest lap Damon Hill

1993 DRIVERS' CHAMPIONSHIP

DRIVER	TEAM	POINTS
Alain Prost	Williams Renault	99
Ayrton Senna	McLaren Ford	73
Damon Hill	Williams Renault	69
Michael Schumacher	Benetton Ford	52
Riccardo Patrese	Benetton Ford	20
Jean Alesi	Ferrari	16
Martin Brundle	Ligier Renault	13
Gerhard Berger	Ferrari	12
Johnny Herbert	Lotus Ford	11
Mark Blundell	Ligier Renault	10
Michael Andretti	McLaren Ford	7
Karl Wendlinger	Sauber	7
Christian Fittipaldi	Minardi Ford	5
JJ Lehto	Sauber	5
Mika Hakkinen	McLaren Ford	4
Derek Warwick	Footwork Mugen	4
Philippe Alliot	Larrousse Lamborghini	2
Fabrizio Barbazza	Minardi Ford	2
Rubens Barrichello	Jordan Hart	2
Eric Comas Larrousse	Lamborghini	2
Eddie Irvine	Jordan Hart	1
Alex Zanardi	Lotus Ford	1

ond, but Senna came to a halt on the very last lap for the third consecutive year and dropped down to fifth. That left Patrese to join the podium, with the British pair Herbert and Warwick claiming fourth and sixth respectively.

On the track, there was plenty of action in Germany, with Berger having a big crash in practice and Warwick rolling his Footwork in the warm-up.

The usual four of Prost, Hill, Schumacher and Senna occupied the front of the grid, and once again it was Hill in the lead off the line. A poor start dropped Prost behind Schumacher, but Senna spun trying to pass the Frenchman and spent the rest of his race fighting through the field. Prost recovered to claim the lead from Hill on lap eight, but was given a stop-go penalty for missing the chicane on the first lap.

Once again, however, it was not Hill's day, and three laps from victory the Briton's Williams suffered a puncture which forced him into retirement. Prost went on to win from Schumacher, with Blundell taking another podium finish for Ligier. Senna's comeback ended with fourth place ahead of Patrese and Berger.

After three races of appalling luck for Hill, Hungary was to be his day, as he took a dominant lights-to-flag first victory. He was helped by Prost's parade-lap stall which sent the pole-sitter to the back of the grid, but he got away well to pull out a clear lead.

Behind him, Schumacher dropped back after a spin and eventually went out with engine failure, and Barrichello had a high-speed off in his Jordan. Senna stopped with a throttle problem on lap 17, and Prost, who was fighting back well, went out of contention with a cracked rear wing support.

Second-generation winner

So Hill, carrying the helmet colours of his late father Graham, stormed home to become the first-ever second-generation Grand Prix winner. Patrese and Berger joined Hill on the podium as his proud mother Bette and wife Georgie looked on.

Belgium was next on the calendar, and Hill was on a roll. Just two weeks after his debut win he took a second victory – this time in front of all his top rivals.

Alessandro Zanardi was injured in a massive crash at Eau Rouge in practice, and Senna almost hit the stricken Lotus as he spun on the scene. Zanardi would be out for the rest of the season, but the racing went on and Prost took the lead as Schumacher dropped from third to ninth at the start. Schumacher also benefited from Prost's pit problems to claim second ahead of the Frenchman, but he could not catch Hill in the end.

Despite the poor performances of their Ferrari team, the *tifosi* were out in droves when the Grand Prix circus arrived in Italy for round 13. But it was

SHORTS

The ongoing saga over regulations concerning the active suspension systems (which had been started when the governing body, FISA, declared they were illegal in Canada) continued when the teams headed to Germany, and they asked FISA to allow the same regulations as they had adhered to all season.

Ayrton Senna raises his fist in victory at the Japanese Grand Prix.

Champion for 1993 Alain Prost discusses details with one of the Williams team at Silverstone.

clear that there was a lack of harmony in the team when Berger and Alesi collided in practice.

Alesi, however, still managed to qualify third, and moved in behind Prost to claim second at the start. Senna, meanwhile, climbed over the slow-starting Hill at the chicane and was forced to work his way up the field, only to retire after hitting Brundle at the same spot. Both Schumacher and Prost went out with blown engines, to leave Hill 40 seconds ahead of a crowd-pleasing Alesi in second.

Fittipaldi clipped the rear of his team-mate Pierluigi Martini's car, and completed a dramatic 360-degree flip as he crossed the line to finish.

Andretti took the final podium place, but it was to be his last race for McLaren as he announced he was returning to IndyCar racing after a difficult debut in Formula One. Sensationally, Prost, who looked set to claim the World Championship at the next round in Portugal, announced his decision to retire at the end of the season.

He would become the second World Champion in succession to desert the series after Mansell's defection to IndyCar racing the previous year, but it paved the way for the dream partnership of Senna and Williams for 1994.

Hakkinen's McLaren debut

However, there were still three races to go in the 1993 season, and McLaren had drafted in test-driver Mika Hakkinen to replace Andretti. He immediately out-qualified Senna to take third on the grid behind the Williams pair, as Hill claimed pole position. But Hill stalled at the start and Prost was blocked by a fast-starting Hakkinen, so Alesi who the field into the first corner. Senna blew his engine chasing Alesi, but Prost took the lead on lap 20, only to lose it to Schumacher when he went in for tyres. Hakkinen crashed to end his McLaren debut in the pit wall, and a problem while exiting the pits sent Berger across the track where he was narrowly missed by Warwick.

So through it all came Schumacher to earn his second career win ahead of the Williams pair of Prost and Hill – and second was enough to secure Prost his fourth world title.

Senna's knockout punch

With the title over, Japan could have been just another race, but it had plenty of action on and off the track – much of it centering around a confident newcomer named Eddie Irvine. The Ulsterman came in as the fifth different driver in the number-two Jordan car, but he was unaccustomed to the ethics of Formula One and would be punished.

Senna took the early lead as Irvine shot up to fifth at the start, but Hill – who had qualified down in sixth – was fighting his way through.

Senna made an early tyre stop, and although there was a sudden rainstorm after he passed Prost for the lead he still beat the Frenchman to victory, with Hakkinen an impressive third in his second race for McLaren.

But when a lapped Irvine decided to re-pass leader Senna, the triple World Champion was so angry that he punched the newcomer at the end of the race. And a controversial debut ended with a point for sixth place after Irvine literally nudged Warwick out of the points.

And so to the final race of the season, and the end-of-term party in sunny Adelaide, Australia. It was the end of a long and successful relationship with McLaren for Senna, and the end of a long and successful career for Prost – and the race was all about the pair who had been rivals at the top of the sport for so long. They lined up alongside one another on the front row, and Senna soon converted his 62nd pole position into a clear lead.

Irvine crashed out on lap one, and Schumacher went out with engine failure nine laps later after passing Hakkinen. Hill tried for second but spun and recovered, but he could not catch Prost for second as Senna held on to take his 41st Grand Prix win.

It had been a dominant year for Prost, and as the newly-crowned Champion bowed out, Senna's thoughts now turned to his own future with the team. But unbeknown to this Brazilian genius, Australia would be his final Grand Prix win.

1993 CONSTRUCTORS' CUP

TEAM (Engine)	POINTS
WILLIAMS RENAULT	168
McLAREN FORD	84
BENETTON FORD	72
FERRARI	28
LIGIER RENAULT	23
LOTUS FORD	12
SAUBER	12
MINARDI FORD	7
FOOTWORK MUGEN	4
LARROUSSE LAMBORGHINI	3
JORDAN HART	3

Damon Hill

CAREER DETAILS

1960	Born 17 September, Hampstead, London
1983	Switches from bikes to cars
1992	Test driver for Williams and F1 debut with Brabham
1993	Promoted to race team at Williams. Maiden F1 win at Hungary
1996	World Champion
1997	Moves to Arrows
1998	Moves to Jordan
1999	Retires

FORMULA ONE RECORD

Year	Team	Wins	Poles	Fast laps	Pts
1992	Brabham	0	0	0	0
1993	Williams	3	2	4	69
1994	Williams	6	2	6	91
1995	Williams	4	7	4	69
1996	Williams	8	9	5	97
1997	Arrows	0	0	0	7
1998	Jordan	1	0	0	20
1999	Jordan	0	0	0	7

DAMON HILL IS THE FIRST SON of a World Champion to win the title himself. Hard work, sheer determination and natural dignity enabled him to achieve his popular success in 1996.

Damon Hill was 15 when his father died and after that, he said he had "no interest at all in Formula One". His enthusiasm for racing was rekindled, but firstly on two wheels, which also gave him a day job as a despatch rider to fund his career. After a brief experience of Formula Ford at the end of 1983, Hill became increasingly addicted to the challenge of racing cars. Brands Hatch supremo John Webb helped his cause and by 1985 he was racing Formula Ford with serious intent.

In 1986 he finished an undistinguished ninth in the Formula Three Championships, having joined Murray Taylor Racing, but went on to have two solid years at Intersport, notching up prestigious wins at Spa and Zandvoort in 1987 and the Grand Prix support race at Silverstone.

Hill moved up to F3000 for 1989, switching after a year from Footwork to Middlebridge where he showed his mettle. While results were hardly headline material, he earned a reputation as a decent racer over the next two years and secured the Williams testing contract while also striving to qualify the tank-like Brabham (succeeding twice). Patrick Head was impressed with his technical feedback and Hill was promoted to the race team for 1993 after Nigel Mansell had departed for Indycars. He could hardly believe his luck. "The first time I drove the FW14 I was like a kid in Santa's grotto," he enthused of his testing break.

Unfazed by Alain Prost as a team-mate, Hill showed maturity to weather early errors and gradually push the Frenchman. He took his maiden Grand Prix win in Hungary, followed by successive wins at Spa and Monza, and finished third in the Championship. The following season he faced Ayrton Senna as team-mate, but the Brazilian's death at Imola thrust Hill into the role of team leader. Just as his father had refocused Colin Chapman after Jim Clark's death, so Damon helped Frank Williams. He saw off Nigel Mansell, won the British Grand Prix (a feat that had eluded his father) and challenged Michael Schumacher race by race to the controversial decisive round in Adelaide.

Boosted with confidence, Hill began 1995 as a title favourite but fell prey to embarrassing errors. "The wonderful thing about being a Grand Prix driver is that you are presented 16 times in a season with a challenge that you can focus on, and it's

Damon HIll in winning form at the Japanese Grand Prix in 1996.

> "He's proved himself to have more integrity in his little finger than most people have in their whole body."

Georgie Hill on her husband.

something that's never more than a fortnight away. It's a tangible goal each time and it's very appealing to live like that. The trouble is your life goes up and down each time," he said.

Unbeknown to him, Frank Williams had already decided to replace him with Heinz-Harald Frentzen at the end of 1996. "If you really want to know why we're replacing Hill, it's because he can't bloody pass people," grunted an anonymous Williams team member.

In the 1995–96 winter Hill had reinvented himself as a tougher individual and his self-esteem rose. After winning the first two races of the season he said: "I am more Damon Hill than the son of Graham now." He won eight of the 16 rounds and eventually secured the title in an emotional finale at Suzuka. The season's achievement had television commentator Murray Walker choking back tears over his microphone, but had not been decisive enough to woo all the paddock sages. "I've never seen anyone go to so much trouble to lose the World Championship," muttered Niki Lauda after Hill's initial failure to clinch the title at Estoril.

"I think Damon has done it the same way as his dad did," said Ken Tyrrell. "I don't think Graham had any great talent, but he won Monaco five times as well as Indianapolis and Le Mans. Damon has slogged away at it. He's not a Clark, a Senna or a Stewart, but he's done a great job."

Too late to find a top seat, Hill accepted a lucrative offer to lend his experience to Tom Walkinshaw's lower-order Arrows team. Apart from a near-win in Hungary, the season was a miserable one for the defending Champion as he and Walkinshaw fell out publicly. He joined up with Jordan for the next two years. After a shaky start to 1998, he brought the team their maiden GP win in a triumphant drive in the wet at Spa.

However, clearly demotivated in 1999, Hill came dangerously close to ruining his reputation. Comprehensively overshadowed by a reinvigorated Frentzen, and uninspired to meet the competition, he was accused of continuing just for the cash. As Eddie Irvine put it, "Damon's retiring like he overtakes. Will he? Won't he? It's not a very good way to walk away, is it?"

Sheer hard work and determination were responsible for Damon Hill's World Championship title.

1994
Double tragedy casts gloom

TALKING POINT

SENNA

The 1994 season, like so many before it, was marred by serious accidents, but this year had an added element of horror, sadness and dismay as the legendary Ayrton Senna lost his life in the San Marino Grand Prix.

The Brazilian, who had won the hearts of millions and was arguably the sport's greatest-ever driver, died after a fifth-lap accident in the third-round race at Imola as he careered into a wall at high speed and suffered fatal injuries.

Brazil mourned its lost son, and Formula One also badly missed the great man. As if Senna's death was not tragedy enough, the 1994 season – and indeed the San Marino weekend – was marred by several big shunts and another fatal crash.

A day before Senna's death, Roland Ratzenberger died on impact after crashing his Simtek at nearly 200 mph at the Gilles Villeneuve curve. His death was the first in the series since Riccardo Paletti had lost his life in 1982.

San Marino had already seen a massive crash involving Rubens Barrichello in a Jordan during Friday's qualifying session. And the Imola race was also marred at the start by a crash involving Pedro Lamy and JJ Lehto. Lamy ploughed his Lotus into the back of Lehto's stalled Benetton and sent debris flying into the crowd, injuring four people.

Karl Wendlinger was also lucky to survive a crash 11 days after Senna's death as he suffered a big accident in practice for the Monaco Grand Prix. Amazingly, the Austrian driver was back racing within five months. And in the next race in Spain, Italian Andrea Montermini's Grand Prix debut was wrecked as he crashed his Simtek heavily and broke his heel, ending his season prematurely.

In a season, which saw Grand Prix racing lose one of its greatest-ever drivers amid scenes of carnage in San Marino, the sport's governing body, the FIA, turned the campaign into one of the most stringent ever. The FIA had promised to be strict in its regulations, but nobody could have predicted the extent to which they were prepared to go, as controversy reigned in the season which saw so much.

Another unusual factor was the way in which most teams opted to use more than the customary two drivers in each outfit. Williams used Damon Hill, David Coulthard, Ayrton Senna and Nigel Mansell, while Benetton employed Michael Schumacher, J J Lehto, Jos Verstappen and the well-travelled Johnny Herbert.

Herbert also drove for the Lotus and Ligier teams in 1994 as the season saw several technical changes in its efforts to become safer. In Monaco, one race after the nightmare San Marino event, the FIA responded to growing unrest concerning safety and announced three sweeping technical changes to make the cars slower and safer.

The three changes involved aerodynamics concerning the turning vanes and wings, the reduction of engine power and aerodynamics concerning the flat bottom of the cars. After the German Grand Prix, the FIA introduced a wooden plank, which was fitted underneath the chassis of each car, and which was measured before and after a race. If it had worn by more than one millimetre, the car was disqualified.

The teams were originally in uproar over the FIA's proposals and the above were the result of compromises and meetings over subsequent weeks. The Grand Prix Drivers' Association was also reformed, with Schumacher spearheading its return, so the drivers could have a bigger say in the safety of the sport.

The cars and the drivers, however, lined up for the season-opening Grand Prix in Brazil without the planks. Senna claimed pole position for the 71-lap race at his home Interlagos circuit, but had Schumacher and the quick-starting Jean Alesi in a Ferrari behind him on the grid and it was Schumacher who cruised to victory after Senna spun out.

Irvine ban

After Mark Blundell crashed his Tyrrell on lap 21, much worse was to follow 13 laps later when Eddie Irvine in a Jordan, Jos Verstappen in a Benetton, Martin Brundle in a McLaren and Eric Bernard in a Ligier were involved in a pile-up. Amazingly, all four drivers emerged unscathed, but Irvine was later charged with dangerous driving by FIA race stewards and was immediately fined $10,000 and banned for one race, later extended to three.

Roland Ratzenberger who died in a crash during practice for the San Marino Grand Prix.

Alesi was injured in testing before the next race at the Aida circuit in Japan, so Ferrari drafted in Nicola Larini. The Italian driver courted controversy immediately as he allegedly let slip to his home pressmen that he had used illegal traction control in practice. Ferrari refuted the claims and so did Larini to the world press.

A crash allowed Schumacher, who was second on the grid, to power through into the lead, and despite attempts from Hill and Brundle to catch him he was unbeatable.

Death strikes Formula One

The next round in San Marino is not remembered for Schumacher claiming his third consecutive win, but for the carnage which took the life of two drivers – Senna

Officials, drivers and medical staff gather to help Ayrton Senna after his horrific crash at Imola.

and Ratzenberger – and nearly claimed a third, Barrichello, over the weekend (see Talking Point).

The race was run in surreal circumstances as the Formula One world waited for news of Senna's condition while Schumacher powered to his third victory of the season.

Senna's crash had come after a period of running with the safety car, deployed after Pedro Lamy's Lotus had ploughed into the stalled Benetton of J J Lehto on the grid. Lehto had come in to replace Verstappen, and was lucky to escape injury along with Lamy.

After Senna's crash, the race was restarted at a set distance of 53 laps. Berger led from the restart from Schumacher, though eventually withdrew on lap 16, complaining of a problem with his Ferrari, but many believe he was thinking of Senna. More drama followed later in the race as Alboreto departed from his final pit-stop and a loose wheel flew off his car, hitting four mechanics, though none was seriously injured.

Arriving in Monaco for the next race, all of the teams' personnel were subdued as the unrivalled master of the principality, Senna, was missing. The sombre mood was not improved in practice on the Thursday as Wendlinger ploughed straight on at the chicane after the Lowens Tunnel. Miraculously, Wendlinger cheated death, but he was in a coma for several days. In the wake of his crash, Schumacher was again the man to beat as he claimed pole position for the 78-lap race. But he did not start from that place on the grid, as the first two places were left empty as a mark of respect for Senna and Ratzenberger.

After the drivers – including the fit-again Alesi – had stood at pole position for a one-minute silence before the race, the event began and Schumacher, as expected, sped into the lead. He was head and shoulders above the rest of the field and won his fourth race of the season by more than 30 seconds.

The first aerodynamic technical changes came into force for the next round in Spain, and the circuit's organizers also heeded the call for improved safety by building a tyre-wall chicane on the track to slow the cars down.

Coulthard arrives

Irvine also returned to the fray after his three-race ban, and Williams decided to replace Senna with the young British driver David Coulthard. Neither made a significant mark in qualifying, as Schumacher once again took pole position from Hill and Hakkinen.

At the start of the 65-lap race, Schumacher once again seemed unstoppable, and Hill and Hakkinen appeared to be consigned to a battle for second place. But on lap 20 the German driver started to slow as his gearbox faltered, and Hakkinen went through, followed by Hill.

Coulthard went out on lap 32 with an electrical fault on his Williams, but eight laps later his teammate Hill took the race lead as Hakkinen came in for a second pit-stop. It was a lead Hill would not lose,

RACE BY RACE DETAILS

ROUND 1 – BRAZIL
Race Michael Schumacher
Pole Ayrton Senna
Fastest lap Michael Schumacher

ROUND 2 – PACIFIC
Race Michael Schumacher
Pole Ayrton Senna
Fastest lap Michael Schumacher

ROUND 3 – SAN MARINO
Race Michael Schumacher
Pole Ayrton Senna
Fastest lap Damon Hill

ROUND 4 – MONACO
Race Michael Schumacher
Pole Michael Schumacher
Fastest lap Michael Schumacher

ROUND 5 – SPAIN
Race Damon Hill
Pole Michael Schumacher
Fastest lap Michael Schumacher

ROUND 6 – CANADA
Race Michael Schumacher
Pole Michael Schumacher
Fastest lap Michael Schumacher

ROUND 7 – FRANCE
Race Michael Schumacher
Pole Damon Hill
Fastest lap Damon Hill

ROUND 8 – BRITAIN
Race Damon Hill
Pole Damon Hill
Fastest lap Damon Hill

ROUND 9 – GERMANY
Race Gerhard Berger
Pole Gerhard Berger
Fastest lap David Coulthard

ROUND 10 – HUNGARY
Race Michael Schumacher
Pole Michael Schumacher
Fastest lap Michael Schumacher

ROUND 11 – BELGIUM
Race Damon Hill
Pole Rubens Barrichello
Fastest lap Damon Hill

ROUND 12 – ITALY
Race Damon Hill
Pole Jean Alesi
Fastest lap Damon Hill

ROUND 13 – PORTUGAL
Race Damon Hill
Pole Gerhard Berger
Fastest lap David Coulthard

ROUND 14 – EUROPE
Race winner Michael Schumacher
Pole Michael Schumacher
Fastest lap Michael Schumacher

ROUND 15 – JAPAN
Race Damon Hill
Pole Michael Schumacher
Fastest lap Damon Hill

ROUND 16 – AUSTRALIA
Race Nigel Mansell
Pole Nigel Mansell
Fastest lap Michael Schumacher

1994 DRIVERS' CHAMPIONSHIP

DRIVER	TEAM	POINTS
Michael Schumacher	Benetton	92
Damon Hill	Williams	91
Gerhard Berger	Ferrari	41
Mika Hakkinen	McLaren	26
Jean Alesi	Ferrari	24
Rubens Barrichello	Jordan	19
Martin Brundle	McLaren	16
David Coulthard	Williams	14
Nigel Mansell	Williams	13
Jos Verstappen	Benetton	10
Olivier Panis	Ligier	9
Mark Blundell	Tyrrell	8
Heinz-Harald Frentzen	Sauber	7
Nicola Larini	Ferrari	6
Christian Fittipaldi	Footwork	6
Eddie Irvine	Jordan	6
Ukyo Katayama	Tyrrell	5
Eric Bernard	Ligier and Lotus	4
Karl Wendlinger	Sauber	4
Andrea De Cesaris	Jordan and Sauber	4
Pierluigi Martini	Minardi	4
Gianni Morbidelli	Footwork	3
Erik Comas	Larrousse	2
Michele Alboreto	Minardi	1
JJ Lehto	Benetton and Sauber	1

Gerhard Berger is frustrated as he runs out of fuel at the German Grand Prix.

as he took a poignant win for a team which had suffered so much after the death of Senna.

The Gilles Villeneuve circuit in Canada hosted the next round of the Championship and, undeterred by his failure to win in Spain, Schumacher returned to the winners' rostrum.

Comeback for Mansell

Mansell made his shock return to the sport for the next round in France at the expense of Coulthard. The reigning IndyCar Champion was back for what was supposed to be a one-off race, before taking part in the final three events of the season.

Hill had another new team-mate, and it inspired him as he beat Mansell to pole position to complete an all-Williams front row, with Schumacher lurking dangerously in third on the grid for the 72-lap race.

The start realized Williams' worst fears, as Schumacher made an amazing dash off the line and powered in front of Hill and Mansell. Hill kept up, but Mansell dropped back as Alesi and Berger piled on the pressure for third place. But Schumacher maintained his lead with Hill in tow and Mansell's race ended in anti-climax, with the transmission failing on his Williams after 48 laps when he was back up to third, which let in Berger for the last podium place.

Despite his failure to win in France, Hill had driven impressively, and after Coulthard returned for the next round in Britain Hill was in no mood to give up the fight to catch runaway Championship leader Schumacher. He claimed pole for the 60-lap event and beat second-placed Schumacher off the grid at the start.

Schumacher ban

Before the start of the race, however, confusion had reigned, with the race stewards imposing a five-second penalty on Schumacher for overtaking Hill on the formation lap. Benetton team members and FIA stewards argued furiously after Schumacher was black-flagged in the race for not observing the stop-go sanction – which Benetton believed was not a stop-go penalty, but one that would be added to his time at the end of the race.

Schumacher ignored the black flags and raced to a second-place finish behind valiant winner Hill. A week later, however, Schumacher was disqualified and banned for two races. Benetton, meanwhile, were fined a total of $600,000 for their part, as the FIA also discredited the team by stating that they suspected Schumacher's car had used a form of illegal traction control at Imola. The authorities could not prove it, so no penalty was officially given, but the huge fine for Schumacher's misdemeanours at Silverstone was seen by the paddock gossips as a way of punishing the team for the electronic aid.

There were bans too for Hakkinen and Barrichello for clashing on the last lap of the British race and again for Hakkinen after he was blamed for a first-lap acci-

SHORTS

Hakkinen had retired with an engine problem on lap 48 in Spain, and that allowed Schumacher to claim a remarkable second place, after which it was revealed he had run for two-thirds of the race in only fifth gear.

dent that wiped him – as well as the two Jordans of Irvine and Barrichello, Blundell, Frentzen and Coulthard – out of the German Grand Prix.

More bans (though suspended) were given after the Spanish Grand Prix (won by Berger) to Alboreto, de Cesaris and Zanardi for their part in a start-line incident and the fact that they all left without explaining their actions to the stewards.

At the next race in Hungary, Schumacher returned with a bang as he powered from pole position to victory in a race which once again displayed his dominance over the rest of the field.

Hill was now 31 points behind Schumacher in the title race, but the British driver was not about to give up the ghost. His determination was rewarded in Belgium as controversy reigned once again. Schumacher cruised to victory at the Spa-Francorchamps circuit, only to be disqualified after the plank under his car was deemed to have worn by more than the stipulated one millimetre.

It was a bitter pill for Schumacher to swallow, as the points he thought he had earned went to Hill, and two days later the FIA upheld Schumacher's two-race ban for ignoring black flags in the British Grand Prix. The punishment had to be taken immediately, and Schumacher missed the races in Italy and Portugal.

In a way the Italian Grand Prix played second fiddle to its own qualifying session, as most of the action occurred in the sessions that would decide a remarkable grid.

Michael Schumacher celebrates his first Championship with the Benetton team.

Pole for Alesi

Alesi claimed the first pole position of his career and, unbelievably, his Ferrari team-mate Berger lined up alongside him on the front row despite a big shunt in practice – from which he was lucky to escape unscathed, while Hill was third. A crash involving Irvine, Herbert, Coulthard, Panis and Comas meant that the race had to be restarted.

Berger was gifted the lead by Herbert and looked set for his second victory of the season until his second pit-stop. As he pitted, Panis also came in and did not park up correctly. Berger was forced to struggle around the Ligier, but lost sufficient time to allow Hill through into the lead. Hill went on to win from a frustrated Berger, while in the aftermath of the race Irvine was given a suspended one-race ban for his part in the opening-lap crash.

Hill was now 11 points behind Schumacher, and in the German driver's enforced absence in Portugal Hill reduced that deficit to just a point as he took a third consecutive win at Estoril.

Schumacher returned to action in Jerez for the European Grand Prix, and spiced up the title run-in by criticizing Hill in the British press. He also claimed pole position from Hill for the 69-lap race and took a win from second-placed Hill that left the gap at the top of the standings at five points with two races to go, in Japan and Australia.

Season finale

The penultimate race at Suzuka was a thriller as Schumacher knew he could claim the World Championship if results went his way. Hill responded with the drive of his life as he beat pole-sitter Schumacher into second place to take the title race to a tense finale.

As the drivers arrived in Adelaide for the final race of the season, Schumacher held a single-point lead over Hill, and nobody could have predicted the finale to come in a race for which Mansell had claimed pole from Schumacher and Hill.

Schumacher soon reeled in Mansell in the early stages, and after he had clipped a wall and damaged his Benetton on lap 35 of the 81 with Hill on his tail, the unthinkable happened. Hill dived inside Schumacher to overtake and Schumacher turned in, smashing the cars together. Schumacher went out immediately, and a few yards later Hill was also out. The Championship had been decided in controversial circumstances. Some believed that Schumacher was at fault for the clash. Others felt that Hill had taken an unnecessary risk, particularly after post-race analysis revealed that Schumacher's car would have been a likely retiree after his earlier scrape with a wall. It was a bad end to the season – the dawn of a new Champion and, sadly, the end of perhaps the sport's greatest ever Champion.

1994 CONSTRUCTORS' CUP

TEAM (Engine)	POINTS
WILLIAMS RENAULT	118
BENETTON FORD	103
FERRARI	71
MCLAREN PEUGEOT	42
JORDAN HART	28
TYRRELL YAMAHA	13
LIGIER RENAULT	13
SAUBER MERCEDES	12
FOOTWORK FORD	9
MINARDI FORD	5
LARROUSSE FORD	2

Michael Schumacher

CAREER DETAILS

1969	Born 3 January, in Hurth-Hermuhlheim, Germany
1991	F1 debut with Jordan. Moves to Benetton
1992	Maiden Grand Prix win at Spa
1994	World Champion with Benetton despite being banned for two races in mid-season
1995	World Champion with Benetton
1997	Stripped of second place in World Championship following incident with Villeneuve
1999	Breaks leg in crash at Silverstone
2000	World Champion with Ferrari
2001	World Champion with Ferrari
2002	World Champion with Ferrari with most wins and most points in a season
2003	World Champion with Ferrari to take overall lead in championship victories with his sixth title

FORMULA ONE RECORD

Year	Team	Wins	Poles	Fast laps	Pts
1991	Jordan	0	0	0	4
1991	Benetton	0	0	0	-
1992	Benetton	1	0	2	53
1993	Benetton	1	0	5	52
1994	Benetton	8	6	8	92
1995	Benetton	9	4	8	102
1996	Ferrari	3	4	2	59
1997	Ferrari	5	3	3	78
1998	Ferrari	6	3	6	86
1999	Ferrari	2	3	5	44
2000	Ferrari	9	9	2	108
2001	Ferrari	9	11	3	123
2002	Ferrari	11	7	7	144
2003	Ferrari	6	5	5	93

WITH A FREAKISH TALENT and uncompromising attitude similar to Ayrton Senna, Michael Schumacher inherited the Brazilian's mantle as the world's best driver and took a record-breaking sixth world title in 2003.

Michael Schumacher has a huge following of fans both in his own country of Germany but also in Italy with Ferrari.

Michael Schumacher, the son of a bricklayer, raced karts from infancy and in due course was crowned German champion. In 1988 he progressed to cars, becoming Champion of the entry-level Formula König series, and competed in Formula Ford where he finished second behind Mika Salo in the European series. In 1989 he was signed by front-running German Formula Three team OTS and finished third, equal on points with team-mate Heinz-Harald Frentzen, just one point behind series winner Karl Wendlinger.

All three were placed by Mercedes sporting director Jochen Neerspasch in his junior-driver scheme in the Sauber-Mercedes Group C programme for 1990, and schooled by Jochen Mass. In parallel to this tutelage, Schumacher raced in German Formula Three. He won five times to dominate the series and also won at Fuji and Macau.

After winning the series in 1991, the German *Wunderkind* finished second in a Formula 3000 car before bursting on to the Grand Prix scene with a sensational one-off outing, qualifying seventh at Spa in a Jordan, while Bertrand Gachot was in jail. Benetton then snaffled Schumacher from under Eddie Jordan's nose – even though his race ended prematurely when his clutch failed at the start. In his first three races for Flavio Briatore's team he finished in the points – and the Benetton team had a star around whom they were to build their future.

The 1992 season was Mansell's year in the overwhelmingly superior Williams, but Schumacher exhibited remarkable consistency as well as speed, and claimed his first Grand Prix win, fittingly at Spa. The following season he won at Estoril, and finished on the podium every time his Benetton lasted the distance.

After rigorous winter dedication the new Benetton B194, powered by the Ford Zetec-R V8 engine, took Schumacher to a 20 points-to-nil advantage over Ayrton Senna in the Williams.

After the tragic events of Imola, Schumacher was left fighting for a Championship he felt had been devalued by the loss of the Brazilian. He won the title, but it was indeed devalued – by the rumblings that Benetton were running illegal traction control. He suffered a two-race ban for ignoring a black flag at Silverstone and was disqualified at Spa for an illegal skid-block, but even so beat Damon Hill to the title after pushing him off the road at the final race in Adelaide.

"He was the champion, no doubt about that, but he had not achieved it in the way that a Champion should," said Hill. "At the time, I couldn't believe that he would do such a thing but, with hindsight, I think I was being a little naive."

The following season saw Schumacher rampant. He successfully defended his title with brilliant wins in Brazil, Spain, Monaco, France, Germany, Belgium, Japan, at the Pacific Grand Prix and at the Nurburgring. Raw speed, canny tactics, superior fitness and superb skills marked him out. "He wins races he shouldn't and, more importantly, doesn't lose races he shouldn't," said technical director Ross Brawn.

Benetton were dismayed when he signed for Ferrari in 1996 for a "massive" retainer and then set about restructuring the sleeping giant. He somehow dragged the reluctant car to wins in Spain, Spa and Monza which it did not deserve.

Things had not advanced considerably at Ferrari the following year as Jacques Villeneuve proved the man to beat in his superior Williams. Schumacher took stunning wins in three wet races – Monaco, Magny Cours and Spa – but his dogged title challenge ended shamefully after an outrageous manoeuvre on the French-Canadian in the decisive race at Jerez. He was subsequently stripped of his points and his place in the Championship.

The World Championship looked a probability in 1998 when he drove magnificently against Mika Hakkinen in the McLaren, but stalling at the start of the final round at Suzuka scuppered his chances. The pressure on the German to deliver for Ferrari in 1999 was peaking, but early shows of dominance at Imola and Monaco were ruined when Schumacher broke a leg on the first lap of the British Grand Prix.

On the 21st anniversary of the last Ferrari World Championship – delivered by Jody Scheckter in 1979 – Schumacher triumphed to add the drivers' trophy to the constructors' one that had made its home in the Maranello stable the previous year. After that, it seemed the silverware would never leave.

In 2001 Schumacher equalled Alain Prost's record tally of 51 Grand Prix victories and won a fourth world title with five races still to go.

But the following year more records tumbled as he won 11 Grands Prix, more than anyone in a season, and claimed the title after just 11 races in a controversial season that turned many fans away from the sport. It won them back with regulation changes in 2003, but not even impressive young talent Kimi Raikkonen could prevent Schumacher snatching a record sixth title in the final race of the year and staking a claim to be the all-time number one in Formula One.

"I don't want to be treated as special because I'm not. I just drive a racing car round in circles a bit faster than anyone else."

From karts to Formula One, Michael Schumacher has planned his career in fine detail.

1995
Schumacher shows title class

TALKING POINT

MANSELL MESS

In the pre-season it was announced that Nigel Mansell would make his expected comeback into the sport, not for Williams – for whom he had driven four races in 1994 – but for up-and-coming McLaren, as team-mate to Mika Hakkinen.

The move was received with contrasting opinions in the media, some deeming it a potential race-winning partnership, while others rated it a match made in hell as two egos collided – Mansell's, and that of McLaren team boss Ron Dennis.

Unfortunately, the latter assessment proved correct, as Mansell was prevented from starting the season because the team had built the cockpit of his car too small. This allowed Mark Blundell to drive the opening races of the season alongside Hakkinen, but even when Mansell finally did get in the cockpit the partnership lasted for just two races.

McLaren spent more than £200,000 redesigning the cockpit to fit Mansell, and by the San Marino Grand Prix, Mansell was ready to race. However, after getting a puncture and struggling with his car, Mansell finished 10th at Imola, and in the aftermath complained about his chariot.

At the next round in Spain, tension was high between Mansell and McLaren and, despite qualifying just one-tenth of a second behind Hakkinen, Mansell gave up 15 laps into the race.

By the next round, the Monaco Grand Prix, Mansell had left the team and Blundell was back alongside Hakkinen. It was a sad end to the career of one of Britain's best ever racers in Formula One.

In the closed season, and throughout the campaign, most teams took the opportunity to change drivers, and Benetton produced one of the biggest surprises as they dropped Jos Verstappen for British driver Johnny Herbert. Herbert would prove a fitting team-mate to reigning champion Michael Schumacher, however, and would silence the critics.

Williams boosted their ranks as the young British hopeful David Coulthard was taken on full-time after sharing duties with Nigel Mansell the previous season. Mansell, meanwhile, had a short and unhappy spell at McLaren, and Mika Hakkinen was left with two other partners in the season: Mark Blundell and Jan Magnussen.

So the season started in the sweltering heat of Sao Paolo as the Interlagos circuit hosted the Brazilian Grand Prix. On arrival, the drivers all had problems with the bumpy nature of the circuit, and this was to prove crucial for the outcome of the race.

Hill took pole for the 71-lap event, but the lead-up to the race was tarnished by fuel fears as Elf announced that the FIA were investigating the fuel of Williams and Benetton.

Amid the investigation, the race got underway and Hill powered into the lead with Schumacher on his tail. Panis was the first driver to retire as he went out in a spin on the first lap, but Hill looked comfortable until disaster struck.

The suspension on his Williams broke – presumably taking a beating from the bumpy nature of the track surface – and Hill's race was over on lap 30. That gifted the lead to Schumacher, and he duly led Coulthard, Berger, Hakkinen, Alesi and Blundell (in for the missing Mansell) to the chequered flag.

However, after the race the FIA ruled that the fuel in both Coulthard's and Schumacher's cars was illegal, and both drivers were disqualified only to be cleared on appeal three weeks later.

Premier pole for Coulthard

Coulthard secured the first pole position of his career at the next race in Argentina and in wet conditions on race day he powered away at the start with Hill and Schumacher in close proximity. But behind the top three, there were problems. Alesi spun his Ferrari and crashed into Salo, who in turn made contact with Panis, Badoer and Herbert. Barrichello spun later in the lap as he was clipped by the damaged car of Badoer.

The race was red-flagged and the drivers involved in the mêlée ran for their spare cars. Barrichello was forced to use a car which was set up for team-mate Irvine, and Badoer was a non-starter as his Minardi team did not have a spare.

At the restart, Coulthard again pulled away and Irvine and Hakkinen clashed, sending the latter out. Irvine retired as well on lap six with engine problems, and leader Coulthard was unlucky 10 laps later when he suffered the same fate.

His retirement gifted the lead to Hill, who took the opportunity to stamp his authority on the Championship early on. Hill took his first win of the season with Alesi in second after he had outshone Schumacher in third.

In changeable conditions at the San Marino Grand Prix, Schumacher started the race well, but as the track dried he came in for slick tyres on lap 10 and, after rejoining the track, spun out almost immediately and crashed into a barrier to leave Hill the eventual winner.

Schumacher arrived in Spain for the next round under a barrage of criticism over his start to the season. It had not been a bad start, but for Schumacher and Benetton it was a surprise to see him seemingly struggling. That was all to change at Barcelona.

The German driver was back to his best as he claimed pole position for the 65-lap race by almost

Jean Alesi wins for Ferrari at the Canadian Grand Prix.

A delighted Johnny Herbert receives his awards at the British Grand Prix.

half a second from his nearest rival. He then proceeded to lead the race almost from start to finish as he lapped nearly a second faster than the rest of the field in the early stages.

Herbert finished second to complete a Benetton one-two, and Berger came in third. Before the Monaco Grand Prix, Mansell had left the McLaren team and Blundell was back.

Monaco mayhem

As usual, the start was chaotic as the 26 entrants powered their way to the Sainte Devoté chicane. Leader Hill and Schumacher got through safely, but Coulthard and the two Ferraris of Alesi and Berger collided and forced the race to be red-flagged as they blocked the track.

All three drivers returned to the pits for spare cars and made the restart, which again saw Hill lead the field – this time safely – through the first chicane.

The race turned on Williams' and Benetton's strategies as Hill came in on lap 24 for the first of two stops. Schumacher, however, stayed out with a single-stop strategy and built up a lead as Hill rejoined in traffic. Schumacher built up a big enough gap so that by the time Hill rejoined after his second stop the German driver was well clear.

In the next round in Canada, history was made as Alesi claimed his first win after 91 Grands Prix. It was a poignant moment for the emotional Frenchman, who profited from a gearbox problem on Schumacher's Benetton to take victory.

Hill seemed on course for a third-place finish when the susceptible hydraulics on the Williams went again, and he was out on lap 50.

Alesi was making no headway on Schumacher when fate intervened and the Benetton's gearbox started to fail. That allowed Alesi past, and he went on to claim his first win, from the Jordan duo of Barrichello and Irvine.

Schumacher shines

After receiving early criticism in the season, Schumacher was now in full swing, as he demonstrated at the French Grand Prix.

Schumacher came in first for a pit-stop, and just when Hill needed a quick lap he got caught in traffic. By the time Hill pitted, Schumacher had made up sufficient ground to be in front by the time the Briton got back out, and it was a lead he would not relinquish.

The British Grand Prix threw up a surprise, as Herbert took his first career win after a controversial incident involving Hill and Schumacher 16 laps from the finish. After losing out in the pit-stops again, Hill seemed to be trailing Schumacher home for another Benetton-Williams one-two, until the British driver made an ambitious overtaking manoeuvre at Priory, hit Schumacher and sent both drivers into the gravel and out of the race.

Schumacher was livid, but more importantly his team-mate Herbert inherited the lead from Coulthard, who then got a 1-second stop-go penalty for pit-lane speeding. That left the way clear for Herbert, who beat Alesi into second place, with Coulthard third.

Fangio – the legend

Prior to the German Grand Prix at Hockenheim, sadness once again descended on the sport with the news of the death of the man whom many view as the sport's greatest-ever driver: Juan Manuel Fangio.

Argentine Fangio died at the age of 84 after a long illness, but after his exploits in the 1950s, when the World Championship was in its formative stages, his record of five World Championships remains the best-ever personal haul.

In Germany, Hill tried to quell stories about a hatred between himself and Schumacher as he walked to the Benetton garage and shook hands with his rival in front of his home crowd on race day.

That, however, was where the niceties ended and Hill was the first to lose out as, pushing hard, he went out of the race on the second lap, spinning through the gravel and into a tyre wall.

RACE BY RACE DETAILS

ROUND 1 – BRAZIL
Race Michael Schumacher
Pole Damon Hill
Fastest lap Michael Schumacher

ROUND 2 – ARGENTINA
Race Damon Hill
Pole David Coulthard
Fastest lap Michael Schumacher

ROUND 3 – SAN MARINO
Race Damon Hill
Pole Michael Schumacher
Fastest lap Gerhard Berger

ROUND 4 – SPAIN
Race Michael Schumacher
Pole Michael Schumacher
Fastest lap Damon Hill

ROUND 5 – MONACO
Race Michael Schumacher
Pole Damon Hill
Fastest lap Jean Alesi

ROUND 6 – CANADA
Race Jean Alesi
Pole Michael Schumacher
Fastest lap Michael Schumacher

ROUND 7 – FRANCE
Race Michael Schumacher
Pole Damon Hill
Fastest lap Michael Schumacher

ROUND 8 – BRITAIN
Race Johnny Herbert
Pole Damon Hill
Fastest lap Damon Hill

ROUND 9 – GERMANY
Race Michael Schumacher
Pole Damon Hill
Fastest lap Michael Schumacher

ROUND 10 – HUNGARY
Race Damon Hill
Pole Damon Hill
Fastest lap Damon Hill

ROUND 11 – BELGIUM
Race Michael Schumacher
Pole Gerhard Berger
Fastest lap David Coulthard

ROUND 12 – ITALY
Race Johnny Herbert
Pole David Coulthard
Fastest lap Gerhard Berger

ROUND 13 – PORTUGAL
Race David Coulthard
Pole David Coulthard
Fastest lap David Coulthard

ROUND 14 – EUROPE
Race Michael Schumacher
Pole David Coulthard
Fastest lap Michael Schumacher

ROUND 15 – PACIFIC
Race Michael Schumacher
Pole David Coulthard
Fastest lap Michael Schumacher

ROUND 16 – JAPAN
Race Michael Schumacher
Pole Michael Schumacher
Fastest lap Michael Schumacher

ROUND 17 – AUSTRALIA
Race Damon Hill
Pole Damon Hill
Fastest lap Damon Hill

1995 DRIVERS' CHAMPIONSHIP

DRIVER	TEAM	POINTS
Michael Schumacher	Benetton	102
Damon Hill	Williams	69
David Coulthard	Williams	49
Johnny Herbert	Benetton	45
Jean Alesi	Ferrari	42
Gerhard Berger	Ferrari	31
Mika Hakkinen	McLaren	17
Olivier Panis	Ligier	16
Heinz-Harald Frentzen	Sauber	15
Mark Blundell	McLaren	13
Rubens Barrichello	Jordan	11
Eddie Irvine	Jordan	10
Martin Brundle	Ligier	7
Gianni Morbidelli	Arrows	5
Mika Salo	Tyrrell	5
Jean-Christophe Boullion	Sauber	3
Aguri Suzuki	Ligier	1
Pedro Lamy	Minardi	1

Schumacher could not believe his luck, and he was not about to waste his chance as he cruised to another victory.

Hill's focus, however, was relentless as he knew nothing less than a win at the next round at Hungaroring would keep him in the Championship race with the devastating Schumacher.

At the start of the race, the Williams drivers got the jump on Schumacher and looked comfortable and Schumacher never got within 10 seconds of the Williams man throughout the remainder of the race.

SHORTS

For the third round, the teams returned to Imola for the San Marino Grand Prix for the first time since the tragedies which had marred the 1994 event, and Mansell joined the fray after his McLaren team at last built a cockpit big enough for the British driver.

Open Championship

Second place was taken away from Schumacher as his car coasted to a halt four laps from the finish so Hill took the chequered flag and clawed back 10 points in the gap at the top of the standings, throwing the Championship race wide open again.

Before the Belgian Grand Prix, Schumacher confirmed the worst-kept secret in Formula One as he announced that from 1996 he would drive for the Ferrari team in a deal that would reportedly pay him $25 million a year.

Schumacher started from 16th and Hill was fifth on the grid, after the two qualifying sessions were hit by a deluge of rain. It didn't make much difference, as by lap 16 Schumacher was leading with Hill second, and that was how it finished – but not without controversy.

During the first stops, fire engulfed Irvine, who was fortunate to get out without injury. As the other drivers came in, Schumacher took a risk and thought the track was going to dry quickly, while Hill stayed on wets. As the drivers rejoined the race, Hill was all over Schumacher, who seemed initially to block his way past.

Eventually, Hill got past Schumacher and opened a gap, but as the track dried the German driver came back and re-took the lead. Just as Hill came in for slicks it started to rain again, as Schumacher stayed out until his scheduled fuel stop.

When he changed tyres the rain was still falling, and as Hill also changed to fresh wet tyres the race looked set for a tense finish, with just two seconds between the two, after an inexplicable period during which the safety car came out because of the conditions.

But it was not to be, as Hill was penalized for pit-lane speeding and forced to observe a stop-go penalty. That virtually gifted the race to Schumacher, while Hill held on for second, but he was now 15 points behind in the Championship.

After the Belgian race Williams launched an official protest against Schumacher's driving style, when he apparently made it difficult for Hill to pass. The FIA did penalize Schumacher, but only in the form of a one-race ban suspended for four races.

In Italy, it was a case of déjà vu from Britain as Schumacher and Hill again crashed out together on lap 23 with Hill attempting to overtake and both went out. It produced an amazing response from Schumacher, who had to be held back by race offi-

Michael Schumacher and Damon Hill battle for first place during the Belgian Grand Prix.

David Coulthard showed that he was gaining ground and claimed his maiden win at the Portuguese Grand Prix at Estoril.

1995 CONSTRUCTORS' CUP

TEAM (Engine)	POINTS
BENETTON RENAULT	137
WILLIAMS RENAULT	112
FERRARI	73
McLAREN MERCEDES	30
LIGIER MUGEN	24
JORDAN PEUGEOT	21
SAUBER FORD	18
TYRRELL YAMAHA	5
FOOTWORK HART	5
MINARDI FORD	1

cials from confronting Hill. The two Ferraris looked like winning and Herbert was left to pick up the pieces for his second win of the season.

Coulthard claimed pole for the 53-lap race from Schumacher, Berger and Hill, but the young Williams driver was soon out of the race as a wheel-bearing went on his car after just 13 laps. He had looked a potential winner, and it was a bitter blow.

Portugal hosted the next round, and, after being linked to a move to McLaren at the end of the season, Coulthard made his mark at Estoril as he won his first Grand Prix in spectacular style.

Maiden win for Coulthard

Coulthard took pole position for the 71-lap race, and duly led from start to finish. Schumacher finished second from Hill in third to open up a 17-point gap in the Championship.

Hill went to the Nurburgring for the European Grand Prix knowing that only a win would realistically keep his Championship hopes alive. Unfortunately for him, it did not happen and, in fact, Schumacher produced a superb drive in variable conditions to win.

As Hill crashed out nine laps from the finish, it left Schumacher needing just three points from the final three races to win his second world crown. Coulthard had claimed pole for the race, with Hill alongside him on the front row.

Storming Schumacher

But Schumacher produced two spells of genius in the damp conditions to reel in his competitors in front of his home crowd, and win a race with a performance that astounded all who watched it – and even some that competed in it.

It was no surprise, then, to see Schumacher make the long journey to Aida for the Pacific Grand Prix and take a victory that sealed the World Championship, and left the world in awe of the latest driver to take the sport by storm.

Coulthard had again claimed pole with Hill in second, but Schumacher passed both with relative ease to take his eighth win of the season. Hill was a distant third, and looked jaded as he was forced to admit defeat.

In the final two races of the season, Schumacher set a record for race wins in a season as he won in Japan. To rub salt into the wound, both Williams failed to finish as Hakkinen at last showed his true potential with a great performance in second place.

In the final race in Australia, Hill finished the season on a high with a well-earned win, but the weekend was marred by a serious practice accident involving Hakkinen.

Hakkinen suffered a puncture on his McLaren and spun into a tyre-wall that was just one tyre deep, before hitting a concrete wall at high speed. Hakkinen smashed his head on the steering wheel and only the swift actions of Professor Sid Watkins at the side of the track saved the Finnish driver's life. Hakkinen went on to make a full recovery.

In fact, only eight drivers finished the race at Adelaide as Schumacher, Alesi, Moreno, Barrichello, Coulthard and Inoue all went out in accidents amidst others with mechanical problems. Behind winner Hill, Panis finished an amazing second for Ligier, while Morbidelli was third in the Arrows. It was a lofty finish to a remarkable season.

Mika Hakkinen

CAREER DETAILS

1968	Born 28 September, Helsinki, Finland
1974-86	Five times Finnish Karting Champion
1987	Formula Ford 1600 Finnish, Swedish and Nordic Champion
1988	GM Lotus Euroseries champion. Second in British Vauxhall Lotus Challenge
1991	F1 debut with Lotus
1993	Moves to McLaren. First podium finish
1994	Survives horrific crash in Adelaide
1997	Maiden Grand Prix win at Jerez
1998	World Champion with McLaren
1999	World Champion with McLaren
2000	Runner-up
2001	Announces decision to take a year off racing
2002	Announces retirement at Monaco Grand Prix

FORMULA ONE RECORD

Year	Team	Wins	Poles	Fast laps	Pts
1991	Lotus	0	0	0	2
1992	Lotus	0	0	0	11
1993	McLaren	0	0	0	4
1994	McLaren	0	0	0	26
1995	McLaren	0	0	0	17
1996	McLaren	0	0	0	31
1997	McLaren	1	1	1	27
1998	McLaren	8	9	6	100
1999	McLaren	5	11	6	76
2000	McLaren	4	5	9	89
2001	McLaren	2	0	3	37

INCREDIBLE RAW SPEED and shrewd guidance ensured Mika Hakkinen was bound for great things. He miraculously fought back from a near-fatal accident to claim back-to-back World Championships.

Mika Hakkinen's successive World Championships with McLaren-Mercedes were all the sweeter for being the fruition of his extraordinarily determined recovery from serious head injuries at the end of 1995.

He was at McLaren for four years before he scored his maiden Grand Prix victory, at Jerez in 1997. Once he had rid himself of a tendency to make the odd rash error, he became a long-term genuine threat.

Hakkinen, the son of a harbourmaster, enjoyed an outstanding junior career, entering the 1989 Formula Three series as winner of Formula Ford titles and the GM Lotus Euroseries champion, where he had outscored team-mate Alan McNish and Heinz-Harald Frentzen. His campaign in British Formula Three was his first career setback, as his team had little experience of this category. He finished sixth as David Brabham won the title.

In 1990, however, he joined West Surrey Racing and stormed to the title, challenged all the way by fellow Finn Mika Salo. He won 12 races that season and should have won the prestigious finale race in Macau, but a last-lap accident handed Michael Schumacher his first major result.

The Finn was snapped up by Lotus and made his Formula One debut in 1991. The car was not up to battling with the front-runners, but Hakkinen impressed with his sublime car control. The following year was better and he strung together some promising results by squeezing every ounce of potential from the Ford-powered Lotus 107.

Then came his big break – though he needed patience to see it as such. Ron Dennis, anxious to find cover for a prevaricating Ayrton Senna, signed the Finn as a reserve. Senna chose to race the whole season, but Hakkinen's chance came when team-mate Michael Andretti failed to cut the mustard and returned to the United States prematurely. In Hakkinen's first race, in Portugal, he out-qualified Senna, the qualifying master. Finishing third in Japan, he had done enough to secure a full-time drive for 1994.

Ford, Peugeot and Mercedes engines in three successive years made this a lean, inconsistent spell for McLaren. Lack of performance from the car

"Deciding the Championship in the last Grand Prix is nerve-racking. I do not recommend it to anyone."

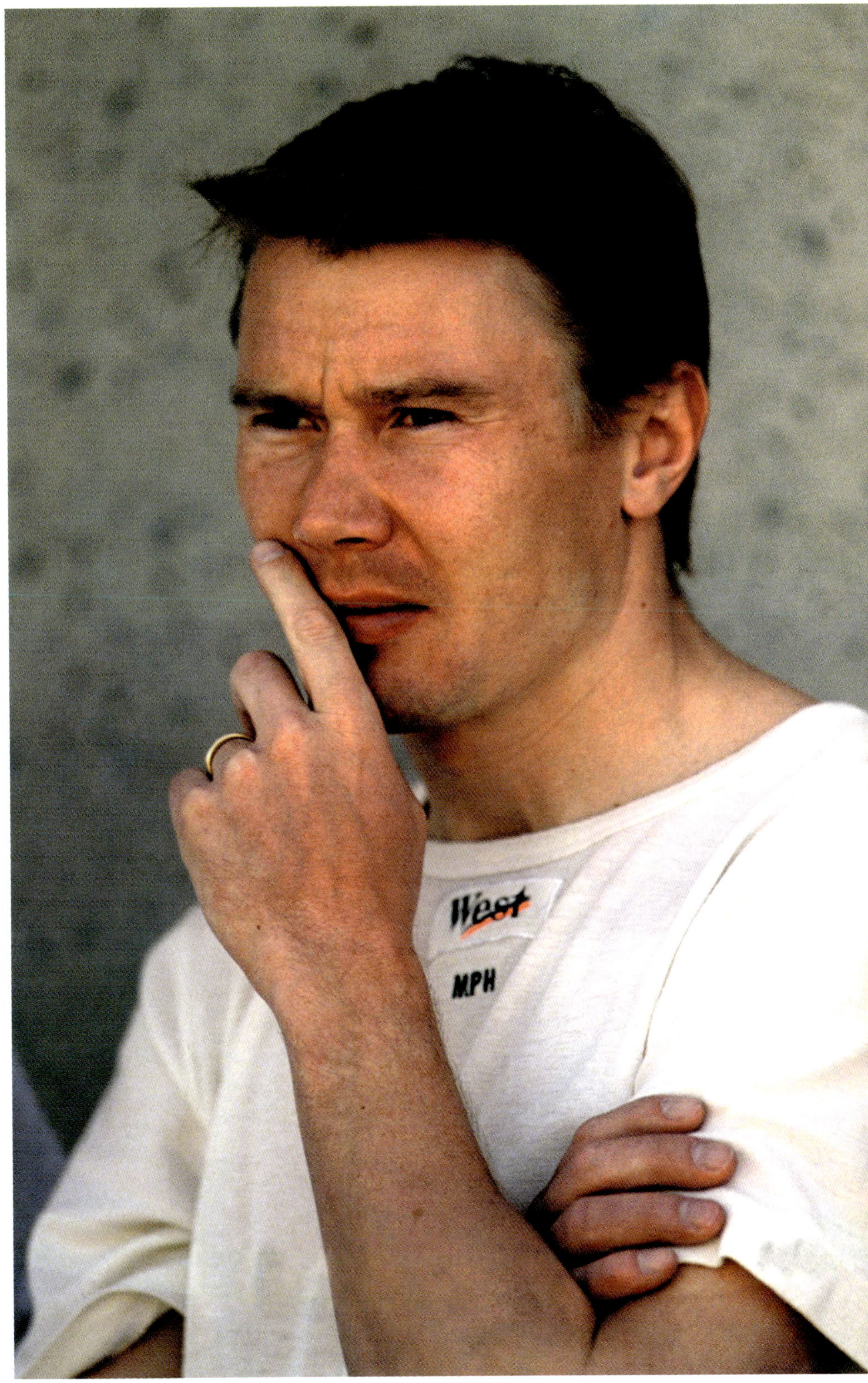

engendered desperation in the ambitious Finn. Rash first-corner moves at Monaco and Hockenheim eliminated him in 1994, the latter earning him a one-race ban and a hot-headed reputation. The next season promised a better future, with second-place finishes at Monza and Suzuka.

The last race of the season, however, nearly claimed his life after he suffered serious head injuries in Adelaide. Prompt medical action and an emergency tracheotomy saved his life and he spent the winter establishing his fitness and mental equilibrium.

His first test session back in the car attracted huge attention. Would his appetite have been diminished? Absolutely not, was the answer, as he proceeded for the next two years to be a front-runner. "Normally it is noisy but everyone was a bit nervous," he said of his arrival for the refamiliarizing test. "When I accelerated, it felt fantastic. I thought, 'This is great, this is fun,' and I did not feel scared any more."

The breakthrough Grand Prix victory continued to elude him until he was gifted victory in the 1997 Jerez season-closer by Jacques Villeneuve. That first experience of the top step of the podium seemed to liberate him, and he never looked back.

Eight wins yielded the title in 1998. The defence of his title was a far tougher contest, in which he twice made nervous mistakes which cost him race wins (both in Italy), but he came back resoundingly to retain his crown in somewhat controversial political circumstances.

"I will be an old man before I understand any of this," he announced, when he was proclaimed World Champion following Ferrari's disqualification in Malaysia in 1999.

"I don't really like it. It is not the way to win a title. It doesn't feel good to me."

Off-form for the beginning of 2000, he lost his crown to an ebullient Schumacher. The 2001 season, too, started appallingly, with the Finn a shadow of his former self. His form picked up in the tail end of the season, with victories in Britain and the US. But after finishing fifth in the Championship, Hakkinen anounced that he wanted to take a year off. His seat at McLaren has gone to fellow "Flying Finn" Kimi Raikkonen and it remains to be seen if Hakkinen will ever return.

A breakthrough victory in Spain in 1997 guaranteed that Hakkinen did not look back until he had won his first crown in 1998.

Previous page: *Hakkinen in action in Japan.*

1996
Hill follows in father's footsteps

TALKING POINT

'THE NEW BOY DONE GOOD'

The arrival of Canadian Jacques Villeneuve in Formula One was heralded as a positive move by the Williams team, but few could have envisaged the mark he would leave on the sport in his first season.

Villeneuve, son of the late Gilles, put his Williams on pole for the opening race of the season in Melbourne, and was only denied victory by an oil leak which allowed his team-mate Damon Hill to reel in what was an impressive lead.

The youngster's talent was shown throughout the season, and he confounded belief as he battled with team-mate Hill and kept him waiting for the title until the final race of the season in Japan.

After claiming two drivers' Championship successes in as many years and helping to achieve Benetton's first constructors' title, Michael Schumacher decided to chance his arm elsewhere, and signed a money-spinning deal to move to Ferrari.

Schumacher had narrowly beaten Damon Hill to the 1995 crown, but his departure from the Renault-backed Benetton team handed the Englishman his best chance of emulating the feats of his father Graham. With the Williams-Renault being the quickest car on the track, Hill did not disappoint.

Schumacher decided to join Maranello-based Ferrari in a new line-up which saw him and Eddie Irvine act as replacements for Jean Alesi and Gerhard Berger. They, in turn, opted to fill the void at reigning champions Benetton left by Ferrari-bound Schumacher and Johnny Herbert's departure to Sauber.

The first race of the season did not go according to plan for the Forti team, as both drivers failed to qualify, but the biggest shock was that the talented Villeneuve was on pole on his debut after out-qualifying his new team-mate Hill.

Villeneuve, who had tested throughout the winter to ensure his first year of Grand Prix racing would start positively, was quickest off the grid after a restart and led until lap 53, when an oil leak forced him to slow down and settle for second place behind Hill.

Jordan jinx

The race began dramatically when Martin Brundle's Jordan launched itself while jostling in the midfield and rolled into the gravel trap halfway through the first lap.

The Briton was lucky to survive after his Jordan split in two on impact, but he climbed out and heroically ran back to the pits to take the restart.

Michael Schumacher's Ferrari spell started less dramatically – but just as disappointingly – when brake difficulties ended his race on lap 32, to leave him watching his old rival Hill cruising to victory ahead of Villeneuve for a Williams one-two.

Irvine made up for the retirement of Schumacher as he finished third for Ferrari, with Benetton's Berger, McLaren's Hakkinen and Tyrrell driver Salo completing the points.

Hill qualified on pole for the next race ahead of Jordan's Brazilian Barrichello, and took the lead at the start as he looked for a second straight win, while Marques made a disastrous start to his Formula One career by spinning off on the opening lap.

Alesi, starting from fifth on the grid, was Hill's only real challenger during the race and the Italian, whose Benetton team-mate Berger retired on lap 26 with gearbox problems, held the lead for two laps during the pit-stop periods. But Hill eventually led him home by almost 18 seconds with everybody else a lap down. Hakkinen finished fourth behind Michael Schumacher, with Salo fifth for Tyrrell and Ligier's Panis sixth.

Hill holds his own

Hill was on a roll, however, and produced another dominant display as he won for the third time in as

Yachtsmen view Olivier Panis' win on screen in the harbour at the Monaco Grand Prix.

many races in the Argentinian Grand Prix, and this time Villeneuve was back to form to challenge him for top spot.

Hill was on pole, with Michael Schumacher alongside him and Villeneuve and Alesi behind. At the off Hill was quickest, and was never headed as he powered through to an easy victory. Hakkinen retired on lap 19 with throttle difficulties, and Michael Schumacher joined him on lap 46 when a rear wing failure brought his race to an abrupt and dramatic end.

At the European Grand Prix in late April, Villeneuve qualified second behind Hill, but made the better start and led Schumacher, who was quicker than the Briton's Williams in front of him. Villeneuve kept his cool to hold off the German in a battle to the line to take the chequered flag for the first time since switching from America.

Williams' perfection

Hill returned to winning ways in the San Marino Grand Prix at Imola in early May as he maintained Williams' 100 per cent start to the season and secured his fourth win in five races. Schumacher put his Ferrari on pole ahead of Hill and the impressive Coulthard, but it was the latter, starting from fourth, who raced into the lead. He remained in front for the opening 19 laps, but lost out as Hill benefited from a quick pit-stop to move ahead.

Coulthard, however, remained in contention along with Schumacher and Villeneuve, before his McLaren developed gearbox problems and he called it a day on lap 44. His departure left Schumacher and Villeneuve as the only men capable of catching Hill.

But Villeneuve suffered suspension problems six laps from the end, and was eventually classified 11th, so it was Schumacher who trailed Hill home, more than 16 seconds down.

Monaco magic

The sixth round of the Championship, in Monaco, produced one of the most enthralling races of the decade as Frenchman Olivier Panis mastered the changing conditions to drive to a remarkable victory, Ligier's first since 1981.

Schumacher was on pole ahead of Hill and Villeneuve, while Forti's Andrea Montermini, who did not qualify in San Marino, was a non-starter after a crash in practice. Hill was quickest off the grid in wet conditions and five drivers crashed out on the opening lap. Schumacher was the most significant of these, while the Minardi duo of Lamy and Fisichella were joined by the Arrows of Verstappen and Jordan's Rubens Barrichello. But engine failure cost Hill a potential fifth win of the season as he exited the race on lap 40. Alesi was left in front, but suspension failure forced him out, with Panis assuming

Rubens Barrichello is upset after crashing out on the first lap of the Monaco Grand Prix with four other cars.

the lead and holding his nerve to head home Coulthard by almost five seconds, with Sauber drivers Herbert and Frentzen third and fourth; amazingly, those four were the only drivers to finish the race.

The struggle for the Forti team continued in the Spanish Grand Prix, as Montermini and Luca Badoer both failed to qualify again, but it was all smiles for Hill, who secured pole position in an all-Williams front row with Schumacher third fastest.

It wasn't to be for long, however, as Villeneuve took the lead with Hill struggling in torrential conditions. Panis failed to build on his Monaco win as damage from an accident forced him to retire on lap two. Villeneuve held his advantage until lap 11, when Schumacher showed his class in the conditions after Hill had crashed out one lap earlier.

Schumacher eased to his first win for Ferrari, more than 45 seconds ahead of Benetton's Alesi, who had used his experience to get the better of Villeneuve. Frentzen, Hakkinen and Diniz ended in the points as the conditions took their toll once again, and only six drivers finished.

A titanic battle between team-mates Hill and Villeneuve in the Canadian Grand Prix in mid-June saw the latter just denied a memorable win at the circuit named after his late father, Gilles, in Montreal.

Hill prevented Villeneuve from starting from pole in front of the Canadian debutant's fanatical home crowd, and the Briton emerged ahead of the rest of the field into the opening corner.

But Hill returned to the lead on lap 36, and remained there to lead home Villeneuve by little

RACE BY RACE DETAILS

ROUND 1 – AUSTRALIA
Race Damon Hill
Pole Jacques Villeneuve
Fastest lap Jacques Villeneuve

ROUND 2 – BRAZIL
Race Damon Hill
Pole Damon Hill
Fastest lap Damon Hill

ROUND 3 – ARGENTINA
Race Damon Hill
Pole Damon Hill
Fastest lap Jean Alesi

ROUND 4 – EUROPE
Race Jacques Villeneuve
Pole Damon Hill
Fastest lap Damon Hill

ROUND 5 – SAN MARINO
Race Damon Hill
Pole Michael Schumacher
Fastest lap Damon Hill

ROUND 6 – MONACO
Race Olivier Panis
Pole Michael Schumacher
Fastest lap Jean Alesi

ROUND 7 – SPAIN
Race Michael Schumacher
Pole Damon Hill
Fastest lap Michael Schumacher

ROUND 8 – CANADA
Race Damon Hill
Pole Damon Hill
Fastest lap Jacques Villeneuve

ROUND 9 – FRANCE
Race Damon Hill
Pole Michael Schumacher
Fastest lap Jacques Villeneuve

ROUND 10 – BRITAIN
Race Jacques Villeneuve
Pole Damon Hill
Fastest lap Jacques Villeneuve

ROUND 11 – GERMANY
Race Damon Hill
Pole Damon Hill
Fastest lap Damon Hill

ROUND 12 – HUNGARY
Race Jacques Villeneuve
Pole Michael Schumacher
Fastest lap Damon Hill

ROUND 13 – BELGIUM
Race Michael Schumacher
Pole Jacques Villeneuve
Fastest lap Gerhard Berger

ROUND 14 – ITALY
Race Michael Schumacher
Pole Damon Hill
Fastest lap Michael Schumacher

ROUND 15 – PORTUGAL
Race Jacques Villeneuve
Pole Damon Hill
Fastest lap Jacques Villeneuve

ROUND 16 – JAPAN
Race Damon Hill
Pole Jacques Villeneuve
Fastest lap Jacques Villeneuve

1996 DRIVERS' CHAMPIONSHIP

DRIVER	TEAM	POINTS
Damon Hill	Williams	97
Jacques Villeneuve	Williams	78
Michael Schumacher	Ferrari	59
Jean Alesi	Benetton	47
Mika Hakkinen	McLaren	31
Gerhard Berger	Benetton	21
David Coulthard	McLaren	18
Rubens Barrichello	Jordan	14
Olivier Panis	Ligier	13
Eddie Irvine	Ferrari	11
Martin Brundle	Jordan	8
Heinz-Harald Frentzen	Sauber	7
Mika Salo	Tyrrell	5
Johnny Herbert	Sauber	4
Pedro Diniz	Ligier	2
Jos Verstappen	Footwork	1

more than four seconds. Schumacher retired on lap 41 with driveshaft failure, and Berger spun off one lap later when in the points.

Alesi's consistency was rewarded with another podium position as he ended almost one minute down on Hill, and Coulthard and Hakkinen finished in the points for McLaren. Jordan driver Brundle scored a point in sixth.

The season returned to Europe two weeks later for the French Grand Prix, and once again the dominance of Williams told, Hill winning from Villeneuve as the duo left the remainder of the field trailing.

Ferrari woes

But for the emerging Ferrari team the race proved a disaster. After claiming pole position, Schumacher was a non-starter when hit by an engine failure on the formation lap. Team-mate Irvine fared little better, starting from the back before retiring on lap five.

With Hill assuming pole position as Schumacher failed to take to the grid, he marched into the lead in front of Villeneuve and was never headed as he extended his Championship advantage over the Canadian to 25 points.

Having won six of the nine races of the season, Hill headed into the British Grand Prix at Silverstone in mid July planning a seventh victory for the adoring home fans. After grabbing pole position from his team-mate, few would have bet against him achieving it. But Villeneuve beat him into the opening corner and he remained in front for the majority of the race as Hill was forced to retire on lap 26 when a wheel-bearing problem forced him out.

Ferrari had suffered another difficult race, with Irvine and Schumacher both retiring in the opening five laps with gearbox problems, while Alesi briefly led, before exiting the race on lap 44 with the same wheel-bearing problem which had ended Hill's race.

The Italian Fisichella was the last of the 11 finishers at Silverstone, but was replaced at Minardi for the next round of the Championship in Germany by compatriot Giovanni Lavaggi. Lavaggi, however, failed to qualify, while the Forti team – which had failed to qualify at Silverstone two weeks earlier – ended its brief Grand Prix spell when a lack of funding meant no engines were available.

Hill down, but not out

Hill may have been looking good for the title, but at Hockenheim news emerged that he was to lose his seat at Williams at the end of the season to Sauber's Frentzen. He ensured his current employers were red-faced by securing pole alongside Berger, but his position within the team had now become very uncomfortable.

Benetton driver Berger made the bigger impact at the start of the race and took the lead, then stayed in front until pitting on lap 23, by which time Hakkinen had retired with gearbox problems.

Berger assumed the lead again after Hill made his routine stop, but three laps from the end the engine in the Austrian's Benetton failed, and he was eventually classified 13th and last. So Hill took a fortunate victory ahead of Berger's team-mate Alesi, with Villeneuve and Schumacher behind them. Coulthard and Barrichello completed the points positions.

Hill's 21-point lead over Villeneuve was reduced when the Canadian won for a third time in his debut season at the Hungarian Grand Prix. Schumacher was on pole and led for the opening 18 laps, before Villeneuve and Hill exchanged the lead three times.

A water-pump problem ended Coulthard's race, and Irvine suffered gearbox failure. Berger was another retirement with engine problems on lap 64, the same lap on which Villeneuve took the lead for the final time as he led home Hill by less than eight tenths of a second. A throttle problem ended Schumacher's race seven laps short, and he was classified ninth.

Villeneuve turned his pole position in Belgium into a race lead in damp conditions before Coulthard took over at the front on lap 15. The advantage then switched between the McLaren of Hakkinen, Ferrari's Schumacher and Villeneuve in

Jacques Villeneuve holds off Michael Schumacher in his successful bid to win the British Grand Prix.

Jacques Villeneuve's win in Portugal kept Damon HIll waiting for his title, but he claimed his reward in the final race in Japan.

1996 CONSTRUCTORS' CUP

TEAM (Engine)	POINTS
WILLIAMS RENAULT	175
FERRARI	70
BENETTON RENAULT	68
McLAREN MERCEDES	49
JORDAN PEUGEOT	22
LIGIER MUGEN-HONDA	15
SAUBER FORD	11
TYRRELL YAMAHA	5
FOOTWORK HART	1

the Williams, before Schumacher moved in front as the circuit began to dry. The German stayed in front to win by more than five seconds from Villeneuve, and the result reduced Hill's advantage to 13 points with three races remaining, as the Briton managed only fifth after a pit-stop mix-up.

Schumacher secured back-to-back wins in the next race, with his first for Ferrari in front of the *tifosi* at Monza. But more significantly the pressure had seemingly got to Hill, now confirmed to be leaving Williams at the end of the season, and he crashed out of the lead to hand victory to the German.

Hill was on pole and led for the opening five laps before spinning off early. Coulthard crashed out on the second lap and gearbox difficulties ended Berger's race on lap five, while Frentzen failed to show the promise that prompted Williams to sign him as he crashed out on lap seven.

Hill had the chance to wrap up the title in Portugal after Villeneuve had failed to score at Monza. And the Briton looked likely to succeed when he led for the first 48 laps after claiming pole position.

SHORTS

Villeneuve's short wait for his first Formula One victory ended in late April at the European Grand Prix, the fourth round of the Championship. The Canadian demonstrated his potential with a calm and collected performance to hold off a determined challenge by Michael Schumacher and halt Hill's run of successes.

Victorious Villeneuve

But Villeneuve produced a remarkable drive to win and take the battle to the final round of the season in Japan. The Canadian overtook Schumacher in a dramatic confidence-filled move and then powered past Hill for a deserved win. Schumacher ended third, with Alesi, Irvine and Berger behind him.

Hill's second place, however, left him needing just one point to become the first second-generation Champion in emulating the achievements of his father Graham. And after starting quicker than pole-sitter Villeneuve at the Japanese circuit of Suzuka – scene of many a dramatic title decider – he did not disappoint as he led from start to finish.

Alesi crashed out on the opening lap and when, on lap 36, Villeneuve lost a wheel from his Williams, the title race was complete. The improving Hakkinen was third, with Berger, Brundle and Frentzen ending in the top six, but Hill refused to buckle under the pressure of Schumacher and he ended his spell at Williams with a win to seal the Championship.

Hill had benefited from the awesome power of the Renault engine in his Williams, and after Schumacher's defection to Ferrari, the season was destined to end with a Williams driver as Champion. It was only thanks to the talent of newcomer Villeneuve that the battle remained open until the final race of the season, but no one doubted that Hill deserved the crown after his two near misses in the previous seasons.

Williams' decision to axe him came as a shock, but the emergence of Villeneuve kept a driver capable of winning the title with the team.

Jacques Villeneuve

CAREER DETAILS

1971	Born 9 April, St Jean-Sur-Richelieu, Quebec
1989	Italian Formula 3
1992	Runner-up in Japanese Formula 3
1993	Formula Atlantic Rookie of the Year
1994	PPG Indy Car (CART) Rookie of the Year
1995	PPG Indy Car champion
1996	Joins Williams and is runner-up in title race
1997	World Champion with Williams
1999	Moves to BAR in team's debut year
2001	Finishes seventh for the second year running
2002	Slumps to 12th with just four points
2003	Quits the sport before the Japanese Grand Prix

FORMULA ONE RECORD

Year	Team	Wins	Poles	Fast laps	Pts
1996	Williams	3	6	78	2
1997	Williams	10	3	81	1
1998	Williams	0	0	21	5
1999	BAR	0	0	0	-
2000	BAR	0	0	0	7
2001	BAR	0	0	0	12
2002	BAR	0	0	0	4
2003	BAR	0	0	0	6

Jacques Villeneuve races to his win in the Spanish Grand Prix at Jerez in 1997.

HE IS THE SON of a legendary father, but the outspoken and free-spirited Jacques Villeneuve achieved his IndyCar and Formula One titles absolutely on his own terms.

Jacques Villeneuve was 11 when his father Gilles was killed in 1982. He was brought up in Monaco, rather than his native Quebec, and steered through adolescence by his former sports teacher Craig Pollock. However, he had spent his formative years travelling the motorsport circuit and was soon lured by the siren call of high-powered engines.

After a trial racing course, he tried his hand in the Italian Formula Three series. For three years from 1989 he failed to impress and in 1992 moved to the Far East, to the Japanese Formula Three series where he scored three victories and finished second overall. An invitation to compete in the 1992 Trois Rivières race in Quebec proved his launchpad. He raced to an outstanding third place and Pollock arranged for him to race in Formula Atlantic in the 1993 season.

He scored seven poles and five wins from 15 starts, but a few crucial errors meant he finished the season third overall. His team took him with them as they progressed to IndyCar racing. Villeneuve stormed the scene, picking up the Rookie of the Year award after winning at Elkhart Lake and finishing a close second in the Indy 500. The following year the self-assured young French-Canadian became, at the age of 24, the youngest driver to win the Indy 500. He took the title with great conviction – and won his passport to the best car in Formula One.

Villeneuve signed a two-year contract with Williams with an option year, and shrewdly spent the winter testing intensively. "When most drivers start racing, nobody knows who they are until they make a name for themselves," he said before the 1996 season. "But when you start racing with a name like mine, everybody knows who you are and expects you to succeed."

His debut was a sentimentalist's dream. He qualified on pole in Melbourne – a track he had never seen before – and could have won the race but for an oil leak. He finished the season runner-up to team-mate Damon Hill, having won

"He is the only one who can give Schumacher some stick. He is like Senna as a person and Prost as a driver."

Bernie Ecclestone

four races at the Nurburgring, Silverstone, the Hungaroring and Estoril (where he executed an exquisite passing manoeuvre, going round Michael Schumacher on the outside).

Formula One had a new star – a tough, aggressive racer who boasted a quirky personal style ("The man is a millionaire but always looks like an unmade bed," as an Australian newspaper noted) and was not afraid to talk about the thrill of danger. "I'm not racing because my father left too early and I have to carry the name and tradition," he said. "I don't really care about tradition. I love this sport because I like being on the edge. When you are riding on that edge you are in a different world. Nothing else exists at all."

In 1997 he delivered the title after slugging out a none-too-pretty campaign with Michael Schumacher. His victory came after the German's outrageous blocking manoeuvre at Jerez. "I spotted him checking his mirror," Villeneuve said afterwards.

"Even though I was 10 or 15 metres behind him, I just went for it and braked very late. I was actually surprised that he hadn't closed the door yet. But it was just a matter of seconds before he decided to turn in on me. But he didn't do it well enough because he went off and I didn't."

With the loss of Renault power units, Williams were not a dominant force in 1998. Villeneuve showed good temperament by dragging the car to points-scoring finishes and two third-place finishes without showing frustration. In 1999, however, he signed for British American Racing, a team founded by his mentor Pollock. The inaugural season was a non-points yielding horror, the 2000 season showed some improvement with seven points finishes, including four fourths, but still no podiums. He finally sprayed the post-race champagne for BAR in Spain in 2001 when he finished third and did so again in Germany that year with another third. But, just when things were on the up, his manager and team boss was ousted by David Richards, the team's performances dropped off and, with the arrival of Richards' golden boy Jenson Button and the imminent requirement from Honda for a Japanese driver, Villeneuve could not care less in 2003 and quit the sport in Suzuka on the eve of what would have been his final race.

As one Australian newspaper put it, he is "a millionaire but always looks like an unmade bed".

1997
Victory for Villeneuve

TALKING POINT

SCHUMACHER'S CRAZY MOVE

After a season-long battle with the superior Williams-Renault package of Jacques Villeneuve, Michael Schumacher undermined his achievements throughout the year by attempting to win the title in the most unsportsmanlike circumstances in Spain.

With a one-point advantage, Schumacher needed to finish ahead of Villeneuve in the European Grand Prix at Jerez. But as the Williams driver tried to pass Schumacher, who was leading, Villeneuve saw the German's Ferrari veer towards him in an attempt to ram him off the road. The move failed and as Villeneuve was crowned Champion, Schumacher was left to contemplate his actions in the gravel trap.

Jackie Stewart congratulates Rubens Barrichello after taking second place at the Monaco Grand Prix.

After serving his apprenticeship in Formula One, Jacques Villeneuve demonstrated the potential he had shown in winning America's IndyCar series. Nobody doubted the talk that he could become a Champion, and the Canadian did not disappoint. His father Gilles had proven himself a front-runner in the sport during the 1970s before his death. And Villeneuve underlined his growing reputation to win the title which had eluded his father.

He benefited from being the number one at Williams after the team had chosen to blood German Heinz-Harald Frentzen in place of newly-crowned Champion Damon Hill. Villeneuve received the full backing of his team, and duly retained the Championship for Renault-backed Williams.

His closest challenger, right up until the final race of the season, was Ferrari's Michael Schumacher. World Champion Hill, however, was left with no option but to move to Arrows. However, he could qualify only 20th in his first experience of the Yamaha-powered Arrows. He didn't race, however, because of throttle problems.

Villeneuve's hopes of starting the season in style were dashed on the opening lap in Melbourne when Ferrari's Eddie Irvine collided with him at the first corner. Sauber's Johnny Herbert was also caught up in the incident as his race ended.

Opposite: Race officials remove the debris of Olivier Panis' car from the track at the Canadian Grand Prix. Panis broke both his legs.

McLaren break their barren spell

Coulthard was trailed home by Michael Schumacher and team-mate Mika Hakkinen as Frentzen disappeared three laps from the end with brake-disc failure. It was McLaren's first win since 1993.

Villeneuve returned to the top of the podium two weeks later in Brazil as he got his Championship challenge on track at Interlagos. He won ahead of Berger, with the improving Panis third.

The domination of the Williams-Renault partnership continued in the third round in Argentina, and resulted in another win for Villeneuve. Just as in Brazil two weeks earlier, Villeneuve got his strategy spot on as he pitted earlier than his rivals and ended in front for the win. This time it was Irvine who pushed him for victory, the Ulsterman losing out by less than one second.

Coulthard and Michael Schumacher tangled in an opening-lap incident which put both of them out. Frentzen's points-less start to the season continued with a fifth-lap retirement through clutch failure. Panis, Barrichello, Fisichella and Hill joined the list of casualties before Irvine held the lead for five laps. Villeneuve returned in front after the pit-stop shake-up and held on for the win.

At San Marino, Frentzen finally demonstrated his potential when he qualified on the front row alongside Villeneuve, but the Canadian made the better impression at the start and led. Berger spun off on lap four, while Herbert and Ralf Schumacher retired before Frentzen moved into the lead on lap 26. He remained in front and won by more than one second from Michael Schumacher after Villeneuve retired on lap 40 with gearbox problems.

Stewart hit form

Michael Schumacher ended Williams' winning run when he dominated in the wet in Monaco, but more significantly the race marked the arrival of the Stewart team as a potential top-five team, with a magnificent drive by Barrichello.

Schumacher led throughout after heading Frentzen off the line, and won ahead of Barrichello by almost a minute. The race was stopped after 62 laps under the two-hour rule, despite being scheduled for 69 laps.

Hakkinen, Coulthard and Hill all crashed out on the opening lap and Herbert and Ralf Schumacher joined the list of retirements in the opening 10 laps. Villeneuve and Alesi were casualties on lap 16 before Frentzen also crashed out on lap 39. Barrichello benefited to finish second in only Stewart's fifth race.

Villeneuve returned to form at the Circuit de Catalunya as he overcame the heat to win the Spanish Grand Prix in late May. The hot conditions posed tyre problems, but Williams survived to hand Villeneuve his third win of the season. It was Panis, however, who made the most impact, as he finished second and pushed Villeneuve for the victory. But Panis' luck ran out in Canada three weeks later when he broke both his legs in a heavy collision with the barriers. The incident brought the race to a halt three laps earlier than anticipated.

The race also marked the debut of the talented Austrian Alexander Wurz, who stood in for Berger – who was suffering from a virus – at Benetton.

Prost opted to sign Italian Jarno Trulli from Minardi to replace the injured Panis, and the Brazilian Tarso Marques filled the vacant seat at the Faenza-based team. Morbidelli's spell with Sauber had lasted just two races, as the Swiss team chose to employ Norberto Fontana instead.

Schumacher won his second race in succession with a dominant performance at Magny-Cours. He led from the off and beat Frentzen to the chequered flag after the two had started from the front row of the grid. Villeneuve made no impression at the front as he finished fourth behind Irvine, while Alesi and Ralf Schumacher occupied the remaining points-scoring positions.

Hakkinen looked likely to end his search for a win in the British Grand Prix at Silverstone, only for engine failure to end his chances when in front. Villeneuve was on pole and took the lead, but Frentzen, who started from the back of the grid, collided with Minardi's Ukyo Katayama on the first lap and went out.

Villeneuve assumed the lead after Schumacher's departure, but a delay during his second pit-stop cost him, and Hakkinen moved in front. The McLaren driver was seemingly home and dry, only for an engine blow-out to end his race seven laps from the end. Alesi ended second behind Villeneuve from 11th on the grid, while Alexander Wurz marked his first Grand Prix finish with a superb third. Coulthard was fourth in his home event, Ralf Schumacher fifth and Hill scored a point for Arrows.

Berger back

Wurz's performance was to be his last of the season as Berger returned to action in dramatic style, holding off a determined challenge by Jordan's Fisichella to win the German Grand Prix at Hockenheim.

RACE BY RACE DETAILS

ROUND 1 – AUSTRALIA
Race David Coulthard
Pole Jacques Villeneuve
Fastest lap Heinz-Harald Frentzen

ROUND 2 – BRAZIL
Race Jacques Villeneuve
Pole Jacques Villeneuve
Fastest lap Jacques Villeneuve

ROUND 3 – ARGENTINA
Race Jacques Villeneuve
Pole Jacques Villeneuve
Fastest lap Gerhard Berger

ROUND 4 – SAN MARINO
Race Heinz-Harald Frentzen
Pole Jacques Villeneuve
Fastest lap Heinz-Harald Frentzen

ROUND 5 – MONACO
Race Michael Schumacher
Pole Heinz-Harald Frentzen
Fastest lap Michael Schumacher

ROUND 6 – SPAIN
Race Jacques Villeneuve
Pole Jacques Villeneuve
Fastest lap Giancarlo Fisichella

ROUND 7 – CANADA
Race Michael Schumacher
Pole Michael Schumacher
Fastest lap David Coulthard

ROUND 8 – FRANCE
Race Michael Schumacher
Pole Michael Schumacher
Fastest lap Michael Schumacher

ROUND 9 – BRITAIN
Race Jacques Villeneuve
Pole Jacques Villeneuve
Fastest lap Michael Schumacher

ROUND 10 – GERMANY
Race Gerhard Berger
Pole Gerhard Berger
Fastest lap Gerhard Berger

ROUND 11 – HUNGARY
Race Jacques Villeneuve
Pole Michael Schumacher
Fastest lap Heinz-Harald Frentzen

ROUND 12 – BELGIUM
Race Michael Schumacher
Pole Jacques Villeneuve
Fastest lap Jacques Villeneuve

ROUND 13 – ITALY
Race David Coulthard
Pole Jean Alesi
Fastest lap Mika Hakkinen

RACE 14 – AUSTRIA
Race Jacques Villeneuve
Pole Jacques Villeneuve
Fastest lap Jacques Villeneuve

ROUND 15 – LUXEMBOURG
Race Jacques Villeneuve
Pole Mika Hakkinen
Fastest lap Heinz-Harald Frentzen

ROUND 16 – JAPAN
Race Michael Schumacher
Pole Jacques Villeneuve
Fastest lap Heinz-Harald Frentzen

ROUND 17 – EUROPEAN
Race Mika Hakkinen
Pole Jacques Villeneuve
Fastest lap Heinz-Harald Frentzen

1997 DRIVERS' CHAMPIONSHIP

DRIVER	TEAM	POINTS
Jacques Villeneuve	Williams	81
Heinz-Harald Frentzen	Williams	42
David Coulthard	McLaren	36
Jean Alesi	Benetton	36
Gerhard Berger	Benetton	27
Mika Hakkinen	McLaren	27
Eddie Irvine	Ferrari	24
Giancarlo Fisichella	Jordan	20
Olivier Panis	Prost	16
Johnny Herbert	Sauber	15
Ralf Schumacher	Jordan	13
Damon Hill	Arrows	7
Rubens Barrichello	Stewart	6
Alexander Wurz	Benetton	4
Jarno Trulli	Minardi/Prost	3
Mika Salo	Tyrrell	2
Pedro Diniz	Arrows	2
Shinji Nakano	Prost	2
Nicola Larini	Sauber	1

Berger claimed pole position ahead of Fisichella, while Villeneuve could only manage ninth. The Benetton driver made an instant impression as he beat Fisichella in the race to the first corner. Villeneuve spun off on lap 33 to join team-mate Frentzen out of the race following his first-lap collision with Ferrari's Irvine. Schumacher ended second to Berger, with Hakkinen third and Trulli producing a magnificent drive to finish fourth for Minardi.

Sauber opted for another change with Morbidelli returning for the Hungarian Grand Prix in place of Fontana. His comeback had lasted just seven laps when engine failure forced him to retire from the race.

Amazing Arrows

Schumacher made the quickest start from pole position, but he lost the lead to Hill – performing out of his skin in his Arrows – on lap 11. The British driver remained in front before Frentzen moved ahead, only for a fuel-valve problem to end his race and hand the advantage back to Hill.

While Hill remained in front, Fisichella and Coulthard retired. But the reigning World Champion was denied a memorable win in the Arrows when his car slowed on the last lap, and Villeneuve was able to pass him for a fortunate win.

Schumacher extended his lead in the Championship with a well-deserved win in the wet in Belgium after Villeneuve paid the price for poor tyre choice in the conditions.

Villeneuve qualified on pole and led the opening four laps, but Schumacher moved into the lead and stayed there, as brother Ralf and Coulthard were casualties of the conditions when they both spun off.

The Canadian finished a distant fifth with Schumacher heading home Fisichella by almost half a minute. Hakkinen ended third, but was disqualified over a fuel irregularity, so Frentzen stood on the podium instead, with Herbert back in the points in fourth and Berger sixth.

McLaren's search for a win was finally ended in the Italian Grand Prix at Monza when a clever strategy put Coulthard out in front during a tight race in which the top eight finishers were separated by just 17 seconds. Benetton's Alesi was a surprise on pole for the race ahead of Frentzen and the impressive Fisichella, and he made a big impact at the start to take the lead. The Frenchman held the lead until lap 32 when Hakkinen, still searching for his first career win, moved ahead. It lasted two laps until the pit-stop sequence left Coulthard out in front after his McLaren team chose to leave him out longer than his rivals.

Coulthard kept his cool at the front to finish less than two seconds ahead of Alesi, while seven seconds separated the entire top six which included Frentzen, Fisichella, Villeneuve and Michael Schumacher.

Prost replacement Jarno Trulli, standing in for Olivier Panis, who was still out, was the star of the show in Austria two weeks later when he qualified third on the grid behind World-Championship-contender Villeneuve and Hakkinen. The Italian even had the temerity to lead for half the race. He made the best start in a Mugen-Honda powered car and beat Villeneuve and Hakkinen – who then retired on lap two with an engine blow-out – off the grid.

Alesi retired on lap 37, and one lap later Villeneuve moved ahead of Trulli and into the lead, while Irvine crashed out on the same lap. Other than through the pit-stop period, Villeneuve remained in front to the chequered flag. The Minardi of Marques

SHORTS

The European season started with the San Marino Grand Prix at Imola in late April, and it marked the arrival of Heinz-Harald Frentzen into the big league as he scored his first-ever win. After a disappointing opening to the season, he finally showed why he had landed a drive with Williams.

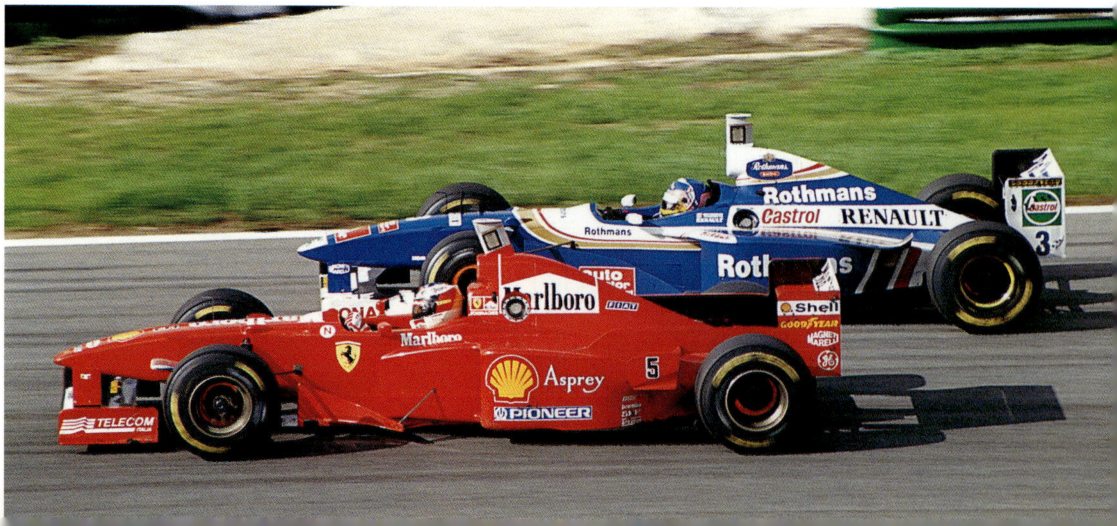

Michael Schumacher tries to take out Jacques Villeneuve at the European Grand Prix in Jerez – it ended in disaster for Schumacher.

Jacques Villeneuve celebrates his win at the British Grand Prix, a foretaste of the Championship crown that was to come.

1997 CONSTRUCTORS' CUP

TEAM (Engine)	POINTS
WILLIAMS RENAULT	123
FERRARI	102
BENETTON RENAULT	67
McLAREN MERCEDES	63
JORDAN PEUGEOT	33
PROST MUGEN-HONDA	21
SAUBER	16
ARROWS YAMAHA	9
STEWART FORD	6
TYRRELL FORD	2

was excluded for being underweight.

The Nurburgring in Germany hosted the Luxembourg Grand Prix in late-September, and Villeneuve moved into the ascendancy in his quest to become World Champion, although his win was only made possible by the demise of the McLarens.

Hakkinen qualified on pole and led the race until lap 43 when another engine blowout forced him into retirement, ironically just one lap after his team-mate Coulthard had exited the race from second place with the same problem. Frentzen ended third ahead of Berger, while the Brazilian Pedro Diniz scored his first point of the year for Arrows from fifteenth on the grid. Panis returned and proved he was over his injuries by picking up a point in sixth.

Villeneuve headed into the penultimate round with a nine-point lead over Schumacher, but the Japanese Grand Prix at Suzuka did not go according to plan for him. He was adjudged to have passed under yellow flags during qualifying, and was banned with a suspended sentence already hanging over his head. He raced under appeal and finished fifth, only to be disqualified and lose the points from the race.

Michael Schumacher, on the other hand, won the race to put himself in the driving seat with a one-point lead over the Williams driver. He had to hold off a spirited challenge from Frentzen, aiming to help his team-mate, to take the chequered flag first.

Villeneuve, on pole, was quickest off the line and led for two laps before Irvine moved in front. The two then exchanged the lead before Schumacher took over at the front, and despite sacrificing his advantage for three laps to Frentzen, to win.

Schumacher shame

Schumacher entered the European Grand Prix at the Spanish circuit with a one-point advantage over Villeneuve and needing simply to finish ahead of the Williams driver.

Qualifying ensured that the battle would continue throughout the race, with Villeneuve on pole and Schumacher alongside him. The German made the better start and led the race until he controversially tried to guarantee the title for Ferrari.

Villeneuve attempted to pass Schumacher on lap 46, and the race leader turned towards the Williams. He tried to damage the car but failed as Villeneuve went through and the manoeuvre left Schumacher stuck in the gravel trap. It was a return to his antics of 1994, but this time he had failed.

Villeneuve led until the penultimate lap when, knowing that third place was enough to secure the title, he allowed McLaren's Hakkinen and Coulthard to pass him. Berger finished fourth on his farewell to the sport, while Irvine and Frentzen claimed the final points of the season.

The win finally ended Hakkinen's bad luck and brought him his first-ever win during a long spell in Grand Prix racing. But the day belonged to Villeneuve, who ensured the title remained with Williams in Renault's final year in the sport.

Schumacher was rapped for his actions and his reputation was tarnished by the incident. He had amazingly lived with the far superior Williams-Renault package, but undermined his performance throughout the season with his move on Villeneuve at Jerez.

David Coulthard

DAVID COULTHARD's privilege has been to race in either a Williams or McLaren in his grand prix career. But he looks destined to rival Stirling Moss as Formula One's most successful driver without a title.

CAREER DETAILS

1971	Born on 27 March, in Twynholm, Scotland
1982–88	Three times Scottish Karting Champion
1989	Winner of both British FF 1600 Junior Championships
1990	McLaren Autosport Young Driver of the Year
1991	Runner-up in British F3 Championship. Winner of Macau GP
1993	Test driver for Williams
1994	Promoted to race driver after Senna's death
1995	Maiden Grand Prix win in Portugal
1996	Moves to McLaren
2000	Third in the World Championship
2001	Runner-up in World Championship
2002	Fifth in the World Championship beating team-mate Kimi Raikkonen
2003	Seventh in the World Championship with 40 points less than his team-mate's 91

FORMULA ONE RECORD

Year	Team	Wins	Poles	Fast laps	Pts
1994	Williams	0	0	2	14
1995	Williams	1	5	2	49
1996	McLaren	0	0	0	18
1997	McLaren	2	0	1	36
1998	McLaren	1	3	3	56
1999	McLaren	2	0	3	48
2000	McLaren	3	2	3	73
2001	McLaren	2	2	3	65
2002	Mclaren	1	0	1	41
2003	Mclaren	1	0	0	51

He came close, as a runner-up in 2001, but in a season dominated by Ferrari he could achieve little more than half the points won by champion Michael Schumacher. After that, Coulthard remained stuck on an unlucky 13 wins and never achieved the credit his hard toil promised or his honourable team commitment deserved.

As a youngster Coulthard was truly a star in the making. With great support from his family, he was racing karts by the age of eight and competing all over the country, his family spending their weekends in their own motor home. Between 1982 and 1988 he was three times Scottish Champion before progressing to cars in 1989, when he dominated both junior Formula Ford 1600 championships.

Already noted as the recipient of the McLaren Autosport Young Driver of the Year award, he joined Paul Stewart Racing to contest the British Vauxhall Lotus Challenge and GM Lotus series. A broken leg forced him out of the final reckoning and he finished fourth overall. Staying with PSR, he moved up to Formula Three, battling all season against Rubens Barrichello but ending as runner-up. He gave his reputation a timely boost by winning both the prestigious international Formula Three races at Zandvoort and Macau.

For the next two years Coulthard floundered in Formula 3000. He struggled to adapt in 1992, but appeared on the podium for the last two races. He finished ninth overall but this newfound momentum continued into 1993 with Pacific and he finished third overall. By this stage the Scot had done some testing for Williams, who signed him as official test driver for 1994. It was back to Formula 3000 for a third year until the horrifying news of Ayrton's Senna death came from Imola, and the inexperienced Coulthard stepped up to the race team.

"It's a terrible time for motor-racing, but you cannot choose when you receive the great chance of your life," he said, on taking over Senna's seat for his first race in Barcelona. "I'm in a tunnel this weekend, there's no doubt about it."

Poised, mature and determined to make the most of his opportunity while backing Damon Hill's title bid, Coulthard scored 14 points from eight races and must have been deeply frustrated at having to surrender his seat to Nigel Mansell in the final three rounds. The question-mark over Williams' commitment led him to sign a contract with McLaren for 1995 but a tribunal decided he would remain at Williams.

It was an inconsistent year, with the Scot troubled by tonsillitis and his own tendency to make embarrassing elementary errors, such as crashing into the wall on the pit-lane entry in Adelaide. He would have won the British Grand Prix but incurred an unfortunate stop-go penalty which put paid to that dream. He had the joy of spraying champagne on the rostrum eight times, once as winner in his first appearance at Estoril.

David Coulthard in action at the Malaysian Grand Prix in 2000.

"The days of Grand Prix drivers lying on the beach between races is long gone."

Coulthard moved to McLaren for the 1996 season, which proved a big disappointment, with just two podium finishes. Worse, he was consistently outpaced by new team-mate Mika Hakkinen. The 1997 campaign started well with a win in Melbourne which suggested McLaren were reinvigorated after three lean years. He won again in Monza and moved over to let Hakkinen take the honours in the season's finale at Jerez.

The same after-you-after-me move was seen in the opening race of the 1998 season as Coulthard upheld a pre-race gentlemen's agreement. However, the controversy it caused and the accusations that the Scot did not have the ultimate winner's instinct unsettled him. Hakkinen got on with the job and Coulthard was yet again left playing his subordinate role.

The season included further controversy when Coulthard slowed in appalling weather conditions at Spa and an unsighted Schumacher crashed into the back of him. "That a Formula One driver should take his foot off the accelerator at a speed of 200 mph is incomprehensible to me," raged the Ferrari driver, who arguably lost his title bid in that moment of impact. "I suspect that it was deliberate. Schumacher came like an animal into the pit, swearing and calling me a f***ing killer. I am not standing for that," retaliated Coulthard.

The mixture of brilliance and error-prone inconsistency continued in 1999 as he finished fourth overall while his team-mate successfully defended his World Championship. In 2000 he moved up to third, with 10 podium finishes, then finally bettered Hakkinen in 2001, when the Finn was questioning his commitment to the sport. He beat his team-mate again when Kimi Raikkonen took Hakkinen's place but 2003 saw the young Finn mature into a Championship contender while Coulthard slumped. The next season saw McLaren slip up. And so second-best would be the best he could hope for in a career that, like so many of his era, saw his talents locked out at a time when Schumacher was rampant.

Coulthard has promised a more ruthless attitude in the future to help him achieve success.

1998
McLaren make their mark

TALKING POINT

FROM NEARLY-MAN TO CHAMPION

Finn Mika Hakkinen had struggled to find his first win in Grand Prix motor-racing, and after he eventually did so in the final race of the 1997 season, the proverbial buses all came along at once the following season. He had been a "nearly-man" with Lotus and McLaren, but Hakkinen delivered the title as he stepped on to the top level of the podium with regularity and saw off the challenge of Michael Schumacher to become Champion. Some doubted he could do it, but Hakkinen proved to everybody that he had what it takes, with his eight wins in the season putting him on top of the world.

Opposite: *Alexander Wurz rolls his Benetton at the start of the Canadian Grand Prix. Luckily he was unhurt and went on to gain fourth place in a spare car.*

Mika Hakkinen won his first Grand Prix in the final race of the 1997 season, but 12 months later the McLaren driver had added another eight to the total as he won the World Championship for the first time to signal an era of McLaren dominance.

McLaren kept an unchanged line-up with Hakkinen being partnered by David Coulthard. The only other major team to do the same, Ferrari with Michael Schumacher and Eddie Irvine, were the closest rivals as the German pushed Hakkinen to the bitter end in another exciting season.

Jordan signed former Champion Damon Hill from Arrows to replace Fisichella and also had a new engine supplier in the form of Mugen-Honda after Peugeot's decision to defect to Prost.

McLaren show their intent

The season started in Australia and McLaren dominated the opening race, sending a warning of their intent to get back to the top. Hakkinen won from Coulthard, with the rest of the field a lap behind.

An engine problem ended Michael Schumacher's race on lap five and nobody else posed a threat to the McLarens. Frentzen was third, Ferrari's Irvine fourth, with Villeneuve fifth and Sauber's Johnny Herbert sixth.

The second round in Brazil proved to be no different. Hakkinen put the Bridgestone-shod McLaren on pole and led all the way as he headed Coulthard home again. Schumacher's Ferrari, with Goodyear tyres, was third with Frentzen fifth, sandwiched between the Benettons of Wurz and Fisichella. Villeneuve struggled home in seventh and his former Williams team-mate Hill was disqualified from 10th after his Jordan was deemed to be underweight.

Schumacher ensured McLaren did not walk away with the season, though, with a superb drive to win in Argentina in April, as Villeneuve's struggle to stay in title contention was already evident without the factory Renault engine.

The McLarens were on pole and Coulthard led for the opening laps. Schumacher muscled his way through on lap five, but Hakkinen got back on top on lap 29 as he looked for a third straight win of the season. Irvine ended the race third, almost a minute down on team-mate and winner Schumacher, with Wurz fourth and Alesi fifth, scoring his first points for Sauber. Coulthard ended sixth after recovering from the incident when sacrificing the lead to Schumacher.

McLaren returned to the top of the podium with

Michael Schumacher on the podium after winning the Argentinian Grand Prix.

another win in San Marino, but this time it was Coulthard who took victory after an intriguing battle with Schumacher.

Aerodynamic enhancement

McLaren introduced an upgraded aerodynamic package for the Spanish Grand Prix in May, and it only helped to enhance their early-season dominance, with Hakkinen leading home a one-two.

With the two on the front row of the grid, Schumacher could find no way through at the start of the race, and Coulthard helped his team-mate as he held up the Ferrari driver. After the first pit-stops, Irvine and Fisichella tangled and retired while in the top six. As Hakkinen increased his advantage lap after lap, Hill disappeared with engine failure to his Jordan, and the McLaren driver eventually beat his team-mate by almost 10 seconds, with Schumacher over 50 seconds behind.

Struggling Tyrrell driver Riccardo Rosset failed to qualify for the Monaco Grand Prix in late May. He had also been outside the 107 per cent time in Spain two weeks earlier, as Hakkinen and Coulthard claimed the front-row positions ahead of Fisichella. Once again Hakkinen headed his rivals in the early stages, with Coulthard behind him. Frentzen was an early casualty and Coulthard joined him on the list of retirements through engine failure. Wurz and Jordan's Ralf Schumacher added their names to the list in mid-race after accidents, before Michael Schumacher lost ground after troubles. He eventually finished 10th, two laps down on winner Hakkinen.

Michael Schumacher ended the McLaren run in Canada as he started a series of three victories in Montreal. The race had to be restarted with Coulthard on pole ahead of his team-mate after Wurz rolled his Benetton. Amazingly, the Austrian jumped into the spare for the second start and finished in the points in fourth. Coulthard took the lead at the start ahead of Schumacher, after gearbox problems ended Hakkinen's race. When Coulthard spun off on lap 18, Schumacher was left in the lead – only for Fisichella to get the upper hand in the pit-stops. The talented Benetton driver stayed there until lap 43, when Schumacher moved ahead to win from the Italian and team-mate Irvine.

Schumacher won for the second race in succession in France, benefiting from being on the front row for only the second time in the season to outpace his McLaren rivals.

The race had to be restarted after an incorrect procedure was displayed, and the event was reduced to 71 laps. Schumacher won the race to the first corner, and he was never headed again.

Hakkinen trailed the German throughout the race, and even lost out for second as Irvine pipped him to land the first Ferrari one-two of the season. Coulthard endured a disappointing race as he ended sixth behind Villeneuve and the impressive Wurz.

And Schumacher added his third straight win in the British Grand Prix at Silverstone in July, but it was a bizarre success, as a mistake by the race organizers and the FIA allowed him to keep his win despite not fulfilling a 10-second stop-go penalty.

Hakkinen and Schumacher were on the front row and duelled throughout the 60-lap race as the McLaren driver headed the field. He remained there until 10 laps from home, when a quick pit-stop put Schumacher in front.

Schumacher, however, was given a stop-go penalty for speeding in the pit-lane on his exit. He failed to fulfil the penalty, and it was expected that an addition would be made to his winning time. The FIA failed to make that addition, and his win was allowed to stand. Hakkinen ended in second place 22 seconds down, with Irvine, Wurz, Fisichella and Ralf Schumacher finishing in the points. Villeneuve ended seventh, with Frentzen spinning off on lap 15 and Coulthard crashing out on lap 37.

Hakkinen back with a vengeance

Hakkinen's disappointment at being denied the win at Silverstone showed in Austria two weeks later, as he stormed to a dominant win ahead of team-mate Coulthard, which increased his advantage in the standings with Schumacher only third.

Fisichella was a surprise qualifier on pole with Sauber's Alesi alongside him, but both were eclipsed by Hakkinen who made a quick start. Coulthard was also impressive during the opening exchanges as he weaved his way through the field after qualifying 14th.

Frentzen again retired, this time through engine failure, and Alesi and Fisichella joined him on lap 21 when they came together. Coulthard moved up to second and then briefly led, before the pit-stops put Hakkinen back in front to win. Irvine was fourth, with Ralf Schumacher fifth and Villeneuve sixth.

RACE BY RACE DETAILS

ROUND 1 – AUSTRALIA
Race Mika Hakkinen
Pole Mika Hakkinen
Fastest lap Mika Hakkinen

ROUND 2 – BRAZIL
Race Mika Hakkinen
Pole Mika Hakkinen
Fastest lap Mika Hakkinen

ROUND 3 – ARGENTINA
Race Michael Schumacher
Pole David Coulthard
Fastest lap Alexander Wurz

ROUND 4 – SAN MARINO
Race David Coulthard
Pole David Coulthard
Fastest lap Michael Schumacher

ROUND 5 – SPAIN
Race Mika Hakkinen
Pole Mika Hakkinen
Fastest lap Mika Hakkinen

ROUND 6 – MONACO
Race Mika Hakkinen
Pole Mika Hakkinen
Fastest lap Mika Hakkinen

ROUND 7 – CANADA
Race Michael Schumacher
Pole David Coulthard
Fastest lap Michael Schumacher

ROUND 8 – FRANCE
Race Michael Schumacher
Pole Mika Hakkinen
Fastest lap David Coulthard

ROUND 9 – BRITAIN
Race Michael Schumacher
Pole Mika Hakkinen
Fastest lap Michael Schumacher

ROUND 10 – AUSTRIA
Race Mika Hakkinen
Pole Giancarlo Fisichella
Fastest lap David Coulthard

ROUND 11 – GERMANY
Race Mika Hakkinen
Pole Mika Hakkinen
Fastest lap David Coulthard

ROUND 12 – HUNGARY
Race Michael Schumacher
Pole Mika Hakkinen
Fastest lap Michael Schumacher

ROUND 13 – BELGIUM
Race Damon Hill
Pole Mika Hakkinen
Fastest lap Michael Schumacher

ROUND 14 – ITALY
Race Michael Schumacher
Pole Michael Schumacher
Fastest lap Mika Hakkinen

ROUND 15 – LUXEMBOURG
Race Mika Hakkinen
Pole Michael Schumacher
Fastest lap Mika Hakkinen

ROUND 16 – JAPAN
Race Mika Hakkinen
Pole Michael Schumacher
Fastest lap Michael Schumacher

1998 DRIVERS' CHAMPIONSHIP

DRIVER	TEAM	POINTS
Mika Hakkinen	McLaren	100
Michael Schumacher	Ferrari	86
David Coulthard	McLaren	56
Eddie Irvine	Ferrari	47
Jacques Villeneuve	Williams	21
Damon Hill	Jordan	20
Heinz-Harald Frentzen	Williams	17
Alexander Wurz	Benetton	17
Giancarlo Fisichella	Benetton	16
Ralf Schumacher	Jordan	14
Jean Alesi	Sauber	9
Rubens Barrichello	Stewart	4
Mika Salo	Arrows	3
Pedro Diniz	Arrows	3
Johnny Herbert	Sauber	1
Jan Magnussen	Stewart	1
Jarno Trulli	Prost	1

David Coulthard caused a pile-up which meant a restart for the Belgian Grand Prix.

The McLarens were less dominant at Hockenheim in the German Grand Prix, but still came away with a one-two, with Villeneuve the closest challenger.

Hakkinen was on pole and Coulthard helped him from the front row as he initially held the opposition back. Again Hakkinen was in front for the entire race – other than through the pit-stops – although he was less than a second ahead of Coulthard at the chequered flag. Villeneuve produced his best performance of the season to finish third, while Jordan's impressive weekend was rewarded with Hill finishing fourth and Ralf Schumacher sixth. A poor race for Michael Schumacher resulted in only fifth place.

Schumacher hauled himself to within seven points of Championship leader Hakkinen with a deserved win at the Hungaroring in August. A tactical masterstroke made the victory possible, and he had his team to thank for the success. After qualifying third behind the two McLarens, Ferrari decided to run Schumacher on a three-stop strategy for the 77-lap race. He treated every lap as a qualifying lap, and duly walked away as the winner from Coulthard.

Spa carnage

Treacherous conditions marred the start of the Belgian Grand Prix at Spa-Francorchamps and Coulthard, second on the grid, sparked a massive pile-up – with the incident being judged serious enough to force a restart. Rosset, Salo, Barrichello and Panis failed to appear for the second start.

SHORTS

The year marked the exit of Tyrrell, whose place on the grid was bought by the new British American Racing team for the 1999 season. Tyrrell failed to go out in the blaze of glory they deserved in the 1998 season's final race in Japan, as Rosset failed to qualify and Takagi crashed out. It was the end of an era for Tyrrell, but the season had signalled the re-emergence of McLaren as a force and, more importantly, thrust Hakkinen to the top of the sport.

Hakkinen, Wurz and Herbert all retired after accidents at the restart, and it was the Jordan of Damon Hill – starting from third – which raced into the lead. He remained in front for seven laps until Michael Schumacher moved ahead of him.

Schumacher seemed ready to walk away with the race, but he approached Coulthard on lap 25 and attempted to lap the McLaren. Coulthard moved offline and slowed, but Schumacher was taken by surprise and ploughed into the back of the McLaren. He lost a wheel and had to retire.

Jordan's maiden win

Villeneuve, Irvine and Fisichella were all involved in accidents and that left Hill to score Jordan's first-ever win. More to the delight of team-boss Eddie

Jordan, his team-mate Ralf Schumacher ended second to secure a one-two.

Michael Schumacher qualified on pole for the Italian Grand Prix at Monza, but it was McLaren who gained the upper hand in the early stages of the race as Hakkinen burst into the lead from third on the grid, with the out-of-sorts Villeneuve a surprise qualifier on the front row. Wurz retired with gearbox difficulties, while a determined Villeneuve spun off. Hakkinen's McLaren was troubled by gearbox problems, and he slowly dropped down the field.

Schumacher won by almost 40 seconds from his team-mate Irvine, as the home *tifosi* went crazy with a Ferrari one-two. Ralf Schumacher produced another assured performance for Jordan to claim third ahead of the struggling Hakkinen.

The result left Schumacher and Hakkinen level on 80 points in the standings, with six wins each for the season, heading into the penultimate round of the Championship, the European Grand Prix at the Nurburgring.

Schumacher qualified on pole, with Irvine alongside him and the McLaren of Hakkinen on the second row with Fisichella. Schumacher made an immediate impact, leading from the off in his homeland. He kept his Ferrari in front for 24 laps, but was then outraced by Hakkinen, whose determination to become a World Champion was clearly evident. The McLaren went ahead on lap 25 and managed to keep Schumacher behind him, winning by more than two seconds to go into the final race of the season with a four-point advantage over his rival. The tension was immense, but the scene was set for a thrilling end to the season at the Japanese Grand Prix. Schumacher was on pole with Hakkinen also on the front row, with little else mattering to the crowd.

Start stalls

Prost's Jarno Trulli stalled on the grid and a restart was ordered, with the race reduced by a lap. Then, amazingly, Schumacher did the same thing, and when the race was started for a third time Hakkinen was left unopposed for the lead, with Trulli and Schumacher starting from the back of the grid.

Hakkinen had just Coulthard and Irvine for company early on as Ralf Schumacher retired with gearbox troubles. It was Irvine who eventually pushed Hakkinen, as Schumacher moved through the field.

Schumacher made it up to third before a major tyre blow-out ended his race on lap 31. His exit handed the Championship to Hakkinen, and the McLaren driver ensured he ended the season on a high by securing the title in style with the race win.

He won from Irvine by more than six seconds, with Coulthard trailing the two home. Hill ended fourth with the Williams duo of Frentzen and Villeneuve finishing the season in fifth and sixth.

The season undoubtedly belonged to McLaren's Hakkinen, as he finally left the book of the sport's nearly-men and joined the growing list of Champions. His eight wins secured the title, and 1998 will be remembered as the making of the placid Finnish driver.

1998 CONSTRUCTORS' CUP

TEAM (Engine)	POINTS
McLAREN MERCEDES	156
FERRARI	133
WILLIAMS MECACHROME	38
JORDAN MUGEN-HONDA	34
BENETTON PLAYLIFE	33
SAUBER PETRONAS	10
ARROWS	6
STEWART FORD	5
PROST PEUGEOT	1

Mika Hakkinen celebrates his first World Championship and a race win at the Japanese Grand Prix.

Eddie Irvine

CAREER DETAILS

1965	Born 10 November, Conlig, Co Down, Northern Ireland
1987	British Formula Ford 1600 Champion. Wins Formula Ford Festival
1990	Third in Formula 3000 Championship
1991	Moves to Japan
1993	Runner-up in All Japan Formula 3000 Championship. Formula One debut for Jordan
1994	Signs for Jordan
1995	First podium finish
1996	Moves to Ferrari
1999	Runner-up in World Championship
2000	Moves to Jaguar Racing
2001	Podium finish in Monaco but retires from 11 of 17 Grands Prix
2002	Podium finish in Italy before retiring at the end of the season

FORMULA ONE RECORD

Year	Team	Wins	Poles	Fast laps	Pts
1993	Jordan	0	0	0	1
1994	Jordan	0	0	0	6
1995	Jordan	0	0	0	10
1996	Ferrari	0	0	0	11
1997	Ferrari	0	0	0	24
1998	Ferrari	0	0	0	47
1999	Ferrari	4	0	1	74
2000	Jaguar	0	0	0	4
2001	Jaguar	0	0	0	6
2002	Jaguar	0	0	0	8

FROM HIS DEBUT, when he was punched by Ayrton Senna, Eddie Irvine has been a colourful presence in Formula One. Indifferent or defiant off-track, he was first and foremost a racer of tenacity.

Eddie Irvine drives for Jaguar in the Monaco Grand Prix in 2000.

Eddie Irvine best summed up his debut in Formula One himself. "What a start to my Grand Prix career," he exclaimed in 1994. "I get punched by Senna in my first race, crash in my second, destroy four cars in my third and get banned from my fourth. People are going to think I'm some kind of nutter."

However, Irvine's strength – both personal and sporting – has been his resilience. He bounced back all the stronger to make impressive progress from Jordan to Ferrari and finally to a multi-million-pound move to Jaguar.

From being a tough and consistent racer, the playboy Ulsterman transformed himself into team-leader material, confidently equating his efforts with Michael Schumacher's and Mika Hakkinen's.

Driving a works Van Diemen, Irvine was both the RAC and Esso Formula Ford 1600 champion and Formula Ford Festival winner in 1987. In the following season he competed in Formula Three and notched up eight podium finishes without ever threatening the dominance of J J Lehto and Gary Brabham. In 1989 he graduated to Formula 3000 with Pacific and in a difficult year earned the admiration of Eddie Jordan, who signed him for 1990. He showed his mettle, winning at Hockenheim and finishing third in the Championship behind Erik Comas and Eric van de Poele.

With no chance of a Formula One drive, he decided to race in the Japanese F3000 series. He was sixth in both 1991 and 1992 and won more races in 1993 than the veteran Kazuyoshi Hoshino to whom he unluckily finished runner-up. Toyota included him in their Le Mans squad in 1993 (finished fourth, setting fastest lap) and in 1994 (came second).

Eddie Jordan invited him to do the last two Formula One races of 1993 – where he made his controversial debut appearances. He had the temerity to re-pass Ayrton Senna, who was attempting to lap him. This attitude was interpreted by the Brazilian as a lack of respect and earned Irvine a physical and verbal battering. The incident also introduced paddock insiders to Irvine's no-nonsense hold on the reality of a situation.

"I've got a nutter's reputation that isn't fully deserved, but if I can intimidate my rivals with it, it's to my advantage."

"The era of one driver saying, 'After you, Claude' is long gone and that is as much due to Senna as anybody else. He started being very aggressive and everybody else has copied him," he argued.

He signed with Jordan as Rubens Barrichello's team-mate for 1994, and immediately found himself labelled a wildman. He showed his resilience on the track with a run of fine late-season performances, and off the track in remaining unimpressed by the Formula One lifestyle compared to Japan. "I miss the camaraderie between the drivers. We all hung out together, and went to the nightclubs and bars after the race," he said. "In F1 everyone just disappears. It's like you're raping a country. You go in, do the race and get out before you get caught."

In 1995 Irvine outperformed Barrichello, outpsyching the emotional Brazilian with his nonchalance. "Eddie is a driver who just drives. It seems to come naturally. Sometimes he doesn't know what gear he's in," mused Barrichello.

The Ulsterman's consistent qualifying speed and scorching starts had erased his former wild reputation, but it was still a surprise when Ferrari announced they had signed him as Michael Schumacher's team-mate in 1996.

Mechanical failures and few testing opportunities saw him end the season 10th in the Championship with just 11 points. However, Irvine realized he could learn from Schumacher and improve his standing as a competent number two. In 1997, he achieved five podium finishes, ending the season seventh with 24 points. In 1998 he became a reliable points-scorer (doubling his season tally to 48) and narrowed the gap between himself and Schumacher.

By 1999 Irvine's every comment about his team-mate suggested impatience with his subordinate role. He won his first Grand Prix in Melbourne and after Schumacher's accident at Silverstone, which sidelined him for seven races, became Ferrari's title contender. He took his challenge to Hakkinen all the way to the final round but finished runner-up and moved to Jaguar Racing on a multi-million-pound three-year deal. A dismal first season brought only 13th place in the championship, while in 2001 the Ulsterman retired from 11 of the 17 Grands Prix but managed to secure the team's maiden podium with third-place in Monte Carlo. That glimmer of hope grew in 2002 but a podium finish alongside former team-mate Schumacher at Monza would prove an emotional swansong before he bowed out of the sport at the end of that year.

A strong and resilient driver, Irvine likes life in the fast lane.

1999
Two in a row for Hakkinen

TALKING POINT

INJURY WINS HAKKINEN THE TITLE

Mika Hakkinen secured a second straight title, but injury seemingly handed him the crown. The injury was not to him, but rather to Michael Schumacher, his arch-rival. Schumacher and Hakkinen were expected to battle until the last race of the season for World Championship honours. But mid-way through the year an opening-lap crash at Silverstone left Schumacher with a broken leg and out of the running. Hakkinen was pushed hard by Schumacher's team-mate Irvine in the German's absence, but in the end the crash in the British Grand Prix effectively handed a second title to the Finn.

Michael Schumacher crashes out of the British Grand Prix and effectively ends his title chances.

Opposite: *The tifosi cheer on Michael Schumacher to a win at the San Marino Grand Prix.*

Mika Hakkinen's success in the 1998 Championship race sparked life into his career, and the McLaren driver continued his upward trend the following season as he landed a second straight title, albeit after a monumental battle with Ferrari again.

Hakkinen had to wait until the final race of the season to wrap up proceedings after seeing off the challenge of Eddie Irvine, whose Ferrari team-mate Michael Schumacher had been left out of the title run-in because of a mid-season injury suffered in a horror crash in the British Grand Prix.

McLaren kept faith with the Hakkinen-Coulthard partnership, and had Mercedes-Benz power on board for another year. Ferrari, likewise, were unchanged for the new campaign.

The season marked the arrival of the new British American Racing team, founded by Adrian Reynard, Rick Gorne and Craig Pollock, and the latter pulled off a major coup with the capture of former World Champion and close friend Jacques Villeneuve from Williams, who was joined by the young Brazilian Riccardo Zonta. German Heinz-Harald Frentzen also followed Villeneuve out of Williams, with Jordan his destination to partner Damon Hill. Ralf Schumacher, the man he replaced at Jordan, ironically replaced him at Williams, and the Grove-based team decided to hand two-times ChampCar champion Alex Zanardi a second chance in Formula One as they aimed to turn around their flagging fortunes.

McLaren miss out

As had happened the previous year, the McLarens of Hakkinen and Coulthard proved to be quick straight out of the box, and both were on the front row of the Melbourne grid for the Australian Grand Prix.

Hakkinen led as Villeneuve crashed out on lap 13, and second-placed Coulthard joined him on the same lap when his gearbox failed. Throttle problems affected Hakkinen's McLaren and he sacrificed the lead to Irvine, who had benefited from his team-mate starting from the back of the grid. The problems cost Hakkinen his place in the race on lap 21. Irvine remained in front, winning by little more than a second from Jordan driver Frentzen, and Ralf Schumacher enjoyed an impressive debut for Williams by finishing third.

Zonta retired nine laps from the end to ensure BAR failed to fulfil their expectations of a win in their first race, and Michael Schumacher had an unhappy start to the year as he finished last of the eight finishers and a lap down on team-mate Irvine.

Zonta, however, was a non-starter in his home event in Brazil two weeks later after he injured his ankle in a shunt during practice.

Hakkinen and Coulthard ensured the difficulties McLaren experienced in Australia did not hinder their progress during the early weekend as they locked out the front row of the grid. But Hakkinen lost the lead on lap three because of gear-selection troubles and then Coulthard retired from the race on lap 22 with the same problem.

Hakkinen recovered from his problems to remain in the running as Barrichello delighted the home fans by leading the race in his Stewart and remaining in the lead until Michael Schumacher moved ahead. But Hakkinen powered back, overtaking Schumacher on lap 38 and going on to win the race by five seconds, as Frentzen continued his impressive start for Jordan in third.

All change

German Michael Schumacher became the third different winner in as many races at the San Marino Grand Prix, but it was thanks to an uncharacteristic error by Hakkinen.

The Finn led during the early exchanges, but crashed into the barrier at the beginning of the start-finish straight, and retired on lap 17. From there, Schumacher and Coulthard duelled and the Ferrari driver emerged on top to send the *tifosi* into ecstasy.

Schumacher signalled his intent to become a three-time Champion in the next race as he dominated the Monaco Grand Prix to end more than half a minute ahead of team-mate Irvine.

BAR none...

In Spain two weeks later, Hakkinen and Coulthard started better than the Ferraris, but Villeneuve, who qualified sixth, impressed in the Supertec-powered car as he held off Michael Schumacher and Irvine to run third for most of the race.

Zonta returned from his broken ankle for BAR in the Canadian Grand Prix, but at the front, Michael Schumacher turned his pole position into the lead after the safety car had been deployed because of an opening-lap incident.. However, he surprisingly crashed out on lap 29 to cost himself the chance of an almost certain victory and hand the lead to Hakkinen, ahead of Coulthard and Irvine who clashed while duelling for second place, both of them losing time and dropping down the field to hand Fisichella his best result of the season with second place.

Two weeks later Frentzen helped Jordan to victory in a wet French Grand Prix – his first win since joining the team. The circuit was wet for qualifying and the grid line-up saw Barrichello and Alesi on the front row. Michael Schumacher started sixth on the grid, Hakkinen lined up 14th and Irvine was way down in 17th place.

Barrichello tussled first with coulthard who went out with electrical problems and then Michael Schumacher to whom he eventually lost the lead on lap 43. Hakkinen recovered from a spin to take the lead on lap 60 but lasted just five laps before Frentzen got the better of him to take the chequered flag. Hakkinen ended second ahead of Barrichello.

Schumacher's shunt

Frentzen's victory sent Jordan heading into their home event, the British Grand Prix, in positive mood and they produced another points-scoring finish, with both the German driver and Hill ending in the top six. For Michael Schumacher, however, the Silverstone race proved to be a disaster when his brakes locked when he entered Stowe corner on the opening lap. His Ferrari was sent hurtling across

RACE BY RACE DETAILS

ROUND 1 – AUSTRALIA
Race Eddie Irvine
Pole Mika Hakkinen
Fastest lap Michael Schumacher

ROUND 2 – BRAZIL
Race Mika Hakkinen
Pole Mika Hakkinen
Fastest lap Mika Hakkinen

ROUND 3 – SAN MARINO
Race Michael Schumacher
Pole Mika Hakkinen
Fastest lap Michael Schumacher

ROUND 4 – MONACO
Race Michael Schumacher
Pole Mika Hakkinen
Fastest lap Mika Hakkinen

ROUND 5 – SPAIN
Race Mika Hakkinen
Pole Mika Hakkinen
Fastest lap Michael Schumacher

ROUND 6 – CANADA
Race Mika Hakkinen
Pole Michael Schumacher
Fastest lap Eddie Irvine

ROUND 7 – FRANCE
Race Heinz-Harald Frentzen
Pole Rubens Barrichello
Fastest lap David Coulthard

ROUND 8 – BRITAIN
Race David Coulthard
Pole Mika Hakkinen
Fastest lap Mika Hakkinen

ROUND 9 – AUSTRIA
Race Eddie Irvine
Pole Mika Hakkinen
Fastest lap Mika Hakkinen

ROUND 10 – GERMANY
Race Eddie Irvine
Pole Mika Hakkinen
Fastest lap David Coulthard

ROUND 11 – HUNGARY
Race Mika Hakkinen
Pole Mika Hakkinen
Fastest lap David Coulthard

ROUND 12 – BELGIUM
Race David Coulthard
Pole Mika Hakkinen
Fastest lap Mika Hakkinen

ROUND 13 – ITALY
Race Heinz-Harald Frentzen
Pole Mika Hakkinen
Fastest lap Ralf Schumacher

ROUND 14 – EUROPEAN
Race Johnny Herbert
Pole Heinz-Harald Frentzen
Fastest lap Mika Hakkinen

ROUND 15 – MALAYSIA
Race Eddie Irvine
Pole Michael Schumacher
Fastest lap Michael Schumacher

ROUND 16 – JAPAN
Race Mika Hakkinen
Pole Michael Schumacher
Fastest lap Michael Schumacher

1999 DRIVERS' CHAMPIONSHIP

DRIVER	TEAM	POINTS
Mika Hakkinen	McLaren	76
Eddie Irvine	Ferrari	74
Heinz-Harald Frentzen	Jordan	55
David Coulthard	McLaren	48
Michael Schumacher	Ferrari	44
Ralf Schumacher	Williams	35
Rubens Barrichello	Stewart	21
Johnny Herbert	Stewart	15
Giancarlo Fisichella	Benetton	13
Mika Salo	BAR/Ferrari	10
Jarno Trulli	Prost	7
Damon Hill	Jordan	7
Alexander Wurz	Benetton	3
Pedro Diniz	Sauber	3
Olivier Panis	Prost	2
Jean Alesi	Sauber	2
Pedro de la Rosa	Arrows	1
Marc Gene	Minardi	1

the gravel and into the tyre barrier. The impact broke his right leg, and it was expected to keep him out for the remainder of the season.

Hakkinen lost his lead during the pit-stop interval when one of his wheels was not put on properly and he had to stop for a second time. His team-mate Coulthard took over in front after Irvine had overshot his crew having been unsighted by Hakkinen's car. By lap 35, Hakkinen's wheel problem had failed to improve, and he decided to retire from the race to leave a straight fight between Coulthard and Irvine, and the McLaren driver won by almost two seconds.

Ferrari chose super-sub Salo to replace the injured Schumacher for the Austrian Grand Prix at the A1-Ring, but it was Irvine who kept the team's hopes of a first drivers' world title since 1979 firmly alive with a narrow victory from Coulthard.

Hakkinen produced the performance of the day, however, as he raced back to third from last place after a collision with Coulthard, but the incident left a question-mark over the relationship between the two McLaren drivers.

Irvine impact

Frentzen's good form was again evident in the German Grand Prix at Hockenheim but the race itself was further evidence that Irvine was a serious title contender as he landed back-to-back wins, albeit thanks to stand-in team-mate Salo.

SHORTS

McLaren returned to winning ways in Spain as Mika Hakkinen ended his disappointing run of form with victory ahead of team-mate David Coulthard. The race, however, more significantly heralded the potential of BAR and Jacques Villeneuve, if not the reliability.

Hakkinen dominated the opening stages of the race as he led from the off, but the Finn lost ground after a refuelling problem during his pit-stop. His team-mate Coulthard had been stuck behind Salo, and his attempts to force a way past resulted in a stop for a new nosecone after touching the Ferrari. Hakkinen's rear tyre failed as he approached Agip Kurve, and he spun off, handing an unexpected lead to Salo, who was in front for just one lap before allowing Irvine to pass him on team orders. The Ferrari pair secured a one-two finish, with Frentzen just five seconds back in third.

McLaren hit back in Hungary as pole-sitter Hakkinen led from start to finish and Coulthard outfought Irvine to give the team their own one-two finish.

The issue of team orders, which had given Irvine victory in Germany as Salo moved over, cropped up again in Belgium in early-August as Coulthard was

The Jordan team go wild as Heinz-Harald Frentzen wins the French Grand Prix.

Johnny Herbert, Jackie Stewart and Rubens Barrichello celebrate a memorable win for the Stewart team at the European Grand Prix

1999 CONSTRUCTORS' CUP

TEAM (Engine)	POINTS
FERRARI	128
MCLAREN MERCEDES	124
JORDAN MUGEN-HONDA	61
STEWART FORD	36
WILLIAMS SUPERTEC	35
BENETTON PLAYLIFE	16
PROST PEUGEOT	9
SAUBER PETRONAS	5
ARROWS	1
MINARDI FORD	1

victorious after McLaren team-boss Ron Dennis refused to use team orders to help one of his drivers. But many criticized the decision as Hakkinen ended up second and lost potential points for his Championship challenge.

Four weeks later, Dennis may well have regretted his decision not to impose team orders when Hakkinen crashed out while leading the Italian Grand Prix at Monza in September where Frentzen achieved his second win of the season.

Victory for Stewart

A rain-affected European Grand Prix at the Nurburgring in late-September produced another surprise result, as Herbert survived the conditions to give Stewart their first-ever Grand Prix win.

Frentzen's form continued with pole position ahead of Coulthard and Hakkinen, and he led in the early stages only to retire on lap 32 with electrical problems as he joined team-mate Hill in the pits. Coulthard then led, but his race ended five laps later when he spun off in the wet conditions, and from there Ralf Schumacher took over at the front, only to lose out during the pit-stop periods.

Fisichella was on course for a win until he was sent spinning out of the race on lap 48, and his disappearance left Herbert in front to ease his Stewart home for a memorable win.

Irvine headed into the penultimate race at the newly built Sepang circuit in Malaysia with an eight-point deficit to Hakkinen, but his hopes of landing the world crown were boosted by the news of Michael Schumacher's return from injury.

Schumacher, who declared his support for the Ulsterman's charge, rubbished suggestions that his injuries might have had a lasting effect on his career by putting his Ferrari in pole position, with Irvine also on the front row. Irvine moved into the lead and Schumacher shielded his team-mate as he charged to a vital victory, leaving Hakkinen frustrated as he failed to find a way past the German.

The order stayed the same at the front but Ferrari were disqualified after the race over an infringement relating to their bargeboards. They contested the decision and the original verdict was overturned to set up a grand finale to the season.

Title rivals Hakkinen and Irvine were separated by just two points, with the final race of the season in Japan set to be a tense thriller, and Schumacher putting his Ferrari on pole again at Suzuka. But Irvine failed to produce his best form in qualifying and ended fifth on the grid, while Hakkinen was quick enough to be alongside Schumacher on the front row.

The McLaren driver was quickest off the grid and held the lead until lap 19, when Schumacher moved in front. But the German's lead was only temporary, and order was restored after the pit-stops on lap 24. With a second world title in his sights, Hakkinen held off the challenge of Schumacher to win the race by five seconds, and Irvine was left to ponder what might have been as he finished third behind his team-mate.

The season had gone to the wire, but not in the way in which pre-season talk had predicted. Michael Schumacher had been expected to lift Ferrari's first crown since 1979. But it was left to his team-mate Irvine to do the job, and it was a case of "so near, but yet so far" for the Ulsterman.

2000
Schumacher back on top

TALKING POINT

BRITAIN'S STAR OF THE FUTURE...NOW

At the start of the year, Jenson Button was unknown. By the end, he was a rising star and, not yet 21, a World Champion of the future. At the start, he told people he would not be changed by Formula One. By the end, he had broken up with his childhood sweetheart, bought a Ferrari and taken an apartment in Monte Carlo. As Johnny Herbert departed the scene, Button broke through to give the British fans more than an ordinary replacement. He was pioneering a new generation and doing it his way.

But as Button moved "on loan" from Williams to Benetton for the 2001 and 2002 seasons, to be replaced by Juan-Pablo Montoya at the BMW-powered Grove-based team, the real question was more about his character and ability to withstand the media pressure than about his talent. No one had expected Button to make the entry he did. No one, that is, except Button himself – and his ever-present father John.

At the start, as the teams assembled in Melbourne, Jackie Stewart was widely quoted saying it was not right for a young driver to make the kind of jump to Formula One that Button had done. He needed more time to prepare and to grow up, said the three-times champion. By the end of the year Button, who scored 12 points to finish eighth, had delivered his own answer with a season which showed it does not matter how old, or young, you are if you have got the talent and the team.

Jenson Button takes advice from a member of the Williams team during his first season in which he finished eighth.

The season started extraordinarily well for Michael Schumacher, and it ended in triumph for both him and Ferrari as the Maranello team celebrated their first Championship double in 21 years in red wigs amid champagne parties in the pit-lane. It was a well-deserved reward for years of hard work, not just the good fortune of one race or one sunny afternoon.

This time, Schumacher and Ferrari had enjoyed it all and the German driver entered the sport's hall of fame as another triple World Champion, adding his 2000 title with Ferrari to the previous two claimed for Benetton in 1994 and 1995.

Flying start

Schumacher started the season in fine style at Albert Park at the beginning of March. Arriving on a crest of confidence after a good winter recovering completely from the broken leg he had suffered at Silverstone the previous summer. But it was the McLarens who were smiling after qualifying, when Mika Hakkinen and David Coulthard, as usual in Melbourne, topped the times and took the front row of the grid. Schumacher was third with his new Ferrari team-mate Rubens Barrichello, signed from the Stewart team (which had transformed into Jaguar following its acquisition by Ford), fourth.

But on Sunday afternoon, it was a different story. Despite the team concentrating on reliability in winter testing, McLaren's two men were undone by engine failures. And once the race settled into a battle for survival behind Schumacher, who took the lead after Hakkinen's exit, there was only going to be one result.

Barrichello came home second ahead of Ralf Schumacher, who joined his brother on the podium by bringing his Williams in third.

In the second round, in Brazil, Schumacher was lucky again, made the most of it, and delivered a second successive victory after which, to their dismay, McLaren saw Coulthard disqualified from second place in scrutineering. Ironically, it was for exceeding the 5mm tolerance which had allowed both Ferraris to be reinstated on appeal after the 1999 Malaysian Grand Prix, and in terms of the Championship, it meant Schumacher led with 20 points and McLaren still had none on the board.

A "home" win

Next stop was Imola for the San Marino Grand Prix, a "home" event for Ferrari, but McLaren were set to spoil the party as Hakkinen took pole once again with Schumacher second and Coulthard third ahead of Barrichello.

Hakkinen led to his first stop, but in a brief middle stint Schumacher, reeled off a series of quick laps, pitted swiftly and came out in front to leave the Finn, hit by difficulties including debris damage to the floor of his car and electrical problems, in runners-up place again.

Two weeks later Silverstone witnessed an Easter weekend of torrential rain and non-stop misery for the British Grand Prix. It mattered little to Coulthard who swept to victory on his home track to announce himself as a title contender.

And it was the Scot who commanded all the attention on arrival in Barcelona for the Spanish Grand Prix. He had made worldwide headlines during the previous week when, at France's Lyons airport, he and his fiancée Heidi Wichlinski survived an air crash in which the pilots died.

He had behaved like a hero, and in the race at the Circuit de Catalunya he drove like one. He had three cracked ribs, much bruising and pain, but did not complain and drove well for second place behind Hakkinen as McLaren repeated the one-two they had enjoyed the previous year.

Next stop was the Nurburgring and the European Grand Prix. Coulthard claimed pole. Schumacher was second, Hakkinen third and Barrichello fourth, confirming once more that the season belonged to just two teams. Hakkinen snatched the lead at the first corner as he shot past the front row men, but Schumacher gave chase and the pair provided a duel to enjoy.

When the rain came, the Ferrari was able to ease away in front, unfussed, until the very late stages when Hakkinen responded. By then, though, it was too late and only a multiple collision involving Eddie Irvine, Jos Verstappen and Ralf Schumacher provided any diversion from Schumacher's progress towards another win and an 18-point lead.

Button out "on loan"

At the Monaco Grand Prix, two weeks later, the paddock was surprised to learn that the impressive young Jenson Button was to be released by Williams at the end of the year to allow the team to bring in Juan-Pablo Montoya. For Button, it was a chilly item of news, but Monte Carlo cared little.

The weather was glorious and the harbour a picture-perfect setting for another famous Coulthard triumph. This time, he was lucky. Schumacher was forced to retire while leading easily, his Ferrari falling prey to its first mechanical failure since Silverstone the previous year after 55 laps.

Schumacher gets a grip

And so to Canada and the Circuit Gilles Villeneuve where Schumacher took the opportunity to dominate and regain a firm grip on the Championship in the incident-packed wet-and-dry race.

Coulthard stalled on the grid, was hit with a 10-second stop-go penalty because his crew came out to help him restart, and then switched to wet tyres from dry too late. This left the German with an easy run home and a 22-point advantage in the title race.

Two weeks later, at Magny-Cours, Coulthard came back with a gutsy performance to claim victory in the French Grand Prix, and followed up by lambasting Schumacher's tactics at the start when he weaved around to stop Coulthard passing.

The Scot continued to give vent to his feelings on Schumacher and his swerving tactics and brought the matter up at the drivers' meeting in Austria prior to the next race at the A1-Ring. But despite backing from Jacques Villeneuve and Schumacher's former team-mate Irvine, no action was taken by the FIA. Irvine had gone public saying Schumacher should stand down from his position as head of the Grand Prix Drivers' Association (GPDA).

Austria nearly overshadowed

The simmering war of words threatened to overshadow all else, but McLaren made sure they were not losing their concentration. Hakkinen claimed pole while Coulthard joined him on the front row and Barrichello led the Ferraris a row back.

Hakkinen led into the first corner, where Schumacher crashed out, and he was still there, followed by his team-mate Coulthard, at the finish.

At last the Championship looked interesting, with McLaren taking the initiative and Coulthard cutting Schumacher's lead to just six points. But after

David Coulthard quenches his thirst after a successful win at the British Grand Prix.

RACE BY RACE DETAILS

ROUND 1 – AUSTRALIA
Race Michael Schumacher
Pole Mika Hakkinen
Fastest lap Rubens Barrichello

ROUND 2 – BRAZIL
Race Michael Schumacher
Pole Mika Hakkinen
Fastest lap Michael Schumacher

ROUND 3 – SAN MARINO
Race Michael Schumacher
Pole Mika Hakkinen
Fastest lap Mika Hakkinen

ROUND 4 – BRITAIN
Race David Coulthard
Pole Rubens Barrichello
Fastest lap Mika Hakkinen

ROUND 5 – SPAIN
Race Mika Hakkinen
Pole Michael Schumacher
Fastest lap Mika Hakkinen

ROUND 6 – EUROPEAN – NURBURGRING
Race Michael Schumacher
Pole Michael Schumacher
Fastest lap Michael Schumacher

ROUND 7 – MONACO
Race David Coulthard
Pole Michael Schumacher
Fastest lap Mika Hakkinen

ROUND 8 – CANADA
Race Michael Schumacher
Pole Michael Schumacher
Fastest lap Mika Hakkinen

ROUND 9 – FRANCE
Race David Coulthard
Pole Michael Schumacher
Fastest lap David Coulthard

ROUND 10 – AUSTRIA
Race Mika Hakkinen
Pole Mika Hakkinen
Fastest lap David Coulthard

ROUND 11 – GERMANY
Race Rubens Barrichello
Pole David Coulthard
Fastest lap Rubens Barrichello

ROUND 12 – HUNGARY
Race Mika Hakkinen
Pole Michael Schumacher
Fastest lap Mika Hakkinen

ROUND 13 – BELGIUM
Race Mika Hakkinen
Pole Mika Hakkinen
Fastest lap Rubens Barrichello

ROUND 14 – ITALY
Race Michael Schumacher
Pole Michael Schumacher
Fastest lap Mika Hakkinen

ROUND 15 – UNITED STATES
Race Michael Schumacher
Pole Michael Schumacher
Fastest lap David Coulthard

ROUND 16 – JAPAN
Race Michael Schumacher
Pole Michael Schumacher
Fastest lap Mika Hakkinen

ROUND 17 – MALAYSIA
Race Michael Schumacher
Pole Michael Schumacher
Fastest lap Mika Hakkinen

2000 DRIVERS' CHAMPIONSHIP

DRIVER	TEAM	POINTS
Michael Schumacher	Ferrari	108
Mika Hakkinen	McLaren	89
David Coulthard	McLaren	73
Rubens Barrichello	Ferrari	62
Ralf Schumacher	Williams	24
Giancarlo Fisichella	Benetton	18
Jacques Villeneuve	BAR	17
Jenson Button	Williams	12
Heinz-Harald Frentzen	Jordan	11
Jarno Trulli	Jordan	6
Mika Salo	Sauber	6
Jos Verstappen	Arrows	5
Eddie Irvine	Jaguar	4
Riccardo Zonta	BAR	3
Alexander Wurz	Benetton	2
Pedro De La Rosa	Arrows	2

the race, a missing official seal on Hakkinen's electronic control unit meant the team were docked 10 points and fined £33,000.

Next up on the calendar was Hockenheim and, amazingly, another non-finish for Schumacher who perished, for the second successive race, on the first bend. But it was not all plain sailing for McLaren as Barrichello decided it was high time he secured his first Grand Prix victory. He executed the feat with aplomb and emotion, bursting into tears on the podium as the Brazilian anthem played for the first time since the death of Ayrton Senna.

Remarkably Barrichello achieved this breakthrough victory after not only starting from 18th on the grid but also having to overcome a bizarre interruption during the race when a safety car was introduced because a spectator, protesting at losing his job with Mercedes-Benz, had wandered on to the circuit.

The next race was on Schumacher's favourite circuit at Spa-Francorchamps, where he had made his Formula One entry in 1991 and claimed his debut victory the following year. Thousands of fans from his home town of Kerpen gathered to support him but Schumacher was to be beaten emphatically by the most thrilling passing move of the season from Hakkinen.

Schumacher had inherited the lead when Hakkinen spun at Stavelot on lap 11, but the Finn recovered and, using backmarker Riccardo Zonta's BAR as assistance, overtook Schumacher to squeeze back into the lead.

Controversy surrounded the sport in the weeks that followed when several team chiefs revealed they were keen for FIA president Max Mosley to resign because they did not approve of his handling of Formula One, its rulebook and the planning for the future. But Mosley confronted them at a meeting in a Heathrow airport hotel and left with his position secure.

Italian tragedy

All this seemed irrelevant, however, when the field left Monza after the Italian Grand Prix mourning the first death in Formula One since the tragic passing of Roland Ratzenberger and Senna at Imola in 1994. Ferrari had seen Schumacher and Barrichello drive to a *tifosi*-pleasing one-two victory, but the champagne spray was replaced by the tears of a World Champion when Schumacher broke down in the post-race press conference.

The man killed was Paolo Ghislimberti, a marshal, struck by a wheel sent flying during a multiple collision on the opening lap at the Variante della Roggia. Barrichello had attempted to go inside Trulli but when Frentzen followed he misjudged the Ferrari's braking and collided, lifting off into the rear of Trulli's Jordan. The impact sent debris spiralling and Frentzen's front right wheel flew with fatal consequences. Coulthard, de la Rosa, and Zonta were also involved.

Amazingly, none of the drivers were injured. Hot words were exchanged, but in the colder light of analysis it was a serious racing accident and one man, who was in the wrong place at the wrong time, paid the price.

Mika Hakkinen takes a rest after winning in Austria.

Michael Schumacher in dashing red wig and the Ferrari team celebrate his third Championship title and Ferrari's first for 21 years.

Title becomes a duel

Coulthard's failure to finish at Monza meant that the title race was reduced to a duel with three rounds to go, defending Champion Hakkinen leading on 80 to Schumacher's 78. McLaren led Ferrari by 131 to 127. The relentless stress of the Championship provided a new twist for the next contest with a trip to the United States and the first race at Indianapolis since the 1950s. The stars and stripes were in full flower, a new infield course had been created within the vast 2.5 mile oval and Formula One was made welcome albeit by a minority of the public.

It was the first United States Grand Prix in nine years and Hakkinen, who made his Formula One debut in the last race in America, wound up third on the grid behind Schumacher and Coulthard who had enjoyed slipstreaming assistance from their team-mates. But the Finn retired from a disappointing race with engine failure whilst chasing Schumacher.

SHORTS

If the actual race at Interlagos was curious and controversial, so too was the qualifying session. Once again, it was dominated by the rapid McLarens with Hakkinen taking pole and Coulthard second ahead of the two Ferraris, but the session was halted three times because wind caused advertising hoardings on the start-finish straight to fall down on the track. Prost's Jean Alesi hit one, but escaped unhurt.

Coulthard led the early laps but was given a stop-go penalty for jumping the lights and that killed off his challenge. All this left Schumacher cruising in front in such dreamy fashion that he briefly lost concentration and spun. But he recovered, and with Barrichello following him home, Ferrari were back on top.

Far East decides prizes

Suzuka, the scene of so many Championship showdowns, was a fitting next stop for the Japanese Grand Prix. Hakkinen refused to bow to suggestions that it was virtually all over and planned to race on while Schumacher said he would race to win, because he wanted it all over as soon as possible. There was to be no carrying on for the sake of a finale in Kuala Lumpur in the final race, and notably both drivers were as sporting towards each other as possible in the circumstances. It demonstrated their quality, their class and their dignity.

When it was all over, and Schumacher was celebrating his third drivers' world title and Ferrari's first for 21 years, Hakkinen was with him in the log cabin. It was almost a mutual appreciation society.

The constructors' crown was still to be decided when the teams headed into the stifling heat and humidity of Malaysia. Johnny Herbert said his goodbyes after 12 happy years in Formula One, but Ferrari claimed the headlines as they swept the board with another Schumacher victory. It was his fourth win in a row and his ninth in 17 outings, and the triumph confirmed the constructors' title for Ferrari. For the red-wigged Ferrari boys it was a celebratory welcome home.

2000 CONSTRUCTORS' CUP

TEAM (Engine)	POINTS
FERRARI	170
McLAREN MERCEDES	152
WILLIAMS BMW	36
BENETTON RENAULT	20
BRITISH AMERICAN RACING HONDA	20
JORDAN HONDA	17
ARROWS	7
SAUBER PETRONAS	6
JAGUAR	4

2001
A class of his own

TALKING POINT

A SEASON OF CRASHES AND DEVASTATION

Just four races after the death of marshal Paolo Ghislimberti at the Italian Grand Prix in the 2000 season, it happened again. Four and a half laps after the cars roared away from the line to begin the new season in Australia, Jacques Villeneuve's BAR collided with the Williams of Ralf Schumacher and was launched into the air. A stray wheel from the car went through a gap in the debris fencing and marshal Graham Beveridge was killed. The incident was a shock to the sport on its opening weekend, and there was almost another tragic incident when, several months later, at the Belgian Grand Prix Brazilian Luciano Burti crashed into the tyre wall at full speed. Observers watched with concern as Eddie Irvine, whose Jaguar had collided with Burti to cause the crash, dragged the tyre wall away from the wrecked car in a desperate bid to save his former team-mate. And amazingly Burti survived, with only bruising on his face to show for the devastating crash. He was out for the season, but returned to become a Ferrari test driver in 2002.

Michael Schumacher wraps up his fourth World Championship at the Hungarian Grand Prix.

Nobody could doubt that Michael Schumacher was the outstanding champion of a 2001 season dominated by Ferrari, but behind the scarlet steamroller, the Formula One story was full of tragedy and intrigue with new heroes staking a claim to replace retiring stars.

Schumacher, winner of a record-equalling nine races, headed towards his fourth drivers' Championship and a place alongside, and then beyond, Alain Prost in the record books. The buzzword of Schumacher's season was perfection.

Breaking records

He overhauled Alain Prost's total of 51 Grand Prix victories and finally outstripped him for career points. Now, other than Ayrton Senna, who as the master of the single lap holds a currently out-of-reach record for pole positions, only Juan-Manuel Fangio is ahead of Schumacher in terms of statistical achievements.

In place alongside him at Ferrari was a new number two, the capable Brazilian Rubens Barrichello, while McLaren continued their long-standing partnership of Finn Mika Hakkinen and Briton David Coulthard.

At Williams there was an exciting new partner for German Ralf Schumacher with confident Colombian Juan Pablo Montoya moving from American CART racing to replace Benetton-bound Briton Jenson Button, who teamed up with Italian Giancarlo Fisichella at the Renault-backed team.

Further down the grid, there were some interesting new faces, with Finn Kimi Raikkonen, 21, sensationally joining Sauber having competed in just 23 single-seater races in his career, and 19-year-old Fernando Alonso joining Minardi.

The year began with Schumacher winning confidently in Australia and then gradually building on that early advantage to extend a lead on his nearest challenger Coulthard.

A tragic fifth-lap incident in Melbourne (see talking point) marred what was an impressive performance for Schumacher, which saw him claim pole, the win, and the fastest lap despite rolling his Ferrari in the first practice session of the year.

Coulthard finished close behind, but only because the champion was driving cautiously, and Barrichello made it two Ferraris on the podium with third as Raikkonen scored a point on his debut when Olivier Panis' fourth-placed BAR was disqualified.

Going for a spin

Moving onto Malaysia, the exciting racing continued and it was enhanced by a dramatic rainstorm which hit the track just after the start and saw five cars spin off as everyone else headed into the pits.

There was chaos in the Ferrari garage as Schumacher was forced to queue behind team-mate

Barrichello while the Italian team searched for the fourth tyre to put on the Brazilian's car. But the team pulled off a stroke of genius by putting intermediate tyres on, as everyone else went for wets, and the pair made up more than a minute to come back and take a one-two finish ahead of Coulthard in third. Somehow it was already looking like Ferrari's year.

At the next race, in Brazil, Schumacher's run of victories was halted by Coulthard, who capitalised on the misfortune of a surprisingly competitive Williams team, benefiting from their new association with Michelin tyres, who had re-joined the sport at the start of the year.

Hakkinen had stalled on the grid and the race went into a safety car period as the marshals removed his stricken car. From the rolling re-start, newcomer Juan Pablo Montoya took the lead from Schumacher in an audacious move at the first corner. The Colombian led until lap 38, when he lapped Jos Verstappen and the Arrows driver smashed into the rear of his Williams. It was double disaster for Williams, who had just seen Ralf Schumacher run into the back of Barrichello. And so Coulthard picked up the pieces and when the rain arrived he beat Schumacher in the pit to keep the lead, and came home just ahead of his rival, with the Sauber of impressive Nick Heidfeld in third.

And brother makes two...

Williams' fulfilled some of their Brazilian promise at the following race, the San Marino Grand Prix at Imola, where Schumacher junior made history by joining his brother on the list of Formula One winners.

Championship challenger Coulthard took pole but, with the Scot bogged down at the start, the Williams of Schumacher made it through into the lead. He was never challenged as he led from first corner to the chequered flag.

Coulthard finished second and was now leading the McLaren challenge as Mika Hakkinen faded away. But Coulthard's team was undone when the new regulations for traction control were introduced at the next race, in Spain, and electronic gremlins left the Scot was motionless on the warm-up lap.

Hakkinen, however, looked set to post his first points finish as he led into the final lap, but the luck was still with Schumacher and Ferrari, as the Finn's Mercedes engine blew as he cruised towards the line. A heart-broken Hakkinen was classified ninth, and Coulthard, who stormed through the pack to claim two points for fifth, could only watch as Schumacher took a fortunate victory ahead of Montoya to extend his Championship lead.

To his credit, however, Coulthard came back fighting to win the next race in Austria as the gremlins hit Hakkinen this time, leaving him sitting on the grid with four other problem-riddled teams. Montoya stormed into the lead, but was chased

Luciano Burti driving for Prost flips over Michael Schumacher's Ferrari at the German Grand Prix at Hockenheim.

RACE BY RACE DETAILS

RACE 1 – AUSTRALIA
Race Michael Schumacher
Pole Michael Schumacher
Fastest lap Michael Schumacher

RACE 2 – MALAYSIA
Race Michael Schumacher
Pole Michael Schumacher
Fastest lap Mika Hakkinen

RACE 3 – BRAZIL
Race Michael Schumacher
Pole David Coulthard
Fastest lap Ralf Schumacher

RACE 4 – SAN MARINO
Race Ralf Schumacher
Pole David Coulthard
Fastest lap Ralf Schumacher

RACE 5 – SPAIN
Race Michael Schumacher
Pole Michael Schumacher
Fastest lap Michael Schumacher

RACE 6 – AUSTRIA
Race David Coulthard
Pole Michael Schumacher
Fastest lap David Coulthard

RACE 7 – MONACO
Race David Coulthard
Pole Michael Schumacher
Fastest lap David Coulthard

RACE 8 – CANADA
Race Ralf Schumacher
Pole Michael Schumacher
Fastest lap Ralf Schumacher

RACE 9 – EUROPEAN
Race Michael Schumacher
Pole Michael Schumacher
Fastest lap Juan Pablo Montoya

RACE 10 – FRANCE
Race Michael Schumacher
Pole: Ralf Schumacher
Fastest lap: David Coulthard

RACE 11 – BRITAIN
Race Mika Hakkinen
Pole Michael Schumacher
Fastest lap Mika Hakkinen

RACE 12 – GERMANY
Race Ralf Schumacher
Pole Juan Pablo Montoya
Fastest lap Juan Pablo Montoya

RACE 13 – HUNGARY
Race Michael Schumacher
Pole Michael Schumacher
Fastest lap Mika Hakkinen

RACE 14 – BELGIUM
Race Michael Schumacher
Pole Juan Pablo Montoya
Fastest lap Michael Schumacher

RACE 15 – ITALY
Race Juan Pablo Montoya
Pole Juan Pablo Montoya
Fastest lap Ralf Schumacher

RACE 16 – UNITED STATES
Race Mika Hakkinen
Pole Michael Schumacher
Fastest lap Juan Pablo Montoya

RACE 17 – JAPAN
Race Mika Hakkinen
Pole Michael Schumacher
Fastest lap Michael Schumacher

2001 DRIVERS' CHAMPIONSHIP

DRIVER	TEAM	POINTS
Michael Schumacher	Ferrari	123
David Coulthard	McLaren	65
Rubens Barrichello	Ferrari	56
Ralf Schumacher	Williams	49
Mika Hakkinen	McLaren	37
Juan Pablo Montoya	Williams	31
Jacques Villeneuve	BAR	12
Nick Heidfeld	Sauber	12
Jarno Trulli	Jordan	12
Kimi Raikkonen	Sauber	9
Giancarlo Fisichella	Benetton	8
Eddie Irvine	Jaguar	6
Heinz-Harald Frentzen	Jordan/Prost	6
Olivier Panis	BAR	5
Jean Alesi	Prost/Jordan	5
Pedro de la Rosa	Jaguar	3
Jenson Button	Benetton	2
Jos Verstappen	Arrows	1

down by Schumacher and the pair banged wheels as they fought a classic battle for the lead into the first corner on lap 15. The beneficiary of this was Barrichello, who assumed the lead ahead of Coulthard but he lost it in the pit stops and was then controversially forced to give way to Schumacher, who stormed back to claim second as Raikkonen took an impressive fourth.

Moving to Monaco, Coulthard was four points behind Schumacher and gave his chances a boost when he qualified on pole. But again he was left stranded on the formation lap with electronic problems, and could only fight back to fifth again. So it was an easy one-two for the scarlet Scuderia again, with Eddie Irvine a surprise third in the Jaguar .

To sign or not to sign

Controversy hit Irvine's team in the paddock at the next race, in Canada, when they claimed to have signed technical guru Adrian Newey. McLaren said he was still theirs and, after a quick reconciliation with team boss Ron Dennis, Newey remained with his team and the faces at Jaguar glowed red.

On track, Jordan driver Heinz-Harald Frentzen missed the race after concussion sustained in a crash in Monaco was made worse by a practice shunt in Montreal - Riccardo Zonta replaced him.

The race was a battle between the two Schumachers, and won by the young pretender when Williams gained the advantage through the only pit stop of the race. Ralf finished 20 seconds ahead of Michael, as Hakkinen picked up third after Montoya had crashed and Barrichello had spun off in sympathy. An engine failure took care of Coulthard, and he dropped 18 points behind in the title race.

The elder Schumacher was back on top of the rostrum when the circus returned to Europe at the Nurburgring after almost squeezing his little brother into the pit wall at the start.

The lead battle between the Schumacher pair and Montoya was close, but Ralf was given a stop-go penalty for crossing the white line coming out of the pits and Michael was able to finish ahead of Montoya with Coulthard a distant third.

Next stop France and it was business as usual for McLaren and Ferrari, with Schumacher storming to another dominant victory and Hakkinen stalling on the grid yet again. Michael Schumacher overhauled his brother in the mid-race pit stops and led him to the finish as Barrichello claimed third and Coulthard's title hopes took another blow when a 10-second pit-lane speeding penalty dropped him to fourth.

Finally, at the next race in Britain, Hakkinen was back, proudly standing on the top of the podium after passing Schumacher on lap five and leading him and Barrichello home in a processional race.

Coulthard retired in front of his home crowd after colliding with Trulli in the first corner to leave him 37 points adrift of Schumacher in the Championship, as Sauber claimed three more points with Raikkonen fifth and Heidfeld sixth.

Juan Pablo Montoya gets his first Grand Prix win at Monza.

Title race over for Coulthard

There was drama at the start of following German Grand Prix, when Luciano Burti took to the air and rolled into the first corner after hitting the slowing Ferrari of Michael Schumacher. Both emerged unscathed and took the re-start, but Schumacher could not win at home this time and left that honour to his brother Ralf, who was handed the lead when his team-mate Montoya had a disastrous pit stop and then blew his engine.

Coulthard virtually waved goodbye to his title bid as his engine let go on lap 28, failing to make the most of Schumacher's second retirement of the season. Barrichello came second and Villeneuve scored a rare podium for BAR.

The Championship was won at the next race, at the Hungaroring, as Ferrari sealed both drivers' and constructors' titles with a dominant one-two finish in an otherwise dull race. Coulthard's consolation third place did little to lift his spirits as Schumacher and Barrichello were joined by team boss Jean Todt to dance on the podium in a champagne celebration.

The emotions were on the other end of the scale in Belgium, where the race was stopped after Burti had an horrendous high-speed crash and was taken to hospital (see Talking Point).

Schumacher took a record-breaking 52nd Grand Prix win after the re-start, finishing ahead of Coulthard and a rejuvenated Fisichella, but the podium was subdued as thoughts turned to the injured Burti.

Mika Hakkinen celebrates only his second win of the season in the United States.

Black days

More bad news was to come as the teams moved to Monza for an emotionally-charged Italian Grand Prix which was almost cancelled because of the terrorist attacks in the United States on 11 September.

Schumacher was clearly hit hard by the emotional turmoil and called for care at the start. With the World Champion effectively out of the picture, the impressive Montoya took his maiden Grand Prix victory ahead of Barrichello and team-mate Ralf Schumacher.

The defiant Grand Prix circus then moved to the United States for the penultimate round of the year and a rejuvenated Hakkinen, who in Italy announced he would take a 'sabbatical' in 2002, claimed the 20th win of a glittering career.

A superior pit-stop strategy moved the Finn ahead of his rivals and he led home Michael Schumacher with Coulthard making it two McLarens in the top three as veteran Jean Alesi scored his first point for Jordan after replacing the sacked Frentzen in Hungary. Ironically Frentzen had taken Alesi's seat at the cash-strapped Prost team.

Although Michael Schumacher won the final race in Japan in style, Williams pair Montoya and Ralf Schumacher briefly led through the pit stops, but Ralf was given a 10-second penalty for missing a chicane and Montoya was left to finish second, three seconds adrift of the master.

Alesi's career came to an end in a collision with McLaren-bound youngster Kimi Raikkonen, and Hakkinen also waved goodbye at the end of the race after giving up his podium finish to allow Coulthard to seal distant second in the Championship.

SHORTS

Instead of sitting back and revelling in his fourth Championship, Michael Schumacher finished off a polished season in style. With his mind back on track after a turbulent month in which he had even thought about quitting the sport, the World Champion ignored the pit stops at Suzuka, to complete a pole-to-flag victory in the Japan Grand Prix.

2001 CONSTRUCTORS' CUP

TEAM (Engine)	POINTS
FERRARI	179
McLAREN-MERCEDES	102
WILLIAMS-BMW	80
SAUBER PETRONAS	21
JORDAN-HONDA	19
BAR-HONDA	17
BENETTON-RENAULT	10
JAGUAR	9
PROST-ACER	4
ARROWS	1

2002
Year of the red steamroller

TALKING POINT

TEAM ORDERS

Team orders caused a major controversy in 2002 as Ferrari orchestrated the racing at the sharp end of the field. When they were not switching drivers to create the best one-two finish for their championship quest – as they did in Austria when Rubens Barrichello moved over for Michael Schumacher – they were forcing the drivers to hold station – as they did in the European Grand Prix when Barrichello finished ahead of Schumacher. Despite the uproar, however, the sport's governing body, the FIA, could do nothing to stop it because, in the regulations, team orders were not banned and had, in fact, been a part of the sport from day one. Their blatant use in Austria, when Barrichello moved over on the final corner, and the subsequent behaviour on the podium that saw Barrichello move up to the top step to receive his second-place trophy, earned them a fine when many had called for a race ban. And only at the end of the season did the FIA strictly confirm that team orders were no more.

Williams' one-two in Malaysian GP... Ralf Schumacher put in a near-faultless performance ahead of Juan Pablo Montoya.

In one of the most one-sided seasons of Formula One ever completed Ferrari romped away with the constructors' championship and Michael Schumacher equalled the great Juan Manuel Fangio's record of five drivers' titles as the men from Maranello re-wrote the record books.

Schumacher's championship win was the fastest ever, secure by the 11th race of the season in France. By the season's end his and team-mate Rubens Barrichello's points tally totalled the same as the rest of the field combined. They were virtually unstoppable.

The red steamroller crushed Formula One's popularity and their controversial tactics, which saw team orders outlawed at the end of the season, drew uproar from traditionalists and new fans alike. Their mastery was majestic, but their domination was damaging.

Hat-trick Down Under

Schumacher started the way he meant to go on when, using his old 2001 car, he avoided trouble in a collision-strewn start in Melbourne and hardly put a wheel wrong as he enlarged his record haul of Formula One triumphs to 54 with a commanding win.

He became the first man to complete a hat-trick of victories in the Australian Grand Prix, but it was not the perfect start for Ferrari as Barrichello was rammed out of the race at the start by Ralf Schumacher's Williams.

Their collision triggered a multiple pile-up that halved the number of cars in the race before the first lap was completed and saw the field reduced to just eight by the end of the race.

Schumacher came home 31 seconds clear of nearest rival Juan Pablo Montoya, who had snatched the lead at one point. Finn Kimi Raikkonen was a further six seconds back in third in his maiden outing for the McLaren-Mercedes team.

And there was delight for local hero Mark Webber, who claimed points in the Australian-owned Minardi team on his Formula One debut and Finn Mika Salo, returning from a sabbatical, gave the Toyota team a points-scoring debut with sixth.

Williams on top

Ralf Schumacher ensured Ferrari's supremacy over Australia was immediately halted when he put in a near-faultless victory ahead of his Williams-BMW team-mate Montoya in a steamy Malaysian Grand Prix in Sepang.

He took his fourth career win from fourth on the grid after Michael Schumacher's Ferrari was knocked out of contention at the first corner of the opening lap by Montoya.

Montoya had to undergo a drive-through penalty for what was described by the stewards as an avoidable collision, but recovered while Schumacher fought back after a front wing change to take another podium finish in third.

Barrichello, who led from that opening lap collision, suffered even greater heartbreak as Ferrari's fairytale of perfection ended in spectacular fashion with an engine failure sending flames and smoke from his car.

Briton Jenson Button looked set to claim his maiden podium in his Renault but faded on the final lap and ended in fourth, with Sauber pair Nick Heidfeld and Felipe Massa, in only his second race in Formula One, fifth and sixth respectively.

Schumacher's new machine

Ferrari responded by rushing in their new car in time for Schumacher to use in the Brazilian Grand Prix and it proved fast and reliable enough to help him fend off a challenge from younger brother Ralf and claim victory number two.

Schumacher came out on top this time after he clashed with Montoya on the first lap for the second successive race as the pair jostled for position in a thrilling opening four corners.

Montoya was not so lucky; he had to pit and dropped down to 20th place before fighting back to finish fifth and furiously stormed off after a post-race altercation with his rival.

Briton David Coulthard secured his first finish of the year with third place, while Jenson Button took his second successive fourth-place finish. Salo claimed more points in his second finish for Toyota.

But there was more heartbreak for Barrichello. Three laps after being waved into the lead by Schumacher to the rapturous cheers of the local crowd he cruised to a halt to post his eighth successive retirement from his home race.

Ferrari on parade

By the time the Grand Prix circus returned to Europe, Ferrari had things well in hand and Schumacher scored a commanding victory with Barrichello claiming the Italian team's first one-two finish of the season.

Schumacher delighted the passionate *tifosi* crowd as he led from start to finish in a processional race where excitement gave way to admiration of a near-polished performance from the scarlet Scuderia.

Ralf Schumacher claimed third for Williams-BMW after a storming start pushed him ahead of Ferrari's Barrichello into the first corner, but he lost the place in the first set of pit stops and was purely outpaced by the Ferrari pair.

Warm temperatures, which suited the Michelin runners, were diminished by cloud and Montoya was forced to finish a lonely race in fourth place, well ahead of Button who beat fellow Briton David Coulthard in sixth.

Michael Schumacher takes the chequered flag to score the first win of the season in the Australian Grand Prix in Melbourne.

RACE RESULTS

ROUND 1 - AUSTRALIA
Race Michael Schumacher
Pole Rubens Barrichello
Fastest lap Kimi Raikkonen

ROUND 2 – MALAYSIA
Race Ralf Schumacher
Pole Michael Schumacher
Fastest lap Juan Pablo Montoya

ROUND 3 – BRAZIL
Race Michael Schumacher
Pole Juan Pablo Montoya
Fastest lap Juan Pablo Montoya

ROUND 4 – SAN MARINO
Race Michael Schumacher
Pole Michael Schumacher
Fastest lap Rubens Barrichello

ROUND 5 – SPAIN
Race Michael Schumacher
Pole Michael Schumacher
Fastest lap Michael Schumacher

ROUND 6 – AUSTRIA
Race Michael Schumacher
Pole Rubens Barrichello
Fastest lap Michael Schumacher

ROUND 7 – MONACO
Race David Coulthard
Pole Juan Pablo Montoya
Fastest lap Rubens Barrichello

ROUND 8 – CANADA
Race Michael Schumacher
Pole Juan Pablo Montoya
Fastest lap Juan Pablo Montoya

ROUND 9 – EUROPE
Race Rubens Barrichello
Pole Juan Pablo Montoya
Fastest lap Michael Schumacher

ROUND 10 – BRITAIN
Race Michael Schumacher
Pole Juan Pablo Montoya
Fastest lap Rubens Barrichello

ROUND 11 – FRANCE
Race Michael Schumacher
Pole Juan Pablo Montoya
Fastest lap David Coulthard

ROUND 12 – GERMAN
Race Michael Schumacher
Pole Michael Schumacher
Fastest lap Michael Schumacher

ROUND 13 – HUNGARY
Race Rubens Barrichello
Pole Rubens Barrichello
Fastest lap Michael Schumacher

ROUND 14 – BELGIUM
Race Michael Schumacher
Pole Michael Schumacher
Fastest lap Michael Schumacher

ROUND 15 – ITALY
Race Rubens Barrichello
Pole Juan Pablo Montoya
Fastest lap Rubens Barrichello

ROUND 16 – UNITED STATES
Race Rubens Barrichello
Pole Michael Schumacher
Fastest lap Rubens Barrichello

ROUND 17 – JAPAN
Race Michael Schumacher
Pole Michael Schumacher
Fastest lap Michael Schumacher

Michael Schumacher crosses the finishing line to take the chequered flag in San Marino.

difficult start to the season continued as he made a total of four stops and dropped down the order with a splash-and-dash at the end.

Fiasco on a wet track

The rain-hit Brazilian Grand Prix was even more chaotic than the first two races and its result was eventually decided, at the FIA headquarters, in Paris, on the Friday after the race, when Jordan's Giancarlo Fisichella was handed a long-awaited win. Raikkonen had been awarded the victory on the day.

The race was stopped 17 laps from the end when Australian Mark Webber, in a Jaguar, crashed heavily on the main straight and Alonso, ignoring yellow flags, ploughed into the wreckage. Both drivers were unhurt. With the results declared two laps before the accident, Raikkonen was deemed the winner.

Fisichella thought he had won and celebrated with his team as his car blazed in the soaking pitlane before the results were declared. After making an appeal, Jordan proved a timing mistake and Fisichella collected the trophy from Raikkonen in a ceremony on the main straight at the next race in San Marino.

Michael Schumacher retired for the first time in 25 races after sliding off, along with seven other drivers, on a river of rainwater flowing across the track at turn three. Barrichello succumbed to technical gremlins, so Alonso finished third but failed to appear on the podium after being taken away on a stretcher.

Fitting tribute

Michael Schumacher finally claimed his first win of the season, in emotional circumstances, when he produced an impressive and composed performance on his Ferrari team's home soil, just one day after his mother Elisabeth had passed away, in a hospital, in Cologne.

Schumacher, who visited her bedside with his brother Ralf on the Saturday night, finished 1.8 seconds ahead of Raikkonen, but, sadly, Ralf Schumacher failed to make it a double family podium tribute when he finished fourth behind Barrichello after starting alongside his brother on the front row.

Ralf took the lead as the field headed into the first chicane but a slow stop handed his brother a lead he would never relinquish in a processional race. Coulthard was fifth with Alonso sixth, Montoya seventh after a fuel filler problem caused him to stop twice in as many laps.

Button claimed the final point for BAR, but Brazilian winner Fisichella, who had been disappointed not to be given a full podium celebration when he belatedly received his trophy, was brought down to earth with a bump as he went home early after his Jordan engine expired midway through the race.

Three in a row

Schumacher gave Ferrari's new F2003-GA machine, named after the late Fiat boss Gianni Agnelli, a victorious debut at the next race in Spain and disappointed the record sell-out crowd when he got the better of local youngster Alonso to secure his third consecutive victory in Barcelona.

Championship leader Kimi Raikkonen failed to travel more than 16 yards after crashing into Pizzonia's stationary Jaguar at the start and his team-mate Coulthard had a disastrous day when he crashed out after hitting Button after a first-lap collision with Trulli.

Montoya finished a distant fourth with Ralf Schumacher fifth, despite several off-track excursions.

SHORTS

Although the outcome of the 2002 season saw Schumacher claim his record sixth title, it was the emergence of two new names at the sharp end of the Grand Prix grid that encouraged some people to believe that his reign could finally be brought to an end in the near future. The German genius had been racing with few rivals since he took control of the sport with his first title in 1994. Damon Hill, Jacques Villeneuve and Mika Hakkinen had all got in his way, but none seemed to be a true great who could beat the man who has become known as the best of the best. Finn Kimi Raikkonen and Spaniard Fernando Alonso, however, showed the potential to become just that as they belied their youth and significant inexperience to take their maiden pole positions and maiden victories. Only time will tell whether they really can maintain their position, then make progress and assume Schumacher's mantle in the years ahead, but their arrival was enough to make the German realise he might finally have some tough competition.

Da Matta was sixth, Webber scored his first points for Jaguar with seventh and Briton Ralph Firman claimed his first world championship point when he finished eighth for Jordan.

Back from the flames

After the early season shake-up, the third successive Schumacher victory, which came in the subsequent Austrian Grand Prix, proved things were getting back to normal as the talented but lucky German calmly overcame a pitlane fire in his Ferrari to become the first back-to-back winner at the A1-Ring.

Schumacher shot into the lead after two aborted starts, but, at his first pit stop, the fuel filler stuck. Fuel spilled out over the engine cover and burst into flames, but the team put out the fire with three extinguishers and Schumacher coolly drove out of the pits after 20.4 seconds to slot into third.

Montoya's engine blew on lap 32 and Schumacher passed Raikkonen in the confusion to take the lead again as the smoking Williams-BMW machine dropped through the pack and Montoya retired. Ferrari fixed their refuelling problems by the second round of stops and Schumacher cruised to the finish.

Raikkonen claimed second to keep himself two points ahead of Schumacher in the championship table and Barrichello finished third. Button was more than half a minute behind in fourth with Coulthard fifth, Ralf Schumacher sixth, Webber overcoming a penalty to claim seventh and Trulli completing the top eight.

End of the hoodoo

Montoya stopped Schumacher's run and ended his Williams team's 20-year hoodoo in the Monaco Grand Prix when he claimed his second Formula One win with an impressive drive to hold off Raikkonen's nose-to-tail challenge and become the first Williams winner in Monaco since Keke Rosberg in 1983.

Button was withdrawn before the race, after spending Saturday night in hospital recovering from a heavy practice crash at the chicane, but he was back at the track to watch as Frentzen escaped injury, but forced the safety car out, when he ploughed into the barriers at the Swimming Pool complex.

Michael Schumacher started fifth and chased hard, but had to settle for third ahead of his brother Ralf, who had started from pole for Williams, but lost out in the first pitstops. Alonso finished fifth ahead of team-mate Trulli with Coulthard and Barrichello claiming the final points-scoring positions.

Cream rises

Schumacher moved ahead in the title race with his fourth win of the year in the Canadian Grand Prix as Raikkonen finished sixth after starting from the pits and suffering a puncture in the race. But there was

Fernando Alonso on the podium after taking second place in his home GP at Circuit de Catalunya.

2004
The stallion prances once more

Michael Schumacher takes his Ferrari for a spin during Promotional Day for the Australian Grand Prix.

A beaming Jenson Button celebrates third place in the Malaysian GP.

The close competition during an intriguing 2003 championship led to predictions that Ferrari would finally be beaten in 2004 and strong pre-season testing times set by radical new cars from both McLaren-Mercedes and Williams-BMW built up expectations that Formula One would be back to its best.

Teams were handed a new challenge when a rule forcing them to use just one engine per weekend was introduced, with a penalty of a 10-grid-position demotion handed out if they suffered a blow-up. Some manufacturers coped well with the changes, others did not – and unsurprisingly Ferrari came out on top.

Early predictions of a Williams or McLaren world champion were rapidly altered when Michael Schumacher clocked up a record-equalling run of five wins from the first five races as the challenge of Ferrari's rivals crumbled when their cars proved slow and unreliable.

Talk of Schumacher winning all 18 races in an expanded calendar that included the first race in the Middle East, in Bahrain, and the first in China, in Shanghai later in the year, was ended by Jarno Trulli's maiden victory in Monaco, but Schumacher remained favourite to race to his seventh title.

Fear of Ferrari

Ferrari opted against going head-to-head with their rivals in pre-season testing as the worked alone at alternative tracks, and when the action got under way in the Australian Grand Prix Schumacher shocked the field with an easy victory ahead of team-mate Rubens Barrichello as the previous year's championship runner-up Kimi Raikkonen failed to even complete ten laps.

Renault claimed the final podium spot with Fernando Alonso, as Ralf Schumacher and Juan Pablo Montoya battled home to fourth and fifth for Williams, Jenson Button was sixth for BAR, Jarno Trulli seventh for Renault and David Coulthard claimed a consolation point for McLaren in eighth.

But the fact that the two Ferraris finished more than half a minute ahead of Alonso, after trading record times around the Albert Park circuit and easing away from the pack at a second per lap, put fear into their rivals of a return to the domination of 2002.

Beating the heat

Schumacher had been tipped to struggle in the heat of Malaysia but, instead, he started from pole, cruised to victory and set the fastest lap of the race to finish ahead of second-placed Montoya as Button kept Barrichello at bay to claim his first career podium with third for BAR.

Trulli finished fifth and his team-mate Alonso climbed up from last on the grid to score a point for eighth. Coulthard was sixth for McLaren but championship hopeful Kimi Raikkonen saw his chances slide away again when he spun on the parade lap and retired with a smoking engine.

Desert storm

Despite a Sunday morning sand storm at Bahrain's state-of-the-art desert circuit, the first race in the Middle East went without a hitch for both the organisers and for Schumacher, who claimed his hat-trick of victories as Barrichello helped Ferrari to their second one-two finish of the year.

Schumacher started from pole and went unchallenged as Button claimed another podium. The expected title contenders suffered again as Raikkonen went out with a spectacular engine blow-up, Ralf Schumacher was punted out by Takuma Sato and Montoya dropped from third to 13th after a problem late in the race.

Trulli finished fourth, with Sato fifth to hand BAR their first double-points finish of the season and move them level on points with Williams. Alonso fought his way up from a first-lap collision to claim sixth place while Ralf Schumacher and Mark Webber claimed the final points.

Three in a row

Schumacher continued his perfect start to the season with victory in front of the Ferrari *tifosi* in San Marino despite starting the race, which marked the tenth anniversary of Ayrton Senna's death, behind Button after the Briton had claimed his first career pole position.

Button recorded his best-ever Grand Prix result with second but Schumacher was able to cruise to his sixth victory at the Imola circuit. Montoya finished third with Renault pair Alonso and Trulli fourth and fifth, Barrichello sixth, Ralf Schumacher seventh and Raikkonen winning his first point of the year in eighth.

Winning numbers

The numbers came up again for Schumacher in Spain when he started from pole for the fourth time in five races and claimed his 75th career victory in his 200th Grand Prix with a dominant win that equalled Nigel Mansell's 1992 record season-opening winning run of five.

Barrichello secured Ferrari's third one-two of the year as the expected threat from Button failed to materialise and he finished eighth after a mistake in qualifying. Renault were 'best of the rest' this time but Trulli finished 32.2 seconds behind, just ahead of home favourite Alonso.

Tonic for the troops

The Monaco Grand Prix threw up just the tonic for Formula One when Trulli won an incident-filled race to claim his maiden Grand Prix victory from his first-ever pole position as the chances of a Ferrari 'redwash' were ended when Schumacher crashed out in the tunnel.

The race was interrupted by two safety car periods, the first coming when Giancarlo Fisichella rolled his Sauber after being blinded by smoke from Sato's blown engine and the second when Trulli's team-mate Alonso crashed in the tunnel as he lapped Ralf Schumacher's Williams.

Michael Schumacher's first retirement in the 19 races, which came when he locked his brakes and collided with Montoya's Williams, left the road clear for Button to finish second with Barrichello third for Ferrari, proving the German was not invincible. And that was it for the first six races of the year...

Juan Pablo Montoya attempts to overtake Michael Schumacher during the San Marino Grand Prix.

A frustrated Kimi Raikkonen climbs from his McLaren and retires from the Malaysian Grand Prix.

The Ones to Watch

CAREER DETAILS

1976	Born 27 August, Queanbeyan, Australia
1991	Began three years in Australian karting
1994	Australian Formula Ford Championship
1995	Fourth in Australian Formula Ford and third in Formula Ford Festival in Britain
1996	Second in British Formula Ford, won the Formula Ford Festival
1997	Fourth in British Formula Three Championship with one win
1998	Second for Mercedes in GT Championship with five wins
1999	Le Mans 24-Hours with Mercedes
2000	Third in F3000 championship
2001	Second in F3000 championship with three wins, Benetton test driver
2002	Formula One debut with Minardi, finishing fifth on his debut
2003	Formula One with Jaguar, best result sixth
2004	Formula One with Jaguar

FORMULA ONE RECORD

Year	Team	Wins	Poles	Fast laps	Pts
2002	Minardi	0	0	0	2
2003	Jaguar	0	0	0	17

Mark Webber

An amiable Australian with a huge natural talent, Webber made an immediate impact when he joined Formula One and has become one of the most respected drivers in the paddock for his pace and his commitment to the sport.

Webber worked his way up the Australian motorsport ladder before moving to Europe and, in a similar career progression to Michael Schumacher, he took in a spell in GT sportscar racing on his way to Formula One.

He first became known for his spectacular flip in the Mercedes at Le Mans rather than his abilities as a future Formula One star, but he showed promise in Formula 3000 when he finished second in the championship to Briton Justin Wilson.

He secured a drive with Minardi, partially because the team owner Paul Stoddart was of the same nationality, and he proved fast and committed despite running in a back-of-the-grid car. He did, however, score points on his debut.

A move to Jaguar took his career up another notch and, despite struggling to better his fifth place finish, his talent and his interest in working on the personality side of the sport has helped push him towards a top-line drive.

CAREER DETAILS

1979	Born 17 October, Espoo, Finland
1991	Began eight years of national and international karting
1999	Competed in Formula Ford and Formula Renault, winning the British winter series
2000	Won the British Formula Renault Championship, tested with Sauber
2001	Made his Formula One debut with Sauber, finishing 10th in the championship
2002	Moved to McLaren and scored his first podium
2003	Finished second in the championship after claiming his first pole and first victory
2004	Had a difficult third season with McLaren

FORMULA ONE RECORD

Year	Team	Wins	Poles	Fast laps	Pts
2001	Sauber	0	0	0	9
2002	McLaren	0	0	1	24
2003	McLaren	1	1	4	91

Kimi Raikkonen

His concentration and determination is what made him known as "The Iceman", and his extreme car control and measured mind gave him the chance to challenge for the championship in only his third year in Formula One.

The new Flying Finn had competed in just 23 single-seater races before his 2001 debut for Sauber, who obtained a special dispensation from the FIA to bring him straight in from a dominant season in the British Formula Renault series.

He overcame a scare on his debut, when his steering wheel came off in his hands, and two fourth places in Austria and Canada convinced McLaren team boss Ron Dennis to sign him up as a replacement for Mika Hakkinen in 2002.

He claimed his first podium on his debut for his new top-level team, almost won in France and finally turned his potential into results the following season in 2003 when he won the Malaysian Grand Prix and challenged for the title.

His consistent performances in what was, in truth, an old McLaren put the title within his grasp but he missed out by just two points and 2004 proved to be a disappointment as the team dropped down the grid.

Fernando Alonso

The young Spaniard was groomed to be a top racer by Renault boss Flavio Briatore and he entered the record books when he became the youngest-ever Grand Prix winner in Hungary in 2003 in only his 30th race.

He spent two years on the car-racing ladder, first in the Euro Open and then in Formula 3000, and signed up with Briatore before making an early debut in Formula One with the back-of-the-grid Minardi team.

A year of testing around the European circuits and working on his PR skills during the race weekends in 2002 helped mature him for his front-running Formula One debut the following year and the tactics worked to perfection.

In the Malaysian Grand Prix he claimed his first-ever pole position and later went on to dominate the Hungarian Grand Prix as he turned a second pole into his first victory. His talent and commitment ensure he should enjoy many more.

CAREER DETAILS

1981	Born July 29, Oviedo, Spain
1988	Started karting in Spain and became Spanish champion in 1994 to 1997
1999	Made his car-racing debut in the Euro Open with Nissan, winning six races and the championship
2000	Finished fourth in Formula 3000 with one win
2001	Made his Formula One debut with Minardi
2002	Spent year testing for Renault
2003	Moved into the Renault race team and finished sixth in the championship with one win
2004	Raced for Renault

FORMULA ONE RECORD

Year	Team	Wins	Poles	Fast laps	Pts
2001	Minardi	0	0	0	0
2003	Renault	1	2	1	55

Jenson Button

Thrown in at the deep end with Williams in 2000, he won a shoot-out for the top drive with the team's Brazilian test driver Bruno Junqueira and did not disappoint in his debut season.

After victory in the British Formula Ford Championship and its associated end-of-year Festival, he was plucked from relative obscurity and climbed into the hot seat despite a solid but relatively unsuccessful season in Formula Three.

He matched and occasionally bettered the pace of team-mate Ralf Schumacher and claimed a best finish of fourth but was then replaced by Juan Pablo Montoya and forced into two difficult years with Benetton-Renault.

His career was saved by long-time family friend David Richards, who signed him up to race for BAR-Honda in 2003, and he won the battle with feuding team-mate Jacques Villeneuve with some strong performances.

Complete with a pop singer fiancée, he quickly became known as the David Beckham of Formula One but he matched the hype with results as he led the team and claimed his first-ever podium in the Malaysian Grand Prix and pole in San Marino.

CAREER DETAILS

1980	Born January 19, Frome, England
1989	Started karting and won five British championships in five years
1997	Won the European Super Cup A kart series
1998	Won the British Formula Ford series and Festival
1999	Finished third, as top rookie, in the British Formula Three Championship
2000	Made his Formula One debut for Williams, aged 20, and collected 12 points
2001	Moved to Benetton-Renault and finished 17th in the championship with just two points
2002	Finished seventh in the championship with 14 points
2003	Moved to BAR-Honda and finished ninth in the championship with 17 points
2004	Raced for BAR and claimed his first Formula One podium and pole position

FORMULA ONE RECORD

Year	Team	Wins	Poles	Fast laps	Pts
2000	Williams	0	0	0	12
2001	Benetton	0	0	0	2
2002	Renault	0	0	0	14
2003	BAR-Honda	0	0	0	17

Index

Page numbers set in *italics* indicate illustrations.